THE PROFESSIONAL STUDENT AFFAIRS ADMINISTRATOR

THE PROFESSIONAL STUDENT AFFAIRS ADMINISTRATOR

Educator, Leader, and Manager

Roger B. Winston, Jr.
Don G. Creamer
Theodore K. Miller
and Associates

Stuart J. Brown
D. Stanley Carpenter
Diane L. Cooper
Benjamin Dixon
Theodore W. Elling
T. Dary Erwin
Donald D. Gehring
Joan B. Hirt
Barbara Jacoby
Steven M. Janosik
Susan R. Jones
George D. Kuh

Marcia B. Baxter Magolda
Dennis C. Roberts
Arthur Sandeen
Sue A. Saunders
John H. Schuh
Michael J. Siegel
Stephen A. Sivo
Auden D. Thomas
M. Lee Upcraft
Dudley B. Woodard, Jr.
Robert B. Young

USA	Publishing Office:	BRUNNER-ROUTLEDGE
		A member of the Taylor & Francis Group
		29 West 35th Street
		New York, NY 10001
		Tel: (212) 216-7800
		Fax: (212) 564-7854
	Distribution Center:	BRUNNER-ROUTLEDGE
		A member of the Taylor & Francis Group
		7625 Empire Drive
		Florence, KY 41042
		Tel: 1 (800) 634-7064
		Fax: 1 (800) 248-4724
UK		BRUNNER-ROUTLEDGE
		A member of the Taylor & Francis Group
		27 Church Road
		Hove
		E. Sussex, BN3 2FA
		Tel.: +44 (0) 1273 207411
		Fax: +44 (0) 1273 205612

The Professional Student Affairs Administrator: Educator, Leader, and Manager

1 2 3 4 5 6 7 8 9 0

Printed by Edwards Brothers, Lillington, NC, 2001.
Cover design by Ellen Seguin.

A CIP catalog record for this book is available from the British Library.
∞ The paper in this publication meets the requirements of the ANSI Standard Z39.48-1984 (Permanence of Paper).

Library of Congress Cataloging-in-Publication Data
CIP information available from the publishers.

ISBN 1-58391-066-2 (case)

Contents

APPENDICES

Preface

The goal of this book is to provide a comprehensive text for advanced master's and doctoral students in college student affairs administration preparation programs and a reference for established professionals who desire to remain current on developments in the field. By "advanced student," we and our associates mean that we made the assumption that readers already possess a basic understanding of the student affairs field (such as history, usual functional areas of responsibility, ethos, philosophical groundings, and professional organizations) and a broad understanding of higher education (for example, history, typical means of organizing, and unique culture).

This volume supersedes the previous graduate student text *Administration and Leadership in Student Affairs: Actualizing Student Development in Higher Education* (2nd edition) edited by Miller and Winston (1991). This volume is not a revision of the previous work, but a totally new work that reflects the changes that have taken place in higher education in the past decade and in the most recent thinking about the purpose, role, and function of college student affairs.

THE STUDENT AFFAIRS ADMINISTRATOR

The book's philosophical perspective focuses upon three roles of the student affairs administrator: (a) as educator who plays a significant role in addressing the institution's academic goals, (b) as leader who can express a vision to guide student affairs practice, and (c) as manager who administers and coordinates student affairs programs and services (and sometimes other essential institutional services such as data processing, campus police, and day care centers). Grounded in student development, learning, leadership, group dynamics, and management theories and in social science research and evaluation methods, today's professional college student affairs administrator is viewed as being in the forefront of student learning initiatives.

Arthur Sandeen, in his book, *The Chief Student Affairs Officer: Leader,*

Manager, Mediator, Educator (1991), focused on the person and function of the chief or senior student affairs administrator and identified four principal roles for the student affairs division head. We, too, see these roles as fundamental for student affairs practitioners at all levels, but we view the mediation function as integral to the leader and manager roles and as often being employed in the educator role as well. Because dealing with conflict and disagreement is embedded in the other roles, we visualize the mediator role as subsumed within the primary roles of educator, leader, and manager. This is not to suggest that we view Sandeen's conceptualization as inadequate or wrong; instead, we have chosen to use a slightly different model in this book.

In this book, *student affairs* is seen as having both formal and informal educational missions. That is, the student affairs division must become an integral part of college students' quests to integrate, make meaning of, and apply classroom learning; to remediate academic deficits and acquire new skills; and to address personal and social development issues. This can be accomplished only through the existence of a partnership between student affairs and academic affairs that focuses on the individual student. The *principal* tenet of this book asserts that the purpose of student affairs administration is to educate, and the criterion for determining success is reflected in how well students utilize the learning opportunities (both formal and informal) available to them within the institution. All other roles are viewed as supporting the fundamental mission of furthering students' academic, social, and personal development.

The basic premise for the book is that the quality of student affairs administrative practice is determined by the successful accomplishment of the dual functions of education and institutional or organizational maintenance, which is necessary for accomplishing the institution's primary mission. An underlying assumption is that the successful accomplishment of these functions is affected by active membership within the campus community and the professional community. Throughout the book, the meaning and attendant responsibilities of being a *professional* are explicated.

Even though the editors of this volume view the educator role as fundamental to student affairs and in many ways the raison d'être for the existence of student affairs, all three roles are crucial. Truly successful student affairs administrators attend to all of these roles with skill and alacrity, although the priority of the roles may change depending on the circumstances. Candor, however, compels the editors to acknowledge that in their combined experience of more than 100 years of practice in and study of the field, they know of relatively few chief student affairs administrators who have been relieved of their positions for failure to fully address the educator role, but many have been fired because of their failures as managers or leaders or both.

TARGET AUDIENCE

This book is intended for two principal audiences. The primary focus is master's level students in student affairs preparation programs. Primarily, the book was conceptualized to meet the instructional needs of student affairs faculty members who teach master's level administration courses or course units. In addition, some faculty may use the book for doctoral-level courses or for in-service education of practitioners as well. The second target audience is composed of entry-level student affairs practitioners, who are faced with increasingly complex administrative responsibilities, and midmanagement and senior practitioners, who can benefit from exposure to current thinking about student affairs practice and can use that knowledge in their own work and when supervising staff.

NOMENCLATURE

As was noted in the two editions of *Administration and Leadership in Student Affairs* (Miller & Winston, 1991; Miller, Winston, & Mendenhall, 1983), student affairs is a field still without universally accepted terminology. We have, therefore, somewhat arbitrarily, though not capriciously, adopted a terminology for this book while also acknowledging that its superiority over other frequently used terms cannot always be assured. This terminology was adopted primarily to avoid confusion across chapters.

- *College* is used as a general term to include all postsecondary educational institutions, be they community colleges or Research I universities.
- *Student personnel* is an anachronistic term that is no longer considered a suitable description for the field. In this book "student personnel" appears only in quotations or in regard to historical references.
- *Student affairs* is used to describe the organizational structure or unit within an institution responsible for students' out-of-class life and learning.
- The administrative head of the institution-level student affairs unit on a campus is interchangeably referred to as *vice president for student affairs, chief student affairs officer, chief student affairs administrator,* and *senior student affairs administrator.*
- *Student affairs administration* or *practice* is viewed as the global or generic term for describing the field of professional endeavor, including all the specialties within the field, such as counseling, residence life, career planning, admissions, and student discipline.
- Names for units within a student affairs division often are the vestiges of history (sometimes forgotten), but many have significance within an institution. Often there is an attempt to create a parallel between academic and student affairs unit names and to have an internal logic for use of particular titles and organizational names. In this book, the overall administrative unit is referred to as the *student affairs division.* Units subsumed within a division are called *departments,* such as financial aid, student activities, or academic assistance/development. Units within departments are referred to as *programs, centers,* or *offices,* such as a student leadership development program (originating from the Dean of Student Office), family housing office (a Depart-

ment of Housing subunit), or African American Cultural Center (a subunit of the Minority Student Services Department).

ORGANIZATIONAL STRUCTURE AND CONTENTS OF THE BOOK

The book is organized into five parts: (I) Foundation and Context, (II) Parameters of Professional Practice, (III) Managing and Administering, (IV) Teaching and Inquiring, and (V) Leading and Visioning. Each part has two or more chapters written by exceedingly experienced and knowledgeable professionals. This book deals with student affairs administration from a perspective not provided by any other publication. This book offers graduate students and practicing student affairs professionals an introduction to the basic knowledge and skills needed by present-day student affairs staff members.

Under Part I, Foundation and Context, there are four chapters. In Chapter 1, Creamer, Winston, and Miller discuss contemporary conceptualizations of student affairs administration, the principal roles of the student affairs administrator as educator, leader, and manager, and what it means to be a professional. Kuh, Siegel, and Thomas, in Chapter 2, describe the cultures of higher education with special attention paid to the perceptions and understandings of the student affairs arena by diverse student and faculty groups and the changing nature of contemporary college student populations and cultures. In Chapter 3, Dixon explains how student affairs administrators are called upon to address daily one of higher education's most persistent and pressing concerns—how to foster multicultural learning communities. Diversity of students, faculty and staff members, and institutions themselves requires the creation and maintenance of welcoming multicultural environments. He proffers a model for use in student affairs practice that effectively addresses many of the challenges presented by an ever-increasing diversity and need for continued change in institutions today. The final chapter (Chapter 4) of Part I is written by Elling and Brown. It identifies the challenges and opportunities that new electronic technologies present to the student affairs field and the accomplishment of its traditional mission, especially on the virtual campus where students and instructors (and student affairs practitioners) are separated in both time and space. The chapter identifies challenges and accomplishments that student affairs administrators now face or will face as educators, leaders, and managers and provides examples of successful practices in the utilization of expanding technologies.

Part II, Parameters of Professional Practice, addresses the legal and ethical boundaries of student affairs practice. In Chapter 5, Gehring describes legal mandates, constraints, and other legal and judicial considerations currently facing those who administer and manage institutions. Consideration is given to the historical evolution of legal aspects associated with the relationship between higher education and its students and to limitations faced by administrators as they function within academic communities. Supporting this chapter in Appendix

A is a short introduction to reading legal citations and conducting research in case law. Professional ethics are addressed by Young in Chapter 6, who examines both the philosophical underpinnings of ethics and what it means to be an ethical *professional*. Supporting this chapter are copies of the American College Personnel Association and National Association of Student Personnel Administrators' statements of ethical principles and standards in Appendices B and C.

Part III, which deals with management and administration of student affairs units, contains four chapters. Sandeen, in Chapter 7, focuses on organizational approaches to the effective administration of student affairs programs and services. Examples of organizational structure alternatives are presented with strengths and weaknesses identified. In Chapter 8, Carpenter deals with staff recruitment, selection, orientation, retention, supervision, development, and evaluation. Strategies for establishing effective approaches to creating quality work environments are presented, as are criteria for evaluating staff members in ways that will increase satisfaction, productivity, and collaboration. Woodard, in Chapter 9, provides an introduction to effective budget management, including alternative budget planning strategies and connecting budgets to program operation. Elementary budget issues, such as how to read a financial or operations statement, are presented as well as more advanced considerations such as how to use the budget for management and program development. In Chapter 10, Janosik and Hirt conclude Part III by providing strategies and approaches that administrators (in all three roles) may use when faced with conflict situations.

Part IV (Teaching and Inquiring) is composed of four chapters. Baxter Magolda (Chapter 11) asserts that effective educational practice requires an understanding of how students learn. She addresses pedagogical principles and approaches that can be used by student affairs practitioners to enhance learning in staff training, policy formulation and implementation, and formal classroom contexts. In Chapter 12, Saunders and Cooper present a model for designing programs based on identified student needs and interests to foster personal development and learning. The chapter also deals with the importance of both understanding and attending to group dynamics when functioning as administrators. In Chapter 13, Schuh and Upcraft explore needs assessment and program evaluation. To respond appropriately to diverse student needs and interests, student affairs administrators must make systematic assessments and then use the information elicited for designing programs and services. Likewise, administrators should evaluate carefully the effects of the programs and services provided to students to determine their effectiveness and cost efficiency. This chapter addresses techniques and strategies for conducting these assessments and using what is learned to improve program design and availability. Chapter 14, written by Erwin and Sivo, addresses outcomes assessment in student affairs, an area of increasing importance in terms of gaining funding and institutional accreditation, and in determining institutional effectiveness. This chapter defines outcomes assessment, provides a conceptual framework for conducting outcomes assessment in student affairs, and offers suggestions for ways that practitioners can combine research on educational environments and diverse students with outcomes data to inform practice of the larger profession.

The concluding part (V) of the book addresses leading and visioning. In Chapter 15, Roberts deals with contemporary leadership theories and their applications, including planning techniques and processes and policy development and implementation. Finally, Jacoby and Jones (Chapter 16) focus on the importance of administrator vision to the effective functioning of organizational systems. Paradigm shifts in higher education and student affairs are identified and discussed, as are issues such as the role of student affairs in dealing with diversity, distance education and other institutional outreach activities, community service, and the creation of learning communities.

ACKNOWLEDGMENTS

Foremost, we wish to thank the twenty-three contributors to this work. Without their creativity, resourcefulness, expertise, cooperation, and good natures, we would never have been able to complete this work in a timely fashion. We also acknowledge both their conscientious work and scholarship, which is evident in the reading of this volume, and the guidance they provided us as we conceptualized the book and sought to bring coherent structure to its presentation.

We also acknowledge Tim Julet and Jill Osowa of Taylor and Francis for their encouragement, support, and occasional nudges through this process.

Athens, Georgia   Roger B. Winston, Jr.
Blacksburg, Virginia   Don G. Creamer
May 1, 2000   Theodore K. Miller

REFERENCES

Miller, T. K., & Winston, R. B., Jr. (Eds.). (1991). *Administration and leadership in student Affairs: Actualizing student development in higher education* (2nd ed.). Muncie, IN: Accelerated Development.

Miller, T. K., Winston, R. B., Jr., & Mendenhall, W. R. (Eds.). (1983). *Administration and leadership in student affairs: Actualizing student development in higher education*. Muncie, IN: Accelerated Development.

Sandeen, A. (1991). *The chief student affairs officer: Leader, manager, mediator, educator.* San Francisco: Jossey-Bass.

About the Writers

Stuart J. Brown is an assistant dean of students at the University of Connecticut in Waterbury. He received a B.A. degree (1979) in political science from Rutgers University, an M.A. degree (1981) in student personnel administration from Teachers College, Columbia University, and an Ed.D. degree (1989) in student personnel administration from Teachers College, Columbia University. Prior to his current position, he was the director of college activities at Barnard College and coordinator of housing at Mitchell College. He has served as the president of the Connecticut College Personnel Association, on the NASPA Region I Executive Board as secretary/treasurer and information technology chair, and is currently the national chair of the NASPA Information Technology Network. He has authored a number of articles on the impact of technology on student affairs. Brown is also the webmaster for the StudentAffairs.com website.

D. Stanley (Stan) Carpenter is professor of educational administration and coordinator of the Student Affairs Administration in higher education (SAAHE) program at Texas A&M University. He earned a B.S. degree in mathematics from Tarleton State University (1972), an M.S. degree in student personnel and guidance from Texas A&M at Commerce (1975), and a Ph.D. degree in counseling and student personnel services from the University of Georgia (1979). Before becoming a professor, he was dean of students at the University of Arkansas at Monticello and assistant director of development at Texas A&M. He served as the executive director of the Association for the Study of Higher Education (ASHE) for 10 years and on the ACPA Media Board for nine years, currently as editor/chair. He has published more than 50 articles, chapters, and reviews. Carpenter is an ACPA senior scholar and received SACSA's Melvene Hardee Award for Contributions to Student Affairs, the Distinguished Service Awards from ASHE, and the Alpha Phi Omega National Service Fraternity.

Diane L. Cooper is an associate professor of college student affairs administration in the Department of Counseling and Human Development Services at the University of Georgia. She received a B.A. degree in marketing management from Miami University in Oxford, Ohio, in 1978; an M.Ed. degree from the University of Missouri at St. Louis in counseling in 1979; and a Ph.D. degree from the University of Iowa in counselor education in 1985. She served for eight years as a student affairs practitioner at the University of North Carolina at Greensboro. Cooper served as the editor for the *College Student Affairs Journal* (1994–1999) and is on the editorial boards of the *Journal of College Student Development* and *Georgia Journal of College Student Affairs*. She edited *Beyond Law and Policy: Reaffirming the Role of Student Affairs* (with James Lancaster, Jossey-Bass, 1997) and is an author of the *Student Developmental Task and Lifestyle Assessment* (with Roger Winston and Theodore Miller, Student Development Associates, 1999), five book chapters, and numerous journal articles. She is currently serving as a SACSA scholar.

Don G. Creamer is professor of higher education and student affairs and director of the Educational Policy Institute of Virginia Tech in the Educational Leadership and Policy Studies Department at Virginia Polytechnic Institute and State University. He received a B.A. degree (1960) in American history and M.Ed. degree (1961) in counseling and guidance from Texas A&M University at Commerce, and an Ed.D. degree (1965) in higher education from Indiana University. Prior to assuming teaching duties, he was dean of students at El Centro College of the Dallas County Community College District and previously served in several student affairs administrative roles at Texas A&M University at Commerce. He is past president of the American College Personnel Association (ACPA) and continues to serve the association through one of its Core Councils. He is alternate director for ACPA on the Council for the Advancement of Standards in Higher Education (CAS), where he actively pursues an agenda for quality assurance in higher education. He is a member of the editorial board of the *Journal of College Student Retention*. He is author of four books, including *Improving Staffing Practices in Student Affairs* (with Roger Winston, Jossey-Bass, 1997). Creamer is an ACPA senior scholar diplomate and holder of the association's two highest awards, the Contribution to Knowledge Award and the Ester Lloyd-Jones Distinguished Service Award. He also received the Robert H. Shaffer Award for Academic Excellence as a graduate faculty member from the National Association of Student Personnel Administrators and the Robert H. Shaffer Distinguished Alumnus Award from the Indiana University Department of Higher Education and Student Affairs.

Benjamin Dixon is vice president for multicultural affairs at Virginia Polytechnic Institute and State University in Blacksburg. He received a B.Mus.Ed. degree (1962) from Howard University, an M.A.T. degree (1963) from the Harvard University Graduate School of Education, and an Ed.D. degree (1977) in education administration with an emphasis on master planning in higher education from the University of Massachusetts. Prior to assuming his post at Virginia Polytechnic Institute and State University, Dixon served as deputy commissioner of education for the State of Connecticut. He was a cofounder of Education/Instruction, Inc., an advocacy/consultant group, and the Diversity Council, a regional organization for major corporations interested in improving their understanding and management of cultural diversity in the workplace. Dixon is a past president of both the Connecticut Association of Pupil Personnel Administrators and the Study Commission for the Council of Chief State School Officers. He has served on the writing or editorial boards for *Consortium Currents* and *Curriculum for the New Millennium*. He was appointed a Ford fellow in 1974 and was a charter member and governor's appointee to the Connecticut Commission on African American Affairs.

Theodore W. Elling is an assistant vice chancellor for student affairs at the University of North Carolina at Charlotte. He received a B.A. degree (1977) in chemistry from the State University of New York at Potsdam, an M.S. degree (1980) in counseling and student development at Radford University, and an Ed.D. (1990) in student personnel administration from Teachers College, Columbia University. Prior to his current position, he was the assistant to the vice chancellor for systems development and research at the University of North Carolina at Charlotte and associate director of residential life at Hofstra University. He has served on the National Association of Student Personnel Administrators (NASPA) Region III Advisory Board as information technology network chair, the SACSA Technology Committee, and the Association of College & University Housing Officers–International (ACUHO-I) Information Technology Committee. He has authored an article on minority student retention issues and serves on the editorial board of the *Student Affairs Journal On-Line*.

T. Dary Erwin is director of the Center for Assessment Research and Studies and professor of psychology at James Madison University. He received his B.S. degree and M.S. degree from the University of Tennessee and his Ph.D. degree in student development and measurement from the University of Iowa. He has previously been affiliated with Texas A&M University and the University of Tennessee. Erwin is a past recipient of the Annuit Coeptis Award of the ACPA and of the Ralph F. Berdie Memorial Research Award of the American Association for Counseling and Development, is past chairperson of the Measurement Services Association, and is currently on the editorial board of *Active Learning in Higher Education*. He is author of *Assessing Student Learning and Development: A Guide to the Principles, Goals, and Methods of Determining College Outcomes* (Jossey-Bass, 1991).

Donald D. Gehring is professor and director of the doctoral program in higher education administration at Bowling Green State University in Ohio. He earned a B.S. degree (1960) in industrial management at the Georgia Institute of Technology, an M.Ed. degree (1966) in mathematics education at Emory University, and an Ed.D. degree (1971) in higher education at the University of Georgia. He was first president of the Association for Student Judicial Affairs, a member of the board of directors of the CAS, and the NASPA Foundation. He is the editor of *The College Student and the Courts*. Gehring is an ACPA senior scholar diplomate, holder of the SACSA Melvene Hardee Award for Contribution to Student Affairs, the H. Howard Davis Award for Outstanding Service to the Association, the recipient of the NASPA Robert H. Shaffer Award for Academic Excellence as a Graduate Faculty Member and the NASPA Outstanding Contribution to Literature or Research Award.

Joan B. Hirt is an associate professor of higher education and student affairs in the Department of Educational Leadership and Policy Studies at Virginia Polytechnic Institute and State University. She received her B.A. degree (1972) in Russian studies from Bucknell University, her M.A.Ed. degree in college student personnel administration (1979) from the University of Maryland, College Park, and her Ph.D. degree (1992) in higher education policy and administration from the University of Arizona. Prior to assuming a faculty position, she was associate director of housing and dining service at Humboldt State University. She is a former president of the Western Association of College and University Housing Officers and former Director of Commission XII of the ACPA. Hirt is an editor (with Steve Janosik, Don Creamer, and Roger Winston, Brunner-Routledge, in press) of a book on supervising new professionals in higher education and a book on the supervised experience in higher education (with Diane Cooper, Sue Saunders, and Roger Winston, Brunner-Routledge, in press). She was the recipient of ACPA's Annuit Coeptis Award for emerging professionals in 1997.

Barbara Jacoby is director of commuter affairs and community service at the University of Maryland in College Park. She is also director of the National Clearinghouse for Commuter Programs. Having received her Ph.D. from the University of Maryland in 1978, she is affiliate associate professor of college student personnel and instructor of French. Jacoby's books include: *The Student as Commuter: Developing a Comprehensive Institutional Response* (ERIC-ASHE, 1989), *Service-Learning in Higher Education: Concepts and Practices* (Jossey-Bass, 1996), and *Involving Commuter Students in Learning* (Jossey-Bass, 2000) in the New Directions for Higher Education series. In addition to holding leadership positions in the ACPA and the NASPA, she serves on the board of directors of the CAS.

Steven M. Janosik is a senior policy analyst and associate professor in the Department of Educational Leadership and Policy Studies at Virginia Polytechnic Institute and State University (Virginia Tech) and codirector of the Educational Policy Institute of Virginia Tech. He received a B.S degree (1973) in business administration from Virginia Tech, an M.A. degree (1975) in student personnel in higher education from the University of Georgia, and an Ed.D. degree (1987) in educational administration from Virginia Tech. Prior to assuming a faculty position, he served as deputy secretary of education for the Commonwealth of Virginia. He has served as editor of the *Journal of College and University Student Housing*, and a member of the executive committee of the Association for Student Judicial Affairs. He is currently a reviewer for the *Journal of College Student Retention* and the *Journal of Counseling and Development*. Janosik has received the Outstanding Research Award from Commission III of the ACPA and the D. Parker Young Award for outstanding scholarship and research in the areas of higher education law and judicial affairs from ASJA.

Susan R. Jones is assistant professor in higher education and student affairs and director of the Student Personnel Assistantship Program in the School of Educational Policy and Leadership at the Ohio State University in Columbus. She received a B.A. degree (1978) in sociology from Saint Lawrence University, an M.Ed. degree (1981) in higher education and student affairs from the University of Vermont, and a Ph.D. degree (1995) in college student personnel from the University of Maryland. Prior to joining the faculty at Ohio State, she was the assistant director of campus programs and student union at the University of Maryland and dean of students at Trinity College of Vermont. She has served on the executive board of the National Association for Women in Education (NAWE) and is currently on the editorial board of the *Journal of College Student Development*. Jones received the ACPA Annuit Coeptis Award for emerging professionals from the ACPA, the Dorothy Truex Emerging Professional Award from the NAWE, and the Salva Dignitate Award from the University of Vermont.

Marcia B. Baxter Magolda is professor of educational leadership at Miami University in Oxford, Ohio. She received her B.A. degree (1974) at Capital University, her M.A. degree (1976) and her Ph.D. degree (1983) from the Ohio State University in college student personnel/higher education. She teaches student development theory and inquiry courses in the College Student Personnel Master's Program. Her books include *Creating Contexts for Learning and Self-Authorship: Constructive-Developmental Pedagogy* (1999, Vanderbilt University Press), *Knowing and Reasoning in College* (1992, Jossey-Bass), and *Assessing Intellectual Development* (1988, ACPA). She edited *Linking Students' Worldviews, Identities, and Learning: Teaching to Promote Intellectual and Personal Maturity*, *New Directions for Teaching and Learning* (Jossey-Bass, in press). She serves on the editorial board of the *American Educational Research Journal*, the Board of contributors of *About Campus*, and is a member of the ACPA Senior Scholars. She was named as one of 40 young leaders in academe by *Change* magazine in 1998.

Theodore (Ted) K. Miller is professor emeritus at the University of Georgia in Athens, Georgia. He received a B.S. degree (1954) in business and English education and an M.A. degree (1957) in guidance and counseling from Ball State University and an Ed.D. degree (1962) in counseling and student personnel services from the University of Florida. Prior to his retirement in 1997, Miller spent 30 years as professor and coordinator of the student personnel in higher education program in the Department of Counseling and Human Development Services at the University of Georgia and was department head from 1993 to 1996. From 1989 to 1992 he was director of the university's Southern Association of Colleges and Schools (SACS) Accreditation Reaffirmation Self-Study. Prior to his tenure at Georgia, he was a head resident counselor at the University of Florida and a counseling psychologist and assistant professor at the University of Buffalo. Miller has been active in professional associations over the years and was president of the ACPA (1975–1976), the CAS (1979–1989), and the Georgia College Personnel Association (1969–1970). He has been the recipient of several professional association awards for contributions to the field of student affairs. In addition to the presentation of numerous national and international keynote addresses, conference programs, and skill-building workshops, he has authored or edited 11 professional books and monographs and upward of 50 book chapters and journal articles.

Dennis C. Roberts is assistant vice president for student affairs at Miami University in Oxford, Ohio. He is also an assistant professor in the Educational Leadership Department. He received his B.A. degree in music (1971) and M.Ed. degree in student personnel administration (1973) from Colorado State University and his Ph.D. in college student personnel (1979) from the University of Maryland. Roberts was the first chair of the ACPA Commission IV Leadership Task Force, which resulted in the publication of *Student Leadership Programs in Higher Education* in 1982. He also served as chair of ACPA Commission IV, was vice president for commissions in 1982–1984, and president in 1985–1986. He edited *Designing Campus Activities to Foster a Sense of Community* (Jossey-Bass, 1989). Roberts was recognized by ACPA in 1990 with the Annuit Coeptis Senior Professional Award and in 1999 with the 75th Anniversary Diamond Award. The University of Maryland Department of Counseling and Personnel Services awarded him the first Thomas M. Magoon Distinguished Alumni Award in 1989.

Arthur Sandeen is professor of higher education at the University of Florida in Gainesville. He earned a B.A. degree in psychology in 1960 from Miami University, Ohio, his M.A. degree in college student personnel administration from Michigan State University in 1962, and his Ph.D. degree from Michigan State in 1965 in administration and higher education. Between 1965 and 1973 Sandeen served as associate dean and then dean of students and associate professor of higher education at Iowa State University. In 1973, he was appointed the vice president for student affairs and professor of higher education at the University of Florida and served in this position until August 1999 when he joined the teaching faculty full time. Sandeen was elected president of the NASPA in 1977, and in 1987 he chaired the committee that wrote the report, "A Perspective on Student Affairs," commemorating the 50th anniversary of the "Student Personnel Point of View." He is the author of numerous articles and book chapters and has written three books, including *The Chief Student Affairs Officer: Leader, Manager, Mediator, Educator* (Jossey-Bass, 1991). He received the Fred Turner Award in 1982 for contributions to NASPA, the Scott Goodnight award in 1990 for outstanding performance as a dean, and NASPA's award for contributions to research and the literature in 2000.

Sue A. Saunders is dean of student affairs at Lycoming College in Williamsport, Pennsylvania. She received a B.S.J. degree (1972) in journalism and an M.Ed. degree (1973) in counseling from Ohio University, and a Ph.D. degree (1979) in counseling and student personnel services from the University of Georgia. She was a member of the faculty in student affairs administration at the University of Georgia and dean of students, executive assistant to the president, and counselor at Longwood College. She served on the ACPA Executive Council as Director of the Core Council for the Generation and Dissemination of Knowledge and as the president of the Virginia division of ACPA, and as the chair of the Virginia Administrative Leadership Commission. Her research focuses on professional development, staff supervision, and the application of student development theory to professional practice. Saunders is a recipient of the Annuit Coeptis and Diamond Honoree awards given by the ACPA.

John H. Schuh is professor of educational leadership at Iowa State University where he is also department chair. Previously he held administrative and faculty assignments at Wichita State University, Indiana University at Bloomington, and Arizona State University. He earned his B.A. degree (1969) in history from the University of Wisconsin at Oshkosh and his M.Ed. degree in counseling (1972) and Ph.D. (1974) degree from Arizona State University. Schuh is the author or editor of more than 150 publications. Among his books are *Educational Programming and Student Learning in College and University Residence Halls*, *Violence on Campus* (with Allan Hoffman and Robert Fenske, Jossey-Bass), the Assessment in Student Affairs (with M. Lee Upcraft, Jossey-Bass) and *Involving Colleges* (with George Kuh, Elizabeth Whitt, and Associates, Jossey-Bass). Currently, he is editor-in-chief of the New Directions for Student Services Sourcebook Series and is associate editor of the *Journal of College Student Development*. Schuh has received the Contribution to Knowledge Award and the Presidential Service Award from the ACPA, the Contribution to Research or Literature Award from the NASPA, and the Leadership and Service and S. Earl Thompson Awards from the ACUHO-I.

Michael J. Siegel is a doctoral candidate in the higher education program at Indiana University in Bloomington and former project manager of the College Student Experiences Questionnaire. He received a B.A. degree in psychology from Wake Forest University (1989) and an M.S. degree in counseling and psychological services from Georgia State University (1992). Prior to his work at Indiana University, Siegel was assistant to the executive vice president at Reinhardt College in Waleska, Georgia, where he also served as an instructor of sociology.

Stephen A. Sivo is an assistant professor of psychology/assistant assessment specialist at James Madison University in Harrisonburg, Virginia. He received a B.A. degree (1987) in psychology from Franciscan University, an M.A. degree (1991) in student personnel services from Northwestern State University of Louisiana, and a Ph.D. degree (1997) in research, measurement, and statistics/educational psychology from Texas A&M University. At James Madison University, he teaches structural equation modeling, multivariate statistics, and advanced measurement theory for the assessment and measurement Psy.D. program. Furthermore, he assists all programs in the division of student affairs with program evaluation and assessment. Prior to his current position he was a psychometrician intern in the Training Center at Pennsylvania Power and Light Nuclear Power facility. He is the author of several peer-reviewed journal articles, the latest of which concern the use of structural equation modeling (SEM) to analyze longitudinal panel data.

Auden D. Thomas is a doctoral student in higher education at Indiana University in Bloomington, where she holds a chancellor's fellowship. She received a B.A. degree (1986) in telecommunications from Pennsylvania State

University and an M.F.A. degree (1990) in dance from Temple University. Prior to pursuing doctoral work, she served as the director of student activities and special projects at the University of the Arts and as the director of student activities/coordinator of student volunteer services at Widener University, and worked in admissions at Carolina Friends School. She is currently project associate with the College Student Experiences Questionnaire Research and Distribution Program at Indiana University's Center for Postsecondary Research and Planning.

M. Lee Upcraft is a research associate in the Center for the Study of Higher Education, assistant vice president emeritus for student affairs, and affiliate professor emeritus of higher education at the Pennsylvania State University. He received both his B.A. degree (1960) and his M.A. degree (1961) in guidance and counseling from the State University of New York at Albany, and his Ph.D. degree (1967) in student personnel administration from Michigan State University. He is a senior scholar diplomate of the ACPA, and the author/editor of more than 100 publications, including his most recent book *Assessment in Student Affairs: A Guide for Practitioners* (with John H. Schuh, Jossey-Bass).

Roger B. Winston, Jr., is professor of college student affairs administration in the Department of Counseling and Human Development Services at the University of Georgia in Athens, where he coordinates the doctoral program in student affairs administration. He received a B.A. degree (1965) in history from Auburn University, an M.A. degree (1970) in philosophy, and a Ph.D. degree (1973) in counseling and student personnel services from the University of Georgia. Prior to assuming teaching duties at the University of Georgia in 1978, he was the dean of men at Georgia Southwestern State University. He has served on the ACPA's Executive Council and the CAS and the National Academic Advising Association's boards of directors, been editor of *ACPA Developments*, and is currently on the editorial boards of the *Journal of College Student Development* and *NASPA Journal*. He is also the editor of the *Georgia Journal of College Student Affairs*. He is author or editor of 10 books and more than 100 journal articles and book chapters; his most recent books are *Improving Staffing Practices in Student Affairs* (with Don Creamer, Jossey-Bass, 1997), *Student Housing and Residential Life: A Handbook for Professionals Committed to Student Development Goals* (with Scott Anchors, Jossey, Bass, 1993), and a psychosocial development assessment instrument, the *Student Developmental Task and Lifestyle Assessment* (with Theodore Miller and Diane Cooper, Student Development Associates, 1999). Winston is an ACPA senior scholar diplomate, holder of the Southern Association for College Student Affairs (SACSA) Melvene Hardee Award for Contributions to Student Affairs, and recipient of the ACPA Contribution to Knowledge Award and the National Academic Advising Association's Outstanding Researcher Award.

Dudley B. Woodard, Jr., is professor of higher education at the Center for the Study of Higher Education, University of Arizona in Tempe, where he previously served as vice president for student affairs. Woodard earned his B.A. degree (1962) in psychology from McMurray College and both his M.A. degree

(1965) in human relations and his Ph.D. degree (1969) in counseling from Ohio University. He is a past president of the NASPA and an ACPA senior scholar. Recent books include *Student Services: A Handbook for the Profession* (3rd edition) with Susan Komives (Jossey-Bass, 1996).

Robert B. Young is professor and chair of the Department of Counseling and Higher Education and director of the Center for Higher Education at Ohio University in Athens. Young earned a Ph.D. degree in higher education from the University of Illinois in 1975, an M.S. degree in counseling from California State University at Los Angeles, and an A.B. in history from the University of Rochester. He is the author of *No Neutral Ground: Standing by the Values We Prize in Higher Education* (Jossey-Bass), and the editor of five books, including *The Essential Values of the Profession*; *Invisible Leaders: Student Affairs Mid-managers* (NASPA, 1990); *The State of the Art of Preparation and Practice* (ACPA, 1992), and *Expanding Opportunities for Professional Education* (ACPA, 1988). He has served on the executive boards of NASPA and ACPA and received the Contribution to Knowledge, Senior Scholar, and senior Annuit Coeptis awards of the ACPA.

PART I

FOUNDATION AND CONTEXT

*P*art I serves as the foundation for this book and for understanding college student affairs administration. Just as with a foundation for a building, Part I assists readers in acquiring a solid, commonly shared understanding of student affairs administration and the milieu in which it operates. As noted in the Preface, the authors have made several assumptions about the readers of this book; that is, they assumed that readers possess a basic understanding of the philosophy and operating principles that underlie student affairs administration and higher education in the United States.

In Chapter 1, Creamer, Winston, and Miller briefly discuss how student affairs functions conceptually fit into the educational schema of an institution and how the renewed emphasis of student affairs practitioners to become more directly involved in students' learning finds expression. The chapter explores the roles of educator, leader, and manager that student affairs administrators are called upon to assume and provides historical and functional context for understanding how they complement, and sometimes conflict with, one another. Each role is examined in detail. The authors identify many kinds of skills and knowledge required of practitioners and describe the scope and function of practice associated with each. Finally, the authors address the question of professionalism: Is student affairs a profession? Can it be? Should it be? And how can practitioners enhance the continued development of the field?

Chapter 2, written by Kuh, Siegel, and Thomas, addresses four important questions: (a) What is collegiate culture and its various properties? (b) What are the core values of the academy and how do those values articulate with the cultures of student affairs, faculty, academic affairs, and other groups? (c) How are changing student demographics and other factors influencing campus culture? (d) What are the characteristics of the "culturally competent" student affairs practitioner as educator, leader, and manager? Only when student affairs administrators possess an adequate level of knowledge about the institutional culture within which they work can they hope to be successful in promoting the personal and educational development of students.

1

Dixon, in Chapter 3, tackles one of the most complex, emotion-laden, and perplexing issues facing American society and higher education today. How can those responsible for higher education attract, retain, and better educate more students of color and other minority culture representatives in our institutions? A heavy responsibility falls on student affairs to help create campus environments that are welcoming to minority students. Dixon points out that all in higher education, but especially student affairs practitioners, must become sensitive to both the pragmatic and the equity and fairness issues for moving toward a more inclusive teaching, learning, and living environment. He posits a useful model for practice called the Equity-Sensitive Perspectives model to guide student affairs practitioners toward achieving these difficult goals.

In Chapter 4, Elling and Brown address another pressing issue for higher education and student affairs: How do we utilize and manage the new electronic technologies to the service of higher education and its students? Change is occurring so rapidly in this arena that institutions have great difficulty in accommodating the change and even greater difficulty in foreseeing how such change may affect educational processes and students' personal development. Equally important, how can institutions obtain the financial resources to upgrade essential equipment and software? The authors offer a primer on the currently most widely used technologies, provide examples of innovative and successful uses that enhance the educational experience, and scan the future to alert us about what appears to be on the technology horizon.

READING SUGGESTIONS

Our suggested approach to reading Part I is to read Chapters 1 and 2 before reading other chapters in the book because they are fundamental to understanding most subsequent sections. Chapters 3 and 4 are relatively independent and may be read in the order prescribed by reader interest or need for information. Because the topics of the latter chapters concern two of higher education's more pressing concerns, it may be wise to read them before moving to other sections of the text.

1

The Professional Student Affairs Administrator:
Roles and Functions

DON G. CREAMER
ROGER B. WINSTON, JR.
THEODORE K. MILLER

<p>any student affairs practitioners have come to understand that for higher education to realize its educational potential and contribute to making its host nations more humane and just, all components of the enterprise must apply principles of student learning as affirmed by the Joint Task Force on Student Learning's *Powerful Partnerships* statement sponsored by the American Association for Higher Education (AAHE), American College Personnel Association (ACPA), and the National Association of Student Personnel Administrators (NASPA):</p>

> Realizing the full benefit [of the application of principles of learning] . . . to the practice of teaching, the development of curricula, the design of learning environments, and the assessment of learning . . . depends upon collaborative efforts between academic and student affairs professionals—and beyond. (AAHE, ACPA, & NASPA, 1998)

Too often, divisions of student affairs in colleges and universities appear to be organizationally separated from other units, such as academic and business affairs, within the same institution. This separation, however, is only palpable on organization charts. The best and most effective institutions fully integrate student, academic, and business affairs in a manner that focuses all resources on a primary goal of higher education—student learning and personal development—and involves every organizational unit fully in the achievement of its mission. Mission statements and the institution's "living mission" (Barr, 2000)

Structural approach

(as demonstrated through language, history, location, purpose, academic programs, and campus governance systems) are crucial guiding directives for student affairs administrators and all other institutional educators and leaders. Student affairs professionals and other educators strive to fulfill the institution's mission through their specialized educational programs and services. Furthermore, all institutional units—including student affairs—participate in multiple organizational roles and serve multiple internal and external constituencies, including, but not necessarily limited to, students, faculty, executive leaders, boards of trustees, legislative bodies and politicians, members of the media, and parents and families.

Such involvement in central institutional functions by student affairs practitioners is not new. Effective institutions have long viewed student affairs professionals as partners in the total educational enterprise. In 1976, for example, Miller and Prince in their now-classic book, *The Future of Student Affairs*, recognized the importance of fully integrating all educational programs and services. They argued that the mission of the institution is to educate the whole student, not only the student's intellect: "Agreement on this principle is manifested in the way personal development goals are woven into the formal academic fabric of the institution and the way all the educators and staff members collaborate to encourage students' growth" (Miller & Prince, 1976, p. 169).

Although fully integrated in higher education, student affairs programs and services function professionally as a distinguishable set of educational and management activities that occur mostly, though not exclusively, outside the formal classroom. The best administrators of students affairs strive continuously to create learning environments that represent seamless opportunities for student learning. These professionals apply the best principles of teaching and learning (AAHE, ACPA, & NASPA, 1998; ACPA, 1996) and employ the best practices of the field (ACPA/NASPA, 1996). *Powerful Partnerships: A Shared Responsibility for Learning* (AAHE, ACPA, & NASPA, 1998) is a call to arms via collaborative educational methods to promote student learning and personal development. The report documented multiple ways to employ collaborative methods and exhibits how higher education professionals of all types have roles to play in the application of learning principles. Likewise, the "Student Learning Imperative: Implications for Student Affairs" (ACPA, 1996) included a similar call, especially to student affairs professionals, to commit to the achievement of the institution's central purpose—to promote student learning and personal development. This report provided multiple avenues that student affairs professionals can use to accomplish their educational goals by remaining focused on learning as a central purpose. Continuing in this vein, *Principles of Good Practice for Student Affairs* (ACPA/NASPA, 1996), later expanded into book form (Blimling & Whitt, 1999), is a report of "best practices" in the field and emphasized the vital nature of active learning and the multiple ways student affairs professionals can work to achieve the institution's and students' goals.

The administration of student affairs programs and services has evolved from marginal or ancillary duties of faculty members to specialized functions central to effective institutions of higher education. These functions provide vital support to college and university students through such traditional programs and services as admissions, student financial aid, new student orientation, advising and counseling, career services, campus activities, recreational sports, health and wellness education, and residential life programs. Many longtime student affairs–provided services have indirectly supported the institution's educational mission, such as maintaining order on the campus, assisting students to deal with the emotional demands of academic life and growing up, providing safe and comfortable housing, and managing the class registration system. These traditional roles have been expanded in recent years to include more intentional efforts to shape the student learning environment and to make the campus a more inviting place for those who have been excluded from or ignored by higher education in the past, such as racial and ethnic minorities; nontraditional-aged students; gay, lesbian, bisexual, and transgender students; commuting students; students with disabilities; and women. In addition, student affairs administrators are expected to address myriad student conditions that mirror the larger societies from which the increasingly diverse student population comes. They are expected to provide far-reaching services and environmental redesign initiatives to remove or lessen barriers to student learning and academic success. Contemporary student affairs administrators also must effectively provide services to the increasing number and diversity of students in part-time status at the institution, for example, or who never come to the campus, such as distance learners.

To accomplish these vital functions, student affairs administrators must perform as educators, leaders, and managers. The professional student affairs administrator must integrate these roles fully to meet the needs of students and their college or university. Further, the professional student affairs administrator must perform these duties in large and small institutions, in public and in private institutions, and in institutions of all types, including community colleges, liberal arts colleges, state and regional institutions, and research universities.

Professional student affairs practitioners can be, and often are, powerful partners (AAHE, ACPA, & NASPA, 1998) with faculty and administrators in making students' educational experiences intellectually stimulating, practically applicable, and personally meaningful. They promote student learning and personal development through the execution of multiple educational activities that are fundamental to the basic purposes of higher education and they execute them using principles of collaborative and active learning.

Other functions that student affairs divisions perform in higher education are essential to organizational efficiency and effectiveness and the institution's educational mission. These functions are best performed by persons who are both knowledgeable and experienced in designing and operating mechanisms that assure the smooth and effective operation of the institution and also promote the educational and personal development of all its students.

Persons who are employed to attend effectively to both the educational mission of the institution and the organization's maintenance requirements in ways that are consistent with the historical values and ethnical principles of the field are known as *professional student affairs administrators*.

This chapter provides a conceptual foundation for the discussions throughout the remainder of this volume by describing student affairs administration as an essential component of higher education's most basic purposes. It also presents an integrated model of the student affairs administrator as educator, leader, and manager and examines the professional stature of student affairs in higher education. Each aspect of this conceptual scheme is briefly described here but is expanded upon in Chapters 2–16.

EDUCATION AS A MORAL ENDEAVOR

First, it is important to underscore the basics of higher education and to describe the relationship of student affairs to those functions. The raison d'être of higher education is to enable individual development in a context of creating and maintaining community rooted in democracy. This view of the purposes of education at all levels is articulated by many educational philosophers and recently in a particularly articulate fashion by the eminent educational philosopher and reformer, John I. Goodlad, in his acclaimed *In Praise of Education* (1997). Thus, higher education, indeed all education, is concerned with two purposes: providing the means for achieving individual goals related to self and insuring that individual development occurs in a context that promotes and sustains a democratic society. Goodlad pointed out that there is considerable tension between these two purposes, but for education to fulfill its most basic function in society, one purpose cannot be promoted without the other. For these reasons, education, and thus the administrative function, is part of a moral endeavor. Education is moral because it is intimately concerned with both the individual and the community. This focus is different from moralistic or self-righteous behavior; rather, it recognizes that all education is moral in that it focuses on these two inextricably intertwined purposes. To imagine it otherwise is to be thinking of something else, according to Goodlad (1997).

As asserted throughout this book, professional student affairs administrators function as educators, leaders, and managers. The educative role must ensure that the college or university functions over which the administrator presides are actively and unswervingly engaged in promoting both individual and community development. In the role as leader, student affairs administrators must marshal resources from the environment—human, physical, and fiscal—and bring them to bear on the tasks and activities within their domain of responsibility. The purpose for these environmental manipulations should always be accomplished to promote the educational mission of the institution, which is development of the individual—mind, body, and character. In the manager role, student affairs administrators must oversee people and resources to ensure that they are directed toward achieving the goals of both the unit and the institution. Often one of the administrator's more important functions is to make sure that there is an adequate infrastructure (for example, space, heat, lighting, trained personnel, and equipment) to accomplish the institution's goals. As Goodlad (1997, p. x) noted, "Since one is educated by the entire surroundings, education is environmentally ubiquitous." When fulfilling these roles, it is vital that student affairs administrators understand that education, no matter its form or host, is concerned with individual and community development. The student affairs administrator must not be swayed from these two essential purposes.

Young (1996) asserted that these purposes also are captured in the most basic values of the student affairs profession—individuation, or a concern for human dignity, and community, and a concern for the establishment of meaningful relationships. These values run through all of education, especially those forms known as liberal or general education that occur in almost all types of colleges, but they especially drive the actions of student affairs professionals who embody educational activities explicitly aimed at promoting these values. Student affairs administrators, acting in their multiple roles of educator, leader, and manager, organize campus resources to achieve these purposes for all students.

Related to this most basic concern for education is a second fundamental purpose of student affairs administration: The student affairs administrator should act as a moral conscience of the campus. Although all members of the academic community—faculty, staff, students, and administrators alike—are expected to exhibit good character in all of their dealings, student affairs administrators have a special responsibility in this regard. Not only must they exhibit strong moral character, but because of their unique relationships with students and others on and off campus, student affairs administrators must also take responsibility to assure that others understand and reasonably adhere to the moral, ethical, and legal expectations of the campus community. Student affairs administrators have traditionally been responsible for monitoring student conduct and administering the disciplinary process. Student affairs professionals fulfill the function of moral conscience in multiple ways, for instance, by (a) serving as a role model of responsible, reasoned, compassionate, and ethical conduct while fulfilling professional responsibilities and in their personal lives; (b) fairly and impartially applying the institution's conduct code and other rules and policies; and (c) challenging unethical, illegal, and unjust behavior or policies wherever encountered.

SCOPE OF STUDENT AFFAIRS ADMINISTRATION

Student affairs administrators occupy many different roles in higher education. Some are entry-level staff members who provide direct educational service to students such as campus activities programmers, residence life staff, academic support personnel, health and wellness consultants, and coordinators of special services and projects for students. Many are midlevel supervisors of complex functional units such as directors of career services, judicial programs, and academic advising. Others are executive-level managers with direct responsibilities for the superintendence of many other educators and staff members and of multimillion-dollar budgets such as deans or vice presidents for student affairs. Some student affairs administrators may be functional specialists, such as financial aid or disciplinary hearing officers, while others may occupy generalist functions such as advisors of student groups or organizations, directors of testing and assessment centers, or academic support providers. Most of these professionals carry out their duties and responsibilities in out-of-class settings (Miller & Jones, 1981), but they have the same commitments to educate students as do faculty members, who execute their educational functions inside class and laboratory settings. In fact, according to Sandeen (1991), "most student affairs leaders define their primary responsibility as educators" (p. 6). These administrative roles continue to grow in number and importance throughout higher education. By virtue of increased numbers and diversity of college students and increased educational functions assumed by institutions, by choice or by government mandate, administrative functions assumed by student affairs professionals in higher education are growing steadily. It is likely that this constant rise in administrative functions will continue. In fact, the responsibilities of creating and sustaining multicultural communities to better prepare college graduates for leadership responsibilities in global societies suggest that the trend toward more diversified roles may accelerate and that educational requirements for these administrators will become even more rigorous.

A MODEL FOR STUDENT AFFAIRS ADMINISTRATION

Today's student affairs administrator is expected to educate, lead, and manage. This concept is depicted in Figure 1.1. The three dominions depicted constitute the principal roles of student affairs administration. Each of these domains or dimensions must be performed well for an administrator to be effective.

THE EDUCATOR DOMAIN

The fundamental domain of student affairs administration as it enters the twenty-first century is education, carried out in an integrated and collaborative manner with faculty and staff members from other major institutional organizational units. Student affairs administration is conducted within institutions of higher learning with rich traditions of transmitting knowledge and culture to students through conventional pedagogical modes, such as lecture, laboratory work, and library research. Even though for most student affairs practitioners teaching occurs outside the traditional classroom most of the time, nevertheless it is committed to precisely the same purposes as the instruction occurring in the conventional classroom.

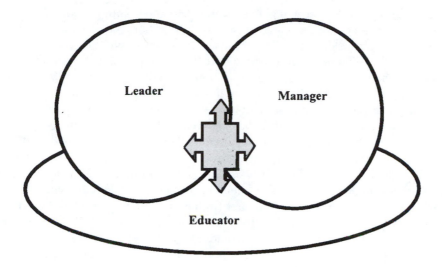

FIGURE 1.1. Domains of Student Affairs Administration

Historical Evolution

Student affairs administrators always have been educators in practice, if not in position title or by popular perception. Their duties and responsibilities, even in the earliest days, were to take on tasks resulting from faculty members' increased emphasis on research and furtherance of their academic disciplines and a concomitant decreased emphasis on students' personal, nonintellective development. Initial efforts to classify these new service providers resulted in assigning them titles such as *appointment secretary* to assist students to obtain employment upon graduation. The first such operation was called a personnel bureau (Yoakum, 1919/1994). Early student affairs practitioners worked to deliver educational services directly to students and to provide individualized attention in the institution's attempt to educate the whole person. They sponsored debate societies, organized and coached competitive events, and guided students in the exercise of civic activities. Such services, later expanded exponentially and into broader arenas of educational responsibility and institutional forms, were designed to enable students more fully to take advantage of institutional resources, but they clearly represented specialized forms of teaching.

The Student Personnel Point of View (*SPPV*, American Council on Education [ACE], 1937) was the first and arguably the most important document to describe the functions of the emerging profession of student affairs and to demonstrate the proper relationships of *student personnel* (the language of the day) to other aspects of higher education. Significantly, this statement articulated the philosophy of American higher education and underscored its commitment to the development of the whole person. By implication, the document recognized and acknowledged the separation between institutions' academic and support service functions and suggested that student personnel were fully devoted to the holistic philosophy of education. Even though the language of the 1937 version of the *SPPV* was couched in *service-oriented* language, its overall message was that student personnel workers were fully committed to teaching that which was needed to ensure that students could take full advantage of the available educational opportunities. Subsequently, the 1949 revision of the *SPPV* employed *needs-oriented* language to expand upon the responsibilities of student personnel workers, but the overarching concepts presented strongly suggested direct educational roles for members of the emerging profession.

Esther Lloyd-Jones and Margaret Ruth Smith (1954) presented this educative theme most dramatically in their book *Student Personnel Work as Deeper Teaching*. They provided explicit examples of how student personnel work was actually teaching in a somewhat unorthodox, unconventional form. They further argued, as the title of their landmark book suggests, that student personnel work was deeper than conventional forms of teaching. It penetrated, in their view, to the core functions of higher education and sought to facilitate whole person development through multiple educational functions, many of them traditionally administrative in nature.

In the late 1960s, following nearly a decade of student unrest on many campuses and radical changes in social and political attitudes on and off campus, questions were raised about the field of student affairs, its basic purpose, and its modus operandi. Significantly, in 1961 (*Dixon vs. Alabama*) the federal courts fundamentally altered the conceptual nature of the relationship between students and public institutions. Dating from the earliest days of higher education in the United States, colleges were seen to have parental-like responsibilities for students. Thus, the concept of in loco parentis (acting in the place of the parent) evolved as a means of describing the nature of the relationship between students and their institutions. Student affairs staff members had the responsibilities of supervising minor students, as do parents, with few restraints on the measures to be used to direct and discipline students (as is still true of parents today). *Dixon vs. Alabama* represented the legal death knell of in loco parentis in that the court ruled that students in public institutions retained all citizenship rights after they enroll. (Even though *Dixon vs. Alabama* did not apply to students enrolled at private colleges—the relationship there is defined by contract—most private institutions adopted policies and procedures closely aligned to those in effect at comparable public institutions.) As a means of establishing other foundations for student affairs work, the field turned its attention toward emerging theories of human development.

These theories offered plausible explanations for the behavior of college students and the processes by which they learned and developed. The rapid adoption of this *student development* point of view, widely perceived as an important adaptation of student services as articulated in the *SPPV*, was aided significantly by publication of *Student Development in Tomorrow's Higher Edu-*

cation (Brown, 1972). Wide-ranging discussions among professionals in the field followed this publication about the implementation of a developmental perspective in student affairs. Significantly, Brown (1972) discussed several roles that should be altered in student affairs if a developmental approach were adopted. One role that he described was that of *student development educator*, in which multiple teaching functions were envisioned for student affairs professionals.

The Brown (1972) monograph was prepared as Phase I under the auspices of the ACPA's Tomorrow's Higher Education (THE) Project, which shortly thereafter spawned the book, *The Future of Student Affairs* (Miller & Prince, 1976). This book, which represented Phase II of the THE Project, articulated an integrated student development model that incorporated several developmental strategies, including instruction as well as goal setting, assessment, consultation, milieu management, and program evaluation. The instructional strategy clearly emphasized the role of teaching in the developmental processes of student affairs programs. Further, numerous exemplary developmental programs, including their educational strategies, were described.

Recently in the evolution of milestone professional documents, *The Student Learning Imperative* (*SLI*; ACPA, 1996) was published by the ACPA and later endorsed by the NASPA. This document represented yet another adaptation for student affairs practice, this time focusing specifically on the outcomes of student affairs programs and services on student learning and personal development. Importantly, this initiative represented another reminder that the work of student affairs practitioners is principally educational in nature. It is, in fact, devoted precisely toward the same goals as their faculty colleagues—promoting learning and personality or self-development using instructional tactics.

The educational philosophy underpinning this domain is pragmatism, or an educational philosophy that links individuals, knowledge, and action (Young, 1996). This philosophy was seen in the *SPPV* statements (American Council on Education, 1937) and emphasizes the development of the whole person rather than intellectual aspects alone. Pragmatism rests, in part, on premises of respect for the uniqueness of the individual and beliefs that experience is the principal source of knowledge. Such philosophical commitments lead naturally to a commitment to student self-direction as a major goal of education where experience is valued and viewed as a predominate source of knowledge. Establishing environments that are conducive to this goal is a major responsibility of student affairs administrators. Learning communities (AAHE, ACPA, & NASPA, 1998; Kuh & Schuh, 1991; Kuh et al., 1991) may serve as examples of such environments by virtue of intentional arrangements designed to heighten student involvement and commitment to learning through self-initiated activities that promote the construction of meaning by the participants.

Skills and Knowledge Used

The teaching-oriented administrator first must be an expert on higher education and must demonstrate keen insight into the campus cultures and work to transmit this knowledge to all staff members of the organization. Campus cultures can be complicated and require comprehension by skilled observers who can translate them into realities upon which other practitioners can base their actions (Chapter 2 in this volume; Kuh & Hall, 1993; Kuh & Whitt, 1988).

Campus cultures are changing in some very important ways (Brown, 1997; Cheatham, 1991; Fried, 1995; Kuh, Whitt, & Shedd, 1987; Stage & Manning, 1992). Almost all institutions of higher learning are working to create multicultural communities. Rhoads and Black (1995) argued that the educator functions should take a critical cultural perspective in these transitions that actively seek understanding of the political, cultural, and economic forces that are shaping current communities. Too often educational environments are oppressive and must be overcome by actively teaching the "practice of freedom" (Rhoads & Black, 1995, p. 418). They envisioned student affairs administrators functioning as transformative educators who play significant roles in structuring and restructuring campus communities. The resulting profound changes heighten the importance of the teaching role for student affairs administrators who need to constantly monitor and translate campus cultures to multiple constituencies.

Brown (1997) described how administrators in student affairs can benefit from acting on disciplines of a learning organization. These disciplines are taken from Senge (1990) and relate to the quality of one's thinking and communication. The first discipline is called *personal mastery* and pertains to the constant examination of self as a means to increase one's personal capacities. According to Brown (1997), who interpreted Senge's five disciplines of a learning organization for student affairs administrators, "the role of leader is to encourage us all to live in the gap between compelling vision and current reality, without either lowering the vision or lying about current reality" (p. 6). Senge (1990) saw this mastery as "the discipline of continually clarifying and deepening our personal vision, of focusing our energies, of developing patience, and of seeing reality objectively" (p. 7). The second discipline pertained to *mental models* or theories held in one's head about how things work. According to Senge, these models are "deeply ingrained assumptions, generalizations, or even pictures or images that influence how we understand the world and how we take action" (p. 8). In effect, leaders help others to comprehend that there are alternative ways of understanding reality. The third discipline is *shared vision*, which Brown (1997) preferred to call *sharing vision* to emphasize the ongoing nature of the visioning process. This discipline is emphasized to enable all members of an organization to agree on a mutually established vision. The fourth discipline is *team learning* or the practice of using data about organizations for improved functioning. The discipline begins with dialogue, according to Senge (1990), and leads to a genuine "thinking together." The fifth discipline is *systems thinking* and calls on leaders to help all members comprehend the organization's big picture and not just its parts. Systems thinking is "the discipline that integrates the [other] disciplines, fusing them into a coherent body of theory and practice" (Senge, 1990, p. 12). Each of these disciplines requires the application of important teaching skills on the part of professional student affairs administrators.

Chickering and Gamson (1991) identified seven principles of good practice for teachers, which apply equally well to student affairs educators: (a) encourage student–faculty contact, (b) encourage cooperation among students, (c) encourage active learning, (d) give prompt feedback, (e) emphasize time on task, (f) communicate high expectations, and (g) respect diverse talents. Student affairs administrators can apply these principles in myriad programs and activities on a daily basis. Blimling and Alschuler (1996) described how these applications can occur in routine student affairs practices such as programming for intentional democratic communities, providing learning opportunities in student government and leadership training, conducting freshman seminars and workshops on time management and study skills, and intentionally creating and sustaining multicultural communities.

The student affairs administrator also functions as a pedagogical specialist in many roles. The administrator determines by what method staff training (Roper, 1996) is to be conducted, for example. All forms of teaching may find relevance in the innumerable activities of student affairs administration, including those typically associated with faculty roles such as lecturing, demonstrating, advising, coaching, modeling, evaluating, collaborating, and facilitating interactions with and among students. Table 1.1 displays these behavioral characteristics of educators more fully.

Teaching always incorporates the transmission of knowledge and increasingly includes the making of personally relevant meaning and the generation of knowledge. This latter activity is often referred to as constructing knowledge and occurs in settings that enable students to engage in active, cooperative, and collaborative learning (Chapter 11 in this volume; Baxter Magolda, 1992; Bonnell & Eison, 1991). These active forms of teaching are especially well suited to student affairs practice and may employ such tactics as case study methods, role-playing, simulations, computer-based instruction, debates, and peer teaching.

Many of the behavioral characteristics of educators are identified in Table 1.1. This list is not intended to be exhaustive, but is intended to assist readers in comprehending the breadth of activities that student affairs administrators as educators have at their command.

Scope and Functions of Practice

Through the administration of a broad range of functions, student affairs professionals educate students in both out-of-classroom and traditional classroom settings. In some instances they teach directly, such as in the education of staff colleagues and paraprofessionals or in continuing orientation courses for new students. In other cases, they teach students more indirectly, through provision of environments suitable for the application of knowledge and for reflections on learning experiences. They also provide environments for expression of interests, a vital aspect of promoting individual development in cultural context, and they make and execute policies that govern the actions of staff members and shape their manner of interacting with students.

TABLE 1.1. Behavioral Characteristics of Educators

Category	Brief Description
Lecturing	Making oral presentations of facts, theories, or information; relating personal experiences; telling how to do something; providing illustrative examples or approaches; reporting research findings
Demonstrating	Displaying behavior or manipulating equipment to explicate a principle, teach a process, or exhibit an approach
Advising	Listening to interests and concerns; aiding in identification of available resources; explaining institutional rules and procedures or laws; initiating cooperative problem solving; challenging unexamined assumptions, beliefs, and prejudices; providing emotional support
Coaching	Showing how to do something; offering suggestions; providing feedback about quality of performance; providing opportunities for practice in achieving mastery; helping perfect an activity; praising exemplary performance (usually done one-on-one)
Modeling	Showing by example; allowing self to be observed
Facilitating	Assisting an individual or group to make meaning of experiences; encouraging expression of feelings and examination of effects on others; encouraging discussion of ideas and exploration of implications; enabling democratic decision making
Learning	Gaining knowledge and skill through study and/or self-analysis; being a life-long learner
Researching	Seeking understanding of facts, theories, or conditions through systematic inquiry
Evaluating	Providing critique of ideas, performance, or product reflecting a comparison with a standard of excellence; correcting mistakes or errors
Collaborating	Engaging jointly with others to accomplish a goal; joining individual or group in solving a problem or learning new material; participating as an equal in collective process
Structuring	Providing assignments or tasks designed to explicate subject matter; creating exercises and opportunities for practice; identifying resources; offering a framework for examination of ideas, beliefs, values, and research methods and findings; creating or reinforcing psychosocial environment conducive to learning

An example of environments intentionally created for learning includes student affairs practices associated with residence halls, in which multiple teaching/learning opportunities are incorporated. Such practices include the provision of first-year seminars, leadership training, and theme houses focused on healthy and productive living or on a social orientation or academic discipline, such as a foreign culture and its language or engineering. Large-scale education of resident assistants, hall directors, and area or community coordinators also occurs in residence halls and serves as an explicit example of the teaching function of student affairs administrators.

Other examples can be taken from specialized environments such as practices common to commuter campuses. Community colleges are illustrative of this type of environment where many structured student affairs practices must be woven into the fabric of academic affairs for them to work well. Students on nonresidential campuses may come to campus for class, then leave for home or work. If they are to be reached by student affairs professionals, they must be encountered in academically related arenas or by electronic means. Academic advising, for example, is often conducted by student affairs professionals in these colleges, and through these practices they educate students directly as they assist in educational planning or fashioning career objectives. Good academic advisors encourage students to participate in nonrequired activities, such as student organizations or in out-of-class programs, which serves to enrich the quality and depth of educational experiences. Cultural and issue-related programs often reach students in these settings best when they are established and coordinated with faculty members whose courses relate to the programming content.

Likewise, the educative role can be observed in campus activities such as in the training of student leaders, organization advisors, and programming councils. They also are seen in the judicial arena where hearing officers teach community values through application of the student disciplinary process. In addition, new student orientation programs often reflect a preparation for future learning. Student affairs administrators acting in the roles of orientation directors teach students and parents about themselves and the richness of the learning opportunities available to them. In all of these activities, student affairs administrators have opportunities to instruct students about self-knowledge and the role of self-direction in learning and personal development. Even though all these activities may be personally meaningful and educational, that will not likely be the case unless they are intentionally planned and executed with educational goals at their foundation.

Perhaps the most pervasive, and arguably the most important, arena for teaching by student affairs administrators lies in the compelling requirements for creating and sustaining multicultural communities on campus. These communities, which operate simultaneously, represent the lifeblood of learning in a cultural context. Unless students can experience multiculturalism in real life, they cannot profit from it nor can they prepare themselves for living in increasingly global societies. This is one of the essential moral components of education—individual learning in the cultural contexts of diverse and democratic societies. (See Chapter 5 in this volume for more details in this area.)

THE LEADER DOMAIN

Student affairs administrators are designated institutional leaders by virtue of their formal placement in the organizational structure. They also serve to create and sustain visions for the campus community and act to shape institutional environments to achieve these visions.

Many scholars in the field of student affairs share this contemporary view of leadership (see Chapter 15 in this volume). Caple and Newton (1991), for example, urged administrators to view leadership as the application of self-organization theory. In this approach to leadership, student affairs practitioners focus their efforts on processes that create experiences for learners and act as catalysts for change rather than as maintainers of change. Caple and Newton also proffered seven propositions for effective leadership that evolved from their examination of the history of leadership theory and its practice in higher education.

They proposed that a leader

1. is aware of his or her role and responsibility within a system and of the connections that relate and affect this position;
2. is able to articulate and act consistently with a clear set of values;
3. demonstrates respect for people through actions that value human dignity;
4. is a model for others;
5. knows when to assert direct or indirect influence and when to distribute power;
6. is aware of the special nature of the system in which she or he is embedded and how this system relates (exchanges) energy with its environment;
7. is able to make transitions to higher levels of order and inspire people to achieve similar levels of functioning.

These propositions represent plausible action guidelines for effective leadership in that they recognize the contextual nature of leading. They suggest that leaders inspire followers to achieve a desirable new state or condition by shaping the environment for learning. This shaping process occurs by building a shared vision, empowering people, inspiring commitment, and enabling good decisions to be made through designing learning processes (Senge, 1990).

Building shared vision requires leadership that allows collective participation by all members of the student affairs staff in activities designed to gain consensus about the operational status of the current organization and the direction it is taking on the basis of its most public goals. Vision is not about buying into a position established by others. Rather, it is about accessing the individual and a collective sense of what matters most (Chapter 16 in this volume; Brown, 1997). Brown also asserted that "vision emerges from the community under the stewardship of good leadership" (p. 7). This form of leadership demands an understanding of the institution's culture and subtleties and skills in translating this understanding to others in clear language that enables them to participate in decision making.

Empowering people and inspiring commitment begins with the manifest value of respecting voices of all members of the organization. Organizations that value ideas and contributions of all members are more productive than are those that choose to limit such participation, and they are healthier in that they can take full advantage of their capacities to achieve goals. Members of such organizations tend to feel empowered to think as well as to act and they develop a sense of ownership by virtue of having their ideas respected. Ownership of ideas leads to a vested commitment by individuals regarding the outcomes of initiatives collectively determined.

Enabling good decisions through designing learning processes refers to creating conditions and procedures within the organization that lead to what Senge (1990) called the *learning organization*. According to Tobin (as cited in Freed, 1997) learning organizations tend to exhibit three characteristics: (a) an openness to new ideas, (b) a culture that encourages and provides opportunities for learning and innovation, and (c) widespread knowledge of the organization's overall goals and objectives and an understanding of how each person's work contributes to them. The effective student affairs leader must be able to create conditions within the organization that enable each of these processes to be fully functioning.

Knowledge and Skills Used

Komives, Lucas, and McMahon (1998) described leadership by its relationship properties. To them, leadership is "a relational process of people together attempting to accomplish change or make a difference to benefit the common good" (p. 68). In effect, relational leadership requires that the leader be self-aware, be open to differences and values in all perspectives, and practice listening skills, building coalitions, and effective civil discourse. Their model of relational leadership incorporates being inclusive of people and diverse points of view, empowering others who are involved, being purposeful in commitments and collaboration to achieve common objectives, being ethical in all conduct, and approaching all tasks from a process-oriented perspective. The skills of effective leaders are similar to the competencies, behaviors, and beliefs associated with postindustrial forms of leadership (Rost, 1991), as described by Rogers (1996), who argued that leadership involves many skills, including

1. understanding, valuing, and nurturing the group process (leaders and collaborators coming together for mutual purposes to bring about change);
2. collaborating and engaging in creative conflict (includes skills for successful community collaboration, or "democratic arts," as defined by Lappé and Du Bois (1994), including active listening, creative conflict, mediation, negotiation, political imagination, public dialogue, public judgment, celebration and appreciation, evaluation and reflection, and mentoring);
3. creating environments based on trust and empowerment (encouraging risk taking and enabling collaborators);
4. encouraging diverse voices (providing the means for all voices to be heard and putting oneself in the place of others);
5. knowing yourself and changing yourself first (reflecting about and beginning change with self);
6. creating and articulating a shared vision (uncovering meaning already embedded in other's minds; Bensimon & Neumann, 1993);

7. understanding and using political processes (employing noncoercive forms of persuasion);
8. developing a multiperspective view (understanding and acting upon the big picture of the organization).

Allen and Cherrey (2000) call for new ways of relating, influencing change, learning, and leading in their analysis of today's networked knowledge era. They contrast this networked orientation with its necessity of taking a whole systems approach to understanding leadership with a fragmented/hierarchical orientation. This leadership orientation is understood from an independent parts perspective, employing distinct boundaries, linear causality, incremental change, simple complexity, and the belief that structures can be controlled. By contrast, the networked orientation assumes a whole system perspective, blurred boundaries, nonlinear causality, dynamic flux, high-level complexity, and the belief that structures can only be influenced. The Internet is an example of a network with these characteristics.

From the networks perspective, leadership requires new ways of relating and influencing change (Allen & Cherrey, 2000). A new way of relating and influencing change "involves the capacity to build and maintain effective cooperative relationships across the boundaries of an organization and between the organization and the community" (p. 8). A new way of influencing change "involves more organic strategies that take into account the non-linear dynamics of the connected systems and its response to force" (p. 9).

Further, Allen and Cherrey (2000) characterize the industrial era with the knowledge era wherein the latter recognizes, among other qualities, that knowledge is the primary resource, that it is both infinite and systemic. Learning in the knowledge era involves "ongoing learning and integration of knowledge needed on both an individual and organizational level" (p. 15). Thus, the new ways of learning "involve leveraging diverse perspectives into collective or shared group intelligence and integrating theory, new capacities, and practice with one another" (p. 16). This latter idea is closely connected with Senge's (1990) notion of a learning organization.

These new perspectives on leadership result in what Allen and Cherrey (2000) call *systemic leadership*, which seamlessly integrates new ways of working and calls on practitioners to reframe assumptions about working and to adopt new roles. (See Chapter 15 in this volume.)

Conscience of the Campus Community

In addition to these pervasive actions of leaders, student affairs administrators also should serve as a conscience of the campus. This is not a responsibility that can be delegated to others, but instead is one that is ideally shared with other administrative leaders, the faculty, students, and other institutional stakeholders.

This ethical role requires the application of broad ethical principles and role modeling. (See Chapter 8 in this volume.) Kitchener (1985) presented the most commonly accepted set of ethical principles applied in student affairs: (a) respect autonomy, (b) do no harm, (c) benefit others, (d) be just, and (e) be faithful. The competent student affairs administrator accepts these principles to guide practice. These principles often are articulated in greater detail in official statements or codes published by professional associations. The "Statement of Ethical Principles and Standards" published by the ACPA (1990) and the "NASP Standards of Professional Practice" (1993) are examples of written codifications provided by professional associations. (See Appendices B & C.) These statements serve to educate practitioners about potential ethical dilemmas by identifying behaviors or situations to avoid or by providing guidelines to minimize the deleterious effects of ethical breaches. They are, however, only one way of "doing" ethics, according to Canon (1996). In addition to applying broad ethical principles and formal codes, student affairs administrators should develop "an informal consensus about standards, generated and supported by a community that holds certain values in common" (p. 108). In this manner, student affairs administrators create individual ownership of the standards of practice to which they are expected to adhere. In this regard, the ethics components of the CAS Standards and Guidelines (Miller, 1999) represent professionwide ethical standards relevant to various student affairs functional areas. (See Appendix B.)

Scope and Functions of Practice

Clement and Rickard (1992) studied elements of effective leadership in student affairs by interviewing nominated leaders in the field. Deductive analyses of interviews identified essential leadership elements, relationships essential to success, challenges, and an ethic of care that pervaded practice by leaders. Although not surprising, certain personal attributes revealed in their study are essential building blocks for leadership. They include *integrity* (involving trust, honesty, loyalty, courage, and risk taking), *commitment* (evidenced by a positive attitude toward working with students, enthusiasm, joy, optimism, and passion for student services work), and *tenacity* (focusing on a strong work ethic, perseverance, patience, and follow-through).

Integrity, commitment, and tenacity are leader traits that suggest omnipresence by those operating in the forefront of organizations or units within them. Such people within organizations are visible translators of the culture who are actively engaged in the work of all members of the organization and who keep the units focused on agreed-upon goals. They model behavior they expect from others and they never give up in their pursuit of productive behavior on the part of all the staff members they lead.

Yukl (1998) identified 14 behavioral characteristics associated with leading. These are briefly described in Table 1.2 and further illustrate the magnitude of leadership knowledge and skills required by the effective student affairs administrator. None of these distinguishable leadership behaviors is mystifying or even especially difficult. It is when they are taken as a whole that they represent a formidable set of behavioral expectations for effective leaders to exhibit.

TABLE 1.2. Behavioral Characteristics of Leaders

Category	Brief Description
Planning and organizing	Determining long-term objectives and strategies, allocating resources according to priorities, assign responsibilities to staff; determining how to improve coordination and effectiveness of organizational unit
Problem solving	Identifying and analyzing work-related problems; acting decisively to implement solutions
Clarifying roles and objectives	Assigning tasks, providing direction on how to do work, clearly communicating responsibilities, task objectives, deadlines, and performance expectations
Informing	Disseminating relevant information about decisions, plans, and activities; answering questions and requests for information
Monitoring	Gathering information about work activities and external conditions; checking on the progress and quality of work; evaluating performance of individuals and units
Motivating and inspiring	Using influence techniques that appeal to emotion or logic to generate enthusiasm, commitment to work tasks, compliance with request for cooperation, assistance, support, or resources
Consulting	Checking with people before making changes that affect them; encouraging suggestions for improvement; inviting participation in decision making; incorporating the ideas of others in decisions
Delegating	Allowing subordinates to have substantial responsibility and discretion in carrying out activities, handling problems, and making important decisions
Supporting	Acting friendly and considerate; being patient and helpful; showing empathy and support when someone is upset or anxious; listening to complaints and problems; looking out for someone's interests
Developing and mentoring	Providing coaching and helpful career advice; doing things to facilitate staff's skill acquisition, professional development, and career advancement
Managing conflict and team building	Facilitating constructive resolution of conflict; encouraging cooperation, teamwork, and identification with the unit
Networking	Socializing informally; developing contacts with persons who are sources of information or support; maintaining contact over time
Recognizing	Providing praise and recognition for effective performance, significant achievements, and special contributions
Rewarding	Providing or recommending tangible rewards for effective performance, significant achievement, and demonstrated competence

Based on and adapted from Gary Yukl, *Leadership in Organizations*, p. 60. Copyright © 1998. Reproduced by permission of Prentice-Hall.

THE MANAGER DOMAIN

The management function of student affairs administration consists of providing oversight to all major functions of student affairs. These functions most often include admissions and recruitment, orientation, registration, financial aid, academic advising and support services, international student services, college unions and student activities offices, counseling services, career development, residence life, services for students with disabilities, intercollegiate activities, child care services, student health services, food services, dean of students services, community service and leadership programs, student judicial affairs, student recreation and fitness programs, student religious programs, special student populations services, commuter student services, and program research and evaluation (Sandeen, 1991).

Schools of Thought

Creamer and Frederick (1991) traced five schools of thought regarding management theory: classical scientific (the best work methods can be developed through science), human relations (people are motivated by needs), behavioral science (workers seek and are capable of finding self-fulfillment on the job), management process (the principles of management are universal), and quantitative (management can be explained by patterns of decisions within the framework of mathematical models). These historical models of management have been replaced by more current models, including total quality management (TQM; Bryan, 1996) or continuous quality improvement (CQI) as it is sometimes called.

According to Bryan (1996), TQM is best understood as a comprehensive philosophy of management in which community members

- are committed to CQI and to a common campus vision, set of values, attitudes, and principles;
- understand that campus processes need constant review to improve services to customers;
- believe the work of each community member is vital to customer satisfaction; and
- value input from customers. (p. 5)

TQM is based on the principles identified by Deming (1986) that are believed to help any organization develop a quality culture. Bryan (1996) summarized Deming's principles in a manner to make them directly applicable to student affairs:

1. Create a constancy of purpose toward improvement of services and programs.
2. Adopt a continuous improvement philosophy.

3. Build quality into processes from the beginning.
4. Develop productive relationships with parents, school educators, and students.
5. Improve continuously the ways in which students and other customers are served.
6. Institute training and development activities and programs for professional, support, and student staff.
7. Initiate educational leadership.
8. Eliminate fear.
9. Eliminate barriers to excellence.
10. Develop a quality culture.
11. Eliminate numerical objectives and quotas.
12. Remove barriers that hinder people in taking pride in their work or in being creative.
13. Institute a comprehensive program of professional development, education, and personal development.
14. Encourage a culture in which staff accepts responsibility for achieving excellence.

CQI works because it incorporates certain themes into practice that are consistent with other leadership and management propositions discussed in this chapter. These themes include values, mission, vision, teams, customers, shared leadership, continuous improvement, process, information, professional development, and empowerment. Perhaps above all, these themes include institutional cultures that embrace quality principles. Repeatedly, it can be seen in effective student affairs administration that these ideas are consistently present in practice.

It should be acknowledged that many management innovations, including TQM and CQI, have been seen by some critics as fads, or management ideas that enjoy brief popularity (Birnbaum, 2000). TQM and CQI work in some institutions better than in others. Many have tried to implement quality principles into their management practice and have found the benefits to be minimal or have even resulted in counterproductive effects. Such failures may have more to do with an inability to embrace quality principles in the institutional culture than with weaknesses in the management ideas themselves. Any management approach should be considered in the context of professional administration in all of its complexity, as is advocated throughout this book.

Aspirational management (Rogers & Ballard, 1995) is another example of a recommended approach to management in student affairs. This approach calls for the application of self-organizing models in student affairs administration and is premised on two features. First, self-organizing models place primacy value in people: "People, values, and customer satisfaction make the organization" (1995, p. 164). This view of people differs from more conventional models that assume that people must be controlled and managed. Second, self-organizing models assume much ambiguity in the external environment and in the organization and strive to create conditions that deal with instability. These new models rely upon open and lateral communication, continuous learning among all members of the organization, flexible and shared roles, and routine, informal, open, shared, and noncompetitive evaluation systems. According to Rogers and Ballard, four processes are necessary to sustain aspirational management: (a) creating a statement of aspirations based on the shared values of organization members; (b) living the aspirations and integrating them into organizational life; (c) providing continuous learning, training, and development opportunities for all members so they can achieve the aspirations; and (d) designing evaluation and reward procedures that reflect, reinforce, and further the aspirations. Taken together, these processes serve to keep managers focused on consensual goals and future conditions and help avoid getting mired in day-to-day issues.

Birnbaum's (2000) recent work, *Management Fads in Higher Education*, offers some salient advice to administrative practitioners in higher education that fits well into the nature of professional administration discussed herein. He writes, for example, that "Higher education does not need more good management techniques; it needs more good managers" (p. 239). He further contends that "Managing in a complex, knowledge-based, interpretive institution is difficult, frustrating, and imprecise. But good management is essential for institutional success, and to be a good manager is a goal worthy of the time and effort of administrators and faculty who are committed to the enduring purposes of higher education" (p. 240).

Knowledge and Skills Used

Student affairs administrators must be knowledgeable about and skillful in the management of human resources, institutional planning, assessment of programs and environments, budgeting, and use of technology and information systems. Each of these functions requires specific application of knowledge and skill crucial to effective administration.

Nothing is more vital to successful management of student affairs functions than the quality of the people employed in their respective roles (Winston & Creamer, 1997). Staff member quality generally is derived from three sources: (a) the quality of preservice education, (b) the correctness of the original decision to hire staff, and (c) the appropriateness and quality of in-service education provided to staff members. Successful student affairs administrators pay attention to hiring and nurturing staff members and recognize that people are the most valuable ingredient in student affairs. (See Chapter 8 in this volume for more detailed treatment of staffing in student affairs.)

Student affairs managers also must be skillful planners. Most healthy organizations are constantly in a state of flux as they adapt to economic or political conditions and change things that are not working well. Student affairs administrators must be able to establish and articulate a vision, involve all staff members in the crafting of plans, and orchestrate necessary changes in operations.

According to Schuh (1996), good planning involves several elements. He presented these elements in simplified form, although each element requires special talent by student affairs administrators to operationalize:

- Initiate the planning process.
- Review the institution's mission statement.
- Develop plans for each unit.
- Assess the environment.
- Develop a vision for success.
- Review preliminary plans.
- Identify alternatives and determine a final plan.

Environmental assessment. Assessing campus programs and environments requires special skill involving complex methods of observation and inquiry. Most approaches to assessing the campus environment are based on Kurt Lewin's (1936) well-known formulation: $B = f(P \times E)$; that is, behavior is a function of the interaction of the person and the environment.

There are four basic models, with some variations, that explain interrelationships between behavior and the context or environment: (a) physical models, (b) human aggregate models, (c) structural organizational models, and (d) perceptual models.

Physical models address how the natural environment (such as climate and topographical features) and human-made structures affect behavior (Strange, 1991). For example, in both very warm and very cold climates, certain kinds of activities are difficult if not impossible. Likewise, some building designs promote frequent communication while others make communication difficult because inhabitants seldom encounter one another.

Human aggregate models postulate that environments are transmitted through people and reflect the collective characteristics of the inhabitants. For example, the offices of advertising agencies generally look quite different from those of engineers because they are composed of different personality types; each of these environments exerts different influences on the people who work there.

Structural organizational models accentuate the importance of goals and purposes of environments; that is, "they have goals, explicit or implicit, that give them direction and, in turn, give rise to organized structures that affect inhabitants' behaviors and attitudes" (Strange, 1991, p. 172).

Perceptual models emphasize the importance of understanding how individuals experience an environment or their subjective interpretations of an environment. This approach rests on the premise that a consensus of individuals characterizing their environment constitutes a measure of climate that exerts an influence on behavior. Using Strange's illustration, suppose that the temperature of a room is 70 degrees Fahrenheit, which can be objectively measured by a thermometer. From the perceptual perspective, the only way to ascertain whether the room is warm or cold is to determine the perceptions of the people experiencing it. In effect, the perception, not the measured temperature, is the reality.

Program assessment.   According to Erwin (1996), the purposes of assessment may be both formative and summative. Formative assessments generally are conducted to determine student needs and program requirements for modification purposes. Summative assessments, on the other hand, generally are conducted for student certification or program funding at the end of an activity or project. Both quantitative and qualitative methods have utility for making judgments about campus culture, student performance, and program effectiveness and require doing four things well: (a) asking good questions, (b) observing and listening carefully, (c) thoughtfully interpreting the information for the people who need it, and (d) moving others to action by sharing what was learned in a simple, understandable fashion (Hanson, 1997).

Budgeting.   Meisinger and Dubeck (1984) held that budgeting is many things: a process, a plan of action, a control mechanism, a way of communicating, a contract, and a political tool. According to Woodward (1993),

> As a process, a budget allows for the participation of constituents in consensus building with regard to levels of funding by program, revenue source, and standards of accountability. As a plan, it is a mechanism for setting priorities for activities consistent with the institution's strategic plan and forecasted resources. The budget is a contract based on commitments reflected in the strategic plan and on receipt of restricted funds from donors, federal agencies, and state appropriations. As a control mechanism, the budget regulates the flow of resources to support each activity in accordance with the approved institutional policies and procedures. As a communication network, the budget allows each department or unit to communicate its objectives, needs, and the resources required to fund them. And finally, a budget is a political tool because it reflects the outcomes of negotiations with different constituents about founding sources and about which activities will be supported and at what level. (p. 245)

A more complete treatment of budgets and financial practices in higher education may be found in Chapter 9 of this volume.

Technology.   The use of technology and information systems enables all student affairs administrators to make data-based decisions. Educational technologies pervade college campuses, in both their instruction and management. No modern student affairs administrator can avoid the use of educational technologies, especially computer-based technologies and the Internet. Information is reasonably accessible for making almost any kind of decision faced by administrators. This ready availability of information makes feasible the achievement of four roles for administrators advocated by Ausiello and Wells (1997). They see the crucial roles as that of architect (constructors of vision, goals, and objectives), facilitator of change (champions of change), educators and learners (teaching one another to enable student affairs divisions to become learning organizations), and policymaker (proactive promulgation of appropriate policies and guidelines) as central to the use of technology and information systems. (See Chapter 4 in this volume for more detailed treatment of the use of technology in student affairs.)

Scope and Functions of Practice

Management essentially is about the stewardship of resources, including people, facilities, money, and information. The management structure must be designed to accommodate educational purposes, the nature of the student body, the size of the institution, the nature of the community, and the relationship of the student affairs functions to other functions in the institution (Sandeen, 1991).

Staffing.   A large part of management pertains to overseeing people who do the work of the organization. Winston and Creamer (1997, p. 1) referred to this responsibility as "staffing practices." They pointed to the essential nature of hiring the right people, inducting new people into the organization, and supervising staff, as well as staff development and performance appraisal.

Central to their model of staffing is supervision of staff, which they maintain requires a synergistic approach involving collaboration and ongoing contact between supervisor and staff member. Supervision of staff is an essential skill. If it is done well, it can substantially boost the productivity of organization units. The place of values in staffing practices was underscored by Winston and Creamer and also by Dalton (1996). Dalton proffered five propositions pertaining to the place of values in human resources management:

1. Employees are individuals with unique abilities and needs that transcend group characteristics.
2. Excellence in organizations requires a high level of regard for and utilization of the talents of organizational members.
3. Fairness and equal consideration in relationships with employees is the bedrock of human resource management.
4. The most powerful motivator of human development is personal challenge, which is created by high performance standards, feedback, and a clear reward structure.
5. Effective organizations have identifiable and shared values and beliefs that provide a common framework of purpose and meaning for employees. (pp. 497–498)

Both Winston and Creamer (1997) and Dalton (1996) argued for maximizing human potential in student affairs administrative units. This requires managers to possess a very clear understanding of individual talents and needs to be able to further nurture their development as individuals and as members of the organization. (See Chapter 8 in this volume for a more detailed treatment of staffing practices.)

Facilities management.   Management of facilities is especially crucial in student affairs administration. Residence halls and college unions are examples of multimillion-dollar institutional investments often designed to enhance learning opportunities for students. Student affairs administrators are frequently assigned responsibility for the aforementioned facilities and others such as athletic and recreational buildings, playing fields, and equipment.

Hallenbeck (1991) pointed out that the physical environment of the campus, especially its buildings, sends constant and powerful messages to all who encounter it. Heilweil (1973) asserted that buildings impose absolute limits on human behavior. If such is the case, then student affairs administrators responsible for facilities management need to examine the messages being sent to the inhabitants and visitors. If the institution truly teaches through its buildings that ugliness is an acceptable price for efficiency, that living is to be separated from learning, then neither what is said in the classroom nor promulgated in promotional materials can truly counter those messages (Hallenbeck, 1991).

Information utilization. Information is power. Although a somewhat overused cliché, it is true nevertheless. Student affairs administrators regularly generate information about students and their learning climates, often through participation in national testing programs such as the Cooperative Institutional Research Project (CIRP) and the College Student Experiences Questionnaire (CSEQ) program. Likewise, many institutional research offices regularly study their campus learning climates and provide data about recruitment, admissions, and enrollment to student affairs administrators. Information from these and other sources can provide significant insight into the nature of enrolled students and is invaluable to student affairs practitioners, teachers, and other administrative colleagues. Good management suggests that data such as these be used constantly. They often require analysis and interpretation and the good manager will routinely make information available to institutional colleagues to allow their full participation in decision making and planning. Today's manager also must learn how to collect and use information accessible via the Internet. Available in multiple forms and in overwhelming amounts, this type of information especially requires analysis and interpretation by student affairs administrators to make it useful to members of the organization.

Yukl (1998) identified nine functions or categories of behavior that are associated with being a manager: (a) supervising, (b) planning and organizing, (c) decision making, (d) monitoring indicators, (e) controlling, (f) representing, (g) coordinating, (h) consulting, and (i) administering. Table 1.3 provides brief descriptions of each of these categories of management duties and responsibilities. Many of these managerial behavioral characteristics are similar to the staffing practices described by Winston and Creamer (1997).

Table 1.3. Behavioral Characteristics of Managers

Category	Brief Description
Supervising	Improving the performance of subordinates by working with them to analyze work behaviors and developing strategies to build on strengths and overcome weaknesses
Planning and organizing	Formulating short-term plans; developing budgets; translating long-term plans into operational goals; recommending and developing policies and procedures
Decision making	Making decisions in unstructured situations with incomplete information; authorizing deviations from policy to meet demands of new situation
Monitoring indicators	Monitoring internal and external factors and forces that may affect unit, division, or institution and students
Controlling	Developing schedules; assessing benefits and costs of programs and services; analyzing operational effectiveness
Representing	Answering questions; responding to complaints; promoting a positive image of the unit, division, and institution
Coordinating	Communicating with internal and external publics; meeting schedules and deadlines; solving problems; maintaining smooth working relationships with peers; mediating disagreements and conflicts between key individuals
Consulting	Keeping current with developments in the field; introducing new techniques and technologies into the organization; acting as an expert advisor or troubleshooter for others in the institution
Administering	Performing basic activities such as locating information on policies and procedures; analyzing routine information, and maintaining detailed and accurate records and documents

Based on and adapted from Gary Yukl, *Leadership in Organizations*, p. 23. Copyright © 1998. Reproduced by permission of Prentice-Hall.

The successful integration of the roles of educator, leader, and manager by the professional student affairs administrator requires the use of multiple and complex skills, knowledge, and personal traits. Recently, Lovell and Kosten (2000) completed a meta-analysis of 30 years of studies addressing these administrator attributes. Not surprisingly, and as noted in the previous discussion, "to be successful as a student affairs administrator, well-developed administration, management, and human facilitation skills are key. Knowledge bases in student development theory and higher education are required. Personal traits that allow one to work cooperatively and display integrity are basic foundations for success" (p. 566).

Professionalism

Student affairs has made enormous strides in recent decades toward achieving professional status. Evidence is abundant that most persons employed in the field are consistently educated in common knowledge and that the field is widely recognized for its vital contributions to higher education. Still, a continuing debate has been conducted over the past 50 years about whether student affairs technically constitutes a "profession" or whether practitioners uphold the tenets of professionalism (Carpenter, 1991; Carpenter, Miller, & Winston, 1980; Winston, 1997); and even whether it is desirable for student affairs practitioners to aspire to professional status (Bloland, 1974; Canon, 1982). As early as 1949, Wrenn tested the field against the criteria of a profession proposed by sociologists and found that it failed to measure up to the accepted standards.

Traditionally, fields such as law and medicine have served as prototypes of what classifies as a profession. Wilensky (1964) and Moore (1970) proposed criteria to be used to determine whether, or to what degree, an occupation was truly a profession: (a) viewing the occupation as a calling; (b) requiring specialized, advanced education; (c) exhibiting a service orientation; (d) possessing a high degree of autonomy in practice; and (e) having an identifiable peer group organization.

The Field as a Calling

To be a calling, an occupation must be pursued full time and attract a cadre of practitioners who persist throughout a lifetime career. Evidence that student affairs is a calling include (a) continuance in the field, sometimes for many years and increasingly for a working career lifetime; (b) acceptance of appropriate norms and standards; and (c) identification with peers as a collective (for example, a professional association). On this criterion there is ample evidence that student affairs qualifies as a profession. There is also disturbing evidence that many new practitioners only stay with the field for a few years after completing their master's degree. Because the midmanagement bottleneck is often tight and requires geographical mobility, many new professionals seek careers in business or other fields that pay more and have greater flexibility to remain "rooted" in a given location (Wood, Winston, & Polkosnik, 1985).

Specialized Training

There are numerous college student affairs administration master's-level professional preparation programs. The field, however, has yet to reach consensus about what constitutes "adequate" preparation for entry into practice. Many programs are either counseling based or administratively based, though a growing number exist that are a hybrid of the two. The CAS has adopted standards that are multidisciplinary in scope and broad based. Although being widely acknowledged, however, these standards provide only for voluntary compliance. In a study of a large sample of student affairs practitioners, Winston and Creamer (1997) found that 98% of all chief student affairs administrators held either a master's (40%) or doctorate (58%); more than two-thirds held their degrees in counseling, higher education, or student affairs. Even though consensus has yet to be achieved about the exact content of professional preparation, there is basic agreement that graduate education directly focused on working with students outside the classroom is appropriate and desirable, if not obligatory.

Student affairs practitioners, however, have yet to establish in the minds of the larger academic community that there is a domain of specialized knowledge that is necessary for the successful practice of student affairs. From the perspective of this criterion, student affairs has made substantial progress in the past quarter century but currently falls short of being a full-fledged profession (Winston, 1997).

It may be argued that the *student development movement* initiated in part with the THE Project (Brown, 1972; Miller & Prince, 1976) was the first major attempt to carve out an area of expertise for the student affairs profession. Recent evaluations, such as that of Bloland, Stamatakos, and Rogers (1994), have argued that this attempt was a failure. If one judges from the quantity or quality or both of data-based research produced by student affairs practitioners, it is difficult to argue against their point. Most of the research done about college students is performed by faculty in student affairs preparation programs or in neighboring disciplines, primarily psychology, sociology, and anthropology (Saunders, Register, Cooper, Bates, & Daddona, 2000). With the more recent guiding approach of student learning, there is little evidence that it will be more successful in carving out an area of expertise for student affairs. If anything, *student learning* is a much more vague concept and one to which virtually everyone in higher education has a legitimate claim. In all likelihood, the field of student affairs will continue to seek to clarify its theoretical base and resultant professional identity in the years to come. Over time, student affairs practice has been viewed by many as an applied social science, and we may well see increased attempts to integrate theory and practice constructs and approaches from other academic disciplines and the corporate community in the near future if attempts to emphasize student learning as a foundation falters.

Service Orientation

Moore (1970) maintained that there are three characteristics of a profession's service orientation: competence, conscientious performance, and loyalty. To be a professional means to be competent as the term "incompetent professional" is an oxymoron. Winston (1999) asserts that "To claim to be a professional means that one holds himself or herself up [to] a high level of generalized and specialized knowledge and skill appropriate to the tasks to be undertaken" (p. 6). As a consequence, professionals must be aware of their limitations and refrain from attempting to perform tasks for which they are not adequately trained or skilled. Likewise, student affairs divisions need to provide adequate professional development opportunities for staff members to enhance the skills and competencies essential for successful practice.

Service orientation also means that professionals are primarily community oriented, rather than function on the basis of self-interest. In effect, professionals place the welfare of clients, charges, or employers above their own interests. The difficulty sometimes comes, however, in determining to whom the student affairs professional owes primary loyalty, or "Who is the client?" Is it the individual student, the institution, or both? If both, how does one resolve conflicts of interests or obligation? The ACPA Ethical Principles and Standards (ACPA, 1990) acknowledges this inherent conflict of loyalties, but it does not provide explicit guidance in how to resolve conflicts when they are encountered.

On the criterion of service orientation, student affairs has made considerable progress over the past half century, but has not fully met this standard. Few student affairs divisions can document that what they do actually makes a difference for students (even for a simple majority of students). There has been active opposition to external pressures to be accountable, especially for using careful, tightly controlled outcomes assessment. Mueller's (1961) question of four decades ago still lacks an answer: "What can student personnel work offer today's youth which he [*sic*] patently needs but cannot receive from any other professional worker in the whole system of higher education?" (p. 522). To be recognized as a profession by other members of the academic community, student affairs professionals must provide a clear, easily understood answer to Mueller's question. This is an important challenge for the next generation of student affairs practitioners.

High Degree of Autonomy

Ambiguity about to whom primary allegiance is owed is caused in part by the fact that student affairs, unlike law and medicine, virtually never functions outside of higher education institutions; that is, student affairs exists and functions almost exclusively within a bureaucracy. When professionals are required to function within a bureaucratic organization, four areas of potential conflict arise: (a) resistance to bureaucratic rules when the rules conflict with the values and purposes of the profession, (b) rejection of bureaucratic standards, (c) resistance to supervision, and (d) conditional loyalty to the organization (Moore, 1970). Which is more important, to support the institution or to support the ideals and standards of the profession as expressed through its professional organizations and statements of purpose and ethics? On this criterion, student affairs practitioners may never fully resolve the ambiguity of being professionals within a bureaucracy, "with or without portfolio." There will always be some level of dynamic tension here. Even medicine, which is often viewed as an exemplar of a *profession*, has lost much of its autonomy with the widespread adoption of managed care health plans.

Identifiable Peer Group

Student affairs does not lack for a sufficient number of professional organizations; currently there are well over 30 such associations. Virtually every functional area has at least one, and sometimes several organizations vying for prac-titioners' membership and loyalty. This very proliferation presents a major ob-stacle to student affairs being recognized as a profession. There is a cacophony of voices claiming to speak for the profession, but the messages often become lost to the academic community, and even more so to the general public.

There are two major generalist professional organizations, the ACPA and NASPA, both of which serve international audiences and are open to practitioners in all functional areas, though neither can legitimately speak for the profession as a whole. Interestingly, the membership of the National Association of Women in Education (NAWE), one of the earliest entries into the professional organi-zation milieu, recently voted in favor of dissolution, largely because of the association's loss of professional identity and purpose. This lack of a unitary voice creates confusion in the minds of others in the academic community and makes it easy to disregard student affairs claims that it is a legitimate and essential player in the process of higher education. Until the field can find a way to bring together a majority of these organizations to speak as one, it will be difficult, if not impossible, to persuasively argue that student affairs is a full-fledged pro-fession.

Impartial observers must conclude that student affairs possesses many of the characteristics of a profession, but has not yet fully reached that goal. Con-sequently, it is necessary to continue to call it an "emerging profession" (Carpenter, Miller, & Winston, 1980).

What Does It Mean To Be a Student Affairs Professional?

If student affairs is a profession, emerging or otherwise, what meaning does that have for practitioners? Student affairs professionals exhibit at least five important characteristics that include (a) theory-based practice, (b) adherence to ethical standards, (c) professional involvement, (d) advocacy for students, and (e) contribution to the educational process.

Theory-based practice. Professionals base practice on theories that explain why they do what they do. This means that practitioners need to be knowledge-able about theories of college student development, program design and imple-mentation, organization development, assessment and evaluation, research de-sign and implementation, interpersonal communication and facilitation, group dynamics, staffing practices, budget development and resource allocation, as well as theories about how gender, sexual orientation, ethnicity, and cultural background affect students and their environments. This is a great deal to be mastered and cannot be accomplished fully during a formal degree program; yet well-designed professional preparation programs provide a solid foundation for a lifetime of professional study. Effective student affairs practitioners must be continuously involved in active learning about the context of and the partici-pants in higher education, and, generally, good formal preparation programs equip them for these lifelong learning activities. Student affairs administrators must conduct and report for peer review the results of serious studies of students' development and learning; they cannot continue to depend on others to do this work for them.

Adherence to ethical standards and principles. Student affairs professionals are knowledgeable of the ethical standards that apply to their work, especially to areas of direct responsibility. They adhere to those standards and take action when they observe others violating them. These expectations sound straightforward; however, new paradigms for today's campuses suggest that universal principles, orderliness, and reversible, linear cause-and-effect relationships may not provide the best perspective for dealing with modern dilemmas. Fried (1997) asserted that new paradigms emphasize "the power of relationships and information in a context of nonlinear interaction" (p. 9) and focus on culture, respect, and interaction. The complexity of decisions facing student affairs administrators cannot be overstated. Many are well recognized, such as whether to employ standards for the awarding of financial aid to people of color that are different from those used for others, and require thoughtful and often collaborative action to obtain an appropriate resolution within the cultural context of a given institution. Other issues, oftentimes driven by crises, tend to be less commonly encountered, but nevertheless are complicated to resolve.

Professional involvement. One cannot be a student affairs professional unless she or he is actively involved in promoting the profession and extending its knowledge base. Student affairs professionals are members of professional organizations that directly relate to their work assignments and are actively involved in furthering the goals of those organizations. Further, student affairs professionals are actively engaged in extending the profession's knowledge base through contributions to the professional literature. Most professional associations support at least one professional journal and many produce periodic monographs and other professionally related publications.

Advocates for students. Student affairs professionals advocate within their work settings for students' interests. They monitor institutional policies and practices to assure that students' best interests are recognized and intervene when students' welfare is being jeopardized. This is especially true when dealing with students and student groups who have been ignored or discriminated against by higher education and society and who may not be skilled in representing their own interests, such as students of color; gay, lesbian, transgender, and bisexual students; students with disabilities; and in some instances women.

Contributors to the educational process. Student affairs professionals evaluate their work to determine if they are contributing to the institution's educational mission. Every position in student affairs should make either a direct or indirect contribution to student learning. If it does not, perhaps the responsibilities should be changed or the position should be transferred to other areas of the institution. It is incumbent upon student affairs practitioners to collaborate effectively with students, faculty and staff members, academic affairs administrators, and other institutional stakeholders for purposes of creating environments that are conducive to student learning and personal development. Student affairs professionals can and should function as major players in the educational endeavors of any higher education institution.

CONCLUSION

Professional student affairs administrators seek to balance and integrate the roles of educator, leader, and manager. Their functions are increasingly central to the effective operations of colleges and universities and they increasingly assume institutionwide educational responsibilities. Student affairs administrators always have striven for civility among students and to provide educational environments capable of meeting the learning and personal development needs of students. Today, these administrators assume those historic roles as well as current and emerging roles such as creating and sustaining multicultural environments capable of helping students to prepare for life and work in societies with global cultural dimensions and the support of distance learners who are often far removed from the campus.

The roles of educator, leader, and manager are complicated in the contexts of postindustrial organizations such as is the nature of today's colleges and universities. All three roles require creative uses of multiple professional talents to originate visions and use active, cooperative, and collaborative strategies to move current establishments toward learning organizations and lifelong learning communities. To be effective in these roles, student affairs administrators must be well educated in the knowledge of the field and must be engaged in in-service education and professional development on a continuing basis. Learning organizations require the employment of lifelong learners in the functional roles of the institution.

While the tasks associated with student affairs administration may be intricate and comprehensive simultaneously, they are doable by well-educated and conscientious professionals. Persons most likely to succeed in student affairs administration, however, are those individuals of unimpeachable integrity who are educated in the knowledge, skills, and attitudes of student affairs, whose values are grounded in respect for individuals, whose commitment to building multicultural communities is unconditional, and whose work ethic is clearly in place.

QUESTIONS TO CONSIDER

1. How does the educator, leader, manager model of professional student affairs demonstrate the centrality of student affairs to student learning and personal development?
2. When are the roles of educator, leader, and manager most likely to conflict for student affairs administrators? What general rules or principles could you recommend for resolving these conflicts?
3. Is it desirable for student affairs to become a profession? What are the pros and cons?

REFERENCES

Allen, K. E., & Cherry, C. (2000). *Systemic leadership: Enriching the meaning of our work.* Lanham, MD: American College Personnel Association/National Association for Campus Activities/University Press of America.

American Association for Higher Education (AAHE), American College Personnel Association (ACPA), & National Association of Student Personnel Administrators (NASPA). (1998). *Powerful partnerships: A shared responsibility for learning.* [On-line]. Available: http://www.aahe.org/assessment/joint.htm

American College Personnel Association (ACPA). (1990). Statement of ethical principles and standards. *Journal of College Student Development, 31,* 198–202.

American College Personnel Association (ACPA). (1996, March/April). Student learning imperative: Implications for Student Affairs. *Journal of College Student Development, 37.*

American College Personnel Association (ACPA)/National Association of Student Personnel Administrators (NASPA). (1996). *Principles of good practice for student affairs.* [On-line]. Available: http://www.acpa.nche.edu/pgp/principle.htm

American Council on Education (ACE). (1937). *The student personnel point of view* (Ser. 1, Vol. 1, No. 3). Washington, DC: Author.

Astin, A. W. (1996). Involvement in learning revisited: Lessons we have learned. *Journal of College Student Development, 37,* 123–134.

Ausiello, K., & Wells, B. (1997). Information technology and student affairs: Planning for the twenty-first century. In C. M. Engstrom & K. W. Kruger (Eds.), *Using technology to promote student learning: Opportunities for today and tomorrow* (pp. 71–95). New Directions for Student Services, No. 78. San Francisco: Jossey-Bass.

Barr, M. J. (2000). The importance of institutional mission. In M. J. Barr, M. K. Desler, & Associates (Eds.), *The handbook of student affairs administration* (2nd ed., pp. 25–36). San Francisco: Jossey-Bass.

Baxter Magolda, M. B. (1992). *Knowing and reasoning in college: Gender-related patterns in students' intellectual development.* San Francisco: Jossey-Bass.

Bensimon, E. M., & Neumann, A. (1993). *Redesigning collegiate leadership.* Baltimore: Johns Hopkins University Press.

Birnbaum, R. (2000). *Management fads in higher education: Where they come from, what they do, why they fail.* San Francisco: Jossey-Bass.

Blimling, G. S., Whitt, E. J., & Associates. (1999). *Good practice in student affairs: Principles to foster student learning.* San Francisco: Jossey-Bass.

Blimling, G. S., & Alschuler, A. S. (1996). Creating a home for the spirit of learning: Contributions of student development educators. *Journal of College Student Development, 37,* 203–216.

Bloland, P. A. (1974). Professionalism and the professional organization. In T. F. Harrington (Ed.), *Student personnel work in urban colleges*. New York: Intext Educational.

Bloland, P. A., Stamatakos, L. C., & Rogers, R. R. (1994). *Reform in student affairs: A critique of student development*. Greensboro, NC: ERIC Counseling and Student Services Clearinghouse.

Bonwell, C. C., & Eison, J. A. (1991). *Active learning: Creating excitement in the classroom*. ASHE-ERIC Higher Education Report, No. 4. Washington, DC: Association for the Study of Higher Education.

Brown, J. S. (1997). On becoming a learning organization. *About Campus, 1*(6), 5–10.

Brown, R. D. (1972). *Student development in tomorrow's higher education: A return to the academy*. Washington, DC: American College Personnel Association.

Bryan, W. A. (1996). What is total quality management? In W. A. Bryan (Ed.), *Total quality management: Applying its principles to student affairs* (pp. 3–15). New Directions for Student Affairs, No. 76. San Francisco: Jossey-Bass.

Canon, H. J. (1982). Toward professionalism in student affairs: Another point of view. *Journal of College Student Personnel, 23*, 468–473.

Canon, H. J. (1996). Ethical standards and principles. In S. R. Komives, D. B. Woodard, Jr., & Associates, *Student services: A handbook for the profession* (3rd ed., pp. 106–125). San Francisco: Jossey-Bass.

Caple, R. B., & Newton, F. B. (1991). Leadership in student affairs. In T. K. Miller, R. B. Winston, Jr., & Associates, *Administration and leadership in student affairs: Actualizing student development in higher education* (2nd ed., pp. 111–133). Muncie, IN: Accelerated Development.

Carpenter, D. S. (1991). Student affairs profession: A developmental perspective. In T. K. Miller, R. B. Winston, Jr., & Associates, *Administration and leadership in student affairs: Actualizing student development in higher education* (2nd ed., pp. 253–269). Muncie, IN: Accelerated Development.

Carpenter, D. S., Miller, T. K., & Winston, R. B., Jr. (1980). Toward the professionalization of student affairs. *NASPA Journal, 18*(2), 16–22.

Chickering, A. W., & Gamson, Z. F. (1991) Seven principles for good practice in undergraduate education. In A. W. Chickering & Z. F. Gamson (Eds.), *Applying the seven principles of good practice in undergraduate education* (pp. 63–69). New Directions for Teaching and Learning, No. 47. San Francisco: Jossey-Bass.

Cheatham, H. E. (1991). Identity development in a pluralist society. In H. E. Cheatham (Ed.), *Cultural pluralism on campus* (pp. 23–38). Washington, DC: American College Personnel Association.

Clement, L. M., & Rickard, S. T. (1992). *Effective leadership in student services: Voices from the field*. San Francisco: Jossey-Bass.

Creamer, D. G., & Frederick, P. M. (1991). Administrative and management theories: Tools for change. In T. K. Miller, R. B. Winston, Jr., & Associates, *Administration and leadership in student affairs: Actualizing student development in higher education* (2nd ed., pp. 135–157). Muncie, IN: Accelerated Development.

Dalton, J. C. (1996). Managing human resources. In S. R. Komives, D. B. Woodard, Jr., & Associates, *Student services: A handbook for the profession* (3rd ed., pp. 494–511). San Francisco: Jossey-Bass.

Denning, W. E. (1986). *Out of the crisis*. Cambridge, MA: Massachusetts Institute of Technology Center for Advanced Engineering Study.

Dixon v. Alabama State Board of Education, 273 F.2d. 150 (1961).

Erwin, T. D. (1996). Assessment, evaluation, and research. In S. R. Komives, D. B. Woodard, Jr., & Associates, *Student services: A handbook for the profession* (3rd ed., pp. 415–432). San Francisco: Jossey-Bass.

Freed, J. E. (November, 1997). *Leading continuous quality improvement on campus: This train is going north*. Paper presented at the annual meeting of the Association for the Study of Higher Education, Albuquerque, NM.

Fried, J. (1997). Multicultural ethical frameworks for a multicultural world. In J. Fried (Ed.), *Ethics for today's campus: New perspectives on education, student development, and institutional management* (pp. 5–22). New Directions for Student Services, No. 77. San Francisco: Jossey-Bass.

Fried, J., & Associates. (1995). *Shifting paradigms in student affairs: Culture, context, teaching, and learning*. Washington, DC: American College Personnel Association.

Goodlad, J. I. (1997). *In praise of education*. New York: Teachers College Press.

Hallenbeck, D. A. (1991). Managing physical facilities. In T. K. Miller, R. B. Winston, Jr., & Associates, *Administration and leadership in student affairs: Actualizing student development in higher education* (2nd ed., pp. 643–671). Muncie, IN: Accelerated Development.

Hanson, G. R. (1997). Using technology in assessment and evaluation. In C. M. Engstrom & K. W. Kruger (Eds.), *Using technology to promote student learning: Opportunities for today and tomorrow* (pp. 31–44). New Directions for Student Services, No. 78. San Francisco: Jossey-Bass.

Heilweil, M. (1973). The influence of dormitory architecture on resident behavior. *Environment and Behavior, 5*, 377–412.

Kitchener, K. S. (1985). Ethical principles and ethical decisions in student affairs. In H. J. Canon & R. E. Brown (Eds.), *Applied ethics in student services* (pp. 17–30). New Directions for Student Services, No. 30. San Francisco: Jossey-Bass.

Komives, S. R., Lucas, N., & McMahon, T. R. (1998). *Exploring leadership for college students who want to make a difference*. San Francisco: Jossey-Bass.

Kuh, G. D. (1996, September–October). Some things we should forget. *About Campus, 1*(4), 10–15.

Kuh, G. D., & Hall, J. (1993). Using cultural perspectives in student affairs. In G. D. Kuh (Ed.), *Using cultural perspectives in student affairs work* (pp. 1–20). Alexandria, VA: American College Personnel Association.

Kuh, G. D., & Schuh, J. H. (Eds.). (1991). *The role and contributions of student affairs in involving colleges*. Washington, DC: National Association of Student Personnel Administrators.

Kuh, G. D., Schuh, J. H., Whitt, E. J., & Associates. (1991). *Involving colleges: Successful approaches to fostering student learning and development outside the classroom*. San Francisco: Jossey-Bass.

Kuh, G. D., & Whitt, E. J. (1988). *The invisible tapestry: Culture in American colleges and universities*. AAHE-ERIC Higher Education Report No. 1. Washington, DC: Association for the Study of Higher Education.

Kuh, G. D., Whitt, E. J., & Shedd, J. D. (1987). *Student affairs work, 2001: A paradigmatic odyssey*. Washington, DC: American College Personnel Association.

Lappé, F. M., & Du Bois, P. M. (1994). *The quickening of America: Rebuilding our nation, remaking our lives*. San Francisco: Jossey-Bass.

Lewin, K. (1936). *Principles of typological psychology*. F. Heider & G. M. Heider (Trans.). New York: McGraw-Hill.

Lloyd-Jones, E., & Smith, M. R. (1954). *Student personnel work as deeper teaching*. New York: Harper.

Lovell, C. D., & Kosten, L. A. (2000). Skills, knowledge, and personal traits necessary for success as a student affairs administrator: A meta-analysis of thirty years of research. *NASPA Journal, 37*, 553–572.

Meisinger, R. J., & Dubeck, L. W. (1984). *College and university budgeting: An introduction for faculty and academic administrators*. Washington, DC: National Association of College and University Business Officers.

Miller, T. K. (Ed.). (1999). *The CAS book of professional standards for higher education*. Washington, DC: Council for the Advancement of Standards in Higher Education.

Miller, T. K., & Jones, J. D. (1981). Out-of-class activities. In A.W. Chickering & Associates, *The modern American college: Responding to the new realities of diverse students and a changing society* (pp. 657–671). San Francisco: Jossey-Bass.

Miller, T. K., & Prince, J. S. (1976). *The future of student affairs: A guide to student development for tomorrow's higher education*. San Francisco: Jossey-Bass.

Moore, W. E. (1970). *The professions: Roles and rules*. New York: Russell Sage.

Mueller, K. H. (1961). *Student personnel work in higher education*. Cambridge, MA: Riverside.

National Association of Student Personnel Administrators (NASPA). (1993). NASPA standards of professional practice. *Membership handbook*. Washington, DC: Author.

Pope, R. L., & Reynolds, A. L. (1997). Student affairs core competencies: Integrating multicultural awareness, knowledge, and skills. *Journal of College Student Development, 38*, 266–275.

Roberts, D. C. (1998, July–August). Student learning was always supposed to be the core of our work—What happened? *About Campus, 3*(3), 18–25.

Rogers, J. L. (1996). Leadership. In S. R. Komives, D. B. Woodard, Jr., & Associates,

Student services: A handbook for the profession (3rd ed., pp. 299–319). San Francisco: Jossey-Bass.

Rogers, J. L., & Ballard, S. (1995). Aspirational management: Building effective organizations through shared values. *NASPA Journal, 32,* 162–178.

Rhoads, R. A., & Black, M. A. (1995). Student affairs practitioners as transformative educators: Advancing a critical cultural perspective. *Journal of College Student Development, 36,* 413–421.

Roper, L. D. (1996). Teaching and training. In S. R. Komives, D. B. Woodard, Jr., & Associates, *Student services: A handbook for the profession* (3rd ed., pp. 320–334). San Francisco: Jossey-Bass.

Rost, J. C. (1991). *Leadership for the twenty-first century.* New York: Praeger.

Sandeen, A. (1991). *The chief student affairs officer: Leader, manager, mediator, educator.* San Francisco: Jossey-Bass.

Saunders, S. A., Register, M. D., Cooper, D. L., Bates, J. M., & Daddona, M. F. (2000). Who is writing research articles in student affairs journals? Practitioner involvement and collaboration. *Journal of College Student Development, 41,* 609–615.

Schuh, J. H. (1996). Planning and finance. In S. R. Komives, D. B. Woodward, Jr., & Associates, *Student services: A handbook for the profession* (3rd ed., pp. 458–475). San Francisco: Jossey-Bass.

Senge, P. M. (1990). *The fifth discipline: The art and practice of the learning organization.* New York: Doubleday/Currency.

Stage, F. K., & Manning, K. (Eds.) (1992). *Enhancing the multicultural campus environment: A cultural brokering approach.* New Directions for Student Services, No. 60. San Francisco: Jossey-Bass.

Strange, C. (1991). Managing college environments: Theory and practice. In T. K. Miller, R. B. Winston, Jr., & Associates, *Administration and leadership in student affairs: Actualizing student development in higher education.* Muncie, IN: Accelerated Development.

Wilensky, H. L. (1964). The professionalization of everyone? *American Journal of Sociology, 70,* 21–23.

Winston, R. B., Jr. (1997). Suppose professional ethics really mattered. *Georgia Journal of College Student Affairs, 11*(1), 4–13.

Winston, R. B., Jr., & Creamer, D. G. (1997). *Improving staffing practices in student affairs.* San Francisco: Jossey-Bass.

Wood, L., Winston, R. B., Jr., & Polkosnik, M. C. (1985). Career orientations and professional development of young student affairs professionals. *Journal of College Student Personnel, 26,* 532–539.

Woodard, D. B., Jr. (1993). Budgeting and fiscal management. In M. J. Barr & Associates, *Handbook of student affairs administration* (pp. 242–259). San Francisco: Jossey-Bass.

Wrenn, C. G. (1949). An appraisal of the professional status of student personnel workers, Part I (pp. 264–280). In E. G. Williamson (Ed.), *Trends in student personnel work.* Minneapolis: University of Minnesota Press.

Yoakum, C. S. (1919/1994). Plan for a personnel bureau in educational institutions. In A. L. Rentz (Ed.), *Student affairs—A profession's heritage: Significant articles, authors, issues and documents* (2nd ed., pp. 4–8). Washington, DC: American College Personnel Association.

Young, R. B. (1996). Guiding values and philosophy. In S. R. Komives, D. B. Woodard, Jr., & Associates, *Student services: A handbook for the profession* (3rd ed., pp. 83–105). San Francisco: Jossey-Bass.

Yukl, G. (1998). *Leadership in organizations,* 4th ed. Upper Saddle River, NJ: Prentice-Hall.

RECOMMENDED READING

Allen, K. E., & Cherrey, C. (2000). *Systemic leadership: Enriching the meaning of our work.* Lanham, MD: American College Personnel Association/National Association for Campus Activities/University Press of America.

Barr, M. J., Desler, M. K., & Associates. (2000). *The handbook of student affairs administration.* San Francisco: Jossey-Bass.

Komives, S. R., Woodard, D. B., Jr., & Associates. (1996). *Student services: A handbook for the profession* (3rd ed.). San Francisco: Jossey-Bass.

2

Higher Education:
Values and Cultures

GEORGE D. KUH
MICHAEL J. SIEGEL
AUDEN D. THOMAS

*M*eredith Skolar, fresh out of a master's degree program, has been on the job for six weeks as assistant dean of residential life at Midwestern State University. Midwestern has almost 15,000 students, about 90% undergraduates. Reporting to the dean of students, Meredith's responsibility, among others, is to oversee the development of a Freshman Interest Group (FIG) program—groups of about 20 first-year students who live with one another in the residence halls, coenroll in two or three courses, and meet together weekly in a peer instructor-led seminar. FIGs at Midwestern are supposed to help students make the academic transition to college life, with the hope of boosting persistence rates. Meredith coordinates the work of the implementation committee, which includes nine people: the dean of students, the associate dean for academic affairs, the assistant registrar, three faculty members (biology, sociology, English), two students (the student government president and the residence halls governor), and Meredith.

Meredith has just returned to her office following what she thinks was an abysmal first meeting of the FIGs committee and sees an e-mail from a colleague from her master's program. She immediately responds:

Date: Mon, 12 June 2000 16:08:29 - 0400
From: Meredith Skolar <mskolar@msu.edu>
To: HYPERLINK mailto: djonathan@asu.edu
Subject: my confusing new job
David: How good to hear from you!!! Wow, you got the job at our alma mater!
Congrats!!!

How am I doing? Midwestern is great but it's a huge challenge figuring out how this place works. It's nothing like ASU. Just today the FIGs implementation committee met. We're trying to do something like the programs we read about last year at Mizzou and Indiana to enhance the living-learning environment. Anyway, I spent most of the meeting trying to figure who was saying what and why. Nobody seemed to agree on how FIGs should be organized or the focus of the program. The academic side of the house definitely has different notions of what this project is about. And the registrar's office wasn't sure they could reserve spaces in courses for FIGs students as they have not typically made arrangements for special courses like this in the past. I expected that students and the res life staff would collaborate on identifying faculty to participate, but the VP for Academic Affairs had already picked them! And then when we talked about program goals it felt like herding cats. My boss really emphasized the social adjustment part, but the faculty people (particularly the guy from Biology) said that they didn't want the academic integrity of the program compromised. The program is intended to enhance student learning, so I am not sure why some of the faculty think it will compromise the integrity of academics at the school. The two student reps didn't seem to see any advantages to FIGs and were mostly worried that they would create cliques on hall floors and work against community building.

Whew! Didn't mean to lay all this on you, David. I'm just really puzzled at the very different perspectives and values at play here. And I'm the one who is supposed to be facilitating this group!!! Got any advice for me?!? Great to be in touch, and I hope we can talk soon. *Meredith*

This vignette is instructive for two reasons. First, the types of people and issues Meredith described exist in some form on almost every campus. Second, it illustrates critical aspects of institutional life that are manifested in the roles, relationships, values, and assumptions that many people find confusing or dismiss as irrelevant. Put another way, some of the most important things student affairs practitioners must learn about their school and job are all but invisible, such as the beliefs and values held by different groups that affect the way they think and the nature of relations among people and institutional priorities, policies, and practices. These aspects of institutional life are very real but not necessarily obvious to most people who live and work there or to others who know the institution well. They are particularly difficult to apprehend for newcomers like Meredith.

Meredith's e-mail intimates that part of what she finds frustrating is the way things are, or appear to be, at Midwestern. Meredith is trying to understand a campus culture that is strange—at least to her. People on the FIGs implementation committee seem to be at odds about the relative value and even the meaning of intellectual development, academic and administrative priorities, social adjustment, and community building. These different perspectives reflect different traditions and values about what matters in higher education (Arnold & Kuh, 1999) and are perpetuated on a daily basis as people do their work without becoming familiar with the institution's history and examining the assumptions and beliefs that undergird its policies and practices.

PURPOSE AND OVERVIEW

The aim of this chapter is to encourage student affairs professionals to become culturally competent practitioners by familiarizing them with the properties and effects of college and university cultures and pointing out how an enhanced awareness of institutional culture can improve the effectiveness of student affairs. Toward this end the chapter is organized around four questions:

1. What is collegiate culture and its various properties?
2. What are the core values of the academy and how do those values articulate with the cultures of student affairs, faculty, academic affairs, and other groups?
3. How are changing student demographics and other factors influencing campus culture?
4. What are the characteristics of the "culturally competent" student affairs practitioner as educator, leader, and manager?

WHAT IS CULTURE?

Culture is a complex and somewhat ambiguous, all-encompassing concept, so it is not surprising that culture can be defined in many different ways. One major view is that culture is the "social fabric of community" (Dill, 1982, p. 304), implying that as groups live and work together they develop distinctive "philosophies, ideologies, values, assumptions, beliefs, expectations, attitudes, and norms" (Kilmann, Saxton, Serpa, & Associates, 1985, p. 5) that shape their thinking and determine to a large extent what they do. In other words, culture is the organizational glue that holds groups and institutions together (Peterson & Spencer, 1990).

At the same time, culture is not something that is "out there" to be accurately described (Martin, 1992) or that exists independent of human thought and action. Indeed, as anthropologist Clifford Geertz put it, "Man is an animal suspended in webs of significance he himself has spun" (Geertz, 1973, p. 5), meaning that people both construct as well as interpret culture. This also implies that culture is not a fixed entity, but is somewhat dynamic and subjective, open to multiple interpretations and meaning making in the flow of social life. Culture is inherently "complex, both a product and a process, the shaper of human interaction and the outcome of it, continually created and recreated by people's ongoing interactions" (Jelinek, Smircich, & Hirsch, 1983, p. 331) and interactions with the external environment.

Collegiate culture is in many ways an expression of an institution's values, which guide how people judge situations, acts, objects, and people (Kuh & Hall, 1993). Some values are espoused and frequently mentioned. But many other values are essentially tacit, guiding behavior almost subconsciously. For example, an art and design college annually features an enormously popular fashion show in which students and faculty model unusual combinations of unconventional artists' materials and found objects, highlighting the importance of visual creativity and originality. One would not likely find such an event on a campus with different values and institutional culture. Indeed, every college or university has its own particular culture manifested as the "collective, mutually shaping patterns of norms, values, practices, beliefs, and assumptions that guide the behavior of individuals and groups [providing] a frame of reference within which to interpret the meaning of events and actions on and off campus" (Kuh & Whitt, 1988, pp. 12–13). Although institutional cultures differ from one another in various ways, culture serves similar purposes on all campuses, the most important of which is that it is "a fabric of meaning in terms of which human beings interpret their experience and guide their action" (Geertz, 1973, p. 145).

Organizational Culture

One important way student affairs educators, managers, and leaders use the concept of culture is as a window through which to view organizational life. Because many features of an institution's culture are tacit, to discover or learn the culture of a campus one must intentionally search for it. In recent decades, anthropological and sociological constructions of culture have been appropriated to better understand the functioning of both for-profit and not-for-profit organizations (including institutions of higher education) to better understand organizational dynamics and improve decision making and other organizational actions. Researchers typically focus on identifying firmly embedded patterns of organizational behavior and the shared values, assumptions, beliefs, or ideologies that, taken together, form an institution's "unconscious infrastructure" (Smircich, 1983), meaning the cumulative product of the interactions between an institution's history, academic mission, traditions, and location and the people who live, work, and study there. These elements also typically determine the nature of organizational structures and services, which may vary widely from one campus to another. Thus, much attention is given to discovering a college's "invisible tapestry" (Kuh & Whitt, 1988), or the values, processes, and aspirations of a college's members, and what people do and how they do it (Tierney, 1988).

In *The Wizard of Oz*, Dorothy's dog, Toto, exposes the Wizard for what he is—not a towering physical and intellectual presence but a meek little man. Discovering that the Wizard is not what people thought changed the way Dorothy made sense of what appeared to her to be strange surroundings. In this sense, using a cultural lens to view colleges and universities takes one behind the scenes, providing a different vantage point on the familiar institutional structures, functions, mission, espoused priorities, and individual personalities, and also gives meaning to these elements as parts of a whole that comprise an institution.

Manifestations of Culture

An organization's cultural properties are revealed in many ways to the culturally competent practitioner. Observable manifestations of culture include campus rituals, symbols, stories, language, sagas, myths, and ceremonies. Memorials, buildings, and campus grounds are examples of physical artifacts. Written documents, publications, and websites are verbal storehouses of campus culture. Stories, sagas, and language identify and unify members of an organization or one of its subgroups. Newcomers to a campus encounter unfamiliar "lingo"—nicknames and abbreviations for campus processes, events, and locations. For instance, the "HUB" (Hetzel Union Building) is the union building at Penn State, and the "WUB" (Warnock Union Building) is one of the dining halls. In terms of campus stories, Indiana University Bloomington lore has it that a female student is not "a real coed" until she is kissed in the well house at midnight. This tale harkens back to a time when women students had an 11:00 p.m. curfew. If a freshman at the University of Michigan walks over the "M" (the metal university seal that is laid in stone in a crosswalk in front of the library), he or she is supposed to fail his or her first test at the university. It is not uncommon to see students trying to push each other onto the seal as they walk to class! Learning such stories and their meaning are essential steps toward becoming enculturated so that what was once strange and unfamiliar is now taken for granted (Whitt, 1993).

Tailgating at football games, the annual fall all-campus convocation, and ceremonies such as commencement are cultural events that both preserve and impart meaning to their participants. Often there are student-generated rituals that take place at colleges and universities that are not sanctioned or recognized by the campus but are nonetheless part of the cultural fabric. At Wake Forest University some students participate in what is called "tunneling," a long-held tradition whereby students take to underground tunnels (built several decades ago as bomb shelter tunnels) in the middle of the night. The tunnels, at various locations equipped with cans of food left by people in case of emergency, lead to buildings around the campus. Tunneling students risked being expelled from school. These and other events lend stability and continuity to the collegiate experience, which enable graduates to return to their alma mater five or ten years later and find many things to be much the same as one remembers them. Indeed, some of the most precious memories many alumni have of their college experience are associated with participating in formal or informal traditions and other cultural events.

Subcultures

Culture in higher education can be manifested at different levels—the institution, the department, the academic discipline, the residence hall, the Greek organization, the athletic team, the theater group, and so on. Subcultures are cultural enclaves, subgroups of institutional members who share common problems, interact regularly with one another, perceive themselves as distinct from other campus groups, and base their behavior on norms and understandings unique to their group (Van Maanen & Barley, 1984). Among the subcultures at a college or university that affect the undergraduate experience are faculty or disciplinary groups, academic administrators, student affairs professionals, and students. Each of these clusters of people have the potential to evolve into subcultures with their own distinctive artifacts, guiding values, and behavioral norms that in the context of the institution's history and traditions work together to shape the larger institutional culture that is host to subcultures. For this reason, it is essential that student affairs professionals become familiar with the principal values held by members of these various subcultures. Understanding the proximal causes of misunderstandings that routinely occur when certain values conflict or are considered less important by various groups will serve well the student affairs educator, manager, and leader.

Faculty cultures.   Several core values determine the identity of the academic profession (Austin, 1990). These include pursuing and disseminating knowledge (engaging in research, teaching, writing for journals and other publications) as the fundamental purpose of higher education, academic freedom, and collegial self-governance (Kuh & Whitt, 1988). Most faculty members ascribe to these foundational beliefs, though differences in interpretations and applications exist by discipline, specialty area, and type of institution (Kuh & Whitt, 1988; Tierney & Rhoads, 1994). The worldview and preferred discovery modes of a Medieval historian are very different from those of a physics or mathematics professor. Although disciplinary cultures differ, institutional cultures also vary by size, type, control (public or private), and location. Research universities, for example, place a higher priority on knowledge production than do teaching-oriented colleges, whereas smaller liberal arts colleges and community colleges are focused on teaching. At the same time that faculty beliefs are somewhat segmented by disciplinary groupings and institutional type, the core academic values mentioned above have a strong integrating effect and yield a differentiated, recognizable academic culture (Kuh & Whitt, 1988) that exerts a powerful influence on the overall culture of an institution.

Administrative cultures.   Administrators compose another fairly large group of professionals on a college campus, but they have received very little attention in the literature as distinctive subcultures (Clark, 1984). Typically administrators are not socialized to the academic ethos in the same way as are faculty members (although some administrators have come through faculty ranks to eventually land administrative posts as deans or vice presidents). As a result they have different interests, duties, and job training. Like other nonfaculty groups, they tend to interact much more with one another than with faculty members (Kuh & Whitt, 1988). Pragmatism drives the administrative work of such widely ranging roles as fiscal managers, facilities directors, and human resource personnel. Efficiency, management, and problem solving are highly valued. The assistant registrar in the opening vignette is a case in point. Her primary concern about FIGs (at least as described by Meredith) focused on the logistical and scheduling difficulties associated with the implementation of the program.

Student affairs professionals. Although the values of student affairs professionals overlap somewhat with those of administrative subcultures, there are distinguishing ideological hallmarks of the profession. These include "a commitment to the development of the whole student including basic and developmental needs, active learning and participation, and the importance of accepting and celebrating human differences" (Love, Kuh, MacKay, & Hardy, 1993, p. 46), which are enacted to support the educational mission. In addition, student affairs professionals advocate for the common good and champion the rights of the individual in the larger institutional context (National Association of Student Personnel Administrators [NASPA], 1989). Meredith intones these values in her e-mail to her colleague from graduate school by referring to the field's commitment "to enhance the living-learning environment."

As with the faculty culture, the student affairs culture is further divided into specialized subgroups, usually along the lines of functional areas. These specialty groups develop their own language and norms that can be discerned by contrasting the purposes, language, publications, annual meeting formats, and foci of their respective organizations. This is perhaps most obvious when attending the conventions of such groups as National Academic Advising Association (NACADA), National Orientation Directors Association (NODA), National Association of Student Personnel Administrators (NASPA), Association of College and University Housing Officers-International (ACUHO-I), American Association of Collegiate Registrars and Admissions Officers (AACRAO), and National Association for Campus Activities (NACA) and comparing the nature and content of sessions, informal hallway conversations, and organized social events. In addition, the skills and interests of people who perform different student affairs functions set them apart "culturally" from other student affairs professionals. For example, a student activities director with a master's degree in business administration (MBA) might oversee the programming budget with an eye toward cost cutting, thus enabling an increased number of activities to be offered to students. A residence hall director with a counseling background might emphasize communication skills and trust building among residents. So it is important to recognize that even within the student affairs subculture, "cultural differences exist among the various types of institutions, departments, and professional associations" (Love, Kuh et al., 1993, p. 50).

Student cultures. As with the other major subgroups on campus, student culture is not monolithic. And, as with faculty, administrative, and student affairs professionals, student cultures are maintained through ceremonies and rituals (Kuh & Whitt, 1988), such as new student orientation and "spring fling" events that mark the beginning and end of each academic year. Subgroups of an institution's student body often have their own rituals. For example, the fraternity and sorority rituals of rush and initiation serve to maintain the distinctive values of the Greek subculture. In another example, the annual masked Halloween ball held by the campus gay, lesbian, bisexual student organization allows the group to publicly present itself and its values. Because institutional history and context affect the "creation, maintenance, and potency of student subcultures" (Kuh & Whitt, 1988, p. 88), a member school of the Coalition of Christian Colleges and Universities would probably not host a Halloween ball of the type noted above.

A college's history and its core personnel—long-time faculty and administrative staff members—tend to be stabilizing influences on collegiate culture. At the same time, students themselves have the greatest overall effect on such things as how students spend their time, how much they study, from whom they take classes, how they perceive the faculty, what they do with their discretionary time, and how they view their overall experience at college (Kuh, 1995; Kuh & Hu, 1999; Love, Boschini, Jacobs, Hardy, & Kuh, 1993). Thus, student culture is a dominant and influential force in virtually every dimension of campus life, including implementing new initiatives in student housing such as FIGs.

On the typical college campus, the academic culture manifested in the values and beliefs of faculty members, administrative and student affairs cultures, and the variety of student subcultures on a college campus coexist side by side. Their interactions contribute to the character of the larger institutional culture (Kuh, 1993). To appreciate the distinctive influence of student affairs on collegiate culture, the history and core values of the field must be understood.

HISTORICAL ROOTS AND VALUES OF STUDENT AFFAIRS

In the colonial college era, a holistic, organic philosophy of education prevailed (Young, 1996, p. 86). Faculty members were purportedly concerned in equal measure with the intellectual, religious, and moral development of their White male students. Following the Civil War aspects of student affairs work began to emerge. This development was brought on by a rapidly growing U.S. population, unprecedented industrial growth, and federal legislation including the Morrill Acts of 1862 and 1890. These changes dramatically altered the nature and purposes of higher education by making it more accessible and expanding the curriculum to include the practical arts needed by the developing nation. Other key factors in the emergence of the profession were the importation of the "university ideal" and its concomitant "intellectual impersonalism" from Germany (Rudolph, 1962). These pervasive influences, especially the German model of education with its emphasis on basic research and the development of graduate school programs to support it, rapidly eroded whatever was left of a spiritual emphasis of college life for students. Over time faculty became much less concerned with students' moral underpinnings and social experiences and much more interested in their own increasingly specialized teaching and research activities.

These developments, coupled with the increased organizational complexity that was a natural by-product of larger colleges and universities, produced potentially alienating learning conditions for students. The institutional response was to create a new category of college personnel that began to appear in the latter decades of the nineteenth century, the dean of students. Student life deans believed that students should be treated as whole persons with individual personalities (National Association of Deans and Advisors of Men, 1943). In 1937 a group of educational leaders drafted *The Student Personnel Point of View*, a treatise delineating the values and functions of student personnel workers (as they were called then). This foundational document remains the most comprehensive articulation of the field's philosophy and functions, even though it was revised in 1949 and again updated and affirmed in 1987 in *A Perspective on Student Affairs* (NASPA, 1989).

Student Affairs Values

The practice of student affairs on a daily basis is influenced by many things, chief among them the personal background, values, assumptions, and beliefs of individual student affairs practitioners and the particular college or university context where one works. Student affairs staff must balance the sometimes competing demands of serving the institution's purposes and responding to the needs and interests of individual students (NASPA, 1989). Student affairs professionals also are expected to endorse institutional values personally as well as professionally, particularly in small college settings where frequent face-to-face student contact between students, faculty members, and student affairs professionals is the norm (Love et al., 1993).

Although the functional duties of a residential life director, counselor, and student activities coordinator differ, certain core values have come to represent and unify student affairs administrators working in these different roles. These values are grounded in four philosophical traditions: holism (the student is a whole person), humanism (belief in human rationality, the possibility of human perfection, and the value of self-awareness and self-understanding), pragmatism (making things work), and individualism (recognition of and appreciation for individual differences in backgrounds, abilities, interests, and goals) (Winston & Saunders, 1991). These traditions give rise to seven values that are essential to the field: service, truth, freedom, individuation, equality, justice, and community (Young, 1997). Other values that are often mentioned in the literature as characteristic of the field include altruism, human dignity, and tolerance (Canon & Brown, 1985; Dalton & Healy, 1984; Sandeen, 1985; Upcraft, 1988). Taken together, these bedrock values are the wellspring of the profession's deep commitment to humanizing the student experience in institutions that can be very impersonal and bureaucratic (Brown, 1972) and the reason the student affairs function is sometimes expected to act as the conscience of the campus by modeling and promoting ethical behavior and doing no harm (Kitchener, 1984). It is no coincidence that the recently published *Good Practices in Student Affairs* (Blimling & Whitt, 1999) articulates well with these values. These espoused values, and the beliefs and assumptions that undergird them, "anchor the work of those in student affairs and make what they do, and how they do it, distinctive and valued" (Lyons, 1990, p. 40). These values are implicit in some of Meredith's comments to her friend, David, especially her belief that the proposed living–learning community at Midwestern State University can be an important vehicle for introducing new students to the campus culture and the academic values that are important for students to learn.

Through a Cultural Lens: Student Affairs and Other Campus Constituencies

How you get there depends on where "there" is, advises a character in Lewis Carroll's classic *Alice in Wonderland*. Using a cultural lens helps practitioners discover existing cultural properties; it also involves reminding oneself of what matters to various campus constituencies. This suggests the culturally competent practitioner should ask, "In the context of this situation at this point in time, in light of the institution's educational purposes and values, what is central, and what is peripheral, to the various campus groups that are directly involved, have a vested interest in, or could be affected by the issue or decision?"

Faculty members, academic administrators, and student affairs practitioners all make valuable contributions to the educational process, yet their core values and priorities sometimes put them at odds with one another. In large part this is because of the different "maps" or mental models (Senge, 1990) they have of the collegiate landscape (Arnold & Kuh, 1999). A "mental model" of the world is a sort of navigational system that guides thought and behavior in an almost unconscious manner. These mental models, or maps, of undergraduate learning and personal development determine what people attend to, what they hold dear, and what they emphasize in their own work with students and others. They essentially determine how one spends time and on what one focuses. And, most important, they dictate the relative value one gives to various facets of the undergraduate experience (Arnold & Kuh, 1999).

Recall that a prime faculty value with respect to student learning is the creation and dissemination of knowledge, and the vehicles through which these values are expressed are teaching, research, and service. For student affairs, a prime value is holistic student development thought to be fostered through students' active participation in various activities and programs (Love et al., 1993). Faculty members believe that learning occurs best through reflective thought, whereas student affairs professionals tend to value doing over thinking and reflecting (Love et al., 1993). These activities and the values they represent are not mutually exclusive, of course, though educators and practitioners sometimes talk and act (especially at national or regional student affairs meetings) as if they were. It is far more productive to view the contributions of faculty members and student affairs practitioners as complementary parts of the complicated process of student development, the yin and yang of "interlocked halves" perceived as "distinct but inseparable, necessary to each other to form the whole, each containing some elements of its opposite" (Blake, 1996, p. 4).

With this perspective in mind, how might Meredith have managed and responded to what transpired during the FIGs planning meeting? Knowing that groups of faculty and student affairs professionals have different mental models of undergraduate education and what matters to student learning (Arnold & Kuh, 1999), she might have framed the issues differently for each of the project's various stakeholder groups (faculty members, the other student affairs practitioners present, students), leading each to see a larger piece of what all share as the central goal of the undergraduate experience—student learning and personal development. Meredith might have contacted another institution with a FIGs program to get guidance and perhaps positive testimonials from faculty, administration, and students on the value of their program. Perhaps she could have consulted some of the literature citing the relevance of FIGs programs to academic learning, thus increasing her chances of persuading the faculty members of the educationally powerful environment that FIGs create, leaving them more favorably disposed to implementing the program.

CAMPUS CULTURE IN TRANSITION

There is, throughout this chapter and in most writings on the topic, a tendency to portray culture as if it were a stable, enduring set of immutable properties. There is plenty of evidence to suggest that campus cultures today may be changing more quickly and to a greater degree than at any time in the past half century. This, in turn, is making campus cultures much more ambiguous and difficult to describe, understand, and manage. Some decades ago it was clear to newcomers how they were to behave in order to succeed—what was valued and what was not. Because of a variety of uncontrollable factors, the institutional ethos at most colleges and universities that once communicated institutional expectations and core values has lost much of its conforming effect on the behavior of both students and professional staff. In this section we entertain some of the reasons for this change and note implications for student affairs educators, managers, and leaders.

There is good reason to view collegiate cultures as essentially stable, changing imperceptibly if at all. Indeed, an important function of culture is to lend continuity and stability to groups and organizations. As intimated earlier in this chapter, culture maintains—for better or worse—key elements of institutional life. It perpetuates cherished values and principles that mark a school's character and that its constituents are inclined to support for various reasons (Kuh, 1993). This is essential to accomplishing daily tasks as well as focusing institutional agents on performing those tasks that are needed to realize the institution's educational mission. The myriad interaction patterns that evolve into normative practices guide the behavior of newcomers and veterans alike and help people learn their organizational roles and responsibilities, a key responsibility of the student affairs professional as educator. In this sense, an institution's culture provides stability in an increasingly complicated, rapidly changing world.

This enduring quality of culture is a major reason why it is so difficult to intentionally change many long-standing institutional policies and practices. That is, people develop routines and any attempt to substantially modify these behaviors and the assumptions on which they are based are typically rebuffed because the familiar response—"That's not the way we do things around here"— is often invoked. Not recognizing the tenacious grip that culture has on institutional policies and practices can frustrate the student affairs leader and manager committed to bring about change. Although all of this is true, institutional cultures do evolve over time. Two sets of conditions are especially ripe for inducing cultural change.

The first is a cataclysmic event (or series of events or circumstances) that is either externally prompted or induced internally by a variety of uncontrollable factors (Peterson & Spencer, 1990) and that has implications for both the manager and leader roles. Because the pace of change in the external environment is unprecedented, it is likely that colleges will have to more quickly reallocate resources that may lead to changes in culturally embedded practices and beliefs. The most obvious of these may be financial threats to an institution, brought about by declining revenue streams, such as shrinking student enrollments. When an institution's existence is at issue (Zammuto, 1986), faculty and staff members are more likely to consider alternative ways of managing their affairs and performing their duties. Other examples of the kinds of institutional responses to enrollment shortfalls include shifting staff resources to add more admissions and financial aid personnel, modifying academic programs to appeal to an expanded range of students, and increasing teaching loads or class sizes so that fewer instructors are needed. No one of these will likely produce significant cultural change, but taken together they can shift over time the ratios of faculty, staff, and students (e.g., fewer tenure-track faculty, more support staff) and the role and functions of student affairs (e.g., from one focused on student welfare and student learning to one more aligned with a recruitment and enrollment management emphasis).

Another influence of the external environment is a heightened need for campus security and safety, which affects the work scope of student affairs professionals as educators and managers. Once a widely accepted article of faith was that the college campus was a protected island where student safety was assured. Student affairs professionals have always known that this was a fiction and have worked tirelessly to make students aware of campus resources available to insure their well-being as well as teach them how to take care of themselves in a new environment. Civil laws have redefined the nature of student–institutional relations and, in the process, affected the culture of many campuses with strictly enforced due process student conduct codes replacing a values-based, developmental approach to handling student discipline. The former insures the protection of an individual's constitutional rights, but it also tends to homogenize and legalize campus cultures.

A second, and more subtle, form of cultural change occurs over a typically longer period of time and concerns interactions between people that influence the larger institutional environment and its subenvironments. Newcomers from a specific historically underrepresented group can have a particularly influential effect when their numbers reach critical mass of the population, estimated to be about 15% (Smith, 1989). This position is consistent with the campus ecology view (Banning, 1989), which views the student experience as a series of transactions between people and their environments, broadly defined to include all forms of physical, biological, and human exchanges between and among students, faculty, staff, and so on. That is, newcomers arrive in substantial enough numbers to begin to gradually change how various institutional events, policies, and practices are interpreted, which can ultimately lead to substantive changes in those events, policies, and practices. For example, as faculty members trained in research university graduate departments come to a campus they expect to engage in scholarship at the same high level as their graduate school mentors even though their new institution may have a different mission. This can create misunderstandings and frustration on the part of both veteran faculty and newcomers. Similarly, new student affairs professionals directly out of graduate preparation programs often are discouraged after a few months on the job with their colleagues who are not as familiar with the recent literature or the priorities and activities of the professional associations.

Over time, the influx of newcomers can challenge and change the status quo. Certain events, for example, that once were considered essential to maintaining the cultural traditions of a school are years later widely viewed as demeaning and offensive because newcomers see them differently than their predecessors. Manning (1993) described one such event, Kake Walk, which was practiced annually at the University of Vermont between 1893 until 1969 and remains embedded in the institutional memory:

> Kake Walk, including the performer's black-face make-up, was a parody of late nineteenth-century minstrel shows. Primarily a fraternity and sorority event, kake walkers would practice their high-stepping routines for months. . . . The racist message of Kake Walk, clearly evident in the re-enactment of slaves' performance to win the cake provided by their masters, was not viewed as being racist in intent by many. . . . Because [it] was declared to be not intentionally racist, it was not easy to eliminate; its racist messages were confounded with positive messages of community, loyalty, unity, and entertainment. (pp. 27–28)

Another factor that can induce cultural change is the increasing diversity of students matriculating to many college campuses. Undergraduate students today differ in many respects from previous cohorts (Astin, 1998; Kuh, 1999). Whereas in the 1960s only about a third of the college age population matriculated to a two- or four-year college, today more than 60% of this age group enroll in higher education within a year following high school graduation. Although earlier generations did not necessarily represent an elite, college-going class, the range of student ability and performance expectations today is considerably expanded. In particular, students' expectations for what college life will

be like appear to be less congruent with those of the faculty and previous cohorts of students.

Along with a wider range of abilities, interests, and expectations, contemporary students also bring with them a much more diverse set of cultural understandings, beliefs, and assumptions about education, college life, and the preferred nature of relations among groups and individuals. The importation of
people from different cultural backgrounds—what Van Maanen (1984) called
cultures of orientation—means that newcomers (students, faculty, staff) will try
to understand their new environment using an interpretive scheme or sense-
making system developed through previous experiences in their cultures of origin. This is not unlike the mental model concept (Senge, 1990) discussed earlier. For example, does the family or others from one's cultures of origin (school
teachers, relatives, neighbors) value attending and graduating from college? Is
college going supported, or congruent with, the family's values and aspirations?
Is college important primarily to get a good job? Or does it hold some other
meaning, such as cultivating aesthetic sensibilities or developing a new
worldview? Is college appropriate for both men and women? What is the student's
(or new faculty or staff member's) mental model (Arnold & Kuh, 1999) of the
institution? Answers to these questions reveal cultural underpinnings that shape
the aspirations of individuals and groups and may occasionally collide with dominant themes in an institution's culture and ultimately challenge accepted practices and ways to thinking and making meaning (Kuh & Love, in press).

This is a particularly confounding set of factors when trying to interpret
the shaping influence of newcomers on the institutional culture and how student affairs professionals can best respond. Although student affairs professionals are expected to be experts on students, and may understand and appreciate the variation and importance of the increasing diversity of students at many
schools, they must also be wise enough to discern how this increased diversity is
clashing with, accommodating, or substantively modifying their institution's
culture. The literature offers little insight into the nature of cultural ambigu-
ities encountered by newcomers (Martin, 1992). But there is enough evidence
to suggest that the experiences of minority students and their level of satisfaction with their college differs qualitatively in ways that a thorough examination
of the campus culture might help elucidate.

Another factor increasing the ambiguity permeating contemporary collegiate culture is the changing nature of the faculty. At all but the most selective
and affluent four-year colleges, a smaller proportion of replacement faculty are
full-time tenure-track hires. One implication of this trend is that, over time,
fewer of the instructional staff will become familiar with an institution's history,
values, and, traditions, and therefore, be able to persuasively affirm, uphold,
and translate the meaning of these cultural properties to newcomers and to
behave in ways that reinforce these valued cultural properties as did their predecessors. This is not to suggest that the activities and behaviors of newcomers,
whether they be full or part time are somehow less valued by, or less valuable

to, the institution. It suggests only that their reduced presence on campus will not allow them to become fully invested in and knowledgeable about the institution's culture or be around long enough to understand its nuances.

Another personnel factor that makes collegiate culture more complicated today is the palpable increased professionalization of almost every group of institutional agents, from academic administrators and student life professionals to building and grounds staff, and so on. As mentioned earlier, almost every student affairs functional area (admissions, orientation, financial aid, career services, residence life, student activities) has its own national professional organization with a distinctive language and other cultural artifacts that can affect how one interprets and performs the educator, manager, and leader roles. These professional groups and their regional and state organizations help advance knowledge and practice in functional areas, but they also tend to segment the student affairs field, making it difficult to communicate and understand the work and the contributions of colleagues in other units. These are not criticisms, but rather points to ponder in attempting to understand the factors and conditions that are increasing the ambiguity associated with what the institution and its various constituents value and what is the most appropriate way to do things in the institutional environment.

Another influence on institutional culture is the increased usage on college campuses of external agents and service providers to perform internal functions. Functions that have been traditionally performed and managed by units within the college are increasingly being outsourced. For example, dining services in residence hall and campus unions are being provided by for-profit firms at some institutions. Similarly, many colleges and universities across the country are entertaining the notion of turning the operation of their campus bookstores and residence halls over to providers outside the campus. In the future, campus culture will be inevitably affected by the ebb and flow of personnel who might have little knowledge of, or concern for, the norms and values that undergird institutional functioning. This has implications for both the leader and manager roles.

Last but certainly not least, long-standing notions about what constitutes learning, including where and how it takes place, are changing. Traditionally, it was assumed that learning was concentrated in laboratories, studios, classrooms, and lecture halls, and—with few exceptions (e.g., study abroad, coop arrangements)—this was a campus-based phenomenon. Today, learning is no longer synchronous and is just as likely to take place off campus as on campus. Desktop computers are all but ubiquitous, making accessible intellectual resources from around the world, not just the host institution (Green, 1996). Information technology (IT) promises to change virtually every aspect of college and university life (Abeles, 1998; Gilbert, 1996; West, 1996) by blurring the lines between privacy and public exposure, which will almost certainly affect student culture, especially on residential campuses. The thoughtful but worrisome observation of one parent points to a substantial challenge facing student affairs educators:

There is a huge lifestyle/living issue that has been created by computers in dorm rooms. Students spend most of their time in their rooms because of computers. This creates cohabitation problems beyond dorm rules and regulations as well as privacy and courtesy dilemmas. What do you do when your roommate is on the computer all night and you need to sleep? Or is playing videos at any time of day or night and you need to study? Where is the private time for students? Dorm rooms are becoming a 24-hour communications terminal. (Rhodes, 1999, p. 11)

The confluence of these and other factors demands that student affairs professionals become skilled cultural practitioners (Lundberg, 1990) with the ability to discover and make sense of sometimes ambiguous, confusing cultural properties.

THE CULTURALLY COMPETENT STUDENT AFFAIRS PRACTITIONER

In this section we describe selected characteristics of culturally competent student affairs professionals in their roles as educators, managers, and leaders. That is, cultural competence is essential to perform any of the three roles effectively. The student affairs *educator* becomes knowledgeable about the campus culture in order to teach those aspects of the culture that newcomers (students, staff, faculty) need to know to function effectively and to develop strategies to change those aspects that are no longer appropriate, given the changing characteristics of students, faculty, and staff or the evolving institutional mission. The student affairs *manager* must be culturally competent in order to do things in ways that are consistent with existing norms and expectations when planning, coordinating, supervising, and making decisions. In this sense a student affairs manager constantly monitors the campus environment and is adept at crossing the cultural boundaries that may exist between various groups. The student affairs *leader* models appropriate value-driven behavior for people throughout the institution (including colleagues in student affairs) by frequently articulating how the contributions of the student affairs division are compatible with core institutional and academic values and advancing the institutional mission of holistic student development using language and behavior appropriate for different subcultures. Finally, in all three roles—educator, manager, and leader—the culturally competent student affairs professional uses knowledge of campus culture to foster collaborative working relations with students, faculty, administrators, and others in order to enhance the institution's educational effectiveness and to help students succeed.

Cultural competence is not a state of *being* that can be mastered, but rather a way of *seeing* and *acting* that is once learned then practiced every day. Emphasizing seeing and acting rather than being is consistent with the idea that culture is constructed by the intersection of the private or personal with the public or social experience. Because meaning making is subjective, culturally competent student affairs educators, managers, and leaders must routinely engage in a process whereby they *discover, observe, reflect, evaluate, act,* and *re-evaluate* the campus environment, various situations, and their actions. This is to say that cultural competence is an acquired way of experiencing the campus as well as an ongoing process of discovery and rediscovery by which one enhances the capacity for creative, appropriate responses to a new or dynamic environment. It offers the possibility of daily renewal, heightened sensitivities and perception, and invigorated responses for new and veteran practitioners alike.

To perform effectively, newcomers must make the strange familiar by learning the institution's norms, language, core values, and other important aspects of the institutional culture (Whitt, 1993). Seasoned practitioners, however, must try to make the familiar strange by continually monitoring the cultural scene, modifying or reinterpreting it as appropriate, such as responding affirmatively to newcomers or assessing how components of campus culture affect, or are experienced by, members of historically underrepresented groups. If Meredith were to use the *discover–observe–reflect–evaluate–act–reevaluate* approach to understand the dynamics of the FIGs implementation meeting and to facilitate her work with this group and elsewhere on campus, she might very well ask herself the following:

What do I need to discover to understand the key elements of the Midwestern University culture that are influencing the beliefs, assumptions, language, and behavior of the members of the FIGs implementation committee?

What cultural properties (norms, values, beliefs, traditions, language, sagas, myths, and so on) do I need to teach and manage when working with the various groups that have a stake in and must be involved in developing the FIG initiative?

Do certain of Midwestern's deeply held values, traditions, and norms conflict with those of newcomers who need to be validated? And, if so, how can I best exercise leadership to help the institution welcome and affirm these newcomers?

What is my mental model of student learning, and how does it complement, or conflict with, the mental models of other FIG implementation committee members?

What tactics might be effective in managing the different mental models that are represented by the faculty members, administrators, and students on the committee?

What other steps can I take by myself and with others to discover and more fully understand the different campus subcultures that will be affected by FIGs?

How can I use my increasing knowledge and understanding of Midwestern's culture to improve my overall effectiveness as a student affairs educator, manager, and leader?

To answer these and related questions, Meredith (and other student affairs professionals) should work through the five-step action plan in order to become culturally competent. As is attributed to Yogi Berra, "You can observe a lot by just watching," but there are other ways that student affairs educators, managers, and leaders can obtain valuable information needed to become culturally competent. One way is to read comprehensive treatises on the topic. In addition to those already mentioned, we recommend Clark (1970, 1972), Kuh (1993), Kuh and Whitt (1988), Martin (1992), Tierney (1988), and Tierney and Rhoads (1994).

1. **Become familiar with the institution's history, traditions, norms, and other cultural properties, including their behavioral implications.**

   The history and traditions of a college or university are the building blocks of institutional culture. Taken together, they affect—for better or worse—how many other cultural properties (beliefs, values, norms) are interpreted. For culturally competent student affairs professionals, knowledge of the institution's history and traditions is a compass that points to ways to handle various situations. It is a daunting challenge for newcomers like Meredith to make sense of the myriad, often ambiguous properties of institutional culture. Meredith must take control over her socialization to Midwestern and become familiar as soon as possible with the norms and values (both espoused and enacted) that guide institutional behavior. She will need this information to teach it to others, including new professional and paraprofessional staff members. As a manager and leader, she must continually monitor and assess the impact that various cultural properties seem to be having on various groups.

   Meredith can use the *discover–observe–reflect–evaluate–act–reevaluate* cycle to learn the institution's history and traditions and determine the extent to which these cultural properties affirm or alienate various groups. She can discover relevant aspects of Midwestern's history by reading historical documents, literature, and other archival material. She can observe the cultural implications of history and tradition in the present by noting their impact on institutional policies and practices and on the behavior of individuals and various groups. Often visiting with campus historians or touring the campus with the institutional architect are good sources of relevant cultural insight. She might then reflect on how various cultural features (for example, sagas, traditions) bear on the present and evaluate their current utility to see how they facilitate or obstruct the attainment of general institutional and specific student development goals. In her leadership role she should then act purposefully to affirm the positive aspects of Midwestern's history and traditions and develop a strategy to be pursued with the help of others to minimize those cultural features that are deleterious to the learning and well-being of certain groups.

   Finally, Meredith must reevaluate her actions in the context of the present and evolving circumstances. Consider Kake Walk at the University of Vermont. Although this event is no longer an active tradition, revisiting it in historical context can illustrate how the *discover–observe–reflect–evaluate–*

act–reevaluate cycle can be used. Meredith should first discover as much as she can about the event—its origins, who participates and why. Then she can imagine observing the event and then reflect on and evaluate how this event might have affected different subcultures on campus. She could reevaluate her interpretation of the various perspectives on this event, perhaps even schedule a campus forum where the residual effects of this tradition can be discussed and how her university can continue to help individual students and various groups deal with this unfortunate aspect of their school's history.

2. **Locate and identify the vehicles through which culture is transmitted.**

As mentioned before, an effective way to transmit culture is to intentionally teach newcomers what is valued and desirable. After becoming familiar with Midwestern's history and traditions, Meredith should identify the various ways and means through which Midwestern intentionally and unintentionally transmits its culture. Who are the primary culture bearers, people who are in a position to influence values and ideas? What are the venues through which values and beliefs are communicated? How can she draw on her knowledge of Midwestern's culture to more effectively manage various aspects of the FIGs planning process?

Most schools stage elaborate orientation and welcome events for new students and faculty members to introduce various aspects of campus life. However, unintended antiintellectual messages are sometimes communicated. Meredith should discover who is communicating what in terms of institutional values. She should also determine the formal and informal ways the newcomers (especially students and student affairs staff) learn about Midwestern—what is acceptable and what is not in terms of behavior, language, dress, and so forth. She should then observe and scrutinize written and spoken communication to be sure the messages being sent to students are those that are intended. She could take note of how people perform in various settings and how various cultural properties are transmitted, by whom, and toward what ends. Meredith should then reflect on what is communicated to determine whether there are better ways of teaching newcomers what they need to know. She should further pay attention to how these norms, values, and belief systems may have become stitched into the institutional fabric, being sensitive to whether the values and beliefs of certain groups are or are not represented. She could consider how to more effectively introduce members of various groups to Midwestern's culture. She should then reevaluate the processes by which the university's culture typically gets transmitted and acculturated in various groups and whether new norms and values are emerging that may be important to validating certain groups, thereby contributing to institutional vitality in the future.

3. **Continuously monitor the values and norms of the various campus subcultures, how they interact with one another, and their impact on the larger campus culture.**

The next step toward cultural competence is to figure out how the various cultural properties work together in shaping institutional policies and practices, articulate with the institution's espoused values, and affect the behavior and performance of different subcultures. One of Meredith's important tasks is to foster symbiotic working relationships among the various members of the FIGs implementation committee. Being able to encourage collaboration among people from different cultural enclaves is an invaluable personnel management skill. She must also assiduously manage the communication during FIGs meetings to minimize potential misunderstandings that are sure to result because of the different mental models operating.

Meredith can begin by discovering the assumptions and normative behaviors that are shared by the committee members as well as the ways that individual members' beliefs and preferences might confound group understanding, strain interpersonal relations, and obstruct progress. She can observe how campus groups interact, communicate, work, collaborate, and get along with one another in meetings, ceremonies, academic environments and social environments. Meredith could then reflect on the content and process of group interactions, noting shared assumptions about norms and behaviors, paying attention to those elements of culture each group contributes to the campus environment, and identifying what groups seem to have in common. She might then evaluate what kinds of interventions and language might best facilitate the group's progress and how to best negotiate in the common interest of those whose views must be represented. She can then perform an act of leadership by developing a strategy that would get all members of the committee to share their goals and expectations for FIGs as they relate to the institution's larger educational mission. In making decisions and setting priorities Meredith should remember to ask, "Whose values and interests are represented and honored, and whose are not?" At this point Meredith would do well to reevaluate her actions, noting whether any changes have occurred in the nature of the understandings that committee members have about FIGs and if any other aspects of Midwestern's culture need attention to move the group forward.

4. **Strive for cultural congruence, both personally and professionally.**

Student affairs professionals are often the first (and sometimes the most sustained) point of contact students have with their college. For this reason, whatever student affairs professionals say and do can validate or invalidate espoused institutional values and norms. In addition, student affairs educators are among the best positioned institutional agents to provide feedback to students as to the appropriateness of their behavior in an academic environment. Thus, Meredith and her colleagues in the division of student affairs at Midwestern are professionally obligated to continuously monitor the degree to which the university's policies and practices are aligned with, and complement, its espoused values. In short, Meredith must ask over and over, "Are we doing what we are saying and saying what we are doing?"

To be culturally congruent, Meredith must discover aspects of her behavior that are more or less consistent with the espoused institutional values and the beliefs and assumptions of the student affairs profession (Lyons, 1990; NASPA, 1989). She can observe how others respond to her when articulating these views in FIGs implementation meetings and other venues and evaluate the situations in which she is more or less culturally congruent. Meredith can use this information at some later point to reevaluate how her actions affect others and solicit feedback about her effectiveness. Of course, reevaluation leads to discovery, observation, and reflection; thus the cycle begins anew.

Meredith can lead the design of the FIGs project by communicating to various campus groups how the FIG experience will contribute to student learning and personal development consistent with Midwestern's educational mission. In this role she must constantly monitor the work of the FIG implementation committee and address any misunderstandings that may emerge about what the program is trying to accomplish on the part of students, faculty members, residence life staff members, and others.

5. **Personify holistic student development in all words and deeds.**

As discussed earlier, student affairs traditionally has championed holistic student development, including the enhancement of intellectual and moral development as well as emotional, social, and physical wellness. In her work with the FIGs implementation committee, Meredith can lead the way by reminding her colleagues and students at every appropriate opportunity of Midwestern's espoused mission of cultivating in students an appreciation for understanding human differences and civic responsibility as well as honing critical thinking skills and obtaining a foundation in a field of study that will prepare them for advanced study in their professional area, graduate school, or a job after college.

Meredith can begin by discovering how other student affairs practitioners, faculty members, and academic administrators perform in this regard, noting who at Midwestern articulates this goal particularly well. In her educator role she can use her knowledge of college student development to teach her colleagues on the FIGs planning committee and members of other campus groups about the changing characteristics of today's students. She can also offer her expertise to the campus assessment committee (Banta & Kuh, 1998). She should then reflect on how her mentors and respected colleagues perform these important functions. Meredith might evaluate the methods by which various activities can be introduced to Midwestern that nurture holistic development and learning for different types of students. She should also determine the extent to which campus events and activities either further or limit the attainment of student learning and personal development.

In her manager role Meredith is now ready to act by designing and implementing programs that address holistic development across different groups, including the FIGs implementation committee. She must emphasize activities that draw on shared beliefs and norms and minimize activities that foster or perpetuate divisiveness. Meredith's effectiveness will depend in large part on her ability to intentionally weave the objectives of the FIGs program into Midwestern's academic mission. After trying out some of these tactics Meredith should re-evaluate the status of her committee's work related to holistic development and see whether other tactics or activities are warranted.

CONCLUSION

Being culturally competent enhances virtually all aspects of the student affairs educator, manager, and leader functions. For example, teaching institutional values to new students is a major responsibility of the orientation director when designing transition to college programs, such as celebrating diversity and becoming aware of the various cultural and performing arts venues that can will help students cultivate an appreciation for the esthetic dimensions of campus life. Student judicial proceedings are occasions to teach students about the role of community in academic settings, emphasizing the institution's values of respecting all individuals and diverse points of view. Programming board members can be challenged to reflect on the values and symbolic messages they communicate by selecting certain entertainers over others. For example, bringing a comedian to campus whose material features racist or sexist jokes is inconsistent with a campus culture that espouses inclusiveness as a value. Simply put, the culturally competent student affairs educator translates and enacts campus values through teaching students and others.

Student affairs managers are responsible for the stewardship of student and institutional resources and deploying those resources in ways that will have the maximum positive impact on student learning and personal development. Campus culture affects every managerial function, from how major decisions are made that affect budget, personnel, and programs to the hundreds of interactions one has on a daily basis with faculty members, students, and others. The culturally competent student affairs manager who has a keenly honed understanding of the way things work enjoys the respect of colleagues and is able to act with confidence in the best interests of students and the institution.

Student affairs leaders articulate a vision for holistic student development and work to create settings where that vision can be realized. Leadership requires mutual respect and persuasive communication skills. The student affairs leader needs a deep understanding of campus culture to take students and the institution in a direction that will enable both to succeed.

In conclusion, many forces are influencing and changing collegiate cultures. For this reason, the skills and knowledge required to become culturally competent are no longer desirable, they are essential. Whether it be a calamitous campus event, the shifting roles of faculty and other personnel, the evolving relationship between institutional environments and their subenvironments, the influence of both internal and external dynamics, or the changing student demographics in the landscape of higher education, students affairs professionals must always be cognizant of the role and importance of culture in their professional practice.

QUESTIONS TO CONSIDER

1. What cultural assumptions do you hold that bear on your work as a student affairs practitioner? Have you been in situations on campus where these assumptions have been challenged or considered suspect by others or resulted in unsatisfactory outcomes? If so, what were the dynamics that led to this situation and how might misunderstandings or disagreements be addressed more productively?
2. If you were designing a staff development workshop to help people with whom you work become culturally competent, what aspects of institutional culture would you emphasize? What kinds of activities would be effective in attaining your goals for the workshop?
3. Identify some key characteristics of your campus culture that are consistent with or affirm the espoused institutional values. What are some enacted cultural elements that are inconsistent with espoused values? Keeping in mind the often conflicting norms, values, and beliefs that campus subcultures bring to bear on institutional functioning, what steps could be taken to make your institution's espoused and enacted values more congruent?

REFERENCES

Abeles, T. P. (1998). Perplexed about technology. *On the Horizon, 6*(4), 14–16.

Arnold, K., & Kuh, G. D. (1999). What matters in undergraduate education? Mental models, student learning, and student affairs. In E. J. Whitt (Ed.), *Student affairs and student learning*. Washington, DC: National Association of Student Personnel Administrators.

Astin, A. W. (1998). The changing American college student: Thirty year trends, 1966–1996. *The Review of Higher Education, 21*, 115–135.

Austin, A. E. (1990). Faculty cultures, faculty values. In W. G. Tierney (Ed.), *Assessing academic climates and cultures* (pp. 3–18). New Directions for Institutional Research, No. 68. San Francisco: Jossey-Bass.

Banning, J. H. (1989). Creating a climate for successful student development: The cam-

pus ecology manager role. In U. Delworth & G. Hanson (Eds.), *Student services: A handbook for the profession* (pp. 304–322). San Francisco: Jossey-Bass.

Banta, T. W., & Kuh, G. D. (1998). A missing link in assessment: Collaboration between academic and student affairs. *Change, 30*(2), 40–46.

Blake, E. S. (1996). The yin and yang of student learning in college. *About Campus, 1*(4), 4–9.

Blimling, G. S., & Whitt, E. J. (Eds.). (1999). *Good practices in student affairs: Principles to foster student learning*. San Francisco: Jossey-Bass.

Brown, R. D. (1972). *Student development in tomorrow's higher education: A return to the academy*. Washington, DC: American College Personnel Association.

Canon, H. J., & Brown, R. D. (1985). How to

think about professional ethics. In H. J. Canon & R. D. Brown (Eds.), *Applied ethics in student services* (pp. 81–87). New Directions in Student Services, No. 30. San Francisco: Jossey-Bass.

Clark, B. R. (1970). *The distinctive college: Reed, Antioch, and Swarthmore*. Chicago: Aldine.

Clark, B. R. (1972). The organizational saga in higher education. *Administrative Science Quarterly, 17*(2), 178–184.

Clark, B. R. (1984). *The higher education system: Academic organization in cross-national perspective*. Berkeley: University of California Press.

Dalton, J., & Healy, M. (1984). Using values education activities to confront student conduct issues. *NASPA Journal, 22*, 19–25.

Dill, D. D. (1982). The management of academic culture: Notes on the management of meaning and social integration. *Higher Education, 11*, 303–320.

Geertz, C. (1973). *The interpretation of cultures*. New York: Basic Books.

Green, K. C. (1996). The coming ubiquity of information technology. *Change, 28*(2), 24–28.

Gilbert, S. W. (1996). Making the most of a slow revolution. *Change, 28*(2), 10–23.

Jelinek, C., Smircich, L., & Hirsch, P. (1983). Introduction: A 'code' of many colors. *Administrative Science Quarterly, 28*, 331–338.

Kilmann, R. H., Saxton, M., Serpa, R., & Associates. (1985). *Gaining control of the corporate culture*. San Francisco: Jossey-Bass.

Kitchener, K. S. (1984). Intuition, critical evaluation and ethical principles: The foundation for ethical decisions in counseling psychology. *Counseling Psychologist, 12*, 43–55.

Kuh, G. D. (1993). Appraising the character of a college. *Journal of Counseling and Development, 71*, 661–668.

Kuh, G. D. (1995). Cultivating "high stakes" student culture research. *Reseach and Higher Education, 36*, 563–576.

Kuh, G. D. (1999). How are we doing? Tracking the quality of the undergraduate experience from the 1960s to the present. *Review of Higher Education, 22*, 99–119.

Kuh, G. D., & Hall, J. E. (1993). Cultural perspectives in student affairs. In G. D. Kuh (Ed.), *Cultural perspectives in student affairs work* (pp. 6–20). Lanham, MD: American College Personnel Association.

Kuh, G. D., & Hu, S. (1999, April). *Learning productivity at research universities*. Paper presented at the annual meeting of the American Educational Research Association, Montreal.

Kuh, G. D., & Love, P. G. (in press). A cultural perspective on student departure. In J. Braxton (Ed.), *New perspectives on student departure*. Nashville: University of Vanderbilt Press.

Kuh, G. D., & Whitt, E. J. (1988). *The invisible tapestry: Culture in American colleges and universities*. ASHE-ERIC Higher Education Report No. 1. Washington, DC: Association for the Study of Higher Education.

Love, P. G., Boschini, V. J., Jacobs, B. A., Hardy, C. M., & Kuh, G. D. (1993). Student culture. In G. D. Kuh (Ed.), *Cultural perspectives in student affairs work* (pp. 59–79). Lanham, MD: American College Personnel Association.

Love, P. G., Kuh, G. D., MacKay, K. A., & Hardy, C. M. (1993). Side by side: Faculty and student affairs cultures. In G. D. Kuh (Ed.), *Cultural perspectives in student affairs work* (pp. 37–58). Lanham, MD: American College Personnel Association.

Lundberg, C. C. (1990). Surfacing organizational culture. *Journal of Managerial Psychology, 5*(4), 19–26.

Lyons, J. W. (1990). Examining the validity of basic assumptions and beliefs. In M. L. Upcraft, M. J. Barr, & Associates (Eds.), *New futures for student affairs* (pp. 22–40). San Francisco: Jossey-Bass.

Manning, K. (1993). Properties of institutional culture. In G. D. Kuh (Ed.), *Cultural perspectives in student affairs work* (pp. 21–36). Lanham, MD: American College Personnel Association.

Martin, J. (1992). *Cultures in organizations: Three perspectives*. New York: Oxford University Press.

National Association of Student Personnel Administrators (NASPA). (1989). *Points of view*. Washington, DC: Author.

Peterson, M. W., & Spencer, M. G. (1990). Understanding academic culture and climate. In W. G. Tierney (Ed.), *Assessing academic climates and cultures* (pp. 3–18). New Directions for Institutional Research, No. 68. San Francisco: Jossey-Bass.

Rhodes, J. C. (1999). *Video survey results*. Unpublished manuscript, Bloomington, IN: Indiana University Office of Enrollment Services.

Rudolph, F. (1962). *The American college and university: A history*. Athens, GA: University of Georgia Press.

Sandeen, A. (1985). The legacy of values education in college student personnel work. In J. C. Dalton (Ed.), *Promoting values development in college students* (Monograph Series No. 4, pp. 1–16). Washington, DC: National Association of Student Personnel Administrators.

Senge, P. M. (1990). *The fifth discipline: The art and practice of the learning organization*. New York: Doubleday.

Smircich, L. (1983). Concepts of culture and organizational analysis. *Administrative Science Quarterly, 28*, 339–358.

Smith, D. G. (1989). *The challenge of diversity: Involvement or alienation in the academy*. ASHE-ERIC Higher Education Report, No. 5. Washington, DC: The George Washington University School of Education and Human Development.

Tierney, W. G. (1988). Organizational culture in higher education: Defining the essentials. *Journal of Higher Education, 59*, 2–21.

Tierney, W. G., & Rhoads, R. A. (1994). *Faculty socialization as cultural process: A mirror of institutional commitment*. ASHE-ERIC Higher Education Report No. 93-6. Washington, DC: The George Washington University, School of Education and Human Development.

Upcraft, M. L. (1988). Managing right. In M. L. Upcraft & M. J. Barr, *Managing student affairs effectively* (pp. 65–78). New Directions for Student Services, No. 42. San Francisco: Jossey-Bass.

Van Maanen, J. (1984). Doing old things in new ways: The chains of socialization. In J. Bess (Ed.), *College and university organization: Insights from the behavioral sciences*. New York: New York University Press.

Van Maanen, J., & Barley, S. R. (1984). Occupational communities: Culture and control in organizations. *Research in Organizational Behavior, 6*, 287–365.

West, T. W. (1996). Make way for the information age: Reconstruct the pillars of higher education. *On the Horizon, 4*(4), 1, 4–5.

Whitt, E. J. (1993). Making the familiar strange: Discovering culture. In G. D. Kuh (Ed.), *Cultural perspectives in students affairs* (pp. 81–94). Washington, DC: American College Personnel Association.

Winston, R. B., Jr., & Saunders, S. A. (1991). Ethical practice in student affairs. In T. K. Miller, R. B. Winston, Jr., & Associates (Eds.), *Administration and leadership in student affairs: Actualizing student development in higher education* (2nd ed., pp. 309–346). Muncie, IN: Accelerated Development.

Young, R .B. (1996). Guiding values and philosophy. In S. Komives, D. Woodard., & Associates (Eds.), *Student services: A handbook for the profession* (3rd ed., pp. 83–105). San Francisco: Jossey-Bass.

Young, R. B. (1997). *No neutral ground*. San Francisco: Jossey-Bass.

Zammuto, R. F. (1986). Managing decline in American higher education. In J. Smart (Ed.), *Higher education: Handbook of theory and research* (Vol. II, pp. 43–84). New York: Agathon.

RECOMMENDED READING

Kuh, G. D., & Whitt, E. J. (1988). *The invisible tapestry: Culture in American colleges and universities*. ASHE-ERIC Higher Education Report, No. 1. Washington, DC: Association for the Study of Higher Education.

Schein, E. H. (1992). *Organizational culture and leadership* (2nd ed.). San Francisco: Jossey-Bass.

Tierney, W. G. (1990). *Assessing academic climates and cultures*. New Directions for Institutional Research, No. 68. San Francisco: Jossey-Bass.

3

Student Affairs in an Increasingly Multicultural World

BENJAMIN DIXON

*T*oday's college student experience differs in a variety of ways from the past. Interestingly, these changed conditions are not mysterious or even unexpected. They range from an extraordinary focus on anything that can claim the "high tech" label, to the growing recognition by higher education that there is still a need for effective "high touch" or relationship/community-building learning experiences for students. The increasing diversity of the college student population and the multicultural world of work evidence this latter condition.

The role of the student affairs administrator in helping colleges and universities effectively address diversity is crucial. This chapter is designed to shed light on the leader, educator, and manager functions of the student affairs administrator who operates in a multicultural environment. In this context, the chapter focuses on the challenges and opportunities student affairs administrators face and the personal competencies and institutional supports they need to be effective. Finally, there is a review of some strategies for creating, along with the benefits for sustaining, an environment where differences are recognized, valued, and embraced.

DRIVERS FOR DIVERSITY AND MULTICULTURAL PERSPECTIVES

The inevitability and impact of dramatic demographic changes in the population of the United States have emerged as major factors in the way many institutions do business, in both the public and private sectors. Universities and

65

colleges, for example, can no longer assume that the population of students entering each year will be largely homogeneous, with similar socioeconomic, cultural, or even linguistic characteristics. For well over a decade these demographic and related changes have been familiar to teachers and administrators in elementary and secondary schools throughout the country. With the K–12 schools as the primary source of their undergraduate students, institutions of higher education must acknowledge these trends as major factors when planning and making projections for the future.

Projections reported in 1995 in a position statement by the Connecticut Association for Supervision and Curriculum Development (CASCD) predicted some of the national trends in student population changes through 2000. The report (Hay & Roberts, 1995) was developed by a panel of education practitioners, K–16, who were commissioned to identify major impacts on the future of education. They cited the following as the most important changes:

- By 2000, the population of the United States will be 52% White, 22% Hispanic, 16% Black, and 10% Asian, and early in the next century, "minorities" as a whole will outnumber Whites.
- Early in the twenty-first century, Hispanics will surpass Blacks as the largest single minority group in the United States.
- Immigrants—both legal and illegal—will account for half of the population growth in the United States by the end of the decade.
- A substantial number of people who practice Islamic and Asian religions will cause conflict with and require accommodation by the Judeo-Christian culture prevalent in the United States.
- Despite the increasing diversity of the general population, there will continue to be geographical concentrations of people of color and poor in urban areas.
- The percentage of Americans in the lower and upper economic classes will continue to increase while the percentage in the middle class declines.

The CASCD position statement, using a 10–15-year time horizon for its projections, not only discussed demographic trends and their educational impacts, but also examined data and information in other areas. Specifically, the report examined the changing family, world of work, the nature of government, complexity of health issues, age of convenience, information technologies, ethics and values, and globalization. Almost all of these trends and impacts can be viewed as spin-offs of the demographic and related cultural changes occurring during the last two decades. The complexity of these trends and impacts warrants closer study by everyone involved in higher education, particularly student affairs administrators who are often seen as the front line of institutional efforts to understand and be responsive to the so-called nonacademic needs of a rapidly changing student population.

Hodgkinson (1999) suggests that diversity of the student population is not a simple Black and White issue. Even though the nation's youth will reflect no majority race by 2025, only 200 of the 50 states' 3,000 counties will evidence this mix. In fact, no type of diversity (for example, race, wealth, religion, disabilities, or age) will be evenly spread across the nation. Complicating the matter further is the impact of late-twentieth-century immigration and mixed marriages. For example, the number of public school students from mixed ethnic ancestry will reach 6 million by 2010, a 58% increase over 1999. Added to this is the dramatic shift in the racial/ethnic make-up of the immigrant population over the past 30 years, where persons from countries of color compose the bulk of this population. As these trends continue, there is the question of who is being "melted" into America's pot, and to what extent. Hodgkinson makes it very clear that the nature of who "we" are in this country is changing:

> Only about 15% of the U.S. population is made up of Germans married to other Germans, Poles married to other Poles, etc. Hispanics and Asians are now completing the same process, as over half of the children of Asian immigrants are marrying non-Asians, and almost half of Hispanic immigrant's children are marrying non-Hispanics. Race is a powerful historical, political, and economic force, but is scientific nonsense. The . . . [2000] U.S. Census will allow people to check as many race/ethnicity boxes as they wish, allowing Tiger Woods [the multiracial professional golfer] to truly *be* a "Cablinasian." (There are a minimum of 3 million school children who are of mixed racial identity in the U.S.) So as race becomes an even more important matter in the nation, the physical characteristics that identify races are diffusing through marriage. (1999, p. 19)

The single most neglected diversity issue for even the more progressive institutions is the inclusion of people with disabilities into the classroom, the workplace, and the community (Yuker, 1987). Spurred on by the successful passage of the Americans with Disabilities Act (ADA), more and more individuals with physical, mental, or medical impairments are presenting themselves as candidates for matriculation in higher education. According to Carnevale and Stone (1995), there are 43 million Americans who are disabled. Only 10%, however, are persons who have obvious physical and visual impairments. The challenge of providing accommodations for persons with either visible or not-so-obvious disabilities can be daunting for any institution. However, as these institutions begin to understand and appreciate the enormous potential of this relatively untapped talent pool, employers will have to begin looking at persons with disabilities as people—not as a disability with a person attached.

Another driving force for diversity and multicultural perspectives in higher education is the changing expectations of the customers. Currently, parents, students, and employers, as well as governmental and private contributors, are becoming vocal about receiving an acceptable return on their investments in education. There is evidence that business leaders, who tend to be highly knowledgeable about the operations and "products and services" of higher education, are raising questions about quality and effectiveness (Immerwahr, 1999). Public institutions in particular are undergoing closer scrutiny on many fronts, including efficiency, standards, and fiscal accountability. (See Chapter 14 in this volume.)

Further, the areas covered by this emerging focus on accountability are expanding to include other issues like the availability of and access to higher education opportunities and diversity. The Kellogg Commission on the Future of Land-Grant Universities (1998) stated that

> The full force of the challenge of maintaining the diversity of our institutions has yet to be felt. We haven't seen anything yet. The face of America will be remade in the new century. We should broaden access because it is the right thing to do. But, if appeals to fairness are insufficient, Americans need to know that access must be broadened because the practical economic need for diversity on our campuses is too compelling to ignore. (p. vi)

A growing number of parents and students are including diversity and multicultural environments on their lists of quality components sought in higher education institutions. This trend is moving so rapidly that collegiate programs incorporating these concepts and other equity principles are being reviewed, rated, and ranked by various entities. One of these organizations is the *U.S. News and World Report* magazine that recently included a "campus diversity" measure in its rankings of higher education institutions (Schneider, 1999, p. 5). In an increasingly competitive higher education environment, diversity can be viewed as another way for an educational institution to distinguish itself from its peers. However, it cuts both ways. If an institution is perceived as less than adequate in its attention to multicultural perspectives and climate issues, or is viewed as consistently unrepresentative of the diversity of this country, it may find itself facing questions of academic quality and organizational effectiveness.

The student affairs administrator as a campus leader, manager, and educator can play important roles in helping the institution meet the needs of students who must acquire the knowledge, skills, and competencies required to function effectively in the work environment. More and more that environment calls for entry-level employees who can demonstrate such abilities as working effectively on culturally diverse teams, or who can appreciate and value, but not be distracted by, difference in the workplace. Companies know that employees without such capacities can become liabilities in terms of legal compliance issues and business competitiveness. This is why General Electric, when spelling out its expectations for employees, includes the statement, "GE leaders . . . always with unyielding integrity . . . have global brains . . . and build diverse and global teams" (General Electric Company, 1999, n.p.). These few words speak volumes about the company's view of its employees, all of whom are expected to behave as leaders. Further, this statement is not a casual idea, but one of the eight core values that form the basis for how the company operates, and by which they assess employee performance and promotability.

Carnevale (1999, p. 6) pointed out several reasons why corporations see benefits in hiring and retaining a diverse workforce. First, diverse work groups are more innovative and flexible by nature. The presence of different points of view or unique perspectives encourages creativity and productive criticism of ideas. Second, a company is more likely to be successful in identifying and hiring good talent from a broader, more diverse, rather than a narrower, labor force. Finally, the emerging global economy and increasing diversity of the U.S. population combine to create a multicultural business environment where excellence in product creation and customer service cannot be achieved with a monocultural, White, male-dominated workforce.

CHALLENGES AND OPPORTUNITIES FOR STUDENT AFFAIRS ADMINISTRATORS

Dynamic demographic changes, along with attendant social, cultural, and economic effects, have propelled higher education into the twenty-first century more or less prepared to meet the changing demands of the workplace and society in general. This reality has pushed companies to be more realistic in their expectations for entry-level, college prepared students to be highly conversant with emerging changes in business practices, in large part because of the volume and rapidity of change. Increasing numbers of business organizations, especially those driven by technology and global economics, are placing higher value on individuals who offer both technical skills and highly developed learning and interpersonal relationship competencies. The challenge for higher education is to meet these demands by reviewing the form and substance, as well as the methodologies, for delivering quality learning opportunities to today's students.

The current debate over content-centered versus student-centered higher education is in large part a direct result of change and its impact on the way business is conducted. According to Blimling and Whitt (1999) the content-centered approach focuses on specialized and professional training, whereas student-centered education concentrates on providing settings where, for example, students learn how to learn and live effectively: "If creating 'ever more powerful learning environments' and bringing students to the center of a community of learners are aims of college, student affairs professionals play an essential role" (p. 13).

Toward an Integrated Role

The challenges and opportunities for student affairs administrators to utilize effective practices to support student success are multifaceted and strongly suggest the viability and necessity of multiple professional roles: educator, manager, and leader. Student affairs administrators must be as adept and competent as educators and leaders as they are as skilled managers. The three roles, or, more accurately, the three-part role of the administrator, can be best understood from an integrative point of view.

This view requires an understanding and appreciation of the power of synergistic models of behavior or, more simply stated, integrated practices. Student affairs administrators who are comfortable using such models to govern their practice are provided greater opportunity for achieving a balance among the three aspects of the job. For example, the types and nature of the issues that arise out of a leader's portion of the role are probably more aligned with those that are common to the educator portion. The manager part of the role focuses more on the manner in which tasks are executed and in what context.

A good example of this can be seen in the area of judicial affairs, where, despite the range of differences in how this activity is organized across various campuses, the fundamental goal is learning and living ethical values in the context of community. The student affairs administrator leader becomes the front-line role model for defining and demonstrating fair, honest, rule-abiding values. The student affairs administrator educator understands that the "do as I do" or "be as I am" approach, while appropriate, may not be sufficient for students to truly learn and internalize these behaviors. Other opportunities for learning, therefore, must be provided. This is why student affairs administrator educators on most campuses assure extensive student involvement in the operation, management, and decision making of the judicial system. The student affairs administrator manager makes certain the legal context, operational support, and the communications and public relations strategies are properly addressed.

In some ways, the student affairs administrator manager function serves as the operational link between the leader as educator or the educator as leader functions. Kotter (1996, pp. 25–27) distinguished the manager function by suggesting that it creates a sense of stability or order by focusing on the processes and attending to the systems that make things happen, especially for the short term. In a multicultural environment it is important that all groups, particularly the underrepresented, see some concrete evidence of the steps being taken to achieve the goals or accomplish the changes promoted by the student affairs administrator leader and educator. For example, the student affairs administrator manager can work with others to eliminate some of the more visible access barriers for people with disabilities (sidewalk curbs and nonautomatic doors, for example). This can go a long way in convincing everyone that the institution is committed to achieving the goals of inclusion espoused by the student affairs administrator leader and for which the student affairs administrator educator is preparing the community to embrace. The key to becoming an effective student affairs administrator is establishing a balance between the domains of educator, leader, and manager.

LEADING, EDUCATING, AND MANAGING WITH EQUITY-SENSITIVE PERSPECTIVES (ESP)

The student affairs administrator's integrated role of leader, educator, and manager is an interdependent set that is greater and more effective than the sum of its parts. Balancing the three roles of the student affairs administrator should be an intentional act. Further, this act or behavior should be based on an integrated model that clarifies the discrete parts of the whole while illustrating the relationships between the parts. The following ESP model illustrates these concepts.

ESP Model

Essentially, ESP is an interdependent, synergistic change management model that focuses on people, processes, and programs in the context of institutional change. It assumes that the most effective or successful activities of an organization feature a balanced application of the principles and concepts of the major parts of the model. ESP suggests an exceptional capacity of an organization or an individual to be sensitive to the impact and the interrelationships of multiple aspects of important large- or small-scale activities. Using student affairs as an example, the model can be used to guide development and evaluation activities for the overall program or for a discrete activity such as services for disabled students. The model also can be used as a planning device prior to initiating an activity. During and following a new activity, ESP can serve as a framework for monitoring or evaluating an activity's effect or goal attainment. Figure 3.1 illustrates the dynamic relationships and interactions between the linked components of the model.

In application of its principles, the components—people, process, program—of the model interact with one another as do the legs of a three-legged stool. A similar relationship can be seen in the three factors within each compo-

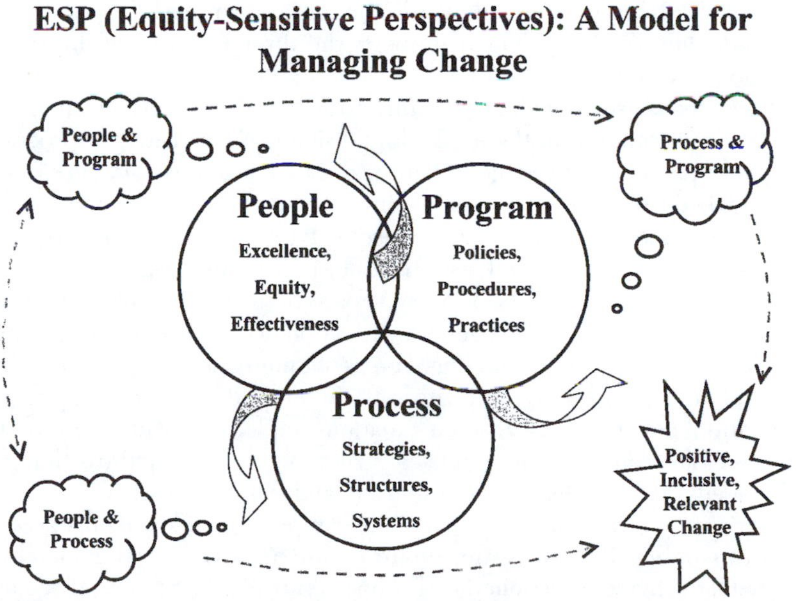

FIGURE 3.1. Integrated Components of a Synergistic Model

nent, for example, people embrace excellence, equity, and effectiveness. If one removed or ignored any of the three components, or a factor within a single component, the integrity and effectiveness of the whole model would be diminished.

The great utility of the ESP model is that its application can be initiated through any one of the three components and still focus appropriate attention on the remaining two components as part of an integrated approach to achieving a desired change. The most effective and welcomed changes in most situations are those where the individuals and groups involved perceive the change to be positive, inclusive, and relevant. This is important because, too often, in the vigorous pursuit of major change we fail to take steps to minimize the unanticipated consequences that can derail our efforts to install or institutionalize that change. Almost equally tragic are the lost opportunities to maximize the benefits of a change that might have been anticipated through a more integrated and coordinated approach.

A good example of a lost opportunity is the initial knee-jerk reactions by many institutions to the costs for providing reasonable accommodations to individuals and groups protected under the ADA of 1990. Carnevale and Stone (1995) cite how employers frequently assume that the cost for providing accommodations for persons with disabilities will be prohibitive; yet there is a wide variety of accommodations that cost very little. Further, if these employers took a more proactive approach, using equity-sensitive perspectives, they may find the cost (for example, cut-outs in sidewalk curbs, automatic opening doors, and voice-activated computers) to be reasonable, given the benefits to both the disabled employee and others in the workplace.

Figure 3.2 describes in key words the concepts in each segment of the ESP model and illustrates how it supports the three-part role of the student affairs administrator.

The effective student affairs administrator attends to each concept in each of the three dimensions of the model for all significant activities or programs. Using multiple perspectives the administrator views, senses, and understands what it will take to achieve successful completion.

Student affairs administrators can use ESP to focus attention on those aspects of specific programs and activities that may be the origin of confusion, limited or questionable results, or missed goals. In the contexts of planning and evaluation it may be viewed as a generic set of organizational effectiveness principles that, when applied, can highlight areas of unintended consequences. This is particularly important for programs developed for and operating in multicultural environments. In such situations, underrepresented groups who do not see how some program policies, structures, or goals address their particular needs often make claims of exclusion and lack of access.

For example, on many majority White campuses, Black students perceive an unwelcoming, if not hostile, environment in terms of the social and cocurricular activities sanctioned and supported by the institution. It seems to matter little if the activities are designed and organized by other students, who

ESP (Equity-Sensitive Perspectives): A Model for Managing Change

Leading/Educating

People =	Excellence	Equity	Effectiveness
	Values/Beliefs, Assumptions, Desires/Needs	Diversity, Access, Fairness	Relevant, Performance-based, Positive Results

Managing

Process =	Structures	Systems	Strategies
	Organizational arrangements	Resources, Delivery mechanisms	Short & long term plans

Educating/Leading

Program =	Policies	Practices	Procedures
	Direction, Responsibility, Accountability	Individual & Organizational behaviors	Expectations, Standards, Guidance

FIGURE 3.2. Application of ESP Model: Student Affairs Administrator Role

are usually White. As long as there is routine inattention to inclusion of minority groups by the majority, climate issues remain volatile. When White male-dominated activities seem to take precedence over the needs of women and people of color, efforts are made by these groups to establish their own programs. Although there is nothing wrong with special gender- or race-based programs, their main reason for existence should not be students' systematic exclusion from mainstream activities because of gender or racial differences.

The probability of unintended exclusions can be minimized if the ESP principles are applied in the planning and development stages of the program. When applied, these principles stimulate certain questions. For example, the application of the ESP principles to a campuswide initiative to reduce alcohol abuse might generate questions in the people component of the model:

1. Do all members of the community believe that the consumption of large quantities of alcohol at parties is necessary to have a good time? (Addresses assumptions and values)
2. Should prevention strategies be applied across all groups, despite evidence that certain groups (African Americans, for example) are significantly below the average in alcohol usage on campus? (Addresses diversity)

3. Whether the answer to question 2 is yes or no, how do student affairs administrators assure that their evaluation of prevention strategies are focused on the most important target group, and how do they leverage the nonabusive behavior of some groups to encourage moderation on the part of other groups? (Addresses effectiveness—relevant and performance based)

Using the process component of the ESP model, the following questions might be raised:

1. What types of resources, if any, should the institution provide to promote alcohol-free activities for students during their unstructured time? (Addresses organizational arrangements and planning)
2. How does the institution respect the privacy rights of students and, at the same time, strongly encourage students to avail themselves of counseling and other support services? (Addresses resources)
3. Given the potential legal liability, should the institution allow students to become involved in prevention activities that target other students, for example, an institutionally sponsored designated driver program? (Addresses delivery mechanisms)

The program component of the ESP model, with its focus on policies, practices, and procedures, suggests the following types of questions:

1. How broadly or narrowly should the institution's policy statement on the use of alcohol be written, given the initiative to reduce alcohol abuse? (Accountability, responsibility)
2. Do institutional practices related to alcohol use on campus reinforce or contradict the goals of this initiative? (Addresses organizational behaviors)
3. Are the published procedures for setting up programs and activities under this initiative clear and based on how the organization actually operates? (Addresses guidance)

Individuals and institutions today need ESP because American society, despite the strong presence of diverse groups, has for far too long operated as if there is a sole perspective. If one had to characterize this perspective, the most appropriate terms would be: White, nondisabled, heterosexual, male, Judeo-Christian, native-born American. The ESP model, if regularly applied, can become a constant reminder that the world is changing and a check on how effectively student affairs administrators are using multiple approaches and multicultural perspectives to help solve some of society's stickier problems.

It is important to note that the ESP model for managing change was designed initially to fulfill a need for a philosophy/system that could assist individuals and organizations in using a holistic approach to managing diversity or difference. This was developed to avoid the weakness found in many other change models. This weakness can be described as change management practices that create, re-create, sustain, or promote institutional supports and individual behavior that have the effect of precluding the full participation of people of color, women, persons with disabilities, and others in society. But this model is not a tool for simply addressing equity and cultural diversity issues alone. Indeed, it is a generic model that can be used for almost any issue involving the need to achieve synergy among people, processes, and programs during institutional change initiatives or organizational effectiveness reviews.

INITIATING CHANGE THROUGH RESEARCH-BASED PROGRAMS AND STRATEGIES

Higher education's obligation to students is to assure that the education provided reflects the real world. Student affairs administrators can help students understand and try out the skills and competencies they are expected to possess when they enter the workplace or the community at large. This is why practica, internships, cooperative education programs, and related opportunities to practice or apply one's knowledge and skill are important. These activities help to extend and enhance the technical knowledge and skill acquired in the classroom. Similarly, many intercultural and human relations competencies can be both acquired and enhanced through programs and learning experiences provided outside the classroom within the student affairs division.

Characteristics of the Multiculturally Competent

Pope and Reynolds (1997) defined multicultural competency as the "awareness, knowledge, and skills" (p. 267) needed to interact effectively with others who are culturally different. People who are competent in this area understand themselves and how a person's values and beliefs can influence their behavior. Specific knowledge of different cultures, in terms of their histories, traditions, and values, is another characteristic of the multiculturally competent person. Multicultural skills are those capabilities, behaviors, and practices that enable the individual to interact effectively and meaningfully with others whose backgrounds are different from their own.

With a focus on students, Howard-Hamilton, Richardson, and Shuford (1999) extended this list of competency categories by adding three other items: attitudes, understanding, and appreciation/valuing. Some of the competencies included in these three categories are the beliefs that:

- one must have pride within one's own cultural group;
- no one group is better than another;
- discrimination because one cultural status is unjust;
- assumptions about an individual cannot be based solely on one's group membership;
- one must take risks in life; and
- cross-cultural interactions enhance the quality of one's life.

Multiculturally competent student affairs administrators are important assets and resources for any higher education institution committed to creating and sustaining a diverse teaching and learning environment. Why? These administrators are more likely to engage in active promotion and support of a diversity initiative. They are more likely to approach their role as leaders, educators, or managers or as multiculturally competent professionals who demonstrate an effective integration of all three domains. Finally, these multiculturally competent student affairs administrators are more likely to seek strong, collaborative relationships with other institutional units, particularly in academic affairs.

The wisdom of this approach is supported by increasing amounts of research on the role of diversity in higher education. Gurin's (1999) following conceptual model of the impact of diversity is particular instructive:

- Structural diversity—primarily the racial/ethnic composition of the student body.
- Classroom diversity—the incorporation of knowledge about the diverse groups into the curriculum.
- Informal interactional diversity—the opportunity to interact with students from diverse backgrounds in the broad campus environment.

All three dimensions described by Gurin are important components of a comprehensive diversity program that student affairs administrators should be aware of, understand, and support. It is in the area of informal interactional diversity, however, that their special contribution to the whole can be made. As community builders and professionals directly involved in student development, student affairs administrators can apply the principles embedded in the ESP model to focus institutional and individual attention on the people, processes, and programs that foster strong inclusive communities. There are many opportunities within traditional student affairs practices through which this can be achieved, including student forums, workshops, leadership training initiatives, residence life programs, advising, learning communities, and student organizations and activities (Blimling & Whitt, 1999).

Diversity Benefits All

Most student affairs administrators have entered the profession with a sincere desire to work directly with students in the areas of personal and career development. Some even imagine the academy, or academic development, as an area within their purview. Those who view student development holistically are very likely to quickly understand the compelling argument that diversity and multicultural perspectives are necessary characteristics for higher education institutions today. Furthermore, emerging research by Hurtado, Milem, Clayton-Pederson, and Allen (1999) shows that the benefits from this focus do not accrue just to members of underrepresented groups, but to the majority as well.

Student affairs administrators who are inclined to be very creative in their programming for diversity would do well to rely heavily on researched-based information to support their request for resources and institutional endorsement of their efforts. Gurin's (1999) study, even though based only on data from the University of Michigan, has much to inform other institutions about the benefits of diversity. For example, in examining the effect of structural diversity on classroom and informal interactional diversity, Gurin found the following:

1. Structural diversity had significant positive effects on classroom diversity and interactional diversity among all students. Attending a diverse college also resulted in more diverse friends, neighbors, and work associates nine years after college entry. This is strong evidence that structural diversity creates conditions that lead students to experience diversity in ways that would not occur in a more homogeneous student body.
2. The results show strong evidence for the impact of diversity on learning outcomes. Students who had experienced the most diversity in classroom settings and in informal interactions with peers showed the greatest engagement in active thinking processes, growth in intellectual engagement and motivation, and growth in intellectual and academic skills.
3. The results strongly support the central role of higher education in helping students to become active citizens and participants in a pluralistic democracy. Students who experienced diversity in classroom settings and in informal interactions showed the most engagement in various forms of citizenship and the most engagement with people from different races/cultures. They were also the most likely to acknowledge that group differences are compatible with the interests of the broader community.
4. Diversity experiences during college had impressive effects on the extent to which graduates in the national study were living racially or ethnically integrated lives in the postcollege world. Students who had taken the most diversity courses and interacted the most with diverse peers during college had the most cross-racial interactions five years after leaving college. This confirms that the long-term pattern of segregation noted by many social scientists can be broken by diversity experiences during college.

There are three points to be drawn from the data upon which these findings are based that make a compelling case for diversity and the integration of multicultural perspectives in both academic and cocurricular programs. First, if the outcomes described in Gurin's report are to be replicated, it is absolutely necessary that a predominantly White institution achieve to the extent possible not only critical masses of people from underrepresented groups, but also critical levels of participation of the members of these groups in important or significant activities of the campus community. Another point to be understood, particularly by student affairs administrators, is that a comprehensive diversity program requires a balance of classroom and informal interactional activities for students. Third, the Gurin data show especially impressive results for Whites.

Virtually all of the relationships between classroom diversity and learning outcomes and between informal interactional diversity and learning outcomes were positive and significant, and none were negative.

Smith and Associates (1997) confirmed several of Gurin's conclusions, using for their study a focus on institutional transformation, education and scholarship, and campus climate. In addition the literature reviewed in their study raises some interesting questions relating to current assumptions about managing diversity in higher education, and how institutions should be altered to assure students are prepared to live, work, learn, and excel in an increasingly complex and multicultural society. Smith observed that:

1. Overall, the literature suggests that diversity initiatives positively affect both minority and majority students on campus.
2. Diversity initiatives have an impact not only on student attitudes and feelings toward intergroup relations on campus, but also on institutional satisfaction, involvement, and academic growth.
3. The evidence grows showing that involvement in specialized student groups, such as ethnic residential theme houses, support centers, and academic departments benefits students of color and others. Indeed, these activities appear to contribute to increased satisfaction and retention, despite prodigious commentary about their negative effect on development of community on campus.
4. Contrary to widespread reports of self-segregation among students of color on campuses, the research finds this pattern more typical of White students than the reverse.
5. We also require more clear analysis of what students need to know and to do to function in a diverse workplace and global society, and what part they can play in developing healthy, respectful communities.

CONCLUSION

Achieving and sustaining quality higher education in the future is dependent on many factors. Diversity and the application of multicultural and equity principles are among those factors. The efficacy of diversity as a key component of a continuing effort to improve educational services and outcomes for a wider proportion of our society is being driven by the inexorable changes in the demographics of America's population. Attending these changes are the social and cultural influences that, despite the efforts of some to promote separation, are transforming America and its institutions. The issue of diversity and improving intercultural relations within our institutions has become more and more of a concern of not only the providers of education, but also the consumers. Business and industry managers have recently awakened to the role diversity plays in their enterprises; similarly, higher education practitioners are becoming more sensitive to the pragmatic as well as the fairness and equity reasons for moving toward a more inclusive teaching, learning, and working campus environment.

Student affairs administrators are clearly on the front lines of most institutions' responses to these trends. As campus leaders, educators, and managers, student affairs administrators need a basic understanding of the interdependent relationship between the classroom and the cocurricular activities that are a significant aspect of the college experience. The ESP change model is one tool that student affairs administrators may find helpful as they engage various aspects of the organization and its operations. This engagement, while centered on student developmental needs, will require close attention to all the people, processes, and programs that are likely to help or hinder the successful building of an inclusive community for all.

Finally, it is important to note that the task of moving beyond affirmative actions toward a society that affirms diversity is in its infancy. Much more research is needed before a collective understanding of the diversity challenge has been established, and before there are solutions that are both effective and applicable on a large scale across many types of situations. In the meantime, student affairs administrators need to be more reflective about the current personal and career needs of the increasingly diverse student body moving through their institutions. Higher education entities should be more intentional and foresighted about what they do today to position themselves as viable institutions of learning for a future population that is significantly different from the one that now exists.

QUESTIONS TO CONSIDER

1. Consider the pluses and minuses of systematically applying equity principles to the mainstream operations of your organization. Which functional areas are most likely to be resistant, and how can they be "brought along" to meet or exceed your organization's expectations?
2. How can the components of quality improvement processes be used to install and institutionalize diversity initiatives or innovations?

REFERENCES

Blimling, G. S., & Whitt, E. J. (1999). Identifying the principles that guide student affairs practice. In G. S. Blimling, E. J. Whitt, & Associates, *Good practice in student affairs: Principles to foster student learning* (pp. 1–20). San Francisco: Jossey-Bass.

Carnevale, A. P., & Stone, S. C. (1995). *The American mosaic: An in-depth report on the future of diversity at work*. New York: McGraw-Hill.

Carnevale, A. P. (1999, Spring). Diversity in higher education: Why corporate America cares. *Diversity Digest*. Washington, DC: Association of American Colleges and Universities.

General Electric Company. (1999). General Electric Company Values Statement. In *1999 annual report*. Cincinnati, OH: Author.

Gurin, P. (1999). Expert report of Patricia Gurin. *Gratz et al. v. Bollinger et al.*, No.

97-75321 (E. D. Mich.) and *Grutter et al. v. Bollinger et al.*, No. 97-75928 (E. D. Mich.). In *The compelling need for diversity in higher education*. [On-line]. Available: http://www.umich.edu/~urel/admissions/legal/expert/gurintoc.html

Hay, L. E., & Roberts, A. D. (Eds.). (1995). *Curriculum for the new millennium: Trends shaping our schools* (2nd ed.). Southport, CT: Connecticut Association for Supervision and Curriculum Development.

Hodgkinson, H. L. (1999). *All one system: A second look*. Washington, DC: The Institute for Educational Leadership and The National Center for Public Policy in Higher Education.

Howard-Hamilton, M., Richardson, B., & Shuford, B. (1999). Promoting multicultural education: A holistic approach. *College Student Affairs Journal, 18*(1), 5–17.

Hurtado, S., Milem, J., Hurtado, S., Clayton-Pederson, A., & Allen, W. (1999). *Enacting diverse learning environments*. ASHE-ERIC Higher Education Report Vol. 26, No. 8. Washington, DC: School of Education and Human Development, The George Washington University.

Immerwahr, J. (1999). *Doing comparatively well: Why the public loves higher education and criticizes K-12*. Washington, DC: The Institute for Educational Leadership and The National Center for Public Policy in Higher Education.

Kellogg Commission on the Future of Land-Grant Universities. (1998, April). *Returning to our roots: Student access*. Unpublished manuscript from a panel discussion at a National Association of State Universities and Land-Grant Colleges (NASULGC) 21st Century Land-Grant Universities, Action Issues Teleconference, Clemson University. Washington, DC: Author.

Kotter, J. P. (1996). *Leading change*. Boston: Harvard Business School Press.

Pope, R., & Reynolds, A. (1997). Student affairs core competencies: Integrating multicultural awareness, knowledge, and skills. *Journal of College Student Development, 38*, 266–277.

Schneider, C. G. (1999, Fall). *U.S. News and World Report* discovers campus diversity: The good news and the bad. *Diversity Digest*. Washington, DC: Association of American Colleges and Universities.

Smith, D. G., & Associates. (1997). *Diversity works: The emerging picture of how students benefit*. Washington, DC: Association of American Colleges and Universities.

Yuker, H. E. (1987). *Attitudes toward persons with disabilities*. New York: Springer.

RECOMMENDED READING

Astin, A. W. (1993). Diversity and multiculturalism on campus: How are students affected? *Change, 25*(2), 44–49.

Benjamin, M. (1996). *Cultural diversity, educational equity, and the transformation of higher education: Group profiles as a guide to policy and programming*. Westport, CT: Praeger.

Richardson, R. C., Jr., & Skinner, E. F. (1990). *Achieving quality and diversity: Universities in a multicultural society*. New York: Macmillan. (ERIC Document Reproduction Service No. ED 327 093)

Sedlacek, W. E. (1995). *Improving racial and ethnic diversity and campus climate at four-year independent Midwest colleges: An evaluation report of the Lilly Endowment Grant Program*. College Park: University of Maryland.

Smith, D. G. (1989). *The Challenge of Diversity: Involvement or Alienation in the Academy?* ASHE-ERIC Higher Education Report No. 5. Washington, DC: School of Education and Human Development, George Washington University.

4

Advancing Technology and Student Affairs Practice

THEODORE W. ELLING
STUART J. BROWN

*B*y 1990, the typical student affairs administrator had daily access to a limited amount of technology that centered on the desktop computer. Not all staff members were lucky enough to have one on their desks, however, so computers were often a shared commodity located in a central section of the office. Although these devices contained fairly powerful word processing, spreadsheet, and desktop publishing software, the programs were not very intuitive or user friendly. E-mail was largely unavailable, and connectivity to other systems was often limited to the departmental local area network. Although access to the institution's student information system was possible, the user interface was arcane enough to discourage widespread use. Files were exchanged between users by saving the file on a diskette and walking it over to the next user. This form of file transport was commonly called "sneaker net." Project collaboration between colleagues occurred in structured face-to-face meetings or over the telephone, and electronic access to information outside of the institution was virtually nonexistent.

In contrast, by 2000 the majority of student affairs administrators and support staff members had a personal computer on their desks. The devices were connected beyond the department to embrace a wide variety of systems across the campus and the Internet, enabling collaborative communication with colleagues around the world by voice, data, text, and video transmission. The software on the desktop and associated application servers was fast, powerful, and intuitive, resulting in easier and more rapid access to information. Files could now be sent to others electronically, and many services that once required the physical presence of staff and students are now located in the virtual domain and accessed over the World Wide Web (the web).

In this chapter we discuss the pervasive and ubiquitous impact technology has on student affairs organizations. The discussion focuses on the issues, trends, and implications for the seasoned practitioner, entry-level staff member, graduate student, and graduate preparation program faculty member as they are exposed to a changing landscape in how services are being delivered and driven by technology.

STUDENT AFFAIRS IN THE TWENTY-FIRST CENTURY: CONNECTED TO TECHNOLOGY

The centerpiece of today's student affairs administrator's office is the personal computer. And why not? For most student affairs administrators the workday most likely begins and ends hunched over the keyboard banging out an e-mail or typing a memo utilizing a word processing program. They may be conducting research via the web or accessing the institution's undergraduate database over the college's network.

The types of computing devices that the student affairs professionals have access to are evolving rapidly. For some, the standard desktop computer is now supplemented by or replaced with a laptop computer. Hand-held computers, also called personal digital assistants (PDAs) are the next wave in portable computing, containing scaled-down word processing and spreadsheet software in addition to an internal cellular modem that provides for Internet connectivity for e-mail access and web browsing. The key word for student affairs in the twenty-first century is *connectivity*, which usually refers to linking up to the Internet. Student affairs administrators concern themselves with how they are connected—telephone modem, cable modem, ethernet, DSL, T-1 lines, wireless—and where these hook-ups lead.

At many institutions, these links are to local area networks that provide access to specialized group applications and databases that also allow for file and print sharing between staff members. The hardware also is likely to be connected to one or more institutionwide conduits called Enterprise Resource Planning Systems (ERPSs) such as student information systems in addition to other campuswide server-based hook-ups that support e-mail and calendars. Last, the device is also connected to the Internet. In short, the technology tool set available to the typical student affairs professional is broad and deep and contains multiple layers of technology.

The value of connectivity cannot be underestimated. Nearly everyone resides in a virtual world where daily tasks are becoming more and more interrelated to these electronic linkages. Without a quick and reliable connection, the world of the student affairs administrator becomes quite small, and student affairs' worth to the institution is marginalized.

Electronic Mail Usage

Just a few short years ago these issues were irrelevant. E-mail addresses, log-on accounts, and passwords were part of an alien vernacular spoken or understood by a select few. Nowadays, e-mail and accessing computer accounts are as commonplace as phone and fax numbers. Electronic mail addresses on business cards and resumes are de rigueur. In a 1997 survey of Internet usage among student affairs administrators, 84% of respondents indicated they used e-mail on a daily basis (Brown & Malaney, 2000). In a similar study, conducted three years previously, that percentage hovered around 35% (Brown & Malaney, 1996). Clearly, electronic mail has become part of the daily lives of most student affairs administrators. The rudimentary functions of e-mail—composing messages, sending, and replying—must now be part of a professional's technological portfolio. E-mail is used to correspond with colleagues, faculty, and students; to conduct academic advising; and to relay information. Research via e-mail has been aided as attached documents, to be viewed and critiqued by fellow professionals, traverse cyberspace.

The advent of e-mail has empowered student affairs administrators to communicate across hierarchical administrative lines within an organization to connect directly with peers and supervisors in other areas. In many respects, this has improved the dialogue within institutions, but because this communication transcends traditional supervisory lines, an increase in interdepartmental friction may also occur.

Growth of the World Wide Web

Although e-mail is currently the most widely used Internet application, the web has the intoxicating power to soon eclipse electronic mail's importance to student affairs practice. The web provides access to an almost limitless amount of information on practically any subject. By utilizing web browsers and accessing page links, student affairs administrators can, for example, easily research how other colleges and universities have crafted their student codes of conduct. They have the ability to review residence hall programming ideas from a plethora of on-line sources, conduct extensive or highly targeted job searches, and peruse vendor and service-provider information at the click of a mouse.

Technological Impact

The impact of the web, however, cannot be solely measured by linkages to outside sources. On-campus web developers, as well as an explosion of "dot.com" companies, are transforming the way services and information are delivered, not only to the campus community, but also to the world at large. Should a prospective student need an admissions application or scholarship form, she or he can download it from the quietude of the personal computer. Individuals seeking institutional contact information can access the institution's web directory for e-mail addresses and phone numbers. Current or soon-to-be students looking for documents related to campus policies or academic requirements can search the on-line catalogue. Entering undergraduates having trouble scheduling site-specific placement exams or registration for their first semester can log on to the campus network to vanquish these mundane tasks. Applicants soliciting a student's view on campus life can read the student newspaper on-line for the undergraduate perspective.

Parents are also part of the higher education equation. For example, the University of Minnesota (UM, 2000a) has developed an extensive website for this group with categories such as "Distance Parenting," where parents of current UM students provide suggestions on a wide range of topics such as academics, residence hall living, and adjusting; "Timely Issues," which succinctly examine issues that can affect undergraduates at different times of the year; "Tuition and Financial Aid News"; "Parents Events"; and even an "E-mail Alert List," which allows parents to sign up to receive electronic notices on special events or news items.

Although most institutions of higher education have translated existing documents into an on-line format and have provided perfunctory information to browsers, other colleges and universities have taken web development to the next level. For example, individuals having difficulty physically setting foot on campus can take a virtual tour of the institution, including visits to residence hall rooms, classrooms, and other facilities. Video downloads of campus life occur through strategically placed webcams that broadcast real-time campus activities. Residence hall room selection is taking place on the web, excising a large headache for residence life personnel by removing the need to staff a room to facilitate the process. One such institution utilizing the web is North Carolina State University, which according to Jim Pappenhagen, assistant director for administration (personal communication, March 28, 2000), runs its fall room sign-up via the web. Students can submit their housing application, including telecommunication and ResNet options, by accessing the web. The forms also have a built-in survey that provides the housing office with student information and preferences. Other colleges, such as the University of Delaware (http://www.mis.udel.edu/main/webinits/elections.html), are enabling undergraduates to cast ballots for student government elections on the web. This removes the need for site-specific locations (and costly ballot machines) or paper and pencil voting methods. Most of all, elections on the web can promise almost instantaneous results. Safeguards are built into the system and can monitor results throughout the day.

Importance of Desktop Applications for Student Affairs

Internet applications—e-mail; on-line discussion groups, such as Listservs; and the web—are currently the flavor du jour for many. Yet student affairs administrators have tended increasingly to utilize an array of software packages for their desktop and laptop computers. Word processing, database management, graphic design, page layout, and presentation software form the nucleus of applications on the typical hard drive. These programs, knowledgeably harnessed and utilized, allow student affairs practitioners to work more effectively and creatively. Campus flyers can be awash in distinctive clipart, font styles, and color. Office manuals and reports can have the look of a typesetter's press by cutting and pasting together various elements and importing graphics, charts, and files from other desktop applications. No longer do overheads need to be somber affairs as presentation programs such as Microsoft PowerPoint bring a visually exciting edge to small or large demonstrations. Likewise, keeping track of organizational expenses and budgets, or leadership rosters and division records, is simplified through the use of spreadsheets and databases, respectively.

These are the standard computer tools of the student affairs professional. Having a thorough understanding of these applications becomes even more crucial today as most, if not all, of the documents created using these programs can easily be stored as hypertext mark-up language (HTML) documents (the coding protocol for web pages). No longer is it a necessity to comprehend the detailed-driven HTML code when a simple "Save As" command automatically translates files into Internet-ready pages.

TECHNOLOGICAL CHANGE AND STUDENT AFFAIRS STAFF

Technology is not a new force in student affairs. It has been embraced within the profession for several decades, and it has changed administrative and service delivery capabilities multiple times and in multiple ways. From the first punch-card-based class registration systems on mainframe computers in the 1960s, to the web-enabled desktop applications of the late 1990s, mainframe, network, and desktop systems have grown in complexity, size, scope, and power. Taken collectively, these systems have radically changed the way the profession conducts its core business of supporting student learning. These changes are dynamic and continue to evolve in regard to how the profession engages in tasks and activities based largely on the technologies available at the time of deployment.

Electronic Innovations

Take, for example, the process of class registration. The first generation of technology to support the registration process required students to stand in a series of lines, usually in a gym or other large hall. Undergraduates picked up a punch card from a faculty or staff member that represented permission from an instructor to register for a given course. The second generation eliminated the punch cards, and the series of lines merged into one long line. Here, students waited their turn to meet with a staff member who would enter the student's desired selections directly into the mainframe system. The third innovation elimi-nated both the long lines and direct staff involvement altogether as telephone registration systems were initiated. The latest generation of registration sys-tems now being deployed allows students to choose classes over the Internet from wherever they have a connection. Consequently, registration can now be virtual, which removes both the student and the registration process from the physical campus.

Each refinement of the registration process has made the system more efficient and more convenient for the student engaged in that effort while it has also removed the direct, visible support of faculty and staff members from the process. This restructuring of administrative tasks and systems is occurring throughout many functional areas.

As the profession enters the new millennium, the specific brand of com-puting tool or platform is less of an issue than it was in the 1980s when often heated debates over which computer or operating system was "the best" cropped up in staff meetings, break rooms, and professional conferences. Strident ad-vances in semiconductor technology, software, programming, and market forces have produced apparatus that perform many of the same functions that were earlier the hallmarks of "other" platforms. Today, more productive discussions can be realized by examining the common operating environment of a depart-ment or office cluster. Clarifying these issues is important to ensure that prod-ucts are easy to learn, promote seamless file and application sharing between users, and are both cost effective and sustainable. Supporting multiple hard-ware platforms and software by different vendors can significantly increase sup-port costs, training time, and user frustration.

In whatever way an office environment is reengineered, benefits must not outweigh a managerial process that emphasizes human support from the sys-tem, a network populated by student affairs professionals. Practitioners, when developing administrative systems, need to remember that the phrase "high tech, high touch" can be a useful developmental tool. Designing systems utiliz-ing a high degree of technological sophistication should not all be done at the expense of reducing or eliminating necessary face-to-face (staff-to-student or staff-to-staff) interactions.

The Changing Staff Role

Technology is also changing staff members' roles in student affairs and shifting communication patterns between departments and individuals throughout the profession. For example, a support staff member in the early 1980s typed office correspondence and maintained membership lists using a typewriter. The de-partmental budget was managed using lined bookkeeping paper. The process of sending a judicial hearing notice to a student involved reading a memo re-garding the alleged transgression and then typing a letter addressed to the stu-dent after the judicial officer's paper schedule calendar was checked to deter-mine an available time for the hearing. In today's environment, the staff member may receive a secured on-line communications report and, after review, append the information to the networked judicial database. Accessing the students' class schedule and the judicial officers' electronic calendar to find a mutually available hearing time then follows this. After this information is entered into the judicial database and after the judicial database queries the student information system for the most current address information, the notice of hearing letter is automatically printed.

A number of judicial processes at the University of Delaware (UD) have been shifted to the web. The Office of Residence Life has shifted its incident report form entirely to the web, which gives the professional staff flexibility and allows it to use student identification photographs to make certain that the correct student is being reported (http://www.mis.udel.edu/main/webinits/judicial.html). From the student's perspective, resolving judicial, academic, or personal problems at UD can be initiated on the web by accessing the Student Problem-solving Action Network (SPAN). Based upon the nature of the problem, SPAN directs students to the department or individual who can best help them address their concern (http://www.udel.edu/SPAN/).

Ensuring that the latest technological innovations are seamlessly integrated into office life requires training. Far too often the introduction of technology is accompanied with little or no training. In a statewide study of faculty and staff employees in four-year public institutions in North Carolina, the average hours provided to employees for training purposes during the previous 12 months was found to be less than one-half hour (University of North Carolina & PricewaterhouseCoopers, 1999). In a regional study of public and private four-year institutions in the Southeast, chief student affairs administrators cited training as the third largest barrier to successfully implementing information technology, closely following funding and technology support (Elling, 1996).

Potential Problems

Other issues surrounding the use of technology center on the student. The current generation of undergraduates entering colleges and universities has coexisted with the Internet during their entire high school experience. Although regular access to technology enables students to support their educational goals, they may also be exposed to disconcerting issues of Internet addiction, pornography, and identity formation. The student affairs practitioner must be aware of these emerging issues and be prepared to provide the necessary support and intervention strategies as needed.

A final critical issue as tomorrow's technology-based programs and services are developed and deployed will be to intentionally build analog and virtual student communities into future systems. One of the most potent forces in a student's collegiate experience is interaction with peer groups (Pascarella & Terenzini, 1991). For institutions with distance learning programs, the need to connect students with one another and to staff and faculty members may play an increasingly important role in student success and retention (Carr, 2000).

For large institutions or those with significant commuter populations, this may involve developing web-based tools to intentionally connect students with the institutional environment.

Using the Web to Build Community

An example of a community-linking mechanism may be found at a UM website (http://www.umn.edu/welcome/index2.html). UM provides entering students with an Internet welcome kit containing information on how to connect to the university's computer network and, in particular, to the campus community.

The University of North Carolina at Charlotte encourages entering freshmen to complete a Get Connected interest survey as a part of its summer orientation program. Before the fall semester, the survey data are merged with student demographic information and the resulting student contact information is sent electronically to each of the 83 participating organizations and services, including registered student organizations, student activities, academic enrichment, and student support programs. By the time new students arrive on campus, they have already received, through the mail, e-mail, or telephone, invitations to participate in a number of student clubs, organizations, programs, and services (http://www.uncc.edu/stuaffairs/fyet989/).

Iowa State's Off-Campus and Adult Student Services Office has created an on-line orientation program (2000) to help connect its populations to the campus. There are links for "Living Options," "Financial Resources," "Clubs and Activities," "Support Services," and "Academic Resources."

Likewise, Florida State University has developed a web-based orientation for students within their distance learning arena (Florida State University, 2000). The institution requires every undergraduate to complete an orientation program, which can be fulfilled on-line. The pages help students "learn how to move efficiently through the University, from enrolling to graduating. [Students] will come to understand what the University expects, from its code of conduct to acceptable methods of paying fees and be introduced to the many resources available, from academic advising to career placement."

THE CHANGING INFORMATION TECHNOLOGY ENVIRONMENT

Previously, "connectivity" was described as a key term. Another apt descriptor is "change." The technological panorama has undergone incredible change and growth over the past few years. This upheaval shows no signs of abating as, seemingly, each day brings pronouncements of new, titillating products from software and hardware manufacturers, e-commerce firms, and state-of-the-art businesses. Yet hardware and software issues are only two aspects of these changes. Distance learning programs, web-based course instruction, and virtual universities are proliferating at an accelerating pace.

Student affairs, as with higher education in general, often has been slow in reacting and adapting to change. Already campuses are being wired so that access to the campus network and Internet backbone will be easily available to students, faculty, and staff members alike. Yet even as these capital projects spread from residence halls to lounges to academic structures, many questions loom. Does the institution *need* to provide universal access? What about the expense? Does the long-term potential for wireless hook-ups to the Internet make the cost of such a gargantuan task worthwhile?

At a more basic level is the very nature of the personal computer. The hardware is becoming less cumbersome, more compact, and increasingly portable while software and separate files may now be shared via networks. Groups, as opposed to individuals, can claim ownership of hard drive content. Even these aspects of the personal computer are metamorphosing as storage space moves to a virtual realm. Soon concern about megabytes and gigabytes on a hard drive will decrease because files will be stored within cyberspace. Consequently, access will become a nonissue as files can be retrieved from any machine linked to the Internet.

Technological Impact on Socialization

The technology landscape is changing the work environment of student affairs administrators. The technological upheaval is altering the very nature of student affairs practice and how members interact with colleagues, undergraduates, and faculty members. Even though the landscape is unsettled, these are crucial questions that must be addressed.

Although specific changes may be years away, certain trends are emerging. The availability of information is becoming less site-bound as web accessed records become retrievable from multiple locations. With infrared systems emanating from laptops and wireless capability growing, the need to be linked via an office computer is less of a concern. The likelihood of electronic mail as a conduit for communication grows daily, as does the web as a user-friendly, 24-hour-a-day vehicle for obtaining needed information and everyday-type forms. Voice and video utilization, still in its infancy, has the power to further personalize and broaden the technology. Can telecommuting be far behind?

A study, released in February 2000, by the Stanford Institute for the Quantitative Study of Society (SIQSS) on the social consequences of Internet activity suggested that as Internet use among individuals rises, social isolationism increases, less time is spent socializing with friends and family, and participation outside the home decreases as do such evening activities as watching television (http://www.stanford.edu/dept/news/report/news/february16/internetsurvey-216.html). A smaller study conducted by Carnegie Mellon University researchers (Kraut et al., 2000) produced similar findings. Director of the SIQSS, and principal investigator of the study Norman Nie observed, "The Internet could be the ultimate isolating technology that further reduces participation in communities even more than television did before it" (O'Toole, 2000).

Student affairs administrators need to be cognizant of these socialization issues and how they impact the undergraduate population, especially as residence hall rooms become technological bastions with voice and data links providing unparalleled access to the curriculum, academic resources, and entertainment possibilities. More emphasis on the promotion of student interaction and face-to-face encounters may be necessary to help combat the cocooning mentality of residence hall members, a mindset that can only increase as the spread of technology continues.

But socialization is a two-way street. Student affairs professionals need to model these behaviors. Preaching involvement and participation away from the computer screen must be followed by more out-of-office, high touch activities by administrators. "Management by wandering around" (Peters & Waterman, 1982) is a proven mechanism within the business sector that facilitates and enhances both face-to-face communication and productivity within an organization. Developing a more visible presence on campus, attending college functions, and maintaining a schedule of student contact can prevent student affairs professionals from becoming prisoners of their computer terminals.

STUDENT AFFAIRS ADMINISTRATORS AS TECHNOLOGY LEADERS

Technological developments and breakthroughs—both via the Internet and personal computers—have occurred with such high-speed frequency over the past few years that keeping up could be a full-time endeavor. In 1993, the text-based tools for accessing the Internet, Gopher and Veronica, were in vogue. Within one year, the information almost totally migrated to web-based functions, and a completely different set of Internet tools, such as Mosaic, Netscape, and Internet Explorer, became accepted as the standard. Page layout applications, clunky in their infancy in the late 1980s, are now sophisticated powerhouses. This fast-paced, everchanging environment provides an opening for student affairs practitioners to become technological leaders on campus. Being on the cusp of the technology revolution affords student affairs practitioners the opportunity to develop into experts in at least one facet of technology. By undertaking this task as a goal, student affairs professionals can become indispensable to the campus community and lead, as opposed to follow, the technology agenda.

The areas for skill expansion are wide open. They can include mastering the HTML code, acquiring a proficiency on off-the-shelf web design products, being able to facilitate workshops on such Internet resources as electronic mail, listservs, and the web or one of the plethora of desktop applications utilized at the institution. The knowledge base does not have to be solely hardware or software oriented. Student affairs administrators can become point people on such topics as Internet addiction and gambling, identity formation in cyberspace, and other developmental concerns. These types of programs have not been fully addressed on college and university campuses and cry out for resident experts to confront them.

Web-based resources can assist in this process. The Counseling Center Village (http://www.ub.counseling.buffalo.edu/ccv.html) is an index website that provides a vast array of web-based services that can be used to research and address developmental issues. The village contains a worldwide listing of counseling center links, a comprehensive self-help materials section, links to virtual pamphlets, and a research network. Similarly, coming up to speed on research related to Internet addiction can be found at websites such as the Center for On-Line Addiction (http://netaddiction.com/).

Participation in the Technology Decision-Making Process

Leadership in the information technology (IT) field does not have to be tackled alone because no one functions in an institutional vacuum. The profession must make it a priority to be included in the IT strategic planning that many institutions are now undertaking. Collaboration with other professional staff and faculty members, in such areas as IT strategic planning and distance learning, can enhance student affairs' role.

It is imperative that the student affairs division has a leading voice when discussions of hardware, software, compatibility, access, and the general direction of the institution are addressed. Decisions put forth by committees will have a significant impact for years to come, and student affairs leaders should be major players in the process. Without direct participation, student affairs risks being left out of crucial planning components or being given a lower priority to resources than warranted.

One structure, which could broaden the student affairs level of involvement in this area, is the formation of a separate technology board to advise the larger institutional group. Expanding the scope and reach of this body would afford more of an association from additional functional units within the division. The net effect would be better thought-through decisions and direction for consideration by the campuswide body. Although data at the national level are limited in this regard, one regional study indicated that where an institutional board devoted to technology planning was in place, 82% of those boards included direct student affairs representation (Elling, 1996). Taking a leadership role in the ensuing distance learning debates can be just as important. Student affairs administrators need to be active participants or risk being left behind the technological juggernaut.

Distance Learning and On-line Student Services

Distance learning education has become a fact of life at most 2- and 4-year institutions. As Lewis and colleagues (1999) pointed out, "About one-third of the nation's 2-year and 4-year postsecondary education institutions offered any distance education courses during the 12-month 1997-98 academic year. Distance learning was more likely to be conducted by public institutions; 78 percent of public 4-year institutions and 62 percent of public 2-year institutions offered distance education courses" (p. iii).

Student affairs professionals, for the most part, have not been members of planning and implementation teams. Questions about the types of student support services needed and their quality have not been properly addressed.

Many institutions have placed a variety of student affairs services on-line, for example, financial aid, registration, and career services. These endeavors have allowed students to be served "better, quicker, easier, cheaper and at times and places more convenient for the student" (NASPA, 2000, p. 1). Yet these systems have not necessarily been produced in concert with those responsible for delivering distance education courses. Needs assessment of any sort is seldom done. Because the number of institutions offering distance education programs and courses is increasing at a dizzying rate, there has been a lag between knowing what the students desire and what is offered.

Student affairs administrators are not cognizant whether these students may need more services or less because of their situation. Practitioners must work with the campus community in developing imaginative, yet cost-effective, services that complement, not replace, structures already in place. So although translating student affairs functions from a brick and mortar campus to a cybercampus can be performed, knowing the types of cyberservices distance education users will need is still a guessing game.

It has been argued that part of the higher education experience is on-campus involvement and its socialization process (Astin, 1985; Boyer, 1987; Kuh et al., 1991). The question that must be examined, primarily by student affairs professionals, is how to incorporate these experiences on-line, off-campus. The "fear is the loss of the socialization function [and limited involvement] associated with college attendance with distance learning students on a cybercampus" (NASPA, 2000, p. 1).

Distance learning, whether via compressed video, the web, or other yet-to-be-developed means, is here to stay. Having the foresight and willingness to work with other members of the campus community to ensure its success is a win-win situation for students, the institution, and the student affairs profession.

IDENTIFYING "BEST PRACTICES" IN ON-LINE STUDENT SERVICES

In addition to taking a leadership role on technological questions within the institutional hierarchy, student affairs professionals need to identify how others in the field are grappling with these concerns. Staying current and identifying the best practices or new methods in which student affairs practitioners are harnessing technological issues can strengthen the profession's role and influence. The initial step is to pinpoint successful models within the technological realm. There are a number of avenues open to student affairs administrators to assist in targeting these programs. First is to utilize the technology of the Internet, primarily web-based search engines. Indicating key words as basic as "student affairs" would yield a plentiful supply of sites to search. Additionally, scouring independent websites such as StudentAffairs.com can produce numerous leads. Contained within the pages of StudentAffairs.com are hundreds of student affairs related websites and on-line discussion group addresses. An electronic journal, *Student Affairs Online* is one of the primary publications providing technology-centered articles and information for practitioners. A variation on this theme is taking a web visit to institutions that have been early leaders in technology development. Arguably the first institution to give students unparalleled access to university information systems was UD. A number of their web initiatives can be accessed at http://www.mis.udel.edu/main/webinits/. Other types of institutions to visit include those with well-developed institutional, divisional, or departmental technology support structures such as Clemson University (http://dcit.clemson.edu/menus/services.html), University of Massachusetts at Amherst (http://www.saris.admin.umass.edu/saris/), and University of Wisconsin Oshkosh (http://www.mio.uwosh.edu/mio/index.html), respectively. Elling (1996) identified that public and private 4-year institutions with a minimum full-time enrollment of 15,000 students were most likely to have technology support staff within student affairs.

Another variation on this theme is accessing what are commonly referred to as "index sites." These sites are often developed by professional associations or individuals who are affiliated in some way with the target group. An example of the former is the National Clearinghouse for Commuter Programs (http://www.inform.umd.edu/CampusInfo/Departments/commute/NCCP/). This organizational site is used to provide members with information, publications, and programs that are of interest to student affairs professionals who are in charge of commuter students. An example of the later type of index site is one that was designed for student affairs research departments to maintain contact with one another and to share research findings over the web (http://www.uncc.edu/stuaffairs/sar/).

Internet Discussion Groups

A second route to exploit is the use of Internet discussion groups. Commonly referred to as Listservs (one of the most widely utilized discussion group software packages), these asynchronous forums can provide a wealth of information. Student affairs professionals participate by subscribing, via electronic mail, to one of the dozens of these Internet bodies. Typically centered on a subject area, such as student activities, academic advising, international students, disabilities, or commuters, messages are routed through the computer server to all members simultaneously, whether that number is 75 or 3,000. Simple queries to one or many listservs can link practitioners to individuals who have developed intriguing programs or furnish leads to be followed up. A sidebar effect could include a discussion or debate over the listserv itself. Although many of these conversations last for a mere handful of e-mail postings, they can provide insight into some of the technological difficulties with which colleagues across cyberspace are struggling.

"Best Practices" Research Through Conferences and Publications

One of the more rudimentary methods of identifying best practices is through conference sessions, both at the regional and national levels. Student affairs administrators look to these gatherings as a way to showcase their wares. By attending these annual gatherings, practitioners can glean information about programs being produced at institutions around the country. Usually, replicating these efforts is not too difficult. Presenters are often more than willing to provide insightful information and advice. If attendance at conferences is not practical, browsing through the program proceedings, either on the web or after the fact, can reveal useful information. Facilitators may even need to be cajoled into adapting their findings to be published on the web after the conference. Fortunately, because many presenters are creating workshops using presentation development software, transforming the material to the HTML code necessary for posting on the web is as simple as the "Save As" or "Publish To" command.

A more amorphous path to ferreting out worthwhile technology-driven programs by student affairs administrators is by perusing journal and magazine articles as well as the science and technology sections of daily newspapers. These periodicals, both from the popular media and the more specialized publications, herald the latest product development—hardware and software—and can stimulate "outside-the-box" thinking on the part of the practitioner. They can also give practitioners a heads-up on emerging trends and hardware and software developments.

Once a list of suitable programs has been identified, the next step is matching the programs with the vision and goals of the senior student affairs administrator and the overall divisional goals. It is imperative to take into consideration the resources necessary to adopt the agenda and policies and understand how these decisions correlate with institutional bearings.

Implementing "Best Practices"

Finally, implementing and then assessing the best practices derived from the identification and research phase needs to occur. Technological development has moved the ability to conduct sophisticated research from the complicated text-based domain of the mainframe down to the desktop. With improved *point and click* interfaces, powerful statistical programs such as SPSS (http:// www.spss.com/spss10/) and SYSTAT (http://www.spss.com/software/science/ systat/) are no longer the sole domain of the statistician and can now be run by student affairs practitioners with a modicum of training and understood with a basic knowledge of research methods and statistics. Departmental databases can provide a rich source of research data. Formerly, linking together of disparate data sources across departments was a time consuming and complicated process. In the digital age, data from one research study can be readily integrated with a number of other data sources to determine a number of research findings pertaining to the academic progress of students. An example of this type of research can be found at the University of North Carolina at Charlotte where multiple data sources were collected, including environmental surveys, program participation data, and academic performance data, to discover factors that enhanced or inhibited freshmen student retention and academic success (Elling, 2000).

A number of student affairs and institutional research departments have well-documented processes on the web regarding how each is organized to conduct outcomes assessment research, program evaluation, and student opinion surveys. A handy index site containing links to these types of research departments and related projects can be accessed at the following location: http://www.uncc.edu/stuaffairs/sarlinks.htm.

Research efforts in student affairs are often enhanced through home-grown product development. The Student Affairs Research Office at the University of Texas at Austin has developed software to deliver web-based survey instruments quickly and efficiently (http://dpweb1.dp.utexas.edu/adsurv/pwst/info.wb). Hanson (2000) explains this: "Random samples of students [can] be identified and contacted via e-mail and invited to participate in the survey administered on the Web. Control of survey participation [is] guaranteed through a firewall of randomly assigned identification numbers and passwords for all participants. The system monitors completed Web surveys in real-time and provides timely reminder letters to non-responders" (p. 2). Yet this time-consuming process can never truly be complete because technological applications are constantly in flux. What is current today can become passé tomorrow. Student affairs administrators, to be true leaders in the information technology field, must continually seek new avenues and new partnerships within the campus community and, possibly, third-party vendors.

STUDENT AFFAIRS PROFESSIONALS AS EDUCATORS

Being a leader in the march toward a more expansive technological universe is important for student affairs administrators. But practitioners are also obligated to be educators—for the students, colleagues, and the entire campus community. These educational endeavors should relate to some of the larger issues within the technology advancement fallout. Administrators must be concerned with the role practitioners play in the development of undergraduates—both on- and off-line. Off-line, student affairs has excelled in its holistic mission of assisting undergraduates as they confront and work through developmental issues faced at a given stage of life. But, the proliferation of technology within offices, student domiciles, and throughout campus lounges and computer labs has empowered parties to convey more via *cybercommunication*—electronic mail, listservs, instant messenger systems, Internet relay chat rooms—than through such old-fashioned channels as in-person meetings and consultations. These new forms of student development interventions have been a tremendous boon to the harried administrator and faculty member. High tech communication, used judiciously, creates enormous opportunities for all parties. Routine information can be funneled quickly and effortlessly. For example, simple academic advising questions may be handled with minimal exertion. Correspondence to multiple destinations is easily executed. The Pennsylvania State University has one of the most complete on-line academic advising models. Its Comprehensive Academic Advising and Information System (CAAIS) is "an expert-based, empirically-grounded advising and information system that is delivered by the latest technologies to supplement student/adviser relationships and to engage students in interactive inquiry for informed educational planning" (http://caais.oas.psu.edu/overview.html). No matter how student affairs professionals choose to communicate, they always need to weigh the benefits between high tech and high touch. Practitioners must understand if the chosen transmission routes are enabling undergraduates to become more outgoing, expressive, and thoughtful, and they need to be aware if technological expediency is hampering the undergraduate's developmental direction. As student affairs administrators, the balance displayed between high tech and high touch is imperative for the growth of undergraduates as technology becomes more a part of campus society. These issues cannot be ignored; practitioners must be cognizant of them as part of the educator role.

Student Affairs Professionals as Community Builders

Recent studies (Kraut et al., 2000; O'Toole, 2000) have demonstrated that higher levels of involvement with certain technologies, such as the Internet, produce a dampening effect on the social intercourse of individuals. More time connected to cyberspace produces less time with family and friends and diminished time interacting with human beings in general. As growth in technological access and utilization at colleges and universities increases, practitioners must strive to assist students to become increasingly involved with the campus community.

Many schools have developed extensive, on-line campuswide calendar systems to keep students informed. The University of Maine, for example, has developed a comprehensive calendar of events (http://calendar.umaine.edu/) that allows users to conduct searches based on a number of query options in addition to listing daily events. This, according to Kim Yerxa, assistant to the dean for communication and technology (personal communication, March 27, 2000), "has been a huge success" and connected undergraduates more to the campus community.

Fostering Face-to-Face Activities

The challenge of facilitating the integration of students into institutional life has been prevalent from the very beginnings of higher education. The problem is magnified today as technology erects barriers to satisfactory participation levels. Student affairs administrators must double their efforts purposely to involve undergraduates in face-to-face activities, to encourage the growth of communities on campus. Those responsible for residential life on campus need to reevaluate the manner in which students are incorporated within the confines of its structures. Student unions should promote opportunities for interaction. Campuses without natural outdoor gathering spots, such as the Low Library steps at Columbia University, should design such communal assembly areas. Campuswide activities that foster a community identity can be developed, such as the University of Connecticut's prefinal-exam Midnight Breakfast for students served by all levels of faculty and administrators.

At the same time virtual neighborhoods should be fostered that help the institution embrace commuter students or the disenfranchised. The obstacle for practitioners is how to harness technology's power and seductiveness while not replacing high touch activities. The University of Minnesota (2000b) has developed its own virtual town—Gopherville—for both commuters and residential students. The site has more than 90 chatrooms divided into 10 different categories. Students can interact with other undergraduates, faculty, and staff. Gopherville also includes information on becoming involved on campus, academic programs, and residence halls.

An exemplary illustration, outside the confines of higher education, is *craiglists* (http://www.craigslist.com), "a virtual bulletin board for the San Francisco Bay Area" (Mieszkowski, 2000, p. 28). According to Craig Newmark, developer of the site, there are some critical components for any virtual community to succeed. First, it must involve people who have the potential to interact with one another while having a shared experience. Second, it must provide browsers a sense of connection, a sense of intimacy, a feeling that "we're in this together." What better way to describe the collegiate experience? Third, the community must be useful. This could include providing such information as a locale for posting ride-share requests, room sharing, or babysitting services, whatever information the community finds beneficial to keep it self-propelling. Fourth, the virtual community must provide a comfortable forum for individuals to have a voice, where anyone can sound off about any subject at length (Mieszkowski, 2000). A common complaint among undergraduates, especially at institutions with large student bodies, is how insignificant they feel. Their voices and concerns go unheeded or are not taken seriously by "the administration." A nonintrusive on-line forum can contribute to an environment whereby students feel empowered to speak their minds—no matter how mundane or trivial the verbiage. Student affairs practitioners, engaged in many of these activities in the brick and mortar world of the campus, are well suited to shepherd the construction of such a virtual community.

Student Affairs in the Classroom

It is common for student affairs practitioners to be extensively engaged in academic-credit-bearing instruction. Student paraprofessionals are trained as resident assistants, orientation leaders, career information assistants, tutors, peer sexuality/health/alcohol and drug educators, and others. Many of these courses are enhanced by creation of web-based instruction sites. (See examples in Chapter 11 in this volume for programs at Miami University.) Many institutions use instructional software, such as WebCT or CourseInfo, as navigational shells in which any digital form of instructional materials may be added. These products enable the creation of sites for courses that include the syllabus, supplemental readings, and Internet links to other information sources and communication between the instructor and students and students with one another.

At the State University of New York at Buffalo, many functional areas of student affairs have created web-based interventions to which students can access to deal with issues such as making a decision about whether to sign up for Greek rush (http://www.greeklife.buffalo.edu/), to get information about careers (http://www.ub-careers.buffalo.edu/career/choose.html), or to begin the acquaintance process with a new roommate in the residence hall (http://www.ub-housing.buffalo.edu/lifehall.html). (For examples of programs developed by master's students in a professional preparation program at the University of Georgia see http://www.coe.uga.edu/echd/student.htm)

Student Affairs as an Academic Support System

A final area in which student affairs administrators can excel in their educator role is in the evolving technology issues that increasingly envelop institutions of higher learning. The campus community is beginning to encounter such volatile questions as Internet addiction (for example, pornography, gambling, overuse), identity formation, the digital divide, and the politics of race on-line, just to name a few. As these concerns become more prevalent, practitioners need to become aware of the issues at hand and become proactive as opposed to reactive in their responses. Whether in graduate preparation, residence life, leadership training, or divisionwide staff development programs, these issues must be addressed. Just as many institutions today provide substance abuse programs and seminars on intolerance and date rape, so must campuses in the future examine technology as a student impact issue, especially those concerned with Internet-related troubles.

Ethical Use and Misuse of Technology

Another set of evolving issues comes under the heading of the ethical use and misuse of technology. Students in the past have tested the behavioral boundaries set for them by colleges and universities. This will continue as students of tomorrow seek to test limits within the digital domain. The use of technology has added another layer of complexity to these testing behaviors that can include copyright infringement, hate speech, harassment, and plagiarism (Petersen & Hodges, 1997). As technology continues to evolve, student affairs administrators will need to maintain their vigilance of how students are using technology to conduct inappropriate, unethical, or illegal activities. To be most effective in this arena, institutions must establish policies designed to govern inappropriate technology usage. Likewise, they need to establish appropriate enforcement procedures and clearly articulated student codes of conduct. Safeguards must be put in place to protect both the student's right to free expression, on the one hand, and the institution's right to protect its systems from damage. Specifically, judicial affairs administrators, working in concert with technology staff and campus security, should develop a coordinated protocol. These plans would be used to research and refer reported incidents of hate speech delivered by electronic means or hacking into administrative systems, for example, to the proper campus authorities for notification, intervention, and adjudication.

Student affairs can take the lead on these issues by collaborating with student leaders, faculty, legal counsel, campus security, and technology center administrators in developing policies and practices designed to encourage appropriate access practices and discourage inappropriate student behavior. Once revised, when codes of student conduct are in place then student affairs practitioners can continue their educative role, acquainting students with the new behavioral standards and consequences.

STUDENT AFFAIRS ADMINISTRATORS AS TECHNOLOGY MANAGERS

Managing technology will be a continual challenge for the student affairs practitioner. With the advent of the Internet, many of the core college and university systems are changing to provide more accessible and convenient administrative and support services. Decisions regarding the design, implementation, support, and funding of these new services and tools are needed. Student affairs managers are the ones who understand the needs of undergraduates and how these services and tools can best be implemented in support of meeting those needs.

As a manager, it will be important for the student affairs professional to learn and understand how their core functions operate. Determining how technology can be tailored to best serve the student body requires an understanding of both the student and the technology. Historically, this type of background was garnered from graduate preparation programs.

Technology Preparation within Graduate Programs

Graduate preparation programs in student affairs have a rich and honorable tradition of training several generations of master's and doctoral candidates in the complexities students face in the collegiate environment. Because of rapid changes in technology, there may be gaps in the level of skill development students receive in their graduate programs that are necessary to succeed as a student affairs professional today. In a recent survey of student affairs preparation programs and Chief Student Affairs Administrators (CSAA), Bowman and Cuyjet (1999) found that 89% of the responding programs indicated they did not have a written goal statement pertaining to the inclusion of technology into the curriculum. The most common technology skills used in graduate programs included working with electronic mail and listservs and accessing electronic research vehicles (such as ERIC, the web, Gopher, and Telnet). In terms of the required use of software in coursework, the most commonly cited were statistical packages (33%), database software (15%), and spreadsheets (14%).

In contrast, CSAAs reported that their practitioners used electronic mail and word processing on a daily basis and, at least occasionally, used databases, spreadsheets, and the web. The researchers summarized that student affairs graduates should enter the profession being able to demonstrate a basic understanding of five areas: (a) electronic mail, (b) the web, (c) word processing, (d) databases, and (e) spreadsheets. The survey indicated that the majority of current programs do not engage graduate students in these areas, especially databases and spreadsheets. Adequate graduate school preparation will be crucial to the successful manager in order to provide them with the grounding in the basic technological tool set necessary to build and maintain administrative support systems for students.

Technology Goals for Graduate Programs

Possible methods for building better technology preparation into graduate programs could include incorporating various technological resources into class projects, integrating guest lecturers from technology-rich disciplines into the classroom, providing students opportunity to participate in technologically oriented campus projects, or by delivering select class sessions utilizing the latest technology. An example of this may be found at the University of Georgia, where a simulated college (Oconee College) has been created and placed on the Internet, including a spreadsheet budget (Winston et al., 1999, 2001). Students have assignments related to managing the budget and initiating change within the context of the simulation (http://www.coe.uga.edu/echd/ocs).

Finally, the goal should be to encourage graduate faculty to actively embrace the learning of new technology with the same intensity as they do for student development theory research and application. "Faculty cannot teach what they do not know" (Bowman & Cuyjet, 1999, p. 13) should not be accepted as a reason for not incorporating technology into the student affairs graduate curriculum.

The outcome would be a student affairs professional competent in a number of technology areas. Practitioners should be proficient in word processing, electronic mail, databases, student information systems, and spreadsheets. They should understand how desktop programs and systems are often linked together to perform routine tasks. Page layout and presentation software are becoming more important for individuals to understand and utilize.

As hardware and software configurations evolve, terminology becomes critical, especially if student affairs administrators seek to comprehend what students are discussing. Practitioners should absorb terms such as RAM, processor speed, MP3, chatrooms, Internet relay chat, and Instant Messenger to name just a few.

Mastering Today's Technology

Last, applications connected to the Internet need to be mastered in order to function in today's world. Electronic mail skills—composing, sending, attaching documents, and replying to messages—is a necessity to carry out day-to-day functions. Understanding the basics of Internet discussion groups such as listservs, can help the student affairs professional perform his or her job. The World Wide Web continues to evolve into an invaluable tool. Knowing the primary workings of web browsers and feeling comfortable executing the various operations will become critical as the web becomes as integrated within student affairs as electronic mail is today. In addition, student affairs administrators need to begin to understand how the web will be changing the way business as usual is conducted. Technology-phobic practitioners will find themselves unable to acquire the necessary competencies to survive in the student affairs realm of the twenty-first century.

The skill set for student affairs managers needs to be at an increasingly higher level as they wrestle with technology questions and solutions. Decisions about how to develop and deploy new applications will be crucial as well as delineating the types of resources, support, and training that are available. A danger for student affairs practitioners arises when applications are deployed without basing them on a foundation of thorough research. Increasing office efficiency, while important, should not be the sole driving force behind application development. Maintaining a purposeful and appropriate level of contact with students is also crucial.

Understanding how technology is changing staff roles is an important dynamic for the successful student affairs manager to address. The tools that are standard on the desktop are transforming secretaries into database administrators, student activities staff members into graphic designers, and work study students into application developers. Electronic mail systems are allowing unprecedented access to staff in other areas of the campus and increasing the exchange of new ideas and information between departments and campuses. Electronic mail has also been cited as the one facet of technology that has had the most influence on management practices in student affairs (Moneta, 1997). As a manager, student affairs practitioners needs to be cognizant of the changing nature of staff roles within their organizations. Position descriptions should reflect adequately the roles and responsibilities that shift in conjunction with technology changes. Serious attention should also be given to developing and maintaining appropriate usage standards for communicating by telephone, electronic mail, and visual methods. Many offices are deploying programs and services on a virtual basis over the Internet. The successful student affairs manager should make certain that these virtual services appropriately reflect the analog (real) versions of the services.

CONCLUSION

Technological advancement has given higher education institutions the opportunity to redefine and posture themselves to prepare the next generation of students to enter the workforce using teaching methods and delivery systems that were simply ideas on a drawing board a few short years ago. Being cognizant of this changing landscape becomes a prime focus for student affairs divisions in the upcoming decade. This will require that the profession actively define who and what it is and what it must do in regard to the development of new types of support systems, administrative applications, and organizational structures.

The student affairs leader of tomorrow must set an example for others by mastering at least one facet of the available technology and becoming familiar with others. The administrator must become a leading voice on the campus for strategic information technology and distance learning planning and collaborative application development, and must become actively engaged in the assessment of the impact of technology on the quality of life on the campus, both physical and virtual. Researching, developing, and promulgating best practices must become the hallmark.

As educators, student affairs practitioners can maintain high touch with students in an everincreasing high tech environment by leveraging technology to encourage the formation and growth of communities both on the campus and in the virtual domain for the distance learner. Collaboration with others on policy development and enforcement issues will continue to raise the visibility of student affairs on campuswide issues.

The student affairs manager must ensure that their organizations provide staff members with the time, resources, support, and training required to perform their roles in this new age. Developing a firm understanding of core administrative functions and how they change over time must be at the heart of this effort. Graduate preparation programs must be viewed increasingly as key players in the effort to produce tomorrow's student affairs managers.

Advancing technology and student affairs practice provides a life-long learning opportunity for student affairs administrators who face continual change and a new set of challenges just over the horizon. The task is massive, but those who accomplish it will reap great rewards for the generations that follow.

QUESTIONS TO CONSIDER

1. How can the use of technology help build community, both within the virtual realm and the brick and mortar world of the college and campus?

2. As the growth in technology continues to spiral upward, what would be some of the potential problems student affairs practitioners face?

3. What should be the role of student affairs in distance learning education?

4. What strategies should student affairs practitioners develop in order to make the use of technology a part of their life-long learning priorities?

5. What areas of technology should be included as a part of the curriculum within student affairs graduate preparation programs?

REFERENCES

Astin, A. W. (1985). *Achieving educational excellence*. San Francisco: Jossey-Bass.

Bowman, R. L., & Cuyjet, M. J. (1999). Incorporating technology: A comparison of preparation program training and student affairs practitioners' expectations. *College Student Affairs Journal, 18*(2), 4–15.

Boyer, E. L. (1987). *College: The undergraduate experience in America*. New York: Harper & Row.

Brown, S., & Malaney, G. (1996). Internet, listserv, and electronic mail usage by student affairs professionals. *Journal of Educational Technology Systems, 25*(1), 79–86.

Brown, S., & Malaney, G. (2000). *Use of electronic mail, listservs and the world wide web by student affairs professionals: A national study of NASPA members*. Unpublished manuscript. Storrs, CT: University of Connecticut.

Carr, S. (2000, February 11). As distance education comes of age, the challenge is keeping the students. *The Chronicle of Higher Education*, pp. A39–41.

Elling, T. W. (1996). *Information technology: Planning for the new dawn*. [On-line]. Available: http://www.uncc.edu/stuaffairs/naspa/index.htm

Elling, T. W. (2000). *Tracking freshmen success*. [On-line]. Available: http://www.uncc.edu/stuaffairs/fyet999/

Florida State University. (2000, March 27). *Online Orientation*. [On-line]. Available: http://www.fsu.edu/~orientat/

Hanson, G. (2000, March). *Assessing students on the web*. Program presented at the National Association of Student Personnel Administrators 2000 National Conference, Indianapolis, IN.

Iowa State University. (2000, March 27). *Online Orientation*. [On-line]. Available: http://www.iastate.edu/~offcampus_info/

Kraut, R., Lundmark, V., Patterson, M., Kiesler, S., Mukopadhyay, T., Scherlis, W. (2000). Internet paradox: A social technology that reduces social involvement and psychological well-being? *American Psychologist, 55*(3). [On-line]. Available: http://www.apa.org/journals/amp/amp5391017.html

Kuh, G. D., Schuh, J. H., Whitt, E. J., Andreas, R. E., Lyons, J. W., Strange, C. C., Krehbiel, L. K., & Mackay, K. A. (1991). *Involving colleges: Successful approaches to fostering student learning and development outside the classroom*. San Francisco: Jossey-Bass.

Lewis, L., Snow, K., Farris, E., & Levin, D.

(1999). *Distance education at postsecondary education institutions: 1997-98* (NCES 2000-013). Washington, DC: U.S. Department of Education, National Center for Education Statistics.

Mieszkowski, J. (2000, Winter). Are you on Craig's list? *Net Company,* 26–34.

Moneta, L. (1997). The integration of technology with the management of student services. In C. M. Engstrom & K. W. Kruger, *Using technology to promote student learning: Opportunities for today and tomorrow* (pp. 5–16). New Directions for Student Services, No. 78. San Francisco: Jossey-Bass.

National Association of Student Personnel Administrators (NASPA). (2000). *Distance learning and student affairs: Defining the issues* (Report of the Distance Learning Task Force). Washington, DC: Author.

O'Toole, K. (2000, February 16). Study takes early look at social consequences of net use. *Stanford Online Report.* [On-line]. Available: http://www.stanford.edu/dept/news/report/news/february16/internetsurvey-216.html

Pascarella, E. T., & Terenzini, P. T. (1991). *How college affects students: Findings and insights from twenty years of research.* San Francisco: Jossey-Bass.

Pennsylvania State University. (2000, March 27). *Comprehensive Academic Advising and Information System.* [On-line]. Available: https://caais.oas.psu.edu/overview.html

Peters, T. J., & Waterman, R. H., Jr. (1982). *In search of excellence.* New York: Harper & Row.

Petersen, R. J., & Hodges, M. W. (1997). Legal, ethical and policy issues. In C. M. Engstrom & K. W. Kruger, *Using technology to promote student learning: Opportunities for today and tomorrow* (pp. 45–58). New Directions for Student Services, No. 78. San Francisco: Jossey-Bass.

University of Minnesota. (2000a, March 27).

A Place for Parents on the Web. [On-line]. Available: http://www1.umn.edu/commpub/parent/

University of Minnesota. (2000b, March 27). *Gopherville Chat Rooms.* [On-line]. Available: http://www1.umn.edu/housing/go4web/gopher.htm

University of North Carolina & PricewaterhouseCoopers. (1999, August 31). *Information technology strategy for the University of North Carolina.* [On-line]. Available: http://www.ga.unc.edu/its/netstudy/PHASE_II/FINAL/ITS_REPORT.pdf, p. 132.

Winston, R. B., Jr., Brown, P. D., Badal, A., Daddona, M. F., Papish, R. A., & Smith, R. L. (1999). *Oconee College: A simulation for the study of higher education.*

Winston, R. B., Jr., Smith, R. L., Marsh, S. R., & Raetz, T. (2001). *Oconee College: A simulation for the study of higher education* (revised). [On-line]. Available (http://www.coe.uga.edu/ocs).

RECOMMENDED READING

Engstrom, C. M., & Kruger, K. W. (Eds.). (1997). *Using technology to promote student learning: Opportunities for today and tomorrow.* New Directions for Student Services, No. 78. San Francisco: Jossey-Bass.

Palloff, R. M., & Pratt, K. (1999). *Building learning communities in cyberspace.* San Francisco: Jossey-Bass.

Smith, M., & Pollack, P. (Eds.). (1999). *Communities in cyberspace.* New York: Routledge.

Western Cooperative for Educational Telecommunications. (2000, October 11). *The guide to developing online student services.* [On-line]. Available: http://www.wiche.edu/Telecom/index.htm

PART *II*

PARAMETERS OF
PROFESSIONAL PRACTICE

*T*he student affairs professional administrator functions in an educational context that both enables and constrains action. Whether administrators are making or enforcing policy, they must be fully cognizant of relevant laws pertaining to higher education if effective function is to be achieved. Likewise, administrators need to be engrained with a fundamental sense of justice, of what is right and fair, if they are to educate, lead, and manage effectively. Professional practice is, of course, constrained by these parameters, but it also is enabled by the same parameters. Ethical administrators who are fully knowledgeable of the laws, regulations, and case precedents affecting practice are more likely to find paths for effective action and to influence and serve as models to others. Even though laws can limit administrators' range of actions available to address problems and issues, they also serve to remind practitioners of the importance of respecting individuals and promoting a sense of fair play within the institution.

In a changing environment for higher education—internally, where its demographics and its relationships among students, their parents, and faculty and staff members are highly complex and multifaceted and, externally, where society demands increasing levels of accountability and offers less trust—knowledge of the law is an essential competency of professional student affairs administrators. Gehring offers a reliable and approachable overview of relevant aspects of law for student affairs administrators in Chapter 5. Beginning with an understanding of legal relationships and essential guarantees in the U.S. Constitution, he addresses both the history of salient legal decisions affecting student affairs and the most compelling current legal issues, such as the First Amendment and cyberspace. The Fourth and Fourteenth Amendments are addressed in detail. Readers are provided the most up-to-date information about the Americans with Disabilities Act, the Family Educational Rights and Privacy Act, the Drug Free Schools and Communities Act, and the Student Right-to-Know and Campus Security Act that is possible in a published document. (Reinterpretation of these laws and prorogation of new regulations occur frequently, often more rapidly than textbooks can go to press.) Contracts, torts, and defamation issues also are addressed. This authoritative chapter provides the most thorough overview of legal issues available today in student affairs literature.

In Chapter 6, Young provides a methodical and carefully considered review of ethical issues in student affairs practice. Beginning with definitions and approaches to ethical practice, he explores faculty and institutional contexts and the inevitability of ethical dilemmas. Young's presentation is designed to help practitioners understand their service obligations and ethical models for professional action. The author explores how professionals can help students learn about ethics and how professionals can use ethics in mediating conflicts, modeling and mentoring, and motivating. He concludes with a concise and comprehensible summary of ethical principles.

READING SUGGESTIONS

These chapters are well placed in the book, proceeding as they do the managing section (Chapters 7 through 10), where direct application of the knowledge provided by Gehring and Young finds particular relevance. Readers may want to explore these chapters immediately following Chapters 1 and 2, which provide a context for applying the legal and ethical parameters of practice.

5

Legal Parameters
for Student Affairs Practice

DONALD D. GEHRING

D uring the past 40 years the environment of the college campus has changed dramatically. While the actual number of students attending postsecondary institutions increased significantly during that time, they were fairly homogeneous in terms of race, ethnicity, sex, age, and socioeconomic status. On the other hand, today's students are as diverse as society at large. Racial and ethnic minorities now populate institutions in ever-increasing numbers. Women outnumber men on most campuses, and the average age of students is increasing on many. Federal financial assistance has brought to campus students from every socioeconomic class.

The campus has changed not only in terms of its demographics, but also in the relationships that exist among students, their parents, faculty, staff, and the institution. These relationships are now much more complex and multidimensional. In loco parentis has been discarded and the Twenty-Sixth Amendment, making 18-year-old students adults, was passed while the legal drinking age was raised to 21. The federal government has also passed a series of redistributive and protective policy laws defining new relationships among students, their parents, and society (e.g., 20 U.S.C. 1232; 20 U.S.C. 1092; 20 U.S.C. 1145). The relationships among students also have become more violent; a loss of civility has been seen on many campuses (Boyer, 1990; Pavela, 1997).

Finally, the society in which colleges and universities exist has seen dramatic changes with respect to postsecondary education. Public accountability is now demanded by taxpayers and institutions no longer enjoy a high trust with society. Evidence of this can be seen in the assessment movement and in the charges that colleges and universities are harboring criminals by protecting them in their "secret" disciplinary processes (Bernstein, 1996). Society has also become more litigious (Caseload Highlights, 2000).

These changes in the demographics, the nature of relationships, and societal attitudes have combined to make a knowledge of the law essential for every student affairs practitioner—from the vice president to the newest entry-level practitioner. Whether the practitioner is acting in the capacity of educator, leader, or manager, a knowledge of the law is imperative.

Student affairs practitioners need not be lawyers to be effective in their roles, but they must have a basic understanding of the legal parameters affecting their work. An understanding of legal mandates, constraints, and the rights of all members of the academic community is imperative in developing campus policies and interpreting them to campus constituents. Nothing will erode the trust essential for leadership faster than implementing policies or developing procedures that violate the rights of others. Knowledge of the law also is important if student affairs practitioners are to serve as positive models for students.

The purpose of this chapter is to provide the practitioner with an overview of the legal parameters involved in student affairs work. This is not intended to be legal advice, and institutional counsel should be consulted whenever legal questions arise. Rather, this overview will assist the practitioner to understand some of the rights, privileges, and responsibilities of individuals and groups so that when they are in jeopardy of being infringed upon counsel may be consulted. Further, this chapter is up to date at the time it is written, but as Justice Cardoza (1921) said, "Law never is, but is always about to be" (p. 126). Thus, continuing professional development in college and university legal issues is essential. Several updating publications such as *The College Student and the Courts* (Young & Gehring, 1985), *Synthesis* (Pavela, 1989–2001) and *Synfax* (Pavela, 1992–2001) are available to help administrators stay abreast of current legal decisions and issues.

UNDERSTANDING LEGAL RELATIONSHIPS

Although the legal relationships that exist among students, faculty, staff, and the institution may seem confusing, there is a way to think about them that can help to untangle this web of confusion. Just as animals and plants are classified in biology, the law, which defines the relationships between constituent groups and the institution, may be classified as the four C's—constitutions, codes, contracts, and contacts (torts).

Constitutional Guarantees

The federal *Constitution* is the highest law in the land and nothing may supercede it. State constitutions may grant more rights than the federal Constitution, but may never provide fewer rights than those granted under the U.S. Constitution (*Washington v. Chrisman*, 1984). Students, faculty, and staff members, even those from other countries, are "persons" and thus enjoy the rights guaranteed by the federal Constitution (*Buckton v. NCAA*, 1977). Individuals who are residents of a particular state also enjoy the rights granted under the state's constitution. Generally the rights guaranteed under state and federal constitutions only serve to protect individuals against actions by the government or its agencies. Thus students, faculty, and staff at private colleges and universities do not have a right to the guarantees found in constitutions.

Statutory Protections

The second C, *codes*, defines the relationships created by various statutes passed by both federal and state governments. The U.S. Code and the several state codes contain laws of that jurisdiction, and practitioners must be familiar with those statutes that pertain to their work. The federal government has been much more active in recent decades in passing both redistributive policy laws that prohibit discrimination and attempt to level the playing field and protective policy laws that mandate specific actions that government believes are necessary to protect individuals from their own conduct (Coomes & Gehring, 1994). State laws vary widely and administrators must be conversant with the laws of the jurisdiction in which they work. Especially important are state alcoholic beverage laws, state open public records, and open meeting laws.

Contractual Agreements

Contracts constitute the third C and define a very important relationship. Faculty and staff have an explicit contract to perform certain functions. These contracts usually incorporate, by reference in the contract, other terms and conditions such as those found in the staff and faculty handbooks. Students, while having explicit contracts for various goods and services such as housing and dining services, also have an implied contract with the institution. This contract implies that the institution will provide an education and award a degree if the student pays tuition and meets academic and behavioral standards. Contracts may be written or oral.

Torts

The fourth C, or *contacts*, represents the final relationship. Unlawful contacts with another's person, property, or reputation are called torts. Tort law also varies from state to state. Each state determines the duty one individual owes another. These duties are derived from statutes or common law (judge-made law). Generally the two torts most common in the context of a college or university are negligence (failure to perform in a reasonable manner or to meet established standards) and defamation (both libel and slander).

Each of these legal relationships is discussed in the following sections. When reading these sections, administrators should understand the limits of the jurisdiction of the courts and what they do. Generally, courts settle controversies between parties, determine the constitutionality of laws, and interpret laws. The decision of a court only extends to its geographic boundary. Thus, the decisions of the Supreme Court of Georgia are not binding on the courts in Ohio. However, Ohio courts are free to adopt the reasoning of the Georgia court. (See, for example, *State ex rel The Miami Student v. Miami University*, 1997, and *Red and Black Pub. Co., Inc. v. Board of Regents*, 1993.) Similarly the decision of one federal court is not binding on another. Only when the decision is that of the United States Supreme Court is every jurisdiction bound to follow the precedent.

THE CONSTITUTION

The Constitution itself simply sets out the branches of the government and the relationships among them. The amendments to the Constitution contain the rights of individuals. The rights guaranteed in the Constitution, however, only provide assurance against government action. For example, the First Amendment only protects individuals against governmental conduct as it provides that "*Congress* [italics added] shall make no law respecting the establishment of religion." Thus, students and staff at private colleges do not enjoy the rights guaranteed under the Constitution unless the institution decides to grant them. As the United States Supreme Court pointed out, the Constitution "erects no shield against purely private conduct" (*Shelley v. Kraemer*, 1947, p. 1180). Private colleges and universities must be shown to be engaged in "state action" for the Constitution to apply to them. The concept of "state action" means that what was originally private action has become so entwined with the state that its actions are now those of the state for all intents and purposes. This is a threshold question in any case claiming Constitutional rights at a private institution. Courts determine whether a private college is engaged in state action by "sifting facts and weighing circumstances" (*Burton v. Wilmington Parking Authority*, 1961, p. 722) or on a case-by-case basis.

Courts have been reluctant to find state action in cases brought against private institutions. The receipt of federal or state dollars is often the first issue raised to show state action, but the courts have held that receiving governmental funds is not sufficient (*Grossner v. Trustees of Columbia University*, 1968; *Torres v. Puerto Rico Junior College*, 1969). Other efforts to bring the actions of private institutions within the arena of state action have also failed (state accreditation—*Berrios v. Inter American University*, 1976; state-approved curriculum—*Rowe v. Chandler*, 1971; state tax exemptions—*Browns v. Mitchell*, 1969; or state grant of powers of eminent domain—*Blackburn v. Fisk University*, 1971).

The First Amendment

The First Amendment provides that

Congress shall make no law respecting the establishment of religion or prohibiting the free exercise thereof; or abridging the freedom of speech or of the press; or the right of the people peaceably to assemble; and to petition the government for a redress of grievances.

The various rights guaranteed under this amendment implicate just about every area of student affairs from the student press to student organizations. Each of the rights guaranteed in this amendment will be discussed as it relates to the management of student affairs.

Religion

The Supreme Court, in the case of *Lemon v. Kurtzman* (1971), fashioned a three-pronged test to determine if the establishment clause of the First Amendment was violated. The test seeks to determine if the state or federal assistance—which need not be financial but can simply be the imprimatur of the government—(a) reflects a clearly secular purpose, (b) has a primary effect that neither advances nor inhibits religion, and (c) avoids excessive entanglement between the government and religion. All three criteria must be met not to run afoul of the establishment clause. As an example, the Eighth Circuit Court of Appeals found that assigning a public university student to do practice teaching at a parochial school did serve a valid secular purpose, but it advanced religion by creating a perception that the state approved the school's religious mission and thereby violated the second prong of the test (*Stark v. St. Cloud State University*, 1986).

Student religious groups on public campuses also create First Amendment issues. When one such group wanted to use space in a building for religious observances the institution said they could not accommodate the request because it would be a violation of the establishment clause to do so. The student group brought suit alleging that if they were not permitted to use the space, it would violate their free exercise rights. The Supreme Court decided the case not on the basis of religion, but as an issue of free speech. The Court pointed out that to allow the use of the room would not violate the establishment clause because the group would only enjoy "incidental benefits" and to prohibit the use of the space would constitute discrimination on the basis of the content of the speech (*Widmar v. Vincent*, 1981). A similar finding was reached when a public university denied activity funding to a campus Christian magazine. The Court held that the denial of funds constituted discrimination based on the viewpoint expressed in the magazine (*Rosenburger v. Rector and Visitors of the University of Virginia*, 1995).

Speech and Press

The freedom of speech and press guaranteed in the First Amendment is not free. Society pays a dear price for it—incivility. It is also not an absolute right.

The exercise of free speech and demonstrations on campus has long been a part of the collegiate experience. In the 1800s student rebellions were precipitated by the clash of aristocratic traditions coming into conflict with newly created democratic ideals (Rudolph, 1990). In the early 1900s students such as Clarence Darrow, Upton Sinclair, and Jack London formed the Intercollegiate Socialist Society to express their concerns and values. Campuses then began to be considered as radical centers of subversive movements (Brubacher & Rudy, 1968). Historian Frederick Rudolph (1990) stated that the most significant characteristics of the 1930s were the use of social protest and the repudiation of the past. The civil rights movement of the 1960s saw speaker bans being promulgated and challenged on campuses across the country (Young & Gehring, 1986).

In each era, student expression has caused administrators to attempt to find a way to stifle hurtful speech or incivility. Yet these types of speech are protected by the First Amendment and are the price paid for the freedom enjoyed. The Supreme Court has ruled that the purpose of the First Amendment is to invite dispute and to stir people to anger (*Terminiello v. Chicago*, 1949). In addition, the Court has said that "If there is a bedrock principle underlying the First Amendment, it is that the government may not prohibit the expression of an idea simply because society finds the idea itself offensive or disagreeable" (*Texas v. Johnson*, 1989, p. 414).

That the First Amendment applies on campus cannot be debated: "It can hardly be argued that either students or teachers shed their constitutional rights to freedom of speech or expression at the schoolhouse gate" (*Tinker v. Des Moines Independent School District*, 1969, p. 506). Protected speech on campus includes symbolic expression, such was wearing arm bands (*Tinker v. Des Moines Independent School District*, 1969; *Students Against Apartheid Coalition v. O'Neil I*, 1987; *University of Utah Students Against Apartheid v. Peterson*, 1986), and speech or expression advocating unlawful activity (*Joyner v. Whiting*, 1973). Remember that although one may *advocate* unlawful activity, one may not engage in such activity without being subject to criminal prosecution.

Indecent speech and incivility also are forms of protected speech. An individual who wore a jacket with the words "F_ _ _ the Draft" in the county courthouse was arrested for disturbing the peace, but the Supreme Court reversed the conviction and quoted Justice Frankfurter saying, "one of the prerogatives of American citizens is the right to criticize public men and measures—and that means not only informed and responsible criticism but the freedom to speak foolishly and without moderation" (*Cohen v. California*, 1971, p. 26). Similar bad taste was exhibited by a student at the University of Missouri two years later, and the institution disciplined her. Again, the Supreme Court held that "The mere dissemination of ideas—no matter how offensive to good taste—on a state university campus may not be shut off in the name alone of 'conventions of decency'" (*Papish v. Board of Curators of University of Missouri*, 1973, p. 670).

Student affairs administrators are by nature sensitive to the needs of students and have a tendency to want to protect students from the incivility expressed by others. The number of institutions that have adopted hate speech codes evidences this. However, these attempts usually conflict with the First Amendment, and the administrators and the institution end up either looking foolish or spending large sums for litigation. Administrators at George Mason University were told by two federal courts that they violated the First Amendment when they disciplined a fraternity for a crude skit demeaning of African American women (*Iota Xi Chapter of Sigma Chi Fraternity v. George Mason University*, 1991). The assistant vice chancellor and director of campus activities at the University of California Riverside were required to take First Amendment sensitivity training as part of a settlement where they suspended a fraternity for distributing a T-shirt that was upsetting to the Latino students on campus (Frammolino, 1993). Probably the most heinous incident involving an attempt to protect individuals from being exposed to hurtful expression involved a march by members of the American Nazi Party. The marchers, dressed in uniforms with swastikas, paraded through Skokie, Illinois, which was populated by many Jews who survived the Holocaust. In its decision to allow the march to take place the court said,

> It would be grossly insensitive to deny, as we do not, that the proposed demonstration would seriously disturb, emotionally and mentally, at least some, and probably many of the Village's residents. The problem with engrafting an exception on the First Amendment for such situations is that they are indistinguishable in principle from speech that "invite[s] dispute . . . induces a condition of unrest, creates dissatisfaction with conditions as they are, or even stirs people to anger." Yet these are among the "high purposes" of the First Amendment. (*Collin v. Smith*, 1978, p. 1206)

In addition to symbolic expression, advocacy of unlawful conduct, indecency and incivility, and pornography are also protected by the First Amendment. However, child pornography is not protected nor is obscenity.

Obscenity is a very difficult standard. To be obscene courts ask whether

> (a) "the average person applying contemporary community standards" would find that the work, taken as a whole, appeals to the prurient interest, (b) whether the work depicts or describes, in a patently offensive way, sexual conduct specifically defined by applicable state law; and (c) whether the work, taken as a whole, lacks serious literary, artistic, political, or scientific value. [citations omitted] (*Miller v. California*, 1973, p. 24)

Obscenity and child pornography are not the only forms of speech that lie outside the protections of the First Amendment. Speech that creates a clear and present danger certainly is not protected by the First Amendment, but the danger must be "present" rather than "probable" (*United States v. Dennis*, 1950). What this means was clarified by the Supreme Court when it observed that "undifferentiated fear or apprehension of disturbance of expression" did not constitute a clear and present danger (*Tinker v. Des Moines*, 1969, p. 508). In deciding if there is a "clear and present danger" the courts look at the context in which the speech is made. The Supreme Court observed that "The most stringent protection of free speech would not protect a man in falsely shouting fire in a theater and causing panic" (*Schenck v. United States*, 1919, p. 52). On one campus, however, the president-elect of the student government association was disciplined for arousing a crowd which, subsequently, made it "costly" for the university to fence off a space previously used by students. Students subsequently confronted police and violence ensued in which one person died and several others were injured. The president-elect was disciplined for his exhortations and not allowed to ascend to the presidency. He claimed he was being disciplined for the exercise of his free speech in violation of his Constitutional rights. The court, however, pointed out that

> Utterance in the context of violence, involving a clear and present danger, can lose its significance as an appeal to reason and become part of an instrument of force and as such is unprotected by the Constitution. (*Siegel v. Regents of the University of California*, 1970, p. 838)

Like a "clear and present danger" speech or expression that incites others to imminent lawless action is not a form of protected speech under the First Amendment. There is a thin line, however, between advocating lawlessness and actually exhorting others to become violent. The former is protected while the latter is not. The Supreme Court noted this difference stating that "the mere abstract teaching . . . of the moral propriety or even moral necessity for a resort to force and violence is not the same as preparing a group for violent action and steeling it to such action" (*Noto v. United States*, 1961, pp. 297–298).

Speech or expression that materially or substantially disrupts the educational process also lies outside the protection of the First Amendment (*Burnside v. Byars*, 1966; *Tinker v. Des Moines*, 1969). However, it must be the speech or expression that creates the disruption. Speech that "stirs people to anger," who then become disruptive, is protected, but the *actions* of the angry people would be cause for disciplinary actions against them. It should, however, be understood that the speech or expression that "stirs people to anger" refers to speech or expression that is directed at the masses and not to a specific individual.

Words directed at a specific individual "which by their very utterance inflict injury or tend to incite an immediate breach of the peace" are "fighting words" and not protected by the First Amendment (*Chaplinsky v. New Hampshire*, 1942, p. 575). Thus, to be "fighting words" they must (a) be directed to an individual and (b) must "have a direct tendency to cause acts of violence by the person to whom individually the remark is addressed" (*Gooding v. Wilson*, 1972, p. 524).

The principles that have been enumerated here as applied to speech and expression also apply with equal force to expression in the campus press. Administrators at public institutions may not censor the content of the student newspaper simply because they are offended by or disagree with it (*Dickey v.*

Alabama State Board of Education, 1967; *Lee v. Board of Regents of State Colleges*, 1969). Censorship may also take the form of withholding funds in addition to excising content. The president of a historically Black state university cut off the funding to his campus newspaper when the editor published segregationist views in an editorial. The president believed this violated the Civil Rights Act of 1964 and the equal protection clause of the Fourteenth Amendment. The Fourth Circuit Court of Appeals, however, held in favor of the editor and restored the newspaper's funding, pointing out that the editor was free, under the First Amendment, to advocate segregation, but he could not engage in the practice of it (*Joyner v. Whiting*, 1973). Student editors are, however, accountable for what they publish and may be liable for defamation (*Mazart v. State*, 1981).

FIRST AMENDMENT AND CYBERSPACE

The Supreme Court has sent a clear signal that it will apply traditional First Amendment analyses to questions about speech and expression on the Internet. The Court has referred to the Internet as a "new marketplace of ideas" and a "vast democratic for[um]" (*Reno v. ACLU*, 1997). In striking down two sections of the Communications Decency Act, which, like many campus speech codes, were overly broad, the Court cited with approval district court Judge Dalzell's opinion in which he stated:

> that the disruptive effect of the CDA on Internet communication, as well as the CDAs broad reach into protected speech not only renders that Act unconstitutional, but would also render unconstitutional any regulation of protected speech on this new medium. (*ACLU v. Reno*, 1996, p. 867)

Thus, those forms of protected speech discussed above—uncivil speech, indecent speech, speech that stirs people to anger or invites dispute, advocacy of unlawful conduct, symbolic expression, and pornography—are protected on the Internet as well. If, for example, an institution permits students to use their servers to set up individual web pages, the same Constitutional protections apply to those web pages as apply to other forms of student expression. Administrators should not be too concerned about legal liability if such protected speech is transmitted over the Internet using their server or even if the server is used to transmit unprotected speech. Internet service providers are simply the pipeline for information being transmitted and, as such, would most likely be immune from third-party liability (*Doe v. America Online, Inc.*, 1998; *Zeran v. America Online, Inc.*, 1997).

Using traditional First Amendment analyses also means that those who are "jamming" or "bombing" the server and thereby causing disruption of the educational process are not engaged in a form of protected speech and may be disciplined. Copyright violations may also result in disciplinary action as well as civil liability. Students and others need to understand that defamation and threats over the Internet could result in civil and criminal liability. Everyone who receives a password to give them access to the institution's server should be required to attend an orientation to Internet use at which these issues are discussed. Ethical issues applied to Internet use should also be discussed. Unauthorized and unlawful use of the server should be included in the code of conduct or a computer use policy (Responsible Use of Electronic Communications, 1996). Finally, administrators should realize that, just as in any other area involving protected speech, reasonable time, place, and manner restrictions may be applied to the exercise of protected speech on the Internet.

EMPLOYEE SPEECH

Student affairs practitioners should understand that although they have a right to free speech under the First Amendment, that right is more limited than it is for students and nonemployees. Employees' speech is protected under the First Amendment only where it is limited to matters of public concern or interest. The Supreme Court upheld the termination of a public employee who, after being transferred to another section, distributed a questionnaire asking coworkers if they had ever been transferred, if they believed it to be fair, and how it had affected their morale. The Court said,

> We hold only that when a public employee speaks not as a citizen upon matters of public concern, but instead as an employee upon matters only of personal interest, absent the most unusual circumstances, a federal court is not the appropriate forum in which to review the wisdom of a personnel decision taken by a public agency allegedly in reaction to the employee's behavior. (*Connick v. Myers*, 1983, p. 147)

What constitutes "speech addressing matters of public concern must be determined by the content, form and context" (*Connick v. Myers*, 1983, p. 147).

Policy Considerations for Campus Speech and Expression

Attempts to control speech on campus, especially hurtful speech, are understandable; however, it must be realized, as the Court pointed out in striking down the University of Wisconsin speech code in *UWM Post v. Board of Regents of the University of Wisconsin* (1991), that

> The problems of bigotry and discrimination sought to be addressed here are real and truly coercive of the educational environment. But freedom of speech is almost absolute in our land and the only restriction the fighting words doctrine can abide is that based on violent reaction. Content-based prohibitions such as that in the UW Rule, however well intended simply cannot survive the screening which our Constitution demands. (p. 1181)

Incivility and other forms of protected speech that are offensive should elicit more speech. Remember that other students and administrators also have the right to speak and can counter incivility with civility and are free to point out the flaws in speech with which they disagree. Long ago Thomas Jefferson pointed out that "We have nothing to fear from the demoralizing reasoning of some, if others are left free to demonstrate their errors, and especially when the law stands ready to punish the first criminal act provided by false reasoning" (cited by Justice Brandeis in *Whitney v. California*, 1927, p. 375).

Campus policy should be crafted in such a way as to respond to behavior rather than to speech. Most institutions also find it useful to designate one space on campus as the "free speech zone." This is usually a place away from classes and the library, where it will not disrupt the educational atmosphere of those buildings. Recall that as a time, place, and manner restriction, it must be in a reasonable place.

Students should be informed of how to initiate complaints about unauthorized or unlawful use of the Internet. Institutions may also decide to restrict the use of their server to "official business" but this would be only an expectation, as it would be almost impossible to monitor (*Loving v. Boren*, 1998). These and the suggestions offered earlier should be helpful in developing campus policies related to free speech.

Assembly and Association

The right of the people peaceably to assemble also includes the right to associate with others (*Student Coalition v. Austin Peay State University*, 1979). Like not prohibiting speech, a public institution may not prohibit students from assembling or demonstrating on campus based on the institution's disagreement with the purpose of the demonstration (*Shamloo v. Mississippi State Board of Trustees, Etc.*, 1980). The First Amendment only guarantees the right to peaceably assemble, and demonstrations that become disruptive may be shut down and those who are disruptive may be disciplined (*Esteban v. Central Missouri State College*, 1969). Reasonable time, place, and manner restrictions may also be imposed on campus demonstrations, but institutions may not impose any prior restraints on students' assembly rights (*Bayless v. Martine*, 1970; *Sword v. Fox*, 1971).

The right of students to freely associate was emphasized by the Supreme Court in *Healy v. James* (1972), a case involving the nonrecognition of a campus chapter of Students for a Democratic Society (SDS). The national organization often reverted to disruption, and when the local group was asked if they too would be disruptive, they responded saying that it was impossible to answer because it would depend upon the issue. When the group was denied recognition, members brought suit. The Court said, "the precedents of this Court leave no room for the view that because of the acknowledged need for order, First Amendment protections should apply with less force on college campuses than in the community at large" (p. 180). There was nothing in the record showing an advocacy directed to inciting lawless action, which would have been a basis for nonrecognition. Denial of recognition of the group was based solely on the institution's disagreement with the organization's purposes. The Court found this reason to violate the First Amendment. Thus, public institutions that have either registered or recognized student groups must allow others to apply for whatever form of recognition they employ. These groups may be required to provide a statement of purpose and the names of their officers (but not members) and sign a statement of compliance with institutional rules and regulations (*Eisen v. Regents*, 1969; *Merkey v. Board of Regents*, 1974).

Once a group is recognized it must be afforded those rights granted to other student groups, but the institution need not assist them in exercising their rights or grant any additional rights (*Maryland Public Interest Research Group Center v. Elkins*, 1977; *National Strike Information Center v. Brandeis*, 1970). Neither must funding to student organizations be equal. Rational decisions about student activity allocations may be made that result in different amounts being allocated to different groups. However, the amount of allocation may not be based on a disagreement with the group's lawful purposes (*Gay and Lesbian Student Association v. Gohn*, 1988).

Although institutions have been permitted to assess and collect mandatory student activity fees to provide a forum for the expression of ideas (*Veed v. Schwartzkoph*, 1973), these fees have recently been challenged. Using activity fees to support political or ideological organizations has been challenged by students who contend that this violates their right of association. They do not want to contribute funds to organizations with which they disagree (*Smith v. Regents of University of California*, 1993; *Southworth v. Grebe*, 1998).

The United States Supreme Court, however, has essentially laid that issue to rest (*Board of Regents of University of Wisconsin v. Southworth*, 2000). The Court rejected the "germane" test established in previous cases involving a bar association and a teacher's union, stating that "It is not for the Court to say what is and is not germane to the ideas to be pursued in an institution of higher education." (p. 4224). The Court made a very powerful statement when it said that if the funds are distributed in a viewpoint-neutral manner,

> The University may determine that its mission is well served if students have the means to engage in dynamic discussions of philosophical, religious, scientific, social and political subjects in their extracurricular campus life outside the lecture hall. If the University reaches this conclusion, it is entitled to impose a mandatory fee to sustain an open dialogue to these ends. (p. 4224)

The right to freely associate also includes the right not to associate. At Washington State University students automatically became members of the student government association when they paid their activity fee. Several students objected, stating that they did not wish to be members of the student government association. The Supreme Court of Washington said the university "may not compel membership in an association, such as ASUW which purports to represent all the students at the university" (*Good v. Associated Students*, 1975, p. 768).

THE FOURTH AMENDMENT

The Fourth Amendment provides, in part, "the right of the people to be secure in their persons, houses, papers and effects against unreasonable searches and seizures shall not be violated, and no warrant shall be issued but upon probable cause." Because the amendment only prohibits *unreasonable* searches and seizures, it would seem to imply that there are *reasonable* searches and seizures.

Reasonable searches and seizures would not require a warrant or probable cause as required by the Fourth Amendment. The most obvious reasonable search and seizure involves the consent of the individual (*State v. Wingerd*, 1974). Contraband that is in "plain view" may also be seized without a warrant without violating the Fourth Amendment (*Washington v. Chrisman*, 1982). State constitutional requirements, however, may raise a higher standard for searches and seizures, and practitioners also should be familiar with those (*Washington v. Chrisman*, 1984).

Room inspections are a reasonable way to ensure that the room is being used and maintained in accordance with university regulations. These inspections, however, should not be a subterfuge for "fishing expeditions." Contraband that is in "plain view" during these routine inspections may be seized and used in disciplinary proceedings (*State v. Kappes*, 1976). The seizure of contraband found during a good faith inventory of a lost item also has been upheld (*State v. Johnson*, 1975).

An emergency may lead to a reasonable search and seizure. In a California case a university librarian had complaints of a foul odor in an area of the library and sent the custodian to investigate. The custodian traced the odor to a particular study carrel and used his master key to open the carrel and remove a briefcase containing small bags of a green-parsley-looking substance. The librarian called the police to identify the substance. The police identified the contents as marijuana that had been treated with a chemical to keep it fresh and, subsequently, arrested the student. The student complained that his Fourth Amendment rights were violated, but the court held that it was reasonable for university officials to seize the briefcase as they had an emergency situation in the library, and it was reasonable for them to call the police who then obtained the evidence in "plain view." The student's conviction for possession with intent to sell was upheld (*People v. Lantheir*, 1971).

In 1985 the United States Supreme Court upheld the warrantless search of the purse of a 14-year-old schoolgirl. The Court found the search and seizure of contraband permissible "when there are reasonable grounds for suspecting that the search will turn up evidence that the student has violated or is violating either the law or the rules of the school" (*New Jersey v. T.L.O.*, 1985, p. 342).

The Court recognized that students had Fourth Amendment rights but that there were also legitimate interests of the school to be protected. Whether a search was reasonable in the context of a school would be determined by the age of the student, the items that are sought, past history, and the degree of individualized suspicion. The Supreme Court has not as yet faced the issue of the Fourth Amendment rights of college students who are adults but whose residence hall room may be their "home," where they have a reasonable expectation of privacy. One federal district court captured the scope of the Fourth Amendment on the college campus when it stated, "The parameters of Fourth Amendment protection on campus have been unclear" (*Morale v. Grigel*, 1976, p. 1001) and remain so.

Although those parameters have been unclear, several state and federal courts have upheld warrantless searches on campus as reasonable and not a violation of students' Fourth Amendment rights. The primary basis for these findings has been that college officials who have "reasonable cause to believe" that the student has contraband in contravention of institutional rules may conduct a search for disciplinary evidence to maintain good order and discipline on the campus. Searches of this type have been upheld for a student's room (*Ekelund v. Secretary of Commerce*, 1976; *Moore v. Student Affairs Committee of Troy State University*, 1968; *Utah v. Hunter*, 1992), suitcases (*United States v. Coles*, 1969), and an automobile (*Keene v. Rodgers*, 1970).

In one federal jurisdiction the court has not permitted a warrantless search of a student's room under the conditions outlined above, but required institutional officials to obtain a warrant (*Smyth and Smith v. Lubbers*, 1975). It also has been held that if police enter a student's room seeking criminal evidence, they must have a warrant and college officials may not delegate to them the college's lower standard of "reasonable cause." For police to obtain a warrant they must meet the higher standard of "probable cause" declared in the Amendment (*Piazzola v. Watkins*, 1971).

Although the weight of precedent seems to allow warrantless searches on campus that are conducted by college officials seeking contraband where there is reasonable cause to believe it is in a particular room or place, the parameters of the Fourth Amendment on campus remain unclear. Policy in this area should be developed only after deliberate consultation with counsel and students. These policies also should be reviewed every few years to be sure student affairs administrators have kept abreast of the developing law in this area.

THE FOURTEENTH AMENDMENT

Two clauses of Section I of the Fourteenth Amendment have particular relevance for student affairs practitioners—the due process clause and the equal protection clause. This section of the Amendment provides, in part, "Nor shall any State deprive any person of life, liberty or property, without due process of law; nor deny to any person within its jurisdiction the equal protection of the laws." The original intent of the Amendment passed by Congress in 1866 and ratified in 1868 was to protect the recently freed slaves, but ever since 1961 when the landmark case of *Dixon v. Alabama State Board of Education* (1961) was decided, the Fourteenth Amendment has been used by students to challenge their suspensions and expulsions.

Due Process

Although the *Dixon* case was not the first decision to find that students were "persons" under the Constitution and thus entitled to due process before being expelled or suspended (see *Commonwealth ex rel Hill v. McCauley*, 1887), it has been referred to as "The classic starting point for an inquiry into the rights of students at state educational institutions" (*Jenkins v. Louisiana State Board of Education*, 1975, p. 999) and "the path-breaking decision recognizing the due process rights of students at state universities" (*Blanton v. State University of New York*, 1973, p. 385). Even the Supreme Court has referred to *Dixon* as the "landmark case" (*Goss v. Lopez*, 1975).

Because of the weight of such support behind it, it is valuable for us to review the words of the *Dixon* court.

> For the guidance of the parties in the event of further proceedings, we state our views on the nature of the notice and hearing required by due process prior to expulsion from a state college or university. . . . The notice should contain a statement of the specific charges and grounds which, if proven, would justify expulsion under the regulations . . . a hearing which gives the Board or the administrative authorities of the college an opportunity to hear both sides in considerable detail. . . . The student should be given the names of the witnesses against him and an oral or written report on the facts to which each witness testifies. He should be given an opportunity to present to the Board or *administrative official* [italics added] of the college his own defense against the charges and to produce either oral testimony or written affidavits in his behalf. (p. 159)

The court also stated that while students were entitled to "notice and *some* [italics added] opportunity for a hearing before . . . [being] *expelled* [italics added] for misconduct" (*Dixon*, p. 158), it also clearly stated that "This does not imply that a full-dress judicial hearing with the right to cross-examine witnesses is required" (p. 159). It is interesting to note that the court only said notice and some opportunity for a hearing was necessary if a student was being expelled or suspended. Even the Supreme Court has said that students being suspended for 10 days were only entitled to "*some kind* [italics added] of notice and . . . *some kind* [italics added] of hearing" (*Goss v. Lopez*, 1975, p. 579). The Court characterized this as an "informal give-and-take between student and disciplinarian" (p. 584).

This does not sound like the formal procedures that exist in many disciplinary systems. The Supreme Court has provided additional guidance concerning due process:

> Considerations of procedures due process may require under any given set of circumstances must begin with a determination of the precise nature of the government function involved as well as the private interest that has been affected by government action. (*Cafeteria & Restaurant Worker's Union v. McElroy*, 1961, p. 895)

The trend seems to be to characterize the nature of the government function in campus discipline as enforcing criminal statutes. Jennifer Markiewicz (1996), writing for Security on Campus (the organization founded by the Clerys after their daughter was raped and murdered at Lehigh University), referred to the student judicial system at Miami University as "private university courts, funded by state money, [which] handle everything from academic dishonesty to violent crimes such as rape and arson. The proceedings and results, however, are the school's dirty secrets" (p. 13). Nina Bernstein (1996), writing on the front page of the *New York Times* also referred to campus judicial systems as dealing with crimes. Even the federal Congress has mandated that colleges and universities keep statistics on students "referred for campus disciplinary action for liquor *law violations* [italics added]" (20 U.S.C. 1092(f)(F)(*i*)(IX)).

Although it is true that one action, such as a rape, may constitute a violation of law (a crime) and also a violation of campus regulations (sexual misconduct), the campus judicial system has no authority to, nor does it, prosecute crimes. It is the job of the county or state's attorney to prosecute crimes. The campus judicial system simply disciplines students who violate college rules. The nature of the government's interest in campus discipline is to maintain good order and discipline in the campus community, not to protect society against criminals.

The courts have consistently said the analogy between student discipline and criminal procedures is not sound (*Norton v. Discipline Committee of East Tennessee State University*, 1969). The Supreme Court of Vermont (*Nzuve v. Castleton State College*, 1975) and four United States Courts of Appeals have each reiterated this principle (*Esteban v. Central Missouri State College*, 1969; *Gorman v. University of Rhode Island*, 1988; *Nash v. Auburn University*, 1987; *Wright v. Texas Southern University*, 1968). Even in the case of irrevocable expulsion, "the disciplinary process is not equivalent to the criminal law processes of federal and state criminal law. . . . The attempted analogy of student discipline to criminal proceedings against adults and juveniles is not sound" (*General Order on Judicial Standards of Procedure and Substance*, 1968, p. 142). If college and university disciplinary procedures are not analogues to criminal procedures, then disciplinary systems must not be dealing with criminals and crimes and thus the nature of the government function is not to protect society from crimes.

In striking the balance between the "nature of the government's interest" (maintaining good order and discipline within the campus community) and the "private interests" (continuing one's education) the First Circuit Court of Appeals tells us that

> courts should not extol form over substance and impose on educational institutions all the procedural requirements of a criminal trial. The question presented is not whether the hearing was ideal or whether its procedures could have been better. In all cases the inquiry is whether, under the particular circumstances presented, the hearing was fair and accorded the individual the essential elements of due process. (*Gorman v. University of Rhode Island,* 1988, p. 16)

The "essential elements of due process," outlined in *Dixon* for expulsions, are fairly straightforward requirements of notice of the charges and an opportunity for a hearing at which the individual can hear the evidence and have a chance to refute it. There is nothing in *Dixon* or any decision by the Supreme Court or any other court that has held that campus discipline includes a general right to be represented by legal counsel, to cross-examine witnesses, or in some cases even to confront them physically, or to appeal the decision. Although there is no general right to counsel (*Dixon v. Alabama State Board of Education,* 1961; *Donohue v. Baker,* 1997; *Gabrilowitz v. Newman,* 1978; *General Order on Judicial Standards of Procedure and Substance,* 1968; *Osteen v. Henley,* 1993), when the college or university is represented by counsel it is only "fundamentally fair" to allow the student the same right (*French v. Bashful,* 1969). Students who are charged with crimes arising from the same set of facts, however, should be allowed to have counsel advise (but not represent) them at the campus hearing (*Gabrilowitz v. Newman,* 1978). The presence of counsel at the campus hearing is "only to safeguard . . . [the student's] rights at the criminal proceeding, not to affect the outcomes of the disciplinary hearing" (*Gabrilowitz v. Newman,* 1978, p. 106). The college may also proceed with its hearing before the criminal trial begins. The Supreme Court of Vermont provided a clear rationale for this principle when it decided the case of a student charged with burglary, rape, and simple assault.

> Educational institutions have both a need and a right to formulate their own standards and to enforce them; such enforcement is only coincidentally related to criminal charges and the defense against them. To hold otherwise would, in our view, lead logically to the conclusion that civil remedies must, as a matter of law, wait for determination until related criminal charges are disposed of. . . . In the instant case, the complaining witness could not have redress for the assault on her, if proven, until the pending criminal charges had run their long course of trial and appeal. (*Nzuve v. Castleton State College,* 1975, p. 325)

In addition, there is no double jeopardy involved in taking action against the student on campus when there will be a subsequent criminal trial (*Kister v.*

Ohio Board of Regents, 1973; *Nzuve v. Castleton State College*, 1975; *State v. Kaukle*, 1997; *State v. Sterling*, 1996; *State v. Wood*, 1996).

Although there is no general "right" to cross-examine witnesses in student disciplinary hearings, if the credibility of a witness is at issue cross-examination may be required (*Winnick v. Manning*, 1972) to provide a "fair" hearing. However, even then the physical confrontation of the witness is not a right. The failure to provide for physical confrontation of witnesses was found not to infringe any Constitutional rights in two separate Supreme Court opinions (*Douglas v. Alabama*, 1965; *Morrissey v. Brewer*, 1972). In a student disciplinary case involving the suspension of a law student who was crawling on his knees under a library table looking up women's skirts, the First Circuit Court of Appeals said that allowing the female student to testify out of sight of the accused because of "her frightened and nervous state did not render the hearing unfair" (*Cloud v. Trustees of Boston University*, 1983, p. 725).

The right to an appeal is also not an "essential element of due process" (*District of Columbia v. Clawans*, 1936; *Reetz v. Michigan*, 1903). The Supreme Court said, "If a single hearing is not due process then doubling it will not make it so" (*Reetz v. Michigan*, 1903, p. 508). However, it is probably wise to have someone review the initial decision as a simple check on the procedures and sanction, but it is not necessary or advised to have multiple levels of appeal.

Finally, students should be given adequate time between the notice of the charges and the hearing to prepare a defense. The hearing should be before an unbiased (it is the burden of the accused student to show bias on the part of the hearing officer or a member of the hearing panel) third person and the decision should be based on substantial evidence or the preponderance of the evidence (*Dixon v. Alabama State Board of Education*, 1961; *McDonald v. Board of Trustees of University of Illinois*, 1974; *Jackson v. Hayakawa*, 1985).

Dannells (1991) has shown that the disciplinary sanctions of suspension and expulsion are not imposed very often, but, rather, "milder forms are clearly the most commonly used" (p. 168). Thus, the "informal give-and-take between student and disciplinarian" (*Goss v. Lopez*, 1975, p. 584) may be all that is required for a hearing.

Due Process in Academic Matters

Whenever the institution decides to expel or suspend a student for failing to meet an academic standard, the Supreme Court has said that it is an academic judgment that does not require a hearing and one in which the courts will not become involved (*Board of Curators v. Horowitz*, 1978). However, an entirely different situation arises when a student is accused of cheating or another form of academic dishonesty. This is not a qualitative academic judgment, but a question of fact. In such instances the student should be provided with the "essential elements of due process" discussed above (Gehring & Pavela, 1994).

Equal Protection

The equal protection clause of the Fourteenth Amendment also has a significant impact on student affairs practice. Of course not everyone is treated equally; for example those under 21 years of age are not permitted to purchase alcohol, whereas those over 21 are allowed. The equal protection clause is designed to ensure that similarly situated persons are treated equally. For example, requiring all female students to live on campus but only requiring first-year men to live on campus would violate the equal protection clause (*Mollere v. Southeastern Louisiana College*, 1969).

Courts apply several basic tests to determine whether there is a violation of the equal protection clause. If there is a classification of individuals who are affected based on race, alienage or national origin (a suspect class), or if their fundamental right (voting, interstate travel, procreation) is infringed upon, then the government (college or university) must demonstrate that it has a "compelling interest" in taking the action and the classification must be narrowly tailored to achieve the compelling interest. This is a very high standard and one that is seldom met. (Compare *Tayyari v. New Mexico State University*, 1980, with *Kovach v. Middendorf*, 1976). If, however, neither a suspect class nor a fundamental right is involved, then the college need only show there is a rational relationship between the classification and the "legitimate" interests of the institution. Requiring all students under a certain age to live on campus for the educational benefits to be derived from campus living would not violate the equal protection clause (*Pratz v. Louisiana Polytechnic Institute*, 1971).

Although sex is not a suspect class requiring a "compelling interest," in recent years the courts have held that if the classification is based on sex, then the government must be held to a higher standard than simply a rational relationship. The area of admissions has been particularly vulnerable to equal protection challenges at single-sex institutions. The courts have held that when classifications are based on sex they must serve an *important* governmental interest and must be *substantially* related to meeting those interests. This is a middle tier test, which is not as high as requiring a compelling interest but requiring more than a mere rational relationship. The male-only admissions policies of the Citadel and Virginia Military Institute were both struck down under this standard (*Faulkner v. Jones*, 1995; *United States v. Virginia*, 1996).

FEDERAL AND STATE CODES

The scope of this chapter does not permit a discussion of every federal law affecting student affairs, nor is it possible to address the specific laws of each of the 50 states that have an impact on student affairs practice. Consequently, this section highlights only the more significant federal laws that have a direct influence on student affairs practice and provides an overview of the trends in state alcoholic beverage laws. Administrators, however, need to become aware of and conversant with their state's laws. These may be found in any county law library or even in the college library. State statutes are indexed, and statutes may be found by consulting the index for key words such as "hazing," "alcoholic beverages," "intoxicating liquors," "colleges and universities," or other topical words.

Although the federal government has been enacting laws affecting education since 1785 ("Federal Education Programs," 1965), only recently has it intensified its lawmaking in this area. In 1964 with the passage of the Civil Rights Act the federal government policy was redistributive; that is, laws were passed to "level the playing field" for what would become protected classes of people. Title VI of the Civil Rights Act of 1964 was followed eight years later by Title IX of the Education Amendment of 1972 and a year later by Section 504 of the Rehabilitation Act of 1973. These three federal statutes were designed to put into effect the government's redistributive policies.

TITLE VI

Title VI prohibits discrimination on the basis of race, color, or national origin in any educational program or activity receiving federal aid (42 U.S.C. 2000(d)). The courts have held that this law applies to any college or university that receives any form of federal financial assistance. Even where the institution received no direct federal aid, but accepted a student who received veteran's benefits, that institution was held to the nondiscrimination standards of Title VI (*Bob Jones University v. Johnson*, 1974). Although the Supreme Court interpreted the nondiscrimination requirements of Title VI only to apply to the specific programs and activities receiving federal aid (*Grove City College v. Bell*, 1984), Congress subsequently defined the term "program or activity" to mean every operation of the college or university (Civil Rights Restoration Act of 1987; *Radcliff v. Landau*, 1989).

Title VI has been operative in both admissions and financial aid, where there have been efforts to overcome past discrimination. These efforts, which have given minority students additional considerations, have been challenged as a violation of Title VI. The earliest "reverse discrimination" case was *Regents of the University of California v. Bakke* (1978). In that case a White male was rejected for admission to the medical school of the University of California-Davis. The university reserved a specific number of spaces in the entering class for minority students, some of whom had lower scores and grades than Bakke. The Supreme Court held that reserving spaces for entering students based on race was a violation of Title VI; however, race could be one of several factors that could be considered in deciding who would be admitted. That rationale was accepted by other courts (*DeRonde v. Regents of University of California*, 1981; *McDonald v. Hogness*, 1979) until recently. In 1996 the Fifth Circuit Court of Appeals struck down the admissions policy at the University of Texas

Law School, which, relying on *Bakke*, used race as a factor (*Hopwood v. Texas*, 1996). The court in this case applied the traditional equal protection test of "compelling" interests and being narrowly tailored and rejected the *Bakke* standard of using race as a factor to diversify the student body. The Supreme Court has refused to review this case.

Financial aid has also been an area where Title VI has come into play. However, in this area, a federal district court held that Georgetown University violated Title VI by implementing a student financial aid policy classifying students on the basis of race, which provided aid to minority students regardless of financial need but not to nonminority students (*Flanagan v. President and Directors of Georgetown College*, 1976). The Fourth Circuit Court of Appeals also was faced with a similar challenge when a Hispanic American student at the University of Maryland attacked that institution's policy of reserving a specific scholarship fund just for African Americans in order to diversify the student body (*Podberesky v. Kirwan*, 1994). This court also applied the traditional equal protection tests and found the university's plan in violation.

TITLE IX

Title IX is modeled after Title VI and prohibits discrimination on the basis of sex in educational programs and activities. The Civil Rights Restoration Act of 1987 also included Title IX in its definition of programs and activities. Thus, this statute also applies to every operation of the institution if the institution receives any federal aid or if it accepts a student who receives any federal aid.

The two most litigated areas of Title IX involve sexual harassment and athletics. Courts have held that sexual harassment is a form of sexual discrimination under Title IX (*Alexander v. Yale*, 1980; *Bougher v. University of Pittsburgh*, 1989). The sexual harassment may be faculty or staff on student (*Alexander v. Yale*, 1980) or student on student (*Davis v. Monroe County Board of Education*, 1999). The harassment can either be a quid pro quo (something for something) (*Alexander v. Yale*, 1980) or a hostile environment (*Patricia H. v. Berkeley Unified School District*, 1993). The Supreme Court held that a college or university can be liable for sexual harassment under Title IX (*Franklin v. Gwinnett County Public Schools*, 1992); however, the standard for liability set by the Court is fairly high.

For both faculty- or staff-member-on-student harassment and student-on-student harassment the courts will require that, to award damages there must be actual notice given to "an official who at a minimum has authority to address the alleged discrimination and to institute corrective measures" and that official fails to take action (*Gebser v. Lago Vista Independent School District*, 1998, p. 292). Complaints of sexual harassment to any official will not satisfy the standard. The complaint must be made to an official who has authority to act. (Compare *Chontos v. Rhea*, 1998, with *Liu v. Striuli*, 1999). In addition, the official, once aware of the complaint, must display a deliberate indifference by failing to take any action. This standard is required by the courts for an award of damages. The Office for Civil Rights, however, only requires that the notice be given to a responsible school official who has the authority to act or the duty to report sexual harassment. If such notice is given and no corrective action is taken, there would be a violation of Title IX jeopardizing the institution's federal funding (65 Fd. R. 213, Nov. 2, 2000).

The Supreme Court holding that institutions could be liable for student-on-student sexual harassment was decided in the context of an elementary school and not a college or university. Although the holding would apply to a postsecondary institution, the Court specifically said that for liability to attach the harasser must be subject to "the school's disciplinary authority" (*Davis v. Monroe County Board of Education*, 1999, p. 1673). The Court then went on to differentiate between schools and colleges:

> A university might not, for example, be expected to exercise the same degree of control over its students that a grade school would enjoy [citations omitted] and it would be entirely reasonable for a school to refrain from a form of disciplinary action that would expose it to constitutional or statutory claims. (*Davis v. Monroe County Board of Education*, 1999, p. 1674)

Gehring (1999), however, pointed out that "This condition obviously raises the issue of whether colleges and universities define off-campus conduct as subject to their code of conduct and how, absent threats, an institution should respond to the exercise of free speech (p. 14).

Many student-on-student sexual harassment complaints will be hostile environment claims. To constitute a hostile environment the harassment must be "so severe, pervasive and objectively offensive, and that so undermines and detracts from the victim's educational experience, that the victim-students are effectively denied equal access to an institution's resources and opportunities" (*Davis v. Monroe County Board of Education*, 1999, p. 1675).

The other major area of Title IX litigation has been athletics. Title IX requires that institutions accommodate the interests and abilities of the underrepresented sex and that schedules, equipment, per diem, coaching, and other services be provided on an equivalent basis for both men and women (U.S. Department of Education, 1979). The case that illustrates these mandates is *Cohen v. Brown* (1996). In that case, several female athletes sued Brown University after the university demoted several women's teams from fall varsity status to club sports. The women argued that they composed 51% of the student body yet only 38% of the varsity athletes and they had an interest in and the ability to participate in the demoted varsity sports. The First Circuit Court of Appeals agreed with the women:

> There can be no doubt that Title IX has changed the face of women's sports as well as our societies' interest in and attitude toward women athletes and women's sports. . . . What stimulated this remarkable change in the quality of women's athletic competition was not a sudden anomalous upsurge in

women's interest in sports, but the enforcement of Title IX's mandate of gender equity in sports. (p. 188)

The Supreme Court has refused to review this decision.

Although there must be gender equity in athletics and proportional opportunities must be available if there is interest and ability, Title IX rules do not require that women be allowed to participate on men's teams in contact sports such as football, boxing, basketball, rugby, wrestling, and ice hockey among others (*Mercer v. Duke University*, 1999).

Although the majority of Title IX litigation has been in the area of sexual harassment and athletics, the Title IX regulations cover many other areas, such as housing, counseling, placement, and rules of conduct, among others. Student affairs administrators should be particularly familiar with these regulations because so much of what is covered involves various student services (34 C.F.R. 106).

SECTION 504 AND AMERICANS WITH DISABILITIES ACT

Much like Title VI and Title IX, Section 504 prohibits discrimination against "otherwise qualified handicapped persons" (20 U.S.C. 749). This law was enacted in 1973 long before the Americans with Disabilities Act of 1990 (ADA). Although the ADA uses the term "qualified individual with a disability" both laws require essentially the same nondiscriminatory practices. The threshold question under Section 504 or ADA is whether the individual is handicapped or disabled. According to the regulations, one has a handicap or disability when he or she has any physical or mental impairment that substantially limits a major life activity, has a record of such impairment, or is considered to have such an impairment. The Supreme Court has held that under the ADA (and the holding would also apply to Section 504) "the determination of whether an individual is disabled should be made with reference to measures that mitigate the individual's impairment including, in this instance, eyeglasses and contact lenses" (*Sutton v. United Airlines*, 1999, p. 2143). The Court emphasized the wording of the law, which is the same for both ADA and Section 504, requiring that the impairment "substantially limits" a major life activity. Thus, if the impairment is corrected, as with eyeglasses or contact lenses, it does not substantially limit a major life activity.

Once it has been determined that an individual has a handicap, it must then be decided whether the individual is "otherwise qualified." Someone is "otherwise qualified" if he or she can perform the essential functions, with or without reasonable accommodation, in spite of his or her impairment (*Doe v. New York University*, 1981; *Southeastern Community College v. Davis*, 1979). To be "otherwise qualified" students must meet the requirement for admission (*Anderson v. University of Wisconsin*, 1988; *Gent v. Radford Univeristy*, 1997/1998).

The requirement that institutions must provide reasonable accommodations for disabled students does not mandate that courses essential to the nature of the degree be eliminated or substituted (*Doherty v. Southern College of Optometry*, 1988/1989; *Ohio Civil Rights Comm. v. Case Western Reserve*, 1996); however, courts will not abide uninformed stereotypes in place of careful assessments of individual students' needs. Boston University's presidential decree that there would be no substitutions for math or foreign language requirements was found to violate both the ADA and Section 504 (*Guckenberger v. Boston University*, 1997). However, where reasoned academic judgment concludes that a particular course is essential to a program and no substitutions will be permitted, "the ADA does not authorize the courts to intervene even if a majority of comparable academic institutions disagree" (*Guckenberger v. Boston University*, 1998, p. 90). Although reasonable accommodations that cause an "undue financial burden" are not required, the courts interpret that term very narrowly. A $15,000 increase in a university's budget for transportation was not found to create an "undue financial burden" when its annual transportation budget was $1.2 million (*United States v. Board of Trustees for University of Alabama*, 1990).

Student affairs administrators should also know that some contagious diseases are considered to be covered under the ADA and Section 504 (*School Board of Nassau County, Florida v. Arline*, 1987). When dealing with such diseases, administrators should engage medical staff, because the test of whether a person with such a disease is "otherwise qualified" requires expert medical advice. In determining if an individual with a contagious disease is "otherwise qualified," the Supreme Court has applied a 4-point test, which asks: (a) How is the disease transmitted? (b) How long will the carrier be capable of transmitting the disease? (c) What is the potential risk to third parties? (d) What is the probability that the disease will be transmitted and cause harm? In two instances where individuals who were HIV positive were dismissed from their medical training programs, the courts applied the above test and found the students were not "otherwise qualified." In both instances the individuals would have been performing invasive procedures where the risk of transmitting the disease was high (*Doe v. University of Maryland Medical System Corporation*, 1995; *Doe v. Washington University*, 1991).

THE FAMILY EDUCATIONAL RIGHTS AND PRIVACY ACT

In 1974, with the passage of the Family Educational Rights and Privacy Act (FERPA or the Buckley Amendment, 20 U.S.C. 1232), the federal government shifted from a redistributive to a protective policy stance toward higher education. Through the enactment of protective policy laws the government is saying it knows what is best and enacts laws to protect individuals. The Buckley Amendment was the first of a long line of protective policy laws and was originally designed to protect student records from unauthorized disclosure. The original language of the law provides that "No funds shall be made available . . . to . . . any institution of higher education . . . which has a policy of denying, or which effectively prevents parents of students attending . . . the right to inspect and review any and all official records " (P.L. 93-380, 438 (a)(1)). Students attending a postsecondary institution, however, have the rights accorded to parents under the law.

Because FERPA was originally written to apply to elementary and secondary education and was never debated in committee, it is one of the most amended protective policy laws. There are also many exceptions both for students' access to their files and for disclosure without a student's consent. There is no private right of action under FERPA (a student whose rights under FERPA are violated may not sue the institution); students may report the violation only to the Office of Family Compliance that administers the law (*Smith v. Duquesne University*, 1985). However, students may initiate a suit under 42 U.S.C. Section 1983 for a deprivation of a federal right (*Lewin v. Medical College of Hampton Roads*, 1996; *Tarka v. Cunningham*, 1989), but this normally results only in nominal damages of one dollar unless the student can show actual damages. Although there is no private right of action and only nominal damages are usually assessed, student affairs administrators must be familiar with the regulations interpreting FERPA because much of their work involves student records.

The most controversial area of FERPA involves the disclosure of disciplinary records. The term "educational records" was substituted in the original legislation for a laundry list of items, including "verified reports of serious or recurrent behavior patterns." (*U.S. Congressional and Administrative News*, 93rd Congress, 2nd Session, 1974, p. 2133). Subsequently, the regulations actually defined disciplinary records as "educational records." In spite of these substitutions and definitions, the Supreme Court of Ohio held that discipline records were not educational records (*State ex rel the Miami Student v. Miami University*, 1997). Ohio followed Georgia in this regard (*Red and Black Pub. Co., Inc. v. Board of Regents*, 1993). Two other courts, however, have held that disciplinary records are "educational records" and thus protected from disclosure (*D.T.H. Pub. Corp. v. University of North Carolina at Chapel Hill, 1998; Shreveport Professional Chapter of the Society of Professional Journalists and Michelle Millhollon v. Louisiana State University in Shreveport*, 1994). The Department of Education subsequently brought suit in federal court to enjoin the Ohio court's order (*United States v. Miami University*, 1998). *The Chronicle of Higher Education* joined Miami University and Ohio State as a defendant in the case. In March 2000 the federal district court issued its decision, which takes precedent over the state courts, holding that disciplinary records are educational records protected by FERPA. The court specifically stated that student disciplinary hearings were not criminal in nature and there was no First Amendment right of access to the record of those hearings. The court also held that the purpose of FERPA was to protect the privacy of student records and rejected the *Chronicle's* contention that disciplinary records are law enforcement unit records (*United States v. Miami University*, 2000).

The Higher Education Amendments of 1998 (P.L. 105-244) amended

FERPA in two substantial ways. Under these amendments, institutions *may* now notify parents of their son's or daughter's violations of campus drug and alcohol rules if the student is less than 21 years of age and has been found responsible for the violation. This requirement, like other requirements of FERPA, is permissive and institutions are allowed to provide this notification but are not required to do so. It is a matter of institutional discretion.

The other amendment provides that FERPA does not protect from disclosure the final outcomes of disciplinary hearings that involve crimes of violence as that term is defined in the U.S. Code (18 U.S.C. 16) or nonforcible sexual offenses (Sec. 915 Higher Education Amendments, 1998). The final results include the name of the perpetrator, the nature of the offense, and the sanction. Because this information is no longer protected by FERPA, public institutions may be required under their state's Open Public Records Acts to disclose the information.

Public records laws do not apply to private institutions, and they would not be required under FERPA to disclose this information. What is troublesome is that once the student newspaper obtains this information and interviews the perpetrator, the name of the victim and witnesses will also most likely appear in the press. This may significantly reduce the number of reports. The other troublesome aspect of this amendment is the potential for a defamation suit by disclosing information to a third person that a student is an alleged perpetrator of a crime of violence or nonforcible sex offense when criminal charges have never been brought nor has a grand jury returned an indictment. Administrators should consult with counsel before disclosing information under this amendment.

There are other troubling aspects to FERPA too numerous for the scope of this chapter to address. Student affairs administrators should read the regulations in their entirety (34 C.F.R. 99), and for an analysis of the law examine Gehring (1994).

DRUG FREE SCHOOLS AND COMMUNITIES ACT OF 1989

Title XII of the Higher Education Act of 1965 required each institution receiving federal funds to file with the Secretary of Education a certificate stating that the institution had a drug and alcohol abuse program. In 1989, however, the Drug Free Schools and Communities Act Amendments (DFSCAA) became law and mandated *specific* actions institutions were required to take with respect to their drug and alcohol abuse programs. The penalty for noncompliance, which the Secretary of Education may unilaterally determine, is not only a loss of federal funding, but also a requirement that all funds paid while the institution was not in compliance be refunded to the government.

The DFSCAA requires an annual notice to students and employees of five distinct items of information. Although the law did not specify that this information be provided in writing, the Secretary of Education unilaterally and without direction from Congress decided that "in order to ensure that each student has access to and can refer to the required materials they must be in writing" (Appendix C, 55 Fed. Reg. 33595 (1990)), even though this method is the least effective method of communicating such information to students (Palmer, Gehring, & Guthrie, 1992) and a very inefficient use of taxpayers dollars (Geraci, Guthrie, Key, & Parrott, 1990). One way for institutions utilizing a computer registration process to accomplish this at little cost is to publish the information in the class schedule, and when students log on a prompt can appear asking them if they have read the DFSCAA information appearing on page X in the class schedule. Those who respond "no" will be given a message telling them to go back and read it and block their registration. Those who respond "yes" will be allowed to continue with registration.

The notice must be provided to every student enrolled for at least one class for academic credit and "merely making the material available to those who wish to take them does not satisfy the requirement" (Appendix C, 55 Fed. Reg. 33595 (1990)). The notice must include the following types of information: (a) standards of conduct prohibiting, at a minimum, the unlawful use, possession, or distribution of illicit drugs and alcohol by students and employees; (b) a description of applicable laws related to unlawful possession or distribution of illicit drugs and alcohol; (c) a description of counseling and treatment programs available; (d) a clear statement that the institution will impose sanctions for violations of its standards; and (e) a description of the health risks associated with the use of illicit drugs and alcohol.

A biennial review of the institution's program is also required by DFSCAA to determine the effectiveness of the program and whether standards are being consistently enforced. Even though there is no set format for the report, it must be a written report available to the Secretary of Education and the public upon request and must be maintained for three years after the fiscal year in which it was created. A discussion of how to conduct the biennial review as well as other information related to the DFSCAA can be found in *A Handbook for Complying with the Program and Review Requirements of the 1989 Amendments to the Drug Free Schools and Communities Act* (Palmer & Gehring, 1992).

STUDENT RIGHT-TO-KNOW AND CAMPUS SECURITY ACT

This law was passed "to provide students and parents with better information in selecting a postsecondary institution" (H.R. Rep. 101-518, 101st Cong., 2nd Sess. (1990)). Under the student right-to-know portion of this law, graduation rates must be "readily available" and must also be provided to each prospective athlete to whom an offer is made. The institution must also provide the graduation rate data for athletes on financial aid classified by race, sex, and sport. Calculation of these data is complex and beyond the scope of this chapter. Administrators should consult the regulations appearing in 34 C.F.R. 668.41.

The campus security portion of the act requires institutions to annually distribute to each student and employee campus crime statistics and various policy statements—generally referred to as a security report. Subsequently Congress passed the Higher Education Amendments of 1992 that included the Sexual Assault Victims Bill of Rights (P.L. 102-325). This legislation amended the Campus Security Act by mandating specific actions by institutions when sexual assaults are reported. Prospective students (anyone who inquires about admission) and prospective employees (anyone who inquires about employment) must be given a notice that a security report exists, and if requested, they can receive a summary of its contents and a copy of the report. Most institutions are not complying with this requirement (Callaway & Gehring, 2000). The security report may be on the institution's website, but the notice to prospective students and employees must be written and contain the exact location of the website.

Crime statistics must be kept on reported murder, manslaughter, arson, robberies, aggravated assaults, burglaries, auto thefts, and sexual offenses. The regulations define each of these crimes. Statistics must also be kept on arrests for liquor, drug, and weapons violations, and the number of crimes in which the victim is selected on the basis of race, gender, religion, sexual orientation, ethnicity, or disability.

Victims of sexual offenses *must* be informed of the outcome of any disciplinary hearing and are entitled to have their academic and living arrangements changed if they request it and if it is reasonably available.

The Higher Education Reauthorization Act of 1998 (HERA98; P.L. 105-244) also mandated that police logs be kept and open to the public. The logs must contain the nature of the offense, as well as the time, date, and location of the offense. Violations of the act may result in a $25,000 fine for each offense, although the Secretary of Education may mitigate the fine. The HERA98 also had some good news for administrators. The amendments specifically stated that the act did not provide a private right of action, and failure to comply with the act could not be used as evidence in any judicial hearing.

There is a great deal in the law and its regulations (34 C.F.R. 668.46-.49) and some of it is troubling (Gehring, 1991b), but this law and these regulations should be required reading for student affairs administrators. The consequences of failing to comply can be expensive and, worse, could result in injury to students.

Statutes Regulating Alcoholic Beverages

Although alcoholic beverage laws are a matter of state jurisdiction, Congress has been concerned about youthful drinking for some time. In 1984 Congress enacted 23 U.S.C. 158 requiring that the Secretary of Transportation withhold highway funds from any state "in which the purchase or public possession in such State of any alcoholic beverage by a person who is less than twenty-one years of age is lawful" (23 U.S.C. Section 158 (a) (1) and (2)). More recently,

HERA98 included a section entitled "Collegiate Initiative to Reduce Binge Drinking and Illegal Alcohol Consumption." Even though this was simply a "Sense of Congress" and not a legal mandate, Congress was suggesting a series of steps for institutions to take to reduce drinking on campus. These steps included appointing a presidential task force to examine academic life on campus and recommend changes and creating alcohol-free zones and housing, a zero tolerance policy for illegal consumption, and vigorous enforcement of campus rules. Although these steps are not a legal mandate it seems inevitable, given the congressional penchant for micromanaging campus life, that it will soon be enacted as law.

State laws regulating alcoholic beverages vary widely. Although individuals over the age of 18 are considered adults, the universal age for purchase or public consumption is now 21. The scope of this chapter does not permit an examination of the laws of each state, but practitioners should become familiar with the alcoholic beverage laws of the state in which they are employed. (See Gehring, 1991a; Gehring & Geraci, 1989; McCarthy & Gehring, 1999, for the alcoholic beverage laws of each state.)

Several states allow minors (those less than 21) to possess alcohol in private residences, whereas others only prohibit consumption in public places. In Ohio minors may not "share in the cost" of alcoholic beverages and in Illinois minors commit a crime if they accept alcoholic beverages as a gift. The sale or gift of alcoholic beverages to a minor or intoxicated person is also generally prohibited, but what constitutes intoxication and how it is determined that a minor was served are questions that have been resolved differently in different states. The misrepresentation of one's age to obtain alcoholic beverages may result in having one's driver's license revoked in several, but not all, states.

Civil liability can result from the sale (known as Dramshop liability) or the gratuitous provision (social host liability) of alcohol to a minor and, in some instances, an intoxicated adult where the individual who is sold or provided with alcohol injures another. Again, the way these laws are interpreted by the courts in the different states varies widely. The clear trend, however, is that states are holding the one who sells or provides the alcohol liable for the injuries to innocent third parties caused by the one who was served (McCarthy & Gehring, 1999).

To teach students about their potential criminal and civil liability and help them make informed decisions, student affairs practitioners must first know the law. Because alcoholic beverage laws are state specific and vary greatly, practitioners need to do research specific to the state in which they practice.

CONTRACTS

In addition to the Constitutional and statutory relationship students have with their institution, they also have a contractual relationship in which both the institution and the student promise to do certain things.

The American Law Institute (1981) defines a contract as "A promise or set of promises for the breach of which the law gives a remedy or the performance of which the law in some way recognizes as a duty" (p. 5). There are several elements to this definition that must be fulfilled if there is to be a contract. These elements include the following: (a) a promise or set of promises; (b) an offer and an acceptance; (c) an agreement of what is to be exchanged by the parties; and (d) an agreement or common understanding of the terms and conditions (*Steinberg v. Chicago Medical School*, 1977).

The terms and conditions of the contract are contained in the publications and other statements of the institution and normally are interpreted by the courts by applying the everyday meaning of words (*Delta School of Business, Etc. v. Shropshire*, 1981; *Warren v. Drake University*, 1989). Courts, however, recognize disclaimers printed in college bulletins and catalogs. Where a nursing student claimed the university breached its contract by failing to follow its procedure outlined in the catalog for grade appeals, the court pointed out that the catalog included the statement that "The provisions of this catalog do not constitute a contract, express or implied, between any applicant, student or faculty member and The University of Texas at Arlington or The University of Texas System" (*Tobias v. University of Texas*, 1991, p. 211). The Supreme Court of Montana also pointed to a similar disclaimer and held that the university was not bound to the curriculum published in the catalog (*Bindrim v. University of Montana*, 1988).

As noted in the disclaimer referred to above at the University of Texas at Arlington, contracts may be either express or implied. Express contracts are those put into specific words. This could include an employment contract, a student's contract for housing and food services, or the disciplinary procedures in a student's handbook. Implied contracts, on the other hand, are not written; rather, what constitutes the promise and what is exchanged is implied. This is illustrated by a case in which a student completed all the requirements for his degree but was denied the degree because the dean believed him to be a homosexual. The student claimed he had an implied contract with the institution to award him his degree if he paid his tuition and met the academic requirements. The court agreed with him:

> The elements of a traditional contract are present in the implied contract between a college and a student attending that college, and are readily discernable. The student's tender of an application constitutes an offer to apply to the college. By "accepting" an applicant to be a student at the college, the college accepts the applicant's offer. Thereafter, the student pays tuition (which obviously constitutes sufficient consideration), attends classes, completes course work and takes tests. The school provides the student with facilities and instruction and upon satisfactory completion of the school's academic requirements (which constitutes performance), the school becomes obligated to issue the student a diploma. (*Johnson v. Lincoln Christian College*, 1986, p. 1348)

Student affairs practitioners should understand that, in addition to implied contracts, oral contracts are also binding. Students were promised they would not be disciplined if they spoke freely about drug use at an institution. When the students admitted their own involvement, however, they were dismissed and subsequently brought a breach of contract suit against the institution. The court, in reversing the students' suspensions, pointed out that the oral assurances contained all the elements of a contract and said, "as agents, the questioners were authorized to make promises. . . . Plaintiffs [the students], by speaking freely, accepted this offer, and a contract was made. The Academy is bound by this agreement" (*Krawez v. Stans*, 1969, p. 1235).

The lesson to be learned about the contractual relationship is not to promise anything you cannot deliver, and to deliver everything you promise. Although courts may forgive minor deviations that do not cause harm, procedures and services outlined in catalogs and handbooks should be followed. It is a good idea to review these documents annually to determine if, during the past year, procedures have been changed or services eliminated. Examine the language in disciplinary codes to ensure that legalistic terms have been eliminated, because if there is a challenge to a disciplinary action, a court will require that the institution conform to the language in its code and procedures (Stoner & Creminara, 1990).

TORTS

The fourth C that defines the relationship between institutions and their students is *contacts*. This word is simply used as a way to remember the fourth relationship, which is an unlawful contact or interference with another's person, property, or reputation—more commonly called a *tort*. The word "tort" comes from the Latin word "torquere," meaning twisted. Because everyone has a duty not to interfere with another's person, property, or reputation, when one does interfere there is a tort or a twisted relationship. More precisely, a tort is defined as a civil (rather than a criminal) wrong, other than the breach of a contract for which the courts will provide a remedy. The remedy is usually damages (money), which may be compensatory (to compensate one for the loss or injury) and punitive (to punish the person who committed the tort).

Student affairs administrators and their institutions are most commonly susceptible to lawsuits arising from the torts of negligence and defamation (or duty). Thus, administrators should be familiar with the elements of both.

Negligence

The tort of negligence requires that there be a legally recognized duty that is breached, causing an injury. Thus, there are four basic elements that must be present for liability: (a) a duty, (b) a breach of the duty, (c) an injury, and (d) a close causal relationship between the breach and the injury. If any one of these elements is missing, there will be no liability.

Duty

Duty is an essential element in negligence, because if there is no duty, then even if there is an injury there can be no negligence. Thus, it is essential that student affairs practitioners understand their duties.

There are several commonly recognized duties student affairs administrators have inherited from English Common Law. The first of these is that administrators are expected to provide proper instruction. This might include how to exit buildings in the case of a fire or where to go if a tornado strikes. Residence hall, student activity, and recreational staff members particularly are faced regularly with providing proper instruction. For example, activity staff members must provide instruction on how to operate lights and other staging equipment (*Potter v. North Carolina School of the Arts*, 1978); recreational staff members have a duty to provide proper instruction to students who are using weights or how to properly adjust ski bindings (*Meese v. Brigham Young University*, 1981).

Proper supervision is another commonly recognized duty, for example. Although college students generally are legally adults and thus require less supervision than minors, "The risk reasonably to be perceived defines the duty to be obeyed" (*Palsgraf v. Long Island R.R. Co.*, 1928). The nature of the activity and the maturity and experience of the individuals will define the amount of supervision necessary. Many institutions have high school students and younger children attending camps and special programs during the summer. These young people are referred to by the courts as "children of tender years" and a heightened duty of supervision is required for them. Institutions may, however, in providing that supervision impose upon these "children" a separate and more restrictive code of conduct than it imposes on its adult students (*Stone v. Cornell University*, 1987).

The third commonly held duty is to maintain equipment in a reasonable state of repair. To do this, regular inspections are necessary to determine if everything is in good working order and appropriately maintained for the activity and use to which it will be put. Recreation staff should inspect playing surfaces regularly (*Drew v. State*, 1989; *Henig v. Hofstra University*, 1990). However, simply making routine inspections is not enough; equipment observed not to be in working order must be repaired (*Shetina v. Ohio University*, 1983). Equipment should never be operated without proper safety equipment, although, in some jurisdictions, adult students are expected to exercise reasonable care in operating dangerous equipment. (Compare *Amon v. State*, 1979, and *Potter v. North Carolina School of the Arts*, 1978, with *Richmond v. Ohio State University*, 1989).

These are not the only duties to be met. Prosser (1971) warns that "'duty' is not sacrosanct in itself, but only an expression of the sum total of those considerations of policy which lead the law to say that a particular plaintiff is entitled to protection" (p. 326). The policy considerations courts consider in establishing duty include the following: (a) the foreseeability of harm; (b) the degree of certainty of injury; (c) the closeness of the connection between the conduct (act or failure to act) and the injury; (d) the moral blame attached to the conduct; (e) the policy of preventing future harm; and (f) the burdens and consequences of imposing duty and the resulting liability for breach.

These considerations are illustrated in the case of *Peterson v. San Francisco Community College Dist.* (1984). The case involved the assault of a female student who had parked her car in a college lot and was traversing the stairs to a classroom building. On the stairway landing there was a large bush where her attacker hid until she approached. Several other women had previously been attacked at the same place, but the college gave no warnings nor did it cut back the bush. In finding the college liable, the court reminded of the policy considerations in fixing duty when it said:

> First, the allegations, if proved, suggest that harm to the plaintiff was clearly foreseeable. In light of the alleged prior similar incidents in the same area, the defendants were on notice that any woman who might use the stairs or the parking lot would be a potential target. Secondly, it is undisputed that plaintiff suffered injury. Third, given that the defendants were in control of the premises and that they were aware of prior assaults, it is clear that failure to apprise students of those incidents, to trim the foliage, or to take other protective measures closely connects the defendant's conduct with the plaintiff's injury. These factors, if established, also indicate there is moral blame attached to the defendant's failure to take steps to avert the foreseeable harm. Imposing a duty under these circumstances also furthers the policy of preventing future harm. Finally, the duty here does not place an intolerable burden on the defendants. (p. 102)

Special Relationships that Create a Duty

Certain special relationships also create a duty to warn or protect individuals from an unreasonable risk of harm (*Restatement (Second) of Torts,* 1965, Section 314A). One special relationship is that of a common carrier to passengers. Colleges and universities operate many common carriers such as buses, vans, and elevators (*Houck v. University of Washington,* 1991). Business invitees create another special relationship with colleges and universities. Invitees are individuals such as students; those who attend plays, athletic events, or other activities; and vendors who come on campus to do business with the institution (*Bearman v. University of Notre Dame,* 1983; *Johnson v. State,* 1995; *Schultz v. Gould Academy,* 1975). The Supreme Court of Nebraska has held that an institution "owes a landowner-invitee duty to students to take reasonable steps to protect against foreseeable acts of hazing . . . and the harm that naturally flows therefrom" (*Knoll v. Board of Regents of University of Nebraska,* 1999, p. 765). The landlord–tenant relationship is yet another special relationship that exists where student housing is provided. A United States Court of Appeals has noted that

> The landlord is no insurer of his tenants' safety, but he certainly is no bystander. And where, as here, the landlord has notice of repeated criminal assaults, and robberies, has notice that these crimes occurred in the portion of the premises exclusively within his control, has every reason to expect like crimes to happen again, and has the exclusive power to take preventative action, it does not seem unfair to place upon the landlord a duty to take those steps which are within his power to minimize the predictable risk to his tenants. (*Kline v. 1500 Massachusetts Avenue Apartment Corporation*, 1970, p. 481)

This principle has also been applied to campus housing (*Miller v. State*, 1984; *Nero v. Kansas State University*, 1993). One who voluntarily takes custody of another also has a special relationship to the other person. In one case, a court held that a student who lived on campus but could not keep a firearm for protection, could not have a dog to warn her of potential dangers, and could not install her own security devices on her room door had surrendered control of her security to the university and the university therefore had a duty to provide reasonable security for her (*Duarte v. State*, 1978). When "children of tender years" come on campus the university assumes custody of them, and this is also a special relationship that raises a duty for their reasonable protection (*Graham v. Montana State University*, 1988).

Generally, however, colleges and universities do not have a custodial relationship with their adult students. As one court has noted,

> The university's responsibility to its students, as an institution of higher education, is to properly educate them. It would be unrealistic to impose upon a university the additional role of custodian over its adult students and to charge it with the responsibility for assuring their safety and the safety of others. Imposing such a duty of protection would place the university in the position of an insurer of the safety of its students. (*Rabel v. Illinois Wesleyan University*, 1987, pp. 560–561)

At least two state supreme courts, however, do not agree with this reasoning. The Nebraska Supreme Court ruled that, based on the relationship between a landowner and student invitees, a university has a duty to protect students from the harm occasioned by hazing when it reasonably knows such activity is taking place (*Knoll v. Board of Regents of University of Nebraska*, 1999). The Supreme Court of Delaware has also held that the university does exercise some control over its students and may be liable where it reasonably knows hazing is taking place and fails to exercise proper supervision (*Furek v. University of Delaware*, 1991). Although these two cases only represent two jurisdictions, they are state supreme court opinions and they have the support of at least some legal scholars (Bickel & Lake, 1994). Practitioners should understand that these courts have only said the university has a duty when it reasonably knows there is a foreseeable danger. If the university acts reasonably to enforce its regulations and acts to provide a reasonably safe environment, it will not have breached its duty and thus will not be liable. Whether the university acted reasonably under the circumstances will be a question decided by a jury.

Finally, if a student affairs administrator voluntarily renders a service to another for her or his protection, the administrator has a duty to exercise due care even though she or he had no obligation initially (*Restatement (Second) of Torts*, 1965, Section 323). The Supreme Judicial Court of Massachusetts applied this duty when it held a college, by voluntarily providing campus police to protect students from the criminal acts of third persons, was liable for the rape of one of its students because it breached (did not perform with due care) the duty it voluntarily undertook (*Mullins v. Pine Manor College*, 1983). However, a special relationship is not created simply by imposing rules of conduct (*Smith v. Day*, 1987).

Breach of Duty

The second element of negligence requires that one breach a legally recognized duty. This may occur by either doing or failing to do something. It does not matter that what was done was accidental if it breaches a duty owed another. An example of this involved a campus police officer who fired a shot at a fleeing student. The officer stated that he had fired a shot into the air after telling the student to stop. When the student continued to run, the officer said he told the student to stop again and fired another shot at the ground. The weapon obviously discharged before it was pointed at the ground because it entered the student's back and killed him. The court held that even though the officer stated that he did not intend to wound the student, his act of firing the weapon was done so negligently; therefore, the jury could find him liable (*Jones v. Wittenberg*, 1976).

Injury

The injury may be either physical or psychological and may be to one's person or her or his property (*Moose v. Massachusetts Institute of Technology*, 1997; *Ross v. Creighton University*, 1992).

Proximate Cause

To be held liable for negligence, there must be a close causal relationship between the injury and the breach of one's duty. In other words, the breach of duty must be the proximate cause of the injury. If there is an intervening variable that caused the injury, there will be no liability. For example, a minor attending a special program at Montana State University was injured in a motorcycle accident after attending an off-campus party. The court found her injuries were caused by the motorcycle operator who had been drinking and failed to look at the road rather than any failure on the part of the university to enforce its rules or properly supervise its young students (*Graham v. Montana State University*, 1988).

Defenses

There are several defenses to negligence. Those who engage in dangerous activity assume the risk of injury. A student who voluntarily assumed the position of "hooker" in a scrum during a rugby practice suffered a broken neck and quadriplegia. The student sued the university, but the court held he had assumed the risk of injury by voluntarily participating in a contact sport. The court pointed out that "It is well settled that 'voluntary participation in sports activities may be held to have consented, by their participation, to those injury causing events which are known, apparent or reasonably foreseeable consequences of their own participation'" (*Regan v. State*, 1997, p. 490). It is not necessary that the individual foresee the exact injury or the way it may occur, but only that he or she is aware of the potential for injury. However, where fraternity pledges are coerced to consume alcohol as part of an initiation, they are not considered to be voluntarily participating and thus do not assume the risk of injury (*Oja v. Theta Chi Fraternity*, 1997).

When an individual's own conduct contributes to his or her negligence the individual may be barred from recovering any damages even where the injury suffered was partly becasue of the negligence of another. This is called *contributory negligence*. In states where there is comparative negligence, the injured individual may only recover that portion of the damages attributed to the negligence of the other person.

Two other defenses are sovereign immunity and charitable immunity. Sovereign immunity is based on the concept that the "King" can do no wrong and is applied to public entities and officials acting in the official scope of their responsibilities. Some states have abrogated their immunity for certain acts through state Tort Claims Acts (*University of Texas-Pan American v. Valdez*, 1993). These laws vary from state to state and administrators should become familiar with their state's Tort Claims Act. Charitable immunity provides immunity to eleemosynary institutions such as churches, private hospitals, and colleges; however, simply being private is not enough. The organization must have a charitable purpose or the exemption from tort liability will not be granted (*Radosevic v. Virginia Intermont College*, 1986). Many states have now abrogated this type of immunity (*Hupman v. Erskine College*, 1984).

Of course the best defense is to fulfill one's duties. *Mintz v. State* (1975) is a case illustrating how an institution met all of its duties even though two of its students died, but the university was not held liable. The case involved a university Outing Club and a canoe excursion. A flashing beacon was placed on a nearby island, a motorboat escort was provided, experienced canoeists were positioned in the stern, life jackets were worn by everyone, and a light was placed in each canoe. Weather forecasts were monitored, but a sudden unexpected storm came up and two students drowned. In finding no liability on the part of the university, the court took note of the fact that the deceased students were 20 years of age, cognizant of the risks, able to care for themselves and not in need of constant supervision, and the university took all reasonable precautions to guarantee a safe outing.

Waivers of Liability

Waivers or exculpatory agreements are an expressed form of assumption of risk in which one person agrees not to hold the other person liable for negligence. Many people believe that waivers are useless, but this is simply not true. As Prosser and Keeton (1984) have noted, "There is in the ordinary case no public policy which prevents the parties from contracting as they see fit, as to whether the plaintiff will undertake the responsibility of looking out for himself" (p. 482). In other words one person may contract with another not to sue the other for negligence for some future injury that may occur. Public policy, however, would not permit exculpatory agreements where the public interest is involved in such areas as common carriers, landlords, public utilities, or other businesses of great importance or practical necessity to the public.

Several conditions must be met if the agreement is to be enforced. First, the agreement must be written, because terms will be construed against the person who drafted it. Thus, it must be carefully drawn. Student affairs staff members are not trained in this area, so counsel should always be involved in drafting the agreement. The two parties must also enter into the agreement freely and openly (*Toth v. Toledo Speedway*, 1989) and must be on equal footing, with neither being at an obvious disadvantage (*Winterstein v. Wilcom*, 1972). Finally, the word "negligence" should be explicitly used in the agreement; although some courts have held it is not necessary if the intent of the parties is expressed in clear and unequivocal terms (*Hine v. Dayton Speedway Corp.*, 1969).

Waivers will not be enforced for willful, wanton, reckless, or gross conduct. A case illustrating the use of waivers in a college setting is *Boucher v. Riner* (1986). In this case a midshipman at the Naval Academy joined a voluntary extracurricular parachute club. He was given instruction, which included the hazards normally associated with the sport, by upper-class midshipmen who were certified by the U.S. Parachute Association. The midshipman signed a waiver before he boarded a plane for his jump. The waiver specifically released the parachute company providing the aircraft and jumpmasters and others from any loss, damage, or injury "whether such loss, damage or injury results from the negligence of the Corporation, its officers, agents, servants, employees or lessors or from some other cause" (p. 487). On his jump he was instructed to execute a turn which brought him into contact with uninsulated power lines and he suffered severe injuries. The court found the midshipman voluntarily joined the club, he was not compelled to sign the waiver, he refused the option of paying an additional $300 to nullify the waiver, he was not in a bargaining disadvantage, and the parachute company was not performing a service of vital importance to the public. Thus, the court held the waiver to be enforceable.

Campus Crimes

Violent crimes on campus have been occurring almost since the establishment of the first institutions of higher education in America. Rudolph (1990) stated that in the 1800s, a student was killed in the dining hall for attempting to take the last trout. Professors were stoned at the University of Georgia and one was killed at the University of Virginia. Smith (1989) and Palmer (1993) have reported that such violent crimes are still present on campuses today. Student affairs practitioners, therefore, should become aware of the liability arising from campus crime and what actions to take to reduce the risk of such liability.

The traditional tort laws discussed above determine the liability for crime on campus. Generally, one person has no duty to warn or protect another against the criminal acts of third persons (*Restatement (Second) of Torts*, 1993, Section 315, 913). However, as Prosser (1971) noted, duty is not sacrosanct. One of the primary elements in fixing duty is foreseeability. The United States Supreme Court has said that foreseeability is "an awareness of conditions that create a likelihood of injury" (*Lillie v. Thompson*, 1947, p. 461). That awareness or foreseeability may thus negate an intervening criminal act (*Gross v. Family Services Agency*, 1998). There is no liability for sudden unforeseen attacks (*Hall v. Board of Supervisors Southern University*, 1981), but administrators should be aware that some courts consider parking lots to be "an especial temptation and opportunity for criminal misconduct" (*Gomez v. Ticor*, 1983, p. 628, quoting Prosser, 1971, p. 174; see also *Issacs v. Huntington Memorial Hospital*, 1985).

Managing the Risk

There is a risk to just about every activity in which student affairs administrators engage, but that should not determine whether they engage in that activity. If the administrators are aware of their legal duties and meet them and generally try to put themselves in the other person's shoes and ask themselves how they would like to be treated, it is likely that the administrator's risk of liability will be reduced.

Specific strategies to reduce administrator risk include inspecting the campus for areas that create a likelihood of criminal attack. Are there spaces that require better lighting? Does foliage need to be trimmed? It is suggested that such inspections be done both during the day and again at night and have someone from another campus do the inspection. There is less chance of rationalizing if the administrator invites others to do the inspections. Having a team of individuals, including students, do the inspection can provide different perspectives. Also inspect buildings. Are there any spaces that create a likelihood of attack? Are the buildings locked? When are they opened? Are those who enter the buildings aware of this? Before beginning a campus safety audit the administrator needs to have assurances that there will be funds available to address deficiencies. Because not all required changes can likely be made immediately, the administrator should have a priority list of the most dangerous areas that need to be addressed first and continue to work on addressing the identified problems each year as funds become available. The worst thing a student affairs administrator can do is to identify areas that are likely to invite criminal activity (foreseeability) and then not do anything to address the problem.

Review campus security reports and police logs required under the Campus Security Act for "hot spots" on campuses to determine what kinds of crimes are taking place on campus and if there are specific areas related to particular crimes.

Personal security educational programs also are required by the Campus Security Act, but even if they were not, students and employees should be provided regular programs on how to create a safer environment on campus for themselves and others. To a large measure a college campus is seen as an idyllic environment, and students, faculty, and staff must be made aware that the campus is not a safe haven free of violent crime and they must assume some responsibility for their personal safety.

The best way to provide a safer campus is for all constituents to work together. Student affairs administrators, including housing, Greek life, counseling, health services, and activities must work with campus police, human resources, and academic affairs if campus crime and its attendant liability are to be reduced.

DEFAMATION

Defamation is defined as a false statement made by one person to another about a third person that holds the third person up to ridicule or contempt. Thus to be defamatory the statement must first of all be false. The truth is the best defense to defamation. In addition, the statement must be made to another person about a third party. Statements made directly to an individual about that individual would not be defamatory. Finally, the statement must hold the person up to ridicule or contempt. There are exceptions to this final requirement. It is defamation per se to accuse someone of being a criminal (*Melton v. Bow*, 1978) or of being unchaste (*Wardlaw v. Peck*, 1984) or of having a loathsome social disease.

Knowledge of the parameters of defamation are important to student affairs administrators because they engage in several activities that are susceptible to defamation—they engage in "shop talk" about students, they are asked to write letters of recommendation, and they teach students. There are two types of defamation. Libel is written defamation and slander is spoken defamation.

As stated earlier, the truth is the best defense against defamation. Administrators should not engage in conjecture about students or draw generalized or stereotyped conclusions about them. For instance, a professor who inaccurately accused a student of being a thief was held to have slandered the student and was held to be liable for damages (*Melton v. Bow*, 1978).

Letters of recommendation should be factual and not judgmental. There is a difference between saying "John has been late with every assignment" and saying "John is lazy and irresponsible." Professional opinions are called for sometimes, but an administrator should state "In my professional opinion" in the communication and the basis should be provided for one's opinion (*Olsson v.*

Indiana University Board of Trustees, 1991). The best defense to defamation is the truth, and when asked to provide a reference, whether listed as such or not, the administrator will be protected from defamation by simply being truthful. There is also a qualified immunity if the administrator, the requestor, and the public have an interest in the topic.

Finally, student affairs administrators are teachers. Students should be taught the parameters of defamation as part of their orientation to the Internet. Damages for defamation increase as the number of individuals to whom the false statement is made increases. When students log on to the Internet their statements may be communicated to literally millions of people. The institution itself will not be liable for what students send over the Internet using the institution's server as long as the server functions as the conduit for defamatory messages and the institution is not aware it is sending specifically defamatory messages (*Zeran v. America Online Inc.*, 1997).

Student editors also need to be taught the elements of libel, because they, and not the institution, will be held accountable for what they publish. A New York court held the editors of a campus newspaper liable for libel when they published a letter in which the authors admitted to being gay. The authors claimed they did not send the letter and were not gay. The court said failing to check the authorship was irresponsible journalism and negated any privilege they may have had (*Mazart v. State*, 1981).

PRIVILEGED COMMUNICATIONS

Student affairs administrators, and others who report violations to the individual to whom such reports are to be made, do not risk defamation even if the charge turns out to be false. Statements enjoy a conditional privilege where "(a) some interest of the person who publishes defamatory material is involved; (b) some interest of the person to whom the matter is published or some other third person is involved; or (c) a recognized interest of the public is involved" (*Vargo v. Hunt*, 1990, p. 627). Conditionally privileged statements are not defamatory. A student who reported a sexual assault to the sexual assault counselor and the chair of the department in which her attacker was enrolled was sued for defamation by the assailant after criminal charges against him were dismissed. The court, however, held that the victim enjoyed a qualified privilege because both she and those to whom she spoke shared a common interest and duty. The duty emanated from the university policy to encourage reporting of incidents of racial or sexual harassment (*Rosenbloom v. Vanek*, 1989).

CONCLUSION

American society has become very litigious and, as this chapter has illustrated, so has the campus community. Every functional area within student affairs is affected by the laws and duties recognized under the legal system. As administrators and managers, student affairs practitioners must be conversant with those laws and duties to ensure students' rights, not to expose them to unreasonable risks, and to protect the institution from liability. As leaders in higher education, student affairs administrators must be proactive in understanding the law and ensuring that programs, policies, and practices are in compliance, thereby serving as role models for students and developing trust. Finally, as educators, administrators must be knowledgeable of the law so that they can help students understand their legal rights and responsibilities.

This chapter can be used as a staff development guide. Case citations used to support the assertions made in the chapter can be used as a basis for study. Most county courthouses and even some college libraries have the publications cited. It is instructive to read the cases and the actual language of the court. Several publications mentioned early in this chapter will assist student affairs administrators to stay current.

QUESTIONS TO CONSIDER

1. Justice Cardozo once said, "Law never is, but is always about to be." What do you think the law will be next?
2. Why do you think First Amendment freedoms are protected so vigorously by the courts even to the point of protecting incivility, indecency, and pornography?
3. Because "The risk reasonably to be perceived defines the duty to be obeyed," what areas of student life do you believe create a reasonable risk and thus could create a duty owed to students by the university?

REFERENCES

American Law Institute. (1981). *Restatement of Contracts 2d.* St. Paul, MN: Author.

Bernstein, N. (1996, May 30). With colleges holding court, discretion vies with fairness. *New York Times*, pp. A1, A16.

Bickel, R., & Lake, P. (1994). Reconceptualizing the university's duty to provide a safe learning environment: A criticism of the doctrine of *In Loco Parentis* and the Restatement (Second) of Torts. *Journal of College and University Law, 20*(3), 261–293.

Boyer, E. (1990). *Campus life: In search of community*. Princeton, NJ: Carnegie Foundation for the Advancement of Teaching.

Brubacher, J., & Rudy, W. (1968). *Higher edu-

cation in transition*. New York: Harper & Row.

Callaway, R., & Gehring, D. (2000). Two year college compliance with the notice requirements of the Campus Security Act. *Community College Journal of Research and Practice, 24*, 181–191.

Cardozo, B. (1921). *The nature of the judicial process*. New Haven, CT: Yale University Press.

Caseload highlights: Examining the work of the state courts. (1999). *National state court caseload trends, 1984–1994*. [On-line]. Available: http://www.ncsc.dni.us/research/csp/csphigh1.htm

Coomes, M., & Gehring, D. (1994). *Student services in a changing federal climate*. New Directions for Student Services, No. 68. San Francisco: Jossey-Bass.

Dannells, M. (1991). Changes in student misconduct and institutional response over 10 years. *Journal of College Student Development, 32,* 166–170.

Federal education programs: Federal aid to education. (1965). *Congress and the nation: A review of government and politics in the post-war years. Vol. 1, 1945–1964*. Washington, DC: Congressional Quarterly Service.

Frammolino, R. (1993, November 11). Suit forces UC Riverside to rescind fraternity penalty. *Los Angeles Times*, pp. A3, A36.

Gehring, D. (1991a). *1990 update to alcohol on campus: A compendium of the law and a guide to campus policy*. Asheville, NC: College Administration Publications.

Gehring (1991b, November). Abreast of the law. *NASPA Forum*, 6–7.

Gehring, D. (1994). Protective policy laws. In M.D. Coomes & D. D. Gehring, *Student services in a changing federal climate*. New Directions for Student Services, No. 68 (pp. 67–82). San Francisco: Jossey-Bass.

Gehring, D. (1999, September/October). Abstract of the law. *NASPA Forum*, 14.

Gehring, D. D., & Geraci, C. (1989). *Alcohol on campus: A compendium of the law and a guide to campus policy*. Asheville, NC: College Administration Publications, Inc.

Gehring, D. D., & Pavela, G. (1994). *Issues and perspectives on academic integrity* (2nd ed.). Washington, DC: National Association of Student Personnel Administrators.

Geraci, C., Guthrie, V., Key, R., & Parrott, D. (1990). *A sampling of responses by higher education to the 1989 Amendments to the Drug Free Schools and Communities Act*. Unpublished manuscript. University of Louisville, KY.

Markiewicz, J. (1996, Fall–Winter). Student newspaper vs. Miami University. *Campus Watch, 2*(1), 13–14.

McCarthy, T., & Gehring, D. (1999). *1999 update to alcohol on campus: A compendium of the law and a guide to campus policy*. Asheville, NC: College Administration Publications.

Palmer, C. (1993). *Violent crimes and other forms of victimization in residence halls*. Asheville, NC: College Administration Publications.

Palmer, C., & Gehring, D. (1992). *A handbook for complying with the program and review requirements of the 1989 amendments to the Drug Free Schools and Communities Act*. Asheville, NC: College Administration Publications.

Palmer, C., Gehring, D., & Guthrie, V. (1992). Student knowledge of information mandated by the 1989 amendments to the Drug Free Schools and Communities Act. *NASPA Journal, 30*, 30–38.

Pavela, G. (Ed.). (1989–2001). *Synthesis* (vols. 1–12). Asheville, NC: College Administration Publications.

Pavela, G. (Ed.). (1993–2001). *Syntax*. Asheville, NC: College Administration Publications.

Pavela, G. (Ed.). (1997). Civility on campus. *Synthesis* 8(4).

Prosser, W. (1971). *Law of torts* (4th ed.). St Paul, MN: West.

Prosser, W., & Keeton, K. P. (1984). *The law of torts*. St. Paul, MN: West.

Responsible use of electronic communications, (1996). *Synthesis* 7(4), 552–553, 561–562.

Restatement (Second) of Torts. (1993). St. Paul, MN: American Law Institute Publishers.

Rudolph, F. (1990). *The American college and university: A history*. Athens: University of Georgia Press.

Smith, M. (1989). *Crime and campus police: A handbook for police officers and administrators*. Asheville, NC: College Administration Publications.

Stoner, E., & Creminara, K. (1990). Harnessing the spirit of insubordination: A model student disciplinary code. *Journal of College and University Law, 1990, 17*(2), 89–121.

U.S. Department of Education. (1979). *Policy interpretation of Title IX and intercollegiate athletics*. 44 Ed. Reg. 71413 (Dec. 11, 1979).

Young, D,. & Gehring, D. (1985). *The college student and the courts* (2nd ed.). Asheville, NC: College Administration Publications.

CASES CITED

ACLU v. Reno, 929 F. Supp. 824 (E.D. Pa. 1996).

Alexander v. Yale University, 631 F.2d 178 (2nd Cir. 1980).

Amon v. State, 414 N.Y.S.2d 941 (A.D. 3rd Dept. 1979).

Anderson v. University of Wisconsin, 841 F.2d 737 (7th Cir. 1988).

Bayless v. Martine, 430 F.~ 873 (5th Cir. 1970).

Bearman v. University of Notre Dame, 453 N.E.2d 1196 (App. Ind., 3rd Dist. 1983).

Berrios v. Inter American University, 535 F.2d 1330 (1st Cir. 1976).

Bindrim v. University of Montana, 766 P.2d 861 (Mont. 1988).

Blackburn v. Fisk University, 443 F.2d 121 (6th Cir. 1971).

Blanton v. State University of New York, 489 F.2d 377 (2nd Cir. 1973).

Board of Curators v. Horowitz, 46 L.W. 4179 (1978).

Board of Regents of University of Wisconsin v. Southworth, 68 USLW 4220 (2000).

Bob Jones University v. Johnson, 396 F. Supp. 597 (D. SC, Greenville Div. 1974).

Boucher v. Riner, 514 A.2d 485 (Md. App. 1986).

Bougher v. University of Pittsburgh, 882 F.2d 74 (3rd Cir. 1989).

Browns v. Mitchell, 409 F.2d 593 (10th Cir. 1969).

Buckton v. NCAA, 436 F. Supp. 1258 (D. Mass. 1977).

Burnside v. Byars, 363 F.2d 744 (5th Cir. 1966).

Burton v. Wilmington Parking Authority, 365 U.S. 715 (1961).

Cafeteria & Restaurant Worker's Union v. McElroy, 367 U.S. 995 (1961).

Chaplinsky v. New Hampshire, 315 U.S. 568 (1942).

Chontos v. Rhea, 29 F. Supp. 2d 931 (N.D. Ind. 1998).

Cloud v. Trustees of Boston University, 720 F.2d 721 (1st Cir. 1983).

Cohen v. Brown, 101 F.3d 155 (1st Cir. 1996); Cert. den. 520 U.S. 1186 (1997).

Cohen v. California, 403 U.S. 15 (1971).

Collin v. Smith, 578 F.2d 1197 (7th Cir. 1978).

Commonwealth ex rel. Hill v. McCauley, 3 Pa. Co. Ct. 77 (1887).

Connick v. Myers, 461 U.S. 138 (1983).

Davis v. Monroe County Board of Education, 119 S. Ct. 1661 (1999).

Delta School of Business, Etc. v. Shropshire, 399 So.2d 1212 (LA App. 1st Cir. 1981).

DeRonde v. Regents of University of California, 172 Cal. Rptr. 677 (1981).

Dickey v. Alabama State Board of Education, 273 F. Supp. 613 (M.D. AL E.D. 1967).

District of Columbia v. Clawans, 300 U.S. 617 (1936).

Dixon v. Alabama State Board of Education, 294 F.2d 150 (5th Cir. 1961); cert. den. 386 U.S. 930 (1961).

Doe v. America Online, Inc., 718 So.2d 385 (Fla. App. 1998).

Doe v. New York University, 666 F.2d 761 (2nd Cir. 1981).

Doe v. University of Maryland Medical System Corporation, 50 F.3d 1261 (4th Cir. 1995).

Doe v. Washington University, 780 F. Supp. 638 (Ed. Mo. 1991).

Doherty v. Southern College of Optometry, 862 F.2d 570 (6th Cir. 1988); cert. den. 493 U.S. 810 (1989).

Donohue v. Baker, 976 F. Supp. 136 (N.D. N.Y. 1997).

Douglas v. Alabama, 380 U.S. 415 (1965).

Drew v. State, 536 N.Y.S.2d 252 (A.D. 3rd Dept. 1989).

D.T.H. Pub. Corp. v. University of North Carolina at Chapel Hill, 496 S.E. 2d 8 (N.C. App. 1998).

Duarte v. State, 148 Cal. Rptr. 804 (Cal. App. 4th Dist. 1978).

Eisen v. Regents, 75 Cal. Rptr. 45 (Cal. App. 1969).

Ekelund v. Secretary of Commerce, 418 F. Supp. 102 (E.D. NY 1976).

Esteban v. Central Missouri State College, 415 F. 2d 1077 (8th cir. 1969).

Faulkner v. Jones, 51 F.3d 440 (4th Cir. 1995).

Flanagan v. President and Directors of Georgetown College, 417 F. Supp. 377 (D.D.C. 1976).

Franklin v. Gwinnett County Public Schools, 503 U.S. 60 (1992).

French v. Bashful, 303 F. Supp. 1333 (E.D. LA N.O. Div. 1969).

Furek v. University of Delaware, 594 A.2d 506 (DE 1991).

Gabrilowitz v. Newman, 582 F.~ 100 (1st Cir. 1978).

Gay and Lesbian Student Association v. Gohn, 850 F.2d 361(8th Cir. 1988).

Gebser v. Lago Vista Independent School District, 524 U.S. 274 (1998).

General Order on Judicial Standards of Pro-

cedure and Substance in Review of Student Discipline in Tax Supported Institutions of Higher Education, 45 FRD 133 (W.D. MO 1968).

Gent v. Radford University, 976 F. Supp. 391 (W.D. Va. 1997); aff'd. 165 F.3d 911 (4th Cir. 1998).

Gomez, v. Ticor, 193 Cal. Rptr. 600 (App. 2nd Dist. 1983).

Good v. Associated Students, 542 P.2d 762 (WA 1975).

Gooding v. Wilson, 405 U.S. 518 (1972).

Gorman v. University of Rhode Island, 837 F.2d 7 (1st Cir. 1988).

Goss v. Lopez, 419 U.S. 565 (1975).

Graham v. Montana State University, 767 P.2d 301 (MT 1988).

Gross v. Family Services Agency, 716 So. 2d 337 (Fla. App. 4th Dist. 1998).

Grossner v. Trustees of Columbia University, 287 F. Supp. 535 (S.D. NY 1968).

Grove City College v. Bell, 465 U.S. 55 (1984).

Guckenberger v. Boston University, 957 F. Supp. 306 (D. Mass. 1997).

Guckenberger v. Boston University, 8 F. Supp. 2d 82 (D. Mass. 1998).

Hall v. Board of Supervisors. Southern University, 405 So.2d 1125 (App. LA 1st Cir. 1981).

Healy v. James, 408 U.S. 169 (1972).

Henig v. Hofstra University, 533 N.Y.S.2d 479 (A.D. 2nd Dept. 1990).

Hine v. Dayton Speedway Corp., 252 N.E.2d 648 (Ohio App. Montgomery Cty. 1969).

Hopwood v. Texas, 78 F.3d 932 (5th Cir. 1996); Cert. den. 518 U.S. 1033 (1996).

Houck v. University of Washington, 803 P.2d 47 (App. WA 1991).

Hupman v. Erskine College, 314 S.E.2d 314 (S.C. 1984).

Iota Xi Chapter of Sigma Chi Fraternity v. George Mason University, 773 F. Supp. 792 (E.D. Va. 1991); aff'd. 993 F.2d 386.

Isaacs v. Huntington Memorial Hospital, 695 P.2d 653 (Cal. 1985).

Jackson v. Hayakawa, 761 F.2d 525 (9th Cir. 1985).

Jenkins v. Louisiana State Board of Education, 506 F.2d 992 (5th Cir. 1975).

Johnson v. Lincoln Christian College, 501 N.E.2d 1380 (IL App. 4th Dist. 1986).

Johnson v. State, 894 P.2d 1366 (Wash. App. 1995).

Jones v. Whittenberg, 534 F.2d 1203 (6th Cir. 1976).

Joyner v. Whiting, 477 F.2d 456 (4th Cir. 1973).

Keene v. Rodgers, 316 F.Supp. 217 (D. Me. ND 1970).

Kister v. Ohio Board of Regents, 365 F. Supp. 27 (S.D. Ohio 1973).

Kline v. 1500 Massachusetts Avenue Apartment Corporation, 439 F.2d 477 (D.C Cir. 1970).

Knoll v. Board of Regents of University of Nebraska, 601 N.W. 2d 757 (Neb. 1999).

Kovach v. Middendorf, 424 F. Supp 72 (D. Del. 1976).

Krawez v. Stans, 306 F.Supp. 1230 (D. E.D. NY 1969).

Lee v. Board of Regents of State Colleges, 306 F. Supp. 1097 (W.D. WI 1969).

Lemon v. Kurtzman, 403 U.S. 602 (1971).

Lewin v. Medical College of Hampton Roads, 931 F. Supp. 443 (E.D. Va. 1996).

Lillie v. Thompson, 332 U.S. 459 (1947).

Liu v. Striuli, 36 F. Supp. 2d 452 (D.R.I. 1999).

Loving v. Boren, 133 F.3d 771 (10th Cir. 1998).

Malley v. Youngstown State University, 658 N.E.2d 333 (Ohio Ct. Clms. 1995).

Maryland Public Interest Research Group v. Elkins, 565 F.2d 864 (4th Cir. 1977).

Mazart v. State, 441 N.Y.S.2d 600 (Ct. Clms. 1981).

McDonald v. Board of Trustees of University of Illinois, 375 F. Supp. 95 (N.D. IL E.D. 1974).

McDonald v. Hogness, 598 P.2d 707 (WA 1979).

Meese v. Brigham Young University, 639 P.2d 720 (UT 1981).

Melton v. Bow, 247 S.E.2d 100 (GA 1978).

Mercer v. Duke University, 190 F.3d 643 (4th Cir. 1999).

Merkey v. Board of Regents, 493 F.2d 790 (5th Cir. 1974).

Miller v. California, 413 U.S. 15 (1973).

Miller v. State, 478 N.Y.S.2d 829 (1984).

Mintz v. State, 362 N.Y.S.2d 619 (App. 3rd 1975).

Mollere v. Southeastern Louisiana College, 304 F. Supp. 826 (W.D. AR Fayetteville Div. 1969).

Moore v. Student Affairs Committee of Troy State University, 284 F. Supp. 725 (M.D. Ala. 1968).

Moose v. Massachusetts Institute of Technology, 683 N.E.2d 706 (Mass. App. 1997).

Morale v. Grigel, 422 F. Supp. 988 (D.N.H. 1976).

Morrissey v. Brewer, 408 U.S. 471 (1972).

Mullins v. Pine Manor College, 449 N.E.2d 331 (MA 1983).

Nash v. Auburn University, 812 F.2d 655 (11th Cir. 1987).

National Strike Information Center v. Brandeis, 315 F. Supp. 928 (D.MA 1970).

Nero v. Kansas State University, 861 P.2d 768 (Ks. 1993).

New Jersey v. T.L.O., 83 LEd.2d 720 (1985).

Norton v. Discipline Committee of East Tennessee State University, 419 F.2d 195 (6th Cir. 1969).

Noto v. United States, 367 U.S. 290 (1961).

Nzuve v. Castleton State College, 335 A.2d 321 (Vt. 1975).

Ohio Civil Rights Comm. v. Case Western Reserve, 666 N.E.2d 1376 (Ohio. 1996).

Oja v. Theta Chi Fraternity, 667 N.Y.S.2d 650 (S.Ct. Tompkins Cty. 1997).

Olsson v. Indiana University Board of Trustees, 571 N.E.2d 585 (Ct. App. In. 4th Dist. 1991).

Osteen v. Henley, 13 F.3d 221 (7th Cir. 1993).

Palsgraf v. Long Island R.R. Co., 162 N.E. 99 (NY 1928).

Papish v. Board of Curators of University of Missouri, 410 U.S. 667 (1973).

Patricia H. v. Berkeley Unified School District 830 F.Supp. 1288 (N.D. Cal. 1993).

People v. Lanthier, 97 Cal. Rptr. 297 (1971).

Peterson v. San Francisco Community College District, 685 P.2d 1193 (Cal. 1984).

Piazzola v. Watkins, 442 F.2d 284 (5th Cir. 1971).

Podberesky v. Kirwan, 38 F.3d 147 (4th Cir. 1994).

Potter v. North Carolina School of the Arts, 245 S.E.2d 188 (NC App. 1978).

Pratz v. Louisiana Polytechnic Institute, 316 F. Supp. 872 (W.D. LA 1970); cert. den. 401 U.S. 1004 (1971).

Rabel v. Illinois Wesleyan University, 514 N.E.2d 552 (Ill. App. 4th Dist. 1987).

Radcliff v. Landau, 883 F.2d 1481 (9th Cir. 1989).

Radosevic v. Virginia Intermont College, 633 F. Supp. 1084 (W.D. Va. 1986).

Red and Black Pub. Co., Inc. v. Board of Regents, 427 S.E. 2d 257 (GA. 1993).

Reetz v. Michigan, 188 U.S. 505 (1903).

Regan v. State, 654 N.Y.S.2d 488 (A.D. 3rd Dept. 1997).

Regents of the University of California v. Bakke, 438 U.S. 265 (1978).

Reno v. ACLU, 521 U.S. 844 (1997).

Richmond v. Ohio State University, 564 N.E. 2d 1145 (Ct. Clms. 1989).

Rosenberger v. Rector and Visitors of the University of Virginia, 515 U.S. 819 (1995).

Rosenbloom v. Vanek, 451 N.W.2d 520 (Mich. App. 1989).

Ross v. Creighton University, 957 F.2d 410 (7th Cir. 1992).

Rowe v. Chandler, 332 F. Supp. 336 (D. Kans. 1971).

School Board of Nassau County, Florida v. Arline, 480 U.S. 273 (1987).

Schenck v. United States, 249 U.S. 47 (1919).

Schultz v. Gould Academy, 332 A.2d 368 (Maine 1975).

Sharmloo v. Mississippi State Board of Trustees, Etc., 620 F.2d 516 (5th Cir. 1980).

Shelley v. Kraemer, 334 U.S. 1 (1947).

Shetina v. Ohio University, 459 N.E.2d 587 (Ohio App. 1983).

Shreveport Professional Chapter of the Society of Professional Journalists and Michelle Millhollon v. Louisiana State University in Shreveport, No. 393, 332 (First Judicial Dist. Ct., Caddo Parish, La. 1994).

Siegel v. Regents of the University of California, 308 F. Supp. 832 (N.D. CA 1970).

Smith v. Day, 538 A.2d 157 (VT. 1987).

Smith v. Duquesne University, 612 F. Supp. 72 (W.D. Pa. Civ. Div. 1985).

Smith v. Regents of University of California, 844 P.2d 500 (Cal. 1993).

Smyth and Smith v. Lubbers, 398 F. Supp. 777 (W.D. Mich. 1975).

Southeastern Community College v. Davis, 442 U.S. 397 (1979).

Southworth v. Grebe, 157 F.3d 1124 (10th Cir. 1998).

Stark v. St. Cloud State University, 802 F.2d 1046 (8th Cir. 1986).

State ex rel the Miami Student v. Miami University, 680 N.E.2d 956 (Ohio 1997).

State v. Johnson, 530 P.2d 910 (Ariz. App. Div. 2 1975).

State v. Kappes, 550 P.2d 121 (Ct. App. Ariz. Div. 1 Dept. A 1976).

State v. Kaukle, 948 P.2d 321 (Okl. App. 1997).

State v. Sterling, 685 A.2d 432 (Maine 1996).

State v. Wingerd, 318 N.W.2d 866 (Ohio App. 1974).

State v. Wood, 679 N.E. 2d 735 (Ohio App. 1996).

Steinberg v. Chicago Medical School, 371N.E. 634 (Ill. 1977).

Stone v. Cornell University, 510 N.Y.S.2d 313 (A.D. 1987).

Student Coalition v. Austin Peay State University, 477 F. Supp. 1267 (M.D. Tenn. 1979).

Students Against Apartheid Coalition v. O'Neil I, 660 F. Supp. 333 (W.D. VA 1987).

Sutton v. United Airlines, 1195 Ct. 2139 (1999).

Sword v. Fox, 446 F.2d 1091 (4th Cir. 1971).

Tarka v. Cunningham, 891 F.2d 102 (5th Cir. 1989).

Tayyari v. New Mexico State University, 495 F. Supp. 1365 (D. NM 1980).

Terminiello v. Chicago, 337 U.S. 1 (1949).

Texas v. Johnson, 491 U.S. 397 (1989).

Tinker v. Des Moines Independent Community School District, 393 U.S. 502 (1969).

Tobias v. University of Texas, 824 S.W.2d 201 (Tx. App., Ft. Worth 1991).

Torres v. Puerto Rico Junior College, 298 F. Supp. 458 (D.P.R. 1969).

Toth v. Toledo Speedway, 583 N.E.2d 357 (Ohio App. 6 Dist. 1989).

United States v. Board of Trustees for University of Alabama, 908 F.2d 740 (11th Cir. 1990).

United States v. Coles, 302 F. Supp. 99 (D. ME N.D., 1969).

United States v. Dennis, 183 F.2d 201 (2nd Cir. 1950); aff'd 341 U.S. 494 (1951).

United States v. Miami University, Case #C298-0097 (S.D. Ohio 1998).

United States v. Miami University, F. Supp. (S.D. Ohio 2000).

United States v. Virginia, 518 U.S. 515 (1996).

University of Texas-Pan American v. Valdez, 869 S.W.2d 446 (Tex. App. 13th Dist. 1993).

University of Utah Students Against Apartheid v. Peterson, 649 F. Supp. 1200 (D. Utah C.D. 1986).

Utah v. Hunter, 831 P.2d 1033 (Utah App. 1992).

UWM Post v. Board of Regents of the University of Wisconsin, 774 F. Supp. 1163 (E.D. Wisc. 1991).

Vargo v. Hunt, 581 A.2d 625 (Pa. Sup. 1990).

Veed v. Schwartzkoph, 353 F. Supp. 149 (D. NE 1973); aff'd 478 F.2d 1407 (8th Cir. 1973); cert. den. 414 U.S. 1135 (1973).

Wardlaw v. Peck, 318 S.E.2d 270 (S.C. App. 1984).

Warren v. Drake University, 886 F.2d 200 (8th Cir. 1989).

Washington v. Chrisman, 455 U.S. 1 (1982).

Washington v. Chrisman, 676 P.2d 419 (Wash. 1984).

Whitney v. California, 274 U.S. 357 (1927).

Widmar v. Vincent, 454 U.S. 263 (1981).

Winnick v. Manning, 460 F.2d 545 (2nd Cir. 1972).

Winterstein v. Wilcom, 293 A.2d 821 (Md. Sp. App. 1972).

Wright v. Texas Southern University, 392 F.2d 728 (5th Cir. 1968).

Zeran v. America Online, Inc., 129 F.3d 327 (4th Cir. 1997).

RECOMMENDED READING

Bickel, R., & Lake, P. (1999). *The rights and responsibilities of the modern university: Who assumes the risk of college life?* Durham, NC: Carolina Academic Press.

Kaplin, W., & Lee, B. (1995). *The law of higher education*. San Francisco: Jossey-Bass.

Paterson, B., & Kibler, W. (Eds.). (1998). *The administration of campus discipline: Student, organizational and community issues*. Asheville, NC: College Administration Publications.

Pavela, G. (1985). *The dismissal of students with mental disorders: Legal issues, policy considerations and alternative responses*. Asheville, NC: College Administration Publications.

Young, D. P., & Gehring, D. D. (1986). *The college student and the courts* (2nd ed.). Asheville, NC: College Administration Publications.

6

Ethics and
Professional Practice

ROBERT B. YOUNG

*M*ark Twain said that his only duty at any time was to do what he believed was right (Ayres, 1987), and the best advice that can be offered in this chapter is, *Follow his lead*. Twain answered any question about *when* student affairs administrators should be ethical; they should "*do right*" at all times, and not just in their professional roles as educators, leaders, and managers. He omitted a few details for student affairs practice, however, such as *what* is right, *where* it is right, *why* people should do right, and *how* to do right. Addressing those concerns requires more time but not more commitment from any reader.

This chapter is directed first to *what* ethics is—to a definition. Then the topic becomes the context of ethical practice, in this case, the *where* of higher education. The next topic is *why* the work of higher education and professions demands ethical behavior. The fourth topic concerns the *how* of ethical practice. It involves using professional codes; reflecting about one's choices; assessing principles and practices; setting ethical missions; helping students learn about ethics; giving voice to the community; mediating conflicts; and modeling, mentoring, and motivating.

WHAT IS ETHICS? DIFFERENT APPROACHES
TO A DEFINITION

Being ethical means more than simply obeying the law. Mark Twain was concerned about more transcendent moral obligations than that. Law is the "ethical minimum" (Chambers, 1981, p. 3) that keeps a society functioning; it is what people *must* do, whereas ethics is what people *should* do. The law and its partners, codes of ethics, describe one's minimal obligations to society and professional service, instead of one's moral opportunities.

Books, chapters, and courses about the law are very popular in America's litigious society. Their popularity has grown from the need to avoid mistakes in the performance of one's duties. Ignorance of the law is no excuse, nor is ignorance of professional codes of ethics, because these codes declare the minimum obligations of practice.

Publications, courses, and documents about legal and ethical codes, however, do not provide sufficient or even stable information. The law and professional codes are not simple, explicit, and coherent; instead, they are "constantly elaborating" to adapt to changing norms, especially in service professions (Ylvisaker, 1983, p. 30). A student affairs administrator will not find easy answers in them when she or he wants to defend herself or himself from trouble. Professional practitioners must rely on other resources, beginning with their ability to understand values as well as circumstances.

In this chapter, ethics is examined from a valuing perspective instead of from a defensive stance. The content focuses on moral values instead of professional codes, even though those codes are very important for practice.

The primary concern is moral self-scrutiny (Wilcox & Ebbs, 1992), instead of protective measures, because student affairs administrators need to work as they *should* and not just as they *must*. Moral values such as caring should incorporate most of the concerns of the law. The law, however, cannot take care of all there is to caring.

Defining Ethics

Doing ethics is more difficult than defining them, but that does not mean that defining ethics is simple. Right after Paul Ylvisaker (1983), former dean of the Harvard Graduate School of Education, declared that the "first commandment imposed upon a contemporary educator [is] 'Be ethical!'" he equivocated, by writing "And what is ethics? I don't ask that cynically. I am not a professional ethicist, but the more I've studied the subject the more I've been persuaded that we are dealing with a remarkably elusive concept" (p. 30).

Three approaches to defining ethics are popular among "professional" ethicists. Kidder (1995) called them rules-based, ends-based, and caring-based approaches to ethics. They differ, but they have similarities too.

Different Approaches. Rules-based ethics comes from the philosophy of Immanuel Kant, who believed that actions are unethical when they cannot be supported with rules of conduct. Whatever a person does in one circumstance must be applied to all circumstances, no exceptions allowed. For instance, if one student is given social probation for an alcohol violation, then all students must receive the same punishment for the same violation. Consequently, student affairs administrators should think carefully before imposing the first sanction.

Ultimately, rules-based thinking affirms the moral equality of people.

Everybody should be treated consistently, and nobody should be used as a means to anyone else's ends. The same sanction is applied to the same action regardless of the circumstances. A student's ethnicity, social status, wealth, or grade point average does not affect the application of the rule.

Kant believed in universal rules of etiquette, but his philosophy of ethics is too strict to be followed all the time. Sometimes rules have to be broken in favor of other rules, because the outcomes of the behavior demand alternative ways of "doing right." If probation is the only sanction for that alcohol violation, then creative sanctions cannot be applied under different circumstances, even if they fit those circumstances better than the original sanction.

The ends-based approach offers alternatives. It measures ethical acts by the amounts of happiness and unhappiness they bring to everyone involved. The guideline is to *do the most good and least harm* to others. The approach is based on the logic that the quantity of ethics is measured by the quantity of happiness that actions generate. In a majority of cases, the happiness of the majority rules.

Americans believe that all humans have inalienable rights to life, liberty, and the pursuit of happiness, but historically the happiness of disenfranchised groups has been slighted for the sake of the majority. The most egregious example is slavery, which hurt African Americans and served the interests of European Americans. Slavery was a legal practice until 1862, but it is impossible to claim that it was ever ethical.

Legal procedures can cement unethical behaviors, in society and on college campuses. Votes often favor the status quo instead of reform. Social programming is generally based on crowd appeal instead of ethical evenhandedness. A coalition of well-established, homogeneous fraternal organizations can use its votes to pass economic sanctions that affect newer, smaller, and diverse fraternities more harshly than its members. The voting seems fair on the surface, but it is ethically shallow, because it does not protect minority interests (Rawls, 1971).

Caring-based ethics offers an alternative to rules-based and ends-based ethics. It rests on the practice of the golden rule: *Do unto others as you would have them do unto you*. This approach is intuitive instead of normative, ethnically persistent (Cortese, 1990), and consistent with feminist theories (Lisman, 1996). It might focus on the relationships involved in an alcohol violation more than weighing the principles or outcomes. Caring ethics is called *virtue* theory to differentiate it from logic-based approaches. Its supporters might believe that good people need to think about ethics as often as bugs need to think about entomology; ethics requires caring actions more than objective discourse.

"Do unto others as you would have them do unto you," but is that not a "rule" that deserves examination? Irrational people might express *caring* in ways that rational people would not want done unto themselves or others. When the meaning of *virtue* or *caring* is examined, then this approach faces the same questions about logic and practice as rules-based and ends-based ethics (Strike & Soltis, 1998). It is not entirely different from the other approaches to defining ethics.

Similarities among the approaches. Strike and Soltis (1998) wrote that the differences in rules-based, ends-based, and caring-based ethics enrich one's knowledge about ethics. These three approaches share compatible, core conceptions of ethics as well; the similarities also enrich one's knowledge of ethics. The first conception is that ethics is not about acts in isolation; people in social situations are always involved in it. Second, ethics is about moral values, and moral values are not selfish in nature. Respecting human dignity, doing the most good and least harm, and caring for others are very generous propositions. Third, each of the three approaches to ethics involves reasoning, whether or not it is used to support Western, non-Western, or universal ideas. Finally, morality might promote "random acts of kindness." (See Random Acts of Kindness Foundation, Retrieved October 29, 2000 from World Wide Web: http:// www.actsofkindness.org.) But all three approaches to ethics are deliberate about what should be done in relation to other people.

The resulting definition for ethics, then, is those deliberate and consistent acts and principles that respect the dignity of all people and promote the greatest good for all concerned. This definition is similar to one that Brown used in his 1990 book, *Working Ethics*, and Lisman (1996) adopted for his book, *The Curricular Integration of Ethics*. The definition is not very original, and that should be reassuring. The meaning of ethics, like ethical behavior itself, should not seem strained. It should seem inherently right.

Inherent Principles in the Derived Definition of Ethics

This definition reflects several principles that have been applied to higher education, and particularly to student affairs administration (Kitchener,1985). The principles are *be just, respect autonomy, do no harm*, and *benefit others*. Being just and respecting autonomy reflect the principles of rules-based ethics. Do no harm and benefit others reflect end-based ethics. In addition, Kitchener has adapted a fifth principle, *be faithful*, to address professional trustworthiness and to reinforce the principle of respecting autonomous people.

These principles have been applied to administrative and educational roles (For examples, see Krager, 1985; Upcraft, 1988, and Chapter 1 in this volume.) The five principles can be found in the 1992 American College Personnel Association (ACPA) *Statement of Ethical Principles and Standards*. (See Appendix B in this volume). They provide a good base for operations, but they must be considered within a context that upholds other values.

WHERE: ETHICS WITHIN THE CONTEXT OF HIGHER EDUCATION AND STUDENT AFFAIRS

Student affairs administrators are not the only ones determining the ethical principles, practices, and priorities of higher education. Other perspectives must be considered, primarily those of the faculty and the host institution. These different perspectives make ethical dilemmas inevitable—and, thus, ethical practice more difficult.

The Faculty Context

Sometimes faculty members embrace different principles than do student affairs administrators (see Chapter 2 in this volume). The American Association of University Professors (1974) published a statement of professional ethics that affects faculty as researchers, teachers, colleagues, institutional representatives, and community members. The values of honesty, competence, and fairness are emphasized because they justify academic freedom and help fulfill the search for truth. Kerr (1994) concurred that competence and freedom are important because the central purposes of academic activity are the discovery of knowledge and its dissemination—in other words, research and teaching.

Several essays were written about ethical teaching; Smith (1996) emphasized fairness, honesty, promise keeping, respect, and responsibility in the teacher–student relationship. Another essayist (Hanson, 1996) described the role of the central virtues of academia as openness to ideas, honesty in evaluations, courtesy, and civil respect. Content competence and pedagogical competence came first in the principles of the Society for Teaching and Learning in Higher Education (Murray, Gillese, Lennon, Mercer, & Robinson, 1996, p. 63), and a fourth author (Rodabaugh, 1996) reiterated the role of fairness as "a preeminent objective of the educational process" (p. 37). These authors placed a high priority on the professor's knowledge of the subject matter and how to teach it. Stupid professors are unethical. Unfair professors are unethical too, because they have more knowledge than their students. According to Churchill (1994), students "are 'other than' teachers by virtue of an asymmetry of power between teacher and student grounded in differences in expertise, experience, and skills" (pp. 150–151).

Faculty ethics are related first to knowledge—to the seeking and speaking of truth—then to students, and finally to the institutions in which they work. Student affairs professionals might alter the priorities by putting students first and everything else far behind. All student affairs administrators, however, understand the need to be competent in correspondence with the values of the institutions that employ them.

The Institutional Context

Winston and Dagley (1985) declared that student affairs administrators represent the interests—and therefore must attend to the ethics—of their institutions as well as their students. This point is supported in the ACPA *Statement of Ethical Principles and Standards* (1992), which declares that "institutions of higher education provide the context for student affairs practice, institutional mission, policies, organizational structure, and culture, combined with individual judgment and professional standards define and delimit the nature and extent of practice" (p. 13). The 1999 *Standards of Professional Practice* of the National Association of Student Personnel Administrators (NASPA) concurred that "Members who accept employment with an educational institution subscribe to the general mission and goals of the institution" (p. 18).

All administrators and faculty must attend to the ethical priorities of their institutions. The standards of the American Association of University Administrators (AAUA, 1994) declared that administrators can represent their institutions within the limits of their appointments and subject to the policies of the institution. Writing in regard to faculty, the Society for Teaching and Learning in Higher Education (Murray et al., 1996, p. 63) listed "respect for institution" as one of nine ethical principles for college teaching.

Chambers (1981) noted that the ethical contract between higher education and society is to teach and study the truth and serve society as a charitable agency. Although this contract is generally applicable, individual institutions are responsible for regulating themselves in the public interest (El-Khawas, 1981). Thus, it is important that all student affairs administrators understand the specific values of their employing institution, as well as those of higher education in general. If they cannot support those values, then ethical practitioners are obligated under the ACPA Ethical Principles and Standards to seek resolution within the institution and to keep performing their duties. If they are unable to resolve the conflict and perceive that institutional values limit their ability to implement professional duties in an ethically responsible way, then the administrators' ethical obligation is to resign from the institution.

The Inevitability of Ethical Dilemmas

Being faced with so many principles and priorities means that ethical dilemmas are inevitable in student affairs administration, and they will not go away. Some of them should not go away, either, because conflict encourages consideration, and ethical deliberation is an important component of student learning.

An ethical dilemma is not a choice between right and wrong, but between two apparent rights (Kidder, 1995). Decisions are especially difficult when the alternatives appear right from different perspectives, and there are contradictory reasons to take conflicting courses of action (Kitchener, 1984). These are dilemmas of principles—when people do *not* know what is right to do—instead of dilemmas of virtue—when people do *not* know if they have the courage to do what is right (Callahan, cited in Ylvisaker, 1983). Both types of dilemmas occur each day, and not in a neutral atmosphere. Whicker and Kronenfeld (1994) reported the obvious: "Ethical dilemmas often become adversarial, pitting colleague against colleague and faculty against administrators. Feelings may run high, political mistakes may be made, perspectives may get muddied, and unmitigated reality may prove elusive. How you deal with ethical dilemmas may affect your career" (p. 4).

Some ethical dilemmas are inherent in society in general, and in higher education and student affairs practice in particular. Student affairs administrators face conflicts of rights and responsibilities whenever they walk into any student government meeting, residence hall facility, or judicial board hearing. These conflicts relate to dilemmas between community and individual welfare. Dilemmas are aroused as well when the virtues of free speech and civility are debated. Free speech allows truth, but it allows many falsehoods as well. Judicial procedures attempt to be fair, but ethical administrators must also be caring to be ethical, which means that they might change procedures in some situations to serve a greater good. It requires awareness of personal and professional value priorities, the ability to understand other priorities, and hard, values-based reasoning to resolve these dilemmas. It also takes stamina and self-esteem to accept that some decisions will be win–lose for students, institutions, staff, or ourselves (Upcraft, 1980).

WHY: ETHICS AND SERVICE

Farago (1981) offered a simple definition of ethical behavior: It "is behavior in which the actor is not motivated by self-interest. Thus, ethical behavior may be motivated by a concern for others or for some ideal" (p. 72). Ethical behavior is borne by the mission of service, by moral commitment beyond one's own self-interest. Student affairs administrators have this commitment to serve, and, thus, they are obliged to be ethical—reasonable, deliberate, and active—in fulfilling their obligations in the higher education community.

The Service Purpose of Higher Education

[Service] is the fundamental purpose of the institution of higher education. The need for services brought colleges and universities into existence, and it will be through their services that they will survive. The significance of a faculty and an administration is measured by their services—to students, to the society, to truth itself. Teaching and research are forms of service, and academic service may take many forms. (Martin, 1977, p. 98)

Higher education, as a social institution, is supported by society because it is more concerned about others than itself. It facilitates growth of people and knowledge. Teaching, research, administration, and other activities are the means and not the ends of the educational enterprise. The institution is only as good as its service. Therefore, work in higher education must be judged on moral grounds, on the good that it generates—one of the conditions of ends-based ethics.

The Service Purpose of Professions

A *profession* is more dignified than other enterprises (Becker, 1956) because it involves expert knowledge, standards of practice, training schools, sanctions, and a service orientation. The "service orientation requires professionals to attend to the needs of individual or collective clients with competent performance, and to serve and develop further capabilities with society in mind" (Young, 1997, p. 12). True professionals use their technical expertise to fulfill their social commitment (Martin, 1977). If they violate the minimum ethical standards of this commitment, then they are subject to sanctions that have been defined by the profession, including the loss of a license to practice. The standards are the "first line of defense" (Kitchener, 1985, p. 18) for professional ethical behavior and both the ACPA and NASPA Standards serve this purpose for student affairs practice.

In a 1984 survey, 91% of a sample of student affairs administrators "strongly agreed" that "student personnel is a profession" (Jacoby, Rue, & Cranston, 1985), voicing an opinion that is at odds with much of the writing about the field. Several authors have asserted that student affairs is an "emerging" profession instead of a full-fledged one (Carpenter, Miller, & Winston, 1980; Stamatakos, 1981; Wrenn & Darley, 1949; Chapter 1 in this volume), but that distinction may be unimportant in regard to ethical practice. Even the skeptics encourage student affairs administrators to be as professional as possible (Stamatakos, 1981), and that means to serve as ethically as possible.

The Service Purpose of Student Affairs Administration

The introduction to the 1999 NASPA *Standards of Professional Practice* stated that the commitment of the association is to "promote student personnel work as a profession, which requires . . . a commitment to service, and dedication to the development of individuals and the college community through education" (p. 18). This connection between the professional status of the field, its service commitment, and student development is not new, however. Years ago, Cowley (1961) identified three types of early student affairs administrators: humanitarians, administrators, and psychologists. He wrote, "Despite the diversity of backgrounds . . . [each of these groups tended] to share a common set of values which [ran] counter to those of impersonalistic professors" (p. 513). They wanted to serve students.

Some of the first deans of women and deans of men were scholars, yet they were not hired for their research skills. Lois Kimball Mathews became the first dean of women at Wisconsin because her teaching put her in contact with male undergraduates, placed her in the intellectual mainstream of the academy, and gave her an educational vision instead of just a focus on details (Fley, 1979). The first meeting of NASPA included seven members of Phi Beta Kappa, professors who were teaching at prominent institutions. At the 1920 meeting, they voiced their concern about the moral decline of students, noting "the close of the war (WW I) was followed by a sentiment of revolt against discipline and the fraternities and sororities are seriously affected by this tendency" (Secretary's Report, 1920, p. 5). That same complaint about student ethics might be made today, but whatever the details of their administrative duties, the early deans were there to help students. They "represent[ed] a point of view—a point of view of the element that gives tone to the whole organization from the one point of the student, the student as an individual, the student as a complete person" (National Association of Deans and Advisers of Men [NADAM], 1943, p. 33). They were advocates for students, men and women so bound to ethical service that they became the moral consciences of their campuses. As is noted in Chapter 1 of this volume, the same mission of professional service guides student affairs administration in the twenty-first century.

HOW: REFLECTION AND THE FUNCTIONS OF ETHICAL PRACTICE

The topic of this section is the how of ethics; it concerns the processes and functions of ethical practice. Ethical reflection is the process. It helps with decision making, so that student affairs administrators can make the best choices before, during, and after problematic situations arise. Ethical reflection involves the use of professional codes and the development of values. The functions include assessing principles and practices; setting ethical missions; helping students learn about ethics; giving voice to the community; mediating conflicts; and modeling, mentoring, and motivating.

Ethical Reflection

Ethics involves those consistent and *deliberated* acts and principles that respect human dignity and promote the greatest good for all. It requires critical thinking, and this sets ethics apart from its parent, morality. Ethics is not simply being good; it involves choosing to do good.

Ethics can be considered to be a rational response to emotional demands and moral impulses, but ethical reflection should precede and follow the onset and resolution of any particular moral dilemma. McGrory (1996) wrote that "The time for serious ethical reflection is in advance of the necessity to make difficult decisions requiring a certain facility in 'doing the right thing,' to develop strengths in the practice of ethical behavior—what St. Thomas Aquinas and Bennett (1995) would call 'virtues' and what Bellah (1985) would call 'habits of the heart'" (p. 106). Ethical administrators always reflect on their decisions of conscience, and they induce systems of personal and professional values from these reflections that guide their choices. The values enable people to make those brave decisions that might not be supported by peers or by administrative rewards; they help them skirt the dangers of moral absolutism or moral relativism. The values are neither "chiseled in stone and delivered like the law to the unwashed multitudes" nor "a matter of taste (sometimes one prefers chocolate, sometimes vanilla)" (Churchill, 1994, p. 146). They are measured guides for ethical behavior. Student affairs administrators must constantly discover, define, and organize them in order to manage those complicated ethical situations when "all that is left is the manager's intuition and the courage to do what he or she believes is right" (Upcraft, 1988, p. 75).

Ethical reflection is not usually intellectual, but it is emphatically rational. If rational reflection is avoided, the ethical criterion to fully consider the interests of others is not met. Ethical people have an impartial, *moral point of view* that considers the interest of all the individuals involved in moral situations (Lisman, 1996). An ethical administrator does not give automatic priority to one student over another, to students over faculty and administrators, or to anyone inside the college to any outsider.

Kitchener's model and the role of professional codes. Kitchener (1984, 1985) developed a multilevel model for making decisions about ethical dilemmas. It begins with the facts of a particular situation, a moral sense of these facts, and intuitive judgments. It then progresses through three levels of evaluation. The first is ethical rules, such as the ACPA or NASPA codes of professional ethics. "The next level, ethical principles, provides a general ethical framework for identifying the critical issues at stake and deciding among them. This is where a student affairs administrator would apply the five principles that Kitchener proposed. [See ACPA Statement of Ethical Principles and Standards, Appendix B of this volume.] At the highest level, ethical theories provide a rationale for deciding when ethical principles are in conflict" (p. 18). The process gets more abstract—and therefore the decision-maker becomes more cerebral—as the complexity of the ethical dilemma increases. Kitchener was concerned that ethical rules can be too general or too specific to help solve many dilemmas; therefore, her "ethical principles both provided a more consistent framework within which cases may be considered and constituted a rationale for the choice of items in the code itself" (1984, p. 46).

The fact that codes are limited does not excuse any student affairs administrator from knowing how to use them well. The codes provide the basic rules of ethics for student affairs administration. Their dos and don'ts comprise a basic list of behaviors, a guide for navigation through uncertain waters, and an objective anchor point when subjective interests are in conflict.

For example, beginning practitioners are concerned about their ethical relations with students. The transition from undergraduate status to professional status is brief, and codes can help clarify issues of professional identity and behavior. Section Two of the ACPA statement described the need to treat students as individuals, to avoid dual relationships, to limit the services that can be promised to students, and to confront students "regarding issues, attitudes, and behaviors that have ethical implications" (p. 13). That list of activities is intuitively obvious, but the standards treat these activities as professional musts instead of maybes. The codes create a sense of certainty about professional behavior, which can support beginning administrators who do not have enough experience to back their will to do right. And when the codes offer insufficient counsel, the ACPA standards offer another resource for ethical reflection. They state, "If [an] ACPA member is unsure whether a particular activity or practice falls under the provisions of this statement, the Ethics Committee may be contacted in writing" (p. 11). The writer will receive "a summary of opinion regarding the ethical appropriateness of the conduct or practice in question" (p. 11).

Additional models of reflection before action. Kitchener's model emphasizes ethical reflection *at the time* people are confronted by ethical dilemmas, and other writers have designed models for decision making at this point. Their models follow a sequence that might typify good decision making of any kind: seeking facts, considering alternatives, weighing consequences, selecting an alternative, acting on it, and evaluating the action. Ethical decision making differs from its counterparts, however, because ethical dilemmas carry a sense of moral responsibility. One's goodness is at stake as well as one's competence. Also, ethical decisions seem involuntary most of the time. They are not sought; they invade a person's life and require a response (Smith, 1996). Ethical decision-making models can be used as structures of logic to deal with these uninvited emotional and moral pressures.

The models emphasize different elements of ethical decision making, and none offers a cookbook of easy answers to complex dilemmas (Lashway, 1996). Instead, each offers different insights about the critical thinking that is necessary in ethical situations.

Brown (1990) generated a series of questions that begins with the facts of the situation, What do we know about it? Ethical people observe what is true or false. Then they ask, What does the situation mean? They make tentative value judgments while asking as well, Why does it mean that? This question is usually answered by assumptions that are taken for granted. The final question is, What should we do? The criterion is whether the responses will be right or wrong. Brown writes that people should answer the final question only after they have used external resources to verify their observations, value judgments, and assumptions. They need to involve other people in the ethical decision-making process.

This same point about inclusion was made by Elfrink and Coldwell (1993) in their INVOLVE model of value-based decision making. The model Includes all values inherent to the situation, Notes the important ones, Views the conflicts, Operationalizes strategies, Lingers in discussions, Votes the best choice, and Evaluates the consequence. Lingering prevents hasty decisions in tough circumstances; it provides the time and input necessary for positive long-term decision making.

Decisionmakers fall into an activity trap when they try to solve a problem before they define it well. The impulse to act prevents them from finding the best solution. Kidder (1995) wrote that many ethical dilemmas are actually *tri*lemmas; they offer win–win solutions that are not evident through win–lose, either–or analysis. Finding these solutions, however, requires time for reflection instead of immediate action.

Although most models focus on the rational process of reflective decision making, Niebuhr (1963) described four moments of discerning judgment that relate to decisionmakers as well as the process. The first moment comes when people respond to an ethical dilemma. Are they closed or open to it, lazy or active about it? A new dilemma is disturbing, and the initial response affects people's ability to judge the facts, much less the solutions that are available. The second moment is interpretation, when people decide which principles or assumptions are important in the situation. Niebuhr suggested being imaginative enough to perceive the entirety of the ethical dilemma. Third, people must be imaginative when they think about responses and discover what Kidder called trilemma solutions. They must balance the consequences and the principles of their judgments. Finally, Niebuhr described participation in a community of solidarity. In religious literature, the metaphor is a household of faith (Vogel, 1991). In such supportive groups, decisionmakers recognize their emotional and spiritual connection to "the community of responsibility they share with all other moral agents and affirm their destiny in relation to their total environment and to the cosmos" (Reynolds, 1996, p. 69). Those lofty words might seem pretentious, but communities of solidarity and households of faith help ethical people in those lonely times when unpopular decisions must be made.

Reflection-in-action and afterward. The authors of the promotional material for the Harvard University Program in Ethics and the Prefessions (1999) contended that ethical principles cannot be applied in a straightforward way to specific problems and policies. When real dilemmas appear, principles are revised as often as they are relied upon. New knowledge arises out of nowhere and decisions are made that conflict with every predictive theory, sometimes for the best. Schön (1987) wrote that unpredicted events challenge one's assumptions. Good decision making requires reflection-in-action, where assumptions are questioned and strategies are formulated that assimilate or accommodate the surprise.

The Harvard program advocated ethical reflection after actions are taken. It seeks to relate professional rules and real experiences to broader ethical contexts and to deep moral assumptions about professional practice. Schön called for less grand reflection-*on*-action, in which administrators examine how their assumptions contributed to the original dilemma. Administrators must use the knowledge that they gain before and during ethical decision making to enrich their specific abilities, and the general character of the profession afterward.

Key points about ethical reflection. Following are the key points about ethical reflection:

1. *Be specific.* Every ethical dilemma involves unique facts and possibilities. Just as the ACPA standards stress the uniqueness of students, so too are the situations and dilemmas that affect them.
2. *Reflect on experience.* People need to reflect on their experiences before and after ethical dilemmas are resolved in order to induce values to guide their behavior during new experiences. Student affairs administrators must

be reflective practitioners who learn from their mistakes as well as their triumphs.

3. *Involve others in the process.* People can generalize their experiences inappropriately to unique situations. Individuals need to get information from others and from their communities to make solid ethical decisions. However, ethical principles must guide what and how other people are involved in the process. A minor situation can worsen and a major situation can become a crisis if information is shared inappropriately.

4. *Understand general ethical principles.* Ethical codes and even laws are not always sufficient to resolve ethical dilemmas. Ethical principles provide a middle ground, a rationale for actions that is neither too specific nor too abstract. The student affairs administrator understands the details of the ACPA and NASPA standards and is aware of the ways the principles can apply to ethical dilemmas.

5. *Test alternative solutions.* All of the facts are gathered, and a full array of solutions is generated before the student affairs administrator tries to resolve an ethical dilemma. He or she looks for win–win possibilities that enhance educational and administrative priorities.

6. *Reflect-in-action.* Some information is not clear before administrators attempt to resolve ethical dilemmas. They must be able to adjust their theories to serve the greatest good and to create new theories for use in later situations.

Functions of Ethical Practice

The functions of ethical student affairs practice often blur distinctions between leadership and management. Ethical student affairs administrators do the right thing *and* they do things right. The functions include assessing principles and practices; developing ethical missions; helping students to learn about ethics; giving voice to the community; mediating conflicts, and modeling, mentoring, and motivating. Assessment, mission development, teaching, and mediation emphasize critical thinking. They activate the ideas of rules-based and ends-based ethics. Giving voice to the community, modeling, mentoring, and motivating emphasize behavior. They emphasize the practice of caring-based ethics.

Ethical leadership and management.   It is familiar practice to define management as doing things right and leadership as doing the right thing, and the reader will find these definitions in other chapters in this book. In this chapter, it seems important to note that "right" is a *moral* adjective in student affairs administration, which means that ethical practice is an integral part of both leadership and management. Perhaps in other fields doing things right might be defined as tidiness and doing the right thing as profit making or ego building, but that is seldom the case in student affairs. Still it is reassuring that so many authors in this book and others have described leaders as doing the *morally* right thing and, therefore, as ethical men and women.

Assessing principles and practices. Assessment builds an administrator's awareness of the moral values in an environment and of practices that fulfill those values. The simplest place to start is with a personal list, for example, by relating ethical principles to work roles. Readers can review the list of behavioral characteristics at the end of Chapter 1 and write down the different functions demanded by their responsibilities. Then they can relate each of those functions to the basic moral principles of ethics: for example, respecting human dignity, helping others, and caring. After they add other principles that are important to them, they can explore the behaviors that are required for ethical performance in each role.

This technique was used in 1985, when Krager applied the ethical principles of respecting autonomy, doing no harm, benefiting others, being just, and being faithful to four administrative roles: planning, resource management, staff development, and evaluation. In 1997, Fried and Sundberg related the same list of principles to four educational roles: interpreter–linguist, translator, transformational architect, and reflective practitioner. They did not want to use traditional role definitions because those definitions got in the way of ethical, educational practice (Sundberg & Fried, 1997).

What is good for individuals can be great for groups and organizations. Banning (1997) developed an Ethical Climate Assessment Matrix that can be used to evaluate any ethical messages that are sent through the art, signs, graffiti, and architecture of a campus. The messages are evaluated according to their ability to transmit (a) Kitchener's list of ethical principles, (b) a list of community values, and (c) elements of community change processes. The list of community values is specifically oriented to the ethical campus. Based on the work of Brown (1985) and the Carnegie Foundation for the Advancement of Teaching (1990), Banning would examined the fulfillment of the values of academic excellence, diversity, provision of a humane environment, and developmental progress for all.

In all these assessment models, the facts of the situation are measured against the criteria of ethical principles. The Krager and Fried and Sundberg models measure principles against role assignments, whereas Banning examines them against visual messages. The facts can be varied according to the needs of the users, but the principles should be fairly consistent and consensual within the system of focus. Acceptance of this technique is related to the simplicity of the models; they do not have to be sophisticated to stimulate critical thinking about ethical practices. The more they have to be explained, the less they will be used.

Such lists help student affairs administrators become more ethical in four ways. First, they help them think critically about their individual work; thus they build one of the essential skills of ethical practice. Second, the lists can be used inductively to teach them more about the ethical principles that guide practice. It is important to gain as much agreement as possible about these principles, whether that is for one person's activity, a department with many people, or an entire campus. Third, these lists can be used deductively to describe and improve practices. Finally, the lists can be used as planning devices, enabling administrators to foresee ethical dilemmas and to plan their priorities when they confront them.

Developing Ethical Missions

Wilcox and Ebbs (1992) suggested using assessments to renew personal and institutional purpose. Audits of an organization's ethical principles and practices can invigorate its mission, vision, and voice. They "increase sensitivity toward consensus building and the processes of setting values" (p. 2). Other leadership authorities expressed similar opinions. To illustrate, Kouzes and Posner (1987) wrote that shared values foster strong feelings of personal effectiveness, promote high levels of company loyalty, facilitate consensus about key goals, encourage ethical behavior, promote strong norms about working hard and caring, and reduce levels of job stress. But Wilcox and Ebbs were not writing about leadership in general, they were writing about ethical leadership in higher education and the idea that moral values should set the mission of higher education. Moral values do not make up the entire mission, but they can guide relationships—among staff, students, faculty, and other people—in every part of it. Moral values generate what Wilcox and Ebbs called "an ethics of ethos," where personal achievement increases "respect for the dignity of the person as an individual and as a member of diverse groups, academic freedom, and a well-thought-out pedagogy" (p. 4).

Talley (1997) brought this point home to student affairs administration when he discussed the relationship between quality management approaches and ethics. He declared that student affairs administrators should use quality approaches to reaffirm basic values and create systems and relationships that respect human dignity. Similar to the assertions in Chapter 1 of this volume, Talley urged student affairs professionals to be the consciences of their campuses, "to remind other administrators and faculty of why the institution exists—its purpose, its mission" (p. 65).

Helping Students Learn about Ethics

The discussion of leadership and management concerned doing the right thing and doing things right, but higher education emphasizes people and ideas more than things. It is a person-intensive environment with a unique intellectual character. Student affairs administrators deal with more things than faculty, but as educational administrators, the main focus is on developing relationships between students and ideas and turning knowledge into improved behavior. Improving student learning is the primary purpose of the field, whether it involves impacting relationships with ideas directly, or indirectly through faculty, other administrators, or campuswide programs and policy.

For most student affairs administrators, this is a counseling role, a management role, and an educational role. It is not often a traditional, in-class, teaching role, but it is still a powerful means to assist learning throughout campus. Rogers (1989) wrote that educational leaders could help students learn about ethics through the curriculum; values pedagogy; advising and personal values clarification; imparting values in institutional relationships; value analysis of the organizational structure in higher education; and values assessment in off-campus social involvement. Classroom activities were only one component in education about ethics.

There are two different tactics to helping students learn about ethics. Caring-based ethics focuses on particular behaviors, whereas rules-based and ends-based ethics focus on general ideas about behavior. Faculty might prefer to begin with rules-based ethics because it seems rational and objective, and student affairs administrators might prefer tangible, caring-based activities. Either is a fine place to begin, because behaviors lead to principles and principles lead to behaviors. And even though student affairs administrators might argue that faculty must remember the real consequences of thought, they too must remember that ethics always "calls for critical analysis and elaboration of the principles, a process that is distinct from both deductive application and case-by-case intuition" (Harvard, 1999). Student affairs administrators must be able to define, voice, and defend the beliefs—even the philosophy—behind their practices.

Values pedagogy.   Lessons about ethics can be learned both in and outside the classroom, and many faculty members prefer to keep them outside. They argue that good behavior cannot be forced down a person's throat, and although students might benefit from discussions about ethical issues, it is more important for them to think critically about other subject matter in the classroom. "Ethics cannot be taught" (Churchill, 1994, p. 147), but even if it could be, ethics would still "be too 'soft' a field to be taught in higher education" (Morrill, 1981, p. 45). Perhaps this explains why few courses on general ethics are available and most professional ethics courses emphasize codes and legal statutes— to protect the licensure of graduates so that they can display their knowledge and skills in a subject matter area.

Faculty members are partially right about forced values. Ethical behavior does not go hand-in-hand with reasoning abilities. However, that does not remove the obligation of faculty to help students think about ethics. The Hastings Project on the Teaching of Ethics (Hastings Center, 1980) reported that all students could and should learn about ethics, primarily by developing analytical skills to deal with ethical issues. Morrill (1981) concurred that ethics was different from other subjects, but it was just as valid a topic of study and it could be taught in an equally valid way.

Morrill (1981) wrote that students needed values *analysis* to study the values inherent to a situation, values *consciousness* to clarify the values in this particular situation, and values *criticism* to discover the conflicts or contradictions within a personal or social system. Values criticism is boosted through values pedagogy, which facilitates critical thinking through dialogue.

Values pedagogy requires students to be active in developing and defending positions, to be challenged about the justifications for their choices, and to confront standards and points of view that counter their personal ones. Students assume the roles of people with contrasting views and wrestle with problems that have no simple solutions.

Values pedagogy can be applied in formal and informal learning situations. Its approach can be used in a student committee meeting or in a debate in the residence halls. Its audience might be individuals who are wrestling with ethical dilemmas, academic groups that are pondering the social implications of their subject matter, or social groups that are determining their agendas. Values pedagogy can also be used in campuswide programming and counter-programming about issues involving ethics.

Giving Voice to the Community

It is not enough to improve individual ethical thinking. Student affairs administrators must do more to bring people and ideas together. Ethics always has contextual consequences; thus, it is important to expand a process like values pedagogy beyond private reflection to active social dialogue.

Strike and Soltis (1998) declared that social dialogue about ethical issues builds community. First, it reinforces a sense of common enterprise and thereby creates a sense of membership. Second, social dialogue improves the process of ethical reflection, because insights are shared. Third, the ethical principles of institutions such as education must be public, and this cannot be the case unless those principles are discussed and debated in a social forum. Fourth, community dialogue provides a context that helps individuals develop sophisticated ideas about ethical issues; it develops critical thinking skills. Fifth, and most important to caring-based ethics, ethical decisions will not be acted upon unless the involved parties agree to them. Even though agreement does not guarantee that the decision is right and the outcomes will do the most good, it makes the *process* good, and that "may itself be a factor that makes the decision morally right" (p. 111).

Mediating Conflicts in Ethical Ways

Typically, at least one of the parties in any conflict believes that his or her ethics have been violated, spawning further suspicion about any people and processes that are involved in mediating the conflict. If the mediator is not well known and trusted by all the parties, then the success of the mediation depends on the perceived ethics of the process.

Mediators must show that they want to help everyone involved in the conflict, and they must demonstrate this value repeatedly. Distrust can overwhelm the process at any time, and mediation fails if distrust is not countered with caring and evenhanded actions. Ethical mediation is evenhanded, but parties with unequal power are rarely able to perceive and accept equal treatment, for example, in conflicts between students and faculty or students and administrators. In these situations especially, mediators have to remember the imperatives of rule-based ethics: equal respect is given to all parties in the conflict and sanctions will be measured by their impact beyond the specific situation.

Modeling, Mentoring, and Motivating

The final functions do not concern the axioms of ethics as much as the adverbs of human living. The discussion of principles is left behind to see what happens when people act unselfishly, sympathetically, benevolently, kindly, generously, courteously, respectfully, charitably, patiently, tolerantly, modestly, and courageously.

Other virtues could be added to that list. Campbell (1949/1989, 1988, 1989) was charmed by the virtues of chivalry—loyalty, temperance, and courage—but these seem to be the values of patrician heroes. These people gained fame as well as grace through goodness. Many would feel more comfortable with "plebeian" heroes who do their moral duties quietly but with equal honor (McCloskey, 1994). Catford and Ray (1991) described this group of people as "everyday heroes." Their processes of thinking might be excellent, but the model of their behaviors is most remarkable; everyday heroes have the courage to do what is right outside the public eye.

Modeling.   Lashway (1996) wrote that "Students of ethics are unanimous on one point: moral leadership begins with moral leaders" (p. 2). He cited the idea of Gardner (1995) that great leaders embody the message they advocate. In short, they model integrity. Campbell agreed that heroes pursue integrity and model it for others. Women and men with integrity are the heroes of the student affairs profession; they are the ones who inspired Brown (1985), Talley (1997), and Creamer, Winston, and Miller (Chapter 1 in this volume) to declare that student affairs leaders serve as the moral consciences of their campuses. This section of the chapter is about the function served by their—and the readers'—personification of ethical leadership.

People who write about leaders often refer to their traits as well as their activities. Whether those traits are created genetically or manufactured later on, they eventually include such things as high energy, intellect, mental health, and integrity (Kotter, 1990); honesty (Lashway, 1996); and honesty, competence, vision, inspiration, intelligence, and fair-mindedness (Kouzes & Posner, 1987). Kouzes and Posner's set of traits is interesting because it was based on a survey. Eighty-three percent of the subjects in their study expected superior leaders to be honest. One might be interested to know what the other 17% expected.

Integrity is not, however, the same thing as honesty. Carter (1996) wrote that integrity requires more than finding and stating the truth. It means acting on the truth even at personal cost. A person might be entirely honest without putting her or his words into action. Carter believed that integrity is not always ethical, even though he admires people who give up their self-interest for the sake of others. Some people are quite truthful about what they will do to further their personal interests, and do it.

Ethical integrity involves three elements (Harvard, 1999). The first is moral reasoning, the critical analysis and elaboration of principles. The second is moral perception, the ability to recognize an ethical issue in a complex set of circumstances, and the third is moral character, the disposition to live ethically in a coherent way over time. The last two elements are needed to see leaders through those acts and emotions that can destroy the rational structures of assessments, planning, mission development, and values pedagogy. The sum of all three elements is "what we mean by moral wisdom, someone who can discern what to do, and also possesses the will to do it" (Lisman, 1996, p. 36).

Historical profile. Twenty years ago, a series of profiles was published about the pioneers in student affairs (Fley, 1979, 1980). The first profile was of LeBaron Russell Briggs, the first dean of men at Harvard. Briggs used himself as an instrument, as a role model, as a prodder, as a cheerleader, as an articulator of high ideals, and as an observer and commentator on student life and the aims of collegiate education. He "mastered the art of becoming a 'beloved' character" (Fley, 1979, p. 27). A Harvard alumnus wrote that he seldom saw the president, "But about Dean Briggs there could be no doubt. He was human, he was intimate, personal, vastly gentle and kind. To me and to my brothers he meant Harvard, and Harvard meant nothing else than Briggs" (Fley, 1979, p. 28). Briggs (1902) wrote, "As an institution of learning, a college must be an institution of truth; as a school of character, it must be a school of integrity. It can have no other justification" (p. 66).

Mentoring: Education from Allies

Campbell (1949/1989) believed that heroes are people who can be relied on. They might be familiar figures or pop up suddenly in the middle of one's struggles. They mentor individuals through dilemmas of principle and virtue. Although these heroes might be older and wiser, their primary role is as comrades who set the environment for learning.

Ethical mentoring differs from other forms. It is not governed by differences in knowledge and experience but by the presumed moral equality of people and the problems that everyone faces. Ethical mentoring is not a relationship that is guided by the transmission and interpretation of information. The mentor does not own the subject matter; he or she is a critical coinvestigator in dialogue with the protégé (Tom, 1984). This is the best way to help a protégé think critically about an ethical dilemma (Baumgarten, 1994).

Ethical mentors might concur with Turnbull (1995), the founder of the Boys Choir of Harlem, who believed that one cannot teach people to act with integrity. Instead, "what's most important is providing an environment in which . . . [one] can learn integrity, an environment where discipline is important, where honesty is important, where courage is important, where love is important, all those things" (p. 10). Mentors offer tools to their protégés instead of answers and advice (Campbell, 1988). They create a learning environment that virtue theorists extol, one that is immediate, that is tangible, and that works.

Krager (1985) related ethical principles to the role of mentoring. She noted that personal and professional sharing distinguishes ethical mentoring from traditional advising. Sharing is related to *respecting autonomy*. In addition, ethical mentors model good behaviors, value holistic human development—their own as well as their protégés—and are committed to *being faithful*. They act "consistently with espoused values across time and situations" (p. 45).

Historical profile. Lois Kimball Mathews was appointed dean of women at the University of Wisconsin in 1911 and authored the first book about the field, *The Dean of Women*, in 1915. In that book, she declared that the dean should not be a disciplinarian or a chaperone for girls—popular roles of the time—but an expert on women's education. The "work of the dean rested on the principle of the right of a woman to the highest possible individual, intellectual, and social development" (quoted in Fley, 1979, p. 37).

Many of her colleagues fought for equality for their students and themselves. At Cornell, Gertrude Martin developed alumnae clubs and peer advising to broaden professional opportunities for women. Mary Bidwell Breed, a chemist, was appointed dean of women at Indiana University in 1901. She decried the Victorian image of women and the segregation of women [and men] into academic fields. Her colleague, Marion Talbot, opposed restrictions in the curriculum, limits on social interaction with men, and parietal rules. Her reasoning? True freedom comes from self-control (Talbot, 1936). Talbot called the first meeting of women deans at the University of Chicago in 1903, her efforts led to the founding of the National Association of Deans of Women in 1916, and later she helped create the American Association of University Women as well.

Motivating

An artist painted an image of an upside-down person who declared, "Most people don't know that there are angels whose only job is to make sure you don't get too comfortable or fall asleep and miss your life" (Andreas, 1994). Morally wise people care so emphatically about ethical behavior that they are not always easy to get along with. These people are not limited to being lawyers, professors, or preachers and do not limit their concerns to codes of behavior. They do not draw too many diagrams on their chalkboards, and they do not sermonize about the right thing to do. They are provocateurs who make others feel more than they may wish to feel and care more than they would like. These people make invisible ethical dilemmas visible, goad laziness into action, and—in retrospect—always seem to be right. They stimulate many human emotions—empathy, caring, disgust, fear, and anguish—and, through that they build appreciation for what good thoughts really are. Morally wise people understand the logic of the *other side*; even worse, they make others acknowledge its sincerity. They tell the myopic to "look at it again," this time with their eyes wide open until they notice people and alternatives on the periphery of their interests. They make the tidy sift through moral mud. Because the worst kind of apathy occurs when issues get too close, morally wise people turn into ethnic aunts and uncles who make nieces and nephews feel guilty about their inaction. At other times they shout "Hands off!" until students are motivated to deal with the issues instead of administrators.

Historical profile.   A 1931 article in *Time* magazine featured the "well-be-loved, well-hated" Tommy Arkle Clark, at the University of Illinois (Fley, 1980). Clark thought that the primary work of student affairs administration was that of developing character, and "character is developed by doing things difficult enough to cut lines in a man's soul" (p. 32). He "looked like Mr. Chips and behaved like J. Edgar Hoover" according to one undergraduate, but when the president turned over one cantankerous student to Clark, his first words were, "Let's go get a soda and talk it over" (p. 33). Clark's efforts for students (and against overly indulgent parents) were dedicated to the principle of respecting autonomy: "He believed that students needed to learn to stand on their own feet and that the best way to learn was to do so" (p. 34).

CONCLUSION

> Socrates is recorded as saying that the unexamined life is not worth living. Why not? In our view the point of this maxim is that to fail to reflect on how one lives is to fail to recognize one's status as a moral agent. It is to refuse to accept responsibility for one's self. In a fundamental way, it is to refuse to be a person. (Strike & Soltis, 1998, p. 113)

Ethical reflection makes morality wise, and it involves the following:

1. Developing one's own defensible definitions of ethics that consider, accept, and perhaps reject attributes of morality and law, and rules-based, ends-based, and caring-based ethics.
2. Understanding one's role within a context of people and ideas. Higher education, the student affairs profession, and institutions place different demands on ethics.
3. Knowing how service demands ethical work.
4. Using structures of logic for decision-making, assessment, mission development, and the mediation of people and ideas.

Reflection without action, however, is empty. An ethical presence is illuminated by actions:

1. Declaring what one believes to be true and acting on those beliefs.
2. Living consistently, words and deeds in harmony across the different dimensions of lives—and over time.
3. Being good friends to others and facilitating their learning, not by intruding on the protégés' search for integrity, but by adding to their environment of self-discovery.
4. Motivating people to make up their own minds and take their own stands on ethical matters. This involves goading and prodding as much as hugging and consoling.
5. Building an ethical community that cares about its members, its voice made stronger by individuals who urge the least as well as the most powerful members to speak, and the most as well as the least powerful to listen.

In conclusion, it is in no way difficult to return to Mark Twain, whose suggestion initiated this chapter. His heart was made sore and his tongue quick by moral hypocrisy. In response to lynchings, he wrote that the "Moral Sense teaches us what is right, and how to avoid it when unpopular" (Twain, 1923/1963, p. 676). To young people, he said, "Always do right. This will gratify some people and astonish the rest" (Ayres, 1987). His beloved Huck Finn asked in moral anguish, "What's the use you learning right when it's troublesome to do right and ain't no trouble to do wrong, and the wages is just the same" (Twain, 1884/1912, p. 129), but Twain still made sure that Huck followed his heart and helped Jim escape from slavery.

Twain would likely have agreed with McGrory that "the glory of the human is still the ability to make moral choices" (1996, p. 107). Perhaps the glory of student affairs administration is still the ability to help students, colleagues, and campuses make such choices, and act on them.

QUESTIONS TO CONSIDER

1. What are your core ethical principles? How do they relate to the ethical principles that have been described in this chapter?
2. What ethical dilemmas occur most often in your specialty area in student affairs?
3. How can the institutional context affect your ability to use your principles to resolve these ethical dilemmas?

REFERENCES

American Association of University Administrators (AAUA). (1994). *AAUA mission statement and professional standards*. [On-line]. Available: http://www.aaua.org/mission.html

American Association of University Professors. (1974). Statement on professional ethics. *Academe, 73*(4), 49.

American College Personnel Association (ACPA). (1992). Statement of ethical principles and standards. In *1997-1998 Member resource directory* (pp. 11–14). Washington, DC: Author.

Andreas, B. (1994). *Angels of mercy*. (Lithograph).

Ayres, A. (Ed.). (1987). *The wit and wisdom of Mark Twain*. New York: Harper & Row.

Banning, J. (1997). Assessing the campus' ethical climate: A multidimensional approach. In J. Fried, *Ethics for today's campus: New perspectives on education, student development, and institutional management* (pp. 95–104). New Directions for Student Services, No. 77. San Francisco: Jossey-Bass.

Baumgarten, E. (1994). Ethics in the academic profession: A Socratic view. In P. Markie (Ed.), *A professor's duties: Ethical issues in college teaching* (pp. 155–166). Lanham, MD: Rowman & Littlefield.

Becker, H. (1956). Some problems of professionalism. *Adult Education, 6*, 101–105.

Bellah, R., Madsen, R., Sullifan, W., Swidler, A., & Tipton, S. (1985). *Habits of the heart: Individualism and commitment in American life*. New York: Harper and Row.

Bennett, W. (Ed.). (1995). *The children's book of virtues: A treasury of moral stories*. New York: Simon and Schuster.

Briggs, L. (1902). *School, college, and character*. Boston: Houghton, Mifflin.

Brown, M. (1990). *Working ethics*. San Francisco: Jossey-Bass.

Brown, R. D. (1985). Creating an ethical community. In H. Canon & R. D. Brown, *Applied ethics in student services* (pp. 67–80). New Directions for Student Services, No. 30. San Francisco: Jossey-Bass.

Campbell, J. (1988). *The power of myth: Conversations with Bill Moyers*. New York: Doubleday.

Campbell, J. (1989). *An open life: Conversations with Michael Toms*. New York: Harper & Row.

Campbell, J. (1949/1989). *The hero with a thousand faces*. New York: Meridan Books.

Carnegie Foundation for the Advancement of Teaching. (1990). *Campus life: In search of community*. Princeton, NJ: The Carnegie Foundation for the Advancement of Teaching.

Carpenter, D. S., Miller, T. K., & Winston, R. B., Jr. (1980). Toward the professionalization of student affairs. *NASPA Journal, 18*(2), 3–7.

Carter, S. (1996, February). The insufficiency of honesty. *Atlantic Monthly*, pp. 74–76.

Catford, L., & Ray, M. (1991). *The path of the everyday hero*. New York: Tarcher/Putnam.

Chambers, C. (1981). Foundations of ethical responsibility in higher education administration. In M. Baca & R. Stein, *Professional ethics in university administration* (pp. 1–13). New Directions for Higher Education, No. 33. San Francisco: Jossey-Bass.

Churchill, L. (1994). The teaching of ethics and moral values in teaching: Some contemporary confusions. In P. Markie, (Ed.), *A professor's duties: Ethical issues in college teaching* (pp. 143–154). Lanham, MD: Rowman & Littlefield.

Cortese, A. (1990). *Ethnic ethics: The restructuring of moral theory*. Albany: State University of New York Press.

Cowley, W. (1961). *An overview of American colleges and universities*. Columbus: Ohio State University.

Elfrink, V., & Coldwell, L. (1993). Values in decision-making: The INVOLVE model. In R. Young, *Identifying and implementing the essential values of the profession* (pp. 61–74). New Directions for Student Services, No. 61. San Francisco: Jossey-Bass.

El-Khawas, E. (1981). Self-regulation: An approach to ethical standards. In M. Baca & R. Stein, *Professional ethics in university administration* (pp. 55–62). New Directions for Higher Education, No. 33. San Francisco: Jossey-Bass.

Farago, J. M. (1981). Academic chivalry and professional responsibility. In M. C. Baca & R. H. Stein, *Professional ethics in university administration* (pp. 63–81). New Directions for Higher Education, No. 33. San Francisco: Jossey-Bass.

Fley, J. (1979). Student personnel pioneers: Those who developed our profession. *NASPA Journal, 17*(1), 23–39.

Fley, J. (1980). Student personnel pioneers: Those who developed our profession. *NASPA Journal, 17*(3), 25–44.

Gardner, H. (1995). *Leading minds: An anatomy of leadership.* New York: Basic Books.

Hanson, K. (1996). Between apathy and advocacy: Teaching and modeling ethical reflection. In L. Fisch (Ed.), *Ethical dimensions of college and university teaching: Understanding and honoring the special relationship between teachers and students* (pp. 33–36). New Directions for Teaching and Learning, No. 66. San Francisco: Jossey-Bass.

Harvard University Program in Ethics and the Professions. (1999). *What is practical ethics?* Cambridge, MA: Harvard College.

Hastings Center. (1980). *The teaching of ethics in higher education.* Hastings-on-Hudson, NY: Author.

Jacoby, B., Rue, P., & Cranston, P. (1985). *The student personnel profession: Is there shared identity within our diversity?* Presented at the Association of College Personnel Administrators convention, Boston, MA.

Kerr, C. (1994, January/February). Knowledge ethics and the new academic culture. *Change,* 9–15.

Kidder, R. (1994). *Shared values for a troubled world.* San Francisco: Jossey-Bass.

Kidder, R. (1995). *How good people make tough choices.* New York: William Morrow.

Kitchener, K. (1985). Ethical principles and ethical decisions in student affairs. In H. Canon & R. D. Brown, (Eds.), *Applied ethics in student services* (pp. 17–30). New Directions for Student Services, No. 30. San Francisco: Jossey-Bass.

Kitchener, K. (1984). Intuition, critical evaluation and ethical principles: The foundation for ethical decisions in counseling psychology. *The Counseling Psychologist, 12,* 43–55.

Kotter, J. (1990). *A force for change: How leadership differs from management.* New York: Free Press.

Kouzes, J., & Posner, B. (1987). *The leadership challenge.* San Francisco: Jossey-Bass.

Krager, L. (1985). A new model for defining ethical behavior. In H. Canon & R. Brown, *Applied ethics in student services* (pp. 31–48). New Directions for Student Services, No. 30. San Francisco: Jossey-Bass.

Lashway, L. (1996, June). Ethical leadership. *ERIC Digest, 107* (ED 397 463).

Lisman, C. D. (1996). *The curricular integration of ethics: Theory and practice.* Westport, CT: Praeger.

Martin, W. (1977). Summary: Teaching, research, and service—let the last be first. In W. Martin (Ed.), *Redefining service, research, and teaching* (pp. 93–99). New Directions for Higher Education, No. 2. San Francisco: Jossey-Bass.

McCloskey, D. (1994). Bourgeois virtue. *The American Scholar, 63,* 177–191.

McGrory, K. (1996). Ethics in teaching: Putting it together. In L. Fisch (Ed.), *Ethical dimensions of college and university teaching: Understanding and honoring the special relationship between teachers and students* (pp. 101–107). New Directions for Teaching and Learning, No. 66. San Francisco: Jossey-Bass.

Morrill, R. (1981). *Teaching values in college.* San Francisco: Jossey-Bass.

Murray, H., Gillese, E., Lennon, M., Mercer, P., & Robinson, M. (1996). Ethical principles for college and university teaching. In L. Fisch (Ed.), *Ethical dimensions of college and university teaching: Understanding and honoring the special relationship between teachers and students* (pp. 57–64). New Directions for Teaching and Learning, No. 66. San Francisco: Jossey-Bass.

National Association of Deans and Advisers of Men (NADAM). (1943, 5 August). *The NADAM shout (Blood, sweat, and tears: News, notes, noise, nosings, and nonsense).* Urbana: University of Illinois.

National Association of Student Personnel Administrators (NASPA). (1999). Standards of professional practice. In *Member handbook* (pp. 18–19). Washington, DC: Author.

Niebuhr, H. R. (1963). *The responsible self: An essay in Christian moral philosophy.* New York: Harper & Row.

Rawls, J. (1971). *A theory of justice.* Cambridge, MA: Belknap.

Reynolds, C. H. (1996). Making responsible academic ethical decisions. In L. Fisch (Ed.), *Ethical dimensions of college and university teaching: Understanding and honoring the special relationship between teachers and students* (pp. 65–74). New Directions for Teaching and Learning, No. 66. San Francisco: Jossey-Bass.

Rodabaugh, R. (1996). Institutional commitment to fairness in college teaching. In L. Fisch (Ed.), *Ethical dimensions of college and university teaching: Understanding and honoring the special relationship between teachers and students* (pp. 37–46). New Directions for Teaching and Learning, No. 66. San Francisco: Jossey-Bass.

Rogers, W. (1989). Values in higher education. In C. T. Mitchell (Ed.), *Values in teaching and professional ethics* (pp. 1–14). Macon, GA: Mercer University Press.

Schön, D. (1987). *Educating the reflective practitioner.* San Francisco: Jossey-Bass.

Secretary's report of the Conference of Deans and Advisors of Men. (1920, February 20, 21). Urbana: University of Illinois.

Smith, D. C. (1996). The ethics of teaching. In L. Fisch (Ed.), *Ethical dimensions of college and university teaching: Understanding and honoring the special relationship between teachers and students* (pp. 5–14). New Directions for Teaching and Learning, No. 66. San Francisco: Jossey-Bass.

Stamatakos, L. (1981). Student affairs progress toward professionalism: Recommendations for action. Parts I and II. *Journal of College Student Personnel, 22,* 105–111, 197–206.

Strike, K., & Soltis, J. (1998). *The ethics of teaching.* New York: Teachers College Press.

Sundberg, D., & Fried, J. (1997). Ethical dialogues on campus. In J. Fried (Ed.), *Ethics for today's campus: New perspectives on education, student development, and institutional management* (pp. 67–80). New Directions for Student Services, No. 77. San Francisco: Jossey-Bass.

Talbot, M. (1936). *More than lore: Reminiscences of Marion Talbot.* Chicago: University of Chicago Press.

Talley, F. (1997). Ethics in management. In J. Fried (Ed.), *Ethics for today's campus: New perspectives on education, student development, and institutional management* (pp. 45–66). New Directions for Student Services, No. 77. San Francisco: Jossey-Bass.

Tom, A. (1984). *Teaching as a moral craft.* New York: Longman.

Turnbull, W. (1995, 17 November). Integrity. *USA Weekend,* p. 10.

Twain, M. (1923/1963). The United States of lyncherdom. In C. Neider (Ed.), *The complete essays of Mark Twain.* Garden City, NJ: Doubleday.

Twain, M. (1884/1912). *The adventures of Huckleberry Finn.* New York: Collier & Son.

Upcraft, M. L. (1988). Managing right. In M. L. Upcraft & M. J. Barr (Eds.), *Managing student affairs effectively* (pp. 65–78). New Directions for Student Services, No. 41. San Francisco: Jossey-Bass.

Vogel, L. (1991). *Teaching and learning in communities of faith.* San Francisco: Jossey-Bass.

Whicker, M., & Kronenfeld, J. (1994). *Dealing with ethical dilemmas on campus.* London: Sage.

Wilcox, J., & Ebbs. S. (1992). *The leadership compass: Values and ethics in higher education.* ASHE-ERIC Higher Education Report No. 1. Washington, DC: ERIC Clearinghouse on Higher Education.

Winston, R. B., Jr., & Dagley, J. C. (1985). Ethical standards statements: Uses and limitations. In H. Canon, & R. Brown (Eds.), *Applied ethics in student services* (pp. 49–66). New Directions for Student Services, No. 30. San Francisco: Jossey-Bass.

Wrenn, C. G., & Darley, J. (1949). Appraisal of the professional status of student personnel work (pp. 264–287). In E. G. Williamson (Ed.), *Trends in student personnel work.* Minneapolis: University of Minnesota.

Ylvisaker, P. (1983). Ethical problems in higher education. *AGB Reports, 25*(1), 28–35.

Young, R. E. (1982, May–June). Faculty development and the concept of "profession." *Academe, 73,* 12–14.

RECOMMENDED READING

Amundson, K. J. (1991). Teaching values and ethics. *American Association of School Administrators' Critical Issues,* Report 24. Arlington, VA: American Association of School Administrators.

Canon, H., & Brown, R. D. (Eds.). (1985). *Applied ethics in student services.* New Directions for Student Services, No. 30. San Francisco: Jossey-Bass.

DePree, M. (1997). *Leading without power: Finding hope in serving community.* San Francisco: Jossey-Bass.

Fried, J. (Ed.). *Ethics for today's campus: New perspectives on education, student development and institutional management.* New Directions for Student Services, No. 77. San Francisco: Jossey-Bass.

Kidder, R. (1995). *How good people make tough choices.* New York: William Morrow.

Kouzes, J., & Posner, B. (1993). *Credibility.* San Francisco: Jossey-Bass.

Moline, J. (1981). Classical ideas about moral education. *Character, 2*(8), 1–6.

Vaill, P. (1991). *Managing as a performing art.* San Francisco: Jossey-Bass.

Young, R. B. (1997). *No neutral ground.* San Francisco: Jossey-Bass.

PART III

MANAGING AND ADMINISTERING

*O*ne of the most important sets of activities carried out by student affairs administrators concerns day-to-day management and administrative responsibilities. Whether those responsibilities concern the operation of a small student support program with few other staff members and rudimentary funding or the maintenance of a large institutionwide student affairs division with many staff members and a multimillion-dollar budget, it is important that the student affairs administrator comprehend the essence of maintaining the organization. They must manage its people, budgets, and programs; formulate and enforce policies; and mediate conflicts on a daily basis. Part III of this text focuses attention on the goals and process of managing in a student affairs context.

Chapter 7, Organizing Student Affairs Divisions, written by Sandeen, who has many years experience as a successful chief student affairs officer, is the lead chapter of this section. He presents a historical perspective of the evolution of student affairs organizations and the forces that influenced the changing purposes, structures, and staffing practices over the years. Further, the chapter explores the changing character of college students, institutional administrators, academic organizations, financial resources, and technology and identifies issues that student affairs administrators will address in the future. Finally, the chapter presents several examples of current organizational structures and provides insight into the ways these structures will likely evolve in the future.

Chapter 8 is entitled Staffing Student Affairs Divisions and focuses on the importance of judicious, skillful selection and supervision of the human resources essential to successful student affairs practice. Carpenter outlines a staffing model specifically tailored to the unique goals and structures within student affairs divisions. Strategies for recruiting, selecting, hiring, orienting, and employing high quality staff members are provided as are recommended procedures for supervising and managing staff members. Finally, he addresses the important issues of professional staff development and performance appraisal.

Chapter 9, Finance and Budgeting, is written by Doug Woodard, who has many years experience preparing and managing student affairs division level budgets. This chapter addresses salient trends that influence resource acquisition and allocation; the management decision-making cycle; budget structures, processes, and approaches; and pertinent advice about managing budgets. The chapter's focus is on comprehending budgetary nomenclature and models and the basic steps involved in developing, planning, prioritizing, implementing, monitoring, and evaluating institutional and program budgets.

The final chapter in Part III is entitled Resolving Conflicts by Janosik and Hirt. This chapter adds a dimension to the administrative process that is too often overlooked in the literature even though it is extremely important to those responsible for managing the work of student affairs staff, administering student affairs programs and service units, and working with students who are involved and invested in the institution's cocurriculum. This chapter reviews the causes of conflict between and among organizations, persons, and groups; conflict resolution strategies; and processes and procedures that administrators can use to manage conflict effectively.

READING SUGGESTIONS

Readers will likely find it helpful to read Chapter 7, Organizing Student Affairs Divisions, early on as they peruse this book because it provides a comprehensive overview of the administrative structures common to the field of student affairs and presents the context within which most student affairs administrators function. The other three chapters in Part III address topics that are relatively independent and can, therefore, be read in any order, depending on the reader's interests and concerns.

7

Organizing Student Affairs Divisions

ARTHUR SANDEEN

M ost colleges and universities in the United States provide support services and related programs to their students. The institutional component most intimately involved in the process is usually referred to as student affairs, student services, or student life, and most institutions are expected by students, parents, and the general public to provide such programs and services. In this chapter, the development of these organizations, the reasons they were created, and their purposes are discussed. Major factors influencing the student affairs organizations are presented and issues affecting student affairs organizations are addressed. Examples and suggestions about future student affairs organizational structures are offered, and recommended readings are included, as well as some questions for further discussion.

THE DEVELOPMENT OF STUDENT AFFAIRS ORGANIZATIONS

When President Charles Eliot at Harvard asked LeBaron Russell Briggs, a young English professor, to assume a newly established dean's position in the college in 1890, Briggs had no job description and no staff. His assignment was vaguely described as "looking after the needs of the students." It was clear that President Eliot was hoping to be relieved of some of the bothersome and timely complaints of the young undergraduate male students, and, thus, the position was created. Dean Briggs, by all accounts, did a marvelous job (Brown, 1926) and became a legend at Harvard and a model for future generations of deans because of his caring and personal treatment of students. But, he did not have to concern himself about how to organize a student affairs division because he was a one-man operation. How, then, did student affairs divisions in all of their current complexity emerge from this quaint and simple model?

The transition from college to university, the growth of coeducation, the increased enrollments, the emphasis upon faculty scholarship, the increased attention to individual differences, and the expectation that colleges should monitor, if not control, student behavior were major factors leading to the development of student affairs divisions as they are known today. As student activities such as sports, student government, and social groups became popular and were encouraged by the colleges as relatively constructive ways to fill students' out-of-class time, various staff members were hired to supervise these functions. With increasing numbers of students, it became apparent that the vocational and psychological needs of students required attention, and persons were employed to specialize in such matters. Similar developments occurred in student health, admissions and registration, housing, academic advising, religious affairs, student unions, and student employment. Eventually, it was logical to bring many of these functions together in some organized fashion, and this led to the creation of student affairs divisions.

In the 1930s, the most influential document ever published in student affairs, *The Student Personnel Point of View* (*SPPV*, American Council on Education [ACE], 1937) was released. Sponsored by ACE, *SPPV* gave increased visibility and support to the development of the field. The document described many of the major functions in student affairs, and many institutions organized their student services and programs in accordance with the functions described in this landmark statement. It also stressed the educational role of student affairs and the importance of cooperation with academic departments in contributing to the learning of students.

To reflect the different expectations for men and women, most institutions established two parallel student affairs organizations based upon gender. Thus, the dean of men and the dean of women positions were created and from about 1910 until almost 1960 these positions reflected the dominant organizational structure in student affairs. The structure was based on the assumption, of course, that men and women required separate attention, including different policies for residences, social rules, and dress codes. This arrangement, considered by most people to be consistent with societal expectations, resulted in organizations with obvious duplication of services and, at times, strained administrative relationships. It also tended to reinforce a secondary role for women, who were excluded from many curricular and professional opportunities, and discouraged their full and equal participation in campus life.

When enrollments exploded after World War II and when the civil rights movement and the women's movement emerged as powerful social forces in American society, the nature of campus student life changed substantially. Most colleges and universities during this time scrambled to accommodate large increases in their student bodies, and in the mad rush to keep up with students and their changing needs, new policies, programs, and services were created rapidly. The 20-year period after World War II resulted in dramatic changes in higher education, and this was especially true for student affairs. It is important to note that the impetus for this change was almost entirely the result of social, economic, and political forces external to the colleges and universities themselves.

The significant changes taking place in American society resulted in new aspirations for social justice, especially in regard to race, gender, and economic background. The civil rights movement, gaining new visibility and support in the late 1950s, signaled a new day for the country, and the American dream of personal achievement being determined by hard work and ability, as opposed to privilege, race, or gender, seemed to be a real possibility. A college education became the almost exclusive vehicle to upward economic mobility and success, and the United States Congress responded to these rising expectations and the need for equal opportunity by establishing federal financial aid programs. These aid programs reflected the public's demand for more access and increased diversity in higher education. In the 1960s, opposition to the Vietnam War, together with the newly acquired voting privileges for 18 year olds, caused millions of college students to question their traditional relationships with the educational institutions they attended. Widespread disruption took place on campuses, and most students rejected the old notion that their college should serve in place of their parents. Within this climate of tremendous enrollment growth and social change, increased demands for services, and a societal concern about how to control student behavior, the organizational structures of student affairs divisions changed as well.

Many departments, such as admissions, housing, registration, counseling, job placement, student union and activities, and student health had become quite large at state universities. Moreover, a whole array of new services had emerged, created largely by student demands, special fees, or new legislation. Thus, departments of financial aid, orientation, academic support services, recreational sports, child care, group legal services, and crisis centers were established. At the same time, it became obvious that the old dean of men/dean of women organizational structure was outmoded and did not fit the current culture of the campuses. The response of many institutions, beginning in the early 1960s, was to create a consolidated student affairs division, headed by a senior administrative officer who reported to the president. The various departments, headed by directors or deans, reported to the senior student affairs officer, and policies, programs, facilities, and services were to be coordinated through this organizational arrangement. This basic structure has now been maintained for the past 35 years and has resulted in greater recognition and influence for student affairs within most institutions. There are many variations of this model, and these will be discussed later in the chapter. The model emerged for a variety of reasons, which are described in the next section.

REASONS WHY NEW ORGANIZATIONAL
STRUCTURES WERE CREATED

The purpose of an administrative structure is to accomplish the goals of the organization. Often, a new or revised structure is created to solve existing problems that were not effectively addressed by the previous one. Of course, the simple creation of a changed organization is not generally sufficient, in itself, to improve services or to solve difficult problems. But new organizational arrangements can create the conditions wherein able leaders can accomplish significant goals. Presidents with the approval of their governing boards established the coordinated, campuswide student affairs division, headed by a senior administrative officer. Because of the proliferation of services, the demands for efficiency, and the need to avoid costly duplication, the necessity for consolidation and coordination became obvious. There were other, perhaps less obvious, reasons as well. Similar consolidations in college and university administration were likewise occurring in academic, business, and development offices. Presidents wanted and needed a manageable number of senior administrators to handle the increasingly large and complex activities of the institution. College and university presidents eagerly accepted the idea of a central management team, and in most instances the senior student affairs officer became part of this team. A major contributor to this newly elevated status for student affairs was the campus turmoil of the 1960s. With so much time and public attention focused on noisy student protesters, student affairs was on center stage and it was necessary to give it high visibility. Indeed, many senior student affairs officers during this period were hired or retained in direct relation to their ability to handle student disruptions effectively. It is not unreasonable to assert that the primary reason the large, consolidated student affairs division, headed by a senior administrator, was created was in response to campus unrest. The coordination of services was essential, but presidents, governing boards, and local, state, and federal governments were very anxious about the campus turmoil and wanted someone to handle these problems. The enhancement of services for students was a useful outcome of this situation, although not necessarily its primary cause. If it was necessary for presidents to elevate student affairs to a central role within the institution to keep the peace on the campus, the appointment of a senior student affairs officer and the creation of a coordinated student affairs division were small prices to pay.

As campus life became more hectic, competitive, and bureaucratic, organizational units often became more independent of one another and the overall institution. This had been true for years with academic departments, but now many colleges and universities, even small institutions, became splintered. The continuing expansion of services required additional staff and facilities and was very expensive. Expansion in student affairs generally met surprisingly little opposition from faculty in the 1960s, as many of them welcomed release from what they considered bothersome advising duties or some vague responsibility for student behavior. Money flowed into most institutions during this decade, and most faculty members knew their best professional opportunities for advancement were in research and scholarship, not in student life. Thus, faculty for the most part acquiesced to the newly expanded role for student affairs organizations during this time. Most did not want to perform support or service functions themselves, and there were enough institutional resources to ensure that specialists without diminishing financial support for faculty could provide these functions. Student affairs organizations flourished and grew rapidly until the mid-1970s. At many institutions, the number of professional staff members in such areas as admissions, financial aid, career planning, and recreation doubled or even tripled. As new needs were identified, new offices were created to address them and were added to student affairs organizations.

When dominant external issues, especially the Vietnam War and the civil rights movement, were diminished considerably around 1975, the expectations for student affairs again began to change. Keeping the peace by resolving difficult student protest issues was no longer so central, and with many colleges and universities feeling the effects of inflation, comparatively flat enrollments, and fewer resources, the emphasis in many student affairs organizations shifted to efficient management of essential services. Thus, student affairs organizations became leaner, relied more upon student fees for support, engaged in entrepreneurial activities, and converted some departments into self-supporting auxiliaries. Senior student affairs officers found that they spent much more time competing with vice presidential colleagues on the campus for resources. The structure of the student affairs organization was largely determined by the press of institutional priorities. Consequently, it became increasingly more important for the senior student affairs administrator to persuade the president about student needs and, often, to find ways to support them within existing institutional resources. It is not surprising that consolidation of departments and the termination of some student affairs functions occurred during this time.

Despite the daunting problems of the period 1975–1990, many student affairs organizations proved themselves to be effective problem solvers and service providers. Moreover, many became significant contributors to the learning of students, via collaboration with faculty and academic departments in a variety of activities, such as retention, academic advising, leadership development, and service learning. As a result, on some campuses the student affairs organization was asked to assume responsibility for such functions as intercollegiate athletics, campus bus services, police departments, academic support services, food services, and large facility management, among others. At some institutions, especially large ones, the division of student affairs included several hundred employees and its budget totaled millions of dollars. Even on smaller campuses (see section on Lafayette College later in this chapter), the organizational structure became quite complex and extensive. The organizational structure of some institutions included major branches addressing student life, enrollment management, administrative services, and auxiliary operations. No longer was the student affairs organization viewed exclusively for student control issues, or even student services; it was a major part of the general management and the

educational program of the institution. On campuses where student affairs organizations were viewed as being incapable of assuming these additional roles,
or when student affairs leaders chose to maintain traditional roles as the sole
focus, their overall impact, especially in educational programs, was diminished.
Moreover, many of these faulty organizations were forced to relinquish some
responsibilities and reporting relationships as a result.

Student affairs organizations during the decade of the 1990s tended to
enjoy better financial times, but were nonetheless subjected to growing scrutiny by presidents, provosts, and the students themselves. Where student affairs organizations did not have the clout or competence to retain such key
functions as admissions, financial aid, or registration, the functions were transferred to another institutional officer, most often the senior academic officer,
often known as provost. In other cases, the entire student affairs division was
transferred from reporting to the president to reporting to the provost or an
executive vice president. This issue is discussed in more detail later; however, it
is clear that such changes have usually occurred because of changed expectations and new perceptions of student affairs by those external to it. The importance of the educational role of student affairs administrators cannot be emphasized enough in any discussion of the organization of student affairs. If staff
members throughout the division are engaged with faculty in collaborative efforts to enhance the learning of students, it is very likely that the student affairs
organization will continue to thrive and be viewed as an important component
of the institution.

The particular form that the student affairs organization has assumed over
the 110 years of its existence has evolved continuously. Its structure, breadth of
responsibility, and reporting relationships has been largely a function of external factors, both inside and outside the institution. There is no such thing as an
ideal or permanent student affairs organization; any existing structure is simply
a reflection of the desires and needs of the institution to meet its goals in a
timely fashion.

PURPOSES OF STUDENT AFFAIRS ORGANIZATIONS

The purposes of any student affairs organization are to support the mission of
the institution and to serve the educational and personal needs of students.
These goals may include creating a supportive campus environment, improving
the graduation rate, reducing student attrition, developing special educational
programs, improving campus racial relations, increasing enrollment, responding humanely to student traumas, developing effective leadership programs,
enhancing the learning environment, or providing efficient services. There are
other goals that could be listed as well; some student affairs organizations may
attempt to do all of these things!

Student affairs organizations may include assigned purposes and functions
that they may actually prefer not to do! They may also believe they should have

responsibility for some purposes or functions that are assigned elsewhere. The student affairs division is rarely the sole determinant of the areas it is obliged to organize and administer. Yet it can be very influential with campus leaders regarding the programs and services it pursues, and, of course, this is a major responsibility of the senior student affairs officer. All members of the student affairs staff can influence the way the organization develops, especially through efforts to contribute to students' education by collaborating with faculty in the various academic departments.

The purposes of the student affairs organization should be clearly stated, understood by everyone, and possible to achieve. They should be consistent with the ability of the staff, the mission of the institution, and the available resources. They should not be so vaguely stated that nothing tangible can be accomplished. It is often wise to focus on a smaller number of achievable goals and to be successful with them than to try to be all things to the campus (Kouzes & Posner, 1995).

At times, the student affairs organization may find its purposes to be in conflict with other institutional programs, standards, or traditions. For example, in its desire to create a welcoming and supportive climate for students, the division may actively support the full participation of gay and lesbian students in campus life; however, the institution may not be willing to support any such actions or policies. Or, within the student affairs organization itself, there may be a conflict regarding the resource priorities given to Greek student groups as opposed to those provided to minority student groups. These conflicts regarding purposes can affect the structure of the student affairs organization, especially when one department is moved to a position of increased authority or provided more resources. When disagreements about purpose occur, cooperation and trust within the organization suffer as well.

Senior student affairs officers must understand the mission of their institutions clearly, as well as the priorities of the president (Sandeen, 1991). It is their responsibility to articulate the purposes of the student affairs organization in a coherent and persuasive manner. When all staff members within the division are engaged in educational efforts, especially with faculty, to enhance learning opportunities for students, the support for student affairs will be increased. The organizational structure of the student affairs division emerges from its purposes and should be designed in a manner to implement them.

FACTORS INFLUENCING HOW A STUDENT AFFAIRS DIVISION IS ORGANIZED

There are many factors that influence how a student affairs division is organized. There is no single organizational model that fits every institution, and changing campus conditions may require a change in a model that has worked quite well for many years. The following discussion explores factors that affect the structure of student affairs organizations.

Institutional Mission and Culture

As previously noted, the most important factor in determining how the student affairs division is organized is the institution's mission and culture (Schein, 1992). A large state university, a religiously affiliated college, a public community college, and a private women's college have very different missions and cultures and these differences should be reflected in how they organize their student affairs divisions. The components of the various divisions will vary, as will the emphasis given to certain functions. The mission and culture of the institution also affects the kinds of staff hired for leadership positions within the organization. One college's mission may be to attract and educate the underprivileged; another's may be to develop religious missionaries; another's may be to prepare students for graduate and professional studies; and yet another's may be to serve the economic needs of the local community. The student affairs organization at these campuses may include components for admissions, financial aid, and academic advising, but the emphasis given to each may differ considerably. Moreover, there may be departments (for example, community service, commuter affairs, multicultural programs, outreach and recruitment, or leadership development) that may have a prominent role at one institution and not even exist at another. Even among public institutions, where the formal, published mission statements may appear similar, there are often distinctive cultural and historical differences, and these often are reflected in their student affairs organizations. One state institution may have a long tradition of leadership development, another a tradition of academic honor, and another may emphasize social service. Despite these differences in mission and culture, the basic roles of education, leadership, and management for student affairs administrators remain crucial for the success of the organization.

As of 1999 there were 4,096 colleges and universities in the United States (*The Chronicle of Higher Education*, 1999), with considerable diversity among them regarding mission and culture. Each of these institutions' student affairs division should be organized to reflect and support its unique mission and culture.

Professional Background of the Student Affairs Staff

Another very important factor affecting the student affairs organization is the ability of the staff itself. The senior student affairs officer must determine this. If there are staff members who do not have the background or professional training to lead departments effectively, and the senior student affairs officer does not have the option of replacing them soon, the organization most likely will require fairly tight controls and very little authority will be decentralized. Much of the planning and policy making will be done from the top of the organization to assure quality, consistency, and credibility. Where there is a high degree of confidence in the professional ability of the staff, and when their actions have resulted in positive outcomes over time, more autonomy and freedom to act will likely be granted to the departments. It is very important for the senior student affairs officer to understand the ability of the staff and the way it is perceived by students, faculty, and others, and then to organize the division in a way that uses staff members' talents most effectively. If staff members are not granted much authority in decision making, their morale and performance may suffer; however, the senior student affairs officer has the responsibility to assure the quality and success of the organization and must make decisions that enable this to happen. When there is a high level of confidence in the staff to contribute to the education of students and the various units are granted considerable autonomy, there are many risks for the organization. Mistakes and poor services can occur, and the senior student affairs officer will be held accountable for them! Balancing the benefits and liabilities of centralized and decentralized organizations is highly dependent upon the professional ability of the staff and the personal style and abilities of the senior student affairs administrator and is crucial to the success of the organization.

Student Characteristics

Student affairs organizations exist to support their institutional missions and to enhance the education of their students. No individual or office on the campus should be more knowledgeable about students and their educational and personal needs than the student affairs staff collectively. An effective student affairs organization reflects this knowledge of students and the varying backgrounds and needs within the student body. Some colleges have assumed that the same organizational approach will work equally well with all students; this almost always results in many students going unnoticed or feeling alienated. The best student affairs organizations work to identify special educational needs within the student populations and create structures that can meet these needs. A student financial aid program may have a central office and standard rules and procedures that can be accessed fully via the World Wide Web. There are likely several groups and students (and potential enrollees), however, who may not be served well by such a model. Setting up small, personalized offices in academic departments, student residences, churches, or shopping centers might be better alternatives for certain students. In another example, a campus may have operated a traditional student union for many years and have found that it is no longer the center of social activity it once was and seems to attract only certain groups of students. A good student affairs staff will understand why and will know where various groups of students go for their social activities. It may adapt the structure of the union to attract a larger variety of student groups, or it may develop new programs on other sites, on and off campus, to help build social communities. As a third example, an institution, such as a community college, that admits large numbers of underprepared students is very likely to have an active academic support services department in its student affairs organization. Indeed, it may be the dominant area of the organization, provided with the best and most visible facilities and the most substantial budget. At a highly selective

college, such a unit most likely would not even exist. All colleges and universities, large and small, have considerable diversity within their student bodies.
The best student affairs organizations will reflect these special populations and
will engage in regular assessment so that they can understand and adapt to the
inevitable changes that occur.

Presidents and Senior Academic Officers

Senior student affairs officers serve at the pleasure of their presidents and, of
course, are expected to support their presidents and their policies and priorities
for the institution. Presidents expect senior student affairs officers to organize
their divisions in ways that meet the needs of the students and do not usually
participate in the day-to-day affairs of the division. The senior student affairs
officer should decide who in the organization would have access to the president, if any. Most senior student affairs officers will reserve this responsibility
for themselves, to ensure that any confusion about policy or other matters can
be avoided. If the president enjoys being with students and is effective in such
settings, the senior student affairs officer can make arrangements for this to
happen. If the president is not interested in meeting often with students or is
not well received by them, however, then other options should be pursued.
Some presidents may want to be involved in admissions, student conduct, residence hall assignments, and registration. Others may expect all such matters to
be handled by the student affairs division and may feel the student affairs staff
is weak and indecisive if they are asked to participate personally in such matters. When a president is confident in the ability of the student affairs division
to handle problems effectively and deliver good services, the impact on the
student affairs organization can be very positive. Their ideas and efforts will be
valued, and more creative efforts may result. It is the responsibility of the senior student affairs officer to understand the style, priorities, and talents of the
president and adapt the organization accordingly. All members of the student
affairs staff, however, can help establish good relationships with the president,
and it is often midlevel or entry-level staff members who are most perceptive
about students' educational needs. Presidents change offices fairly often, and
there are frequently important differences from one administration to another.
What was assumed to be a good practice for a previous president may be viewed
as a poor idea by a new one.

Typically, the provost (executive vice president or chief academic administrator) has responsibility for the majority of the institutional budget and, other
than the president, occupies the most influential position on campus. When the
student affairs division reports directly to the provost, there may be better opportunities for collaboration with academic programs, easier and more rapid
access to decisions, and less of a perception by others that student affairs is a
separate entity that is concerned only with "nonacademic" matters. On the other
hand, this reporting procedure may limit direct opportunities to convince the
president about student needs and issues. There also may be a perception among

students and faculty that the student affairs division is not a full member of the institution's management team and that the division might suffer from an unequal status with academic, business, and development affairs. But, as Barr argued (1993), one frequently has to look beyond formal reporting lines to understand how organizations actually work. She described dual reporting, whereby the senior student affairs officer reports to the provost but sits as a member of the institution's management team, headed by the president. Even when the senior student affairs officer reports directly to the president, most of the contact and decisions may be made with the provost, as the president may be away from the campus frequently. Other major institutional officers, such as those leading business, research, and development, also may report to the provost, who increasingly may act as the institution's chief internal operating officer. The key factor is leadership. Wherever the student affairs organization reports, its role in enhancing learning opportunities for students should be central to all its efforts.

Even though presidents and provosts rarely dictate the structure of the student affairs organization, their personalities, academic priorities, and personal strengths and weaknesses have a major impact on what the student affairs organization does and how it conducts business. They also have a strong influence on the departments and functions included in the student affairs division. The senior student affairs officer is responsible for earning the trust and support of presidents and provosts, which is crucial to the success of the organization.

Academic Organization

How the institution organizes academic programs and how extensive they are can have a major influence on the student affairs division. On a relatively small campus, without graduate or professional schools, it is likely that each student affairs office will serve all students. On larger campuses, some services and programs may be decentralized into the graduate school and to professional colleges such as medicine, law, and veterinary medicine. These colleges may handle such functions as admissions, registration, financial aid, student conduct, and career placement. Sometimes there are joint appointments between the central student affairs division and the colleges on these matters, and such arrangements can lead to effective coordination and collaboration. They may also be essential to assure consistency in policies, staff salaries, and professional advancement opportunities. Senior student affairs officers may spend a good deal of time negotiating with individual colleges that seek more autonomy in such areas as placement policies or student conduct procedures. These interactions often test the skill and authority of senior student affairs officers and the organizational structures they have established. The colleges, and especially the professional schools, may have extensive resources and considerable power on the campus, and the student affairs division may have to adapt its own organizational structure to accommodate these factors. There may be a time when the senior student affairs officer must ask the president or provost to settle a jurisdictional dispute between a professional school and the student affairs division. However, if this is done too often, it may be a signal to the president that a more basic organizational or personnel change might be necessary.

Financial Resources

Both the amount and the source of financial resources available can have an important influence on the way a student affairs division is organized. The student affairs staff may make a compelling case for programs and services that everyone, including the president, agrees would improve student life; however, they cannot be implemented because there are insufficient funds to support them. Even on campuses with large endowments, there are rarely enough resources to fund all of the good ideas suggested by staff and faculty. Facilities also may affect the organization of the student affairs division, especially if there is a central building dedicated to student services functions. When various departments are scattered throughout the campus (for example, when they are located in college offices or in separate buildings) the challenge of bringing them together as a functioning whole is difficult. It is rather easy to draw an organizational chart that describes reporting lines and interactions; it is much more difficult to get various offices actually to work together in harmony, especially when they are physically distant from one another.

Student fees support student affairs divisions entirely or in part. The student affairs division may be dependent on these fees for operating funds, facility expansion and renovation, program support, and staff salaries. Many student affairs functions, including admissions, housing, orientation, student health, food service, recreation, and child care are funded in this manner. If the students have some degree of control of these fees, such as deciding annually how much a fee will be, or which priorities should be supported, the student affairs organization can be directly affected. Such arrangements, although now very common, present real dilemmas for the student affairs staff who may enjoy enthusiastic support of student leaders one year and be viewed as the enemy the next, depending on a campus issue or a clash in personalities. It certainly can be argued that a dependence on student fees for support will assure that the student affairs organization will be responsive to real student needs. It can also be argued that current students are very limited in what they see as important educational programs from one year to another and that professional staff members should not be captives of the political whims of young, or inexperienced students. If students vote down support fees for a Hispanic/Latino cultural center or a special sexual assault counseling unit despite the urgings of student affairs staff members, there is an obvious impact on the organization. Funding via student fees can be a double-edged sword for student affairs leaders. On one hand it may result in financial resources that would never have been possible from the institution's general fund, but on the other hand it may result in a dependency on annual student politics that seriously restricts the freedom of the division to build a first-rate student affairs program. Whatever the amount or source of financial resources available to student affairs, all staff members have the responsibility to use them in ways that ensure the success of the organization. Most important, the educational and leadership role of student affairs on the campus must be emphasized, and the quality of students' learning experiences should not be subjected to the unpredictable nature of student fee support.

Technology

Just 10 years ago, only a few campuses used electronic mail; the Internet was virtually unknown; and conducting essential campus services on the World Wide Web was rare. Now, all of these technological developments are common on campus and are taken for granted by students and their parents. After surveying large groups of students, Levine and Cureton (1998) suggested that students may expect their relationship with their institutions to be similar to the one they have with their bank—instant access to all services with a card or personal identification number, 24 hours a day! Technology has had an enormous influence on how student affairs divisions are organized and how they make their services available to students. Students on many campuses can sit at a computer anywhere and, with adequate identification and financial resources, apply and be accepted for admission, apply for and check the status of their financial aid, pay their tuition and housing bills, order and pay for their semester's books, and communicate directly with employers and schedule on-campus interviews. All of this has happened during the past decade, and it is logical to assume that even more dramatic technological developments will be available in the next few years. Within this rapidly changing environment, student affairs divisions may need to rethink their organizational structures. Traditional departments and qualifications of new staff members might need reconsideration. Educational programs might be devised via technologies that increase learning opportunities for students outside the classroom. These are issues being discussed on every campus now as student affairs organizations struggle to find a balance between the easy accessibility and efficiency of technology and the educational and developmental needs of students. Student affairs staff members know that for most campus functions, because of technology, it is no longer business as usual. It is their job to organize divisions efficiently and to deliver services and educational opportunities to students without such previous obstacles as waiting lines, restricted availability, or uncooperative employees. They are keenly aware of the growing competition from private companies, many of which are eager to provide traditional campus services for a fee. But they also are aware that vital student affairs programs such as values development, leadership training, and community service cannot be effectively learned except through face-to-face interaction and involvement. Moreover, a student may receive information about admissions, curricula, financial aid, and employment over the Internet, but there are very important decisions that students have to make about such matters that require extended thought and interaction with

faculty and staff—either face-to-face or electronically, and at this point the electronic interface seems far less effective than the interpersonal encounter for
most students.

The student affairs division is now extremely dependent on technology,
and, at times, may be influenced too heavily by it. The need to address students'
educational needs more effectively through the wonders of technology will only
become more challenging in future years. (See Chapter 6 in this volume.) As a
result, the organizational structure and ways of delivering educational programs
will certainly change. (See Chapter 12 in this volume.)

Legislation and Court Decisions

At the state and federal level, legislation has been enacted that directly affects
student affairs and how it is organized. The most obvious example is financial
aid legislation, which has transformed higher education by making college accessible to virtually everyone. The state and federal legislation regarding financial aid has created large new departments on nearly every campus, and no
other student affairs office is more crucial to the success of the institution.
Moreover, amendments to financial aid legislation over the years have mandated institutions to develop new policies, programs, and services in areas unrelated to financial aid. Drug abuse counseling, voter registration, and campus
disruption penalties are examples. Student affairs divisions have been significantly influenced by legislation and court decisions regarding campus security,
privacy of records, student conduct rules, use of student activity fees, and alcohol abuse. Student conduct records have been defined as noneducational in
nature by at least one state court and thus are open to public view. Some states
are now requiring parental notification when under-age-21 college enrolled students violate alcohol laws or policies. These legislative and court decisions have
policy, staff, and fiscal impacts on the student affairs organization. New resources
are needed to fulfill the requirements of the laws, and often this means changes
have to be made in the student affairs organization as staff members are transferred from what they had been doing to new, mandated activities. Obviously,
this can easily disrupt the overall student affairs program, as the new requirements are frequently not activities the institution would have chosen to do on
its own. Student affairs leaders must establish the educational and leadership
needs of their students as the primary criteria in making any organizational
changes.

Legislation and court decisions affecting student affairs organizations confirm the litigious nature of American society in 2000. Much of the legislation
passed during the 1990s seems to assume that college students over the age of
18 are not considered adults by society and that the public expects institutions
of higher education to revert to assuming an in loco parentis relationship with
students. If this conservative trend continues, the changes for student affairs
organizations will be dramatic. New staff and new programs will be needed to
meet the public's expectations to monitor students' behavior and to report be-

havioral infractions to parents. Such a fundamental change in the student–institution relationship would have a profound impact on the quality of student life and on the ability of students to learn to take responsibility for their own actions. Student affairs leaders will serve their institutions and students well in the next several years by becoming informed participants in this important debate. The educational needs of students should be the basis for policy decisions at the institution, as opposed to a temporary political fad.

ISSUES THE STUDENT AFFAIRS ORGANIZATION SHOULD ADDRESS

Effective student affairs organizations have lean structures, are responsive to changing needs, open to new ideas, committed to student learning, and in touch with their various constituencies. They are also aware of the sometimes-conflicting expectations that students, faculty, staff, the larger community, and institutional leaders have for them. The following discussion reflects some of the key issues student affairs organizations should address to serve the educational needs of students effectively.

Span of Control

As student affairs organizations have grown, both in size and function, a basic organizational problem must be faced; that is, how many departments should report directly to the senior student affairs officer? Many senior administrators want to be personally involved in guiding the operations of each department, and this model can work well when the number is manageable. But some student affairs divisions now have as many as 15 different functional units—from the bus system and bookstore to the women students' program—and have found it advisable to have some departments reporting to associate senior student affairs officers, thus adding another administrative layer to the structure. This can free the senior student affairs administrator to work directly with only 3 or 4 administrators who are responsible for various parts of the student affairs division. The second tier administrators can give more focused and personal attention to the departments, but this structure can also make some staff members feel disconnected and can lead to isolation and poor communication within the division. An alternative to this model is to consolidate the 15 departments into 6 or 7 and retain the direct reporting relationship to the senior student affairs administrator. Such consolidation, however, may not work well, as 2 or 3 departments merged into one may result in confusion for students and a lack of coherence for staff. The span-of-control issue is an important one for the student affairs organization, even on smaller campuses, and each institution should review its staff organization periodically to assure that it is functioning effectively. Again, the primary criterion used to guide the student affairs staff is how the organization will affect the education of students.

Participation in Decision Making

Most student affairs professionals want to have a role in deciding what educational programs and services are provided, and the policies that guide the division. Moreover, most student affairs organizations recognize this and find it to be a strong asset. Divisionwide committees, task forces, and study groups have been created to review budgets, policies, and programs. Senior student affairs administrators must decide how extensive the participation in decision making will be in their divisions. They must find a balance between the benefits of staff involvement and the obvious need to get things done in a timely fashion. The student affairs organization needs to be responsive and agile to keep up with student issues and problems and can damage its reputation by spending too much time studying a problem. Students who are angry about financial aid delays deserve to have their problem solved quickly and will not be satisfied by being told that a committee is reviewing the matter. Neither will the president be satisfied by this response. And after the president receives 10 letters complaining about dirty residence halls, it is time to clean them up, not to study the problem further. But there are many important issues, such as how to use institutional scholarship funds, where to place a new recreational facility, how to assign students to residence halls, how to fund a major leadership development initiative, or how to integrate honors students into Greek houses that invite wide participation by staff. Moreover, their involvement will likely lead to better decisions and ones that will be more readily understood and accepted.

The student affairs division should model the type of student involvement in decision making it advocates for the rest of the campus. Students from all parts of the campus should be invited to participate at all levels of decision making in the division. Such involvement is usually a positive educational experience for the students and frequently produces new ideas and valuable insights.

Consistent Messages

The student affairs organization should demonstrate through action that it has integrity and consistency. If the senior student affairs administrator announces a policy, then the division as a whole should act on it. Students, faculty, parents, and others must see that the organization does what it says it will do and what it believes. This is important for the professional staff in the organization as well. If the organization is to be effective, staff members must know how much autonomy they have and that their decisions will be respected by the senior student affairs administrator. Moreover, if the student affairs organization grants authority to student government groups, but then ignores or regularly overturns their decisions, negative relations and distrust will quickly result. Faculty members must also be able to rely upon the student affairs organization when they need assistance with a difficult student, when they would like to collaborate on an educational program, or when they encounter a student who has cheated on an exam. The ability of the student affairs organization to respond in a reliable and consistent manner to students and faculty is very important to its success.

Dual Authority

Some student affairs divisions may have dual reporting relationships. Admissions and student financial aid may jointly report to student affairs and the senior academic officer; the student health service may be shared by student affairs and the medical school dean; the housing department's maintenance and rent collection may be handled by business affairs, whereas programming, discipline, and general operations report to student affairs; the child care center may be shared by student affairs and the College of Education or family services; and the fund-raising office may be a joint effort between student affairs and the development office. Such organizational arrangements can be confusing to students and staff alike if there is a reluctance by leaders to communicate effectively or to be responsive to problems. Student affairs staff members should work closely with their administrative colleagues to assure that departments operating under a split authority relationship give consistent and timely messages to students and staff. At times, these dual authority departments have serious personnel, financial, and operational differences that may have to be resolved by one division taking over the office entirely. Such organizational problems are often difficult, but they must be confronted and solved to assure that good services, consistent policies, and effective educational programs are provided.

Evaluation

The student affairs organization is highly visible because of the very nature of its work. Much of it affects the lives of students and their families, and, thus, a variety of people have the opportunity to formulate opinions about it. A student may have a good experience with admissions, financial aid, housing, and the food service, but if that same student was treated poorly in the student health service, questions may be raised about the quality and performance of the entire student affairs division. Some faculty may view the student affairs organization in a very limited fashion, believing it must be doing well if students are not being disruptive. Parents may have yet another set of views about student affairs, with an emphasis on personal security for their offspring. Some campus administrative units may scrutinize student affairs departments primarily on the basis of their fiscal health. Student affairs organizations cannot escape the varying perceptions and expectations that these diverse groups have of them and must understand the potential impact such informal and sometimes vocal evaluations can have on their activities. Most student affairs staff members have very different notions about how their work should be evaluated. To explain their views, they should describe the purposes of the organization for the public in ways that are easily understood. If the student affairs organization does not have confidence in what it does and responds defensively to those who criticize it, its insecurity as an organization will become obvious and will become a significant liability. The emphasis should be upon the contributions the student affairs program is making to the learning of students.

Isolation

As student affairs organizations become increasingly professionalized and specialization continues to develop, the very dangerous problem of isolation can occur. This problem may be exacerbated when most student affairs staff members work in a building specifically designed for them. Staff members may become very comfortable interacting almost exclusively with one another, speaking their own professional language and sharing concerns that are largely known only to them. Such physical and psychological isolation, although unintentional, can seem very attractive and secure. It, however, is a sure way of death for student affairs organizations. The strength of any student affairs organization rests in the relationships it develops with faculty, other administrators, student groups, and local community members. Outreach, collaboration, and joint ventures should be the norm. As with other issues facing the student affairs organization, the senior student affairs administrator must ensure that such isolation is avoided. Staff members in every office should be expected to be visible and active participants in both campus and community life. The student affairs organization is not an entity unto itself. Its purpose is to serve the educational needs of students, and this is best done by active engagement with students and faculty.

EXAMPLES OF ALTERNATIVE STUDENT AFFAIRS ORGANIZATIONAL STRUCTURES

As noted through out this chapter, the organizational structure of student affairs divisions is affected by many factors, especially the size and mission of the institution. Following are some concrete examples of organizational structures in markedly different kinds of institutions.

The University of Texas at Austin

The main campus of the University of Texas, located in Austin, is presented as an example of a large, public institution with a highly developed professional student affairs organization. Its structure is intended to combine the advantages of both centralization and decentralization. The senior student affairs administrator reports directly to the president. There are 14 separate departments in the division, 5 of which are responsible directly to the vice president.

The University of Texas enrolls more than 48,000 students on its Austin campus and has one of the largest and most extensive student affairs programs in the country. Moreover, the campus itself is large, and the student affairs facilities are purposely located in a variety of areas for student convenience. The current vice president, James Vick, who developed the structure, believes that it represents an effective compromise between a completely flat model and a strongly decentralized approach. He indicated that the 10 people reporting to him keep him very busy, but he believes this direct involvement enables him to stay well informed about issues and remain accountable to both staff and students. The structure works well, he added, because of the strong, experienced professional staff members who lead each of the departments (James Vick, personal communication, August 3, 1999).

The structure at the University of Texas is also organized to enhance learning opportunities for students, with strong emphases upon community service and leadership development. Vick stresses the importance of collaborating with faculty on programs and policies that improve educational opportunities for students.

Figure 7.1 displays the student affairs organizational chart of the University of Texas at Austin.

The University of Missouri at Kansas City

The University of Missouri at Kansas City is cited as an example of a midsized urban public university with an extensive student affairs program and organization. The senior student affairs officer has the title of vice chancellor for student affairs and enrollment management, reflecting the strong institutional emphasis on recruitment, selection, and retention of students.

Although all of the departments report to the vice chancellor, there is an assistant to the vice chancellor position, and this aids in the coordination and direction for the division.

Of special note at the University of Missouri at Kansas City is the liaison relationship between student affairs and the student support offices in each of the institution's 13 colleges and schools. This academic–student affairs link provides many opportunities for collaboration and cooperation in handling student issues and problems, and for enhancing learning experiences for them.

The senior student affairs administrator noted that he has created what he calls "cluster management teams" (Gary Widmar, personal communication, August 10, 1999) in the division. These are enrollment management, student leadership and development, and auxiliaries. This cluster approach is designed to ensure cooperation and coordination among closely related departments and to improve the overall quality and efficiency of services. The student affairs organizational chart of the University of Missouri at Kansas City is displayed in Figure 7.2.

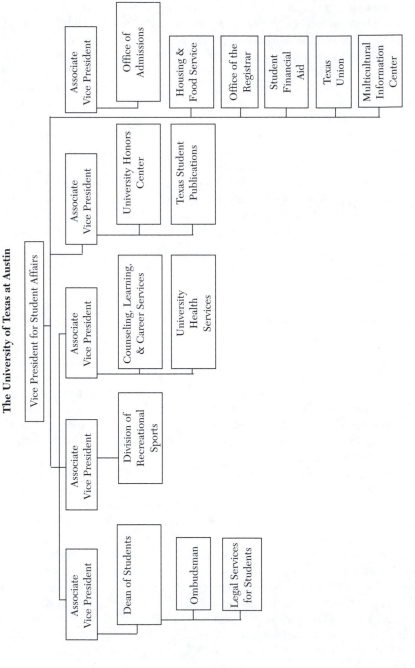

The University of Texas at Austin

Vice President for Student Affairs

Associate Vice President
- Dean of Students
- Ombudsman
- Legal Services for Students

Associate Vice President
- Division of Recreational Sports

Associate Vice President
- Counseling, Learning, & Career Services
- University Health Services

Associate Vice President
- University Honors Center
- Texas Student Publications

Associate Vice President
- Office of Admissions
- Housing & Food Service
- Office of the Registrar
- Student Financial Aid
- Texas Union
- Multicultural Information Center

FIGURE 7.1.

University of Missouri at Kansas City

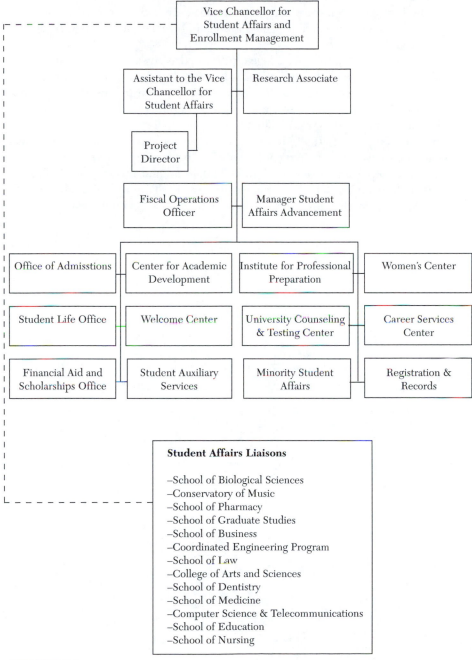

FIGURE 7.2.

Santa Fe Community College

Santa Fe Community College, located in Gainesville, Florida, enrolls more than 14,000 students in a wide array of programs designed to prepare students for further higher education and for positions in business, technology, health careers, and government service.

Santa Fe Community College is presented as an example of a comprehensive community college where the academic and student affairs functions have been effectively combined and coordinated. Patricia Grunder serves as the vice president for educational services and reports directly to the president. This organizational model was developed, according to Grunder (personal communication, August 21, 1999), to integrate the major curricular and cocurricular functions of the college in the institution's effort to educate the whole student.

Also reporting to the senior student affairs administrator is the director for research, planning, and performance assessment. The student affairs division works very closely with this office and with applied technology and arts and

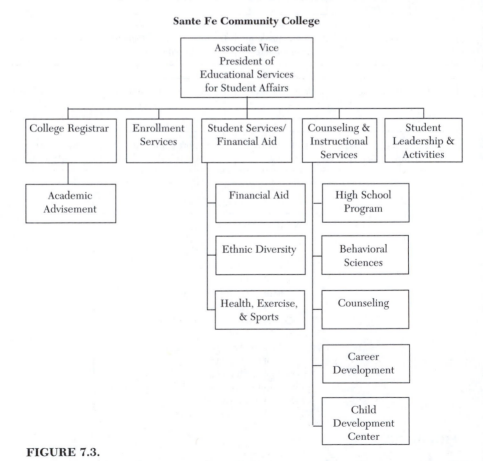

Sante Fe Community College

FIGURE 7.3.

sciences divisions to develop systematic assessments of their academic and cocurricular programs.

The structure at Santa Fe Community College places the student affairs division within the same organization as all of the major academic and applied technology programs. As a result, there is very little separation between academic and student affairs staff members and good coordination and cooperation are assured in their joint reporting relationships to the vice president for educational services. Santa Fe's organizational chart is displayed in Figure 7.3.

Lafayette College

Lafayette College is a highly selective liberal arts and engineering institution, located in Easton, Pennsylvania. Its enrollment is 2,200 students. Herman Kissiah, dean of students, is the senior student affairs administrator and has been in that position for nearly 30 years.

Kissiah reports to the president of the college and works very closely with the provost and the dean of the college, who have responsibility for the admission, financial aid, and the registrar offices. Because the college is relatively small in comparison to the other institutions described earlier, there is frequent interaction with the faculty and very little separation between academic and student affairs matters. Dean Kissiah has the advantage of an extended tenure in his leadership position. He has made adjustments in the organization over these years, depending upon the priorities and style of the president, the nature of student issues and problems, and the abilities and professional aspirations of the staff. "Especially at a small college, the actual 'paper structure' of the organization is probably not as important as the quality of the relationships the staff develops with students and faculty," Kissiah said (personal communication, August 5, 1999). The student affairs organizational chart for Lafayette College is presented in Figure 7.4.

THOUGHTS FOR FUTURE STUDENT AFFAIRS ORGANIZATIONAL STRUCTURES

Student affairs organizations are dynamic, not static, and should be flexible and responsive to the changing needs of both students and the institution. Even though a current administrative arrangement may be comfortable to the staff, student affairs leaders should not assume that any given structure is permanent. Services and programs can be delivered in a variety of ways, and it is very likely that many student affairs organizational structures will look different in 2010 than they do in 2000. Presented herein are some considerations student affairs leaders should reflect on as they contemplate future organizational structures.

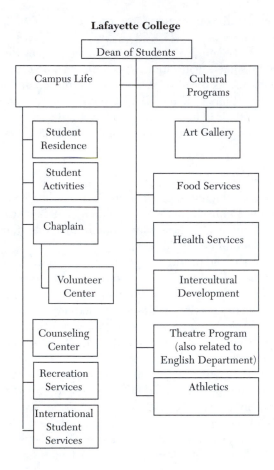

FIGURE 7.4.

Institutional Mission

Governing boards are quite properly directing their institutions to be more focused, that is, to define clearly who they are and what they are trying to do. Higher education is still lagging behind the corporate world in this regard, but the trend is unmistakable. Student affairs leaders should be active participants in this conversation and will benefit from revising and reshaping organizations to reflect more sharply defined institutional missions. Whether the mission relates to public service, international understanding, technological competence, vocational preparation, social activism, or intellectual excellence, the student affairs organizational structure always should reflect the dominant emphasis of the institution. Student affairs leaders should regularly ask themselves this question: "Does what we are doing and how we are organized help advance the mission of the institution?"

Technology

This topic was discussed earlier, but a few additional thoughts are offered here. Technological changes are happening so fast that it is difficult for student affairs leaders to know what hardware and software systems to buy for such major functions as financial aid, admissions, and registration. There is the ever-present fear that a major financial investment may result in a system that does not work or that will be obsolete by the time it is installed. Because the stakes are so high for institutions and their students, student affairs leaders should consult widely with colleagues within and without the campus to educate themselves about technology. Otherwise, they and their organizations will simply become passive recipients of whatever developments occur outside of student affairs, and their organizations will be changed by others in ways they can neither predict nor control. At this point in time, no other issue causes student affairs leaders more financial or organizational anxiety than does technology.

Outsourcing of Services

Student affairs leaders are being approached by companies who assert that they can provide effective and timely services at a lower cost than the institution is now paying. These "privatization" claims are being made for student health services, housing programs, counseling services, student publications, and registration programs. It is likely that similar offers soon will be made regarding admissions and student recruiting. It is already common for such functions as food services and bookstores to be outsourced; it is very likely that outsourcing will become more common in the future. It has become virtually standard practice in large corporations who want to focus energy and resources on their key activities as opposed to matters considered ancillary to their real business. Many student affairs leaders believe strongly that what they do is crucial to the institution's educational mission. They should not be defensive about the possible outsourcing of services; instead, they should be working to assure that each of their departments is functioning effectively and is contributing to the institution's educational goals and to student learning. The competition is already here, and student affairs leaders should view it as a challenge to improve the educational quality and operational efficiency of their organizations. If student affairs leaders can function effectively as educators, other institutional officers will view their programs as viable entities.

Assessment and Accountability

At all levels of higher education, the public, expressed through legislative action, governing boards, parents, and employers, is demanding evidence of the actual benefits to students of the college experience. There is currently a strong emphasis on assessment in higher education (Upcraft & Schuh, 1996; see also Chapters 13 and 14 in this volume) and although much of it may rely on reputational factors, or be conducted simply to satisfy external constituencies, some of it is genuinely carried out to improve the quality of students' educational experiences. Student affairs leaders must not rely entirely on others to construct accountability and assessment programs for them. When they do, the programs may focus on matters that have minimal relevance or use for the improvement of student life. Rather, student affairs administrators should take the lead by using some of the excellent materials already available to them and find ways to conduct systematic assessment programs within their divisions. However, much of the activity in this area is defensive in nature, there being a fear that "negative data" might result in the elimination of a program or department. Student affairs administrators can contribute to a more professional approach to assessment by taking the lead with genuine assessment programs that can improve the quality of education and the learning of students.

Growing Departmentalism

Student affairs as a profession has advanced in very impressive ways during the past 35 years. Most persons now working in the field have completed graduate degree programs and there are increasing numbers of outstanding, well-educated new professionals entering the field annually. At the same time, many of the services and programs have become better defined and developed, as standards of good practice (Blimling & Whitt, 1999), professional functions and standards (Miller, 1999), and other useful guides have been published. This enhanced definition has resulted in the creation of more than 30 national professional associations within the student affairs field that focus upon somewhat specialized student affairs functions. Student recreation, health, unions, judicial programs, orientation, housing, and career counseling, among many others, now have active professional associations with publications, conferences, regional officers, workshops, and journals. For the most part, this is a healthy development, reflecting efforts to improve the quality of services and providing excellent professional growth opportunities for the people working in each specialty. But there are serious concerns among student affairs leaders that this proliferation of professional organizations is splintering the field, encouraging departmental isolation, and making communication more difficult among various student affairs functions on the campus and throughout the country. Student affairs professionals, whether they work in counseling, student aid, admissions, or housing, have a great deal in common, and it is these similarities, not differences, that should be emphasized. Student affairs leaders will do well to assess this situation on their own campuses and encourage participation by staff in professional association activities, but the overall student affairs organization must function as a whole, not as a collection of autonomous, separate departments. It is very important that student affairs administrators take leadership in ensuring that the coordination of their educational programs and services is maintained.

The Search for Resources

Student affairs staff members know that their ability to secure financial resources is essential for any success they might achieve. Indeed, most of them spend considerable time attending to this very task. Funds to support student affairs functions come from a variety of sources, depending on the nature of the institution. Some may come from student fees, some from rent on facilities, some from program charges, some from entrepreneurial activities, and some from tuition or the institution's general fund. Most student affairs staff members are aware that there will rarely be enough financial resources to do all the things they consider necessary for students' education and, as a result, have followed the lead of their academic colleagues by establishing fund-raising units of their own. Most often, these offices are established in conjunction with the institution's development program. This relatively new trend has significant organizational implications for divisions of student affairs and for senior student affairs officers in particular. Deciding what staff to hire for this program, how to pay them, and where they will concentrate their efforts are all-important questions to address. Most institutions that have established such programs have discovered that they require considerable time and effort and frequently require staff members to be away from the campus to meet with donor prospects. If this is done, adjustments will have to occur within the student affairs organization for it to continue to meet its other obligations effectively.

Additional Challenges

Especially on larger campuses, many colleges and professional schools have established student support programs and services. These academically based programs often provide excellent opportunities for the student affairs organization to establish cross-functional teams and connections. By focusing on specific groups of students (for example, graduate students, dental students, or Hispanic students in the physical sciences), support programs can be developed that engage student affairs and faculty from a variety of areas, regardless of formal reporting responsibilities. The most effective student affairs organizations in the future will be relatively seamless, able to respond quickly to changing needs and conditions, and will not be encumbered by traditional reporting lines to accomplish their objectives. Higher education and student affairs administrators, in this regard, will be following examples set by leaders in business and management (Nanus, 1992; O'Toole, 1995). Because of the increasing emphasis upon student learning and personal development as well as student learning communities, it is both desirable and likely that student affairs administrators will increasingly work very closely with both faculty members and academic affairs administrators. In view of the rapid innovations in technology, which will inevitably lead to many traditional service functions being offered via the Internet or by outside contract, student affairs leaders will benefit from building strong alliances with academic teaching and learning programs. This will require increased levels of flexibility on the part of student affairs administrators, and the traditional departmental structures currently in place on most campuses may need to be reconfigured. Consequently, it may be useful to envision a student affairs organizational structure for the future that is focused not on traditional services or support programs, but on desired student learning and personal development outcomes. Such an organization would need to be quite fluid and include professional staff and faculty members from several areas. Such a reconfigured organization might even constitute a newly created component of the institution that replaces the traditional student affairs division. Such a new organization could also become a part of the provost's office, assuring the creation of effective links with the institution's colleges and academic departments. In addition to these possible changes, student affairs leaders will benefit by demonstrating that they can be successful fund raisers, problem solvers, fiscal managers, and institutional spokespersons. With the guidance of their presidents, they should also be active with their governing boards, helping them understand the changing nature of student life and diversity and their importance in achieving educational excellence and the institution's mission.

CONCLUSION

The primary purposes of a student affairs organization are to support the mission of the institution and contribute to students' learning. The organizational structure does not exist to make the lives of its staff members more comfortable. It is a structure that continues to evolve, and this dynamic aspect should be viewed as an asset, not a liability. There is no standard structure that can fit all institutions equally well, and an organizational model that worked effectively 10 years ago may need significant realignment to be effective today. Student affairs administrators should view the organizational structure as a vehicle for carrying out their education, leadership, management, and service goals. The emphasis should be upon quality of education as experienced by students and continuing efforts should be made to integrate the various units within the division into a coherent whole. The student affairs profession, while still relatively young, has progressed significantly in the past four decades and with effective leadership will continue to be a vital contributor to the education of students in years to come.

QUESTIONS TO CONSIDER

1. Who should initiate change in the student affairs organizational structure? What are the consequences if the change is initiated from outside the organization?
2. How can current student affairs leaders and their staff adjust to changes that may alter the basic ways they have conducted their work for many years?
3. Assuming student affairs organizations will continue to evolve, how should graduate programs in the profession be changed to prepare future leaders for the new challenges in higher education?

REFERENCES

American Council on Education (1937). *The student personnel point of view* (Ser. 1, Vol. 1, No. 3). Washington, DC: Author.

Barr, M. J. (1993). Organizational and administrative models. In M. J. Barr & Associates, *The handbook of student affairs administration* (pp. 95–106). San Francisco: Jossey-Bass.

Blimling, G. S., & Whitt, E. J. (1999). *Good practice in student affairs: Principles to foster student learning.* San Francisco: Jossey-Bass.

Brown, R. W. (1926). *Dean Briggs.* New York: Harper & Row.

The Chronicle of Higher Education. (1999). Almanac of higher education. Washington, DC: Author.

Kouzes, J. M., & Posner, B. (1995). *The leadership challenge: How to keep getting extraordinary things done in organizations.* San Francisco: Jossey-Bass.

Levine, A., & Cureton, J. S. (1998). *When hope and fear collide: A portrait of today's college student.* San Francisco: Jossey-Bass.

Miller, T. K. (Ed.). (1999). *CAS: The book of professional standards for higher education.* Washington, DC: Council for the Advancement of Standards in Higher Education.

Nanus, B. (1992). *Visionary leadership: Creating a compelling sense of direction for your organization.* San Francisco: Jossey-Bass.

O'Toole, J. (1995). *Leading change: Overcoming the ideology of comfort and the tyranny of custom.* San Francisco: Jossey-Bass.

Sandeen, A. (1991). *The chief student affairs officer: Leader, manager, mediator, educator.* San Francisco: Jossey-Bass.

Schein, E. A. (1992). *Organizational culture and leadership: A dynamic view.* San Francisco: Jossey-Bass.

Upcraft, M. L., & Schuh, J. H. (1996). *Assessment in student affairs: A guide for practitioners.* San Francisco: Jossey-Bass.

RECOMMENDED READING

Balderson, F. E. (1995). *Managing today's university: Strategies for viability, change, and excellence.* San Francisco: Jossey-Bass.

Bolman, L. G., & Deal, T. E. (1997). *Reframing organizations.* San Francisco: Jossey-Bass.

Hesselbein, F., Goldsmith, M., & Beckhard, R. (1996). *The leader of the future: New visions, strategies, and practices for the next era.* San Francisco: Jossey-Bass.

Kouzes, J. M., & Posner, B. Z. (1993). *Credibility: How leaders gain and lose it; Why people demand it.* San Francisco: Jossey-Bass.

8

Staffing Student Affairs Divisions

D. STANLEY CARPENTER

S tudent affairs administration, like any complex societal and human endeavor, is a confluence of people and context. Whether the merge is happy or not at any given college or university depends mightily upon such disparate components as geography, reputation, mission, history, and resources—the things that make campuses unique. Also crucial on any campus are the procedures and policies surrounding the interactions of the people who compose the organization and its structure. Taken together, we can think of these as staffing practices and this chapter is concerned with such systems in the area of student affairs.

Nothing is more important to effective practice in student affairs administration than the people who serve the students and manage the institution. Accordingly, it is fitting that significant attention be paid to the principal issues of staffing, namely, recruitment and selection, position orientation, supervision, continuing education and development, and performance appraisal. This chapter is designed to discuss these important issues following the lead of the Winston and Creamer (1997) Staffing Model (WCSM).

A MODEL OF STAFFING PRACTICES IN STUDENT AFFAIRS

There is little literature available that directly and specifically addresses staffing issues in student affairs, particularly in theory-based and/or data-based ways. There are strands that touch on individual aspects, such as recruitment, retention, and burnout of staff members, professional preparation, and competencies for entry-level, midlevel, and senior level professionals, and nuggets buried in general handbooks for practice and books and chapters on functional practice areas. A full treatment of the literature is beyond the scope of this chapter, but the reader is referred to Dalton (1996), Lovell and Kosten (2000), Windle (1998), and Winston and Creamer (1997), for relatively recent compilations. Dalton (1996) is also a good example of writers who have captured parts of the staffing picture but leave specificity to individual practice. He noted the demise of traditional organizational theory and suggested that modern human resource management is concerned with "(a) helping employees master the specific competencies necessary for success in their assigned duties . . . (b) helping employees understand and cope—professionally and personally—with the culture and requirements of their work environments . . . [and] (c) helping employees engage in continual learning, professional development, and personal renewal" (pp. 495–496).

Winston and Creamer (1997) provide the only comprehensive treatment of student affairs staffing issues, which forms the foundation for this chapter, augmented by further research, background, and experience of the author. In skeletal form, Winston and Creamer (1997) states that

> Staffing practices involve interrelationships among recruitment and selection, orientation, supervision, staff development, and performance appraisal.
>
> Staffing practices reside within and are shaped by the culture of the institution.
>
> The institution is susceptible to multiple environmental forces that influence staffing practices in both obvious and subtle ways. (p. 19)

The value of this conceptualization lies not in its uniqueness or revelatory power, but rather in its codification of tacit knowledge and in urging the profession to new levels. Especially important to note is that the processes of staffing do not stand alone. Proper recruitment and selection carries the seeds of orientation, for example, which should foreshadow job requirements, an expectation for professional development, and knowledge of the performance appraisal approach. Supervision, done with sensitivity and commitment, will point unerringly to needs for staff development. Such development, in aiding professional growth, will clearly have consequences for future supervision as well as performance appraisal. And no performance appraisal methodology can be defended that does not begin with the supervisor making expectations clear, following through with help as needed, and providing resources and time for further learning (staff development). These five processes can be studied individually, but they cannot stand alone in any conceivable real-world environment. It is when administrators deal with them as separate entities that they fail.

Appropriate staffing practices in student affairs may vary in small ways, but they tend to have much in common. The attempt here is to identify best practices, guided by theory, context, experience, and professional values. But before explication of staffing practices, it is necessary to situate present-day student affairs practice within its contexts. To accomplish this end, organizational, societal, and theoretical issues are examined. Recognition and understanding of these constructs are crucial to effectiveness in facilitating student learning and development.

THE CONTEXT OF HIGHER EDUCATION

Birnbaum (1988) suggested that higher education institutions look so much like other corporate, business entities that inappropriate comparisons are invited. Likening for-profit corporations or special interest foundations to colleges, for example, is a fruitless enterprise because no true basis for comparison exists. Colleges and universities are unique organizations in several ways. According to Birnbaum (1988), they often exhibit characteristics very different from "traditional" organizations:

- Unclear goals or large numbers of often conflicting goals
- Lack of a common metric (such as bottom line profit or loss) to measure success
- Incompatibility of administrative practices and power with faculty governance and influence
- Multiple internal and external constraints imposed by federal and state regulation, the nature of external funding, and (paradoxically) decentralization induced by increased specialization of fields, accreditation requirements, and the need to respond to external constituencies
- Inflexibility of resources making reallocation of significant dollars virtually impossible in the short term
- Confusion of organizational levels, roles, prestige, and rank—technical, managerial, and institutional levels of activity may be performed by virtually anyone in the organization and organizational rank is not necessarily related to personal or professional prestige
- Low visibility of role performance—most interactions with students, for example, are not observed by the public or by supervisors
- Little differentiation in work activities, but large differentiation by expertise. (pp. 3–4)

For these and other reasons, customary corporate accountability systems do not work well for higher education, even though regents, legislators, and alumni sometimes wish they would and occasionally attempt to impose them.

Kuh (1996) discussed higher education organizations as bureaucracies, collegia, and political arenas, the so-called conventional models, and then posited postconventional views of organizations (pp. 270–271). Likewise, others have described alternative models, including the organized anarchy model (Birnbaum, 1988; Cohen & March, 1974), cultural models (Bolman & Deal, 1991; Tierney, 1988), and emerging models such as organizations considered as entities that are self-referential (Wheatley, 1992), that are cybernetic in that they can change based upon monitored inputs (Birnbaum, 1988), that learn (Senge, 1990), that can be understood with metaphors such as the brain and the hologram (Morgan, 1986), and that practice double-loop learning in order to rise above historical strictures and respond to new challenges (Kuh, 1996). Such organizations, to be successful, must be responsive to both internal and external climates and environments by definition.

The conventional models tend to differ from the postconventional ones in that they are comparatively static—they reach an equilibrium and inertia dictates that change is slow. Postconventional notions are thought to be more appropriate for modern, rapidly shifting, information-rich environments. But the most interesting aspect of higher education organizations is that many, if not *all* of the models frequently are operating simultaneously as systems interact with subsystems and supersystems. Collegial departments coexist with bureaucratic finance offices, which impact political budget negotiations, which reflect varying emphases on research and teaching, which cause problems with cultural tenets and restrict necessary adaptation and change, leading to pressure upon academic departments to respond to their environments. If that sounds inefficient and paradoxical, it is! It is also complex and wonderful and human—the things that make higher education a rich human tapestry. Consequently, successful student affairs administrators must be able to tolerate, and manage, ambiguity.

THE CONTEXT OF STUDENT AFFAIRS

The very name of the field, student affairs, suggests a useful vagueness. Student affairs administrators are involved in activities ranging from the mundane (for example, counting mattresses, providing shelter and food, reviewing quality of locks) to the highly esoteric and enriching (for example, spiritual development, student self-directed learning, service learning). A routine day may encompass budget meetings, student group advising, and consoling a student in academic difficulty dealing with personal losses of a hundred different kinds. In short, student affairs administrators inhabit the interstitial spaces of higher education, facilitating student learning, adjustment, and growth.

The most interesting questions about the field, then, concern its relative place in the higher education cosmos. Is the practice of student affairs supplemental or complementary? Is it cocurricular, extracurricular, acurricular, anticurricular, or does the field have its own curriculum? Is student affairs a support service or "the other education?" Does the student affairs division "merely" support the academic mission of the institutions, or does it make it complete through avenues of application? These are important questions, and the answers vary from campus to campus. For the purposes here, however, it may be enough simply to assert that the editors and authors of this book believe that the profession of student affairs has an important, distinct place on campus and in the lives of students.

Personal growth, learning, and development are worthy goals for students, and student affairs administrators contribute to them. Hence, it makes good sense to learn as much as possible about the mechanisms and dynamics of such facilitation and to practice in the best ways possible. As a crucial characteristic of quality educational practice, staffing should proceed according to professionally sanctioned best practices.

In this vein, Creamer and colleagues (1992), held the following:

- Certain skills and competencies are required for practice in student affairs no matter how one enters the field.
- Practitioners enter student affairs from a variety of backgrounds that include professional preparation programs, related degree programs, unrelated degree programs, and no formal academic training.
- Practitioners are at unique levels of professional development.
- We believe that . . . quality professional practice requires lifelong continuing professional education . . . and, . . . continuing professional education can take place in many forms and arenas. (Winston & Creamer, 1997, pp. 361–362)

Detailed discussions of the nature of the need for continuing professional education, who should provide it, and in what form are available elsewhere (Bryan & Schwartz, 1999; Carpenter, 1998; Creamer et al., 1992). It suffices to note that the WCSM fully contemplates and supports the essential nature of and need for lifelong learning for student affairs professionals. Indeed, attention to continuing professional development is a requirement for appropriate supervision and performance assessment. Finally, although experience in similar positions may win out over professional preparation in many job searches, surely it cannot be argued that experience augmented by continuing professional education is preferable to a single year's experience repeated multiple times.

OTHER CONTEXTUAL ISSUES

Having considered separately the contexts of higher education organizations and student affairs as a field, I find it useful to examine their nexus, adding some shifts in the wider environment.

Professionals in Organizations

Although by no means universal, there is wide acceptance that student affairs work is a professional undertaking, at minimum an "emerging profession" (Carpenter, Miller, & Winston, 1980, p. 21). As such, the values of the professional culture are quite likely to conflict with values and practices of other parts of the organization, often causing friction among them. Young (1996) wrote that the duty of student affairs administrators is to reflect institutional, administrative attitudes while at the same time respecting the individuality and wholeness of students. Hirt and Creamer (1998) noted that competition among colleagues for program resources works against what should be productive collaboration. Staffing decisions can be adversely affected by institutional or governmental personnel classification schemes that fail to recognize the professional culture of student affairs (Winston & Creamer, 1997). These and other examples argue for increased emphasis on articulating the aims and goals of student affairs to all constituencies of higher education.

Unclear Training/Educational Requirements

Even within the field of student affairs there is disagreement about what is the best training and background for entering the profession. Creamer et al. (1992) noted that a variety of levels of preparation precede service in professional roles, including no formal preparation at all! Carpenter (1998) decried the fact that one could actually become a senior student affairs officer with no appropriate education or experience. Indeed, there is no consensus as to what constitutes entry-level professional preparation, although there are significant efforts in this direction by the Council for the Advancement of Standards in Higher Education (CAS) (Miller, 1999). Commission XII of the American College Personnel Association (ACPA) has adopted the CAS Standards in principle and is striving to move preparation programs toward voluntary compliance with the standards, and there are rumblings of program registry in lieu of accreditation (Carpenter, 1998; Creamer et al., 1992). For now, only professional conscience, institutional precedent, and the job market appear to dictate preparation standards.

Organizational/Institutional Restrictions

In addition to job classification systems and pay scales that do not match up with professional preparation and needed abilities, institutional and extrainstitutional forces and factors intrude on student affairs practice and staffing in a variety of ways (mentioned here only cursorily, but treated extensively in other places in this book). Student affairs professionals are often major players in enrollment management, being asked to serve underrepresented populations, but not given extra resources to do so. Many colleges and universities allege and even aver diversity goals but fail to understand the support needed by students with nontraditional backgrounds in a largely homogeneous environment. Legislative mandates with respect to students with disabilities, campus security reporting, student records management, alcohol and drug education, and even hazing are passed along to student affairs divisions as "part of the job," but with no new resources (Hirt & Creamer, 1998). New technology is becoming available on campuses, which aids in some routine tasks but does not obviate student contact and in some instances causes new advising needs (Walther

& Reid, 2000). Finally, the complexity and time requirements of academic advising may have largely outgrown faculty time and ability, requiring student affairs practitioners to take on the task, as is common practice on many community college campuses.

Consumerism versus Professionalism

Because of an increased emphasis on quality of services and pressure on economic resources, student affairs divisions are stretched in unprecedented ways (Woodard, 1998). Added to these stresses, students are increasingly consumeristic, demanding services—and curricula—that meet their perceived needs. The duality of functional and educational purposes brings with it a potential conflict. Students may not know what is best educationally and indeed may not wish to undergo inconvenience for the purpose of development, at least not without explanation. If the institution is focused on enrollment numbers rather than quality of educational experience, student affairs professionals may become caught between their professional ethics and the expectations of employers or putative clients.

New Educational Modalities

Hand in glove with the consumer movement is the rise of new technologies. Although there are early experiments (Schwitzer, Ancis, & Brown, in press; see also Chapter 4 in this book), the impact of distance learning upon student affairs practice is virtually unknown. The odds are that the focus will shift from education to services for such students, which may lead to parallel though unequal degree programs.

Demographic changes on campuses impact both the perceptions about and the realities of educational equity. Particularly when dealing with so-called nontraditional students, such as those who are older, married, parents, or working full time, the challenges for student affairs are many and vexing. The problem is compounded by the fact that the appropriate level of service or educational intervention is unknown.

Further, there is evidence (Schwitzer, Ancis, & Brown, in press) that higher education is not serving the nontraditional or place-bound students well. For-profit educational institutions are proliferating, offering a model that lacks many of the "frills" that some consider are offered by student affairs. It is possible that there will eventuate a brave new world of information packets for sale in the absence of campuses, student organizations, residence halls, and faculty and staff personal interaction. Although unlikely for traditional students in the near term, nontraditional students increasingly are becoming a fertile market for such enterprises. Perhaps the most disturbing thing about these emerging challenges is that they were not anticipated and planned for, leading to the question that can be asked with wonder or disgust, "What next?"

LENSES FOR THIS CHAPTER

With all the vicissitudes and opportunities manifest on campuses and in the profession, the guiding principles of student affairs require attention. When discussing the core values of student affairs, Winston and Creamer (1997) examined Young's (1993a, 1993b, 1996) work and concluded that the essential values are human dignity, equality, and community. They also stated that "the connection between the quality of staffing practices in student affairs and the quality of educational services delivered to students is direct and powerful" (p. 12). These concepts form the basis for the recommendations that follow. Somewhat more specifically, all decisions, procedures, and practices are guided by attention to these same beliefs.

Moral and Ethical Dimensions

All human beings are intrinsically valuable and worthy of respect. All professional and personal actions are to be conducted with honesty, openness, empathy, and dignity. Actions should be guided by, among other considerations, professional ethical codes (for example, ACPA, 1993; National Association of Student Personnel Administrators [NASPA], 1992–1993). Actions have impact upon and should consider the values and importance of both individuals and institutions.

Diversity

Student affairs professionals and the divisions they lead are committed to equity in all decisions and actions. Equality does not mean identical treatment and opportunity, but rather calls for fundamental fairness, taking into account historical, societal, and other contextual factors. Diversity of viewpoints, backgrounds, personal characteristics, and cultures are of intrinsic value to the educational mission of colleges and universities (Winston & Creamer, 1997).

Empowerment

All members of the academic community are entitled to appropriate avenues of expression and action. People must be free to decide for themselves. Consequences of choices should be made clear and all relevant information should be made available in a timely and comprehensive way (Winston & Creamer, 1997).

Professionalism

Student affairs practice should be conducted as a professional service. That is, staff members should be conversant with best practice in the profession, as well as recent research, theories, and thinking. Student affairs educators are expected to share their expertise and research with others in professional ways and to participate in and submit to peer review as appropriate. Service to the profession is expected, such as leadership in professional associations and active mentorship (Winston & Creamer, 1997).

Personal/Professional Growth and Development

All members of an academic community are expected to be on a journey in search of constant improvement—improvement of educational practice, of wellness, of emotional health, and of self. All institutional procedures, policies, and actions should recognize these journeys and be designed to facilitate them.

The "provinces" of educator, leader, and manager are detailed in the first chapter of this book. For the purposes of this chapter, elements of each role are viewed as essential for peering through the lenses noted above. The student affairs educator teaches these concepts in myriad ways, being aware of current thought, assessing and filling gaps in knowledge, and practicing them in their daily work. The student affairs leader advocates for these principles without compromising them, while guiding others with the strength of vision and example. The student affairs manager ensures that processes, procedures, policies, and budgets align with the principles, for theory becomes ephemeral if practice does not match.

Having examined the contexts and the values of student affairs practice, as well as a model for staffing practices, this discussion now turns to the specifics of staffing.

RECRUITMENT AND SELECTION OF STAFF MEMBERS

If the many horror stories that practitioners report are to be believed, no process is more fraught with ethical peril than recruitment and selection. This is curious, given that selection of the correct candidate, the one that possesses the requisite background and abilities to perform the job and also fits into the environment, is crucial to the success of any organization. Further, few other activities are more likely to result in negative and damaged reputations. If the word goes out that a hiring institution is less than open or actually dishonest in recruitment dealings, the quality of possible hires can be drastically affected. More than one institution has found itself on a surreptitious "blacklist" and it is difficult to recover from such a designation, not to mention possible sanctions from professional associations or accrediting bodies. Of course, in such a scenario, those who suffer most are the institution's students, because the quality of student affairs practice will inevitably be affected adversely. Hence, ethics, attention to diversity, professionalism, empowerment, and a balanced professional and personal growth orientation must be strictly and scrupulously adhered to. Student affairs educators must see to it that all involved in the recruitment and selection process know their roles and follow the rules. Leaders need to model openness, ethicality, and responsiveness. And managers should make sure that procedures are clear, available for review, and adequately funded to allow these most important decisions to flow smoothly.

The key elements of recruitment and selection include (a) providing a position analysis/description, (b) charging the search committee, (c) advertising the position, (d) screening the candidates, (e) interviewing the finalists, (f) checking recommendation(s), and (g) negotiating with/hiring the successful candidate.

Provide Position Analysis/Description

Quite often, an open position provides opportunity for student affairs leaders to reorganize—or at least realign—duties and responsibilities. Consequently, in all fairness every hire should have a direct connection to the vision and mission of the institution, division, and functional area involved. Sometimes it is obvious that the current nature of the position should be maintained, such as when a residence hall director has moved on or when a director of career development is needed. At other times, however, priorities may change. For example, perhaps a position needs to be changed to reflect the needs of commuter or other nontraditional students or to encompass a new emphasis on service learning and voluntarism. The proper way to make such decisions is openly and in a participative manner. All persons who may be directly affected should have a voice in the process, and a designated person should convene the process and prepare and submit the final recommendation to the top levels of the organization. Students should be consulted, as should other affected constituencies, such as academic and business affairs. Human resource departments are usually adept at position analysis and can be valuable in determining comparable duties, titles, and pay scales. Of course, sometimes government or institutional rules conflict with professional values by declaring certain positions "nonprofessional" or "nonfaculty" and restrict salaries and qualifications in ways that may not be responsive to market considerations in the student affairs field. Ideally, human resource departments can intervene and possibly even adjust the situation.

After the position analysis is complete and priorities set, a position description is written, usually by the position's supervisor, and approved at the division and institutional human resource office levels. Position descriptions should include (a) duties of the position situated in the context of the institutional and divisional visions and missions; (b) specific, job-related goals, expectations, and work activities; (c) evaluation criteria and procedures; (d) administrative location and title of the position; (e) required credentials, qualifications, and professional development experience; (f) any unusual conditions of employment; and (g) any special or atypical conditions regarding the position. It is to the advantage of the employer that the position description be as complete and open as possible, because this statement provides the best way for a potential employee to judge both fitness and interest. Additionally, the position description saves time and effort for the search committee and the ultimate hiring officer, because it indicates screening criteria and critical competencies.

Impanel, Charge, and Empower the Search Committee

The size and diversity of the search committee are directly related to the administrative level of the position. For entry-level positions, three to five persons may be optimal, with departmental representation, one external professional, and one or more students, along with a representative from another constituency directly affected, depending upon the nature of the position. For a chief student affairs–level position, on the other hand, the committee is usually much larger, with a broadly diverse representation of groups both inside and outside the institution. There is a wide range of options in between these two extremes. Search committee composition, then, should reflect function—there should be adequate familiarity with the job and expertise to evaluate professional credentials; diversity—both culturally and organizationally; institutional culture, tradition, and precedent—it may be a given that every committee include a faculty member, for example; affected constituencies; campus politics; and successful experience—some members of the search committee should previously have successfully participated in a comparable search assignment.

Ideally, the search committee members should be experienced enough to carry forward the process with minimal supervision, but the ideal is seldom reached for various reasons, such as personnel changes that require new or less experienced members. It is wise to avoid "going to the well" too often, thereby maintaining a reservoir of good will. Position changes, changes in law or human resource regulations, and market changes all demand that the officer appointing the search committee pay attention to training and a clear charge. Whether formal or informal training is initiated, the key procedures and considerations for the search committee should be written and reviewed before each search.

The search committee should be involved in every step of the search from reviewing the position description for clarity and proposing changes to it through recommending which candidates are best "qualified." Depending upon organizational custom or preferences of the hiring officer, the committee may recommend one top candidate, a ranked list, or an unranked list, any of which would be "acceptable" to the committee. It should be noted that committees sometimes bridle at having to submit unranked lists and may rebel. Therefore, this issue should be clearly joined very early in the process and any uncomfortable member accommodated or removed.

Advertise the Position

The position announcement/advertisement contains the same information as the position description, in somewhat less detail, plus more information about the institution and division, an equal opportunity statement appropriate to the institution, minimum and desirable qualifications and credentials, some indication of remuneration, and a clear idea of application requirements, including any statements or reference letters or both required. Reference checks may not be useful for all candidates in the early stage because careful examination is usually limited to finalists. The best advertisements contain not a deadline date, but a date for first consideration, with the search being left open thereafter until filled. Advertisement venues and procedures vary among institutions, level of position, and resources available for search purposes. Some institutions have affirmative action judgments to consider, state laws or policies requiring local newspaper advertisement, strictures on amount of money for ads, and the like. Care should be taken to ensure that a diverse pool of prospective candidates sees the advertisement. The *Chronicle of Higher Education* is the current gold standard, but a host of other professional publications may be appropriate in specific instances and to get the word out to minority candidates. ACPA and NASPA, as well as many other professional associations, have well-organized placement operations. There is a growing number of specialized and general websites available for both position and candidate listings. At this writing the value and popularity of these is unknown, but they are likely to become increasingly more useful over time. As a supplement to widespread advertisement, typical sources of candidates (such as preparation programs and large student affairs divisions) should be contacted by letter, phone, and e-mail.

Screen Candidates

One of the most frequent complaints about search processes is that candidates submit applications and receive little or no response in a timely fashion. This is professionally unacceptable, ethically reprehensible, and poor public relations practice. Each application should be acknowledged and logged and candidates notified of any delays or changes in status. The pool of candidates should be monitored for quantity, quality, and diversity. If an appropriate pool is not being gathered, further steps should be taken. Above all, if a candidate is removed from the pool for any reason, he or she should be notified in a timely fashion, often interpreted to mean within three to five days following the decision.

Screening criteria and procedures should be clear, consistent, relevant, and meaningful to all committee members, and all candidate data should be treated with extreme sensitivity and confidentiality. Discussions about candidates should remain within the committee room, to be reported only to those who need to know. Discussions should be conducted professionally and in accordance with statutes and regulations.

Depending upon the level of the position and the initial charge, the committee will be called upon to make a recommendation to the convening officer via a list of finalists. In higher-level positions especially, it is common to compile a list of three to five finalists to be invited to campus. Sometimes, especially for lower-level positions or in times of resource constraints, the candidates will need to be ranked, with the top candidate invited in and offered the job if a fit is clear and, if not, the next candidate on the list invited and so on. In any case, references should be checked carefully before candidates are brought to the campus, not, as is frequently the case, as the last function of the committee or as an afterthought prior to a job offer. If references are gathered before the candidate visits, remaining questions can be addressed and evaluated. Also, the actual list of finalists may change based on references. In almost all cases, reference checks should be made by telephone by a person knowledgeable about the field and the position being filled. Members of the committee who are not knowledgeable about student affairs probably should not be enlisted to check references by telephone, or perhaps reference checks can be done by pairs of committee members—one of whom is knowledgeable and experienced.

Interview the Finalists on Campus

Ideally, the search committee coordinates the finalists' visits to the campus, making arrangements for or ensuring smooth reimbursement for travel, lodging, and meals (in my opinion it is never appropriate to make reimbursement contingent on acceptance of an offer). Candidates should be either personally guided or provided clear directions to interview locations and should be given a full itinerary prior to or immediately upon arrival. The itinerary should include the names and titles of persons to be seen and a description of each larger session such as candidate presentations. The itinerary should have "white space" in it, allowing the candidate to have some down time or to tailor the visit to personal taste, suggesting interviews not contemplated by the committee. The candidate should be interviewed by all persons, or representatives thereof, with whom the position typically interacts. There should be an interview with the prospective supervisor, including discussion of expectations and evaluation processes, and the reporting authority one level up in the organization. For any conceivable student affairs position, there should be some contact with students, preferably in the absence of staff members. One facet of the visit should involve a short community tour, highlighting quality-of-life issues such as local schools, shopping, recreation, and residential options. The visit should be in the nature of a reciprocal interview—the candidate is interviewing the institution and vice versa. The tone should be respectful of the candidate and upbeat, but honest, comprehensive, and open, especially about potential challenges of the job. No one is served well by dashed expectations, least of all the employing organization. The interview is, after all, the beginning of the orientation and supervision process. Accordingly, special features of the campus and community culture, or work environment (e.g., expected dress, hours) should be clearly communicated. Visits should last from one to three days, depending upon level of position, and at the upper levels it may be appropriate to invite a spouse or partner as well.

Check Final Recommendation(s)

The search committee should conclude its work by overseeing a structured process of interview feedback, probably involving forms to be completed on each candidate by all who had personal contact. The committee should then make decisions on the finalists corresponding to its charge. If it is to make a single recommendation, it should be forwarded with a list of commendations and concerns. More likely, the committee will be asked to prepare a ranked or unranked list, with notations of strengths and weaknesses of each individual included thereon. Unacceptable finalists should not be included on any list, even, for example, if the charge was to submit three candidates when only two are acceptable. The committee must have the courage to make hard decisions. Following the recommendation process, the search committee's work should be thanked, scolded, or otherwise recognized and dissolved.

Negotiate with and Hire the Successful Candidate

Negotiation should be conducted with the officer of the organization empowered to make the hiring decision. This simple dictum is easily stated, but often violated. Nothing should be offered or implied that is not possible. Conditions and terms of employment should be laid out openly and completely. Adequate time to make a decision should be allowed. The amount of time will vary according to the level of position and the status of the candidate in other searches, if any, but in no case should it be less than one work week. Negotiations should reflect reasonable openness with regard to salary and benefits, within the context of institutional guidelines, starting date, title, special considerations (e.g., partner placement, temporary living quarters, moving expenses), and professional development resources. Of particular importance in the negotiation phase is confidentiality of financial terms, both for the benefit of the candidate's privacy and for the health of the organization. Many times, in order to meet the market, new employees are offered significantly better remuneration packages than existing employees who might consider themselves comparable. This can be corrosive and can be avoided through the use of discretion on all sides. The negotiating officer should make himself or herself reasonably available for discussions and questions during the time between offer and decision. Nonselected finalists should be notified as soon as possible of the hiring decision. Although it is not necessary to communicate that an offer has been made to someone else, it is imperative to notify unsuccessful candidates as soon as an offer is accepted.

Final Notes

Two ticklish issues deserve mention in the context of recruitment and selection of staff. First, internal candidates must walk a tight ethical line. Of course, they must play no formal role in the search or selection process, but they must also be careful not to interact with staff members inside or outside of the hiring unit in any way that causes discomfort or could be misconstrued. No matter how tempting or how close their contacts, they must avoid gathering information regarding the selection outside of normal employer–candidate contacts. And finally, they must separate strictly their current job performance from any candidacy issues.

Similar, but slightly different, issues arise when staff members are involved in the selection of supervisors, especially direct ones. All members of the search committee and anyone in an interviewing capacity should keep the interests of the institution, division, and unit uppermost in mind, separating out perceived personal advantage. No staff member who is uncomfortable doing so should be "forced" to participate in a hiring process for a supervisor.

The recruitment and selection process is difficult to carry out professionally, but it is also fraught with very real legal peril. Legal issues include whether the institution is private or public, the type and nature of contracts, and applicable nondiscrimination statutes and regulations. Student affairs professionals must also balance these very real legal constraints with equally compelling needs and ethical requirements in the field for affirmative action and other methods of ensuring staff diversity. Issues and strictures may vary by state, by institutional status with regard to Justice Department action, because of court decisions, or for other reasons. Hence, administrators are left with a situation in which hiring organizations in neighboring states may be subject to different laws and have varying restrictions, even though both regard affirmative action as a responsibility. Readers are advised to access campus human resource offices for guidance and applicable affirmative action procedures. Likewise, reference to the writings of Gehring (1993; Chapter 5 in this volume), Hollander and Young (1991), Kaplin and Lee (1995), and Winston and Creamer (1997) for a broader treatment of legal issues is suggested.

ORIENTING STAFF TO NEW POSITIONS

Purchasing a new vehicle is fun and exciting and the new owner cannot wait to drive it away. Most will simply locate the major controls and proceed on their way. It would be more advisable to carefully read the owner's manual and discover any idiosyncrasies in advance, but that is not the way it generally goes. Fortunately, driving is usually routine and strange situations, like a fuel pump lock out after a minor collision, do not occur until the new owner has had some time to learn. But what if it did on the first trip? This is, simplistically, the problem with asystematic and informal orientation for new staff in student affairs. Everyone wants the new person to "drive" quickly, and everyone hopes that no untoward situation requiring extensive local knowledge happens too soon.

Student affairs divisions that would be aghast if new students did not receive an extensive orientation routinely fail to orient new staff members properly and in a formal way (Winston & Creamer, 1997). A proper orientation is ethically necessary, both to assure optimum professional practice, thereby protecting student clients, and to attend to the personal and professional growth of the new employee. A quality orientation program responds to diversity by highlighting differences and similarities, both personal and organizational, between what the employee has been used to and the current environment. Further, it empowers the newcomer by providing ample information. Without such, it is more difficult to connect with the culture—a complicated prospect in any case

(Whitt, 1990), but even more difficult without help. The student affairs educator views new staff orientation as a challenge and a responsibility to teach. The leader understands the importance of the orientation process to the success of new staff members, as well as the opportunities for boundary spanning, intraorganizational sharing, and relationship building. The manager knows that smooth functioning during a staff transition depends heavily upon the sharing of information and the comfort level of the incoming employee.

An effective staff orientation program involves attention to operative philosophies and procedures, organizational cultures, and professional and personal expectations.

Operative Philosophies and Procedures

Colleges and universities share overwhelming similarities in appearance and structure, but they are also quite different in both subtle and obvious ways. It is important that new organizational participants spend time learning the philosophies and procedures of their departments, divisions, and institutions. The mission, vision, and goals provide crucial clues to student affairs practice. Liberal arts colleges are quite different in focus from land-grant research universities, and both are dissimilar in many respects from community colleges or comprehensive regional universities. These differences impact long-range and short-term activities and programming alike. Private institutions may have points of view that vary significantly from public ones. Technically oriented institutions look different from humanities oriented ones. Even different programs and colleges within a college or university may have significant dissimilarities. The new employee should be oriented extensively to both the macro- and the microcontext for practice in terms of guiding statements and beliefs. Many of these will be written but will require interpretation. Others, though unwritten, may be environmentally ingrained by constant enactment and repetition. Most importantly, the new staff member must be guided to understand the connections between operative philosophies and his or her specific role.

Although philosophies and goals may be somewhat common among institutions, paperwork is not. Reporting requirements, specific forms, employee benefits procedures, payroll accounting, and many other things are site specific and must be learned by the new employee. Procedures on compensatory time may be quite structured or quite informal, depending upon the employee's level, or may vary by individual office, for example. Paperwork and specific procedures are not terribly exciting and may seem trivial to the new person, but few things distinguish the experienced from the "green" like forms. A person who cannot get the hang of filling out and signing time sheets or travel vouchers properly may be marked as incompetent and hence unworthy of professional respect. Conversely, learning quickly and conforming to the (seemingly petty) rules implies efficiency and commitment and may be a precursor to earned authority.

Organizational Culture

Following the rules, whether the largest ones concerned with institutional vision or the smallest ones like filling out time sheets, is in and of itself not adequate for optimal performance in a student affairs role. Individuals must understand and operate within a shared culture. Procedures, organizational charts, and goals that illustrate official thinking beg the question, "How do things really work around here?" A new employee who fails to understand, accept, and be accepted by the culture will not remain long on the job or, at best, fail to grow into a productive member of the organization. Accordingly, orientation for new staff should focus on appropriate behavior. A partial list of topics would include (a) how decisions are made at the department, division, and university levels; (b) what relationships exist between and among subordinates and superordinates, staff and students, various offices, student affairs staff and faculty; (c) office hours staff members are expected to maintain: (d) the existence, if any, of a dress code both within and beyond work hours and for meetings with other offices or the entire division; (e) the formal and informal proscriptions on romantic relationships with other staff, faculty, or students; (f) the ways diversity is recognized, celebrated, or tolerated; (g) the behaviors that make people "look" successful or unsuccessful in this work environment; (h) the "community" nature of the institution and level of "family friendliness" within the division; (i) the major issues and controversies extant in the department, division, and university; and (j) the "hidden" agendas and unwritten survival rules that tend to exist. Ideally, new staff members should have conversations around these issues and others with peers, supervisors, subordinates, organizational colleagues from other offices, students, and faculty or administrators outside the student affairs area. Two very good guides to making a transition to a new position and culture are available in the literature. Whitt (1990) used the analogy of taking a trip to suggest getting advance information, inventorying personal baggage, being open to adventure, taking side trips, and so on in a way that teaches many lessons about cultural integration. Hyde and Carpenter (1992) enlisted the concept of Aristotelian virtue, the golden mean, to discuss ways to take advantage of one's experience and background without angering the locals unduly. For example, it is inappropriate to continually refer to the "way we did it at Past U.," but equally untoward never to use one's previous experiences. The golden mean is to transfer what has worked before to the new context as needed and with modifications.

Personal/Professional Expectations

What many people have the most trepidation about when moving into a new position is organizational fit. This is why interviews are conducted on campus and why so much is at stake for both the new employee and the employing entity. The receiving organization can be very good at what it does and the employee can be an excellent professional and yet the two combined may be a bad fit. Such considerations should have been resolved during the hiring process, but there is work to be done even after arrival on campus. Organizational and personal ethical expectations and interpretations are good places to start. Next, the new hire is likely to want specifics on job performance appraisal processes and supervisor attitudes. Is latitude given for decision making or is the supervisor a hands-on manager? Is supervision sporadic or scheduled? What are the formal rules and the informal practices? Is the position description all encompassing or just the beginning of the job? Is there room for growth or simply no time to even accomplish the stated jobs? What are the professional growth opportunities and what support is available for such? Do the organization and the supervisor allow for the vagaries of personal fitness, family duties (e.g., spouse, children, or parents), community service, religious commitments, or the myriad other things that busy professionals seek to fit into their lives? Such questions call for substantive conversations with many different people over a period of time. The questioning itself should be supported and answers provided honestly and without prejudice. If the new employee does not ask, the "old timer" might well want to introduce the matter at an appropriate time.

Suggestions for Ongoing Orientation

Orientation for new employees begins with information provided prior to and during the on-campus interview. Time should be allotted to discuss potential living arrangements, fringe benefits, and community features. After selection and before the reporting date, a contact person should be appointed to keep in touch and send necessary information to facilitate a good transition. Things to be considered are residence arrangements, utilities, institutional paperwork, and family issues such as schools, day care, and special medical needs. Information that has not been made available previously on the institution, the department, and the division should be sent and questions answered as they arise. Careful and cheerful preemployment help will ease the "first day jitters" that are the dark side of excitement about the new position.

The first day.   Few enjoy being the "new kid." Hence, the goal of the orientation program should be to integrate the recent hire as quickly as possible by easing predictable transition problems. Ideally, on the first day of work someone should meet the new employee at home and accompany him or her to work. If mass transit is involved, this will help with often-complicated systems. If the employee will usually drive to work, parking and travel directions are thus obviated. The first morning's appointments and meetings should be arranged in advance. The day should begin with a short period of time to find and adjust to the new office, followed by an introductory meeting with the immediate circle of fellow employees. This might involve a department or even a larger unit depending upon the size of the institution. If, for example, the position is in an office of two professionals and one support staff member, then the meeting should include the supervisor and perhaps members from other departments that are directly concerned with similar issues. The size of the group should not be overwhelming, but should be large enough to engender the feeling that the new employee is not flying solo. Two or three peer-level employees should be assigned to be available to the new person all day for questions and directions. The morning should conclude with some time in the new office for unpacking and familiarization, followed by lunch with the supervisor and the two "helpers." Usually, the afternoon will be taken up with meetings with the human relations department, which will go more smoothly if the employee has had information available in advance. At the end of the day, the employee should have the opportunity to check directions to home and ask any further questions, including queries about health and retirement plan choices and so on.

The first week.   The new employee should spend half of each day on the job and the remainder meeting people on and off campus who are directly and indirectly connected with the work required of the position. Clearly, this would include individual and groups of students in as timely a fashion as is feasible. Most of these meetings should have been scheduled in advance of the new hire's arrival on campus, with some built-in flexibility for unanticipated activities. The supervisor and his or her immediate superior should make contact with the new employee two or three times during the first week to ensure that things are going well and to answer newly acquired questions. An invitation to an intact social group (e.g., dinner club, church group, softball team) should be arranged during the first week for the second or a subsequent week, depending upon employee interests and divisional contacts. This social engagement should involve the family if that is a consideration. For persons with younger children, opportunities for similar-age children to meet and interact is often helpful.

The first month.   Meetings with relevant contacts should continue but with decreasing frequency, unless demanded by the job. Monitoring of social adjustment and access should continue with someone available at the peer or supervisory level with similar interests to advise and guide the employee about local opportunities. At this point, the supervisor should schedule a relatively formal meeting to discuss professional evaluation issues and procedures. There should be a one-month debriefing session conducted by the supervisor to discuss met and unmet expectations as well as both pleasant and unpleasant surprises in an open and nonevaluative way. The supervisor should meet less formally with the new employee about once per week, and part of each meeting should be allotted to openly discuss the growing working relationship.

The first year.   Every college and university has annual milestones, such as significant campus traditions, evaluation periods, holiday and break periods, peak workload periods, and graduation. Because these are handled differently in each venue, the supervisor or peers assigned as facilitators should brief the new employee well in advance about what to expect. Formative evaluation sessions should be conducted by the supervisor on a quarterly basis, leading to the annual evaluation. Additionally, the supervisor and new employee should meet bimonthly to discuss transition issues and to facilitate adjustment difficulties. Orientation should not end after the formally scripted period. After one year, most adjustment should be well underway if not complete, but the supervisor should be alert for any special circumstances that require additional time, especially if any maladaptive behavior has been observed. Some institutions have a probationary period for all employees of three or six months. Where such a period exists, its passage should be duly noted as a part of the orientation process.

Summary comments. The WCSM considers orientation of new employees to be an integral part of supervision, performance appraisal, and professional development. Elements of these should be woven into the orientation fabric in ways that link initial experiences with desired professional development and outcomes. A good beginning will not ensure a successful career in a given position, but it is clearly a prerequisite.

It should be noted that the above discussion assumed that the new employee came to the new position from outside of the hiring organization. Because many hires occur from inside, some of the suggestions will not apply, such as the personal and family adjustment monitoring. However, allowing and making time to meet people in the new role, paying attention to adjustment issues, and facilitating a new conception of the professional self are all good ideas for anyone, no matter their tenure in the organization, when a change is made. The attempt here was to be comprehensive. Employers would do well to err on the side of doing more, rather than risk not doing enough.

SUPERVISING AND MANAGING STAFF

From a traditional, simplistic perspective, supervision might appear to be antithetical to the lenses used in this chapter. Because these reflect core values of student affairs, a reconceptualization is needed. The moral aspect of supervision involves more than simple honesty, moving into empowerment and promotion of personal and professional growth, while also considering the needs and goals of the organization. It is not ethical to simply apply a mindless boss–employee mentality; rather, a student affairs supervisor is open to a variety of nuances dictated by diversity of all types and resulting in shared responsibility. The student affairs educator knows that supervision is necessary and makes it a learning experience for all. The leader ensures that the organization works for everyone and vice versa through creative supervision. The manager accomplishes more with happy, motivated employees than by cracking the whip.

The WCSM defines supervision in higher education as "a management function intended to promote the achievement of institutional goals and to enhance the personal and professional capabilities of staff" (Winston & Creamer, 1997, p. 186). However, the authors go further and state that, for student affairs work, "a radically different perspective on supervision is proposed. Supervision is . . . a helping process, which is designed to support staff as they seek to promote the goals of the organizations and to advance their professional development" (p. 194). This implies that supervision continues throughout a career and that supervision is a collaborative enterprise. Winston and Creamer (1997, p. 196) call their model "synergistic supervision," the components of which follow.

Dual Focus

The supervisor is concerned not only with essential unit and institutional functions, but also with the personal and professional well-being of subordinates. Responsibility and decision making are shared to the full extent practicable, so that all come to feel ownership in tasks and unit identity. The supervisor realizes that developing employees, both professionally and personally, benefits the unit, the division, the institution, and the student clients. Supervisees experience a pleasant work environment that is responsive to their needs and goals and come to understand that success for the unit will enhance their personal growth as well.

Joint Effort

Supervision is a cooperative venture, a collaboration in goal setting and strategizing between and among the supervisor and coworkers. A commitment to shared effort is essential. The traditional breakdown of "management and labor" simply will not work, especially among student affairs professionals, whose goals and progress are not always clear.

Two-Way Communication

Concomitant to joint effort is meaningful dialogue around personal and work styles and processes. Open, direct feedback and a more-than-typical depth of knowledge of nonwork and professional activities are key characteristics of synergistic supervision. Supervisors must work to create a comfortable, nonpunitive environment.

Focus on Competence

Synergistic supervisors do not look for weaknesses, but concentrate on strengths, both present and needed. Where present, the strengths are capitalized upon through appropriate coordination of duties, delegation of responsibilities, and clear and open mutual recognition. Where absent and needed, the supervisor and the supervisee cooperate in assessment and plan for development through reading, formal and informal coursework, and professional association involvement among others. The WCSM suggested that staff competence be thought of in four areas: knowledge and information, work-related skills, personal skills, and attitudes. Positive attitudes are considered to be as essential to job performance and work environment as any of the foregoing. This is further evidence of the need for organizationwide commitment in order for the model to succeed.

Growth Orientation

Clearly, employees of different ages and career stages have different needs that must be taken into account in the synergistic supervision model. Just as professional practice in student affairs requires knowledge of student learning and development theory, the supervisor must understand adult and professional development concepts and how they are applied. But a growth orientation means much more. Time is not spent on correcting employees or creating elaborate systems to assure compliance to top-down rules. Rather, accountability springs from shared ownership of activities and results. Hence, professional and personal goals, development, and growth are somewhat merged. This makes for a more satisfying work environment, but also complicates supervision because many more variables and contexts must be taken into account. In this case, however, the complex model is the better one because, as is true with college students, nothing is ever simple in supervision, or in life.

Proactivity

Traditional supervision models often have relied upon a "gotcha" mentality. When employees made mistakes, they were "caught" by supervisors and "punished" or corrected. With synergistic supervision in place, this would theoretically never occur. Employees and supervisors would have scanned the environment for imminent problems well in advance and have a jointly constructed plan in place for dealing with them. Employees would have no need to hide activities or issues and supervisors would have highly current information about coming storms. Supervisory meetings, then, take the form of update and brainstorming sessions. Such sessions should be integrated common occurrences, free of fear and trepidation.

Goal Based

Synergistic supervision does not discard the brain to soothe the heart. Things have to be done in student affairs offices and projects must be completed. Mutually arrived upon goals, established within the context of unit, divisional, and institutional planning mechanisms, help by creating written, specific expectations and measures. Winston and Creamer (1997) recommended that individual goals be set every six months for subsequent six-month, year, and five-year periods, then monitored in meetings held for that purpose at two-month intervals. The goal-setting and monitoring processes should be taken seriously, but also be flexible to reflect rapidly changing circumstances.

Systematic and Ongoing Processes

Effective communication and shared responsibility are the hallmarks of synergistic supervision. They are only possible within the context of a systematic program of information sharing, updating of expectations, and the absence of continual crises. The model requires a fundamental commitment to group process among the participants and a true sharing of authority and power by the supervisor with the group. Staff meetings, as traditionally understood, are not adequate, because scheduling and announcements are not the point. Rather, all members of the unit should regularly engage in a meaningful discussion of progress, potential problems, and shifting priorities.

Holism

Staff members are whole people, no less than students. As such, they deserve support for their personal goals as well as their professional ones, because after all is said and done, the two are inseparable. Synergistic supervision suggests that this is as it should be.

Supervising Support Staff

Not all of the employees of a student affairs unit are professionals in terms of educational preparation or position responsibilities. Early career professionals, in particular, sometimes wrestle with the difficulties of supervising personnel with disparate jobs, backgrounds, and values. Examples include student workers, custodial workers, clerical workers, and student paraprofessionals. In general, the components of the model laid out above will work equally well with most full-time employees (Saunders, Cooper, Winston, & Chernow, 2000), except that they may desire more structure and less input into job descriptions and conditions—not zero input, just less. Considerations for supervising support staff include the following.

1. Time matters—a lot. Do not ask hourly and wage employees to work more than their assigned hours without a clearly understood way to compensate them for the extra work either with overtime pay or compensatory time. Not only are there serious legal and regulatory issues at play, but also the nature of these jobs is such that "requiring" extra work is unethical and inappropriate.
2. Use a team approach whenever possible. As in the WCSM, these employees want to feel that they are part of a larger whole. They should be given input into decisions as appropriate, but they may not be qualified to make student affairs or hiring decisions and therefore should be listened to carefully, but not be given a "vote." It should be noted that, especially in the case of long-time employees, they may be very astute and helpful in their comments.
3. Treat every person with respect. Menial labor does not imply that the person doing it is any less worthy of dignity than anyone else. Mistreating others diminishes one's self. Modeling respect will have impact unitwide.

4. Insofar as possible, give discretion and decision-making power to the person doing the job. Clerical and custodial personnel tend to know their jobs better than their bosses. Step in only when your confidence has been shown to be undeserved.
5. Be very clear in communicating expectations for job performance and check often for understanding. Hold regular meetings for the purpose of reevaluating working conditions and communicating upcoming relevant events.
6. Involve all workers in the life of the unit. Celebrate life events with professionals and nonprofessionals alike.
7. Listen!

Conclusion

Three things deserve further emphasis. First, each employee exists within his or her own context and must be treated accordingly. New professionals need more direction and may have to learn to trust the synergistic supervision process. Experienced employees may need less time in supervision. Second, although dealing with ineffective staff members is never pleasant or easy under any schema, at least with synergistic supervision all the cards are on the table. If the performance problem is acknowledged as a shared issue, then it can be attacked with commitment from both sides and with as little resentment as possible. Genuine dialogue, monitoring, renewal, and professional development are not just things that one has to fail in order to receive, but rather are normal, ongoing features in the lives of all employees. Hence, persons who are unproductive do not feel singled out or that the condition is a permanent one. Third and finally, synergistic supervisors understand that individuals are just that, with varied needs and priorities. Things that are small in the context of life issues may loom large if inappropriately focused upon. Subtle (or even conspicuous) differences in religious customs, headwear, taste in jewelry, hairstyles, or a hundred other things are probably not important unless they pose a threat to health or safety.

STAFF DEVELOPMENT

Staff development and continuing professional education in student affairs is like tending a lawn—most people do it and regard it as a good thing, but few know exactly why. The WCSM holds that staff development is tightly coupled with supervision and performance appraisal and hence subject to the same ethical/moral imperatives to further professional and personal growth. Organizations need to empower staff members to seek professional development opportunities by committing resources to the endeavor, but individuals also need to keep in mind the needs of the division and the institution. Neither should hold sway, or, rather, both should, in a negotiated process allowing for diversity of learning styles, activities, cultural aspects, and motivations. The student affairs educator recognizes that this process is precisely analogous to the field's stance with students. The leader keeps up to date, supports continuing professional education via resource allocation, and is active in broad-scale professional activities. The manager realizes that the changing face of practice requires new skills, new knowledge, and renewal generally.

Staff development, according to the WCSM, can be encapsulated in the following aspects.

Dual Purposes of Staff and Organizational Development

As in the synergistic supervision conceptualization, developing a staff member ideally contributes to the organizational mission and goals. However, in practice this requires negotiation and a long-term perspective. A person performing a given role may need specified skill training that may not always be of interest or preferred. This should be balanced with a later opportunity to branch out in directions that may be peripherally related to function, but of more intrinsic appeal.

Developmental Plan

The primary problem with staff development activities that are decoupled from other staffing processes is a randomness or lack of intentionality. Job functions, short- and long-term staff member goals, and organizational needs at all levels should be joined in a developmental plan. For example, if budget management skills are required for a particular position, the incumbent might be encouraged and supported in taking a course on higher education finance. Not all of the material learned will be strictly related to current job function, but enough will and the rest may help the division and the person later or in a different context.

Process and Product

Student affairs professionals do not expect students to learn facts in isolation. Indeed, the theory of the field recognizes the potency and synergy of many different kinds of cognitive and experiential learning interacting in marvelous and unpredictable ways. Similarly, the very action of assessing, intentionally planning, and then executing developmental goals across a staff creates a cultural parallel to the larger purpose of the organization. Both destination and journey are important.

Anchored in Day-to-Day Work

Sometimes the connections between the need for staff development and changing position requirements are obvious, other times less so. However, if staff development is viewed as being linked to supervision and performance appraisal and if communication lines are intact, then the relationship between professional development over time and the specific mission will be clear. If the link is not in evidence, then a reassessment is needed. If the model is working, the mechanism for this link is already in place. This may sound circular, but in reality is profound. It bespeaks a fundamental change in the way that many student affairs units do business.

Multifaceted, Everchanging

Humans change constantly. Likewise, organizations also have shifting needs, priorities, and forms. Staff development that depends upon traditional forms exclusively is virtually doomed to failure in that attendance is not enough— learning requires reflection and practice. Also, staff development may not require "attendance" in a traditional sense. Many people think of professional development as attending conferences at various levels. However, a creative, focused staff development plan can include self-teaching activities, cross training with other offices, readings, discussion groups, and many other options. A flexible plan will be limited only by the creativity and needs of those involved.

Recognition of Maturation and Growth

Staff development occurs at the nexus of individual professional and personal goals and the needs of the unit, division, and institution. Consequently, recognition of age- and experience-related differences are givens. Clearly, individual staff members will have varied interests, short- and long-term goals, dreams, abilities, and backgrounds. It makes little sense to expect allied professionals (such as nurses or accountants) to undergo the same updating activities as persons who have extensive preparation in student affairs theory. But it may make sense to give allied professionals a basic grounding in such theory and student affairs professionals a short course on student health or alcohol and drug education. New professionals require different kinds of activities than do seasoned ones. For example, midmanagers may need specialized training related to job function, whereas entry-level staff members need additional orientation to a functional area. Some may be happy to stay in their current positions forever; others may want to enhance their skills to prepare for a move up in responsibilities. And all staff members will be dealing with the vagaries of lifelong personal development. Taken as a whole, staff development can be seen as a tapestry, rich and full of color. At the individual level, the pattern is less clear. What is clear is that individual and organizational vitality depend upon continuing development in complex and negotiated ways.

Organizations and their members will either change over time or lose their effectiveness. Consequently, the most important question concerns whether the change will be intentional or random, systematic or haphazard, purposeful or by chance. As recognized in developmental theory (Evans, Forney, & Guido-DiBrito, 1998) a student affairs unit may sometimes be in disequilibrium and therefore facing developmental crisis. Perhaps its members are young and in-experienced as a group or good at interacting with students but ineffective as managers. Similar to the demands of developmental theory, the initial step is to recognize the issue and then plan how it can be addressed. Likewise, organizations may need special help. Consultation at a propitious time can be an effective palliative for an organizational crisis. But only staff development can truly restore balance.

PERFORMANCE APPRAISAL

The final piece of the WCSM puzzle is performance appraisal and it is the weakest area in practice (Creamer & Winston, 1999; Winston & Creamer, 1997). If good supervision and staff development processes are in place, then performance appraisal ought to follow naturally, as an outgrowth of ongoing conversations and activities. Yet too many managers appear to consider it as an innocuous waste of time at best or a major irritant and threat at worst. Given its potential impact and its theoretical significance to any staffing model or practice, performance appraisal must be conducted sensitively, ethically, and professionally. Done properly, it is an empowering process for organizations and employees alike, recognizing diversity in styles, cultures, abilities, and developmental needs. The student affairs educator understands clearly the place of consistent, honest data in any learning process. The leader insists on accountability and gives and accepts solid, helpful feedback. The manager acknowledges the necessity of periodic benchmarks and seeks a workable system with few unintended consequences.

The complexity of most student affairs positions and the contested nature of the goals of higher education make performance appraisal problematic at best. The WCSM approach calls for integration of performance appraisal with other staffing functions, especially supervision and staff development. Hence, the components of successful performance appraisal include the following.

Dual Purposes of Evaluating Job Performance and Staff Improvement

The dynamic tension between institutional and individual needs is at play here. Part of the problem with performance appraisal is that it is often perceived as an imposed process. That is, there are regulations and timelines and forms attached, unlike supervision and staff development, which are less formally structured by the institution. Similar to annual reports, which are relatively simple to prepare if appropriately formatted records are kept, performance appraisal needs not be intimidating if operationalized as a normal part of the supervision process. If there is no fear because the clear overriding purpose is staff development and improvement, then evaluation loses its hoary facade.

If there is a consistent failure to meet certain "standards" or goals and the supervisor(s) and employees are convinced that they have done everything possible to correct the problem, then the issue is one of improper expectations and the solution is to change goals or realign job descriptions. Thus, an "imposed" institutional process can be rendered individually meaningful through synergistic supervision and an active staff development program. Unit and division goals are likewise served through constant scrutiny and attention.

Productivity and Reward Structure

Even when used synergistically, performance appraisal continues to be fraught with difficulty when, as so commonly occurs, it is tied directly to reward structures such as promotion and salary. In resource-poor student affairs environments, salary increments are scarce and often contested. Hence, openness and patience in the ideal model may fall prey to a "look good" orientation for employees and a "productivity now" mode for supervisors. When raises and rewards are episodic, variable, competitive, and zero-sum structured, they are detrimental to a negotiated supervision, development, appraisal schema. True, rewards will almost invariably be considered one of the things that stimulate employee development, but only one, and therefore should be kept in proper perspective throughout the institution. Unions and labor contracts add a whole new dimension to performance appraisal, especially with regard to productivity and rewards (indeed, they impact all the components of the WCSM). A full treatment of the impact of unions is beyond the current scope here, but use of the principles of collaboration, teamwork, and reciprocal information flow advocated here should enhance labor–management relations and facilitate shared goals. The collectively bargaining agreement may specify how staff are to be dealt with in specific situations and that agreement must supercede recommended practices here.

Contextual Standards

Things change. Goals set six months ago may seem ludicrous in retrospect. Staff changes resulting in realignment of duties, realization of barriers not previously obvious, and any number of time-consuming disasters can radically impact expected performance. Consequently, the supervisor/evaluator must take the entire context into account when appraising performance. This is reasonably feasible to accomplish in the WCSM because of the constant communication that makes the issue irrelevant by the time the formal evaluation conference occurs.

Participative and Interactive Appraisal

It makes little sense on the one hand to posit a system of interaction in supervision and staff development and on the other impose an appraisal process from the top down. Even when a prescribed institutional process is in place, there should be a humane, thorough, and stakeholder-owned process extant in the division and unit. Even a prescribed process should be open to negotiation, which is the essence of synergism.

Attributes of Clarity, Openness, and Fairness

Ethics, a growth and improvement orientation, attention to variety and diversity of views and cultures, and professionalism all demand a transparent, equitable performance appraisal system. There should be no surprises. However, it must be recognized that any human system is fallible. It is conceivable that one or more of the values of clarity, openness, and fairness may be abrogated by complex events in rare cases. Even when this happens, if the overall staffing model is positive and consistent, the damage should be minimal.

Ongoing Review of Position and Performance

Like all aspects of the WCSM, performance appraisal requires time, energy, and commitment. It is easier to complete meaningless forms once a year and treat them as if they have meaning (the current practice in many institutions) than to enter into a constant state of negotiation and adjustment. Nevertheless, complex systems and processes require flexibility and vigilance.

Appraiser's Leadership Attributes

Perhaps more than the other components of the staffing model, successful developmental performance appraisal requires trust in the evaluator, the leader. Consistent example and effectiveness over time gain this trust. The exact mechanism may matter less than the perception of the person who wields it, however accurately. No one likes to have their shortcomings recognized, so the complete administrator must work diligently to maintain effective working relations with all who must be evaluated.

Workable Formats that Avoid Systematic Bias

Everyone in an organization knows when the appraisal system is not working. Supervisors, those evaluated, and those using the data all come to participate with disdain and work around the bad process. Clearly, there have to be better ways or at least ways that all can agree are better. The WCSM principles will result in a member-owned system if followed properly. It will also forbid systematic bias of illegal, unethical, or senseless types. Of course, the best plan will not be effective if used wrongly. Supervisors must be careful to look for patterns in their own evaluation results and debrief themselves with peers and supervisors, as appropriate.

A good performance appraisal system considers context, rejects bias, fits the organizational culture, and is integral to other staffing practices. It is ongoing, consistent, and genuine. Both formal and informal practices are honored.

Rewards are distributed as fairly as possible, but they are not, in and of themselves, the point. Rather the goal is to get the organization's work done in a way that is respectful of employees and their personal and professional needs without sacrificing hard-minded cost effectiveness. Finally, according to Creamer and Winston (1999) "designing and sustaining effective performance appraisal systems may be more a matter of will than of procedure. Many systems may work" (p. 261). Integrity and follow-through are key.

Conclusion

With the foregoing as backdrop, this discussion turns once again to Winston and Creamer (1997) as a final note:

> The quality of educational programs and services provided by a student affairs division depends on the knowledge, skills, commitment, and professionalism of the staff who create and deliver them.
> Staffing practices directly affect the quality of the work performed and the satisfaction, emotional well-being, and personal and professional growth of all involved.
> Staffing practices are embedded in the institutional and division cultures.
> Organizations that value their members and demonstrate concern for their personal and professional welfare increase the probability of producing excellence. (p. 275)

Student affairs administrators in their roles of educators, leaders, and managers are quite knowledgeable about how to facilitate students' learning and development. Nevertheless, as has been postulated herein, simply applying similar principles of holism, respect for the individual, community consciousness, celebration of diversity, and freedom of personal choice would go a long way toward improving staffing practices in most institutions of higher learning.

The nature of student affairs work is changing. The line between student affairs and academic affairs is rapidly blurring as the need for seamless student experiences is seen as more important. Innovations in first-year orientation courses, supplemental instruction, academic advising, retention programs, services to "nontraditional" students, and the like are creating new roles for student affairs professionals and requiring new skills and knowledge. Predicting the future of campus work would be foolish and futile, but it is clear that old structures have not been effective for a while and will become less so. Only a dynamic staffing model stands a chance of keeping up. Used properly and with commitment, the WCSM and its components can provide a useful environmental scanning function as an added bonus. Student affairs work is fundamentally about recognition of developmental opportunities and strategies for growth. Nowhere is that more true than on today's campuses and in today's student affairs divisions.

QUESTIONS TO CONSIDER

1. Think about situations in your career in which you have been a supervisor and in which you have been supervised. Have you always been pleased with the outcome(s)? What concepts or approaches from this chapter might have helped make things better or more productive?
2. At several points in the chapter, an analogy is drawn between staffing practices and facilitating student development. Can you think of other ways that we should "practice what we preach" in student affairs work? Are attention to personal growth, choices, and consequences necessary for productivity in a work environment or simply frills?
3. A critical piece of the chapter's approach to staffing practices is attention to both individual and institutional needs and goals. Can these ever conflict in ways that are impossible to resolve? What would/should happen then? What are examples?

REFERENCES

American College Personnel Association. (ACPA). (1993). Statement of ethical principles and standards. *Journal of College Student Development, 34,* 89–92.

Birnbaum, R. (1988). *How colleges work: The cybernetics of academic organizations and leadership.* San Francisco: Jossey-Bass.

Bolman, L. G., & Deal, T. E. (1991). *Reframing organizations: Artistry, choice and leadership.* San Francisco: Jossey-Bass.

Carpenter, D. S. (1998). Continuing professional education in student affairs. In N. Evans & C. Phelps (Eds.), *The state of the art of preparation and practice in student affairs* (p. 159–176). Washington, DC: American College Personnel Association.

Carpenter, D. S., Miller, T. K., & Winston, R. B., Jr. (1980). Toward the professionalization of student affairs. *NASPA Journal, 18*(2), 16–23.

Cohen, M. D., & March, J. G. (1974). *Leadership and ambiguity: The American college president.* New York: McGraw-Hill.

Creamer, D. G., & Winston, R. B., Jr. (1999). The performance appraisal paradox: An essential but neglected student affairs staffing function. *NASPA Journal, 36,* 248–263.

Creamer, D. G., Carpenter, D. S., Forney, D. S., Gehring, D. D., McEwen, M. K., Schuh, J. H., Winston, R. B., Jr., & Woodard, D. B., Jr. (1992). Quality assurance in college student affairs: A proposal for action by professional associations. In R. B. Winston, Jr. & D. G. Creamer, *Improving staffing practices in student affairs* (pp. 353–370). San Francisco: Jossey-Bass.

Dalton, J. C. (1996). Managing human resources. In S. R. Komives, D. B. Woodard, Jr., & Associates, *Student services: A handbook for the profession* (3rd ed., pp. 494–511). San Francisco: Jossey-Bass.

Evans, N. J., Forney, D. S., & Guido-DeBrito, F. (1998). *Student development in college: Theory, research, and practice.* San Francisco: Jossey-Bass.

Gehring, D. D. (1993). Understanding legal constraints on practice. In M. J. Barr & Associates, *The handbook of student affairs administration* (pp. 274–299). San Francisco: Jossey-Bass.

Hirt, J. B., & Creamer, D. G. (1998). Issues facing student affairs professionals: The four realms of professional life. In N. Evans & C. Phelps (Eds.), *The state of the art of preparation and practice in student affairs* (pp. 47–60). Washington, DC: American College Personnel Association.

Hollander, P. A., & Young, D. P. (1991). Legal issues and employment practices in student affairs. In T. K. Miller, R. B. Winston, Jr., & Associates, *Administration and leadership in student affairs: Actualizing student development in higher education* (2nd ed., pp. 212–231). Muncie, IN: Accelerated Development.

Hyde, S., & Carpenter, D. S. (1992). No trespassing: What every alien should know. *NASPA Journal, 29,* 149–152.

Kaplin, W. A., & Lee, B. A. (1995). *The law of higher education: A comprehensive guide to legal implications of administrative decision making* (3rd ed.). San Francisco: Jossey-Bass.

Kuh, G. D. (1996). Organizational theory. In S. R. Komives, D. B. Woodard, Jr., & Associates, *Student services: A handbook for the profession* (3rd ed., pp. 269–294). San Francisco: Jossey-Bass.

Lovell, C. D., & Kosten, L. A. (2000). Skills, knowledge, and personal traits necessary for success as a student affairs administrator: A meta-analysis of thirty years of research. *NASPA Journal, 37,* 553–572.

Miller, T. K. (Ed.). (1999). *The CAS book of professional standards for higher education.* Washington, DC: Council for the Advancement of Standards in Higher Education.

Morgan, G. (1986). *Images of organization.* Newbury Park, CA: Sage.

National Association of Student Personnel Administrators (NASPA). (1992–1993). Standards of professional practice. In *Member Handbook* (pp. 17–18). Washington, DC: Author.

Saunders, S. A., Cooper, D. L., Winston, R. B., Jr., & Chernow, E. A. (2000). Supervising staff in student affairs: Exploration of the synergistic approach. *Journal of College Student Development, 41,* 181–192.

Schwitzer, A. M., Ancis, J. R., & Brown, N. (in press). *Promoting student learning and student development at a distance: Student affairs concepts and practices for televised instruction and other forms of distance learning.* Washington, DC: American College Personnel Association.

Senge, P. M. (1990). *The fifth discipline: The art and practice of the learning organization.* New York: Doubleday/Currency.

Tierney, W. G. (1988). Organizational culture in higher education: Defining the essentials. *Journal of Higher Education, 59,* 2–21.

Walther, J. B., & Reid, L. D. (2000, 4 February). The allure of the Internet. *The Chronicle of Higher Education,* p. B4.

Wheatley, M. J. (1992). *Leadership and the new science: Learning about organization from an orderly universe.* San Francisco: Berrett-Koehler.

Whitt, E. J. (1990). "Don't drink the water?" A guide to encountering a new institutional culture. In E. J. Whitt (Ed.), *College student affairs administration* (pp. 516–523) (ASHE Reader Series), Needham Heights, MA: Simon & Schuster.

Windle, L. M. (1998). Skill performance assessment and need for further professional development of student affairs mid-managers (Doctoral dissertation, Texas A&M University, 1998). *Dissertation Abstracts International, 59,* AAT 9831004.

Winston, R. B., Jr., & Creamer, D. G. (1997). *Improving staffing practices in student affairs.* San Francisco: Jossey-Bass.

Woodard, D. B., Jr. (1998). Societal influences on higher education and student affairs. In N. Evans & C. Phelps (Eds.), *The state of the art of preparation and practice in student affairs* (pp. 3–20). Washington, DC: American College Personnel Association.

Young, R. B. (1996). Guiding values and philosophy. In S. R. Komives, D. B. Woodard, Jr., & Associates, *Student services: A handbook for the profession* (3rd ed., pp. 83–105). San Francisco: Jossey-Bass.

RECOMMENDED READING

Carpenter, D. S. (1998). Continuing professional education in student affairs. In N. Evans & C. Phelps (Eds.), *The state of the art of preparation and practice in student affairs* (p. 159–176). Washington, DC: American College Personnel Association.

Creamer, D. G., & Winston, R. B., Jr. (1999). The performance appraisal paradox: An essential but neglected student affairs staffing function. *NASPA Journal, 36,* 248–263.

Saunders, S. A., Cooper, D. L., Winston, R. B., Jr., & Chernow, E. A. (2000). Supervising staff in student affairs: Exploration of the synergistic approach. *Journal of College Student Development, 41,* 181–192.

Wheatley, M. J. (1992). *Leadership and the new science: Learning about organization from an orderly universe.* San Francisco: Berrett-Koehler.

Winston, R. B., Jr., & Creamer, D. G. (1997). *Improving staffing practices in student affairs.* San Francisco: Jossey-Bass.

9

Finance and Budgeting

DUDLEY B. WOODARD, JR.

*P*rofessional student affairs administrators believe that their work is important and central to institutional mission and priorities; therefore, the institution should adequately fund their programs, interests, and activities. Although these professionals invest themselves in being informed about theory and contexts, which impact on their program development, they do not always show the same commitment to being informed about the mechanisms of finance that enable or inhibit their program implementation. Many practitioners view oversight of the constantly changing mix of revenue, politics of allocation, and accountability and control measures designed to insure financial integrity as being the responsibility of the student affairs budget control officer or even the departmental administrative assistant. The budget is after all "only numbers" and pretty dry and dull stuff when compared to fostering human development, promoting community, or responding to individual urgencies. The budget is perceived as an "out of sight, out of mind" abstraction that only requires focused attention once a year during budget preparation season. It is not until requests for increased allocations are denied, accounts are overspent and frozen, or audits underway that many in student affairs pay heed to the budget.

Is this a cynical view or a too frequently accurate description of attitudes in student affairs? *The budget is the single most important work tool the student affairs administrator uses in developing and implementing activities to meet agreed-upon program activities and outcomes.*

The dramatic changes in sources of revenue and the external pressures for accountability require the student affairs administrator to rethink priorities, restructure functions, develop effective and efficient work performance measures, and demonstrate outcomes. Central to these changes is developing and implementing budgets designed to achieve these objectives. Using the budget effectively requires being a professional student affairs administrator who possesses the knowledge and skills to balance and integrate the roles of educator, leader, and manager. (See Chapter 1 in this volume.) Budgeting is not just about sound management. It requires professionals who have the leadership capacity to create and sustain a vision for the educational organization and to educate staff about the social, political, and economic dimensions of budget development and management. The relevance of budgets to student affairs work and to the broader institutional and societal goals must be explicitly communicated and emphasized.

This chapter addresses (a) some of the trends that have influenced resource acquisition and allocation; (b) the management decision-making cycle and budget structures; (c) budget processes and approaches; and (d) budget advice. The focus is on the student affairs administrator developing an understanding of budgetary terms and models as well as the basic budgetary steps of planning and setting priorities, developing and implementing, controlling and monitoring, and evaluation.

TRENDS INFLUENCING RESOURCE ACQUISITION AND ALLOCATION

To understand the budget structure and process, it is important to trace some of the trends that have changed the higher education finance landscape. The shifts in federal and state policy, along with changes in economic conditions during the last 30 years, have generated new or enhanced approaches to acquiring resources and devising ways to allocate those resources. Moreover, the changing regulatory environment has required institutions to identify resources to meet new compliance standards; the demographic context and the political climate have introduced more uncertainty in projecting resources to fund required and necessary instructional support services for higher education institutions. This section describes some of these trends that have led to a reconceptualization of how resources are acquired and allocated. An effective student affairs administrator works diligently to stay informed of local, regional, and national trends that will likely influence the preparation and implementation of succeeding budgets.

Student Purchasing Power

The moving of need-based student financial aid from institutional block grants to direct aid to students (Slaughter, 1997) gave students new purchasing power to select which institution they would attend. In effect, the "United States adopted a student-as-consumer or market model for post-secondary student aid financing" (p. 1). This simple change had a profound impact as for-profit and not-for-profit institutions began treating students as consumers and marketing their institutions to take advantage of this shift in purchasing power.

Another important change in student purchasing power was the federal government's influence in developing a new financial aid policy based on high tuition and high financial aid (Lopez, 1993). The idea was "to keep the private sector competitive with the public sector and to reduce public costs by making users who were able to pay cover a larger share of their costs" (Slaughter, 1997, p. 5). In effect, high-income students were receiving the benefit of a state subsidy, creating an inequity and further straining state budgets. By charging students the *real cost* of an education, some of the revenue was diverted to grants for needy students and the remainder to the operating fund (Lopez, 1993). This policy worked until the grant program for middle-income students was sharply cut back during the Reagan administration and yearly tuition increases exceeded inflationary increases. Revenues, therefore, were insufficient to support the high financial aid policy and students were forced to increase borrowing and hours spent working. In retrospect, these two changes had a profound and lasting effect on the financing of higher education and patterns of attendance.

Resource Competition

The massification of higher education in the United States occurred at a time of increasing fiscal constraints and competition for state and federal resources from other state agencies such as health and public safety. Moreover, the growth in federal entitlement programs reduced the discretionary budget of the federal government, leaving less for financial aid and support for research and training contracts. It is clear that the continuing competition for state and federal dollars, especially in terms of financial aid assistance, will persist for the foreseeable future. Both public and private institutions need to identify sources, other than tuition, to support student services and programs.

Federal Mandates

There have been several far-reaching federal mandates over the past 30 years that have had serious budgetary implications. For example, the Americans with Disabilities Act (ADA) required institutions to expend funds to improve access for disabled employees and students and to modify classroom and teaching conditions to accommodate physical, emotional, and learning disabilities. Other federal mandates such as Title IX, which bans discrimination based on sex, Family Education Rights and Privacy Act (also known as the Buckley Amendment or FERPA), Freedom of Information Act, copyright laws, and affirmative action have real costs associated with compliance and have forced institutions to reallocate resources to meet the requirements of these statutes. (See Chapter 5 in this volume for discussion of several of these mandates.) Many of these statutes have provided new opportunities for individuals who have been marginalized by higher education. The cost of these programs, however, has had the effect of shifting dollars from one source to another, rather than increasing revenues for institutions. In other words, institutions were instructed to "do more, with less, for more students," thereby eroding the funding base of higher education.

Entrepreneurialism

Another trend during this time was a change in federal policy that began to promote "technoscience" as central to the national economy. This emphasis led to legislative changes that permitted partnerships with industry, resulting in the creation of industrial and research parks, promotion of privatization through spin-off companies, and emphasis on commercial ventures (Slaughter, 1997). Colleges and universities began to capitalize on commercial efforts to generate new revenue and privatized traditionally operated college and university functions as a cost saving measure. Faculty members in research universities were encouraged to increase grant-writing activities and use their academic capital (Slaughter & Leslie, 1997) to develop partnerships with companies and create private ventures to transfer technology and research product findings into commercially viable goods and services. Faculty members in community colleges and four-year institutions were encouraged to seek training grants and set up partnerships with local industry to train individuals for the workforce. Many of these institutions engaged in these entrepreneurial ventures as a way to generate new resources to replace funding reductions and to meet escalating costs. These market-driven funding activities have changed how professional administrators and faculty members spend their time. Consequently, several significant changes have occurred in day-to-day operations, including (a) curricular changes to reflect new agreements with external partners; (b) continued underfunding of academic and student service areas not in a position to profit from the marketplace; and (c) less time devoted to advising and teaching activities.

Globalization

The globalization of the economy is another trend that has influenced the flow of monies into institutions. Thurow (1991) described this as a new era: "U.S. colleges and universities—and our schools especially—need to realize that we have entered a new economic era, where educated, hard-working people will be the critical resource" (p. 23). Knowledge capital is the new currency and is being driven by a technoscience/information-based economy. Those institutions that move their products closer to the marketplace and are more responsive to it will be the beneficiaries of this type of economic growth. The cost of participation in this rapidly expanding global economy may be the abandonment of institutional core principles and values in exchange for another set of principles and values more reflective of global economy market values.

These trends have dramatically altered the financing of higher education in all sectors. For example, many private institutions have developed market niches and used technology effectively to generate additional tuition revenue from industry by accommodating the training needs of their employees. Community colleges use distance learning to educate students in remote parts of a state or offer state-funded certificate programs to retrain the unemployed. And public four-year and research universities have aggressively moved into the marketplace, raising money to replace reduced funding through outsourcing, commercial activities, and partnerships with industry. These are a few examples of how the higher education finance landscape has changed, and a new reality for revenue generation, priority setting, and budgeting has emerged.

MANAGEMENT CYCLE AND BUDGET STRUCTURE

Most postsecondary institutions use the budgetary and accounting standards recommended by the National Association of College and University Business Officers (NACUBO, 1997) to organize fiscal operations. (Because budgets tend to have their own language, a glossary of budgeting terms appears in Figure 9.1.) These standards allow for budget comparison among and between institutions, as well as the development of systems support to operationalize planning and to make resource allocation decisions. The NACUBO standards serve as a blueprint for the management of institutional resources and the development of budgets to implement institutional plans on how to wisely invest and spend those resources. This section addresses (a) the budget function in the context of the management process of planning, implementing, controlling, and evaluation, and (b) the operating and capital budgets, including standardized budget categories and sources of revenues.

Management Cycle

The role of budgeting in higher education is to implement institutional priorities through organizational structures and activities and the behaviors of its members. The budget is a projection of financial resources and an expenditure plan based on institutional priorities and mandates designed for control and accountability to the agencies that provided the funds. Budgeting is one of the key elements of the ongoing management cycle. This management cycle usually consists of four components: (a) planning, (b) budgeting, (c) operating and controlling, and (d) evaluating (Rachlin, 1999).

Strategic planning takes into account both internal and external factors that influence the decisions and directions of the institutions. Environmental scanning helps decisionmakers understand the needs of prospective students and the communities they serve. Through the strategic planning process, the institution identifies short- and long-term strategic priorities that reflect the mission and core principles of the institution. These strategic priorities become the centerpiece of the budget development plan. For instance, a community college may want to serve an increasing number of students interested in information technology. This becomes a strategic direction and resources are allocated to fund this initiative.

Once institutional priorities are identified and agreed upon, a financial and expenditure plan is developed. The financial plan is a realistic assessment of likely revenues that can be allocated to meet the ongoing functions/activities

BUDGET DEFINITIONS

The following list represents some of the frequently used budgetary terms. Term usage may vary depending on type of institution, geographical location, and mission. Familiarity with these terms and meaning derived from the local context are important to understand in the development and monitoring of budgets.

Accountability: Once the budget has been approved, designated individuals are responsible for making certain that expenditures reflect the approved plan or that the appropriate authority has approved changes.

Authorization and Appropriations: "Authorization legislation is usually a prerequisite for subsequent appropriations or other kinds of budget authorization . . . and appropriations permit agencies to incur obligations and to make payments for specified purposes" (Wildavsky & Caiden, 1997, p. 337). Most states have enacted legislation for spending money from the state treasury for the cost of higher education, but each year the legislature decides whether to fund at the authorized level or at a lesser amount.

Auxiliary: Services or programs that are financially self-supporting. Housing and food service operations are examples of enterprises that are frequently operated as auxiliary services. Some services or programs may be "mixed" enterprises in as much as they are funded partially through appropriations and partially through auxiliary activities. Health services and student unions are two examples of areas that are frequently "mixed" in this way.

Benefits: These include health, life, disability, and other insurance; vacation days; compensatory time; and pension plans. These are actual costs and must be included in the budget plan.

Budget: It is a spending plan that reflects the organizational structures, activities, and behaviors of the institution and its members. It is a projection about financial resources and an expenditure plan based on institutional priorities and mandates. The expenditure plan is designed for control and accountability to the agencies that provided those resources.

Budget Base: This is the starting point. The point may be last year's level of funding, or it may be zero-based funding, which justifies everything requested for the next fiscal year. It is the base to which "increase (or decrease) factors are applied to calculate the total funds and revenue targets for the next fiscal year" (Maddox, 1999, p. 258).

Budget Components: Most institutions have three budgets: operating, capital, and cash. The operating budget is "revenue received and expenses incurred." The capital includes "construction, building renewal projects, purchases of equipment, major computer software, etc."; cash flow "includes all receipts and disbursements of cash during the year" (Maddox, 1999, p. 60).

Cycle: Budgets are usually a three-cycle activity—closure and auditing of the previous year, the current year, and preparation for the next fiscal year.

Funding Sources: These include state and federal appropriations, contracts and grants, tuition and fees, gifts, financial aid, auxiliary revenue, and other sources.

Mandates/Fixed Costs: These are items for which there is little flexibility in funding for the next fiscal year. Examples include compliance with federal mandates like the American with Disabilities Act or the cost of utilities.

Restricted and Unrestricted Funds: Restricted funds are determined by the requirements of the legislature, grants, or donors. Unrestricted funds can be applied according to the priorities set by the institution.

Roll-up: This is an activity designed to show budget activity at the lowest function, such as a department. Each successive roll-up shows the budget activity at the next level, such as college or division.

Variance: This is the difference between approved expenditure level and actual expenditures.

FIGURE 9.1. Budget Definitions

of the institution and any new initiatives reflective of priorities. The expenditure plan translates the institution's strategic plan into financial terms to accomplish the goals and objectives contained in the plan (Rachlin, 1999, p. 23). Once the budget has been approved, designated individuals assume responsibility for its implementation and for making certain that expenditures reflect the approved plan. This is the operations and control phase of budgeting.

The fourth function of the management cycle is evaluation. The evaluation plan helps to determine whether the expenditure plan was sufficient to carry out the various activities/programs and whether these activities/programs were successful in meeting desired strategic priorities or goals. In other words, the monies may have been spent according to the expenditure plan, but the programs and activities may not have achieved the objectives of the strategic priority. Unfortunately, evaluation is the most likely step in this management cycle to be ignored or accomplished poorly. A sound ongoing evaluation process helps decisionmakers make the necessary changes to successfully implement the strategic plan. Careful execution of the evaluation portion of the cycle also enhances the credibility of the student affairs administrator.

This dynamic process of planning, budgeting, implementing, and evaluating is illustrated in Figure 9.2. It is an open system in which both internal and external factors influence the planning process and the development of the budget. For example, economic conditions, political climate, state and federal entitlement programs, competing agencies, college attendance rates, and the demographic characteristics of the population are some of the external factors that institutions have to take into account when developing strategic directions and revenue projections. Internal factors such as fixed costs, mandated requirements, teaching load, contract agreements, class size, and changing interests of students also play an important role in influencing decision making and resource allocation. Identifying these internal and external factors and the nature of their influence on the management cycle is fundamental to sound planning and decisionmaking.

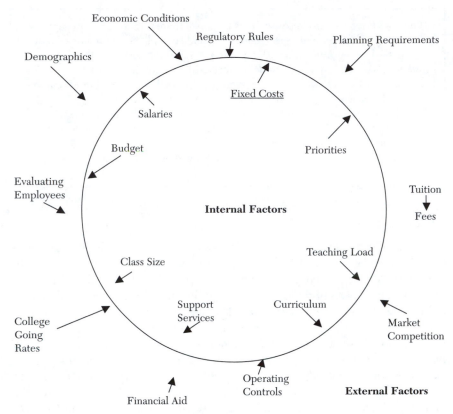

FIGURE 9.2. External/Internal Influences of the Planning and Budgetary Process

Budget Format

Generally, there are two types of budget spreadsheets—the current operating budget and the noncurrent operating budget (capital budget). The 12 expenditure functions recommended by NACUBO (see Table 9.1) are (a) educational and general, (b) instruction, (c) research, (d) public service, (e) academic support, (f) institutional support, (g) operations/plant maintenance, (h) scholarships/fellowships, (i) hospitals (if applicable), (j) independent operations, (k) auxiliary services, and (l) student services. The major sources of revenue are state/county/local appropriations, tuition and fees, auxiliary income (residence halls, bookstore, food service), endowment earnings, private/state/federal contracts and grants, and capital endowments (gifts designated for capital projects).

All institutions do not use the same budget format. Most use the NACUBO functions where appropriate, although variations are found that generally are a function of institutional type and size. Some institutions will collapse everything into a single-purpose budget, whereas other institutions may have several budgets reflecting the complexity of the institution.

The operating budget is the institution's expenditure plan for instructional

TABLE 9.1. NACUBO Financial Accounting and Reporting Definitions

Categories	Definitions
Educational and General	All expenditures that are not auxiliary enterprises or independent operations; instruction, research, public service, academic support, institutional support, operation and maintenance of plant, scholarships and fellowships, auxiliary, and student services.
Instruction	Expenditures for credit and noncredit courses; academic, vocational, and technical instruction; remedial and tutorial instruction; and regular, special, and extension sessions.
Research	Expenditures for activities specifically organized to produce research, including individual and/or project research; institutes and research centers; and separately budgeted departmental research.
Public Service	Expenditures to provide noninstructional services beneficial to individuals and groups external to the institution; community service programs; cooperative extension services; consulting; reference bureaus.
Academic Support	Expenditures for support services to instruction, research, and public service; retention, preservation, display of educational materials; audiovisual services and technology; course and curriculum development.
Institutional Support	Expenditures for management and long-range planning; governing board; planning and programming; legal services; fiscal operations; administrative data processing; space management; employee/personnel records; procurement, storerooms, safety, security, printing, transportation; community and alumni relations.
Operations/Plant Maintenance	Current operating funds for maintenance and operation of the physical plant; grounds and facilities; fire protection, utilities, and property insurance.
Scholarships/ Fellowships	Expenditures for scholarships and fellowships; grants to students, trainee stipends, prizes, and awards from selection by the institution or from an entitlement program; funds may be restricted or unrestricted.
Hospitals	Expenditures associated with patient care, operations of a hospital; nursing and other professional services, general services, administrative services, fiscal services, physical plant, institutional support.
Independent Operations	Commercial enterprises operated by the institution but not established to provide services to students, faculty, or staff or to provide support to one or more of the institution's missions.
Auxiliary Services	Essentially self-supporting activities; residence halls, food services, intercollegiate athletics, college stores, faculty clubs, faculty and staff parking, faculty housing, hospitals, hotels, and convention facilities.
Student Services	Expenditures from registrar and admissions offices; activities contributing to students' emotional and physical well-being and intellectual, cultural, and social development outside the context of the formal instruction program; cultural events; intramural athletics; student organizations; student health service.

Adapted from *Financial Accounting and Reporting Manual for Higher Education,* Release 97-6. National Association of College and University Business Officers, 1997. Reproduced by permission of the National Association of College and University Business Officers.

activities, academic support, research, public service, institutional support, student services and auxiliary activities. Each expenditure category is broken down into several object codes such as personnel and employee benefits (see Table 9.2). The example illustrated in Table 9.2 is for a student affairs department in a small college. The left-hand column lists all the expenditure categories and the top row indicates the expenditure purposes. For example, most of the personnel costs are assigned to student support. However, some personnel costs are assigned to research and instruction because this department has student affairs professionals who teach a freshmen seminar and others who are actively involved in a funded research project on student violence.

The capital budget is an institution's expenditure plan for new and replacement equipment, infrastructure projects, construction of new buildings, or renovation of existing space. Many student affairs administrators do not receive a capital budget; rather, any capital expense such as equipment appears as a line item in the institutional operating budget. When capital budgets do exist in student affairs, they are typically for the purpose of construction or renovation of auxiliary facilities. These capital budgets are often funded through budgeted transfers from operating revenues. The sources of funding for the capital budget are the same sources listed in the operating budget.

In the case of New College, most of its instructional revenue comes from tuition and fees while the state supports academic and student services. In addition, some instructional activities are funded from the college's endowment. A donor may have endowed an academic chair or funded the entrepreneurial program in the business college. Colleges and universities identify the source of funds so that the money is used for the designated purpose(s). Funds are usually classified as restricted or unrestricted. Restricted funds may be used only according to the prescribed purposes of the appropriation, grant/contract, or donor. Unrestricted funds may be used for purposes that the institution deems appropriate; yet some institutions will place restrictions on how these funds may be used. For example, in some colleges, unrestricted funds may not be used for faculty travel or the purchase of alcohol.

Some other examples will help to illustrate the variation that exists among sources and uses of revenue. A community college may or may not receive state support but usually does receive county and local support as a way of keeping tuition costs affordable for the populations it serves. Building project costs for private institutions usually come from a combination of gifts and revenue set aside to service debt. Public financing of capital projects comes from several sources. Some institutions receive state funding, whereas others are required to fund capital projects by using tuition and fee monies, gifts, endowment earnings, or grants. Many community college capital projects are funded from local/state bonding authority or state funds. The operating and capital budgets are usually printed every month so the budget unit manager can reconcile expenses and revenue and determine if, for example, expenditures are occurring at a rate that will lead to a budget deficit. This allows the manager to make corrections to avoid an overexpenditure. It is increasingly the case that budget information is

TABLE 9.2. New College 2000-2001 Budget

	Current Operating						Noncurrent Operating						
	Sources of Funding						Sources of Funding						
	State county local	Tuition fees	Auxiliary	Endowment	Contracts grants	Capital endowment	State county local	Tuition fees	Auxiliary	Endowment	Contracts grants	Capital endowment	Total
Instruction													
Academic support		11,200		8,000									
Research			18,000		23,000								
Public service													
Instructional support	198,968												
Student service													
Auxiliary													

Student Life Office

Account	FTE	Instruction	Research	Public service	Academic support	Student support	Institutional support	Phys. plant operations	Student fin. suppt.	Independent operations	Total
Personal services											
State funds	5.0	16,000					111,000		6,400		133,400
Local	.5		18,000								18,000
Allocations											
Other											
Employee benefits											
State funds		3,200	3,600				32,200		768		39,768
General operations											
State funds		1,500					18,500				20,000
Travel in-state											
State funds							2,700				2,700
Travel out-of-state											
State funds							6,400				6,400
Capital investment											
State funds							5,500				5,500
Student support											
State funds							4,400				4,400
Other							2,000				2,000
Total		20,700	21,600				182,700		7,168		232,168

available on-line, thus providing access to more current and timely information. These reports, whether printed or on-line, are one of the several tools available to managers to monitor and control expenses according to the approved budget plan. Other tools for responsible fiscal oversight are internal audits and a strong cash management program.

BUDGETARY PROCESSES AND APPROACHES

Most observers (Breneman, 1993; Johnstone, 1998; Leslie, 1995) do not foresee any radical changes in the funding of higher education during the next decade. Rather, they see a continuing pattern of turbulence, dissatisfaction, cost-saving measures, increased productivity, cost-saving technology, and the generation of new and increasing sources of revenue on the periphery (for example, new professional programs, distance learning, and partnerships with the private sector). As Breneman (1993) points out, this pattern has been the *new reality* of the past 20 years and will continue for the foreseeable future. Changes in federal and state policy, competition for funds by other social agencies, increased enrollments, a shift in the mix of financial aid, and an increasing reliance on partnerships with the private sector have created this new reality.

These profound changes in the funding of higher education have led to a reconceptualization of the budgeting process and budgeting techniques. Selection of a budgeting technique such as zero-based budgeting or responsibility-centered budgeting may fit an institution's need; however, whatever the choice of technique, the budgeting process must be managed. This next section discusses a process for management and some of the budgeting approaches used in developing an institution's budget.

Budgetary Process

The budget process is usually thought of in three phases: (a) budget development; (b) budget monitoring, tracking, and adjustments; and (c) analysis of final results (Maddox, 1999). These activities overlap during the budget cycle and, according to Maddox, "budget development takes place before the budget year in question starts; monitoring and adjustment occur throughout the budget year; final results are analyzed after the year ends" (p. 27). During the budget development phase, five specific methods of tying the budget process to the strategic planning process of the institution may be used:

> (a) the budget process should be organized so that all elements likely to compete for institutional resources can be considered at the same time; (b) financial data should be organized according to the logic of decision making as well as the logic of control, and resources that support a broad objective should be identified with that objective; (c) program data, such as the number of students enrolled, should be provided along with financial data for each program; (d) in addition to the budget year, financial and program data should

be provided for several years into the future; and (e) the budget process should be closely coordinated and integrated with institutional planning and control processes. (Lasher & Green, 1993, p. 429)

There are basic steps managers need to take in preparing the student affairs division or departmental budgets. First, managers must make certain they understand the institutional mission and priorities and the connection of divisional and departmental priorities to those of the broader institution. This tight coupling of priorities should enhance the chances of receiving funding for the proposed budget activities. Second, it is important to understand the historical development of budgets and how the institution and external funding agencies have responded to budget requests. In other words, the lessons learned from previous budget cycles must be taken into account. Third, an understanding of the current and future financial status of the institution and its sources of revenue is important to gauge the parameters of the budget request. The timing of when to ask for more or for less is tied to the current and projected financial status of the institution. And fourth, the division should develop budgetary guidelines that will assist in the preparation of the budget regardless of the fiscal climate, including (a) workload factors and measurable outcomes; (b) criteria to evaluate contributions of each program; (c) criteria for restructuring and reallocating funds; and (d) expectations for generating sources of revenue. Whatever the guidelines, they should be developed and agreed to in consultation with staff. This will bring integrity to the process by demonstrating the principles that will be used in making final decisions.

Once the institutional parameters and divisional budgetary guidelines have been established, the chief student affairs officer, in consultation with department heads, should decide on the steps in the budgetary process. Woodard (1993) described seven distinct steps in preparing the divisional budget request:

Establish assumptions and constraints.   This is the data-gathering stage of understanding how enrollment will likely change, how the stock market has affected the institution's financial portfolio, what the outlook for the state economy is, or what the fixed costs such as federal mandates are. Assumptions about sources of revenue, enrollment, program offerings, and constraints like mandated requirements and fixed costs must be understood and shared with all individuals responsible for developing the budget.

Create guidelines and timetable.   Written guidelines that describe institutional assumptions, priorities, and constraints should be sent to department heads. Further, the format for developing the budget should be explicated and a reasonable time line should be established for submitting the departmental budgets.

Hold hearings.   Schedule hearings for each department. This should be a public hearing and faculty members, student leaders, and staff should be invited to participate. This is a time for the department head to make his or her case and be questioned by the users of the services and programs as to the effectiveness and efficiency of the department and soundness of new plans and directions. A public hearing will help individuals be more sensitive to the community's needs and perceptions on how well these needs are being met.

Develop alternatives. Each department should develop alternative scenarios as a way to respond to new opportunities or difficult financial challenges. The development of these scenarios will often lead to new ways of thinking about an issue/program and cost-saving measures.

Debate with central staff. After the public hearings and departmental budgets have been prepared, the central staff (management team) of the division should have an open and vigorous discussion informed by the principles/guidelines agreed to in preparing the budget requests. This kind of debate will deepen understandings about each department's requests, trigger ways of meeting objectives through reallocation and reconfiguration, and develop an overall rationale for presentation to the president and cabinet members.

Stay informed and keep others informed. The budget process is organic, and there are changes daily either in institutional parameters or in external parameters/constraints. Keep staff informed of these changes and the likely impact on budget requests. This will help control rumors and prepare individuals to make adjustments as required.

Once the budget has been approved, many managers fall asleep at the budget control switch and concentrate more on program implementation and service. The first task in managing the budget is to make sure that spending corresponds to approved expenditures and that revenues are consistent with projections. A system should be agreed to and an individual should be identified as being responsible for monitoring revenues and expenditures. This should be done on a monthly basis, and audits of expenditures should be made each month. For example, telephone calls should be audited to make sure there is no unauthorized use of the office telephone. There are times that budget adjustments will need to be made. A process should be devised for dealing with this contingency. Moreover, someone should be continually scanning for cost-saving measures, and these should be used as a way of reducing expenditures and freeing up resources for other purposes or unanticipated expenses. Line managers should not wait for the business office to call to discuss unapproved expenditures or expenditures that have exceeded an approved level. If necessary, a plan for meeting these unapproved expenditures, as well as any necessary changes, should be made in consultation with the institutional business office. Finally, managers should do a year-end analysis to understand expenditure patterns and any variances. This information will help with the preparation and development of a plan for generating resources for the next budget.

Usually there is a mix of budget models in designing the budgetary approach for an institution. The budget approach and process will depend on the context and type of institution. A clear understanding of institutional priorities and financial resources, broad-based participation, measurable outcomes, and responsibility and control for allocated resources will lead to greater account-ability and furtherance of institutional objectives.

Administrators new to an institution should seek a budget maven or guru, that is, someone who is willing to offer unbiased advice and who is familiar with the institution's formal rules, but even more importantly, someone who under-stands the informal, unwritten budget rules. One's maven may be an *astute* support staff person who has accumulated a wealth of valuable knowledge about the institution's budgeting process or a seasoned professional either inside or outside of student affairs.

All budget systems have unwritten rules or practices, the violation of which can have serious repercussions. For instance, at some institutions it is custom-ary for vice presidents for student affairs to be very conservative in allocation of supply and equipment funds until near the end of the fiscal year. Near the end of "good" years—that is, where there have been few unexpected expenses—departments may expect to have funds released to purchase computers or other needed equipment. Generally, this practice will not be written into any budget procedures manual. It is, nonetheless, essential to be mindful of these informal guidelines.

Budget Models

During the 1970s, incrementalism was the major budget approach. This is a bottom-up approach in which managers play the role of advocate by "attempt-ing to maintain their base and gain small increases; . . . it concentrates on the parts not the whole" (Rubin, 1988, p. 23). Thus, the changes were marginal and budgeting essentially became a balkanized approach to the allocation of re-sources. During the 1980s, attempts were made to make the budgetary process more rational. This was done by using "program budgeting, management by objectives, and zero-based budgeting approaches which focused on tying allo-cations to outcomes and allowed for internal reallocation of revenue to new programs and needs" (p. 19). These approaches resulted in what Wildavsky and Caiden (1997) called dissensus; that is, decisions were made politically rather than on the merits of priorities or program needs. These budgets relied on conventional planning techniques, which frequently resulted in 5- and 10-year plans that did not take into account or fully appreciate the changes in state and federal policies and marketplace needs. The 1990s ushered in the era of an-other budget reform, "in response to increasing demands for accountability and reduced public revenues" (Lasher & Green, 1993, p. 442). The strategy shifted from funding formulas to accountability and productivity. State legislatures, funding agencies, and governing boards became actively involved in tying allo-cations to measurable outcomes and productivity indicators. (See Chapter 14 in this volume.) This reconceptualization of the budgetary process has led to new budgetary approaches such as cost-centered and responsibility-centered budgeting.

Budget models can be divided between conventional models and emerging models. Although most institutions and funding agencies use a mixed approach, the current emphasis is on using models that are founded on broad-based participation, productivity indicators, and measurable outcomes. The following models represent the array of budget approaches, and any one or combination of models can fulfill the requirement of establishing an annual budget.

Conventional Models

Conventional models include incremental, zero-based, formula, cost-centered, and program budgets.

Incremental. This is one of the oldest approaches to budgeting and assumes that resources from one budget cycle to another will only change modestly. The approach further assumes "basic objectives of the institution, the department, or the program have not changed markedly from the current year, and that they will continue into the next year" (Lasher & Green, 1993, p. 442). This model of budgeting is easily implemented, but it does not force the institution to examine "priorities in a way that encourages annual reallocation, reductions, and elimination of programs" (Woodard & von Destinon, 1999, p. 12).

Zero based. Zero-based budgeting builds in an annual review of each department's performance, cost benefits, and relationship to the institution's strategic plan. Each year everything must be justified or discontinued through the use of cost–benefit analysis (Schuh, 1990). This justification process should yield budgets that are responsive to changing conditions and are based on results; however, the approach can be very time consuming and divisive. Line managers may feel pressure to constantly defend their activities and programs. It can foster a kind of seige mentality among budget unit managers whose departments are not directly connected to the institution's present initiatives.

Formula. Formula budgeting is a way of allocating or appropriating dollars to an activity based on quantifiable workload measures. "Each formula manipulates certain institutional data based on mathematical relationships between program demand and costs to derive an estimated dollar amount to support future program operation" (Lasher & Green, 1993, p. 443). This approach seems objective and equitable and reduces conflict because individuals understand the basis of funding. It is frequently used by state-level agencies and is generally not used by institutions to allocate funds. Formula budgeting is a political process, and unless the state has a strong revenue position, debate centers on how much and to whom. As Woodard and von Destinon (1999) observed, "formula budgeting is widely used but its utility should be in question since it does not encourage program assessment or respond in a timely way to emerging needs or recognize differences among institutions" (p. 336).

Cost centered.   Cost-centered budgeting is used mostly for auxiliary units or academic units that generate, through grants and contracts, most of their revenue. The principle is that every unit/department pays its own way. This type of budgeting works more successfully with "units that are relatively independent in the sense that the instructional and research programs are self contained" (Meisinger & Dubeck, 1984, p. 188). These units generally pay an administrative or overhead charge for institutional services and retain any excess funds at the end of the year. Any deficits are taken from anticipated revenues for the next year.

Program.   Program budgeting is a way of linking strategic planning elements to resource allocation. The objective is "to carefully review program priorities as part of a complex institutional system" (Muston, 1980, p. 80). It focuses on a clear and detailed description of program activities and the cost effectiveness of those activities in terms of attaining desired objectives. The institution's strategic plan is used to establish priorities and a cost–benefit analysis study is done. The cost–benefit analysis is used to determine alternative ways of reaching the goals and objectives through an examination of resources required for each program activity and the estimated benefits to be gained (Woodard & von Destinon, 1999). This is a time-consuming process and the costs of gathering data and the subsequent analysis can be considerable. Some potential problems of this approach are defining outputs of higher education, quantifying program activities, determining cost–benefit ratios, and calculating cost benefits of alternative programs (Schuh, 1990).

Emergent Budgeting Models

Budget models that fall under the emergent paradigm include participative, responsibility-centered, and performance budgets.

Participative.   This approach to budgeting works best in an institutional setting with a history of shared governance and is built on the collegial decision-making model. It is a bottom-up approach and can be effective with broad-based participation. Participative budgeting usually involves the appointment of a campuswide committee that holds hearings and makes its recommendations to the president. It is an open process and "takes time to prepare 'user-friendly' communications materials for the campus, organize meetings and other vehicles for obtaining reactions, and respond to questions and suggestions" (Chabotar, 1995, p. 22). The process can be educational and may develop a broad-based understanding of institutional priorities and state and/or institutional financial status. It is viewed as fair because the committee usually establishes principles to guide its work and widely communicates these principles.

Everyone knows the priorities and the rules by which decisions will be made. On the other hand, it is a time-consuming process and does not work in environments that have a history of rancor and dissent. "Success depends upon careful orchestration and relentless honesty, as well as on remembering that a budget is a plan, a presentation of institutional values, and a political document in which almost everyone has both a stake and role" (p. 29).

Responsibility centered.   Responsibility-centered budgeting has evolved as a way to devolve centralized planning and decision making and to make each academic/service unit financially responsible for its own activities. Three principles serve as the basis for responsibility-centered budgeting: (a) All cost and income attributable to each unit should be assigned to that unit; (b) incentives should be used to increase revenue and reduce costs; and (c) each unit is taxed to meet institutional fixed expenses (Lasher & Green, 1993). Revenue is assigned to the units that generate it, and the unit can allocate dollars according to unit principles and needs as long as the agreed-to instructional/service requirements are met. This approach has been primarily used with academic units but can be applied to student academic and support services. The major advantage is that each unit can control its destiny by enhancing revenue, implementing cost-saving measures, or increasing productivity. The major disadvantage is that it can lead to the segmentation of units by creating competition for "students and resources, making it difficult for them to work toward a common vision or to set academic goals" (Stocum & Rooney, 1997, p. 52). The marketization of academic units, for example, encourages units to seek out opportunities to generate income while moving these units further away from the core mission of the institution. Moreover, some academic/service units have less capacity to generate recourse because of the nature of their work or the conditions of the marketplace. These units do not fare well under this model.

Performance.   Performance-based budgeting is similar to responsibility-centered budgeting, but it is tied to outcome measures and performance indicators. Some states have shifted their funding allocations (or some portion thereof) based on measurable outcomes such as graduation rates, competency-based indicators, and placement. In large state systems, allocations are tied to board-approved outcomes, increases in productivity, and cost-saving measures. This allows for redistribution of resources among institutions based on achievement of board approved performance measures. Similar to program budgeting, "there is disagreement regarding definition and measurement of performance measures. It is often difficult to identify appropriate, measurable criteria on which to judge performance. There is not always a proven relationship between the cause and effect of the criteria and the measures used as proxies for the desired accomplishments" (Lasher & Green, 1993, p. 448). Aside from the issues of defining and agreeing on performance indicators, there is great interest in moving institutions to some form of budgeting based on outcomes as a way of demonstrating public accountability.

ADVICE TO PRACTITIONERS

The budgetary process is an ongoing function that requires the active participation of all levels of student affairs administrators. Like any good recipe, a pinch here and a dash there can make a considerable difference in the outcome. The advice given below comes from the experience of several individuals who have been part of this changing landscape. Their insights on the budgetary process may help avoid pitfalls and make a difference in the development, implementation, monitoring, and evaluation of the budgetary process.

Forest or the Trees

Do not get bogged down by planning jargon or the belief that there is only one right way to plan. Planning is designed to help develop the big picture and make key decisions using all the information available that will lead to informed priority setting and decision making. Planning is not separated from implementation and the people who have to carry out a plan must believe in it and be committed to its goals, schedules, and costs (Finney, 1994).

Assumptions

Start a discussion on what assumptions are being made about the budget process. Is it a fair and rational process or is it a power-based political process? Is it designed to meet institutional mission and the needs of the people the institution serves? Does it reflect agreed-upon institutional priorities?

Signposts

Continually practice environmental scanning and keep a pulse on trends and likely changes. A budget is not static. Adjustments based on new information should be made before it is too late to make corrections.

Penny Wise and Pound Foolish

Spending a lot of time to save a nickel on printing costs, for example, may not be a good investment of time. Instead, spend more time examining the large items that may yield greater savings or greater effects.

Cooperation, not Competition

The budget process should not be viewed as a gladiator game but rather as an opportunity to support the institutional mission and priorities through activities and programs that are connected to the mission and priorities. In some cases, this means scaling back on activities, reallocating resources to new initiatives, or enhancing existing programs.

Revenue Sources

It is imperative that one understands likely future sources of revenue and how the mix of these revenue sources will affect the budgetary process. The "show me the money" attitude moves one from being a collaborator to being a gladiator.

Develop Alternatives

Acting as if the budget is like a poker game such as Texas Hold 'Em does not work very well in a collegial environment. Develop budgetary alternatives and be prepared to discuss alternatives as a way of helping to balance needs, priorities, and anticipated revenue.

Productivity

Simply stating that "we are working harder and longer" does not cut it! Increased productivity does not mean working longer. Rather, it means understanding how professionals spend their time and, as a consequence, redefining how one should spend time in order to meet program initiatives/objectives. Developing measurable workload indicators is a prerequisite to this activity.

Performance

Clearly specify expected outcomes and design a process at the beginning stages to assess and evaluate program objectives. Designing an evaluation program as an afterthought generally will be met with skepticism and undermine a unit's credibility.

Delete to Protect

All programs are not created equally. In difficult times and in rational times, it is necessary to delete some programs to protect others. It does not make sense to weaken high-demand successful programs to protect underserving less successful programs unless such a program has been targeted as an institutional priority.

Politics

The budgetary process is a political process. It is important to understand who one needs to inform and lobby to for approval or support of proposals. What is important in being political is to be ethical and to reinforce the core principles of the profession.

Original Sin

Do not withhold information from one's superior or others. If the original revenue projections were wrong or expenses are more than anticipated, do not delay. Think about how to address the problem. Many practitioners hope things will work out when planning has gone awry. But things do not just work out, in most cases, unless there is intentional intervention.

Human Stress

Financial stress leads to human stress. Just as horses start nipping at one another when the trough is empty, so do humans. Look for signs of stress induced by financial issues and find ways to address stress before it becomes a destructive force.

SUMMARY

This chapter described the changing higher education financial landscape and budget assumptions, terms, models, and approaches. In order to meet the needs of students and other community members and advance the interests of the student affairs staff, an understanding of the budgeting process and how to use it is a prerequisite for success.

The student affairs professional combines all three roles of leader, educator, and manager during the budgetary cycles. As a leader, the student affairs professional helps to create and to sustain a vision and translates the vision into budgetary priorities. The leader is responsible for articulating priorities and gaining consensus and support for these priorities. As a manager, the student affairs professional is responsible for making certain that the budgetary process is understood, fair, and that different constituencies have a voice in the process. The manager has the oversight responsibility for the implementation, monitoring, and evaluation of the budget. As an educator, the student affairs professional uses the budgetary process as a way to educate faculty, students, and external constituents about the programs, activities, and needs of the student affairs unit and how these programs and activities are responsive to institutional mission and priorities. The budgeting process is an opportunity for the senior student affairs professional to work with new professionals in developing an understanding of how the budgeting process works and the skills required for building, securing, and implementing budgets.

QUESTIONS TO CONSIDER

1. What are the initial steps one should take in preparation for developing a budget for the next fiscal year?
2. What are some of the budgetary constraints in student affairs?
3. What are the major budgetary components?
4. Describe a system for implementing, monitoring, and evaluating the budget.
5. Why do you think most people only pay lip service to the budgetary process except during the initial request and allocation stages?

REFERENCES

Breneman, D. W. (1993). *Higher education: On a collision course with new realities.* AGB Occasional Paper Series No. 22. Boston, MA: Association of Governing Boards.

Chabotar, K. J. (1995). Managing participative budgeting in higher education. *Change, 27*(5), 20–29.

Finney, R. G. (1994). *Basics of budgeting.* New York: American Management Association.

Johnstone, D. B. (1998). Patterns of finance: Revolution, evolution, or more of the same? *Review of Higher Education, 21*, 245–255.

Lasher, W. F., & Green, D. L. (1993). Qualitative and quantitative approaches to academic culture: Do they tell us the same thing? *Higher education: Handbook of theory and research, 9*, 428–469.

Leslie, L. (1995). What drives higher education management in the 1990s and beyond? The new era in financial support. *Journal for Higher Education Management, 10*(2), 5–16.

Lopez, M. (1993, April 7). High tuition, high aid won't work. *The Chronicle of Higher Education*, p. A13.

Maddox, D. (1999). *Budgeting for not-for-profit organizations.* New York: John Wiley & Sons.

Meisinger, R. J., & Dubeck, L. W. (1984). *College and university budgeting: An introduction for faculty and academic administrators.* Washington, DC: National Association of College and University Business Officers.

Muston, R. A. (1980). Resource allocation and program budgeting. In C. Fox (Ed.), *Applying management techniques* (pp. 79–91). New Directions for Student Services, No. 9. San Francisco: Jossey-Bass.

National Association of College and University Business Officers. (1997). *Financial and reporting manual for higher education* (Release 97-6). Washington, DC: National Association of College and University Business Officers.

Rachlin, R. (1999). *Handbook of budgeting.* New York: John Wiley & Sons.

Rubin, I. S. (1988). *New directions in budget theory.* Albany: State University of New York Press.

Schuh, J. (Ed.). (1990). *Financial management for student affairs administrators.* Alexandria, VA: American College Personnel Association.

Slaughter, S. (1997). Who gets what and why in higher education? Federal policy and supply-side institutional resource allocation at public research universities. ASHE Presidential Speech.

Slaughter, S., & Leslie, L. (1997). *Academic capitalism: Politics, policies, and the entrepreneurial university.* College Park, MD: University of Maryland Press.

Stocum, D. L., & Rooney, P. M. (1997). Responding to resource constraints: A departmentally based system of responsibility centered management. *Change, 29*(5), 51–57.

Thurow, L. (1991). Planning for the new world economy. *Planning for Higher Education,* *20*(1), 17–23.

Wildavsky, A., & Caiden, N. (1997). *The new politics of the budgetary process* (3rd ed.). New York: Addison Wesley.

Woodard, D. B., Jr. (1993). Budgeting and fiscal management. In M. J. Barr & Associates, *The handbook of student affairs administration* (pp. 242–259). San Francisco: Jossey-Bass.

Woodard, D. B., Jr., & von Destinon, M. (1999). Budgeting and fiscal management. In M. J. Barr, M. K. Desler, & Associates, *The handbook of student affairs administration* (2nd ed., pp. 327–346). San Francisco: Jossey-Bass.

RECOMMENDED READING

Barr, J. M. & Desler, M. K., Associates (Eds). *The handbook of student affairs administration* (2nd ed.). San Francisco: Jossey-Bass.

Slaughter, S., & Leslie, L. L. (1997). *Academic capitalism: Politics, policies, and the entrepreneurial university.* Baltimore: The Johns Hopkins University Press.

Wildavsky, A., & Caiden, N. (1997). *The new politics of the budgetary process* (3rd ed.). New York: Addison Wesley.

Woodard, D. B., Jr. (Ed.) (1995). *Budgeting as a tool for policy in student affairs.* New Directions for Student Services, No. 70. San Francisco: Jossey-Bass.

10

Resolving Conflicts

STEVEN M. JANOSIK
JOAN B. HIRT

*T*he higher education enterprise is an extremely complex organization that responds to a vast array of constituents. These include external groups such as governmental agencies at the federal, state, and local levels and commercial vendors and service providers of all descriptions. Constituents closer to the institution include parents, students, alumni, the faculty, and staff members. These individuals, groups, and organizations interact with the institution on a frequent and regular basis. Not every interaction results in agreement.

Student affairs professionals are primary players in these interactions and are often called upon to resolve unmet needs and conflicts. Knowing how to resolve conflict is an important skill for the professional student affairs administrator.

This chapter is divided into three major sections. The first section reviews the concept of conflict and its causes. Conflict between organizations, persons, and groups is examined. Special attention is paid to conflict resulting from diversity issues. The second part focuses on conflict resolution strategies and how the strategies may be used by student affairs administrators who serve as educators, leaders, and managers. The final section deals with the processes used to resolve conflict effectively.

DEFINING THE CONCEPT OF CONFLICT

Conflict among individuals, groups, and organizations is nothing new, and higher education, as an organization, has not been immune (Holton, 1995b). From the creation of the earliest colleges, disagreements about who should teach and what students should learn have been commonplace (Cowley & Williams, 1991). On occasion in Europe during earlier years the ruling nobility, churches, and governments closed and destroyed schools, and those who taught in them were forced to leave town over such conflicts. Even today, students are expelled, faculty and administrators fired, and institutional affiliation and monetary support lost because of unresolved conflicts.

Before a conflict can be managed, it must be understood (Holton, 1995b). This is not as simple as it may at first appear, because the concept of conflict has no single definition and conflict takes many forms.

In their classic definition, March and Simon (1958) defined conflict in organizations as the "breakdown in the standard mechanisms of decision making, so that an individual or group experiences difficulty in selecting an alternative" (p. 112). Others suggest that conflict is an "interactive state in which behaviors or goals of one actor are to some degree incompatible with the behaviors or goals of some other actor or actors" (Tedeschi, Schlenker, & Bonoma, 1973, p. 232). Finally, Rahim (1992) defined conflict as an interactive process manifested in incompatibility, disagreement, or dissonance within social entities including individuals, groups, or organizations.

After reviewing various definitions of conflict, Barron (1990) concluded that several common elements could be identified:

1. Conflict includes *opposing interests* between individuals or groups;
2. Such opposing interests *must be recognized* for conflict to exist;
3. Conflict *involves beliefs* by each side that one party will thwart the goals of the other;
4. Conflict *is a process* that develops out of existing relationships and reflects past interactions and the context in which they took place;
5. Conflict *implies action* by one or both sides that does in fact thwart the goals of the other party. (p. 199)

For entry-level administrators, this definition of conflict may appear anathema at first. Most administrators are trained to respect differences and resolve conflicts so as to meet the needs of all parties. It may be difficult to adjust to the notion that conflict is an inevitable and natural part of organizational functioning. Yet most entry-level administrators are likely to deal with conflict in many settings. For example, consider the current debate on curbing alcohol consumption among students from the perspective of an advisor to Greek organizations. It is likely that there will be a contingent of students who favor policies designed to control the consumption of alcoholic beverages among fraternity and sorority members. There also are likely to be individuals who strongly oppose such measures, arguing that prohibition is not appropriate and will only drive drinking underground. It is equally likely that past interactions among chapters will influence how the issue of alcohol is viewed, and that members of some chapters will take actions specifically designed to thwart the desires of other chapters' members. It is essential, therefore, that new administrators recognize the inherent role conflict plays in organizations and appreciate the learning that can occur when conflict is acknowledged and addressed when working with students and others.

It is important to emphasize one additional point in this discussion having to do with threshold. Conflict does not necessarily occur simply because there is disagreement, difference, or incompatibility. For conflict to occur, it must exceed a threshold level of intensity before the parties experience or become aware of (recognize) any conflict. In other words, the incompatibilities, disagreements, or differences must be recognizably serious before parties experience conflict. Likewise, there are differences in the threshold of conflict awareness or tolerance among individuals. Thus, some individuals may become involved in a conflict sooner than others under similar circumstances (Rahim, 1992).

Causes of Conflict

Some suggest that economic issues are the primary cause of conflict in higher education (Malveaux, 1994). Even though the stresses caused by inadequate resources may be a significant factor, it would be an oversimplification to think that the cause of conflict is unidimensional. In fact, there are many sources of conflict in all types of organizations.

Holton (1995a) suggested that conflict derives from three different sources: (a) conflict over resources, (b) conflict over needs, and (c) conflict over values. For Holton, conflict over resources occurs when individuals want something that is scarce. Travel funds is an area over which conflict frequently arises. There always seems to be more requests for travel than resources can accommodate. For example, most campuses employ numerous residence hall directors. Many of these practitioners desire to attend one of the national professional conferences, which occur annually. Yet few departments have sufficient funding to support all those who wish to attend. Moreover, residence halls continue to operate during conferences, and some staff members need to remain on campus to manage the daily operations. The conflict among staff members that can arise over who is selected to attend and who is funded for that attendance is seemingly inevitable.

Conflict over needs includes the need to belong, to be recognized, and to possess power and status (Holton, 1995a). These conflicts are difficult to resolve because of their intangible nature. For many new professionals, conflicts over needs may emerge when new policies and programs are introduced. Entry-level professionals, for example, are frequently those who work most extensively with students. They often work nontraditional hours and observe students during evening and weekend hours when higher-level administrators are not on campus. Higher-level administrators, however, are typically charged with assessing student needs and designing policies and programs to address those needs. Such policies and programs are often developed with limited input from entry-level staff, though new professionals are usually charged with carrying out policies or implementing programs. This can create conflict for entry-level administrators who may believe that their understanding of student needs goes unrecognized or unappreciated in the development of policies and programs.

Conflict over values includes disagreement about mission, goals, and directions of the organization (Holton, 1995a). It also may include disagreements over personal style. Consider the issue of advising style in a community college advising center. Some new professionals may focus giving information on curriculum and college policy, whereas others devote more energy to degree choice and vocational interests. The two groups may experience conflict over which value is more important.

Looking at conflict through the Holton (1995a) model is particularly helpful given the purpose of this book. Managers may be able to address conflicts over resources by stretching them, using creative financing, and developing rationale allocation processes. Such action may go a long way in reducing conflict over resources.

In another arena, leader skills may be required to resolve conflicts of needs because leaders help to shape the environment in which individuals interact. Higher-level administrators who actively pursue input from entry-level staff members when designing new policies and programs may address the conflict of needs by acknowledging the expertise that those practitioners possess about students.

Finally, educators may be able to respond to conflicts over values by defining the organization through vision and the articulation of a strategic plan or any set of *jointly* agreed upon goals. In the above example, it may be important for supervisors to discuss the hierarchy of values in terms of policy enforcement within the organization so that their vision of the organization can be shared.

Slaikeu and Hasson (1998) outlined a comprehensive list of 10 causes of conflict. These can be conceptualized in two groups: sources of conflict that are driven by individuals and sources of conflict that are driven by organizational issues.

Denial is the first source of conflict. Denial occurs when people are unaware of their own behavior or that difference exists. This denial or absence of response can add to the differences perceived by others. Skill deficits is another cause of conflict. Some people are poor communicators or negotiators, and this lack of skill can create conflict with others. A third cause, lack of information, can occur when professionals misunderstand information or possess incorrect information.

Other sources of conflict that are driven by individuals include conflicting interests or values. This typically occurs when individuals have differing needs for structure. Some may have greater tolerances for risk or ambiguity than do others, and these differences may serve as a source of conflict. Psychopathology, such as character disorders, acute stress, clinical depression, and other forms of mental illness may affect 10% to 20% of the workforce, including higher education. Behavior connected with psychopathology can create conflict in the workplace. Yet another cause of conflict may result from personality style. Individuals have a wide variety of personal preferences. Some people are aggressively confrontational and extremely candid. Others hide their feelings. Some persons prefer a quiet, well-ordered workstation. Others prefer music or clutter. Differences such as these in work habits and interpersonal style can create conflict.

Two final sources of conflict that relate to individuals in the Slaikeu and Hasson (1998) model may be more elusive. Selfishness, greed, and the desire for power can lead to clashes between competitors or those who fight for fairness. Evil intent, although much less common than the other sources of conflict, does occur on occasion. Sometimes individuals are motivated simply to do harm.

The second group of sources of conflict focuses more on organizational issues. As previously noted, scarce resources are frequently the source of conflict in organizations. When two or more persons want the same thing, conflict frequently results. Organizational deficiencies can also create conflict. Good people often disagree with one another because they receive mixed messages from their supervisor. Reporting to multiple supervisors also can be a source of conflict for employees. Given this overview of sources of conflict, it is interesting to see how these sources play out in organizational settings.

Conflict in Organizations

Identifying the source of the conflict provides clues to managers, leaders, and educators about how the conflict might best be resolved. Similarly, understanding the direction of the conflict may also help predict behavior of those involved. Tucker (1999) suggested that conflict in organizations tends to move in one of three directions: downward, lateral, and upward.

Downward conflict occurs when a subordinate engages in conduct that a superior defines as unacceptable. Consider the example of the entry-level academic adviser who dresses informally when seeing students in the office and continues to "advise" undergraduate students at "group meetings" held at local bars after the office closes. Instead of discussing the matter with the academic adviser, the director issues a memo to the staff member reminding her to dress professionally and to refrain from meeting with students in social settings. The tone of the memo clearly communicates that failure to comply with its content may have negative consequences. Because of the existence of a vertical relationship and the power held by the supervisor, the threat of discipline often is used to resolve the conflict in an autocratic manner. This type of conflict can be reduced by clearly establishing expectations and maintaining open communications (Tucker, 1999).

Lateral conflict occurs when a party defines the behavior of a peer as being unacceptable. For example, one student organization advisor may believe in personally completing the paperwork necessary for a group's upcoming program, whereas another advisor believes that students alone should perform those tasks. Amicable resolution of this type of conflict depends upon two factors: (a) the communication and problem-solving skills of the participants, and (b) the quality of the relationship. If coworkers can express themselves in a clear and constructive manner, the likelihood of resolving the conflict increases. Similarly, the more positive and closer the relationship, the greater the chance that the individuals will invest themselves in finding a mutually acceptable solution (Tucker, 1999).

Finally, upward conflict occurs when a subordinate disapproves of the conduct of a superior. Consider the situation of the new coordinator of multicultural programs who overhears her supervisor telling an off-color joke. Rebellion, resistance, and resentment are likely outcomes when the conflict is ignored or left unresolved. This type of conflict can be reduced when the *distance* in organizational hierarchy is reduced (Tucker, 1999).

By becoming aware of these perspectives, student affairs administrators in their roles as managers, leaders, and educators can do a great deal to reduce the potential for conflict.

Conflicts between Persons

Interpersonal conflict refers to the manifestation of incompatibility, disagreement, or difference between two or more interacting individuals. The previous example of two academic advisers who differ in terms of their priorities for advising students illustrates this type of conflict that may affect the behavior and attitudes of parties toward each other. If the conflict becomes intense, the parties move away from a congenial and trusting relationship and redirect their energies toward the goal of *winning*. As the immediate goal of each party to win or control the situation grows, the interest in finding a solution to the problem becomes increasingly less important to those involved. In other words, the parties become less prepared to contribute to organizational goals effectively (Rahim, 1992).

Conflict between Groups

Intergroup conflict refers to the collective incompatibility or disagreement between two or more divisions, departments, or subsystems in connection with tasks, resources, or information. It is important to distinguish between group actions that prompt intergroup conflict and group attributions that lead to the same outcome. Actions on the part of group members may send fairly clear signals to members of other groups about potential conflicts. At other times, however, people attribute attitudes or behaviors to groups that may not accurately reflect the group's values. Conflicts that arise from inaccurate attributions can be troubling. Additionally, because group conflict implies that each member of a group is in conflict with those of another, quite often the actual dispute is carried out between group representatives (Roloff, 1987). It should be noted that intergroup conflict is virtually inevitable in complex organizations.

Complex organizations create different subsystems with homogeneous tasks and distinct goals to increase organizational effectiveness. Although these systems develop distinct norms, orientations, and attitudes, they are required to work with each other to reach common organizational goals. This interdependence of the subsystems on tasks, resources, and information is often a major source of conflict. In the private sector, classic examples of such conflict occur between management and labor, between sales and marketing, and between headquarters and field staff. In higher education, examples of intergroup conflict include discord between faculty and administration, "town and gown," student affairs professionals and student leaders, and central office and area staffs.

The development of a social identity within a group fosters loyalty and encourages between-group comparisons. It may also create competition. These factors may lead to the development of a *win–lose* mentality where the desire to maintain the perceived differences between groups is given greater priority than achieving a common goal.

Conflict Resulting from Diversity

Despite recent controversy over affirmative action, most colleges and universities strive to attract a diverse student body and workforce. Most agree that a diverse academic community more accurately reflects the larger society and enhances students' learning experiences. Bringing students and institutional staff members together who possess different skills, experiences, values, and worldviews often adds to the quality of the decisions made and work produced. However, these differences also may result in conflict. Student affairs administrators, in their roles as educators, leaders, and managers, must keep these diversity issues in mind at all times.

Age. In the 1970s, the phrase "traditional-age college student" had a well-defined meaning. It was used to categorize a group of students between 18 and 25 years of age. For decades, most students attending residential four-year institutions fell into this age group. This is no longer true for these types of institutions and never has been true for community colleges and other commuter campuses. Today, the average age of college students on a four-year residential campus may be closer to 27 and 29 on commuter college campuses (U.S. Department of Education, 1999). This wide age variation and accompanying value systems today's students bring to campus can be expected to provide a breeding ground for conflict.

Some like to suggest that "if a person under the age of 30 is not a liberal, he or she has no heart. If a person over 50 is not a conservative, he or she has no brain." Although meant to be humorous, such statements illustrate an important point. Those who lived through different historical periods or who have had greater life experiences may well possess different values than those without such experiences. Persons over 50 years of age may have a strong sense of duty to country, may be especially loyal to the organization, and may defer to a chain of command or authority more easily than younger persons. Younger persons may be more inquisitive and may feel more comfortable in an informal work environment than older persons. Such differences based on age and experience may form the basis for conflict. Indeed, Zemke, Raines, and Filipczak (2000) identify four generations represented in contemporary organizations. They suggest that understanding the values and ethos of each of these generations may enable people to avoid some conflicts that result from differences in age.

Gender.   Gender role stereotypes can also form a basis for conflict. Women often are assumed to be nurturing, domestic, and noncompetitive, whereas their male counterparts are viewed as logical, judgmental, and goal oriented. Women are thought to be more liberal as a group, and men are thought to be more conservative (Best & Williams, 1997). Actions based on these stereotypes (or actual differences) can lead to interpersonal conflict.

Cultural values.   Certain cultural artifacts such as etiquette, values, language, traditions and customs, food, dress, musical tastes, belief systems, and worldviews of participants may take center stage in conflict. According to Thiederman (1991), these artifacts are not distinct from one another but tend to overlap and influence one another. For example, the value some ethnic groups place on respecting authority is directly responsible for the preferred etiquette of addressing superiors by their last names, such as Dr. X or Professor Y. Other ethnic groups may find these customs strange and behave differently, giving rise to potential conflict between groups.

Misunderstandings occur when individuals are not aware of these cultural differences. The American who associates a hearty handshake with strength and fortitude might incorrectly perceive the gentle handshake of the Asian as a sign of weakness or indecisiveness. Such cultural differences result in different values that influence how people respond to others and the workplace, especially when uneducated about cultural differences.

These values affect behavior in four important ways. First, values dictate felt needs. Managers cannot accurately assess the needs and expectations of subordinates without first understanding their culturally specific needs and desires. Without such understanding, efforts to motivate productivity and cooperation can be seriously impaired.

Second, values dictate what is defined as a problem. An Asian American staff member might feel good about his or her reluctance to complain when dissatisfied or to ask questions when confused. The European American manager, on the other hand, may see these behaviors as problems reflecting a lack of openness or an unwillingness to learn.

Values also dictate how problems are solved. A Filipino American worker might solve an interpersonal conflict by asking for a transfer to another department in an effort to avoid the loss of harmony that would result from a direct confrontation. A native-born colleague could regard this solution as cowardly and evasive, preferring instead to deal, in typical "American" fashion, with the problem directly.

Finally, values dictate expectations of behavior. Hispanic American workers may expect a supervisor regularly to take time to chat and get to know them as individuals—to learn about their families, home lives, and interests. To behave differently can leave workers with an impression of coldness, which is not conducive to the building of productive harmonious relationships (Thiederman, 1991).

Addressing Diversity

The first steps toward addressing differences within the higher education community may be the most difficult. As educators, leaders, and managers, student affairs administrators must help everyone in their organization acknowledge differences and commonalties. Student affairs administrators acting in their role as manager, for example, should encourage staff members to become aware of and set aside stereotypes that may be positive or negative in the way they characterize individuals and always limit individuals in inappropriate ways. Student affairs administrators acting as educators can help employees learn about the cultures and values of others, communicate respect, share their own culture and values, and reassure employees that everyone experiences diversity. Student affairs administrators acting as leaders can set a standard for conduct by modeling open, inclusive attitudes and actions toward all organizational constituents.

Positive Conflict

For most administrators, conflict carries a negative connotation and is something to be avoided, even if the costs are considerable. This is not always desirable, however. Conflict is natural, inevitable, and, in some circumstances, healthy. Indeed, conflict can hold productive potential. How conflict is handled and resolved often determines if the conflict is helpful or harmful. Handled properly, conflict may produce several functional outcomes between persons, groups, and organizations, including improving organizational decision making. Conflict may be viewed as an opportunity to:

1. provide opportunities to identify alternative solutions;
2. force individuals to search for new approaches;
3. lead persons to synergistic solutions to common problems;
4. require people to articulate and clarify their positions;
5. stimulate innovation, creativity, and growth;
6. improve individual and group performance.

Tjosvold (1991) suggested that administrators who value diverse points of view and experiences, seek *win–win* solutions that are good for themselves and their colleagues, empower each other to feel confident and skillful, and take stock in and develop their abilities to turn the disaster of escalating conflict into positive conflict.

Wanting to manage conflict is not enough, however. Student affairs administrators must believe that positive conflict is possible and that they possess the skills necessary to create positive outcomes. People need an intellectual roadmap and accompanying strategies and procedures to make conflict constructive. They also must believe that their coworkers and colleagues are committed to dealing with conflicts successfully. One person cannot manage conflict alone. A conflict-positive culture enables those involved to use differences in the culture to promote a common mission.

Strategies for Resolving Conflict

To this point in the chapter, conflict has been defined and causes for discord have been identified. The remainder of the chapter is used to discuss strategies for resolving conflicts.

According to Slaikeu and Hanson (1998), human beings have four distinct options for dealing with conflict: (a) avoiding, (b) using power plays, (c) going to higher authorities, and (d) collaborating. As managers, student affairs administrators may choose from several management styles to address conflicts that arise. These styles include (a) avoiding, (b) dominating, (c) obliging, (d) compromising, and (e) integrating (Rahim, 1992). In addition, each style embodies two dimensions, concern for self and concern for others (Blake & Mouton, 1964; Rahim & Bonoma, 1979; Thomas, 1976).

Avoiding the conflict.   One conflict resolution option is simply to avoid the conflict in the first place. This management style illustrates a low concern for self and others. Although this may seem at first glance to be an inappropriate response, avoiding the conflict may be the best strategy when the issue is trivial or where the potential dysfunctional effects of confronting the other party outweigh the benefits of resolving the conflict. Temporarily avoiding a conflict also may be an appropriate strategy when a cooling-off period is needed. Before making a decision to avoid the conflict, however, student affairs administrators should ensure that their behavior demonstrates a high concern for doing the right thing, not necessarily the easy thing. It would be inappropriate, for example, to use this management style when the issue is important to one or more parties, when the parties are unwilling to wait, or when prompt action is required.

Dominating the conflict.   In this option a supervisor imposes a solution to the conflict and illustrates high concern for self and low concern for others. This intervention may be appropriate when the issue is routine or when a speedy action is required. It also may be an appropriate course of action when the supervisor is invested in a particular outcome and the other parties involved do not have the expertise to make technical decisions or subordinates are overly assertive. Supervisors may be compelled to use this style of management when others have already decided upon an unpopular course of action higher up in the organization. Obviously, this strategy has a variety of negative consequences and is not advised when the issue is complex, when parties involved in the conflict have equal power, or when the decision does not have to be made quickly.

Obliging the other party.   Obliging involves yielding to the other party's point of view or solution. This style option illustrates a high concern for others and low concern for self. Obliging or accommodating can be employed successfully when administrators are convinced that alternatives proposed by the other parties have greater merit, when administrators think they have made errors, when a person has less power than the other party, or when yielding may result in an exchange of something else at some future date. Employing this strategy would be inappropriate when the other party is clearly wrong, acting in an unethical manner, violating the values of the institution, or acting illegally or contrary to published policy.

Integrating.   The conflict resolution strategies reviewed thus far involve a *win–lose* approach. Even if a supervisor refuses to address a conflict, the other parties involved will feel as if they have not won because no decision was made.

Integrating is analogous to mediation. Here, a mutually acceptable solution to the conflict is sought. To use this strategy successfully, one must have sufficient time to problem solve. Commitment from all parties must be established. Such a strategy is inappropriate when the task is simple, when a decision must be made quickly, when parties are unconcerned about the outcome, or when the parties involved do not have the skills to problem solve. This approach exhibits high concern for self and others.

Compromising.   Although integrating may be the most managerially satisfying strategy because it treats all parties with maximum respect, it may not be practical in every instance. In some instances it may be necessary to compromise when consensus cannot be reached and a temporary solution to a complex problem must be sought. Solutions to conflicts using a compromise strategy, however, may not sufficiently address the issue. As suggested by the term *compromise*, this approach illustrates an intermediate concern for self and others.

General Processes for Resolving Conflict

Problem solving, mediation, and arbitration represent three general strategies for resolving conflict. They overlap somewhat with strategies just described but deserve special attention because of their widespread use in conflict resolution.

Problem solving.   Palmer and Burton (1996) suggested a seven-stage model for dealing with conflicts in the workplace. These steps are designed to help colleagues take a constructive approach to solving their own problems.

The first step in the process is to identify the problem. In this stage, the goal is to understand the issues and behaviors that are involved in the conflict.

Palmer and Burton (1996) suggested that the parties involved should try to visualize the problem through the use of charts and graphs. Such a strategy encourages a person to describe the issues more accurately and in more depth. If the problem is complex, the conflict or problem should be subdivided into its components and dealt with in smaller parts.

Once the problem has been identified, individuals can set goals for themselves that will help them act to resolve the conflict. These goals must be defined in specific terms that attend to behaviors. They must be realistic goals that are substantial. That is to say, the achievement of the goal will provide the individual with a real sense of progress toward resolution. Focusing on behaviors that will solve the problem makes it relatively easy to verify when the goal has been achieved.

After the conflict has been identified and goals that have the potential for resolving the conflict have been developed, alternative methods for achieving these goals should be explored. This is the third step in the process.

The model's fourth step involves considering the consequences of the various alternatives. The pros and cons of each alternative should be weighed carefully. Obviously, some alternatives will have a greater probability of success. Some may be easy to achieve but may be less likely to resolve the problem.

Deciding on a best course of action is the model's fifth step. Taking action is the sixth step, and, finally, evaluating the success of the strategy selected completes the process.

Obviously, there will be many conflicts where individuals are not willing to act on their own to resolve the problem. In these situations, different strategies must be employed to achieve resolution.

Mediation.   Mediation and other conciliatory methods have increased in popularity in recent years. These processes involve a neutral *third party* who assists disputants in finding a mutually satisfactory resolution to the conflict. The third party may be an individual, a team of mediators, or a panel of arbitrators. Regardless of the number of people engaged in the process, listening is crucial if such processes are to be successful.

Holton (1995c) identifies three parts to the mediation process: (a) identification of the conflict, (b) identification of solutions, and (c) implementation of the solutions.

In this approach, identification of the conflict involves six steps:

1. Identify all of the parties involved in the conflict.
2. Identify the specific observable aspects of the conflict.
3. Determine when the conflict occurs.
4. Determine where the conflict occurs.
5. Determine if there have been previous attempts to resolve the conflict.
6. Determine the consequences if the conflict is not resolved.

Once this information has been determined, the conflict can be understood. Then the parties involved can begin to identify possible solutions.

Identifying solutions that may be acceptable to the parties directly involved in the conflict also involves several steps. Mediators should encourage the development of a positive attitude and establish the ground rules for communication with all of the parties involved. Once this process has been completed, the mediator should identify the interests of the parties directly involved. With their help, the mediator then develops alternatives and identifies the criteria to be used to evaluate these alternatives. Finally, the mediator helps the parties weigh the solutions against the criteria.

Once a mutually acceptable solution or solutions are agreed to, the proposed solutions still must be implemented. Too often, this part of the process is neglected or forgotten. If a solution is to be implemented successfully, one must first develop a specific course of action. In some instances, it may be helpful to identify a third party to monitor the progress accomplished via the action plan. Finally, those involved in the conflict should agree on how conflicts should be handled in the future (Holton, 1995c).

Arbitration.   In some cases, individuals may not be willing or may not have the skills to resolve conflicts. In other instances, mediation may fail to result in a mutually acceptable solution. When this occurs, arbitration may be used to settle the dispute. In arbitration, a neutral third party is empowered to reach a binding decision or solution on behalf of the disputants (Stitt, 1998).

Stitt (1998) suggested that disputes be dealt with directly. In his model, DIRECT is an acronym for a framework for designing an appropriate arbitration system. He argued that any successful system "must provide an opportunity to: (a) Diagnose the conflict, (b) use Interest-based processes to find mutually acceptable solutions, (c) use a Rights-based process as a last resort, (d) use Exits and re-entries when appropriate, (e) use Creativity to solve conflicts and, (f) use Training and evaluation to develop the skills of the organization's arbitrators and assess the effectiveness of the arbitration process" (p. 24).

Diagnosis is the first component of the process or system. This step allows the arbitrator to identify the conflict facing the principals and the approach to be taken in settling the dispute.

In the second part of the system, the arbitrator focuses on the interests of the disputants. What do they want? What do they have in common? What are they willing to trade? If the arbitrator is successful, a mutually acceptable solution will be found at this stage.

If an interest-based solution cannot be found, an arbitrator may seek to resolve the conflict through a determination of rights. This is an exercise in determining who is right and who is wrong based on an objective evaluation of the facts. Clearly, the use of this rights-based approach produces winners and losers.

Stitt (1998) suggested that any conflict resolution system or process should be flexible enough to allow for exits and reentries. Cool-down periods should be used when emotions run high and prevent parties from working to resolve the issue in good faith. Appropriate and temporary solutions might also be negotiated as interim steps in finding a final long-term solution to the conflict.

Stitt (1998) also advocated the use of creativity to solve problems. Brainstorming and looking beyond precedents may help arbitrators think more freely as they search for effective, albeit novel, solutions.

Finally, Stitt suggested that arbitrators be trained in effective mediation and communication skills to enhance their effectiveness. Further, he recommended that those who are affected by it evaluate the results of the arbitration process on a regular basis to determine its effectiveness and level of support.

CONCLUSION

Conflict is an inevitable fact of organization life. Blake, Mouton, and Williams (1981) suggested that the "inability to cope with conflict constructively and creatively leads to increased hostility, antagonism, and divisiveness, clear thinking disintegrates, and prejudice and dogmatism come to prevail. This is the antithesis of the university norm of 'reasoned discourse' (p. 5)." Clearly if student affairs administrators are going to serve as effective managers, leaders, and educators, they must sharpen their listening and clarifying skills. They must be able to cope with emotions. They must be able to brainstorm and suggest alternatives. They must be able to explore and discuss consequences. Most importantly, they must be willing to make decisions. Modeling these behaviors and teaching them to others is one way student affairs professionals can serve as managers, leaders, and educators. In the final analysis, it is the most effective way to reduce and resolve conflict in higher education settings and to turn conflict into an effective agent of change.

QUESTIONS TO CONSIDER

1. Having read this chapter, what skills do you think are most important in resolving conflict? What skills do you already possess that would aid in addressing conflict? Which skills do you need to acquire?
2. Conflict is inevitable, and, as the authors discuss, some conflict can be positive. Place yourself in the role of supervisor and then define instances of positive conflict. How would you use this type of conflict to move your department or organization forward?

REFERENCES

Barron, R. A. (1990). Conflict in organizations. In K. R. Murphy & F. E. Saal (Ed.), *Psychology in organizations: Integrating science and practice* (pp. 197–216). Hillsdale, NJ: Erlbaum.

Best, D. L., & Williams, J. E. (1997). Sex, gender, and culture. In J. W. Berry, M. H. Segall, & C. Kagitcibasi (Eds.), *Handbook of cross-cultural psychology* (pp. 163–212). Boston: Allyn & Bacon.

Blake, R. R., & Mouton, J. S. (1964). *The managerial grid.* Houston: Gulf.

Blake, R. R., Mouton, J. S., & Williams, M. S. (1981). *The academic administrator grid: A guide to developing effective management teams.* San Francisco: Jossey-Bass.

Cowley, W. H., & Williams, D. (1991). *International and historical roots of American higher education.* New York: Garland.

Holton, S. A. (1995a). Conflict 101. In S. A. Holton (Ed.), *Conflict management in higher education* (pp. 1–11). New Direction for Higher Education, No. 92. San Francisco: Jossey-Bass.

Holton, S. A. (1995b). It's nothing new! A history of conflict in higher education. In S. A. Holton (Ed.), *Conflict management in higher education* (pp. 11–18). New Direction for Higher Education, No. 92. San Francisco: Jossey-Bass.

Holton, S. A. (1995c). And now. . . the answers! How to deal with conflict in higher education. In S. A. Holton (Ed.), *Conflict management in higher education* (pp. 79–89). New Direction for Higher Education, No. 92. San Francisco: Jossey-Bass.

Malveaux, J. (1994). Restructuring the academy: Ten years of Black issues. *Black Issues in Higher Education, 11*(4), 68.

March, J. G., & Simon, H. A. (1958). *Organizations.* New York: Wiley.

Palmer, S., & Burton, T. (1996). *Dealing with people problems at work.* New York: McGraw-Hill

Rahim, M. A. (1992). *Managing conflict in organizations.* Westport, CT: Praeger.

Rahim, M. A., & Bonoma, T. V. (1979). Managing organizational conflict: A model for diagnosis and intervention. *Psychological Reports, 44,* 1323–1344.

Roloff, M. E. (1987). Communication and conflict. In C. R. Berger & S. H. Chaffee (Eds.), *Handbook of communication science* (pp. 484–534). Newbury Park, CA: Sage.

Slaikeu, K. A., & Hasson, R. H. (1998). *Controlling the cost of conflict: How to design a system for your organization.* San Francisco: Jossey-Bass.

Stitt, A. J. (1998). *Alternative dispute resolution for organizations: How to design a system for effective conflict resolution.* New York: John Wiley & Sons.

Tedeschi, J. T., Schlenker, B. R., & Bonoma, T. V. (1973). *Conflict, power and games: The experimental study of interpersonal relations.* Chicago: Aldine.

Thiederman, S. (1991). *Bridging cultural barriers for corporate success: How to manage the multicultural work force.* Lexington, MA: Lexington Books.

Thomas, K. W. (1976). Conflict and conflict management. In M. D. Dunnette (Ed.), *Handbook of industrial and organizational psychology* (pp. 889–935). Chicago, IL: Rand McNally.

Tucker, J. (1999). *The therapeutic corporation.* New York: Oxford University Press.

Tjosvold, D. (1991). *The conflict-positiver organization: Stimulate diversity and create unity.* Reading, MA: Addison-Wesley.

U. S. Department of Education. (1999). *The digest of educational statistics, 1998.* (NCES Publication 1999-032). Washington, DC: U.S. Government Printing Office.

Zemke, R., Raines, C., & Filipczak, B. (2000). *Generations at work: Managing the clash of veterans, boomers, xers, and nexters in your workplace.* New York: American Management Association.

RECOMMENDED READING

Domenici, K. (1996). *Mediation: Empowerment in conflict management.* Prospect Heights, IL: Waveland Press.

Moore, C. W. (1996). *The mediation process: Practical strategies for resolving conflict.* San Francisco: Jossey-Bass.

Potter, B., & Frank, P. (1996). *From conflict to cooperation: How to mediate a dispute.* Berkeley, CA: Ronin.

PART *IV*

TEACHING AND INQUIRING

*T*he student affairs practitioner's role as educator requires that she or he promote learning outside the traditional classroom and laboratory through both formal and informal instructional strategies. In addition, the model of professional practice in student affairs, as well as many other professional fields, is that of the scientist–practitioner. This model requires that practitioners be knowledgeable and skilled as administrators, but it also mandates that their work be based on well-tested theory and sound research. Professional practitioners, therefore, have an obligation to contribute to theory building through thorough methodologically sound research. In other words, professional student affairs administrators must not only promote the instructional aspects of students' out-of-class life, but also must attend to the search for new knowledge and strategies for enhancing student learning and personal development through the cocurriculum. Consequently, administrators must be knowledgeable of both instructional and inquiry methods and strategies. As is clear throughout the book, the educational responsibilities of student affairs administrators go well beyond the mere transmission of knowledge and skills and into the realms of assessment, evaluation, and research. All have their rightful place in the student affairs arena, and administrators need to be knowledgeable about all of these educationally relevant components.

Part IV is composed of four chapters, two that focus primarily on educational and instructional processes and two that focus on inquiry. In Chapter 11, "Enhancing Learning," Baxter Magolda provides an in-depth examination of the theoretical and pedagogical foundations of education for student affairs administrators to contemplate. From Lloyd-Jones & Smith's (1954, p. 12) view that personnel work reflects deeper teaching to Tomkins's (1996, p. xvi) call for holistic education, the chapter focuses on reshaping the student affairs administrator's educator role. That requires a conceptual shift of student affairs' educational involvement from complementary to coordinate status via learning-centered practice. This educational overview is followed in Chapter 12,

"Programmatic Interventions: Translating Theory to Practice," wherein Saunders and Cooper provide a model of intentional program development that reflects a deliberate and purposeful approach based on student development and learning theory and the assessment of student needs and campus environments. This highly practical chapter emphasizes programmatic strategies that student affairs administrators can use to enhance student learning and personal development.

Needs assessment and program evaluation is the focus of Chapter 13 by Schuh and Upcraft. This chapter uses a case study approach to illustrate principles and identify salient steps in developing needs assessments and systematic approaches to program evaluation. Further, the chapter demonstrates how needs assessment can be used to establish developmental interventions and how program evaluation can be employed to determine the effectiveness of those interventions. Chapter 14, written by Erwin and Sivo, is entitled "Assessing Student Learning and Development in Student Affairs: A Nuts and Bolts Introduction" and, as the title notes, is designed to provide student affairs practitioners with practical information about the assessment processes important to student affairs administration. The chapter presents a short historical overview of assessment in higher education; distinguishes among assessment, evaluation, and research; and presents sequential steps to guide assessment practice.

READING SUGGESTIONS

Because Chapter 11 presents an overview of the teaching and learning process, readers are encouraged to read it as a follow-up to Chapters 1, 2, and 7. Chapter 12 deals with program interventions and is focused on applications that fit well following Chapters 5 and 6, respectively. Chapters 13 and 14 focus on assessment and evaluation and should be read together—each complements and sometimes illustrates concepts that cut across topical areas.

11

Enhancing Learning

MARCIA B. BAXTER MAGOLDA

*T*he student affairs profession has a long history of endorsing holistic education to prepare students for participation in a democratic society. Early philosophical statements (reviewed in Chapter 1) underscored attention to all aspects of students' development. Esther Lloyd-Jones, a pioneer in the field, called the educational work of student affairs professionals "deeper teaching":

> student personnel workers should not so much be expert technicians as they should be educators in a somewhat unconventional and new sense. Student personnel workers have many opportunities through their work to contribute to the development of students, to help them learn many lessons and skills of vital importance for their fulfillment as whole persons within a democratic society. (Lloyd-Jones & Smith, 1954, p. 12–13)

Although student affairs professionals accepted the charge of helping students achieve fulfillment as whole persons within a democratic society, they did so largely in the areas of personal and social development, leaving intellectual development to the faculty. Contemporary advocates of holistic education emphasize the integration of the personal, social, and intellectual dimensions. For example, Tompkins wrote,

> A holistic approach to education would recognize that a person must learn how to be with other people, how to love, how to take criticism, how to grieve, how to have fun, as well as how to add and subtract, multiply and divide. It would not leave out of account that people are begotten, born, and die. It would address the need for purpose and for connectedness to ourselves and one another; it would not leave us alone to wander the world armed with plenty of knowledge but lacking the skills to handle the things that are coming up in our lives. (1996, p. xvi)

Student affairs professionals have steadfastly focused on helping students handle the things that are coming up in their lives. They have recognized in recent years, however, that functioning effectively in the complex, evolving, and inter-dependent democratic society of the twenty-first century requires integrating the intellectual, personal, and social dimensions of development. *The Student Learning Imperative* (American College Personnel Association [ACPA], 1994) articulated this integration in identifying the hallmarks of an educated person as cognitive complexity, a coherent sense of identity, an appreciation of differ-ence, and the practical skills to apply knowledge in everyday life. This docu-ment also challenged the profession to refocus on student learning as its pri-mary mission.

Student affairs' philosophical foundations, augmented by extensive research in the three dimensions of student development, are congruent with contem-porary trends in education and pedagogical reform. A paradigm shift is under-way from a teaching-centered approach, in which educators deliver instruction and transfer knowledge to students, to a learning-centered approach, in which educators create conditions to produce learning and elicit student discovery and construction of knowledge (Barr & Tagg, 1995). The learning-centered approach is *not* a shift to a student-centered approach where students take cen-ter stage. Rather, as Palmer (1998) pointed out, it is a shift to subject-centered education in which educators and students are equally accountable to the sub-ject being learned. Although the learning-centered approach was advanced by John Dewey and Jean Piaget decades ago, contemporary educational theorists are further defining the forms it might take. Proponents of this shift recognize that being *armed with plenty of knowledge* is not sufficient in the twenty-first century; rather, students need to know how to construct knowledge and engage in lifelong learning. Our educative role is to help them learn this process.

Central to the learning-centered approach is the idea that knowledge is socially constructed. Advocates of constructivism in education rely on Piaget's concept of equilibration, the same concept that is the foundation for the cogni-tive family of student development theories. When one encounters discrepan-cies between his or her way of structuring the world and experience, one is prompted to bring the two back into balance. Similarly, learning begins with students' understanding of their experience and engages them in remaking meaning of their experience. Student experience is thus the foundation from which learning proceeds, yet educators have a responsibility to guide the re-making of meaning. Bruffee (1993) spoke to this joint effort between educator and learner in his scholarship on collaborative learning—a concept that has always been central to student affairs work: "Collaborative learning assumes . . . that knowledge is a consensus among the members of a commu-nity of knowledgeable peers—something people construct by talking together and reaching agreement" (p. 3). Educators are members of the knowledge com-munities students want to join, but students need to become fluent in the knowl-edge community's language to do so. The educator, in order to help students make this transition, needs not only to be knowledgeable in her or his community, but also be able to converse in the students' community. Students' experience is the source of the educator learning to converse in the students' community. As students become members of the knowledge community, they talk together and reach agreement on deciding what to believe. This kind of student participation must be coaxed from students who have been socialized to ignore their experience in traditional education. Feminist pedagogy, described by writers like Hooks (1994), Ladson-Billings (1995), and Noddings (1991), emphasizes respecting and caring for students to empower them to find their own voices, learn from their experience, and learn in connection with others. Palmer called this "making space for the other, being aware of the other, paying attention to the other, honoring the other" (1998, p. 46). Proponents of narrative in teaching advocate making space for the other—the student—by inviting his or her stories to become central to the learning process. Hopkins (1994) wrote, "We are storytelling creatures. We do not just tell stories; we live them, create them, define ourselves through them. Our narratives are the expressive, temporal medium through which we construct our functioning personae and give meaning to our experience" (p. xvi).

Acknowledging student experience and mutual construction of knowledge are also at the core of liberatory, empowering, and critical pedagogy. Freire's (1970/1988) vision of liberatory education was aimed at helping students use academic lenses to reflect on problems in their own lives so that they could reorganize knowledge and society, think critically to discover meaning in the world and experience, see and challenge domination in society, and act to transform society based on that critique. Shor (1992, 1996) provided wonderful illustrations of problem posing, or situating academic learning in students' real lives, and joint teacher–learner dialogue to coinvestigate subject matter. Critical theorists emphasize building curriculum and learning around students' cultural backgrounds while engaging them in a critique of social and political systems that marginalize their culture. These pedagogies are particularly important in student affairs work toward promoting a multicultural campus and appreciation of diversity. (See also Chapter 3 in this volume.)

This paradigm shift creates a context in which the student affairs profession can reshape its educational role and influence. Within direct student affairs practice, articulating specific learning goals that integrate the dimensions of development, connecting students' lived experience with those goals, and engaging in mutual knowledge construction with students can help student affairs educators enhance learning. As members of the campus academic community, student affairs professionals can help faculty enhance learning in the curriculum by sharing their expertise in holistic student development with faculty who must understand how learners construct knowledge to implement learning-centered forms of pedagogy.

This chapter is intended to aid student affairs professionals in reshaping their educative role. An overview of students' holistic development, with intellectual development and learning in the forefront, forms the foundation for envisioning learning-centered practice. Pedagogical principles to promote holistic development and learning are then illustrated in the contexts of staff train-ing, administration, and formal classroom teaching. Particular attention is paid to how these principles create educational practice that includes diverse learn-ers. Finally, notions of how student affairs educators can assist faculty in en-hancing learning in the curriculum are explored.

LEARNING AND INTELLECTUAL DEVELOPMENT

Understanding how students learn and think can often be best achieved, as Perry (1970) suggested, by hearing what they have to say on the matter. Listen-ing to Dawn's narrative helps access key dynamics in holistic student develop-ment and its relationship to learning. Dawn is a participant in a 13-year longitu-dinal study on learning and intellectual development (Baxter Magolda, 1992, 1999a). As a sophomore, she explained what she was doing to learn:

> I'm starting to use the material more to my advantage. Reading through my notes that night after I've been in class, just to start to plant it in my head. A lot of little study habits to learn the material that I have to, using 3 × 5 index cards and rote memory type things. One of the big things I picked up was paraphrasing my notes, sorting out all the garbage and getting right down to what's really important. I picked all these things up in a study skills class.

Dawn's approach to learning was typical of most of her peers. It demonstrates that she viewed learning as memorizing the material given to her by authorities. Contrast this with her comment in an interview four years after college gradu-ation:

> How do you know things? That's a question I've pondered a lot. Sometimes the only answer is you just know—a feeling, an intuitive thing. Something in your body or mind says it is right—a feeling to go on. If you go on it, you apply more technical skills—act on it, testing it out. If the results are right, the feeling is right. This is a whole other can of worms. I trust what I feel as far as knowing things, or thinking things. Knowing they are right or wrong—a physical response—my stomach twinges, or a satisfied feeling comes over me. It goes beyond the realm of factual information.

At this point, Dawn learned through exploration, using both technical skills and her own feelings. Knowledge was no longer the truth to be memorized as it was in her sophomore year; rather it is uncertain and known through her own pro-cess of determining what is right or wrong.

Dawn's narrative illustrates the connections among learning, intellectual development, and identity development. How she learns is grounded in how she constructs knowledge, or her intellectual development. Because as a sopho-more she believed knowledge was certain, learning was simply a matter of plant-ing the material in her head. How she constructs and uses her knowledge is also closely related to her sense of self. We hear no sense of Dawn's identity as a sophomore; at age 26 she trusts her own feelings in knowing and thinking and can use technical skills to test out her intuitions. Both her intellectual and her identity development evolved to more complex forms over time. Dawn's experience illustrates what King and Baxter Magolda (1996) called a *developmental perspective on learning,* which includes the following basic propositions: (a) what individuals learn and claim to know is grounded in how they construct knowledge, (b) how they construct and use their knowledge is closely tied to their sense of self, and (c) the process by which individuals make meaning of their experience improves in a developmentally related fashion over time. Understanding students' holistic development and its evolution over time helps educators create learning contexts that promote both learning and development.

Intellectual Development during College

Since William Perry (1970) first described male college students' intellectual development, student affairs educators have worked to apply to student affairs practice insights about how students think. Although no one theory can describe all students' intellectual development, collective research in this arena offers possibilities and overarching patterns of development that are typical in college. Longitudinal studies indicate that the early college years often yield assumptions that knowledge is certain and known to authorities. The uncertainty of knowledge in some areas usually evolves during college, yielding less reliance on authority. Making one's own choices about what to believe after evaluating relevant evidence can emerge near the end of college but generally emerges after college. In-depth descriptions of this evolution are available elsewhere (Baxter Magolda, 1992; Belenky, Clinchy, Goldberger, & Tarule, 1986; King & Kitchener, 1994; Perry, 1970). For the purpose of this chapter, a brief overview based on a longitudinal study of young adults' development from age 18 to 30 (Baxter Magolda, 1992, 1999a) serves as the foundation for promoting learning in student affairs contexts. Two longitudinal participants' stories are used as case examples to illustrate the trajectory of intellectual development.

Absolute knowing. Dawn's sophomore comment about planting material in her head illustrates absolute knowing, or the assumption that knowledge is certain and known to authorities. These assumptions were prevalent in participants' first two years of college. Dawn used the receiving pattern within absolute knowing, focusing on taking information in from those around her. By contrast, Andrew used the mastery pattern within absolute knowing, focusing on activity aimed at mastery of the material. He explained how he learned best during his freshman year:

> I like to participate and talk and get involved. When there is no input from students, you have a tendency to get bored and drift off. You don't learn that way. If you're interested, you're going to learn no matter what. A lot of teachers

that get you involved will make you think without actually letting you know that you're thinking about something.

Andrew expected the teacher to facilitate this involvement and to make him think. Neither Andrew nor Dawn sensed any connection between themselves and their learning process. Their sense of themselves as knowers was limited to acquiring authority's knowledge.

Transitional knowing.   Absolute knowing decreased substantially by the junior year, replaced by transitional knowing in which understanding took precedence over memorizing. Participants discovered controversy in many areas of knowledge, prompting the assumption that although some knowledge remains certain, other knowledge is yet to be determined. The focus on understanding prompted different approaches to learning, as Dawn described in her junior year:

> I think I would prefer an essay exam because it's so easy to do rote memorization, but when you really have to take a chance, stop and think, and put down what you know and how it all works together, I think you learn more than you do from reading a question and being able to spit out the answer.

Similarly, Andrew advocated essay exams as a sophomore:

> If you just have multiple choice you are just regurgitating the information. You're not relating. And an essay allows the chance to correlate two things and really test whether you understand what's going on. On a multiple choice you can memorize a definition , but can you take that definition and relate it to what it really means? So I prefer a combination of both, really, half and half.

Both students focused on the process of learning given uncertainty of knowledge. Dawn exhibited the interpersonal pattern in her focus on connecting to the material to learn how it all works together. Andrew exhibited the impersonal pattern in his focus on correlating ideas to test his understanding. Transitional knowing opens the door for students to construct knowledge in the uncertain areas, a dynamic that invites the self into the knowing process. Dawn hinted at the start of this process:

> I always felt like, "Well, I'm not going to say anything to the professor about that because he's the professor and I'm just a student." It's almost like they have painted a God-like image; you can't disagree with them at all. But I think now I've learned after a while that you can disagree with them. If anything, I think that could lead to more learning. I listen to what they have to say because I'm not going to be close-minded. But I take into account they might have some very good points, which I can end up adopting. So I kind of weigh things out and make my own decision from there as to what I believe is the right or the wrong choice.

Dawn's willingness to make her own decision came in part from her change of assumptions about knowledge and in part from greater confidence in herself. She explained:

> There have been a lot of things outside of academics that have helped in making me become more outgoing. Theater helped that immensely. And I have much more self-confidence than I did when I came here. I think finally fitting into that group has helped me so much.

Dawn found self-confidence through her connection to and acceptance from others. By fitting in with the theater group, she found a context in which her sense of self could begin to emerge. The sense of self became more central in independent knowing, which occurred for some participants near the end of college and for the majority after college.

Independent knowing.   As participants increasingly encountered uncertainty in areas of knowledge they previously viewed as certain, they shifted to the assumption that most knowledge was uncertain. I called this independent knowing because participants assumed that every person was free to hold their own beliefs. Dawn described this way of thinking in her senior year interview:

> In Chinese history, we talked about Confucianism. The way I might interpret a Confucian poem could be definitely different than the way the guy that sits next to me could interpret it, and if I took the time to stop and listen to how he interpreted it, it might give me a better understanding of the way the government works with the state philosophy being Confucianism. I would be more likely to choose my own ideas just because they're mine. But I would understand and respect the views of someone else.

Dawn regarded others as a resource for expanding her learning. Her bent toward connection to others is apparent in her explanation of the effect of learning from others:

> Social interaction, whether it be for fun or having a serious conversation, for me personally is such a good way to learn, just learn about everything, anything. Any person we come into contact with has a lot to teach us. It opens up so many different things and you really start to see the world beyond—it breaks your tunnel vision. You are not just set in one direction. You can kind of be a little more free about things.

Dawn was open to new perspectives, a characteristic typical of independent knowers who have discovered that they can decide for themselves. She used the interindividual pattern within independent knowing, focusing on connecting with others in learning. In some instances she kept her own ideas and in others broke out of her tunnel vision. In contrast, Andrew used the individual pattern in independent knowing. In his junior year, he reported,

> I found the perfect style that I like in the classroom. It was a discussion class. We read and we talked, and he got us involved. He knew how to get you involved. He would press you. He was always questioning. I gained more out of that class than I did any other. We studied a new and controversial economic theory. I like to hear both sides and then make my own decision. I like somebody to challenge me and make me defend where I'm coming from. I think if you have different ideas, you have to weigh them for yourself. And then you really, truly know where you stand. He encourages you to debate it and disagree with him as long as you can defend your position and know where you're coming from.

Andrew focused on being pushed to clarify his thinking rather than on hearing others' perspectives. His comment about defending positions hints at a more complex way of knowing—contextual knowing—that is yet to come for him.

Contextual knowing. Contextual knowing occurred rarely for participants during college, yet understanding it is essential because it represents what many in the academic community expect of college students and graduates. As a senior Andrew was beginning to realize that making wise decisions meant weighing evidence in a context:

> With a lot of things there is no clear-cut answer. I'm a finance major, and the reason I chose finance over accounting is that in accounting there are rules. You memorize the rules, then you're given different things, and you apply the rules to them. And it's kind of clear-cut. Occasionally you don't know, but that's about as exciting as it gets. With finance there is no right answer. You're not given a bunch of figures and there's going to be one right answer. There's always the idea of the risk-return trade-off. You can always get a good rate of return, but do you want to accept that much more risk? If you were able to quantify risk, then are you willing to take one more percentage rate in return? So there is not ever an exactly right answer. You have to come up with alternatives and make a decision on what you feel is comfortable.

Dawn's comments about how one knows (quoted earlier) also reflect contextual knowing. Her use of technical skills, her body, and her mind to decide what to believe represents using multiple forms of evidence to self-author her own views. Contextual knowers seek relevant information, use it in its appropriate context, trust people they judge to be experts to provide insight, and trust themselves to put all this information together to arrive at a wise and reasonable decision. It is this way of knowing and ability to self-author one's views that educational practice should foster. Promoting self-authorship requires a development perspective on learning and new forms of educational practice.

PROMOTING LEARNING IN STUDENT AFFAIRS CONTEXTS

The gap between absolute or transitional knowing and the goal of self-authorship is wide. Bridging the gap requires intentionally building a bridge from students' current development to the development needed to achieve self-authored learning. Kegan (1994) described this bridge as simultaneously welcoming students' current meaning making and inviting them to remake meaning in a new way. Although this sounds straightforward enough, educators find it complicated by uncertainty regarding how to identify students' current meaning making, working with groups of students who exhibit variations in meaning making, and the fact that students change their meaning making in the course of educational experiences. Promoting learning in student affairs contexts is complicated by the need to simultaneously insure safety and civility on campus.

Rather than offer recommendations for working with each way of knowing, I offer three principles that guide educators in creating the necessary connections with all levels of meaning making. Understanding the four ways of knowing helps interpret the possible meaning of student reactions, enhances patience with perspectives far from the educational goal, and aids in the constant effort to connect to students' meaning making. The principles, however, offer a framework through which to welcome and challenge multiple ways of knowing simultaneously. In doing so, the principles also create conditions that include diverse learners by welcoming all experience and perspectives into the mutual construction of knowledge.

Three Principles

The three principles emerged first from experiences longitudinal participants described as having promoted their self-authorship (Baxter Magolda, 1992). The effectiveness of these principles for promoting learning and self-authorship was confirmed via observation of three college courses in which these principles were mainstays (Baxter Magolda, 1999b). The three work in concert with one another to welcome students' current meaning making yet invite them to remake meaning in new ways. The principles are consistent with the learning paradigm discussed earlier in the chapter.

The first principle, *validating students as knowers*, stems from the belief that students are capable of learning and constructing knowledge. Being viewed as capable of constructing knowledge conveys to absolute and transitional knowers that educators expect them to play a role in constructing knowledge. Supporting their attempts to explore, evaluate, and synthesize perspectives helps them learn the knowledge construction process. Students from diverse backgrounds are validated when their views are included in the process. Student affairs contexts in which students are expected to play an active role in organizing and decision making offer opportunities to validate their capacity as knowers.

The second principle, *situating learning in students' experience*, involves using students' experience as the starting point for learning. Rather than begin with abstract knowledge and perspectives removed from their everyday lives, learning begins with their perspectives, or how they make meaning of their experiences in the context of the focus of learning. For example, exploring alcohol abuse would begin with students' interpretations of this phenomenon rather than abstract statistics about the dangers of alcohol abuse. Situating learning in students' experience helps draw them into the learning process, conveys that their experience and interpretations are valuable (the first principle), and connects learning to their current meaning making, again including all learners regardless of prior experience.

The third principle, *mutually constructing meaning*, invites students to remake meaning through joint dialogue with educators. Educators contribute their perspectives and knowledge to this dialogue and invite students to consider how their perspectives and existing knowledge relate. The educator who learns from students that one major cause of alcohol abuse is peer pressure might engage students in weighing the costs of peer disapproval against the physical dangers of alcohol abuse. She might then engage the students in exploring new ways of making sense of peer pressure or new ways to gain peer approval without the dangers of alcohol abuse. What is important here is that students are invited into the dialogue as genuine partners with legitimate perspectives and are viewed as capable of readjusting those perspectives in light of new information. Because a predominant perspective is not imposed, student perspectives are less likely to be marginalized.

The three principles can be used in both curricular and cocurricular settings. Student affairs educators have substantive opportunities to engage students in meaningful learning contexts. The principles can be used in working with student organizations, paraprofessional staffs, educational programming, service learning, policy, and formal teaching settings in which student affairs professionals engage. Examples of the principles in three of these settings follow to illustrate their implementation.

The RA Institute: A Staff Training Example

Student affairs staff members spend extensive time training paraprofessional staff, student organization leaders, and peer educators. These contexts are ideal opportunities for student affairs professionals to implement their educative role in promoting student learning. The RA Institute, a form of residence life training for veteran resident advisors (RAs) at Miami University, illustrates use of the three principles to promote learning and achieve staff training goals simultaneously. The institute offers multiple tracks, each of which offers the opportunity to explore an issue in-depth in a site relevant to the issue. For example, a Wilderness Leadership Expedition focused on leadership and team building in the context of climbing, hiking, and orienteering. Similarly, a Service Learning track offered intense interaction with foster children to focus on reciprocal learning and social justice. The architects of the institute grounded their work in the three principles for promoting intellectual development as well as Pfeiffer and Jones's five steps of experiential learning: experiencing, publishing, processing, generalizing, and applying (Blystone, Conlon, Kooker, Marriner, & Wigton, 1996). Continued development of the institute incorporated contemporary principles advanced by the profession as well as Miami's liberal education and leadership commitment goals (Dutton, 1997).

The design and implementation of the institute both embody the three principles. RAs choose the track in which they wish to participate and help design the track in the spring prior to its implementation in the fall preservice training period. Their involvement in decision making about the experience validates them as knowers who are capable of making good choices about their own development as paraprofessionals. The mutual construction of meaning that takes place between the participants and the track coordinators, who are graduate students or full-time staff members, gives the RAs practice in constructing knowledge as well as strengthening commitment to the training endeavor. RAs' participation in designing the experience also situates learning in their experience as they establish goals relevant to the issue. The institute's goals address RAs' personal development in addition to the development of their residents. The brochure introducing the institute states, "The RA Institute is an opportunity to cultivate a renewed sense of commitment and to promote the personal development of yourself and your residents" (Miami University Office of Residence Life and New Student Programs, 1997). Choosing one's track and participating in shaping it includes and welcomes the experience of all RAs. Emphasizing self-reflection and personal development as a goal validates RAs as knowers.

The implementation of each track demonstrates the three principles in conjunction with the experiential learning model. Immersion in a meaningful experience stands at the core of each track. For example, the Miami Tribe track traveled to the Miami Indian Tribe reservation in Oklahoma to learn about the culture of the tribe; the Discrimination and Oppression track visited the Holocaust Museum, among others, to study their topic. Other tracks involved immersion in local experiences. Thus learning is situated in students' experience, giving them a concrete foundation from which to explore the issue, their beliefs about it, multiple perspectives, and ways to apply what they are learning to themselves and their work.

Throughout these experiences, intentional discussions occur to make meaning of the experience. These follow the experiential learning cycle of publishing, processing, generalizing, and applying. RAs share their reactions to the experience and work collaboratively to make sense of it. The Institute brochure explains: "You will be challenged to remove yourself from your comfort zone and to explore new concepts and thoughts. . . . You will engage in critical dialogue with fellow RAs and gain a fresh, new perspective from your peers" (Miami University Office of Residence Life, 1997). Although students are welcomed as they are, via validation as knowers and situating learning in their experience, they are also invited to stretch through mutual construction of meaning with peers. For example, the Civic Responsibility and Enrichment track included collaboratively devising ways to help RAs and residents become civic leaders. The processing phase of the discussion illustrates what Kegan (1994) called an *evolutionary bridge*. It welcomes students' current perspectives, yet invites them to remake those perspectives in light of new perspectives. This process of mutual construction of knowledge bridges the gap between initial ways of making meaning and more complex ones.

Validation, situating learning in RA experience, and mutual construction continue as the RAs work to generalize the meaning of the institute content to their RA work and create ways to apply this meaning in everyday interactions with undergraduate students in their halls. Their learning is enhanced by focusing on application to their work, in which they already have at least one year of experience, and on emphasizing that they are trusted to make reasonable meaning of what they have experienced. For example, the Exploring Sexual Identity Issues track focused on learning to be an ally and supporter of student exploration while developing sensitivity to the needs of residents.

Participants in the RA Institute reported that they acquired new knowledge about how to make their community programming meaningful, gained confidence in their ability to work with others, gained personal insight and fulfillment, and felt a part of a community as a result of the institute (Blystone et al., 1996). They appreciated the opportunity for intense critical thinking and reflection and being challenged to rethink their beliefs (Jardis & Wigton, 1999). The institute, in place since 1996, continues to expand because of these positive outcomes.

The tenets inherent in the RA Institute are transferable to multiple contexts. Service-learning contexts can embody these principles (see Rhoads, 1997, for examples), as can student leadership programming. Educational programming could follow this process, in design, implementation, or both. For example, the University of Nevada, Las Vegas, Alcohol Awareness Intervention Program uses these principles in workshops for violators of alcohol policy. Although the participants do not help design the program, they do have a choice regarding participation. The workshop is set in participants' experience, validates their interpretation of their situation, and invites mutual construction of meaning through comparing their drinking behavior with models of student alcohol use and abuse. The workshop emphasizes their personal choice and goals regarding alcohol use. Eighty-five percent of the program participants had no alcohol violations after participation (T. D. Piper, personal communication, October 4, 1999). Use of the principles offers hope that student learning can occur simultaneously with efforts to create inclusive, safe, and civil campus environments.

Establishing Relationships with a Greek Community: A Policy Example

The relationships between the institution and Greek communities are often strained because of disagreements about appropriate behavior and community responsibility. In response to this situation at the University of Nevada, Las Vegas, the student affairs staff and alumni who served as Greek chapter advisors began a process to define an effective relationship between the university and the Greek community. The resulting Statement of Relationship Between the University of Nevada, Las Vegas, and the Social Greek Letter Fraternities and Sororities illustrates how the three principles can be used in policy development and implementation.

To begin this process, the staff members and Greek alumni advisors collaborated to study the Greek chapters, learn about effective relationships at other institutions, and attempt to draft parameters of the desired relationship. A draft statement was shared with the Greek community as a starting point for developing a policy statement. The statement advanced the view that fraternities and sororities were a valuable component of the undergraduate experience because they contribute to student learning through activities that support students' academic, personal, and social growth. The process of further developing the statement was intended to elaborate the expectations of the Greek community and the university in promoting student learning. Over the course of one year, the discussions resulted in a statement ratified by the Greek community and the creation of a committee for fraternity and sorority recognition. This committee oversees the continual process of determining university recognition of Greek chapters.

In establishing the recognition process, both the university and the Greek community desired self-governance within the Greek community. The university additionally wanted accountability on the part of the Greek community to adhere to University, federal, and state laws; policies on racial equity and sexual harassment; expectations for safety of housing; responsible fiscal and property management; and sustained effort to promote student growth. Self-governance was assured through the make-up of the Committee for Recognition, which is dominated by alumni chapter advisors and student leaders in the Greek community. Staff members, particularly those in Greek affairs, participate on the committee but are not the majority. Self-governance and accountability were assured through the process by which chapters acquire recognition.

Each year the Committee on Fraternity and Sorority Recognition conducts a Goal and Chapter Review process in the spring term. The decision to focus on chapters' goals rather than merely their existence is consistent with the perspective that they are active contributors to student learning. To begin, each chapter was asked to create a starting document to assess their current status and desired development in areas inherent in their founding documents and the university mission. These included (a) academic achievement, (b) chapter development, (c) leadership and campus involvement, (d) organizational and fiscal management, (e) philanthropy and community service, and (f) the role of alumni advisers. Each year thereafter, chapters established goals in these six areas in the context of their starting document. They submit goals and plans to achieve them in writing and then personally present them to the recognition committee, who in turn judges progress and awards chapter excellence, full recognition, or probationary status. The university provides staff, advisors, leadership development, facilities, and general operational resources to those chapters achieving recognition.

The creation and implementation of this policy illustrate the three principles in numerous ways. Initially the Greek community's voice was validated in the partnership formed to create this policy. Rather than impose expectations, the university engaged members of the Greek community in wide-ranging discussions to merge the desires of the university and the Greek community. The mutual construction of expectations that resulted represents the mutual construction of meaning. Using its founding ideals as the criteria for recognition also validates the Greek community. Asking chapters to assess their own progress and set goals to meet the expectations of the relationship situates learning in their experience. Rather than be held to an imposed standard, their progress is judged in the context of their chapter history. The process is structured to offer recognition for progress on each criterion so that everyone can achieve excellence. This approach supports their current experience, yet invites them to stretch further to achieve excellence. As such, it is an example of Kegan's (1994) evolutionary bridge—a means of connecting our desired goals for students and their current meaning making. It is inclusive, inviting excellence in numerous forms. Because progress is judged in the context of the chapter's history, diverse chapter goals are welcomed. Finally, interorganizational support provides additional opportunities for validation and mutual meaning making. Because the Greek chapters collaborate on the recognition committee, ties across chapters are strengthened. Offering rewards and recognition on each criterion and rewarding everyone who shows progress reduces competition among chapters and fosters collaboration and mutual support.

Three cycles of goal setting and review have occurred since the ratification of this statement. Staff members report that the Greek community has genuinely implemented this relationship to the point that the university has reopened discussion of building Greek housing, a consideration that had been discontinued prior to this relationship policy. Staff members identify particular positive outcomes, including stronger individual chapters, greater collaboration across chapters, mechanisms to support chapters that are struggling, less adversarial interactions among the university and Greek community, and stronger responsibility on the part of Greek chapters regarding behavior of their members (T. D. Piper, personal communication, October 4, 1999). For example, a recent incident between members of two fraternities resulted in immediate action on the part of their chapters, including an apology to the Greek community and action against the perpetrators. These reactions help assure the university that incidents are problems associated with individuals rather than systemic problems in the Greek community. These outcomes reveal that the perceived risk in trusting a student community is often a lower risk than adopting a controlling approach. The university's interest in accountability was met, the Greek community receives support from the university, and students learn how to set goals and achieve them in their organizations. Thus student learning is promoted simultaneously with meeting safety and civility needs. Using the three principles to develop and implement policy does require a shift in core assumptions about students and authority. Students must be viewed as capable of participating as partners in decision making and authority must be shared. These assumptions and principles can be used in numerous policy arenas—residence life (see Piper, 1997 for a description of such a policy for community standards), career services, student activities, and registration services.

A Diversity Seminar: A Classroom Example

Student affairs staff are increasingly finding themselves in the classroom teaching courses related to paraprofessional staff training, leadership, peer education, career exploration, and appreciation of diversity. Helping undergraduate students appreciate diversity is an ongoing challenge on most campuses in part because the goal inherently involves developmental complexities that most college students have yet to achieve. Kegan argued that appreciating diversity requires

> a mind that can stand enough apart from its own opinions, values, rules, and definitions to avoid being completely identified with them. It is able to keep from feeling that the whole self has been violated when its opinions, values, rules, and definitions are challenged. (1994, p. 231)

This kind of mind represents Kegan's fourth order, in which people make meaning from an internally generated system or ideology and recognize that others do the same. This kind of mind represents complex forms of knowing in which people self-author their beliefs rather than adopt those of authority or significant others. Research on young adults suggests that these kinds of minds are not prevalent in the college years (Baxter Magolda, 1992; Kegan, 1994; King & Kitchener, 1994). Thus guiding students to appreciate diversity is an ideal context for student affairs educators to use the three principles to promote development and appreciation of diversity simultaneously.

Miami University offers a diversity seminar, conceptualized and taught by both faculty and student affairs staff, that embodies the three principles and thus bridges the gap between students' initial meaning making about diversity and the seminar's overall goal of creating a comfortable environment in which all people can learn, teach, live, and work. Although the seminar is part of a larger initiative called the Mosaic Project, which involves a living–learning community, the seminar component illustrates use of the principles in a classroom setting. The seminar uses a holistic approach to appreciating diversity, focusing on "three areas of learning: cognitive (the acquisition of facts, understanding of frameworks and the critical evaluation of concepts), affective (exploration of attitudes and beliefs), and skill building (knowledge to action)" (Scott, 2000). These three areas reflect the cognitive, intrapersonal, and interpersonal dimensions of student development. The specific goals and format of the seminar reveal its consistency with the three principles.

Validation of students as knowers is communicated initially through the syllabus. The syllabus states that the seminar is "designed to create an environment where students learn to strive to learn from each other in an atmosphere of positive engagement and mutual respect, and to educate each other on the existence and effects of racism, ageism, homophobia, religious intolerance, and other forms of invidious prejudice" (Scott, 2000). This statement expresses value in students learning from one another, emphasizes a supportive atmosphere, and implies that students have knowledge from which to educate one another. Validation as knowers is also evident in an emphasis on personal reflection. One of the stated goals of the seminar is "to enable participants to reflect upon their relationship to difference." The format of the course allows "participants to engage their peers and faculty/staff instructors in reflective discourse about diversity." The primary assignment for the course is a journal in which reflection is a key focus. The journal is described as an" informal space" in which students can critically process issues from the seminar, continue the discussion beyond the seminar session, and "work out and through issues and ideas of diversity." The syllabus notes that journal entries should include students' own personal reactions and interpretations of discussion, readings, and materials introduced in the class. It notes that no right or wrong answers exist; it also stresses that there are "no consensus views that you must adhere to or agree with per se." Students are expected to explain their views and to think critically about the material, yet they are invited to "feel free to use your imagination and intuition with reasoning and thought to explore the issues and their impact on you." These parameters directly communicate validating students as knowers. Thus the seminar discussions and journals both validate students as capable of constructing knowledge about diversity issues. They also welcome diverse personal perspectives, creating an inclusive learning environment.

Situating learning in students' experience occurs in numerous ways in the seminar. Using their insights in engaging with peers and instructors to educate each other inherently implies that their experiences are welcome. The journal process also places learning squarely in students' experience, particularly in the invitation to explore the impact of issues raised in class on their lives. In addition, readings, videos, and resources introduced in the class create experience from which to analyze diversity issues. For example, in the introductory session Peggy McIntosh's (1989) "White Privilege: Unpacking the Invisible Knapsack" is used. McIntosh highlights the daily circumstances that White people take for granted, such as finding a band aid to match their skin. Reading and discussing these assumptions creates a concrete experience from which students can begin to explore the subtleties of privilege. Similarly, a short video creates an experience from which students can begin to conceptualize how difference mediates aspects of their lives. Using tools such as these as discussion starters offers students an experience from which to begin exploration. The seminar emphasizes discussion over lecture, another indication that students' experience is a central component of the seminar. Welcoming student experience is another dimension of creating a learning environment that includes all students via their diverse experiences.

The discussion focus of the seminar embodies the third principle, mutual construction of meaning, as do the overall design and guidance for students regarding their journal entries. The journal guidelines illustrate the approach of the seminar director and instructors to helping students make meaning:

> Although journal entries are to be your own responses/reactions, and involve your own critical reflections, you are encouraged to discuss seminar content with other members of the seminar, with those not involved in the seminar, with faculty/staff in and out of the seminar, and with the seminar director. You are also encouraged to include any supplemental material which you feel adds support to your reactions. (Scott, 2000)

These statements highlight the importance of dialogue with others, integration of supplemental material, and critical reflection in deciding what to believe. In the context of the overall design's emphasis on reflecting on one's relationship to difference, the message to students is to self-author their perspectives. Yet the perspectives of the instructors and others via readings, videos, and external resources challenge students to consider various issues. For example, the seminar strives "to enhance participant experience, knowledge, and understanding of the positive aspects and contributions difference and diversity make in the academy and society" (Scott, 2000, p. 2). The topics of the seminar, such as the meaning and role of diversity in society and academia, race and ethnicity, gender, sexual orientation, age, physical abilities/qualities, religious beliefs, and geographic and economic differences, most likely challenge the views of students with limited experience with diversity. The overall aura of the seminar, however, is not to tell students that they need to change their views. Rather, it is to engage students in joint meaning making, trusting that exposure to new experience and new perspectives, coupled with a supportive atmosphere for reflection, will yield more complex understandings of diversity. The tone of invitation to explore is evident in the course description, the format of the course, and the provision of a web page with additional resources and links regarding diversity issues. The overall tone of diversity as an asset rather than a barrier also invites students into the topic. (For more information about the diversity seminar, visit the website at http://www.cas.muohio.edu/~diversity)

The diversity seminar has been successful in its first two years of implementation. Student evaluations report that students felt the seminar provided basic knowledge about difference, enhanced their ability to think critically about it, increased their comfort with discussion and evaluating differences, and provided foundations to evaluate characteristics of groups different than themselves (Scott, DeLue, Holcomb, Chester, & Minor, 1999). Students also reported feeling uninhibited in the discussion and were able to talk freely about difficult matters without fear of negative reaction. Focus group interviews revealed that students valued the safe atmosphere of the seminars and the opportunities to engage with people from diverse backgrounds (Scott et al., 1999).

The ways in which this seminar uses the principles can be transferred easily to other contexts that focus on appreciating diversity, such as educational programming, leadership development, staff training, or service learning. It can also be transferred to other courses to achieve both subject mastery and self-authorship. (See Baxter Magolda, 1999b, for examples.)

STUDENT AFFAIRS ROLE IN ENHANCING THE CURRICULUM

Enhancing learning in the cocurriculum is the profession's primary role. However, students' holistic development—the intertwining of their cognitive, intrapersonal, and interpersonal growth—requires that the curriculum implement the learning paradigm as well. Student affairs professionals have an extensive array of expertise in students' intellectual development and pedagogical principles to promote it to offer faculty as they transform the curriculum from an instruction to a learning paradigm.

Academic and student affairs partnerships are being developed at many institutions and on the national level. A recent report cosponsored by the American Association for Higher Education, the American College Personnel Association, and the National Association of Student Personnel Administrators (1998) endorsed a shared responsibility for learning and outlined 10 areas for collaboration. These areas stemmed from 10 principles about learning that frame learning consistent with student affairs holistic philosophy, constructivist perspectives, and the development perspective elaborated in this chapter. Although the report's extensive recommendations and examples are beyond the scope of this chapter, highlighting their core emphases illustrates how such collaboration can extend the use of the three principles for promoting student development and learning. For example, collaboration to help students make connections takes the form of giving them responsibility for solving problems. Giving them responsibility for leadership creates compelling conditions for learning. Designing opportunities to help students apply their knowledge stimulates the active search for meaning that leads to knowledge construction. Opportunities for reflection create a developmental process for learning. Campus cultures that spawn collaboration help students learn to relate to others. These notions, elaborated far more extensively in the report, center on inviting students to be genuine partners with educators in learning in all aspects of their college experience.

Collaboration in these forms hinges on the same core assumptions underlying the learning paradigm and the three principles to promote intellectual and holistic development. They are, however, new assumptions about the role of authority and students and the nature of knowledge and learning. Viewing knowledge as constructed by the learner alters the role of authority and learner. This requires a shift in educational practice that is more substantive than including more discussion in class, staff training, and programming efforts. It requires the fundamental transformation to genuine partnership with students evident in the example of staff training, policy, and teaching in this chapter. Trusting students to participate in cocurricular decision making and curricular knowledge construction means abandoning ultimate control.

Abandoning ultimate control is perceived as risky. Risk is seen as minimal when the educator role is in the forefront, as is the case in the classroom example. The worst-case outcome is less learning than desired. The perceived risk is slightly higher in the staff training example because shortcomings that emerge from training can play out in staff performance. Risk is perceived as highest when the manager role comes to the forefront, such as in policy development, because problems emerging from these settings are of greater magnitude. For example, hazing incidents or alcohol abuse, phenomena student affairs professionals generally attempt to control via traditional authority, can be life threatening. The risk to safety and civility must be weighed against the potential for education. Regardless of the role the student affairs professional adopts—educator, leader, manager—she or he must constantly weigh the short-term risks involved in meeting long-term educational goals.

Although maintaining order and helping students develop self-authorship may be perceived as conflicting, in most cases these goals can be achieved simultaneously. The three principles described here do not advocate giving total authority and control to students. They advocate engaging students mutually with professionals in decision making. Professionals do not abandon positions that protect students' physical and mental health in this process. Instead, they mutually construct systems to protect and enhance the quality of student life while helping students learn to become positive contributors to productive communities. Engaging and understanding students' perspectives on campus issues helps educators envision systems that do enhance campus life and simultaneously help students understand how individual choices are mediated by community membership.

The evidence stemming from innovative attempts to implement the learning paradigm suggests that the perceived risk is well worth taking. The lack of significant progress on campus problems that endanger safety and civility also suggests that new approaches are warranted. Student affairs is in an ideal position to participate in these innovations and the collaboration to extend them because contemporary thinking is moving toward student affairs' original philosophy. If student affairs can recover this approach and model it for the university community, the profession will make a major contribution to enhancing student learning that extends far beyond the cocurriculum.

QUESTIONS TO CONSIDER

1. What assumptions do I hold about students' capacity to learn? What assumptions do I hold about my role as an educator?
2. What are the basic tenets of my philosophy of educational practice? How do these manifest themselves in my student affairs work?
3. How do I (or can I) implement the three principles in this chapter to bridge my expectations to students' current ways of making meaning?

REFERENCES

American Association for Higher Education, American College Personnel Association, & National Association for Student Personnel Administrators. (1998). *Powerful partnerships: A shared responsibility for learning.* Washington, DC: Authors.

American College Personnel Association (ACPA). (1994). *The student learning imperative.* Washington, DC: Author.

Barr, R. B., & Tagg, J. (1995, November/December). From teaching to learning—A new paradigm for undergraduate education. *Change,* 13–25.

Baxter Magolda, M. B. (1992). *Knowing and reasoning in college: Gender-related patterns in students' intellectual development.* San Francisco, CA: Jossey-Bass.

Baxter Magolda, M. B. (1999a). The evolution of epistemology: Refining contextual knowing at twentysomething. *Journal of College Student Development, 40,* 333–344.

Baxter Magolda, M. B. (1999b). *Creating contexts for learning and self-authorship: Constructive-developmental pedagogy.* Nashville, TN: Vanderbilt University Press.

Belenky, M., Clinchy, B., Goldberger, N., & Tarule, J. (1986). *Women's ways of knowing: The development of self, voice, and mind.* New York: Basic Books.

Blystone, C., Conlon, M., Kooker, D., Marriner, N., & Wigton, K. (1996, November). *Resident Assistant Institute: Past traditions and new directions for RA training.* Paper presented at the Great Lakes Association of College and University Housing Officers Conference, Oshkosh, WI.

Bruffee, K. A. (1993). *Collaborative learning: Higher education, interdependence, and the authority of knowledge.* Baltimore, MD: Johns Hopkins University Press.

Dutton, K. (1997). *The returning RA Institute: Crossing boundaries of student learning through resident assistant training* [Brochure]. Oxford, OH: Miami University Office of Resident Life and New Student Programs.

Freire, P. (1970/1988). *Pedagogy of the oppressed.* New York: Continuum.

Hooks, B. (1994). *Teaching to transgress: Education as the practice of freedom.* New York: Routledge.

Hopkins, R. L. (1994). *Narrative schooling: Experiential learning and the transformation of American education.* New York: Teachers College Press.

Jardis, A., & Wigton, K. (1999, March). *New directions for resident assistant training utilizing experiential learning opportunities.* Paper presented at the American College Personnel Association meeting, Atlanta, GA.

Kegan, R. (1994). *In over our heads: The mental demands of modern life.* Cambridge, MA: Harvard University Press.

King, P., & Baxter Magolda, M. (1996). A developmental perspective on learning. *Journal of College Student Development, 37,* 163–173.

King, P. M., & Kitchener, K. S. (1994). *Developing reflective judgment: Understanding and promoting intellectual growth and critical thinking in adolescents and adults.* San Francisco: Jossey-Bass.

Ladson-Billings, G. (1995). Toward a theory of culturally relevant pedagogy. *American Educational Research Journal, 32,* 465–491.

Lloyd-Jones, E. L., & Smith, M. (Eds.). (1954). *Student personnel work as deeper teaching.* New York: Harper Brothers.

McIntosh, P. (1989, July/August). White privilege: Unpacking the invisible knapsack. *Peace and Freedom Journal,* 10–12.

Miami University Office of Residence Life and New Student Programs. (1997). *The 1997 Miami University resident assistant institute* [Brochure]. Oxford, OH: Author.

Noddings, N. (1991). Stories in dialogue: Caring and interpersonal reasoning. In C. Witherell & N. Noddings (Eds.), *Stories lives tell: Narrative and dialogue in education* (pp. 157–170). New York: Teachers College Press.

Palmer, P. J. (1998). *The courage to teach: Exploring the inner landscape of a teacher's life.* San Francisco: Jossey-Bass.

Perry, W. G. (1970). *Forms of intellectual and ethical development in the college years: A scheme.* Troy, MO: Holt, Rinehart, & Winston.

Piper, T. D. (July/August 1997). Empowering students to create community standards. *About Campus,* 22–24.

Rhoads, R. A. (1997). *Community service and

higher learning: Explorations of the caring self. Albany: State University of New York Press.

Scott, R. (2000). *IDS 151 Diversity Seminar* [On-Line]. Available: http://www.cas.muohio.edu/~diversity/151Outin.htm

Scott, R., DeLue, S., Holcomb, T., Chester, B., & Minor, R. (1999, June). *The Mosaic program: A model for diversity seminars and a focused learning community for first-year students*. Paper presented at the 12th Annual Conference on Race and Ethnicity in American Higher Education, Memphis, TN.

Shor, I. (1992). *Empowering education: Critical teaching for social change*. Chicago: University of Chicago Press.

Shor, I. (1996). *When students have power: Negotiating authority in a critical pedagogy*. Chicago: University of Chicago Press.

Tompkins, J. (1996). *A life in school; What the teacher learned*. Reading, MA: Addison-Wesley.

RECOMMENDED READING

Baxter Magolda, M. B. (2001). *Making their own way: Narratives for transforming higher education to promote self-development*. Sterling, VA: Stylus Press.

Baxter Magolda, M. B. (Ed.). (2000). *Teaching to promote intellectual and personal maturity: Incorporating students' worldviews and identities into the learning process*. New Directions for Teaching and Learning, No. 82. San Francisco: Jossey-Bass.

Kegan, R. (1994). *In over our heads: The mental demands of modern life*. Cambridge, MA: Harvard University Press.

King, P. M., & Kitchener, K. S. (1994). *Developing reflective judgment: Understanding and promoting intellectual growth and critical thinking in adolescents and adults*. San Francisco: Jossey-Bass.

12

Programmatic Interventions: Translating Theory to Practice

SUE A. SAUNDERS
DIANE L. COOPER

*P*rogramming for and by students is ubiquitous on U.S. campuses of all types (two-year, four-year, public, private, residential, and commuter). One simply needs to quickly walk through a student union to see a multitude of flyers for such varied and diverse programs as a ballroom dancing class, a speaker on multiple forms of intelligence, a series of foreign films focusing on alienation, a presentation by student peer educators on AIDS prevention, an information session on sorority rush, a meeting of the nontraditional students' organization to mobilize support for improved child care, or the announcement of a website that promotes stress reduction. Yet the quantity, variety, or even the popularity of programming efforts does not guarantee that these events, however well intentioned, will help student affairs professionals fulfill their educational, leadership, and management roles.

The purpose of this chapter is to describe a model of intentional program development based on an understanding of student development and learning theories and the assessment of student needs and local environment. If student affairs administrators are to effectively implement their educative function and to promote individual and community development, program planners must identify learning and development outcomes that guide the program design throughout the process. Even though learning can occur as a result of serendipitous or random student events, reliance on such causative factors cannot possibly yield the positive educational outcomes that will result from an intentional and purposeful approach.

DEFINING PROGRAMMATIC INTERVENTIONS

The term "programmatic intervention," as used in this chapter, is an elaboration of Barr and Keating's (1985) definition. A programmatic intervention is a planned activity with individuals or student groups that is theoretically based and has as its intent the promotion of personal development and learning.

The specific purposes of such interventions can be to teach skills, to enhance knowledge, or to change behavior or attitudes. If student affairs administrators are to ensure that individual development occurs in a context that supports a democratic society (Goodlad, 1997) however, then the skills taught, information delivered, and attitudes addressed must be those that enhance the common good. A key theme of the *Student Learning Imperative* (SLI; American College Personnel Association [ACPA], 1994) is that all efforts of student affairs administrators, including programmatic interventions, should have as their ultimate purpose to foster students' development of "a coherent integrated sense of identity, self esteem, confidence, integrity, aesthetic sensibilities, and civic responsibilities" (p. 1).

Programmatic interventions can take a variety of forms. Even though administrators often categorize formally structured events as programs, less formal events, such as assisting a student organization resolve an unforeseen conflict, share many of the same characteristics. Therefore, the information presented in this chapter can be used for both formal and informal programming initiatives.

There can be great variety in the duration and target audiences of programmatic interventions. They can range from one-time events to a series of programs for the same target audience (such as a leadership development series for freshmen women) or a series of activities organized around a specific theme (such as alcohol awareness week or Black history month) but with different target audiences. With the advent of distance learning approaches, an increasing number of programmatic interventions occur over the Internet. Some of these interventions are highly interactive, providing opportunities for students to converse on-line. (See Chapter 4 in this volume.)

The program focus can vary and may emphasize enhancement, prevention, or remediation. The foci identified here were drawn from Winston, Bonney, Miller, and Dagley's (1988) model of Intentionally Structured Groups. Even though the foci are not mutually exclusive, determining the intervention focus can assist planners in program design. Enhancement programs help students who are functioning effectively to enrich their skills or knowledge. Typically, enhancement programs are those that deal with normal developmental concerns. A series of workshops designed to identify internship experiences that will strengthen one's opportunities in the job market is an example of an enhancement focus. Interventions with a prevention focus are designed to anticipate problems and to teach skills, knowledge, or attitudes that will prevent or lessen the negative effects of potentially problematic life situations. For example, programs that teach students how to avoid or prevent sexually transmitted diseases represent a prevention focus. The remediation focus is designed to help students deal with existing problems, or to change behavior that has prevented them from being successful. Programs that deal with the grief and death of a fellow student or acquiring more effective study skills are examples of the remediation focus.

The responsibility for initiating and implementing programmatic interventions also varies. For example, student affairs administrators can initiate design of programs without the involvement of students in the planning phase. At times of crisis or if local circumstances such as an immediate safety concern mandate quick response, it may not be possible to involve students in planning. It is preferable, however, to "do with students rather than doing for students" (Manning, 1994, p. 96), primarily because the learning opportunities for student program planners are so rich and plentiful. Students who are partners with student affairs administrators in designing programmatic interventions have unique opportunities to develop critical thinking and problem-solving skills. In addition, because these students are involved with administrators in ways that reduce the impediments of power and status, considerable learning and development is likely to occur as a result of role modeling.

THEORIES THAT INFLUENCE PROGRAMMATIC INTERVENTION

Knowledge of the specific elements of student development theory is critical to designing programs that will be effective and appropriate for a targeted group of students. In the last two decades, a plethora of theoretical conceptions have been developed and many have been effective when used by program planners. The theories that have provided the greatest utility are the psychosocial theories, which focus on the content of human development; the cognitive-structural theories, which focus on how people think and make decisions; the typology theories that provide understanding about the influence of individual differences on learning and development; and person–environment interaction theories that deal with how the environment exerts influence on students' development. Rather than reiterating all of the theories that can be useful, this chapter summarizes the basics of psychosocial and cognitive-structural theories and focuses on typological and person–environment theories; specifically, the implications of Kolb's (1984) typological theory of experiential learning and Astin's (1984) involvement theory that delineates environmental conditions that foster development.

Psychosocial Development Theories

If administrators desire to impact developmental milestones that can be positively affected by programming, it is important to be conversant with the elements of psychosocial theories (such as those of Chickering & Reisser, 1993) and with the identity development models that focus on populations not fully represented in earlier theoretical constructions, such as Josselson's (1987) pathways of women's identity, Cross's (1995) conceptions of African American identity, Cass's (1979) model of homosexual identity formation, and Helms's (1995) White and people of color racial identity models. Suppose that the coordinators of freshman residence halls desire to initiate a series of programs to promote positive racial identity development and better understanding and cooperation across racial and ethnic groups. Helms's (1995) model would indicate that many students in the early years of college are in the first stage, the contact stage, and express satisfaction with their racial status but are oblivious to their participation in racism and oppression. If program planners desire to make a positive change, however, they could establish programs where ethical dilemmas about racial privilege were presented in a way that would allow students to express opinions and feel that they would not be overwhelmed by hostile confrontation from those who see the impact of racial privilege more vividly. Discussing historical films about the ethical dilemmas faced during the civil rights movement and the implications of these activities in the everyday lives of students could be a way to promote movement toward the second status in Helms's model, *disintegration*.

Cognitive-Structural Development Theories

Psychosocial theory examines the changes that occur in thinking, feeling, and behaving as one matures. In contrast, cognitive-structural theories focus on the ways individuals think and make decisions. These theories are concerned with the development that occurs in individuals' assumptions about their experiences and environments (Evans, Forney, & Guido-DiBrito, 1998). The theories developed by Perry (1968), Kohlberg (1969), Gilligan (1982/1993), King and Kitchener (1994), and Baxter Magolda (1992) have implications for the ways in which program designers structure and deliver content. (See also Chapter 11 in this volume.)

If a student activities program advisor decided to design and facilitate a series of workshops on leadership skills for sophomore women who wanted to become active in campus organizations, the theory of Baxter Magolda (see Chapter 11 in this volume) would have utility for determining the degree of structure and the quality of interpersonal relationships to be fostered in the sessions. Assuming that the majority of women in the workshops could be classified as *transitional knowers*, participants would be individuals who accepted that some knowledge is uncertain, and who believed that it is important to emphasize how learning can be applied to current and future practical situations (Baxter Magolda, 1992). With this population, the most effective workshops would emphasize how participants can apply these skills to their organizations, and would offer multiple opportunities to practice skills and to discover that the workshop facilitator does not have all of the answers. Because Baxter Magolda's research indicates that women are more likely than men to use an *interpersonal knowing* pattern during the transitional knowing stage, it would be important for workshop planners to develop support networks among participants, to foster the sharing of ideas among peers, and for the workshop facilitators to demonstrate care for students.

Involvement Theory

Astin's (1984, 1985, 1993) work provided a conceptual framework for understanding the factors in a program that would facilitate development. He defined involvement as the amount of physical and psychological energy a student devotes to the educational experience. Although related to the terms *vigilance, motivation,* and *effort,* involvement connotes a more comprehensive construct that focuses on behavior—on action, rather than on internal psychological states. Involvement has both quantitative and qualitative components. Even though the amount of time spent is important, the level of activity and energy or quality of the investment one devotes to an activity is the key.

For example, suppose that two nontraditional-aged community college students are attending a series of workshops on how to handle multiple responsibilities of work, family, and school. Each of the students attends the five weekly workshops that last two hours each. One student attends all of the sessions, listens quietly to the presenters, and does not participate in the recommended exercises, such as creating a time log, that occur between sessions. The other student has to leave several of the workshops before the closing activities, but she engages the presenters in a dialogue, spends time outside the workshops thinking about implications of the material for her schedule, takes responsibility for talking with her children about how they can take on additional chores around the house, and actively converses with other participants in the workshop experiential exercises. There is an obvious difference in the level of involvement of the two participants. Winston and Massaro (1987, p. 171) define "intensity of involvement" as a means of combining both time on task and personal investment. In this example, the second participant has a higher intensity of involvement, and therefore one can hypothesize that her personal development and learning will be affected to a greater degree than that of the first participant.

Astin (1985) hypothesized a symbiotic relationship between the theories of student development—such as those of Chickering and Reisser (1993), Kohlberg (1969), and Perry (1968)—and involvement theory: "The theory of student involvement . . . differs qualitatively from these developmental theories. Whereas they focus primarily on developmental outcomes (the 'what' of student development), the theory of student involvement is concerned more with the behavioral mechanisms of processes that facilitate student development (the 'how') of student development" (pp. 142–143).

If administrators who create programmatic interventions desire to foster high involvement intensity among participants, several critical conditions are necessary (Winston & Saunders, 1987). These conditions assist students in developing enthusiasm and increase commitment to their own growth. Perhaps the greatest challenge for promoting high intensity involvement is to create incentives for students and groups to make active commitments to their own growth and learning. Oftentimes students will participate in a program simply because it sounds like fun, or could be a way to meet other students, or is seen as a first step to building a more impressive resume. Consequently, the learning and personal development outcomes that may have inspired administrators to create the intervention in the first place become divorced from its implementation. In such instances, the opportunities to learn something challenging or to take responsibility for applying the learning beyond the program are viewed as burdens or mere requirements. Astin (1984) noted that "one of the challenges confronting student personnel workers [*sic*] these days is to find a 'hook' that will stimulate students to get more involved in the college experience" (p. 305).

Making outcomes explicit. Program planners should clearly identify the developmental and learning outcomes that students can achieve as a result of participating in the intervention. It is not sufficient for administrators to simply identify outcomes; they must communicate them in ways that students can comprehend and, more importantly, value and feel enthusiastic about. All too often planners either fail to think through carefully the developmental outcomes or communicate and reiterate those thoughts to students. The title of and marketing materials for the program have relevance for communicating the learning and developmental outcomes to prospective participants. Outcomes should be explained in ways that are appealing to students, and planners can include experiential activities that clarify the fundamental purposes of the program. Student members of a planning team often are the best resources for designing creative outcome explanations that heighten enthusiasm for participating in the program.

In some instances, program planners may take time at the beginning of an intervention to explain the purpose and probable outcomes but then never address these topics again. Program facilitators should ask participants to evaluate their own learning and development periodically and in different ways during the course of the program. This principle of redundancy is crucial to highlighting the importance of learning outcomes.

Meaningful encounters between administrators and students. Several research studies (Astin, 1993; Baxter Magolda, 1992; Pascarella & Terenzini, 1991) pointed to the positive developmental effect of student relationships with faculty members and administrators. The research suggested that students tend to pay more attention to the outcomes of their experiences when administrators spend time discussing with students their growth and learning. Simply having institutional staff members talk to students regularly about their growth and learning progress fosters a greater degree of reflection, thus encouraging students to "actively watch themselves in the process of learning and develop learning strategies that constantly monitor their learning effectiveness" (Cross, 1996, p. 6)—in other words, helping students learn how to learn and develop.

Winston and Saunders (1987) advocated an intrusive approach to advising Greek organizations that has implications for the student affairs administrators who design and facilitate programs. An administrator who is intrusive would actively recruit program participants and discuss with individuals the developmental benefits of participating in a particular activity. An intrusive program facilitator would seek to assist and encourage involvement by passive, reticent, or even rebellious participants. A facilitator who frequently asks, "What are you learning from this experience and how can we work together to make it a more powerful developmental experience?" sends a subtle, but powerful, message that learning and development is a process that requires reflection and modification.

Developing campuswide incentives for involvement in learning and development. Program planners will be most successful in encouraging learning and development if they are part of a campus environment that values student growth. It is indeed difficult to be a "lone ranger" who desires to make interventions educationally productive when others are unenthusiastic about the idea. Influencing the values and priorities of a student affairs division or student social climate is a challenge for administrators. Creamer, Winston, and Miller (see Chapter 1 in this volume) described leadership skills and competencies that can be used to encourage climatic change that focuses on learning and development.

Learning Theory

Kolb (1981) developed an experiential learning theory that also includes a typology of four distinct learning styles. Program planners and facilitators who wish to maximize learning and developmental outcomes need to recognize differential patterns and preferences in student learning. Planners can then better ensure that the program design meets the needs of the wide variety of prospective student participants.

Failing to take into account various learning styles can mitigate against optimal outcomes. For example, suppose that Jose and Jennifer are in a program designed to help resident assistants (RAs) deal with interpersonal conflicts that occur among residents. The facilitator of the workshop is a staff psychologist who has completed extensive research projects on conflict management and designs the workshop to emphasize his theoretical model. At the close of the workshop, Jose raves about the content of the workshop, indicating that it gave him a deeper understanding of how conflict begins and the phases of resolution. Jennifer, on the other hand, is highly critical, stopped listening to the workshop less than halfway through the session, and chose instead to work on her incident reports. Jennifer thought that she was coming to the workshop so that she would learn exactly how to manage the problems on her floor. She wanted to understand the "nuts and bolts" steps she should use for roommate conflicts and felt that the workshop was generally a waste of time. She was looking for a recipe book.

Kolb's (1981) theory of experiential learning describes learning in a way that individual styles can be understood. Kolb sees all learning as a four-stage cycle (Figure 12.1). Concrete experience, such as attending a workshop, provides as basis for the student's observations and reflections about what the experience means. A student then uses these reflections to create an idea or generalizations (theory) that can be applied to a larger range of experiences than one isolated event. From the generalizations, a student can identify implications for action, which can be tested in new situations.

Effective learners need four different competencies: concrete experiences (CE), which involves unbiased involvement in learning activities; reflective observation (RO), which requires thinking about one's experience from multiple perspectives; abstract conceptualization (AC), which includes formulating generalizable ideas or theories related to the event; and active experimentation (AE), which incorporates new ideas into future actions (Evans, Forney, & Guido-DiBrito, 1998). Kolb (1981) found, however, individuals developed some of these skills more fully than others, and thus individuals tend to prefer certain types of learning. Kolb described four types of learners: (a) convergers, (b) divergers, (c) assimilators, and (d) accommodators. Convergers, who have as their dominant abilities AC and AE, prefer situations where there are single correct answers and like to be involved in problem solving, decision making, and practical application of ideas. Jennifer, in the example outlined above, could be classified as a converger. Divergers, who have as their dominant abilities CE

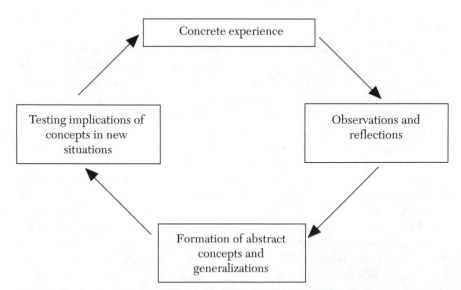

FIGURE 12.1. Experiential Learning Model. Reprinted from Kolb: "Learning styles and disciplinary differences," in *Modern American College,* by A. W. Chickering. Copyright © 1981 by Jossey-Bass. Reprinted by permission of Jossey-Bass, Inc., a subsidiary of John Wiley & Sons, Inc.

and RO, tend to be highly imaginative, enjoy observing and reflecting, and can generate multiple alternative solutions to problems. They tend to enjoy interacting with others and are interested in understanding others' feelings. Assimilators, whose dominant abilities are CE and AE, focus on ideas rather than people. They tend to evaluate the quality of ideas based on logic rather than practicality. They have the ability to create theories by integrating ideas. In the example above, the workshop facilitator and Jose could be classified as assimilators. Accommodators, whose strengths are CE and AE, are action-oriented. They rely on information from others rather than on theories, tend to be very adaptable in new situations, solve problems intuitively, and are at ease in group decision making.

Understanding varied learning styles is especially important if program planners desire to create interventions that include and embrace diverse cultures and ethnic groups. Anderson (1988) and Anderson and Adams (1992) elaborated on Kolb's model discussing the potential impact of ethnicity on learning styles. They asserted that many majority students are assimilators and are comfortable with the abstract theory, impersonal and rational argument, independent learning, and inductive reasoning that characterizes the most traditional college teaching and programmatic interventions. On the other hand, when discussing the general style preferences of African American, Hispanic, and Native American students, Anderson and Adams (1992) indicated that "generally, the pattern that emerges is that these students demonstrate competence in social interactions and peer cooperation, performance, visual perception, symbolic expression, and narrative or verbal skills" (p. 21). Applying Kolb's (1984) theory to a one-time program or short-term workshop presents numerous challenges. Time does not permit assessment of individuals' learning styles or incorporation of this knowledge into program design. The best approach is to vary the activities so that the preferences of all learning styles may be employed successfully. Forney (1991) developed an example of a job-hunting workshop that outlined learning activities designed to meet the needs of each of the four Kolb learning styles. Information about available resources, recommended job-hunting strategies, along with an opportunity for students to obtain feedback about their own plans, would be congruent with the assimilators' learning style. Group discussion about how one could implement the information in personal situations along with attention to individual questions and concerns is congruent with accommodators because of the attention to action, with convergers because of attention to individual situations, and with divergers because of group interaction. If the workshop facilitator conducted a tour of the career library and job vacancy notices, this could connect with the accommodators' preference for hands-on experience and the convergers' inquisitiveness. Those with a diverger or assimilator preference would likely value opportunity for follow-up after they had reflected on the career search process.

It is important to recognize that one must use typology theory with caution. Even though Kolb's theory provided a scheme that allows program planners to be more responsive to the diverse ways of learning, no theory can account for all of the nuances of individual styles of learning and problem solving. Furthermore, generalizing information about ethnic or gender group differences to individuals goes well beyond the strength of current research in this area and frequently may obscure the more important individual differences.

Concepts, Skills, and Approaches that Foster Programmatic Intervention

To plan and facilitate programs that will foster positive learning and development outcomes requires that student affairs administrators have skills in the educative, leadership, and managerial domains that are outlined in Chapter 1 of this volume. Because programming often occurs in groups, the excellent program planner and facilitator will have a solid grasp of the principles of group dynamics and related group theory. With the ever-increasing use of technology as a way to impart information and to foster learning and development, those interested in programmatic interventions should have an understanding of resources both on-line and on-site that can assist in building interventions on the Internet. In light of these important needs, ways in which group dynamics' principles can positively affect programmatic interventions and resources for building Internet-based interventions are outlined in the following section.

Group Dynamics

Group dynamics is the study of behavior in groups and includes research about the interrelationships between individuals and groups, how groups develop over time, the ways in which groups make decisions, and the roles that individuals play within a group context. Because many programmatic interventions are implemented over an extended period of time or occur with student groups and organizations that have life spans that precede and continue after the programmatic interventions, it is important that the basics of group dynamics be understood. Even when program planners are designing a one-time program, the principles of group dynamics can be employed to heighten interest and to strengthen the intensity of involvement.

Development of groups. Napier and Gershenfeld (1989) wrote that "in work groups, social or political groups, sports teams, and classroom groups, a predictable pattern of group evolution emerges in which each stage has certain definite characteristics" (p. 470). Understanding this evolutionary process can be helpful to planners so that the timing of activities is consistent with the life stage of the group. For example, in the beginning for most groups composed of persons who are unacquainted with each other, members are on their best behavior, and are reluctant to express controversial views or self-disclose meaningful personal information. For working with groups in this stage it is important for planners to create a comfortable climate where ground rules for confidentiality are established and where the facilitator explains her or his qualifications to lead the group. For example, suppose that planners of a workshop on racial diversity prepared an exercise to be used in the early part of the first session designed to encourage individuals to share their life experiences about being advantaged or disadvantaged or being of a certain race or ethnic group. It is often tempting for planners with a short time frame to expect a group to *jump into* exercises that require discussion of controversial issues, such as racial diversity, without attending to the preliminary stages of group development. Yet trying to move a group to more intense self-disclosure before the early, formative stages of group development are accomplished will likely fail. If participants are overly challenged before they are ready, several undesired consequences are likely to result, such as conflict and disagreement that goes unresolved or individuals keeping mum and refusing to participate openly but expressing their opinions privately with trusted members of the group, often outside the group setting.

There are many different conceptions outlining the stages of group development, including those by Bach (1954), Bonney and Foley (1963), Napier and Gershenfeld (1989), Schutz (1958), and Winston et al. (1988). Tuckman (1965) and Tuckman and Jensen (1977) reviewed several articles about the behavior of groups over time and determined five general stages that exist for groups that emphasize task completion and those where the agenda focuses on social and interpersonal exploration. These stages are (a) forming, (b) storming, (c) norming, (d) performing, and (e) adjourning.

In the forming stage, individuals try to determine their niche in the group; decide what others, including the facilitator, expect of them; and decide what a commitment to the group will mean. According to Komives, Lucas, and McMahon (1998), successful resolution of the forming stage involves the creation of open, trusting relationships among members where inclusion is valued. Group identity-building exercises, modeling of inclusive and respectful modes of discussion are effective tools that facilitators can use in this stage.

In the second stage, storming, the "honeymoon" is over, the group begins to get down to work, and differences of opinion emerge. In this stage, there are typically resistant members who may not have as much investment in the program as others or there may be members with conflicting opinions about the goals of their involvement. To increase the intensity of involvement, program facilitators need to encourage individuals to discuss expectations for the program and of other members of the group. If participants are to engage actively in the intervention and to make a personal investment, they need to have the opportunity to shape the group's purpose and desired outcomes. For example, if a program facilitator sees her role as being in control of the intervention, imparting information, and having students participate in cursory exercises, the storming stage will likely be avoided. It is also likely however, that an overly structured program where the facilitator is primarily concerned about task completion will not engender the intensity of involvement that will lead to significant behavior or attitude change necessary to realize developmental outcomes. Facilitators can assist in the storming stage by mediating conflict, insuring respectful conversation, and by revisiting expectations—their own and the participants'.

The third stage, norming, occurs only when storming has resulted in a relatively clear direction that members can accept. In the norming stage, groups develop cohesion, where individuals feel that they are a part of a group and where they allow themselves to be influenced by the facilitator and other members. In this stage members agree on how they will function and they establish patterns to complete tasks efficiently and effectively. Groups develop their own cultures about such things as whether it is acceptable to deviate from the facilitators' agenda, whether programs start on time or 10 minutes late, or whether it is appropriate to have private conversations during the program. Even though the facilitator has considerable influence about student behavior during programs, the norms established by the group or even the norms of the campus environment have a strong impact on students' actions and their degree of involvement. Facilitators can positively impact the norming stage by encouraging the group to create a motto or logo that makes its identity visual. Facilitators can also encourage open discussion of norms and whether these help or hurt students' learning.

In the performing stage, the group understands its roles and responsibilities; focuses on task completion, and operates at a high level of interpersonal interaction. Conflicts tend to be less frequent during this stage. When a program continues with the same participants over a long period of time, such as RA continuing education, facilitators will need to make sure that the group is renewed and may need to revisit the norming stage to ensure that the program purposes are clear and fresh.

The final stage, adjourning, is self-explanatory, but many facilitators forget to build "saying goodbye" into the planning. The final stage presents an excellent opportunity for group members to reflect on what they have learned and what changes they may make as a result of participating in the program or workshop. It is yet another opportunity to explore the developmental and learning outcomes that were designed for the program and have students discuss whether they have been achieved. Establishing closure for the group experience is important to assure that members are able to and comfortable about discontinuing and leaving the group.

A variety of resources contain experiential activities that can be adapted for use during this stage and those that precede it. Some of these include *Promoting Student Development Through Intentionally Structured Groups* (Winston et al., 1988), *Joining Together: Group Theory and Group Skills* (Johnson & Johnson, 1997); and *A Handbook of Interactive Exercises for Groups* (Barlow, Blythe, & Edmonds, 1999).

Group roles. Even in a very short term program, participants are likely to adopt familiar interaction patterns that are common to many group settings. For example, John is attending a program on acquaintance rape in which one of the exercises asks students to brainstorm stereotypes placed on victims and perpetrators. John's preferred role in a group is to use humor as a way to get attention. In this group, he uses his "comedic" talents to contribute funny or bizarre stereotypes, such as victims always dress like Shania Twain (the country music performer), in ways that the group is distracted from work. In this same group, for example, Ishmal is constantly trying to seek harmony, attempting to integrate opinions and explain away group members' objections to John's distracting comments. It is important for group planners and facilitators alike to recognize the common roles that are likely to emerge, to allow adequate time for addressing conflicts that arise from roles, and to have the skills to productively manage conflict.

There are numerous conceptions of group roles (Benne & Sheats, 1948; Blocher, 1987; Knowles, & Knowles, 1959; Lifton, 1966). Winston and colleagues (1988) blended the descriptors of Benne and Sheats and Blocher to develop descriptions of common group roles that are productive and those that are unproductive. Examples of productive roles include the following.

> *Information seeker:* Asks for clarification of suggestions made both for their factual adequacy and for their pertinence to the problem being discussed.
> *Opinion seeker:* Asks not primarily for the facts but for clarification of the values involved.
> *Initiator:* Suggests a changed way of regarding the group problems or goals, new procedures for the group, or new ways of organizing the group for the task ahead.
> *Interpreter:* Interprets feelings expressed by members of the group or interprets the significance of nonverbal behavior.
> *Supporter:* Agrees with and accepts the contribution of others; understands and accepts other points of view, ideas, and suggestions.
> *Coordinator:* Points out relationships among ideas and suggestions, tries to pull divergent ideas together, or tries to coordinate the efforts of the members in accomplishing tasks.
> *Energizer:* Prods the group to action or decision and attempts to stimulate the group to increased levels of activity or commitment.
> *Harmonizer:* Attempts to mediate differences between members, reconcile disagreements, or relieve tension in conflict situations through humor or denial of conflict. (Winston et al., 1988, p. 47)

Examples of nonproductive group roles include the following:

> *Aggressor:* Attempts to deflate the status of other members, jokes aggressively, attempts to take credit for others' contributions, belittles other members' contributions.
> *Resister:* Constantly reacts negatively to most ideas, opposes proposals for no reason, recycles rejected proposals or ideas repeatedly, is obstinately negative in general.
> *Recognition seeker:* Frequently calls attention to herself or himself, often by boasting, bragging, or acting in bizarre or unusual ways.
> *Comedian:* Attempts to make everything into a joke; may interrupt activities

to tell jokes or humorous stories or to act in unusual ways to generate laughter.

Dominator: Tries to assert authority or superiority by manipulating members or the entire group; may use flattery, act in an authoritarian manner, interrupt others' contributions, or insist on always having the last word.

Victim: Attempts to elicit sympathy from others in a variety of ways, such as through excessive self-deprecation and expressions of insecurity or inadequacy.

Expert: Treats group members as an audience in order to demonstrate "superior" knowledge, acts as a junior psychoanalyst interpreting everyone's acts and feelings according to some theory; tends to over-intellectualize all experiences in the group. (p. 48)

Dealing with group conflict.   If the facilitator desires to create a climate that promotes involvement and discussion, it is likely that conflict will occur. Conflict can be expected to emerge during the storming stage, especially when a program is designed as a series of events or multiple sessions with the same group. In addition, when working with an intact group (such as a sorority chapter, student government committee, or academic club), the conflict of the storming stage that is occurring in the life outside the group may carry over to a one-time program. For example, suppose that a student affairs administrator is facilitating programs on academic success for executive councils of sorority chapters. If the group is in the storming stage following a hotly contested election of new officers, the student affairs administrator may find resistance to sharing personal problems about time management concerns, or he or she may find that certain members are being highly critical of others with no provocation. Even in programs that occur only once with individuals who cannot be classified as a group, facilitators may find that role conflict occurs because individuals are likely to adopt roles with which they are familiar and comfortable. Participants who seek attention in unproductive ways in other groups are unlikely to adopt the harmonizer role in a one-time event.

How might a facilitator prevent unproductive conflict or deal with it when it arises unforeseen? The first step is to recognize that some degree of conflict is inevitable when students are personally invested in a programmatic intervention. An absence of disagreement and an unquestioning acceptance of all that the facilitator or program planner designs may mean disengagement (a very low intensity of involvement) rather than satisfied, motivated participants. Even though it is often tempting for facilitators and program planners to ignore the universality of conflict, failure to deal with controversy and disagreements forthrightly is likely to result in participants disengaging from the intervention. If facilitators and program planners can view conflict as a natural opportunity for greater growth and creativity rather than a troublesome distraction, the potential positive outcomes will increase.

Conflict is troubling not only because it is distracting, but also because it can lead to individuals becoming defensive and less participatory, can escalate and become entangled with unrelated issues, and can become a negatively reinforcing cycle (Bothwell, 1983). Setting ground rules is one strategy that has proved useful in decreasing some of the liabilities and risks of conflict. Lappe and Du Bois (1994) pointed out that ground rules can promote an "environment 'safe' for differences" (p. 251). Ground rules highlight the ways in which civility and inclusivity are promoted (Komives, Lucas, & McMahon, 1998) as well as the more procedural elements such as starting time, duration, that participation in exercises is voluntary, and confidentiality of sessions, if appropriate (Winston et al., 1988).

Sometimes, however, conflict will emerge even when ground rules are in place. One important principle in dealing with unforeseen disagreement over ideas is to allow participants to have some time to explain their opinions and try to help them see where there is common ground. If the conflict seems to be role conflict related, it would help for the facilitator to encourage those who are engaging in productive behaviors and to turn the attention away from individuals who are distracting the group (Jacobs, Harvill, & Masson, 1994). Finally, for programs where the group may evolve to the storming stage, such as a semester-long series of development sessions for a crisis line center staff, and need time to develop productive norms, it is important to revisit the notion that conflict is natural and can be productive. It could be helpful for the group to reflect on their primary purposes and ways in which they desire to work together.

USE OF TECHNOLOGY FOR PROGRAMMATIC INTERVENTIONS

It is clear that the Internet is changing the ways that people learn and acquire information. Effectively designed websites can serve as tools to advertise programmatic interventions, to assess needs for certain programs, to evaluate program effectiveness, to deliver program information, and to serve as the primary delivery methodology for student groups or individuals. (See Chapter 6 in this volume.) Many institutions have established elaborate websites to aid students in career and financial planning, to help students learn study strategies, and to provide information about stress management, among others. Many of these sites have links with other existing services, such as JobTrak (http://www.jobtrak.com/) for the career services area, and some provide opportunities for interaction via chatrooms or associated e-mail listservs. A list of many student affairs related websites and listservs can be accessed through http://www.studentaffairs.com/. Some institutions have chosen to create websites that meet the particular needs of their students but also incorporate information from other sites. Kansas State University Counseling Center, for example, has created websites (http://www.ksu.edu/ucs/topics.html) on helpful topics that contain information about relaxation, depression, and time management, among others. These websites also contain specific information about the services of the Counseling Center, links to websites at other institutions, and, in the case of the stress management topic, relaxation exercises are included in an audio format. Graduate students in the College Student Affairs Administration Program at the University of Georgia learn how to create a basic website to augment or to take the place of more traditional programmatic interventions. These websites (http://www.coe.uga.edu/dev/echd/csahand.htm#Intentional) are designed to address particular issues that a functional area (such as residence life, international student affairs, health promotions) has determined are important to address.

It is beyond the scope of this chapter to teach practitioners how to design web pages or how to use the Internet to access programming ideas from around the world. If administrators are interested in learning more about Internet interventions, they should consult Chapter 6 in this volume and should take one of many continuing education courses on website development or engage in collaborative learning with a colleague from the information technology or distance learning centers on their own campuses.

RAISING AND ALLOCATING FUNDS FOR PROGRAMMATIC INTERVENTIONS

On many campuses, funds for some programmatic interventions come from student activities fee accounts. For example, it is typical that the major campus lecture series draws its funds from student government allocations, and the expenses for the small-scale residence hall programs are funded through the student residence hall council. Because student organizations often retain control of some of these fee allocations, it is important that administrators collaborate effectively with students in order to obtain funding. Student groups that are given authority to manage activity fees typically do not appreciate an administrator telling them how they *should* spend "their" money. Administrators who desire to tap student-controlled activities fees are well advised to consider the following:

- Students should be actively and visibly involved in planning the intervention.
- Students should be in the forefront of explaining the intervention to the funding organization.
- The intervention's rationale should include specific information about how the program will benefit students, and it should be appealing and understandable to student decisionmakers. (The use of student development and learning theory jargon should be avoided because it may be an impediment.)
- Because student organizations sometimes have limited funds and may see their roles as providing social rather than educational programs, it is important that administrators and student planning teams gain funding approval early in the planning process.

Even when funds for programmatic interventions come directly from institutional operating funds, it is important that administrators initiate comparable steps to justify allocations that they would use in seeking funds from student-controlled activities fees. Visible student involvement in program planning gives upper-level administrators reassurance that students will participate or, at the very least, that student leaders will not complain about a capricious allocation of funds. Again, seeking funding early in the budget process is imperative.

When requesting funds for any programmatic intervention, it is important that program developers clearly articulate the goals for the program, justify it in common terms, specify the evaluation methodology, and report back to the allocation source an honest assessment of the effectiveness of the program. It is often helpful when requesting large allocations to be sure that the intervention is supported by (a) the experience of other institutions that offered similar interventions, (b) results of local needs assessments, and (c) student affairs or other professional literature. When requesting funds, it is also important to provide an executive summary of less than one page and a thorough outline of how the funds will be spent.

APPLYING THEORY TO PRACTICE IN PROGRAMMATIC INTERVENTIONS

A number of program planning models exist that are designed to assist administrators in considering ramifications of their programming efforts. These models provide a theoretical basis for program development, implementation, and evaluation. Each planning model will briefly be discussed in terms of how it addresses the program development process.

The Colorado State CUBE model. One of the most often cited programming models (Morrill, Oetting, & Hurst, 1974) was actually introduced as a programming model based on a classification system in counseling outreach programs. The CUBE, as it denotes, is a three-dimensional model that includes the (a) target of an intervention or program, (b) purpose of the intervention or program, and (c) method of delivery for the intervention or program. Using this model, a student affairs administrator working alone or in a group can consider who should receive the benefits of the program (individual, primary group, associational group, or institution) and define the goal of the intervention as being preventative, remedial, or developmental. The remaining part of the CUBE, the methods used to deliver the program (direct, training and consultation, or media), can be assessed and designed. See Figure 12.2.

Hurst and Jacobson (1985) modified the CUBE to incorporate Drum's (1980) seven dimensions of student development. This modified CUBE model may be more useful for student affairs practitioners because it includes environmental factors in addition to administrative issues. See Figure 12.3.

The WICHE Eco-mapping model. The Western Interstate Commission on Higher Education (WICHE) was the research group that sanctioned the pro-

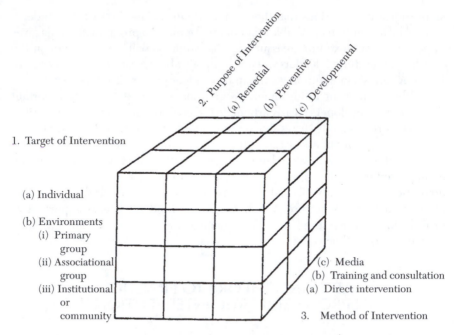

FIGURE 12.2. Dimensions of Intervention for Student Development
Reprinted from *Dimensions of Intervention for Student Development*, by W. H. Morrill, and J. C. Hurst. Copyright 1980 by Weston Morrill. Reprinted by author's permission.

gram development model devised by Moore and Delworth (1976). This model's focus was on the role of the program planning team and the steps it must follow to initiate program implementation and evaluation. This model assumes that the planning team first decides upon the target of the intervention (the term associated with this step is "germinal idea") and the purpose the program is designed to accomplish. Use of the CUBE model can be very helpful to planning team members for these initial steps. The five linear steps in this model include the following:

1. *Initiating the program.* Tasks involved in this step are putting together the program planning team, considering needs and available resources, discussing any foreseeable constraints, identifying target groups and purposes of interventions, and selecting the program.
2. *Planning program goals, objectives, delivery systems, and evaluation.* Once the program concept is clear, goals and objectives are set, and any necessary training is designed and implemented. A plan is also put in place to evaluate the goals and objectives of the program.
3. *Pilot program.* A version, usually on a much smaller scale, of the program is conducted and evaluated.

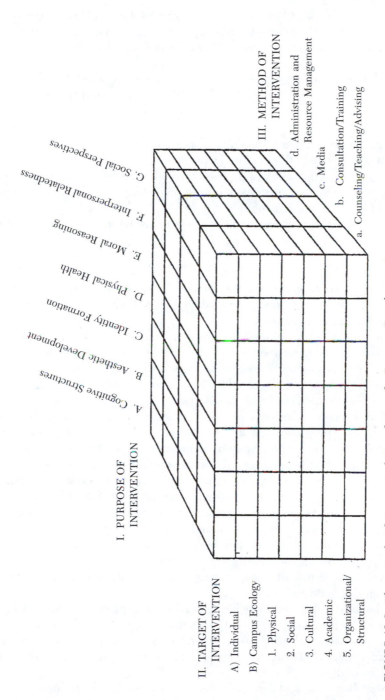

FIGURE 12.3. Theoretical and Conceptual Foundations for Program Development

Reprinted from "Theories underlying student's need for programs," by J. C. Hurst and J. K. Jacobson, in *Developing Effective Student Service Programs: Systematic Approaches for Practitioners*, by M. J. Barr, L. A. Keating, and Associates, pp. 113–136. Copyright © 1985, by Jossey-Bass. Reprinted by permission of Jossey-Bass, Inc. a subsidiary of John Wiley & Sons, Inc.

4. *Program implementation*. Based on experience gained in the pilot program, a full program is initiated.
5. *Program refinement*. An extensive evaluation of the training and outcomes is implemented. Here consideration is given to continuing the program, and if continuation is agreed upon, further offerings are scheduled.

The Barr and Keating model.   This model (Barr & Keating, 1985) was based on both the CUBE and WICHE models. The model is based on three assumptions:

1. Practitioners must have the skills to take a theoretical perspective and apply that perspective to the design of a program.
2. Program development will proceed through a thoughtful consideration of the programming context, goal setting procedures, development of a plan, and method of implementation.
3. All three of the components of the process must be congruent for successful programming to occur.

The Barr and Cuyjet model.   More recently, Barr and Cuyjet (1991) proposed a six-step program planning process model that incorporated components of the previous models discussed but placed added emphasis on goal setting and environmental assessment.

In step one, they outlined five assessment areas to be considered by program planners: (a) current operation, (b) student characteristics, (c) needs, (d) institutional environments, and (e) resource environment. The current operation assessment refers to a consideration of those activities and programs currently in place within the institution. Often, considerable time and money can be saved through a thorough review of programs currently available. Sometimes the only programmatic attention needed on a particular topic is better marketing of a current intervention or providing consultation to augment its strategies to meet the needs of a different population. Barr and Cuyjet (1991) recommended a review of the current student population's characteristics and needs. For example, who attends the institution, what skill deficiencies exist, and where students live and congregate on campus that might be a good intervention site. Particular attention should be given in this step to the needs of students of color and/or other identifiable groups or subpopulations.

Step two, goal setting, focuses on the writing of clear objectives. This step also expresses the importance of stating clear expectations about what the program intends to do and *not* do.

The third step in this model explores the actual planning process. Components include the configuration of the planning team, consideration of the theoretical approaches to be addressed, determination of the extent of the program, design for training of staff members to implement the program, and discussion about the budget.

Step four is the actual program implementation. Several processes, such as preparing publicity, selection of the programming location, and design of the program evaluation, are included.

Postassessment processes compose the model's fifth stage where the evaluation data are analyzed and outcomes are measured. Based on the evaluation the program may be modified for future offerings. Here are important questions to answer in this stage: Did we complete the program within our budget? Did the program have any unanticipated outcomes? Were positive relations formed among participants and other parts of the institution? Did the program contribute to the creation of community? Finally, an administrative decision is made about the next step: continuation, modification, or abandonment.

Cuyjet (1996) added another element to the assessment process of the Barr and Cuyjet (1991) model in his most recent discussion of program development. He cautioned student affairs practitioners to consider past programming efforts, to examine "what has been tried before, and determine why past programs succeeded or failed" (p. 404).

Although still other programming models are available, those discussed above are most commonly referred to in the literature. What emerges from examining these models is the need for student affairs practitioners to develop assessment and evaluation skills and an understanding of group dynamics to facilitate the creation of programmatic interventions that address real needs, that are carefully evaluated, and that promote involvement rather than passive acquisition of knowledge.

ASSESSMENT AND EVALUATION OF PROGRAMMATIC INTERVENTIONS

In these days of shrinking resources as well as demands from external publics that institutions demonstrate that their interventions result in learning and skill acquisition, it becomes increasingly important for administrators to ensure that programs meet important student needs— not simply student desires—and that systematic evaluation be conducted to document effects. Chapters 13 and 14 in this volume focus on assessment and evaluation and provide models that have utility in relation to programmatic interventions.

Because of the importance of needs assessment to the success of programmatic interventions, there are several points to consider when beginning to plan a program.

Needs Assessment

Data collected prior to the planning process will help define what students or other target audiences need, what program components should be included, when the program should occur, and how it should be delivered and by whom (Hanson & Yancy, 1985). Assessment of programming effectiveness can also provide useful information regarding program continuation.

Cooper and Saunders (2000) pointed out that to accomplish effective needs assessment for programmatic interventions, a number of skills and abilities are essential. Even though most of these skills can be acquired during graduate programs, one must keep up with new assessment and program development principles and, in particular, new technologies in order to stay current. Often, those asked to be in charge of program assessment are midlevel student affairs administrators who have not taken a research or measurement course in several years, if at all. Some institutions are fortunate enough to have an assessment specialist dedicated to the student affairs division and available to assist with design and implementation of evaluation studies. At many institutions, however, no staff members have expertise in measurement and design. Fortunately, most campuses have faculty, institutional research, or academic assessment office staff members who have expertise in designing and conducting studies. In addition, workshops about the techniques involved in student affairs assessment often are available at national, regional, and state professional conferences. Also noteworthy, the American Association for Higher Education (AAHE) offers an annual assessment forum designed for academic and student affairs professionals to share exemplary programs and to explore techniques.

Understand Institutional Priorities and Values

Upcraft and Schuh (1996), noted that the purpose of most program assessments is to ensure that the organizational mission and goals are addressed. For example, the organizational goals relevant to a particular program might be to promote increased understanding of various cultures, create community, provide a campus of critical thinkers, or seek to achieve some combination of comparable goals.

The values of an organization also impact the purpose and structure of assessment. Upcraft and Schuh (1996) stated that "values drive not only *what* we choose to assess, but also *how* we choose to do so. When questions about the organizational mission and values are skipped over, assessment threatens to be an exercise in measuring what's easy rather than what is needed" (p. 22). For example, when developing an assessment to determine whether an expensive, time-intensive program to increase the number of students involved in volunteer efforts in the community is having a desired outcome, it is important to consider the organizational context. Within this context, an administrator would be wise to raise the following questions:

- Does the institution see itself as having special responsibilities for the surrounding community?
- Will attention to this effort result in a reduction of time and resources available for other equally worthy efforts?
- Will increased participation by students in the program assist in achieving the institution's goal of improved retention?

Cooper and Saunders (2000) noted that "understanding the institutional priorities and values requires the ability to gain access to both the explicit and implicit priorities and values. Typically, one can easily read the explicit priorities and values in the institution or organization's mission statement or in the values reflected in its strategic plan. Understanding implicit priorities and values requires more skill and is more susceptible to bias because of limited information or individual preferences. For example, a housing professional who wants to assess the effectiveness of residence hall social programs might be unaware of the chief student affairs administrator's and president's priority to emphasize educational interventions. Consequently, even if the social programs are judged to be highly appealing to students and influential in promoting students' willingness to continue to live in residence halls beyond the freshman year, social program resources might be reduced in the interest of promoting more educational efforts.

Understanding campus politics and the implicit values held by various stakeholders becomes even more crucial when a student group is planning a program that might be of a controversial nature or contains material that could be seen as antithetical to the institutions' stated values. At times, program material could be seen as highly offensive or potentially hurtful to various subpopulations. Let us suppose that a student programming board is using its allocated programming funds to sponsor a speaker who purports that the Holocaust was a hoax perpetrated by liberals interested in preventing a resurgence of Nazism. Even though the student group argues that this speaker will encourage constructive dialogue about the Holocaust, faculty members are incensed that student programming funds are being used to broadcast base untruths about history. Local citizens from Jewish, Roman Catholic, and Protestant congregations are planning a silent protest at the event to draw attention to their opposition. Several Jewish students have reported to the dean of students that they fear that the speaker will give support to some "closet" anti-Semitic students on campus. Balancing students' autonomy with the ethic of benefiting others requires that advisors have a clear understanding of their own values along with a trusting, open relationship with their student advisees. It is also critical that program advisors think through and communicate to student leaders sources of potential opposition to a controversial program. Even though student groups will not always make popular or even wise decisions, it is part of a professional's responsibility to reason with students, educating them about potential consequences of their actions. At times, it is also necessary for an advisor to take a strong stand, based on his or her own professional ethics, and openly share advocacy or opposition to a group's decisions.

Cautions in assessing needs for programmatic interventions Not only must administrators understand organizational values and student needs, effective programmers must have a clear picture of the dynamics of the organizations and groups with which they work. For example, on some campuses individuals external to the traditional classroom, such as academic advisors, parents, or even the college president, are interested in assessment of programs designed to increase student learning. At these institutions, it would be wise for multiple stakeholders to be involved in the program planning process designed to address that construct.

When assessing group processes, we must consider a number of factors. The *halo effect* is a group dynamics concept where, for example, students enrolled in an alcohol education workshop facilitated by an attractive program facilitator may be more likely to judge the handouts to be very well written, even though an external reviewer might observe typographical errors and problems with layout. To counteract the halo effect it is helpful to obtain assessments other than simple self-reports (Nisbett & Wilson, 1978), such as assessing students' knowledge or having professional peers review workshop materials.

The *Hawthorne effect* is a concept from group dynamics research (Mayo, 1945) postulating that individuals who are aware that someone is assessing them are inclined to change their behavior in ways that will present a favorable impression to the observer. If, for example, students know that their responses to an opinion questionnaire about a particular program will have an effect on the continuation of that program, their responses might be either more positive or negative than if they were sharing opinions with peers who had no influence on program decisions. To counterbalance the Hawthorne effect, one must view assessment results cautiously, recognizing that the process of assessment itself can affect results.

If an assessor sought to assess whether social fraternity members perceived a need for programs on responsible drinking, it might be tempting to query only Greek students. This approach, however, would be flawed because the assessor assumed that only Greek students are affected by irresponsible drinking, when, in fact, drinking irresponsibly may be affecting students across affiliation boundaries. Students in the Habitat for Humanity or Psychology Club could be experiencing as many problems with alcohol at their functions and may also need programming around this topic.

Cooper and Saunders (2000) noted that the assumptions an assessor makes affects the design, implementation, analysis, and interpretation of the results of an intervention effort. Consequently, all elements of assessment are vulnerable to unintended bias. One way that this often occurs is when data are analyzed with no attention being paid to interaction effects. So single categories, such as race or age or gender or residential status, are analyzed as individual grouping variables in ways that may mask reality. For example, Asian American male commuter students may exhibit behavioral characteristics that are more similar to those of other commuter students than they are to those in their ethnic or gender groups who live on campus.

It is necessary to recognize the importance of the political environment in which the programmatic intervention will take place, because even the best-designed program can fail if the designer does not take into account aspects of the political process when assessing the need for the program. This can be as obvious as conducting a program on a socially controversial topic on which the institution's president has taken a firm stand, or conducting alcohol education programs on a football game day. More often than not, however, the politics are subtle and difficult to ascertain. Brown and Podolske (1993), when discussing political models of program evaluation, noted that skills needed to assess this aspect of the environment range from "being a good observer, thinker, and politician to possessing high-level consultation, negotiation, research design, and measurement abilities" (p. 217). Organizational support will more likely occur when an accurate assessment has been made of the politics surrounding program planning initiatives.

INTEGRATING THEORY INTO PLANNING AND IMPLEMENTATION

The following is a checklist of what administrators need to remember after having assessed student needs and the campus environment and identifying specific learning and developmental outcomes for the intervention. Although relatively simple in construct, these caveats are essential to achieve successful programmatic interventions. (Evaluation of interventions is discussed in detail in Chapter 13 of this volume.)

Planning

- Select a planning team that is inclusive of multiple stakeholders and involves a selected group of students as coplanners.
- Identify conditions and constraints that may affect program implementation. Determine, for example, if students' schedules will permit a weekly series of programs or if they will be more likely to attend a weekend retreat. Funding, physical facilities, availability of materials, and the relationship of the target groups to one another and to the institution are some of the conditions that may shape the program design. These conditions should be identified early in the process. A force-field analysis (as described in Johnson & Johnson, 1997) is a systematic way to identify conditions that could conceivably affect program design.
- Obtain agreement on pedagogies. The planning team should come to an agreement about the multiple types of learning models that will be employed. For example, some program topics, such as fire safety strategies, lend themselves to information transmittal where short lectures about ways to exit a building or demonstrations of how to use the fire extinguisher may predominate. On the other hand, topics such as racial diversity could incorporate small group discussions about personal experiences or experiential exercises that encourage students to identify with racial groups other than their own. To meet the different learning styles likely to be present among participants, it is important to incorporate a variety of approaches into the mix.

- Review the skills and preferences of facilitators. It is important that facilitators are competent in and feel comfortable with implementing various program activities and educational strategies.
- Create or select activities. As stated earlier, there are numerous resources that describe experiential exercises appropriate for programmatic interventions. Oftentimes, however, program planners can modify exercises so that they better fit the local conditions. The goals for exercises should be to promote involvement and not to demonstrate that the program planners can create elaborate, overly complicated, or dramatic exercises (that can often simply intimidate participants). For each activity, program planners should identify the outcomes that participants could achieve from the discussion, experiential activity, lecture, demonstration, and the like. Even though this planning process step may be time consuming, it serves as a double check that selected activities do, indeed, address the purposes of the program. This step also can guide formative and summative evaluation of the program.
- Create an agenda for program sessions. When creating an agenda, it is important to recognize the group's developmental stage in the sequence of activities. Furthermore, if planners desire to foster personal investment, adequate time needs to be allotted for discussion, reflection, revisiting purposes of the group, and dealing with conflict. All too often, program planners judge their effectiveness on how much activity they can pack into a program rather than on the basis of how well participants understand, incorporate, or apply the information. Determining an appropriate sequence of activities is crucial to maintaining a program that promotes involvement. The planning team needs to fully discuss proposed sequences and critique them.
- Identify referral resources that students can access for further information and assistance. For program topics such as acquaintance rape, eating disorders, dating violence, or hate crimes, some student participants may have had experiences that left them with unresolved issues. Attendance at such an educational program may heighten a student's interest in receiving counseling about the topic and the names and addresses of counselors or health educators or both should be provided. Often in student affairs, administrators rely on short-term interventions to cover a wide variety of information. Giving students handouts summarizing pertinent points covered in the program along with suggestions for additional resources (such as books, websites, other programs) provides further opportunity for them to continue their learning and development.

Implementation

- Define responsibilities for implementing the program. Knowing who does what is crucial for ensuring successful implementation. Because most programs will be implemented by groups of practitioners and students, it is important that accountability be maintained. Timelines, which specify target dates for completion of tasks, should also be constructed.

- Make arrangements for facilities, publicity, and supplies. The physical location selected for a program can clearly enhance or detract from its success. On most campuses the most conducive programming space is at a premium, so it behooves those implementing an intervention to make arrangements early.
- If more than one person is facilitating the program, establish the terms of collaboration. Two facilitators are often better than one, except when both try to be the lead facilitator simultaneously. "Because there are two leaders present, they may feel the need to earn their keep, and thus they may intervene too frequently, which has the effect of stifling member participation" (Winston et al., 1988, p. 204). So it is important that facilitators determine who is doing what at each stage of the program. The person who is not leading/facilitating can observe group dynamics or contribute as a participating group member. The nonleading facilitator can provide important feedback about how the program is going and how it might be modified. Critiquing cofacilitator behavior can be a most instructive process if done with objectivity and fairness.
- Recognize that one can never perfectly "work the plan." If a facilitator is observing and listening to participants, it is highly likely that her or his agenda will be modified. Good facilitators concentrate on what they are hearing and seeing as well as what they are saying. A group of participants may need more explanation than was planned, an individual may want to debate a point that was brought up during an exercise, and another person may seem suddenly disengaged and could benefit from encouragement to participate. All of these observations require modifying the plan. Occasionally, a planned discussion or exercise simply does not work and should be cut short.
- Identify what worked, what did not, and why. Facilitating programs is a common activity among student affairs administrators, and often activities for one program can be modified for another. Some facilitators find it helpful to write their own comments about the effectiveness of particular program activities so that the next time they facilitate a program, they retain their evaluative comments. These informal evaluations can be particularly useful when planning subsequent programs.

AN EXAMPLE OF PROGRAM PLANNING. CASE STUDY: A PROGRAM TO INCREASE KNOWLEDGE ABOUT SEXUAL HARASSMENT FOR FRESHMAN WOMEN

To illustrate the programming methodologies outlined herein, a case study is provided as an example of a one-time approach to programming where a specific target population (freshman women) was identified, a purpose established (to provide information useful for identifying sexual harassment), and a method of delivery selected (holding the program in a residence hall that houses many freshman women).

A committee of student affairs administrators has been meeting over the past several months to discuss concerns raised about incidents of sexual harassment on campus. This has taken a variety of forms, including faculty-on-student, staff-on-student, and student-on-student harassment. During the group discussions, a number of possible programmatic intervention responses were discussed. It was decided that a brief program at orientation would serve as one intervention, because the message that harassing behaviors are not tolerated on campus could be delivered to all entering students, men and women alike. Assuming men would be less likely to attend a voluntary program at a later date, the brief orientation program was implemented to reach the male students who are more frequently perpetrators of harassing behaviors than women. The committee also decided that a program was needed for freshman students (particularly women) early during their first term on campus. Because more than 95% of the first-year students live on campus, the residence halls were selected as the most desirable place to deliver the program.

The program was developed by a team whose members possessed expertise on the topic of sexual harassment. The team consisted of a counseling center psychologist, the director of the women's center, the dean of students, an assistant director of housing, and a representative of the institution's legal staff. They met several times to write a script to be used by program presenters and served as trainers of the assigned program presenters. They also designed an assessment instrument to be used at the end of the program to determine what the participants learned from the intervention. The survey also included questions about the effectiveness of the program and elicited ways to improve the program in the future.

The original committee had decided that senior RAs, selected by their area coordinators, would be trained to deliver the program using the script that had been created. The original script was modified by the RAs with the help of the trainers to make it more applicable to the lives of 18–19-year-old women.

The freshmen women were invited to attend the program during the residence hall orientation conducted by the RAs. The vice president for student affairs allotted funds for pizza and soft drinks as an incentive for students to attend. Following the program, the RA facilitators distributed and collected the assessment instruments. These were collected and sent to the student affairs research office for data entry and analysis. The final complete report was distributed to the original committee as well as the team who had written the programming script. A modified report was also provided to the RA facilitators to give them feedback about their performance.

The original committee and the team that wrote the program script met to review the assessment information and plans were put in place to modify the program format for the next year. It was decided that the vice president for student affairs would maintain a record of all reported sexual harassment issues for the academic year. Over the coming years, it was anticipated that the number of sexual harassment incidents reported would actually increase because students would be better educated about the issue.

This case study illustrates how the principles of this chapter can be incorporated into a seemingly simple program plan. Staff involved with the planning process represent a variety of areas of expertise. The workshop involves students in the early planning stages and relies on student assessment data for future program improvement. In addition, the principles of Astin's (1985) involvement theory are incorporated by using upper-class students as presenters of information.

QUESTIONS TO CONSIDER

1. Does the student affairs program with which you are most familiar follow the planning models outlined in this chapter when it develops new programs? If not, what are some alternative program development approaches that you would recommend for staff members to consider in the future?
2. Identify one of the intervention programs with which you are most familiar that is offered on campus and analyze its strengths and weaknesses. Are there ways you could recommend to improve the program's delivery?
3. How does the student affairs department with which you are most familiar currently evaluate the effectiveness of its programs? What strategies would you recommend that might be used to change their evaluation plan to better incorporate outcomes measurement?
4. Are the programs offered in the student affairs department with which you are most familiar generally meeting the learning and developmental needs of the constituent groups they are intended to serve? If not, what strategies can you suggest that would promote a more systematic approach in program planning for the future?

REFERENCES

American College Personnel Association (ACPA). (1994). *Student learning imperative*. Washington, DC: Author.

Anderson, J. (1988). Cognitive styles and multicultural populations. *Journal of Teacher Education, 39*(1), 2–9.

Anderson, J. A., & Adams, M. (1992). Acknowledging the learning styles of diverse student populations: Implications for instructional design. In L. B. Border & N. V. N. Chism, *Teaching for diversity* (pp. 19–33). New Directions for Teaching and Learning, No. 49. San Francisco: Jossey-Bass.

Astin, A. W. (1984). Student involvement: A developmental theory for higher education. *Journal of College Student Personnel, 25,* 297–308.

Astin, A. W. (1985). *Achieving educational excellence: A critical assessment of priorities and practices in higher education.* San Francisco: Jossey-Bass.

Astin, A. W. (1993). *What matters in college.* San Francisco: Jossey-Bass.

Bach, G. R. (1954). *Intensive group psychotherapy.* New York: Ronald.

Barlow, C. A., Blythe, J. A., & Edmonds, M.

(1999). *A handbook of interactive exercises for groups.* Boston: Allyn and Bacon.

Barr, M. J., & Cuyjet, M. J. (1991). Program development and implementation. In T. K. Miller, R. B. Winston, Jr., & Associates, *Administration and leadership in student affairs: Actualizing student development in higher education* (2nd ed., pp. 706–739). Muncie, IN: Accelerated Development.

Barr, M. J., & Keating, L. A. (1985). Introduction: Elements of program development. In M. J. Barr, L. A. Keating, & Associates, *Developing effective student service programs: Systematic approaches for practitioners* (pp. 1–14). San Francisco: Jossey-Bass.

Baxter Magolda, M. B. (1992). *Knowing and reasoning in college: Gender-related patterns in students' intellectual development.* San Francisco: Jossey-Bass.

Benne, K. D., & Sheats, P. (1948). Functional roles of group members. *Journal of Social Issues, 2,* 42–47.

Blocher, D. H. (1987). *The professional counselor.* New York: Macmillan.

Bonney, W. C., & Foley, W. J. (1963). The transition stage in group counseling in terms of congruity theory. *Journal of Counseling Psychology, 10,* 136–138.

Bothwell, L. (1983). *The art of leadership: Skill-building techniques that produce results.* New York: Simon & Shuster.

Brown, R. D., & Podolske, D. L. (1993). A political model for program evaluation. In M. J. Barr (Ed.), *The handbook of student affairs administration* (pp. 216–239). San Francisco: Jossey-Bass.

Cass, V. C. (1979). Homosexuality identity formation: A theoretical model. *Journal of Homosexuality, 4,* 219–235.

Chickering, A. W., & Reisser, L. (1993). *Education and identity* (2nd ed.). San Francisco: Jossey-Bass.

Cooper, D. L., & Saunders, S. A. (2000). Assessing students and environments. In D. Liddell & J. P. Lund (Eds.), *Powerful programming for student learning: Approaches that make a difference.* New Directions for Student Services, No. 90. San Francisco: Jossey-Bass.

Cross, K. P. (1996). New lenses on learning. *About Campus, 1* (1), 4–9.

Cross, W. E., Jr. (1995). The psychology of Nigrescence: Revising the Cross model. In J. E. Ponterotto, J. M. Casas, L. A. Suzuki, C. M. Alexander (Eds.), *Handbook of multicultural counseling* (pp. 93–122). Thousand Oaks, CA: Sage.

Cuyjet, M. J. (1996). Program development and group advising. In S. R. Komives, D. B. Woodard, Jr., & Associates, *Student services: A handbook for the profession* (3rd ed., pp. 397–413). San Francisco: Jossey-Bass.

Drum, D. J. (1980). Understanding student development. In W. H. Morrill, J. C. Hurst, & E. R. Oetting (Eds.), *Dimensions of intervention for student development* (pp. 14–38). New York: Wiley.

Evans, N. J., Forney, D. S., & Guido-DiBrito, F. (1998). *Student development in college: Theory, research and practice.* San Francisco: Jossey-Bass.

Forney, D. S. (1991). Learning style information: A support for service delivery, Part I. *Career waves: Leading ideas for career development professionals, 4*(1), 2–3.

Gilligan, C. (1982/1993). *In a different voice: Psychological theory and women's development.* Cambridge, MA: Harvard University Press. (Original work published in 1982)

Goodlad, J. I. (1997). *In praise of education.* New York: Teachers College Press.

Hanson, G. R., & Yancey, B. D. (1985). Gathering information to determine program needs. In M. J. Barr & L. A. Keating (Eds.), *Developing effective student services programs: Systematic approaches for practitioners* (pp. 137–157). San Francisco: Jossey-Bass.

Helms, J. E. (1995), An update of Helms's White and People of Color racial identity models. In J. E. Ponterotto, J. M. Casas, L. A. Suzuki, & C. M. Alexander (Eds.), *Handbook of multicultural counseling* (pp. 181–198). Thousand Oaks, CA: Sage.

Hurst, J. C., & Jacobson, J. K. (1985). Theories underlying students' needs for programs. In M. J. Barr, L. A. Keating, & Associates (Eds.), *Developing effective student service programs: Systematic approaches for practitioners* (pp. 113–136). San Francisco: Jossey-Bass.

Jacobs, E. E., Harvill, R. L., & Masson, R. L. (1994). *Group counseling: Strategies and skills* (2nd ed.). Pacific Grove, CA: Brooks/Cole.

Johnson, D. W., & Johnson, F. P. (1997). *Joining together: Group theory and group skills.* Boston: Allyn and Bacon.

Josselson, R. (1987). *Finding herself: Pathways to identity development in women.* San Francisco: Jossey-Bass.

King, P. M., & Kitchener, K. S. (1994). *Developing reflective judgment: Understanding and promoting intellectual growth and critical thinking in adolescents and adults.* San Francisco: Jossey-Bass.

Knowles, M., & Knowles, H. (1959). *Introduction to group dynamics.* New York: Association Press.

Kohlberg, L. (1969). Stage and sequence: The cognitive developmental approach to socialization. In D. A. Goslin (Ed.), *Handbook of socialization theory and research* (pp. 347–480). Chicago: Rand McNally.

Kolb, D. A. (1981). Learning styles and disciplinary differences. In A. W. Chickering (Ed.), *The modern American college: Responding to the new realities of diverse students and a changing society* (pp. 232–255). San Francisco: Jossey-Bass.

Kolb, D. A. (1984). *Experiential learning: Experience as the source of learning and development.* Englewood Cliffs, NJ: Prentice-Hall.

Komives, S. R., Lucas, N., & McMahon, T. R. (1998). *Exploring leadership: For college students who want to make a difference.* San Francisco: Jossey-Bass.

Lappe, F. M., & Du Bois, P. M. (1994). *The quickening of America: Rebuilding our nation, remaking our lives.* San Francisco: Jossey-Bass.

Lifton, W. M. (1966). *Working with groups: Group process and individual growth.* New York: Wiley.

Manning, K. (1994). Liberation theory and student affairs. *Journal of College Student Development, 35,* 94–97.

Mayo, E. (1945). *The social problems of industrial civilization.* Cambridge, MA: Harvard University Press.

Moore, M., & Delworth, U. (1976). *Training manual for student service program development.* Boulder, CO: Western Interstate Commission for Higher Education.

Morrill, W. H., Oetting, E. R., & Hurst, J. C. (1974). Dimensions of counselor functioning. *Personnel and Guidance Journal, 52,* 354–359.

Napier, R. W., & Gershenfeld, M. K. (1989). *Groups: Theory and experience.* Boston: Houghton Mifflin.

Nisbett, R. E., & Wilson, T. D. (1978, Summer). *News from groups Institute of Social Research,* Ann Arbor: University of Michigan, pp. 4–5.

Pascarella, E. T., & Terenzini, P. T. (1991). *How college affects students: Findings and insights from twenty years of research.* San Francisco: Jossey-Bass.

Perry, W. G., Jr. (1968). *Forms of intellectual and ethical development in the college years: A scheme.* New York: Holt, Rinehart & Winston.

Schutz, W. C. (1958). *FIRO: A three-dimensional theory of interpersonal behavior.* New York: Holt, Rinehart and Winston.

Tuckman, B. (1965). Developmental sequence in small groups. *Psychological Bulletin, 63,* 384–399.

Tuckman, B., & Jensen, M. (1977). Stages of small group development revisited. *Group and Organizational Studies, 2,* 419–427.

Upcraft, M. L., & Schuh, J. H. (1996). *Assessment in student affairs: A guide for practitioners.* San Francisco: Jossey-Bass.

Winston, R. B., Jr., Bonney, W. C., Miller, T. K., & Dagley, J. C. (1988). *Promoting student development through intentionally structured groups: Principles, techniques, and applications.* San Francisco: Jossey-Bass.

Winston, R. B., Jr., & Massaro, A. V. (1987). Extracurricular involvement inventory: An instrument for assessing the intensity of student involvement. *Journal of College Student Personnel, 28,* 169–175.

Winston, R. B., Jr., & Saunders, S. A. (1987). The Greek experience: Friend or foe of student development. In R. B. Winston, Jr., W. R. Nettles, III, & J. H. Opper, Jr., *Fraternities and sororities on the contemporary college campus.* New Directions for Student Services, No. 40. San Francisco: Jossey-Bass.

RECOMMENDED READING

Claar, J., & Cuyjet, M. (2000). Program planning and implementation. In M. J. Barr, M. K. Desler, & Associates, *The handbook of student affairs administration* (2nd ed., pp. 311–327). San Francisco: Jossey-Bass.

Herron, D. B. (1997). *Marketing nonprofit*

programs and services: Proven and practical strategies to get more customers, members, and donors. San Francisco: Jossey-Bass.

Liddell, D. L., & Lund, J. P. (Eds.). (2000). *Powerful programming for student learning: Approaches that make a difference.* New Directions for Student Services, No. 90. San Francisco: Jossey-Bass.

13

Needs Assessment and Program Evaluation

JOHN H. SCHUH
M. LEE UPCRAFT

Assessment and evaluation in student affairs are not new concepts as attested to on page 552 of Mueller's classic 1961 text *Student Personnel Work in Higher Education*, but this aspect of the portfolio of student affairs administrators has become increasingly important during the past three decades (Upcraft & Schuh, 1996). The growing importance of assessment and evaluation in student affairs is a consequence of calls for greater accountability in higher education (Wingspread Group, 1993, for example). Conducting business in higher education as usual is outdated (Balderston, 1995), which means that institutions either must be able to demonstrate how their programs make a difference or face a reduction in resources. Pascarella and Whitt (1999) concluded that "Although the press for assessment and accountability affects all aspects of a college or university, there is some evidence that student affairs is particularly vulnerable" (p. 100). Consequently, student affairs practitioners must be able to measure the effectiveness of their services and programs. Creating high quality assessments and evaluations will help student affairs practitioners meet the challenge of accountability.

Developing appropriate skills in the assessment and evaluation arenas has become central to the student affairs practitioner's role. Erwin (1996), for example, asserted that "Each of us should be able to supply evidence about the usefulness of our programs and services—for our own use, for administrative use, or for use by external audiences and the public" (p. 416). The development of these skills becomes essential for the person desirous of mastering one of the essential behavioral characteristics listed in Table 1.1 of Chapter 1 of this volume.

An issue that needs to be addressed early in this chapter is whether assessment and evaluation skills should be a part of the repertoire of all student affairs practitioners, or if these areas of responsibility are better assigned to specialists in the student affairs division or office of institutional research. Our view is that individual practitioners as well as student affairs divisions are served best if as many staff members as possible understand and implement assessment and evaluation projects. Erwin (1996) observed, "Student affairs professionals who know more about assessment and evaluation techniques and strategies are more marketable and more valuable to their institution than those who do not" (p. 429). The press of accountability in higher education requires that staff be able to conduct assessments and evaluations on a routine basis and integrate these activities into their annual work routine. Our desire is that as many student affairs practitioners as possible undertake assessment so that their work can reflect the following: "Rather than relying heavily on large-scale assessment projects that often seemed unrelated to regular instructional activities, faculty, staff, and students have developed a variety of assessment approaches that closely reflect everyday campus activities" (Palomba & Banta, 1999, p. xii).

One of the major problems we have encountered as we worked with various groups of student affairs administrators on assessment and evaluation issues is that frequently they and their staffs do not have well-developed skills in these areas. The direct result is that they have difficulty initiating assessment and evaluation programs, which are essential elements of students affairs programs. Providing leadership in developing assessment and evaluation, in turn, becomes an elusive skill not present in the portfolio of many student affairs administrators. This chapter is designed in part to begin to remedy this problem. Palomba and Banta (1999) urged that one or more people provide leadership for campuswide assessments, but they also observed that assessment requires leadership at the division and department level. This chapter provides appropriate background in support of student affairs practitioners providing that kind of leadership.

To cover all aspects of assessment and evaluation would take multiple volumes. Accordingly, this chapter covers two important aspects of these integral processes: needs assessment and program evaluation. More specifically, the chapter has two purposes: to identify salient steps in developing a needs assessment and to discuss a systematic approach to program evaluation. This chapter demonstrates how needs assessment can be used to determine appropriate interventions in student affairs and how program evaluation can be employed to determine the effectiveness of these interventions. Other aspects of assessment such as outcomes assessment are presented in the following chapter.

Although in some quarters the terms *assessment* and *evaluation* are used interchangeably, for purposes of this chapter they are viewed as separate processes. Assessment is defined as "any effort to gather, analyze, and interpret evidence which describes institutional, departmental[/]divisional, or agency effectiveness" (Upcraft & Schuh, 1996, p. 18) while evaluation is viewed as "any effort to use assessment evidence to improve institutional, departmental, divisional, or agency effectiveness" (p. 19). Definitions of needs assessment and program evaluation are provided in later sections of this chapter devoted to these topics.

To provide context for discussion, a short case is described to illustrate essential principles. The analysis of case studies can be very useful in linking theory with practice (Stage, 1993).

CHANGING ENROLLMENT STRATEGIES AT EASTERN SLOPE COLLEGE

Eastern Slope College (ESC) has been experiencing traumatic times. This state-assisted institution has suffered dramatic cuts in state appropriations the past four years. A demoralized legislature and hostile governor who has won two terms by landslides on a platform of reducing income taxes have reduced ESC's appropriations by a cumulative total of 30%. As a consequence, ESC has been forced to reduce course offerings, lay off staff and untenured faculty, and eliminate programs. A popular president resigned in exasperation, and this act has caught attention of the politicians. They have promised that they were through cutting ESC's budget and indicated that appropriations would increase in the future if enrollments grew.

The governing board decided that it needed to attract a president with experience in building enrollments. Fortuitously, the president of an institution in a neighboring state was an ESC alumna with close ties to the region. This president had a remarkable record at building enrollments, and the board was able to attract her with a plea to her loyalty to ESC. She agreed to accept the offer but understood that substantial work needed to be undertaken to get ESC back on track.

The new president developed an enrollment management strategy that had three elements. The first was to examine the institution's efforts at retaining students. She commissioned a blue ribbon committee to examine retention and to present recommendations targeted to improve ESC's retention rate by 5%.

The second element was to begin an aggressive recruiting campaign overseas. The president had a number of excellent relationships with institutions in the Far East and she personally began the work of cultivating relationships with those who could be helpful in sending transfer students to ESC for the final two years of their work.

The third element was the development of a program designed to take ESC's academic programs off-campus to communities in the region. Many adult students had graduated from community colleges within a 50 mile radius of ESC, but had not completed their formal schooling. Much of this had to do with job and family responsibilities. ESC's new strategy was to offer degree completion programs in these communities at night and on the weekend. The president made it clear that any services offered on ESC's main campus would have to be available to the students enrolling at the remote sites. As chair of implementation committee, how would one determine what the students enrolled at the remote sites would require from ESC?

NEEDS ASSESSMENT

Needs assessment, for the purpose of this chapter, is defined as "the process of determining the presence or absence of the factors and conditions, resources, services, and learning opportunities that students need in order to meet their educational goals and objectives within the context of an institution's mission" (Upcraft & Schuh, 1996, p. 128). Kuh (1982) observed that needs assessment "has greatest utility when viewed as a problem-focused strategy" (p. 202).

Kuh observed that distinguishing between student needs and wants is a problem associated with needs assessment. For example, if the food service needs of resident students were to be assessed, one might find that what students want would be something similar to a fine restaurant, but what they needed and could afford would be something more modest.

Gall, Borg, and Gall (1996) defined a need as "a discrepancy between an existing set of conditions and a desired set of conditions" (p. 698). A serious problem they pointed out was that not all members of a particular group have the same needs. This observation is particularly appropriate for institutions of higher education. Seniors, for example, are likely to have very different needs related to job placement than freshmen. Freshmen, on the other hand, have different needs for campus information than do juniors. So an important strategy in developing needs assessment is to make sure that needs of selected populations are desegregated from the entire group.

Needs assessment is a crucial element in the development of programs, activities, and services in higher education. In the circumstance related to ESC, what students report they will need in the way of support is crucial in developing specific interventions. Rossi, Freeman, and Lipsey (1999) described the value of needs assessment: "From a program evaluation perspective, needs assessment is the means by which an evaluator determines if, indeed, there is a need for a program and, if so, what program services are most appropriate to that need. Such an assessment is critical to the effective design of new programs" (p. 119). If no needs are identified, then there is no point in developing any new programs.

An assessment model developed in 1996 by Schuh and Upcraft has been used in a wide variety of training programs and other activities. This model has been found to be quite effective and is introduced here as an approach that has utility for needs assessment:

1. **What is the problem?**
   The first issue to be faced, and that which is most important, is to determine the problem to be assessed. In this case, what must be established is what prospective students report they will need from ESC in the way of support services to complete their academic degrees.

2. **What is the purpose of the assessment?**

The purpose of the assessment is to determine what students will need from ESC to complete their degrees. This assessment is not concerned with academic programs or actual courses offered. Rather, it will identify support mechanisms the college can provide to ensure that students will enroll in degree completion programs and finish their degrees. Because no support programs are in place at this time, it is necessary to determine which programs to initiate and which to forego.

3. **What data are needed?**

ESC needs to develop a rationale for initiating a series of services for adults that will provide support for them to complete academic degrees at remote sites. Data to support this rationale need to be generated.

4. **What is the best assessment method?**

Use of multiple methods is the most appropriate way to conduct assessments. In this instance it is recommended that a quantitative study with a sample of potential ESC degree completion students be conducted and that this activity be followed by a series of focus groups. In most situations, the use of multiple methods is the most effective way to conduct needs assessments. It would not be wise to base the determination of needs solely on the responses to a mailed questionnaire or a focus group of 10 students.

5. **Who should be studied?**

One of the easiest questions to answer in this situation is who to study. In this case, individuals whose names have been placed on a list of potential students identified by the office of admissions and recruitment will become the sample. This office has identified 5,000 individuals who potentially could be a part of this program. This list was developed based on collaboration with communities that would be served by the ESC degree completion program and the State Office of Workforce Development.

6. **How should the data be collected?**

A variety of ways are available to collect the data. Quantitative data typically are collected through the use of mailed surveys. Most typically, however, this approach will yield a low response rate and can take a considerable amount of time to complete (Rea & Parker, 1997). Consequently, ESC opts for collecting quantitative data via a telephone survey involving a random sample of the 5,000 potential adult students. According to Rea and Parker (1997), choosing a random sample of 586 would result in a confidence level of 99% with a confidence interval of ±5%.

Another option is to collect data using the World Wide Web, a technology that is improving in sophistication and effectiveness. A web-based survey can be particularly effective on college campuses where students routinely are assigned electronic mail addresses and have easy access to computers. This might be a less effective technique when dealing with the nonstudent population with which this example deals. Wortman (in press) provided more information about web-based data collection. For the qualitative data, focus groups could be conducted with some of the people who participated in the telephone interviews. Interviewing will continue until the point of redundancy is reached, "and then just one more time for safety" (Lincoln & Guba, 1985, p. 219).

7. **What instrument(s) should be used?**

Identifying a good instrument can be a significant problem, because there are advantages and disadvantages to using either a commercially prepared standardized instrument or a campus-based questionnaire (Ory, 1994). Generally, a commercially prepared instrument should be used because such instruments normally will include psychometric information. Without psychometric information, the validity and reliability of an instrument is unknown and therefore suspect. For this study, an option would be to use the *College Student Needs Assessment Survey* from the American College Testing Program (1989). An alternative would be to develop an instrument specifically for the study.

More information on specific instruments is available at several websites:

- Commission IX of the American College Personnel Association. (2000, October 29). Available: http://www.acpa.nche.edu/comms/comm09/ dragon/dragon-index.html
- Educational Testing Service. (2000, October 29). Available: http:// www.ets.org/hea
- Noel Levtiz. (2000, October 29). Available: http://www.noellevitz.com
- American College Testing Program. (2000, October 29). Available: http:/ /www.act.org

Based on what is learned from the quantitative data, several focus groups will be conducted. These will be designed to generate additional information from the potential students, including answers to such questions as how and why. Among the questions that might be asked in a focus group would be the following:

- How interested are you in attending ESC?
- At this point, what problems stand in the way of your attending ESC?
- What do you think you will need from ESC in the way of academic support services?
- What specific needs do you have that ESC should address for you to enroll in a degree completion program?
- What has not been discussed about your attending ESC that you think we should know?

8. **Who should collect the data?**

The data can be collected by a variety of people. Typically, members of the student affairs staff or perhaps some faculty, students, and even graduates might be involved in the collection process. Using members of the staff to collect data can be problematic, especially if they have a stake in the results. In those cases, using staff exclusively would be a mistake. The use of a combination of insiders and outsiders (such as faculty and students) would be much more prudent. Training will need to be done with all the people involved in data collection, as there are specific skills to collecting data. (See, for example, Krueger, 1998.)

9. **How should the data be recorded?**

The data can be recorded directly from the telephone conversations by the interviewer into computer databases. A variety of computer programs are available for this process. (See Moore, in press.) Recording data during the interviews can be done by tape recording the interviews as well as having an assistant moderator take notes, which should be transcribed as quickly as possible after the interview has been completed.

10. **How should the data be analyzed?**

Several statistical programs can be used to analyze the quantitative data. Certainly, frequency distributions and measures of central tendency should be computed. More sophisticated analyses can be computed based on gender, ethnicity, or other demographic characteristics. The constant comparative method often is used because it can be applied to "any kind of qualitative information, including observations, interviews, documents, articles, books and so forth" (Glaser & Strauss, 1967, p. 104). Themes, patterns, and trends will be sought in analyzing the qualitative data. Software programs also are available to analyze qualitative data (Merriam, 1998).

11. **How should the data be reported?**

We recommend using a variety of reports in reporting assessment data. Executive summaries can be provided for those who are not central to the process of developing programs based on the needs assessment. Reports that are more complete can be prepared for those who will be in the decision-making process. A complete report certainly should be prepared for the president because of her deep involvement in the decision making and implementation of the programs for the remote sites. Other useful ideas on disseminating results are provided by Jacobi, Astin, and Ayala (1994).

12. **How should the data be used in the evaluation process?**

Finally, the data from the needs assessment will be used to frame the evaluation of the process. If it is determined that certain support programs need to be implemented, they will be focused on during the program evaluation process.

PROGRAM EVALUATION

For the purpose of this chapter, program evaluation is defined as "the use of social research procedures to systematically investigate the effectiveness of special intervention programs" (Rossi, Freeman, & Lipsey, 1999, p. 4). Program evaluation can be tied directly to needs assessment. That means that the programs implemented as a result of a needs assessment can very logically become the focus of the program evaluation. In fact, program evaluation results are not very useful unless they can be related to needs (Lenning & MacAleenan, 1979).

The program evaluation, then, is focused on the extent to which the programs implemented have been successful.

At this point, it is important to issue a caveat about the information provided in this portion of the chapter. Substantial volumes have been written about program evaluation, and space limitations simply do not allow for a complete discussion of this topic. The approach presented here is a straightforward model that can be applied to a variety of student affairs settings. Nonetheless, it is important to note that Worthen and Sanders (1987) have presented five alternative educational evaluation models, and Shadish, Cook, and Leviton (1991) provided substantial detail about various theoretical approaches to program evaluation. Rossi, Freeman, and Lipsey (1999) pointed out that program evaluations can reveal problems with the underlying assumptions about the impact of a program itself, resulting in what they termed "theory failure" (p. 78). The reader who seeks more information about theoretical models, undergirding evaluation, alternative evaluation models, or program theory should consult these resources.

Evaluation can occur at two points in the development of programs. In some cases, programs will be evaluated as they are being implemented. This type of program evaluation is defined as *formative*, meaning it "seek(s) to identify the potential problem areas before they escalate" (Brown, 1979, p. 21). The other type of program evaluation is *summative*, which has been defined as evaluations that are "typically conducted at the conclusion of a program cycle and are intended to provide information about the program to an external audience as well as the program staff" (Brown, 1979, p. 21). Either form of evaluation can be implemented depending on the intent of the evaluation. Brown (1979) drew the following distinction between formative and summative evaluations: "The key determinants for choosing between formative and summative evaluation are the purpose of the evaluation and the intended audience" (p. 22). Brown recommended using a formative evaluation if the staff is the audience for the evaluation, while he suggested using a summative evaluation if the audience is external to those responsible for implementing the program or activity.

One other element of evaluation needs to be considered integral in the process according to Brown and Podolske (1993). They asserted that politics plays a crucial role in the evaluation process, an observation with which Schuh and Upcraft (1998) concur. Those conducting evaluations are urged to make sure that they understand the political process in which the evaluation is being conducted. Brown and Podolske (1993) concluded that "it is essential not only to understand that politics and value judgments are a part of the evaluation process, but that this awareness be incorporated into evaluation planning" (p. 228).

If a decision to continue or eliminate a program depends on an evaluation, the political nature of the evaluation becomes obvious. In situations like this, the powerful political ramifications of the evaluation should be recognized, and the evaluation adjusted accordingly. That will include such factors as the questions that are asked, the people involved in collecting the data, how the data are analyzed, and especially how the final reports are crafted.

Determining Program Viability

Pillinger and Kraack (1980) identified six factors related to determining program viability.

Essentiality.   Is the program central to the department's mission as well as that of the student affairs division and the institution? The further away a program moves from being central to the institution's mission, the more vulnerable it becomes. To insure program viability, student affairs practitioners should be very certain before developing new programs to make sure that they are central to an institution's core.

Quality.   Is the program well done? This does not mean that the program needs to be expensive or consume huge amounts of resources, but it does mean that the program reflects the expectations of the institution across all of its programs, academic or otherwise. Quality can be measured by a variety of criteria, among them the *CAS Standards and Guidelines* (Miller, 1999), that identify minimal criteria for students services and programs.

Availability.   Is the program available to those it is intended to serve? The evaluation should make sure that the program serves the population for whom it was intended. The evaluation should include an inquiry related to those individuals for whom the program was intended but never used it. Determining why intended users do not participate in the program is an important element of the evaluation. Even if a program serves its users very well, if it does not penetrate the potential users to a great extent, it could be deemed to be ineffective.

Need or demand.   This element was discussed previously. If the need stays constant, then making sure that the program is delivered is crucial. If the need changes as a consequence of the institution eliminating service to a certain group of students, then the program will have to be adjusted, or perhaps eliminated. A good example of this is the decline in the breadth of programs that currently serve students who are veterans. At one time, many institutions had departments that provided services to students who had been members of the armed forces. With the decline in the number of students qualifying for federal veteran's benefits and the elimination of the draft, the need to provide widespread support for these individuals has declined drastically.

Efficiency.   Is the program cost effective while at the same time providing high quality services and programs? Simply providing programs that are inexpensive is not good enough. Programs must represent good value for the resources expended, and the programs need to be competitive with similar programs offered by other colleges and universities or private enterprise.

Outcomes.   Finally, the program can be evaluated in terms of its ability to achieve its stated goals. If a program is designed to attract and retain students,

does it? Do retention programs result in more students persisting to graduation? Do leadership enhancement programs result in students' developing skills
they would not have developed without the program? These questions and others cut to the heart of all programs. Programs need to accomplish their stated
purposes. A carefully crafted evaluation will help determine if that occurs.

Assume that the needs assessment conducted for the prospective students
at ESC revealed that students required three things for them to enroll in degree completion programs: touch tone phone registration; courses offered at
night and on the weekend; and a child care program so that students would
have a safe and secure place to leave their children while in class.

PROGRAM EVALUATION EXAMPLE

For the purpose of this chapter a description of how to conduct an evaluation of
the child care center intervention is presented. This evaluation is discussed in
the context of a program evaluation model developed by Rossi, Freeman, and
Lipsey (1999, p. 75), which in many respects is quite similar to the assessment
model introduced earlier. The model consists of 10 steps.

1. **What is the program to be evaluated?**

    Each of the three programs needs to be evaluated to determine their
    effect on enrollment patterns in the degree completion programs at ESC.
    The child care program is the first evaluated because its population is most
    easily identifiable, and, according to anecdotal evidence, it is working quite
    well. This is in keeping with suggestions for starting projects of this type
    (Schuh & Upcraft, 2001) in that it is recommended that assessment efforts
    begin with fairly simple projects that have the potential to yield positive
    results (Wehlberg, 1999).

2. **Why is the program being evaluated?**

    This program is being evaluated because it was initiated to support
    students' enrolling in degree completing programs at ESC. Therefore, a
    determination needs to be made as to whether the child care center facili-
    tated enrollment. Additionally, the program has required that the parents
    of the children who attend the child care center pay a fee to the center.
    From a cost effectiveness perspective, the parents' views on the costs asso-
    ciated with child care also need to be evaluated:

    1. Did offering on-campus child care facilitate and sustain student enroll-
       ment at ESC?
    2. Was the program cost effective from the perspective of the users?

    Clearly, the first question is the most crucial, but the second also is impor-
    tant so that the program can be sustained or modified over the long term.

3. **How are people to be prepared for the evaluation?**

    Many people have an investment in the child care program, not least of whom are the administrators who conceived the program and the staff who implemented it. If the evaluation turns out to be negative, the center might be closed or new leadership sought. In this respect, the evaluation is summative (meaning at the end of the program), and it also has political dimensions because of the employment implications with which it is associated.

4. **What are the main issues/questions with which the evaluation has to deal?**

The primary question associated with the evaluation is the extent to which having a child care program facilitated enrollment of students completing their degree through ESC. The secondary question has to do with whether the child care center is cost effective for parents. Do they report that they are receiving their money's worth for the care provided?

5. **Who will do what?**

For an activity of this type, a combination of insiders and outsiders should be used. We recommend that individuals from the student affairs division, some faculty members, and perhaps some students who use the child care center form the core of the evaluation team. Additionally, it may be possible to include members of the child care center staff in the evaluation, but they will need to be part of team efforts and not collect data on their own because of the obvious political implications of the project. We suggest that several faculty members who are neutral about the child care center (they have no affiliation with it) also are involved to assure both the fact and appearance of impartiality.

6. **What are the resources needed for the evaluation?**

For the sake of this evaluation, assume that a combination of telephone data collection will be used along with focus groups. A sample telephone questionnaire and interview protocol are included as Figures 13.1 and 13.2. Help will be required for developing an instrument to administer using the telephone and help will be needed in developing an interview protocol for use with focus groups. Assistance also will be needed in collecting information. Consequently, consultation help is necessary for the evaluation. Perhaps faculty members of ESC could help in these areas.

Other help that might be necessary could include identifying computers and software to use in the telephone collection process. This approach can involve entering data at the time it is collected. A bank of computers with the appropriate software will be necessary. Additionally, a modest honoraria may be needed for those collecting the data, especially if they are students who volunteer time to participate in this phase of the evaluation process.

Resources also might be necessary to help in the qualitative phase of the data collection process. If teams of individuals are used to conduct the focus groups, those who are not full-time ESC employees will need to be paid an honorarium as well. Refreshments often are served when focus groups are conducted (Morgan, 1998) and require an expenditure of funds.

Good evening. We are calling this evening to learn more about your level of satisfaction with the child care program at Eastern Slope College. We would like to ask you a few questions about the child care center and this process should not take longer than 10 minutes. Our goal is to improve services at the center and we want to assure you that your answers will be confidential. If you do not wish to participate in this survey, please let me know and we will stop the interview right now. OK? Let's move ahead.

1 Just to confirm this, you did use the services of the child development center this past
    year?   Yes____   No____

2. Which nights each week did you use the center?

    Monday_____
    Tuesday_____
    Wednesday_____
    Thursday_____
    Friday_____

3. How many children did you have enrolled in the center? _____

4. What was the age of the child you had in the center? _____

5. I'd like to ask you some specific questions about the center. Your choice of answers will include excellent (5), very good (4), average (3), below average (2), and poor (1). OK? Here goes.

    How would you rate the quality of the staff? _____
    How would you rate the friendliness of the staff? _____
    How convenient were the operating hours? _____
    How would you rate the quality of the physical facility? _____
    How would you rate the cleanliness of the physical facility? _____
    How would you rate the snacks served at the center? _____
    Given the quality of service, how would you rate the price you paid for child care?
    _____

6. Let me ask you one last question. If Eastern Slope did not operate the child care center, could you have attended the college? Yes_____ No_____

FIGURE 13.1. NESC Child Care Program Evaluation: Telephone Questionnaire

Additionally, transcription of notes and tape recordings, if the groups are audiotaped, will require clerical staff resources if not separate financial support.

7. What data need to be collected?

    The data that need to be collected are obvious. First, it must be determined if students enrolled and continued in their degree completion program in part because of the child care center. Another way of looking at this issue is to ask the following question: If the child care center were not available, would you have enrolled in classes at ESC? The second aspect of

We appreciate your coming today to participate in this discussion about the college's child care center. Your participation is voluntary and you may leave at any time. When we prepare our final report, we will not attribute any information to specific individuals, meaning that we will keep your responses confidential. Do you have any questions? OK. Let's begin.

1. Why did you choose to attend Eastern Slope?

2. Were your expectations for your college education met? If not, why not?

3. You enrolled a child or several children in the child care center. Was this an important factor in your being able to attend Eastern?

4. What did you like best about the child care center?

5. What would you recommend to improve the quality of care at the center?

6. Is there anything else you would like to tell us about the child care center?

FIGURE 13.2. ESC Child Care Program Evaluation: Focus Group Protocol

the data required is to determine if parents thought charges for child care represented appropriate value for them.

One other aspect of the process might be completed as well. Presumably, some individuals who would have been eligible to participate in the child care programs chose not to do so. It would be very useful to determine why. Identifying these students might be difficult, although financial aid information will include the number of individuals in a student's family, and presumably students with eligible dependents could be identified. It is also possible that the resources are not available to add this dimension to the evaluation. Nonetheless, exploring the question of nonuse by eligible students would provide an important addition to the study.

8. **How will the data be analyzed?**

Data from the quantitative aspect will be analyzed by developing frequency distributions and measures of central tendency (means, standard deviations, and so on). Computerized programs can be used to aid in this process, and in some cases with the appropriate computers and software the data can be inputted as it is collected and analyzed almost immediately (Moore, in press). Data from the qualitative aspect of the evaluation can be analyzed using the constant comparative method (Merriam, 1998). This means, in effect, that as data are collected the investigators analyze them.

9. **What will be the reporting procedure?**

A wide variety of ways are available to report evaluation data. Palomba and Banta (1999) indicated that reports can take various forms, depending on the needs and interests of the audience. They advise that "report writers often need to prepare different reports for different audiences" (p. 318).

We suggest that primary stakeholders should receive complete reports, whereas those individuals who are less directly involved in the decision-making process that will result from the evaluation can receive abridged versions of the report. It is common to promise to provide reports to participants in evaluation studies. In this case, an option to consider is to place a copy of the report on a website and inform the participants of the address of the site.

10. **How will the report be implemented?**

This final step is to decide whether to continue the childcare program in its present form, modify it, or eliminate it. Many people have a stake in the future of the program, including senior administrators who initiated this program to facilitate enrollment, parents who used the center and as a consequence were able to enroll in classes, and the staff members. The final step in the process is to decide what will happen next, and to a great extent, but not entirely, that will depend simply on the findings of the evaluation.

CONCLUSION

This book is dedicated to presenting, describing, and analyzing the professional roles of student affairs practitioners. We concluded in 1996 (Upcraft & Schuh) that "Assessment is now a necessity that demands our highest priority" (p. 323). To that is added program evaluation, because it is clear that the efficacy of many programs, services, and activities in student affairs will depend on these processes and it behooves student affairs administrators to incorporate them into their work on a regular basis.

QUESTIONS TO CONSIDER

1. What strategies will you use in defining the nature of the problem in preparing for a needs assessment?
2. What are the barriers you are likely to encounter in developing a program evaluation?
3. What ethical dilemmas might you encounter in developing an assessment, and a program evaluation?
4. What strategies will you employ in communicating the results of a needs assessment, and a program evaluation?

REFERENCES

American College Testing Program. (1989). *College Student Needs Assessment Survey.* Iowa City, IA: Author.

Balderston, F. E. (1995). *Managing today's university* (2nd ed.). San Francisco: Jossey-Bass.

Brown, R. D. (1979). Key issues in evaluating student affairs programs. In G. D. Kuh (Ed.), *Evaluation in student affairs* (pp. 13–31). Cincinnati, OH: American College Personnel Association.

Brown, R. D., & Podolske, D. L. (1993). A political model for program evaluation. In M. J. Barr & Associates, *The handbook of student affairs administration* (pp. 216–229). San Francisco: Jossey-Bass.

Erwin, T. D. (1996). Assessment, evaluation, and research. In S. R. Komives, D. B. Woodard, Jr., & Associates, *Student services: A handbook for the profession* (3rd ed., pp. 415–432). San Francisco: Jossey-Bass.

Gall, M. D., Borg, W. R., & Gall, J. P. (1996). *Educational research: An introduction* (6th ed.). White Plains, NY: Longman.

Glaser, B. G., & Strauss, A. L. (1967). *The discovery of grounded theory: Strategies for qualitative research.* Chicago: Aldine.

Jacobi, M., Astin, A., & Ayala, Jr., F. (1994). Increasing the usefulness of outcomes assessments. In J. S. Stark & A. Thomas (Eds.), *Assessment & program evaluation* (pp. 695–705). Needham Heights, MA: Simon & Schuster.

Krueger, R. A. (1998). *Moderating focus groups.* Focus Group Kit 4. Thousand Oaks, CA: Sage.

Kuh, G. D. (1982). Purposes and principles for needs assessment in student affairs. *Journal of College Student Personnel, 23,* 202–209.

Lenning, O. T., & MacAleenan, A. C. (1979). Needs assessment in student affairs. In G. D. Kuh (Ed.), *Evaluation in student affairs* (pp. 185–201). Cincinnati, OH: American College Personnel Association.

Lincoln, Y. S., & Guba, E. G. (1985). *Naturalistic inquiry.* Beverly Hills, CA: Sage.

Merriam, S. B. (1998). *Qualitative research and case study applications in education.* San Francisco: Jossey-Bass.

Miller, T. K. (Ed.). (1999). *CAS: The book of professional standards for higher education.*

Washington, DC: Council for the Advancement of Standards in Higher Education.

Moore, B. (2001). Telephone surveys. In J. H. Schuh, M. L. Upcraft, & Associates, *Assessment practice in student affairs: An applications manual* (pp. 83–100). San Francisco: Jossey-Bass.

Morgan, D. L. (1998). *Planning focus groups.* Focus Group Kit 2. Thousand Oaks, CA: Sage.

Mueller, K. H. (1961). *Student personnel work in higher education.* Boston: Houghton Mifflin.

Ory, J. C. (1994). Suggestions for deciding between commercially available and locally developed assessment instruments. In J. S. Stark & A. Thomas (Eds.), *Assessment & program evaluation* (pp. 597–602). Needham Heights, MA: Simon & Schuster.

Palomba, C. A., & Banta, T. W. (1999). *Assessment essentials: Planning, implementing and improving assessment in higher education.* San Francisco: Jossey-Bass.

Pascarella, E. T., & Whitt, E. J. (1999). Using systematic inquiry to improve performance. In G. S. Blimling, E. J. Whitt, & Associates (Eds.), *Good practice in student affairs: Principles to foster student learning* (pp. 91–111). San Francisco: Jossey-Bass.

Pillinger, B. B., & Kraack, T. A. (1980). Long range planning: A key to effective management. *NASPA Journal, 18*(3), 8–17.

Rea, L. M., & Parker, R. A. (1997). *Designing and conducting survey research* (2nd ed.). San Francisco: Jossey-Bass.

Rossi, P. H., Freeman, H. E., & Lipsey, M. W. (1999). *Evaluation: A systematic approach* (6th ed.). Thousand Oaks, CA: Sage.

Schuh, J. H., & Upcraft, M. L. (1996, December). *Assessment in student affairs.* Baltimore, MD. Workshop sponsored by the National Association of Student Personnel Administrators.

Schuh, J. H., & Upcraft, M. L. (1998). Facts and myths about assessment in student affairs. *About Campus, 3*(5), 2–8.

Schuh, J. H., Upcraft, M. L., & Associates. (2001). *Assessment practice in student affairs: An applications manual.* San Francisco: Jossey-Bass.

Shadish, W. R., Jr., Cook, T. D., & Leviton, L. C. (1991). *Foundations of program evaluation:*

Theories of practice. Newbury Park, CA: Sage.

Stage, F. K. & Associates. (1993). Linking theory to practice: Case studies for working with college students. Muncie, IN: Accelerated Development

Upcraft, M. L., & Schuh, J. H. (1996). *Assessment in student affairs: A guide for practitioners.* San Francisco: Jossey-Bass.

Wehlberg, C. (1999). How to get the ball rolling: Beginning an assessment program on your campus. *AAHE Bulletin, 51*(9), 7–10.

Wingspread Group on Higher Education.

(1993). *An American imperative: Higher expectations for higher education.* Racine, WI: Johnson Foundation.

Worthen, B. R., & Sanders, J. R. (1987). *Educational evaluation: Alternative approaches and practical guidelines.* New York: Longman.

Wortman, T. (2001). Web-Based data collection. In J. H. Schuh, M. L. Upcraft, & Associates, *Assessment practice in student affairs: An application manual.* San Francisco: Jossey-Bass.

RECOMMENDED READING

Nichols, J. O. (1995). *A practitioner's handbook for institutional effectiveness and student outcomes assessment implementation.* New York: Agathon.

Palmoba, C. A., & Banta, T. W. (1999). *Assessment essentials.* San Francisco: Jossey-Bass.

Percy-Smith, J. (Ed.). (1996). *Needs assessments in public policy.* Philadelphia: Open University Press.

Rossi, P. H., Freeman, H. E., & Lipsey, M. W. (1999). *Evaluation: A systematic approach* (6th ed.). Thousand Oaks, CA: Sage.

Schuh, J. H. (1996). Planning and finance. In S. R. Komives, D. B. Woodard, Jr., & Associates, *Student services: A handbook for the*

profession (3rd ed., pp. 458–475). San Francisco: Jossey-Bass.

Schuh, J. H., & Upcraft, M. L. (1997, February). *Assessment in student affairs: A guide for practitioners.* Savannah, GA. Workshop sponsored by the National Association of Student Personnel Administrators.

Schuh, J. H., Upcraft, M. L., & Associates. (2001). *Assessment practice in student affairs: An applications manual.* San Francisco: Jossey-Bass.

Upcraft, M. L., & Schuh, J. H. (1996). *Assessment in student affairs: A guide for practitioners.* San Francisco: Jossey-Bass.

14

Assessing Student Learning and Development in Student Affairs:
A Nuts and Bolts Introduction

T. DARY ERWIN
STEPHEN A. SIVO

*P*eter Drucker, a successful predictor of trends in higher education, recently forecasted this future: "Thirty years from now the big university campuses will be relics. Universities won't survive. . . . Such totally uncontrollable expenditures, without any visible improvement in either the content or the quality of education, means that the system is rapidly becoming untenable. Higher education is in deep crisis" (cited in Lenzner & Johnson, 1997, p. 127).

Contentions such as Drucker's bode ill for higher education in general. They raise a number of important questions for student affairs administrators to contemplate. For example, can student affairs administrators demonstrate the educational value of what they do with students? Are student affairs practitioners prepared to document the degree of student learning and development from the programs and services they conduct? Can student affairs professionals furnish credible evidence not only to colleagues but also to external constituents and oversight groups?

Assessment is the process of documenting student learning and development. Although college impact studies exist in the literature (Feldman & Newcomb, 1969; Pascarella & Terenzini, 1991), single institution or specific program impact studies useful for policy-making purposes were infrequent until the 1980s (Erwin, 1989, 1990).

As the new millennium begins, institutions, institutional programs, systems of higher education, faculty, and student affairs professionals must be able to define, measure, and report credible assessment results in an aggregated way about their respective educational programs and services. Certainly, the availability of assessment evidence can benefit individual students through direct feedback and through continued programmatic improvements. Today, however, that is not enough. Educators cannot respond solely to one another; they must provide convincing evidence of effectiveness to an expanding sphere of interested parties. With the press from the outside for change, impact evidence is more crucial than ever for justifying the existence of a given unit, whether just an office in student affairs, the whole division of students affairs, or the institution itself.

This chapter briefly describes assessment's historical context; defines and differentiates among assessment, evaluation, and research; and highlights the sequential steps of assessment practice using student affairs examples. The chapter also serves as an introduction to emerging student affairs administrators as they begin to acquire the skills and knowledge essential to implementing assessment studies that are so necessary for their careers.

HISTORICAL PERSPECTIVE

The value of college was widely accepted as a given until the 1980s when a series of reports about higher education were published that challenged previously unquestioned assumptions: (a) the inattention to undergraduate education (Southern Regional Education Board, 1985), (b) the shortcomings and lack of evaluation of student learning (American Association of Colleges, 1985), and (c) the states' funding priorities emphasizing quantity over quality (Burke & Serban, 1998). In response to these criticisms and questions, many states began to require data that focused on student learning (Nettles, Cole, & Sharp, 1997); accreditation groups refocused their institutional reviews toward student learning (Wingspread Group on Higher Education, 1993); and the nation's governors became interested in college outcomes (Alexander, Clinton, & Kean, 1986).

The lead states in setting assessment policies in the 1980s were Tennessee, Missouri, Florida, New Jersey, South Dakota, Virginia, and South Carolina. Generally, assessment data were requested about basic skills, the undergraduate major, general education, and student affairs. Subsequently, some states requested reports concerning the effectiveness of technologically delivered instruction versus traditionally delivered instruction (typically the lecture) (Russell, 1997).

Higher education professionals within the United States have tended to focus on assessment primarily to improve programs and services. Outside of higher education, however, the demand for data is increasing for accountability purposes such as funding. Moreover, accountability issues in higher education are not limited to the United States; assessment is becoming international in scope (Desruisseaux, 1994; Erwin, 1997, 1999; Gaither, 1998).

Performance Funding

Tennessee took the early lead in using assessment results for accountability by awarding up to 5.45% of institutional instructional budgets based on several quality criteria. These criteria ranged from scores on the American College Testing Program's College Outcome Measures Project (ACT-COMP) Test, a test of general education, knowledge, and skills, to alumni satisfaction surveys (Nettles et al., 1997).

One way to gauge the importance of assessment is to follow the distribution of money. That is, identify the number of states awarding resources according to assessment activities and results and the manner in which they do so. Even though many educators espouse the use of assessment results for program improvement internal to the institution, which is certainly important, the emerging student affairs professional should also heed the external emphasis on assessment and plan accordingly.

In 1998, Burke and Serban reported that 26 states tie state funding or budgeting to some type of institutional performance. By 2003 we predict that 35 or 70% of the states will use performance funding/budgeting approaches. It behooves the institution's president, and subsequently other campus educators, to focus on various areas of institutional performance, particularly student outcomes. Because of the recent dire predictions for lower funding (Healy, 1999), higher education may find the competition for state monies even more severe.

WHAT IS ASSESSMENT?

Some nomenclature definitions may be helpful before launching into a discussion of assessment practice. Traditionally, outcomes were meant to be actual assessment results (Dressel & Associates, 1961), whereas objectives were seen as the expected statements of learning. Aspects of learning are typically conceived as knowledge (for instance, wellness or American history), skills (for example, interpersonal communication or writing), and development (such as open mindedness or career decidedness). Development may be considered as cognitive or affective or both, such as personal characteristics (see also *The Student Learning Imperative*, American College Personnel Association [ACPA], 1996).

As mentioned earlier, assessment is a "process of defining, selecting, designing, collecting, analyzing, interpreting, and using information to increase students' learning and development" (Erwin, 1991, p. 15). It is mostly confirmatory in nature; that is, it determines if students are learning and developing in expected ways (that is, meeting educational objectives).

In contrast, research about students is typically concerned with the creation and refinement of theory. For example, Pascarella and Terenzini's (1991) classic work *How College Affects Students* is a review of student impact research about the field.

Both qualitative and quantitative data are useful in conducting research.

Creswell (1998) classified five traditions of qualitative inquiry: (a) the biography, (b) phenomenology, (c) grounded theory, (d) ethnography, and the (e) case study. Qualitative methods are best suited for (a) theory development, (b) variable discovery, (c) hypothesis generation, (d) organizational structure, and (e) new phenomena development (Borg & Gall, 1989). Quantitative data are typically required and reported in assessment studies, particularly for accountability purposes. Assessment is typically included as a part of evaluation, which is broader in nature. Assessment is usually associated with education, or student learning and development. Evaluation may include both educational and noneducational foci. Readers may also be familiar with the evaluation terms of *formative*, using results for improvement as the process progresses, and *summative*, using results for accountability purposes at the end of the process.

One other distinction may be useful. Outcomes are the results or degree of student learning or development or both and are usually the dependent or criterion variables in statistical analyses. Inclusive of variables about the campus environment can help understand why some students score or rate higher or lower on learning or development or both. From a statistical view, environmental variables are usually the independent or treatment variables. Examples of environment variables include participation versus nonparticipation in a student affairs program or service; student engagement in a task, such as hours spent studying; or type of involvement in a student affairs program, such as a major leader, minor officer, participant, or nonparticipant.

IMPLEMENTING THE ASSESSMENT PLAN

Assessment is best practiced as an ongoing, cyclical endeavor. Evidence of program effectiveness should be continually revisited, because (a) professionals need to know whether favorable program results are a one-time finding, and (b) every program or service requires continual updates and improvement. Although implementing an assessment plan is more fluid than a set of steps may suggest, providing steps that charter the general assessment process can be useful. Consider the following assessment steps:

1. Establishing learning and developmental objectives that fulfill program goals.
2. Planning the design of the study.
3. Selecting or constructing assessment methods.
4. Implementing the assessment study design.
5. Analyzing or evaluating assessment information.
6. Summarizing how the information will be used.

In practice, these steps are not always followed sequentially. For instance, a career planning and placement (CPP) director may involve her office in constructing a test to assess students who participate in a career planning workshop designed to help students narrow the range of their career interests. As the team attempts to develop questions organized around a set of objectives, they may discover that the objectives are more vague than originally thought. In response to this awareness, the CPP director may decide to back up and review the objectives again to see whether more specificity is possible before the remaining steps are taken.

Establishing Learning Objectives That Fulfill Program Goals

What do student affairs administrators want to accomplish in their programs? How will students benefit from participating in a program or service? Answering these questions will assist in identifying the goals of a student affairs program. The goals of a program broadly define what the student affairs administrator intends to accomplish with a program or service. Because initial goals are typically stated in broad terms, each goal is usually broken down into several objectives. Whereas a goal amounts to a general intention of a program, each objective should be (a) clear, (b) specific, (c) focused, and (d) measurable. Objectives are written to operationalize the abstract intention of a goal. By explicitly expressing what an institution or unit specifically intends to do to attain a goal, objectives represent a concrete commitment to a course of action. Writing objectives can be difficult because the process forces the staff to think through exactly what student benefits are expected. The process can be demanding if disagreements occur among staff members or if the staff is unsure about the scope of their work. The absence of clear and specific objectives can communicate that staff members are unclear about their work, particularly to outside reviewers. Often these discussions produce program changes before any data are collected.

Writing useful and meaningful objectives can require much labor and time. The most strenuous challenge before administrators who are writing objectives is ensuring that the stated set of objectives accurately and fully captures the true content of a goal. In practice, no set of objectives will fulfill such an expectation, and so they should be continually revisited, studied, and refined. It is important not to thwart the implementation of an assessment plan because the objectives require further refinement. Nevertheless, using notably unfocused objectives, perhaps labeled as "preliminary," should be avoided in practice as well.

A useful parallel exists between research and assessment, despite the different motives underlying each activity. In a research investigation, a theory should give way to a set of specific, empirically defined hypotheses in which each construct under investigation is defined in terms of observable phenomena. In assessment, a program/service goal gives way to a set of specific empirically defined objectives in which each aspect of student learning and development is defined in terms of observable phenomena. Both researchers and educators must, at some point, commit to empirical definitions that relate constructs to various indicators. In assessment practice, methods such as rating scales, questionnaires, inventories, and tests are by far the most common indicators used.

Sivo (1997) offered tips about developing objectives for a program:

1. Identify objectives that completely represent each of the identified program goals.
2. Enumerate the objectives: one concept for one objective. Avoid complex sentences. A sentence with more than one idea can be subdivided into more than one objective. Be specific and clear.
3. State in terms of intended outcomes. State the objectives in terms of how the *students* participating in the program will benefit *not* how the program will benefit.
4. State the objectives in the present tense.
5. Use action verbs to begin each objective.
6. Make sure the action verb is concrete and suggests something assessable (for example, use words such as identify or enumerate or describe instead of learn or know how to, are familiar with, can explore, or are aware). Consider, for example, "what is 'familiar'"?
7. Make sure people outside the office or department can read the objectives and understand them.
8. Concretely identify students' behavior that is expected to change.
9. Develop student learning outcome objectives that address change or learning in addition to the perceptions and feelings of the people benefiting from the program. Otherwise, program impact will not be completely demonstrable. Even though it is important to know whether students perceive benefits from student learning initiatives through surveys, journals, or focus groups, the student affairs administrator should also collect evidence that student learning has actually occurred.

As an example of how the foregoing tips might be applied when developing an objective, consider the following hypothetical situation. A director of judicial services decides to write an objective concerning a program designed to educate students who have been found guilty of alcohol-related offenses by requiring that they participate in an alcohol abuse class. Generally, one goal of the program is to increase student awareness of the long-term legal, social, and health consequences of alcohol abuse. So the director writes the following objective addressing the health risk component of the program: *Students will indicate that they have become more aware of the consequences of alcohol abuse.* This objective suggests that the director expects students to report that they have become more aware of the alcohol-related health risks as a result of the program.

Reflecting on the ninth tip, the director is reminded that the intended objective should focus on student learning rather than perception. What would prevent, even inhibit, students guilty of alcohol-related offenses from deceiving the director because they want to be perceived as having changed? After all, an honest negative response might invite another mandatory workshop experience.

Suppose that the students were honest. Even if the students accurately report their self-perception, the director would have no evidence that they are now more aware of the health risks than they were prior to the training. Students sometimes believe they have learned more than they actually did, whereas others learned more than they thought. Either way, student perception, although important, is not sufficient evidence.

Focusing the objective on student learning rather than on student self-perception, the director rewrites the objective: *This program will increase the students' awareness of alcohol abuse.* On the surface, this objective seems direct and clear. Yet the word "awareness" in the objective does not clearly indicate what exactly the program attempts to accomplish. Reflecting upon the sixth tip, the director asks, "How am I going to know whether a student's awareness increases?" The term "awareness" is much too vague. How does one demonstrate that awareness or learning was acquired? What specific student behavior(s) can be observed to change within the context of the program to suggest that such has occurred? Clearly, student behaviors were sufficient criteria for mandating that the students attend the workshop in the first place. What behaviors are going to demonstrate that the students no longer need to attend the workshop? Stated in terms of the behavior that the students are expected to evidence, the objective becomes: *Identify the health risks associated with long-term alcohol abuse.*

Designing the Study

Collecting credible evidence to demonstrate program effectiveness requires a study design that is clearly conceived and implemented. The particular design, once identified and endorsed, dictates both how the data will be collected and how the participants will be chosen. Although it is beyond the scope of this chapter to define fully any one of the designs ordinarily used in student affairs assessment, a number of practical suggestions are offered. See Cook and Campbell (1979) or Bracht and Glass (1968) for a more complete discussion of design issues. The most commonly used assessment study designs include the following:

1. One group pretest/posttest design
   Pretest ⇒ Program delivery ⇒ Posttest
2. Pretest/Posttest comparison group design (randomly assigned to either condition)
   Program participants: **Pretest ⇒ Program delivery ⇒ Posttest**
   Nonprogram participants: **Pretest ⇒ No program delivery ⇒ Posttest**
3. Posttest only comparison group design (randomly assigned to either condition)
   Program participants: **Program delivery ⇒ Posttest**
   Nonprogram participants: **No program delivery ⇒ Posttest**
4. Posttest only static-group comparison design (no randomization)
   Program participants: **Program delivery ⇒ Posttest**
   Nonprogram participants: **No Program delivery ⇒ Posttest**

5. Pretest/posttest nonequivalent comparison group design (no randomization)
   Program participants: **Pretest ⇒ Program delivery ⇒ Posttest**
   Nonprogram participants: **Pretest ⇒ No program delivery ⇒ Posttest**

Designs 2 and 3 are different from the other designs in that they involve random assignment. Random assignment, or randomization, simply means that participants are randomly included in the program or not included in the program. The benefit of randomly placing a group of students in a program is that, more than likely, they will be similar to the students not included in the program. So if the students in the program outperform the students not in the program on the posttest, some evidence that the program has had an impact on participants will have been acquired. More evidence over time should be gathered before a professional can be confident that the program fosters student learning or development.

Consider the design issues that a hypothetical assistant director of the student counseling center must face when desiring to know how much students have learned by participating in an eight-week assertiveness training workshop. Originally, the assistant director planned to administer an instrument concerning the principles of assertiveness to the students upon their completion of training. The students are expected to score high. After discussing the plan with a colleague, the colleague points outs that at least some of the students who elect to participate in the workshop are likely to be already aware of some of the issues concerning assertiveness. How will the assistant director truly know how much of a difference the workshop actually made? In response, the assistant director proposes to administer the test to the student participants before the training begins in addition to afterward. The assistant director believes that any change that will occur over time can be attributed to the program. However, the same colleague points out that the students who participate are likely to develop some assertiveness skills as a result of their other university experiences, not just the workshop. For instance, professors encourage students to speak up and ask questions when they do not understand. Moreover, professors teach students to give and respond to criticism. Outside the classroom, students participate in organizations in which the exercise of assertiveness is encouraged. How will the assistant director know that the change in the scores over time is because of the training workshop and not some other typical university experience? In response, the assistant director decides to have a comparison group consisting of students who are similar to those who will participate in the workshop. Both the program participants and the nonprogram participants (that is, the comparison group) will be given a pretest and a posttest. Both groups of students may change over time, but the program participants are expected to change at a greater rate.

The assistant director's decision to include a comparison group was crucial because programs designed to accelerate student learning or development in areas such as assertiveness, leadership, self-confidence, or academic autonomy are very susceptible to *maturational effects*, not change because of a program or service (Pascarella & Terenzini, 1991). Maturational effects refer to natural human development that would have occurred over time even if program participation had not occurred. For instance, as students mature, social, intellectual, emotional, and moral development are likely to occur solely as a natural process without intervention by any educator. So when student affairs professionals decide to facilitate development through a program they must demonstrate that the change that occurred was truly accelerated as a result of the program. One of the best remedies for demonstrating program effectiveness, in such cases, involves including a comparison group. A comparison group consists of people who do not participate in the program but are otherwise very similar to the program participants.

What happens if a comparison group of students cannot be found? One alternative for the assistant director is to give all the students who elect to participate in the workshop a pretest, and then randomly assign them to one of two groups. One group could be designated as participants in the first of two sequential workshops, although the posttest would be administered to both groups at the end of the first workshop. This approach, however, assumes that enough students have elected to participate in the workshop.

When randomization is not convenient or possible, a "quasi-experimental" assessment study design may be chosen (that is, designs 1, 4, and 5). Student affairs professionals usually choose a quasi-experimental design because program participants are typically self-selected. Students who choose to participate in a program are likely to be different from nonparticipants because participants (a) are typically more interested in the program content area and/or (b) already have some knowledge of the content area. Even without more knowledge than their comparison group counterparts, participants by virtue of their interest alone might outperform nonparticipants because of a heightened receptivity to program instruction. In other words, differences found between the performances of the program participants and the comparison group may be more attributable to interest level than program effectiveness.

Fortunately, participants are not as much of a concern for an assessment study as they are for a research study as long as the design of the study is sound in other aspects. The best quasi-experimental study, in such cases, would be the pretest–posttest nonequivalent comparison group design (design 5). If the pretest performances of the two groups are not very different, evidence of the group equivalence at the time of the pretest may be assumed. Even if a moderate difference exists between the two groups from the beginning (particularly when the program participants are outperforming the nonparticipants), evidence of program effectiveness can be tentatively argued when the increasing slope of change over time for the program participants far exceeds that of the nonparticipants. Generally, pretests are very useful in establishing that students who choose to participate in the program truly did benefit. High posttest scores do not sufficiently suggest program impact when pretest scores are not collected because students who choose to participate in a program probably already have an interest in the subject matter of the program. This interest also makes it probable that they possess some knowledge about that subject matter before their participation in a program. Pretest scores provide the student affairs professional with information about how knowledgeable or developed a student is before program participation.

Given that a student affairs administrator has selected an assessment method sensitive enough to detect change over time, any observable change presented as evidence will be questioned if the design of the assessment study is improper. Educated consumers of higher learning know better than to assume program effectiveness just because promising program results are promulgated. For more information about establishing internal and external validity of a study and identifying and/or minimizing the concerns associated with each design, see Cook and Campbell (1979).

Selecting or Constructing an Assessment Measure

Selecting an assessment measure is usually far easier than constructing one. Yet a locally constructed assessment measure has the potential to be much more suitable for the program and more likely to collect evidence demonstrating positive program impact. Measures created at some other institution, administered to some unique group of students, possibly far in the past, often are not as sensitive as homegrown measures when it comes to detecting a program's impact. Occasionally, an off-the-shelf measure is much broader in defining a construct than providing what a student affairs professional needs. Often a program one or two semesters in length cannot have enough impact to advance scores on off-the-shelf measures. A much more narrowly defined measure, organized around a program's specific objectives, is better disposed to detect change for a given program. Indeed, the program may fail. Nevertheless, not considering the advantages of a measure tailored to detect the impact of a specific program might be shortsighted.

Sivo (1998, 1999) suggested that when creating an assessment method, keep these principles in mind:

1. Involve as many experts and program stakeholders as possible in writing the questions (but not the intended student participants).
2. Write more questions than needed, so that when the stakeholders and the student affairs professionals review the final set, poor or redundant questions can be pruned away. One rule of thumb: Attempt to write at least one-and-one-half times as many as needed.
3. When developing a test, write questions for which the correct answer cannot be reasoned by common sense alone, so that students will not do well on the pretest without truly knowing the correct answers. To detect change over time and thereby demonstrate program impact, the students have to move from a state of not knowing to a state of knowing. Questions that are too easy will fail to detect change over time, unnecessarily lengthen the measure, and waste time.

4. Write questions for which the correct answer is likely NOT to be known by the program participants prior to entering the program.
5. After the question-writing task is complete, one may elect to have students who are not program participants review the questions to make sure that the questions are written at an appropriate reading level and with sufficient clarity. Document all comments that are made and consider further revision.

Many books address the issue of measure construction, and, in particular, principles to consider when writing questions. Widely cited principles to consider when writing either multiple choice or Likert-type questions include the following:

1. The incorrect choices on tests should be plausible. (*The most important principle.*)
2. The correct choice on tests should be about the same length as the incorrect choices. No other superficial clues should distinguish the correct answer from all of the other answers.
3. Terms are better tested when placed in the stem of a question. Optional answers to the questions would be composed of correct and incorrect definitions.
4. Avoid choices such as "none of the above," "all of the above," "both A and B," or "either A or C."
5. Do not use the following: not, only, many, some, few, always, seldom, never, all, none, or rarely.

To learn more about measure construction, see Allen and Yen (1979), Osterlind (1989), Erwin (1991), or Crocker and Algina (1986). Gable and Wolfe (1993) have a useful text concerning the development of measures assessing the affective domain.

A number of factors should be considered before a preexisting measure is adopted to assess a student affairs program. First, does the author of the measure define the construct in question in the same manner as the student affairs administrator? For example, the administrator may wish to assess leadership skills using a leadership measure. Keeping in mind that multiple definitions of leadership exist, the administrator may want to examine whether the author of the measure defines leadership similar to the institution's treatment. Moreover, they may want to evaluate the items on the measure to determine how much the substance of the program will actually address the content of the measure. Second, how much more broadly does the measure assess the construct in question than the program intends? Third, to what degree have both the author and independent investigators demonstrated that scores on the measure are reliable and valid for the specific group of students to be assessed (for example, sophomores, Asian Americans, disabled students, or inner-city students)? Fourth, how many other researchers, at institutions other than the author's, report using the measure successfully? Many books address the issue of measure selection. To learn more about choosing a measure that gives reliable, valid, and appropriate scores for a particular group of people, see Anastasi (1988).

Implementing the Assessment Study Design

Implementing the assessment study design primarily involves undertaking a data collection strategy that fulfills what the design specifies. The assessment study design only considers the frequency and timing of the data collection, as described above. Practically, any strategy for collecting the data must also consider the nature of the program or service that is being provided. The manner in which the service is delivered affects how the design is implemented in practice. Consider the following questions:

1. At what time or during what meeting should the pretest be administered?
2. At what time or during what meeting should the posttest be administered?
3. Will all of the program participants or service recipients be administered the pretest and posttest as a single group?
4. Who will serve as the comparison group?
5. Will the comparison group receive the pretests and posttests at the same time and/or place as the program participants or service recipients?

Ideally, data are collected from the program participants and the nonprogram participants under controlled conditions, at the same time and place. In reality, this is not always feasible, and alternatives must be considered. Sometimes pretest data may be taken from a larger administration of the assessment method, such as a new student orientation period. After the data collection period is complete, the program participant data may be extracted. Moreover, after a comparison group has been identified, its data may be drawn from the existing pool as well. Using the data collected during the orientation period would allow staff members to be concerned solely with posttest data collection.

Often, student affairs administrators weave the pretest and posttest administration into the fabric of the overall program or service. Program participants or service recipients may be told ahead of time that the pretest and posttest administration is a vital part of the program. In fact, the results can be used to provide feedback regarding personal development or knowledge acquisition.

Whenever pretest and posttest data are to be collected, obtaining identifying information so that pretest and posttest information may be linked is imperative. A credible comparison of change over time requires that an accurate link be made between the pretest and posttest scores. Forgetting to collect some form of identifying demographic information to establish such a link is one of the biggest oversights that can occur.

Protecting student anonymity is often an issue that dissuades one from collecting student identification. Particularly when the results do not concern a sensitive matter, the students can be told that the purpose of the data collection is program improvement. Whenever a student affairs administrator considers protecting anonymity to be a wise decision, other novel ways of linking pretest and posttest data may be formulated. For instance, students might be asked upon each administration to write their top five favorite animals, their mother's maiden name, their birthday, or some combination of personal facts that would reduce the likelihood of more than one student reporting the same thing.

Analyzing or Evaluating Assessment Information

Once the data are collected, the results must either be scanned or keyed into a computer database. In part, the statistical software package chosen governs the form in which the data must be entered. Data are often entered into a micro-computer spreadsheet or mainframe. After the data entry is complete, the data should be thoroughly checked for accuracy. Sometimes there are too many data to check every case, and so a random, but reasonably extensive, check for accuracy can be undertaken instead.

Decisions must be made with regard to missing data. For example, will student records be deleted when the information collected from them is incomplete? For a complete discussion on strategies about treating missing data, see Roth (1994).

The assessment designs introduced earlier may be used not only as an indication of what data collection strategy will be employed but also serve to suggest various statistical procedures for a given circumstance. If only one assessment method is administered, a univariate statistical procedure is most likely to be an appropriate approach to analyzing a data set. Univariate statistical procedures include the *t* test, the dependent *t* test, analysis of variance (ANOVA), repeated measures ANOVA, and multiple regression. When more than one assessment method is used to collect data on the same construct (e.g., more than one measure of leadership), a multivariate statistical procedure is most appropriate. Multivariate statistical procedures include multivariate regression, multivariate analysis of variance (MANOVA), repeated measures MANOVA, and canonical discriminant analysis.

Statistical procedures often used for assessment studies include the following:

1. *One group pretest/posttest design*: dependent *t* test, repeated measures ANOVA, repeated measures MANOVA.
2. *Pretest/posttest comparison group design*: repeated measures, ANOVA, repeated measures MANOVA.
3. *Posttest only comparison group design*: *t* test, ANOVA, linear regression, multiple regression, multivariate regression, MANOVA, and discriminant analysis.
4. *Static-group comparison design*: *t* test, ANOVA, linear regression, multiple regression, multivariate regression, MANOVA, and discriminant analysis.
5. *Nonequivalent comparison group design*: repeated measures ANOVA, repeated measures MANOVA.

The conditions under which each of the aforementioned statistical procedures is used are reviewed below. Generally, t tests, ANOVAs, and MANOVAs are used whenever the student affairs professional wants to compare two or more groups of people, most often program participants and nonprogram participants. The t test compares only two groups on one assessment score or rating, ANOVA compares two or more groups on one assessment score or rating (and requires additional pairwise tests to determine which groups differ from one another), and MANOVA and canonical discriminant analysis compare two or more groups on more than one assessment score or rating, all of which must be adequately correlated (conceptually/empirically related). Dependent t tests and repeated measures ANOVA or MANOVA are used when the same program participants take the same assessment measures over time, usually before program participation (pretest) and after program participation (posttest). Dependent t tests are used when program participants take one assessment method on two occasions. Repeated measures ANOVA is used when program participants (and perhaps nonprogram participants) take one assessment method on two or more occasions. Repeated measures MANOVA is used when program participants (and perhaps nonprogram participants) take more than one assessment method on two or more occasions. Linear, multiple, and multivariate regression may be used instead of the t test, ANOVA, and MANOVA, respectively, when the assumptions of the latter procedures are not met (equal numbers for the groups compared and equal variances for the groups compared).

Although discussing the interpretation and reporting of statistical output is beyond the scope of this section, the reader is strongly encouraged to review the results of the APA Task Force on Statistical Inference (1999) because therein current standards (the inception of which were provoked by a stimulating controversy) are issued.

Summarizing How the Information Will Be Used

Sivo (1998, 1999) indicated that a discussion concerning the use of assessment study results may be broadly split into two general categories: (a) how to use results that suggest program effectiveness; and (b) how to use results that suggest program deficiency.

When results suggest that a program has fulfilled its outcome objectives, program continuance is a common way to use the assessment results. Nevertheless, a number of other considerations of result use may be entertained as well (Sivo, 1998, 1999). Each of these considerations may take the form of a question:

1. Can the program be expanded to include more content and have yet an even greater impact?
2. Should the program be made more widely available so that more people may benefit?

3. Can the assessment method(s) be broadened in terms of the scope of their inquiry?
4. Should other assessment method(s) be added?
5. Should the assessment method(s) be improved in terms of quality so that evidence of program impact is more profound?
6. Should more funding be allocated or pursued or both so that program expansion and impact may be amplified?

When results suggest that a program has not fulfilled its outcome objectives, program discontinuance should be considered. Assuming that the objectives of the program are still valued, another program designed to fulfill the same objectives could be implemented. Sivo (1998, 1999) has indicated that if the original program is to be retained, a number of questions guiding the use of program results should be asked:

1. Should the purpose of the program be clarified?
2. If the program attempted to accomplish too much, can it be refocused so as to magnify its more salient aims and features?
3. How well coordinated/executed was the program delivery?
4. Which components of the program need to be improved to heighten program effectiveness, or what aspects of instruction are weakest?
5. How suitable, reliable, and valid were the assessment method(s) for this particular program, given the demography of the recipients/participants?
6. Are more resources needed to fulfill the intentions and secure the impact of the program?
7. To what degree is the program targeted toward the intended people?

CONCLUSION

This chapter reviewed several public policy issues surrounding the importance of conducting assessment studies for improvement and accountability purposes. In addition, a process for assessment was outlined and briefly described in a series of steps. This discussion was intended as an introduction, and the wise emerging professional will seek other courses and practical assessment experiences to prepare for the challenges ahead.

Many institutions and similarly units in student affairs have resisted studying the impact of their programs and services. Issues are raised about cultural bias in assessment instruments and using students as human subjects. For some people too, accountability is viewed as a fad; for others, assessment is a fear prohibiting action. Similar to knowledge about technology, greater knowledge of assessment can assist one in pursuing a vision of education and in demonstrating the value of particular programs and services.

The issue of reducing assessment method bias is conceptually and technically complex. Statistical techniques, such as differential item functioning, are now covered in many doctoral-level assessment courses (Erwin, 1999b). However, method bias is secondary to the basic issue of whether an unsubstantiated particular program and service should be offered at all. Certainly, ACPA's Ethical Standards (1993) and the Council on the Advancement of Standards in Higher Education (CAS) standards (Miller, 1999) require evidence of effectiveness before program delivery. Good judgment suggests likewise: Who would not want a received service to be deemed effective before committing to its use?

This volume contends that student affairs administrators, to be successful, must function as educators, leaders, and managers, and the information about quality permeates all three roles. Educators have a clear purpose of "evaluating" by "providing feedback . . . with a standard" (Creamer, Winston, and Miller, Table 1.1). In all likelihood, the next phase of assessment and evaluation will be the setting of standards on learning outcomes, much like what is occurring in K–12 education.

Chapter 1 also stressed the importance of leadership and vision. Essentially, most of the behavioral characteristics in Table 1.2 are steps in the assessment process (Erwin, 1991). True leaders utilize information in long-term planning and decision-making processes.

Successful managers employ information about effectiveness for organizational improvements (Brown, 1997). The postsecondary education managers of the future will refer to "digital dashboards" such as are currently under design by Oracle that will provide performance indicators of efficiency and effectiveness on a dynamic basis at their desks.

Similarly, the professional reasons for conducting assessment studies are mounting. Now claims are being made that collegiate education can be delivered via technology, particularly the World Wide Web (Bankirer & Testa, 1999). Does this imply that outside-of-class on-campus experiences have little educational value? Student affairs is poised to reassert the value of personal development, but only with credible evidence, not simply public relations or unsubstantiated claims. In the opening chapter of this volume, Creamer, Winston, and Miller noted that student affairs professionals conduct their work as a "moral endeavor" with a "moral conscience." Surely it is the student affairs administrator's duty to ensure that only effective programs and services are offered to students.

The tradition of student affairs is long and heralded, but its future faces change in higher education. This destiny will be partially determined by the value shown through empirical evidence. Educators must communicate credible evidence clearly and convincingly. It is a responsibility that student affairs administrators should face firmly and with resolve.

QUESTIONS TO CONSIDER

1. What are some examples of educational (that is, learning and development) objectives particularly found in offices of student affairs?
2. What are some credible ways of assessing those constructs?
3. What must professionals do in student affairs to respond to calls for accountability outside of higher education? Describe an assessment plan including at least 3–4 learning or developmental objectives, possible assessment instruments, and ways of collecting that assessment information.
4. What are approaches that student affairs professionals might use to represent their value through presentations of assessment evidence to state officials, acrimonious boards, and the public?
5. What ethical and professional obligations do student affairs practitioners have for assessing their progress and services?

REFERENCES

Allen, M. J., & Yen, W. M. (1979). *Introduction to measurement theory*. Monterey, CA: Brooks/Cole.

Alexander, L., Clinton, B., & Kean, T. H. (1986). *Time for results: The governors' 1991 report on education*. Washington, DC: National Governors Association.

American Association of Colleges. (1985). *Integrity in the college curriculum: A report to the academic community*. Washington, DC: Author.

American College Personnel Association (ACPA). (1993). Statement of ethical principles and standards. *Journal of College Student Development, 34*, 89–92. [On-line]. Available: http://www.acpa.nche.edu/pubs/prncstan.htm

American College Personnel Association (ACPA). (1996, March/April). Whole issue, The student learning imperative: Implications for student affairs. *Journal of College Student Development*. [On-line]. Available: http://acpa.nche.edu/sli/sli.htm

Anastasi, A. (1988). *Psychological testing* (6th ed.). New York: Macmillan.

APA Task Force on Statistical Inference. (1999). Statistical methods in psychology journals: Guidelines and explanations. *American Psychologist, 54*, 594–604.

Bankirer, M. W., & Testa, A. (1999). Update on assessment at Western Governor's University. *Assessment and Accountability Forum, 9*(1), 13–14, 18.

Borg, W. R., & Gall, M. D. (1989). *Educational research: An introduction* (5th ed.). New York: Longman.

Bracht, G. H., & Glass, G. V. (1968). The external validity of experiments. *American Educational Research Journal, 5*, 437–474.

Burke, J. C., & Serban, A. M. (1998). *Current status and future prospects of performance funding and performance budgeting for public higher education: The second survey*. Albany, NY: The Nelson A. Rockefeller Institute of Government, Public Higher Education Program.

Cook, T. D., & Campbell, D. T. (1979). *Quasi-experimentation: Design & analysis issues for field settings*. Boston: Houghton Mifflin.

Creswell, J. W. (1998). *Qualitative inquiry and research design: Choosing among five traditions*. Thousand Oaks, CA: Sage.

Crocker, L., & Algina, J. (1986). *Introduction to classical and modern test theory*. New York: Holt, Rinehart, and Winston.

Desruisseaux, P. (1994; December 7). Assessing quality. *The Chronicle of Higher Education*, pp. A41–42.

Dressel, P. L., & Associates. (1961). *Evaluation in higher education*. Boston: Houghton Mifflin.

Erwin, T. D. (1989). New opportunities: How student affairs can contribute to student assessment. In U. Delworth, G. R. Hanson, & Associates, *Student services: A handbook for the profession* (2nd ed., pp. 584–603). San Francisco: Jossey-Bass.

Erwin, T. D. (1990). Student outcome assessment: An institutional perspective. In D. G. Creamer (Ed.), *College student development: Theory and practice for the 1990s*. Alexandria, VA: American College Personnel Association.

Erwin, T. D. (1991). *Assessing student learning and development: A guide to the principles, goals, and methods of determining college outcomes*. San Francisco: Jossey-Bass.

Erwin, T. D. (1997). Developing strategies and policies for changing universities. In S. Brown (Ed.), *Facing up to radical change in colleges and universities*. London: Kogan Page.

Erwin, T. D. (1999a). Assessment and evaluation: A systems approach for their utilization. In S. Brown & A. Glasner (Eds.), *Assessment matters in higher education: Choosing and using diverse approaches*. London: Open University Press.

Erwin, T. D. (1999b). A doctoral program for assessment and accountability. *Assessment and Accountability Forum, 9*, 11, 12, 18.

Ewell, P. T. (1998). *Examining a brave new world: How accreditation might be different*. Paper presented at the second annual meeting of the Council for Higher Education Accreditation, Washington, DC.

Feldman, K. A., & Newcomb, T. M. (1969). *The impact of college on students*. San Francisco: Jossey-Bass.

Gakle, R., & Wolfe, M. (1993). *Instrument development in the affective domain*. Boston: Kluwer Academic Publishers.

Gaither, G. H. (Ed.). (1998). *Quality assurance in higher education: An international perspective*. San Francisco: Jossey-Bass.

Healy, P. (1999, 27 July). Report warns of a coming drop in states spending on higher education. *The Chronicle of Higher Education*, p. A38.

Lenzner, R., & Johnson, S. S. (1997, 10 March). Seeing things as they really are. *Forbes*, pp. 122–128.

MacTaggart, T. J., & Associates. (1998). *Seeking excellence through independence: Liberating colleges and universities from excessive regulation*. San Francisco: Jossey-Bass.

Miller, T. K. (Ed.). (1999). *The CAS book of professional standards for higher education*. Washington, DC: Council for the Advancement of Standards in Higher Education.

Nettles, M. T., Cole, J. J. K., & Sharp, S. (1997). *Benchmarking assessment, Assessment of teaching and learning in higher education for improvement and public accountability: State governing, coordinating board, and regional accreditation association policies and practices*. Ann Arbor, MI: Center for the Study of Higher and Postsecondary Education, University of Michigan.

Osterlind, S. J. (1989). *Constructing test items*. Boston: Kluwer Academic Publishers.

Pascarella, E. T., & Terenzini, P. T. (1991). *How college affects students: Findings and insights from twenty years of research*. San Francisco: Jossey-Bass.

Roth, P. L. (1994). Missing data: A conceptual review for applied psychologists. *Personnel Psychology, 47*, 537–560.

Russell, T. L. (1997). *No significant difference phenomenon*. Raleigh, NC: Office of Instructional Telecommunication.

Sivo, S. A. (1997, November). *Assessment study design and measurement methods*. Paper presented at the 11th Annual Virginia Assessment Group Conference, Virginia Beach, VA.

Sivo, S. A. (1998, November). *Structuring the assessment design and measure: Issues and procedures*. Paper presented to participants at the 12th Annual Virginia Assessment Group Conference, Waynesboro, VA.

Sivo, S. A. (1999, March). *Structuring the assessment design and measure at private universities: Issues and procedures*. Paper presented at the Virginia Assessment Group Spring Conference in Longwood, VA.

Southern Regional Education Board, Commission on Educational Quality. (1985, July 3). *Access to quality undergraduate education*. Reprinted in the *The Chronicle of Higher Education*, pp. 9–12.

Wingspread Group on Higher Education. (1993). *An American imperative: Higher expectations for higher education*. Racine, WI: Author.

RECOMMENDED READING

Erwin, T. D. (1996). Assessment, evaluation, and research. In S. R. Komives, D. B. Woodard, Jr., & Associates, *Student services: A handbook for the profession* (3rd ed.). San Francisco: Jossey-Bass.

Erwin, T. D. (1998). *Definitions and assessment methods of critical thinking, problem solving, and writing. Report produced for the Student Cognitive Outcomes Working Group of the National Postsecondary Edu-*

cation Cooperative. Washington, DC: U.S. Department of Education. [On-line: Available: http://nces.ed.gov/npec/evaltests/].

Erwin, T. D. (1999). A doctoral program for assessment and accountability. *Assessment and Accountability Forum*, 9, 11, 12, 18.

Schuh, J. H., & Upcraft, M. L. (2001). *Assessment practice in student affairs: An application manual*. San Francisco: Jossey-Bass.

PART *V*

LEADING AND VISIONING

*T*he final part of *The Professional Student Affairs Administrator: Educator, Leader, and Manager* explores two essential and closely related organizational functions. As this book's title implies, student affairs administrators are challenged and charged to provide leadership for the student affairs division and its subunits and to share with faculty, students, and other administrators in the overall leadership of the institution. In addition, the student affairs administrator is responsible for helping develop and communicate a vision of student learning, organizational functioning, and institutional mission that serves as an organizational and professional guide for the division's staff at all administrative levels and for the college's students. In effect, administrators at all levels who have not developed a well-articulated vision will falter because they lack a clear conception of what they are attempting to accomplish. To say that the purpose of student affairs is to *enhance the personal and educational development of students* is insufficient, unless there is a clear understanding by staff members as to how the agreed-upon purpose is to be played out within the context of the institution's culture and organizational structure. The effective student affairs administrator must articulate through word and deed a vision of student affairs as a profession, as an organizational component of the college or university, and as a contributor to society. A leader with a vision can help the organization accomplish great things. An administrator who lacks either leadership skills or a comprehensible vision to which others are willing to show allegiance is doomed to mediocrity at best, or abject failure at worst.

Part V includes two chapters that articulate the essence of good leadership practice. The concepts and constructs of *leader*, *leading*, and *leadership* continue to evolve as social institutions mature and become more complex. Roberts, in Chapter 15, examines leading and leadership, including an analysis of nomenclature and an exploration of the changing circumstances that affect alternative interpretations of good leadership. Roberts offers an emerging perspective about leadership assumptions and the ultimate purposes of leading that provides a foundation for achieving purposeful and complementary coordination in an increasingly global and complex world. Case examples of both routine and unique leadership dilemmas that student affairs administrators face in the course of their daily work are also provided.

Chapter 16, the final chapter in the book, was authored by Jacoby and Jones and is entitled "Visioning the Future of Student Affairs." It emphasizes the perspective that visioning is a process rather than a product and that it is dynamic rather than static. This chapter discusses the process of visioning, how vision in student affairs is anchored in its history and core values, how vision is created and sustained, and how vision can be used to address and anticipate the future.

READING SUGGESTIONS

As with Chapter 7 that dealt with organizing student affairs, Chapter 15 presents a broad overview of leading and leadership and readers may wish to read it shortly after reading the organizing chapter. Because leadership is not complete without established visions and visioning the future, Chapter 16 both concludes this book and sets the stage for comprehending and considering the future of student affairs and is therefore a chapter to be read after having digested earlier chapters.

15

Leading

DENNIS C. ROBERTS

*E*vidence of the study and analysis of *leading* as a subject area has been with us for as long as humans have been able to write. Whether the analysts are ancient or contemporary, one thing remains consistent—leading is as complex and illusive a subject as anyone might pursue. The problem is that the most coveted wish for many would-be leaders is to understand simply and fully what to expect when attempting to lead.

It is assumed from the beginning that most who study and practice in the field of student affairs administration recognize that there are frequent and consistent expectations that student affairs administrators must be capable of being expert leaders. In fact, the editors of this book began by expressing the view that the raison d'être of higher education is to provide "the means for achieving individual goals related to self and insuring that individual development occurs in a context that promotes and sustains a democratic society" (Chapter 1 in this volume, p. 6). By definition, everyone charged with facilitating learning among students is engaged in forms of leading. To empower democratic participation among students is to engage them in life-changing experiences and to lead them in discovering their full potential.

How one can successfully lead is continually shifting and changing. Clearly, shifts in worldview, educational reform, and self-understanding heavily influence how leaders think about leading. It takes an astute and focused educator to stay abreast of these changes that can so quickly undermine one's ability to lead others. Whether changes occur in information technology, multicultural views of community, or increased skepticism about politics, student affairs administrators must stay abreast of these dynamics by altering their views and potential practice of leading.

This chapter explores a number of issues about leading and leadership. It begins with an analysis of nomenclature and an exploration of the changing circumstances that affect the concepts. An emerging perspective is offered about assumptions of leadership and the ultimate purposes of leading. Following this

perspective on leadership, achieving purposeful and complementary coordination in an increasingly complex world is explored. The chapter closes with case
examples of both routine and unique leadership dilemmas one might face in
student affairs administration.

LEADING AND LEADERSHIP

One of the problems encountered by anyone attempting to understand leadership is that those with whom they interact will invariably possess varying paradigms of leadership. Most often, these paradigms are unexamined and implicit,
which results in assumed, but often conflicting, understandings of leadership
and its dynamics. When competing, unexamined paradigms are active on any
given issue or in an organizational environment, the likely outcome is conflict
that results in a loss of credibility and trust. For that reason, the discussion of
leading is initiated by exploring examples of commonly accepted paradigms of
leadership—paradigms that coexist among those with whom student affairs administrators interact.

Great Man Theories

A widely held view is that only individuals with special talents and abilities are
able to lead. This view was advocated by many during the formative years of the
twentieth century, and it is commonly referred to as the "great man" theory of
leadership. Even today there are those who intentionally, or without reflection,
affirm this view without considering the consequences of such assumptions. If
one believes that leading is the purview of a privileged few capable and heroic
individuals, then it must be assumed that either some are born with these traits
or that they are developed in specific individuals as a result of particularly influential and catalytic experiences. Either assumption results in the creation of an
elite core of leaders who are the ones to whom others must turn for vision,
guidance, and other critical resources.

Rost (1993) was one of the first to challenge the "great man" perspective of
leadership as well as other prevailing notions. His review of dominant theoretical conceptualizations of leadership included reference to three broad classes
of inquiry and theorizing.

The first class of inquiry was the *leader behavior* models. He included in
this class the "seven habits" model of Steven Covey (1992). In addition, he included Bennis and Nanus's (1985) four strategies (visioning, communicating,
trusting, and learning). Kouzes and Posner's (1995) 10 principles of leadership
have been among the most popular of these models, but Rost (1993) similarly
dismissed its claims. In Rost's estimation, these analyses of leading suffer the
same problems—they are "so general as to be meaningless or the lists are so
specific as to be impossible to put into practice in the countless episodes of
leadership any leader encounters in her/his career" (p. 94).

Leader Styles

The second class of inquiry was the *leader styles* models. Rost (1993) proclaimed that these models were "surface oriented, shallow, unauthentic, manipulative and nondevelopmental" (p. 95). The research substantiating the styles models, and the admonition in some theories that they should be varied according to situational dynamics, was "based on sloppy research" and assumed "that all managers and administrators are leaders, an assumption that is patently false" (p. 95).

Personality Traits

The third class of leadership theory is the *personality characteristics and traits* view. Rost's (1993) critique was that the findings were so inconsistent that the only real agreement reached among these numerous inquiries was that "leaders need a bit of intelligence" and "must have some physical stamina, and some psychological balance" (p. 96). He also warned that the most dangerous outcome of a characteristics and traits view of leadership is the gift- and talent-development programs found in many schools and at colleges and universities.

Leadership Phenomenon

Rost (1991) pioneered the critique of most views of leading and leadership that were prevalent in the twentieth century. He did so with a cynical definition that "Leadership is great men and women with certain preferred traits influencing followers to do what the leaders wish in order to achieve group/organizational goals that reflect excellence defined as some kind of higher level effectiveness" (p. 180). This definition captured many of the unexamined assumptions held of leaders and leadership. The flaws and absurdity of them achieve full impact when combined in one statement like that which he proposed.

As a result of critical analysis, Rost (1993) went on to propose a definition of leadership that was not related to an individual as a leader but, instead, focused on the phenomenon of leadership that could be exhibited by anyone. He defined leadership as "an influence relationship among leaders and their collaborators who intend real changes that reflect their mutual purposes" (p. 99). This revolutionized many people's thinking. Rost's critical redefinition resulted in a shift in focus requiring more serious attention to the dynamics of interpersonal conduct and the exchange and sharing of leadership among many.

It is important to understand that the purpose of deeply analyzing and critiquing what is meant by leading is not to undermine certain successful acts of leading that have, in fact, made a significant difference in various institutions and communities. The point is that fertile opportunity may be found by examining the possibility that leading is not limited to a person, role, or heroic act. By looking at it differently, as in the Rost conceptualization, leading we can broaden the definition of to include leadership—*the action exhibited by anyone as a process of engaging others to make a difference through mutual work toward a shared outcome*. Ultimately, regardless of the reader's perspective or that of others, this examination should have made the point that, when there is discussion of leading or leadership, the conversants may or may not be talking about the same thing. Consequently, it is crucial to recognize this potential for misunderstanding.

CHANGING CIRCUMSTANCES THAT IMPACT LEADERS AND LEADERSHIP SUCCESS

Concepts of leading and leadership require contextual grounding. By examining why previous views of leading implied a heroic phenomenon and why this may be changing can provide helpful rationale and support for the historic paradigm shift currently in process.

When twentieth-century influences that shaped it most profoundly are examined, it is impossible to ignore that a hallmark of the century was the rise in industrialization. The late nineteenth and early twentieth centuries were times of incredible expansion of productivity, commerce, transportation, and communication. The United States was at the center of much of the transformation that changed the very circumstances of work, living, families, and communities. Mass production techniques, and the need for their use in winning two successive world wars, quickly catapulted the United States into a dominate position on the globe. The scientific advances that allowed for the expansion of mass production were dependent on routine and repetitive actions of workers. This required a large populace of unskilled or semiskilled laborers and a smaller number of elite managers and leaders. It was in this historic context that heroic notions of leaders emerged, and rightfully so.

What characterizes the present day? More citizens have higher levels of education in the United States and throughout the world than ever before. Technology, automation, and robotics have replaced many unskilled and semiskilled laborer positions in industry and agriculture. Advances in various forms of technology and communication transform everyday functioning (see Chapter 6 in this volume). For example, the personal computer on your desk and the operating systems that make it function are being redesigned at this very moment, even if you purchased the equipment and software yesterday. Information that used to be stored in libraries or encyclopedias is now available through convenient Internet connections. The contemporary and routine functions of business and technology shrunk the planet to proportions requiring greater understanding of everything from economics to culture. A global community now exists. Diversity in the United States and throughout the world is recognized like never before (see Chapter 5 in this volume). It has always existed, but environments of privilege have previously kept many from seeing the natural diversity that truly exits. These are simply the changes that loom most visibly over the landscape of the world and its inhabitants.

What do these changes imply for higher education and student affairs work? They mean that student affairs administrators must find ways of reconceptualizing fundamental beliefs about how organizations function and, more particularly, how leadership is manifest. Postindustrial models of leadership can and should be adapted to student affairs administration. For a variety of reasons, fundamentally broadening or shifting the paradigm of leadership is essential to future success. Three of the most compelling reasons to change how leadership is viewed include (a) understanding leadership as a shared relationship allows for broader talent development; (b) shifting paradigms of leadership in education will match the emerging practice in other segments of life experience; and (c) dismantling the assumption of privilege in leading will provide greater opportunity for all. Further exploration of the implications of these points follows.

Understanding Leadership as a Shared Relationship

The emerging consensus about leading is that it is becoming less and less important while increasing attention should be focused on leadership. Mathews (1995/1996) advocated for the practical abolition of the concept of leader when redefining the responsibility of leadership as being the creation of "leaderful communities." The rationale for that view was that there are so many issues in the world that need attention that there is little possibility for their resolution unless the goal of leadership becomes that of sharing the responsibility for decisions and actions by encouraging leaderful involvement among all.

Further, Mathews indicated that there are a variety of circumstances that make it difficult for society to shift its paradigm toward shared and leaderful communities. Among these is the fact that notions of heroic leadership have led many leaders to believe that they are superior and above those they lead. As the leader role is elevated above others, the role of stakeholders, contributors, and participants is marginalized and trivialized. Consequently, the bottom line is that restricted and constricting views of leadership are perpetuated because individuals fear change. To have an idea that something is wrong about the way leadership is viewed, developed, and practiced is disconcerting, but many will continue to retreat into previous and familiar strategies, whether or not they have utility.

Change in Education Will Complement Broader Societal Change

Creating leaderful communities through interaction with students and colleagues is both consistent with the emerging understanding of leadership in business and community settings as well as consistent with views of learning in the academy. From its very inception, student personnel work (as it was called then) was characterized by a different view of learning. Rooted in the pragmatist philosophy of Dewey (1916), student personnel work was conceived as "Viewing students holistically, believing in the potential of all students, and relying on rich experiences, both in and out of classrooms" (Roberts, 1998, p. 19). Lloyd-Jones and Smith (1954, p. 12) reiterated the innovative relationship they espoused for student personnel workers' relations with students when they "set forth the view that student personnel workers should not so much be expert technicians as they should be educators in a somewhat unconventional and new sense." Fried (1995) urged that Dewey's philosophy of pragmatism be revitalized in student affairs work as she explained that "Dewey's pragmatism is a process oriented approach to learning in which life becomes the laboratory and every thinking person a scientist" (p. 102). Rhoads and Black (1995), although they did not recognize the direct descent of student personnel philosophy from Dewey, advocated for a concept of transformative education whereby student affairs administrators might adopt concepts similar to those in the historic tradition of democratic progressive education as espoused by Dewey. Baird (1996) advocated, "Thus student affairs professionals can play a powerful, if unorthodox, role in their institution's life. As co-creators and maintainers of a culture of responsibility and respect, they can become the leaders of the emerging campuses of the new millennium" (p. 529).

Recently, Allen and Cherrey (2000) authored a "systemic" view of leadership, proposing that the information era and technology that fuels it are changing the way that leadership becomes manifest. Their proposition is that leadership must begin to "incorporate the systemic dynamics of an organization." If these systemic variables are embraced, leadership will begin "to faciliate the development of shared learning, influence change in different ways, relate ideas and people in ways that cross boundaries, and use new forms of cohesion that help organizations retain direction and coherence without control" (p. 21).

While Baird (1996) and Allen and Cherrey (2000) appeared to propose unorthodox, new, and unfamiliar roles, these might more appropriately be recognized as the revival of the commitments outlined in the early student personnel movement and the admonitions made by Lloyd-Jones and Smith in 1954 (p. 12).

The evidence is overwhelming that student affairs is descended from the innovative ideas of education that Dewey initiated and which are often expressed in other theories and paradigms. Constructivism, postmodernism, phenomenology, feminism (Fried, 1995), and others bear similarity to the kind of learning advocated from the birthing of student personnel work. Although this philosophy may not have been fully understood or embraced by student affairs practitioners in early years, it now finds rebirth as contemporary institutions struggle to accommodate the demands of increasingly diverse students, changing environments, and the chaotic and exponential explosion of new knowledge.

Mathews's (1995/1996) admonition in regard to leaderful communities in work and public affairs holds equally well in educational environments. There is little hope to deal effectively with campus challenges unless the goal of leadership becomes one of shared responsibility for decisions and actions. Sharing responsibility means including all voices of fellow professionals, academic colleagues, and students, regardless of position, authority, or power.

Dismantling Privilege in Leading Provides Opportunity

A major practical consideration when enacting a commitment to shared leadership is that, under this new model, power and authority are derived from and used for new and different purposes. Prior views of the privilege of authority and leadership frequently assumed that with title and responsibility came an assumed expectation that the leader has the final say in determining the outcome. This is the quintessential "the buck stops here" perspective. This statement is both an acceptance of the mantle as well as a presumption of who is calling the shots. Notice that the language here, used deliberately to accentuate the point, is focused on resources and control. Once shared leadership is adopted, it becomes very difficult to pull rank under circumstances where suddenly leaders want to recapture the privilege of making decisions unilaterally. Reestablishing leadership in one source will most assuredly be recognized for what it is—inconsistent with a commitment to shared leadership and enacted when the circumstances and costs/benefits are no longer convenient or desired.

Leading, within this context, is the moment or venture when an individual responds to the call to lead. Every individual has the opportunity to initiate leadership and it is the dynamic interplay of roving leadership that creates the best and most appropriate outcome. In such a model, leadership gains credibility or respect from expertise, creativity, innovation, and collaboration. It is not enough to use one's title; it is the ability to forge new understandings and better strategies that improve the desired condition of the community or group.

SHARED LEADERSHIP AND ITS IMPACT ON OTHERS

If student affairs administrators seek to share leadership more broadly, they must work from a definition that reflects a mutual influence relationship in which all individuals and groups can exercise self-determination and make a contribution by doing so (Rost, 1993). This new definition means that the process of proposing problems, working toward their resolution, and pursuing change will be manifest in at least the following five ways:

1. *Individual journey and discovery of what is valued.* All members of a community or organization are expected to determine what they value most. Rather than functioning as automatons dragging through repetitious habit, all student affairs practitioners are expected to cultivate critical thinking and reflection capabilities that prevent mishaps or, better yet, forge new and exciting possibilities.
2. *Leadership of colleagues.* Shared leadership assumes that it is not only the person in a position of authority who can provide feedback, suggest change, or question a practice. In the new paradigm of shared leadership everyone can fairly be expected to be self-monitoring and to care enough for colleagues to address problems.

3. *Leadership of those supervised.* Leadership, not management, is required in supervisory relationships. Although still required at some level, management is a less important concern than is leadership. In effect, leadership of those supervised takes on the function of facilitating, encouraging resourcefulness, problem posing and solving, and empowering responsibility. Under such conditions, managerial issues tend to be resolved by the individuals directly involved rather than orchestrated through managerial intervention.

4. *Leadership with and through academic colleagues.* As the tradition of student personnel work mandates, student affairs staff members are educators in a somewhat unconventional and innovative sense. In fact, the type of educational expertise that comes naturally to student affairs administrators is exactly the kind of deeper teaching that so many academic faculty seek. Engaged learning, experiential application of theory, service learning, advising, mentoring, and habits of reflection are only a few of the unconventional teaching roles in which student affairs administrators should have expertise.

5. *Institutional leadership by focusing on students' learning.* Ultimately, the founding philosophy and purposes of student personnel work have remained an anchor for the emerging student affairs profession in higher education. Because these views tended to be on the margin, however, it allowed student affairs administrators to see the dynamics of learning in ways that many other academic colleagues have not been able to see. Now the opportunity to advocate for the return of student learning to the center of the higher education enterprise is more possible.

ACHIEVING COLLABORATIVE SYNERGY

As Mathews (1995/1996) indicated, and as the experience of modern day colleges and universities demonstrates, there are myriad issues and concerns that command attention. If those in positional leadership do not engage a broader cross section of citizens and contributors, the number of problems and challenges will only grow, and expand beyond manageable proportions. It is this spiraling dilemma that may convince even those who adamantly resist the idea of collaboration to give it a try.

Another dynamic that most administrators must recognize is that the chaos of a changing world is growing at a frightening pace. Wheatley (1999) theorized that a principle of physics can help one understand chaos more effectively and fully. She proposed that what may appear as chaos in the immediate surroundings is actually quite orderly and predictable when viewed from a distance. The problem is that most student affairs administrators are so close to the daily dilemmas and crises that they fail to comprehend that even these problems can be understood when placed in a context. Achieving purpose and order by this means can be powerfully complemented by another idea, even when surrounded by chaos. One can see relationships and complementarity only when one is able to comprehend the connections among apparently disparate ideas. Jaworski (1999) proposed that the communication of one's views and wishes needs to be a greater focus of leadership. The work begins within oneself by examining the concerns of both work and private lives. Then, as these concerns are honed, individuals begin to broadcast their concerns so that others see this conviction. When others hear or observe this, they assess their own concerns and compare them with those expressed through leadership of this type. In essence, synchronous waves are created through sharing concerns with others, thereby creating ripple effects that have the potential to move toward resolution of others' concerns through mutually beneficial strategies.

When Wheatley and Jaworski's ideas are combined, the world becomes much more interconnected and manageable. In particular, Wheatley indicated that, because of the complexity of the modern world, increased numbers of individuals seek ways to connect with others. In her view, the human species has always sought to connect, but structures established in the industrial era interfered with continuing this very natural and basic striving. Individual autonomy, organization, and hierarchy separated people in ways that fit the needs of the industrial era. The question now is, do industrial models of specialization, independence, and hierarchy work in the modern day? Realistically, there is still chaos in the world and there are incredible challenges that require attention. However, if there is a perceived semblance of order and a comprehension that others also care deeply about mutual issues, individuals become empowered to act rather than being put off by the daunting task of attempting to make a difference. One example of this phenomenon was demonstrated through the collaboration of academic and student affairs staffs and resulted in the creation of the Powerful Partnerships model (Potter, 1999). It is no secret that many educators in colleges and universities are struggling to understand how they can be more effective. Too often and in too many ways, academic and student affairs–trained staff members pursue resolution of this challenge independent of one another. The Powerful Partnerships model stands in contrast to autonomous and solo conceptualization and action. This model is the result of a group of faculty and staff working together with the one grand objective of finding those things that can be done jointly to improve the quality of student learning. The committee members reviewed research, reflected on experience, and consulted numerous other colleagues to identify a set of principles that faculty could use in classroom settings and student affairs staff members could use in cocurricular settings. The combination of principles from both arenas gave birth to the idea of powerful partnerships that can be used to enhance student engagement in learning.

In this example, Wheatley's notion of removing oneself far enough to see the orderliness of chaos and Jaworski's communication of intention and concern combine to establish a synergy, or synchronicity, of purpose and initiative that far transcends the action that could be achieved by either faculty or student affairs staff alone. By doing this, ways are found to understand complex problems, individuals become more connected in their mutual work, and all learn to deal with confusing and difficult issues more effectively while assuming shared ownership and leadership.

A PERSPECTIVE FOR LEADERSHIP IN STUDENT AFFAIRS

The following perspective for leadership in student affairs administration was constructed on the basis of the preceding discussion and insights it suggested. This perspective is designed as a catalyst for readers to reflect on their own views of leadership and how those views relate to daily experiences of leadership. If anything can be confidently asserted without question, it is that reflection about one's leadership is one of the keys to success and effectiveness in that leadership.

During the last decade, the study of leadership has moved away from quick fixes and prescriptive models. The *dress for success, one minute,* and *how to win friends and influence people* strategies failed to deal with the deeper issues of personal development, group interaction, and vision that are so important to leadership. This perspective provides a framework of how student affairs administrators can approach their own responsibilities in leadership in the context of a changing world and changing models of leadership. These ideas are applied at the same time that they reflect the deeper theoretical work of such authors as Heifetz (1994), Wheatley (1999), and Jaworski (1999). The *perspective* is stated as personal assumptions or beliefs because leadership is, in essence, a very personal commitment.

Student Affairs Leadership

Leadership emanates from many places—from multiple settings within student affairs, other administrative areas, faculty colleagues, students, and elsewhere. More profoundly, one's leadership responsibility is to stimulate thoughtful responses among all those with whom one has contact to create leaderful communities (Mathews, 1995/1996) on campus and beyond.

As leaders within the higher education community, student affairs administrators emerge from a philosophical lineage that calls for students to become their best selves by being fully involved in the many and varied opportunities for learning. Fulfilling the goal of the pragmatist philosophy of Dewey (1916) is essential to improving the learning and the usefulness of what is learned for all students. This unique philosophy locates student affairs administrators in institutions in ways that allow them to be a part of, yet separated from, the core work of the institution, thus allowing them to see it globally (Allen & Garb, 1993; Fried, 1995). The view from the margin provides an opportunity to see potential changes that will result in constant improvement of institutions while preserving the institution's core mission and purpose.

Leadership under these assumptions requires that student affairs administrators possess philosophical commitments including:

- a vision of professional service to the world,
- recognition of the healing potential in all,
- support of the natural inclination to connect and collaborate, and
- release of the freedom to make a difference in the world by answering the
  call of the heart.

A vision of professional service to the world is necessary to stay focused on
what is important, even at times when it is easy to become distracted by inconvenience, thwarted attempts at change, and uncertainty. If student affairs administrators are able to remain attentive to the aims of instilling a commitment
to personal development, respecting others, and cultivating a lifetime of inquiry, they will be serving the world in significant and profound ways. Sometimes the simple reminder that these are among the administrator's purposes
renews the energy and commitment to one's work.

Recognition of the healing potential in all comes from a belief in the power
of community. Communities throughout history have been a source of support
and healing to their members. In the modern day, many specialists (such as
physicians, counselors, and clergy) have emerged to handle the task of *healing*.
History provides startling examples of how communities can prevent personal
crises and take care of their own, without special expertise. The challenge is to
engage in a serious commitment to community, with appropriate consultation
of those with special expertise but without abdicating one's own responsibility.
Good relationships are profound healers of many things.

Supporting the natural inclination to connect and to collaborate allows
individuals to see others as resources. It does not undermine excellence and a
desire to achieve. It is simply reconceived as something other than competition
for finite resources resulting in winning or losing. Group work has been a natural part of human experience, but the emergence of scientific method and rationality gave the impression that learning was an act of autonomous intellectual effort. Renewed interest in interdisciplinarity and crossdisciplinarity provides
ample evidence that knowledge is interconnected and that collaboration is likely
to produce better results than independence.

*Release of the freedom to make a difference in the world by answering
one's heart* reinforces the critical role of personal centeredness and conviction
as the source of one's best work and contribution to the world. Professionals
who are burned out and exhausted are usually that way because they have lost
their passion for their work. Their purpose is ill defined. Answering one's own
heart renews and reminds one of the potential influence each has in work and
community.

Seeking to work and live consistent with these beliefs allows student affairs
administrators to model the best traditions of education. Specifically,

operationalizing these beliefs will provide student affairs administrators a more effective way to

- focus on what is important,
- maintain balance,
- more effectively utilize the talents of others,
- serve as a custodian for the history and future of their institutions,
- stand as a conscience for the institutions they serve.

This perspective and its commitments are elaborated on and demonstrated in the following examples. The cases include examples of both routine responsibilities that demand leadership on a regular basis and examples that require the exercise of different forms of responsibilities. Regardless of the type of situation, leadership is required.

STUDENT AFFAIRS LEADERSHIP IN ACTION

There are innumerable responsibilities and tasks that are a part of most student affairs professionals' daily duties. Other chapters in this book provide helpful insight into the roles of manager and educator and all the discreet skills and insights required to be successful in each. The leadership roles played by contemporary student affairs administrators are equally complex. The following, however, is not intended to be exhaustive. What is presented is a focused examination of how effective leadership can improve three critical processes that are likely to command a significant portion of any student affairs administrator's energy. These three processes are planning, policy development, and program implementation.

Planning

Some approaches to planning assume that the world is predictable and controllable. This assumption is not embraced here. In fact, much experience indicates just the opposite (Wheatley, 1999). Some would say that because of its commitment to intellectual inquiry and freedom of thought, the academic community is inherently anarchic. It is the role of administration to harness the anarchy to allow faculty, staff, and students to identify ways to relate their needs and desires to one another so that an adequate proportion of the community can achieve its objectives. By doing this, planning achieves some modest degree of directionality and purposefulness in complex organizations.

Effective leadership in planning should be pursued with a full awareness of presses from the broader environment. For instance, a specific initiative, such as a cocurricular leadership development program, will be more effective if the plan is conceived with full consideration of the mission and purpose of the institution, the focus and priorities of the academic program, and the strengths and challenges inherent in students' out-of-class experiences. Effective leadership in planning also must consider (a) macroinstitutional-level issues, (b) other divisional (academic)-level issues, and (c) the nature and substance of students' engagement in their learning.

As planning unfolds, leadership can come from a wide variety of faculty, staff, and students. For the positional leader orchestrating the process, it is crucial to engage a broad cross section of individuals who either are, or could develop into, stakeholders. Stakeholders will only emerge if they see themselves in the planning. In other words, they must believe that issues they see as important are being addressed through the planning initiative.

A process in which the author was involved revealed that a faculty, staff, and student planning team was not only concerned about student leadership development, but also was concerned about the quality of the interactions among all members of the community. The belief was that helping students to learn about leadership would be impossible unless they experienced interaction that demonstrated a commitment to inclusive and empowering leadership throughout their contacts with all aspects of the University. As this emphasis emerged, it was clear that the idea of student leadership development could complement and, in fact, would be enhanced greatly by addressing some of the broader organizational climate issues. Through the process of planning, all those participating in the process became deeply committed stakeholders, and a more innovative and influential leadership development program was created.

In general, for a planning process to be most successful, the leadership approach must be inclusive and must recognize that there are many complex dynamics that affect the outcome. By allowing full participation and seeking to enfold stakeholders' concerns, the quality of the plan can be enhanced beyond expectation.

Policy Development

Effective policy development may be one of the most difficult challenges of leadership. The fact that policy is needed is an indication that there is dissention in the community about the ways members conduct themselves or the ways they handle business. If norms and values to which all adhere are shared throughout the institution, policy is unnecessary.

The key to effective leadership in policy development is to guide a group through a process that helps them determine their essential points of agreement. Then policy in the area of dissention is extracted from the core agreement. Many policy initiatives are undone or undermined because the core and shared purpose was never identified. The shared purpose may be related to historic legacy, the surrounding environment, or the press of new issues on the community.

A great example of difficult policy development pertains to illegal and abusive alcohol consumption among students. Behavior of students in fraternities and sororities represents another area of difficult policy development. Efforts are underway on many campuses today to develop policies in these challenging arenas. Too often, however, the attempt to create or revise policy on alcohol use is conducted in the aftermath of a crisis. Crises sometimes help achieve the level of urgency that forces a community to deal with a problem, but no one realistically wants to wait for a crisis to achieve the teachable moment.

Consider this example. In the absence of a crisis, a Panhellenic president has, over the last several months, introduced the need for a more restrictive and actively enforced alcohol policy. This was achieved by beginning with a series of meetings related to examining issues of general health, effectiveness, and credibility for Greek organizations. A survey of faculty perceptions of these organizations was implemented. Assessment information was reviewed to determine the motivations of those students considering Greek affiliation. And, most importantly, a symposium celebrating the founding values of fraternal organizations was staged. These initiatives, and others, set the stage to ask a very basic and core question—"As Greeks, what do we stand for and what value-added experience do we hope to provide for our members?"

The intuitive understanding of the Panhellenic president involved was masterful. She knew that she had to find the core shared perspective to have a chance of extracting an agreement on such a loaded question as the presence of alcohol in Greek organizations. Rather than impose her views or rely on the frequent, "They're going to make us deal with this" strategy, she focused on the core values of Greek organizations and the concerns and threats that they face in the contemporary environment. She also demonstrated that leadership on such issues can come from a variety of places and that student leadership can sometimes accomplish outcomes that student affairs professionals would struggle mightily to achieve.

Program Implementation

Program quality is a crucial issue for all student affairs professionals. Every event planned, document published, and statement made has the potential to fracture credibility, which is difficult to reestablish once it has been fundamentally damaged. The credibility issue is why most administrators feel compelled to make sure that their programs are as flawless as possible. But what happens when it comes to program initiatives that are substantially or primarily the responsibility of students?

Effective leadership in program implementation, even in the face of high expectations for quality, requires focus on what is important. It is easy to look at the one simple and obvious end product—the program. However, assessing the deeper and probably more influential and long-lasting outcomes is much more complex. Although they are difficult to keep in mind, what students learn about teams and leadership and how they learn to be responsible and accountable are key learning outcomes in programming. In addition to the learning by students participating in planning and delivering programs, student affairs administrators who work with them also have the potential to learn the importance of taking risks, being flexible, and being open to change. These attitudinal insights can make administrators' positions both more enjoyable and educational.

An example of student initiative occurred when students took action to avoid an end-of-the-year calamity similar to one that took place the previous year. As happens on many campuses, spring weather arrived and drew students outside. Then a wonderful spring night near the end of the semester led to an off-campus party in a commercial area. This event ignited a spontaneous and out-of-control event in the local community. In this particular instance, several hundred students became involved in successive nights of revelry, bringing media coverage and community concern. The aftermath was exhausted students and staff members and the local media turning what was a fairly innocuous street gathering into a riot.

The student affairs administrators knew that prevention of a repeat second annual gathering would be difficult to accomplish the following spring. A number of other campuses that experienced similar disturbances were contacted for advice and a meeting was called to compare notes. There were no answers by the time students returned for fall semester and discussions began immediately as student leadership discussed what could be done to prevent a repeat occurrence. Student leadership suggested that on the anniversary of the previous event, the city streets should be blocked off, all-night entertainment booked, food provided, and a distant and subtle police presence provided in case something should happen. When the idea emerged, administrators' immediate response was, "No way, it will never happen! There's just too much risk."

Through many successive meetings and negotiations, the "Red Brick Rasta" was born, complete with entertainment, food, and lots of celebration far into the morning hours. The city council provided all the ordinance abatements to make it possible, the police cooperated, the administration assisted with the resources and celebrity appearances, and one of the best morale-producing and loyalty-building events ever seen was created.

This example may seem trivial, but it avoided untold numbers of wasted hours responding to negative behavior It also avoided media sensationalism and developed a spirit among students that they could take action and find appropriate ways to celebrate the end of the school year. The student affairs administrative staff had to swallow hard and be patient through all the negotiations with others who, at first encounter, were skeptical or even hostile. But as student leaders were challenged to stay the course, the event was a great success. The kind of leadership exhibited in this instance was that of support, encouragement, and perseverance. Students were in the front positions and the administration was there to provide resources, to council, and to demonstrate trust.

These three examples demonstrated a different kind of leadership that many student affairs professionals are afraid to test. They each fulfill the kind of leadership that assumes that all are capable of taking responsibility. They also demonstrate that leadership is shared—it is not the province of a small, select group. Each of these cases, whether in planning, policy development, or program implementation, reinforces what is known about the world. Most environments are chaotic and unpredictable, but they can be understood and ordered, when administrators know what it is they seek as an outcome and when they broadcast that purpose actively to others so that they can become connected and add their purposes and goals to the mix.

There are other situations that may be characterized as special opportunities or challenges. These frequently involve unique circumstances or individuals. Administrators may not have seen the problem before, at least not in its current form, and they will need to determine which leadership strategy is likely to be most effective under the circumstances. Two examples of this kind of leadership challenge include dealing with young professionals and managing entrepreneurial urges.

Dealing With Young Professionals

Young professionals tend to exhibit high energy, enthusiasm, and eagerness to apply the knowledge they have acquired recently in their preparation programs. Honestly, many colleges and universities hire young professionals because they are willing to spend long and erratic hours on the job, because they are hungry for opportunity and advancement, and because they are inexpensive to employ compared to senior professionals. However, the leadership challenges in guiding young professionals are frequently far greater than working with experienced staff members.

One of the primary challenges with young professionals is that many are relatively unclear about the motivations and core philosophies that guide their work in student affairs. A typical response for being in student affairs is that they simply relished their undergraduate involvement and leadership experiences and that they love working with people, especially young people. In addition, many young student affairs administrators swear that they learned much more outside of class than they did in class and that they want to help other students have the same experience.

Under these circumstances, how can leadership be provided that brings the young professional along to a more sophisticated understanding about learning organizations, about their role therein, and about work worth doing? How can young professionals be taught to survey the broader environment of which they are a part? How can the point be made that, if practitioners seek credibility, they must understand and respect the core purposes of the institutions they serve? What is the big picture that student affairs administrators are attempting to fulfill?

Leadership of young professionals requires setting expectations that establish the context of work, the place of student affairs in a higher educational setting, and the delicate transition in moving from student to professional status. This kind of context setting comes naturally for most experienced professionals, but student affairs has a distinctive culture that must be communicated to young administrators and it cannot be assumed that graduate preparation achieved the level of inculturation necessary to be successful. Another dimension of this challenge is that the experience of many young practitioners is relatively narrow. Their world is composed of issues that are close to the person's experience and must be understood as deeply held personal beliefs. However, although personal conviction is important to guide one's work, employment does involve an institution, an organization, and a profession. Service to these three commitments requires a balancing act and young student affairs administrators need help to understand.

When young administrators speak of the value of their undergraduate cocurricular experiences as being transcendent to the academic, what type of leadership intervention is required? It is suggested that such a point of view is reflective of imbalance and incomplete understanding of one's education. Young professionals should be pressed to examine more deeply what responsibility they undertook to translate what they learned in class to their out-of-class experience. Likewise, they should be challenged to contemplate what they did with their cocurricular learning that helped transform and improve their classroom experiences. By raising such questions, young practitioners will begin to consider and hopefully understand the philosophical roots of student affairs practice and begin to realize their critical importance as transformative educators. The leadership needed is to help all colleagues understand the educationally purposeful role they can potentially and should play. Student affairs administrators need not be passive and marginalized. The point is, what can be done to increase and broaden the understanding among colleagues about the institutional issues on which student affairs contributions can be of help? Effective leadership in these circumstances is primarily about anchoring the young professional in relevant historical and cultural contexts, expanding their viewpoint, and nurturing commitment and pride in their work.

Managing Entrepreneurial Urges

Many effective student affairs administrators entered the field because of the perceived novelty and spontaneity it provided. Student affairs practice is, in many ways, a kind of entrepreneurial center within the more complex and bureaucratic higher education setting. Because it is organizationally smaller than most other administrative divisions and frequently lacks the personnel and fiscal resources that others have, this entrepreneurial spirit is often refined and rewarded.

Entrepreneurial behavior is generally highly desirable. The special leadership challenges that it can present, however, involve issues of coordination, cooperation, and collaboration. Study of the entrepreneurial personality reveals that such characteristics as independence, persistence, risk taking, and creativity are key to success in entrepreneurship. What might be expected if a student affairs staff is populated with natural entrepreneurial types or that the environment encourages innovation, application of ideas from other areas, new approaches to old problems, and piloting and testing? How about competition, divisiveness, one-upmanship, and inadvertent or deliberate undermining of one another's initiatives? Further, how about high staff turnover and difficulty maintaining programs over the long haul? As one can easily discern, entrepreneurism has both its advantages and challenges and should be viewed as a two-edged sword.

The key to effective leadership in student affairs environments where entrepreneurial behavior is valued is to harness it for mutual benefit and to help those with entrepreneurial leanings to see the benefit of collaboration and synchronicity. Entrepreneurs are often characterized as headstrong, exploitive, and insensitive to others' needs and interests. What can be done through effective leadership to help entrepreneurs understand that their likelihood of success is greatly enhanced by an openness to others' ideas and, indeed, linking to their aspirations and dreams? This view has to be taught as an authentic and deep commitment, not as a canned strategy to one's own success.

Although competition can stimulate new approaches and innovations, it is debilitating when the spirit of competition descends to delighting in others' failures. Obviously, competition need not include the demise of others, but, under some circumstances, the secret desire to outdo someone else may lead to extreme divisiveness or unwillingness to support someone else's project. This tendency must be checked through leadership that portrays success that lifts the collective as desirable while solo and egocentric success is discouraged.

Appealing to humans' inherent interest to see things that they create maintained, the entrepreneur can be encouraged to consider the long-term benefit of sticking with the task. Not only can good, creative employees be encouraged to continue their current position, they ultimately can be encouraged to pursue additional innovative tasks. Through effective leadership and encouragement, the entrepreneur can grow to see a task through to its end, to see the importance of developing something that lasts, and can engage others so that innovations will be embraced and maintained over time, regardless of the presence of the original innovator who created it.

The Bottom Line

These examples reflect the kinds of challenges one might expect to arise in relation to routine responsibilities as well as in idiosyncratic relationships and supervision. Obviously, there could be many more. Each of these opportunities potentially requires a unique and purposeful act of leadership. The point is that the leadership that is most likely to be successful is one that assumes shared responsibility, maintains focus on the ultimate purposes of education, and calls for understanding oneself and learning to deal with others and their aspirations more effectively.

CONCLUSION

This chapter explored leadership, its meaning and purpose, which is crucial to achieving the student affairs administrator's objectives in higher education.

The assertion that leadership is undergoing a paradigm shift was addressed specifically as well as implied throughout the chapter. A shift in paradigms, regardless of where it occurs, means that there are multiple and conflicting realities present at the same time and in the same environment. Most institutions of higher education are still characterized by bureaucracy, control, power, competition, and the resulting divisiveness they create. This is part of the reality of working in the higher education environment. However, many student affairs departments, units, and perhaps even the division itself may be attempting to modify the way they function. The astute administrator will work diligently to understand the dynamics of both types of environments and work for the benefit of students in both. Any student affairs administrator who does not maintain an awareness of supervising administrators who expect unquestioning compliance with directions and unfailing adherence to the rule that there be no surprises is likely to experience a short tenure under that supervisor. On the other hand, when responsibility and creativity are expected, the successful employee will respond by taking initiative, requesting appropriate clarification and guidance, and then forging ahead without the need for constant checking and affirmation.

As this chapter indicates, there is considerable evidence that the paradigm and climate on many campuses is shifting. Student affairs administrators will hopefully be a part of bringing a more inclusive and empowering campus to reality. Student affairs administrators are granted a great opportunity in the roles they play as they work with others to improve the quality of living and learning in these unique educational settings. The key is to stay focused on the transcendent purposes of one's work and to provide leadership in ways that include and engage others in every way possible.

QUESTIONS TO CONSIDER

1. What can I do to provide opportunities to foster leadership that will be effective in student affairs practice for the future?
2. How do changing student demographics impact the practice of leadership and the strategies that are most likely to influence positive student learning?
3. How can technology and its growing presence in our many interactions be used to deepen, rather than fragment, the relationships that are crucial to creating "leaderful" communities both on campus and elsewhere?

REFERENCES

Allen, K. E., & Cherrey, C. (2000). *Systemic leadership: Enriching the meaning of our work.* American College Personnel Association (ACPA) and National Association for Campus Activities (NACA). Lanham, MD: University Press of America.

Allen, K. E., & Garb, E. L. (1993). Reinventing student affairs: Something old and something new. *National Association of Student Personnel Administrators Journal, 30*(2), 93–100.

Baird, L. L. (1996). Learning from research on student outcomes. In S. R. Komives, D. B. Woodard, Jr. & Associates, *Student services: A handbook for the profession* (3rd ed., pp. 515–535). San Francisco: Jossey-Bass.

Bennis, W., & Nanus, B. (1985). *Leaders: The strategies for taking charge.* New York: Harper & Row.

Covey, S. R. (1992). *The seven habits of highly effective people.* New York: Simon & Schuster.

Dewey, J. (1916). *Democracy and education.* New York: Macmillan.

Fried, J. (1995). Border pedagogy: Reshaping our ideas of teaching and learning. In J. Fried & Associates (Eds.), *Shifting paradigms in student affairs: Culture, context, teaching, and learning* (pp. 97–136). Washington, DC: American College Personnel Association.

Heifetz, R. A. (1994). *Leadership without easy answers.* Cambridge, MA: The Bellknap Press of Harvard University Press.

Jaworski, J. (1999, June). Keynote address at the Conference of the National Association for Community Leadership and Greenleaf Center for Servant Leadership—Navigating the future: Servant-leadership and community leadership in the 21st century, Indianapolis, IN.

Kouzes, J. M., & Posner, B. Z. (1987). *The leadership challenge: How to keep getting extraordinary things done in organizations* (2nd ed.). San Francisco: Jossey-Bass.

Lloyd-Jones, E. M., & Smith, M. R. (1954). *Student personnel as deeper teaching.* New York: HarperCollins.

Mathews, D. (Fall 1995/Winter 1996). Why we need to change our concept of community leadership. *Community Education Journal,* pp. 9–18.

Potter, D. L. (May/June, 1999). Where powerful partnerships begin. *About Campus, 2*(4), pp. 11–16.

Rhoads, R. A., & Black, M. A. (1995). Student affairs practitioners as transformative educators: Advancing a critical cultural perspective. *Journal of College Student Development, 35,* 413–421.

Roberts, D. C. (May/June 1998) Student learning was always supposed to be the core of our work—What happened? *About Campus* (4)2, pp.18–22.

Rost, J. (1991). *Leadership for the twenty-first century.* New York: Praeger.

Rost, J. (1993). Leadership development in the new millennium. *The Journal of Leadership Studies, 1*(1), 91–110.

Wheatley, M. J. (1999, June). Keynote address at the Conference of the National Association for Community Leadership and Greenleaf Center for Servant Leadership—Navigating the future: Servant-leadership and community leadership in the 21st century, Indianapolis, IN.

RECOMMENDED READING

Allen, K. E. & Cherrey, C. (2000). *Systematic leadership: Enriching the meaning of our work.* Lanham, MD: University Press of America.

Caple, R. B., & Newton, F. B. (1991). Leadership in student affairs. In T. K. Miller, R. B. Winston, Jr., & Associates, *Administration and leadership in student affairs: Actualizing student development in higher education* (2nd ed., pp. 111–113). Muncie, IN: Accelerated Development.

Yukl, G. (1998). *Leadership in organizations.* Englewood Cliffs, NJ: Prentice-Hall.

16

Visioning the Future of Student Affairs

BARBARA JACOBY
SUSAN R. JONES

*H*istorically, student affairs came into existence largely because college presidents and faculty members did want to deal with what they perceived to be messy issues related to the lives of their students outside the classroom. Someone had to be responsible for regulating student behavior, discipline, and the myriad personal problems that always arose. Student affairs administrators' initial function was basically to *react* to issues as they occurred and to put in place mechanisms to maintain order. Over time, the essentially disciplinary function of student affairs was broadened by the addition of responsibilities to operate facilities, provide services, and administer programs that were supplemental to the academic core. What enabled the student affairs profession to rise above its original narrow and rather negative role to become a vital partner in the higher education enterprise is *vision*. The profession has, since its beginnings, been blessed by generations of visionary leaders who realized that the field has a critical and unique role to play in facilitating student learning and development, a role that is vital to the academic mission of higher education (Nuss, 1996). This chapter discusses the process of visioning, how vision in student affairs is anchored in its history and core values, how vision is created and sustained, and how to use vision to address and anticipate the future.

Vision is related to, but different from, other foundations of good practice such as mission, goals, and strategic plans. *Vision* focuses on the future; it is defined as "anticipating that which will or may come to be" (Flexner, 1987, p. 2126). Vision is about *why* we do what we do. Mission statements are about what we do and focus appropriately on the present. Goals, objectives, and strategic planning are about how we achieve, or plan to achieve, our mission.

This chapter is titled "Visioning" to emphasize that it is a process rather than a product, that it is dynamic rather than static. The next section elaborates on the visioning process, how vision is created and sustained. It is important at this point to clarify the distinction between visioning and imaging. Whereas visioning is taking an active role in anticipating and shaping the future, imaging focuses more on packaging and positioning. In other words, visioning is creating, and imaging is concerned with marketing what has been created.

Visioning is an essential element of student affairs work. If student affairs administrators cannot clearly articulate a vision—how they anticipate the future and their role in shaping it—how can they expect others to understand and appreciate what they do and can do? Student affairs administrators work for and with multiple publics: students, faculty, provosts, presidents, other administrators, parents, governing boards, elected officials, community leaders, and external funders. Engaging in the process of visioning and ensuring that student affairs' vision is understood by all of the above individuals is necessary if student affairs' administrators are to be the players and resources that they deserve to be—and must be—to be full partners in the learning enterprise. If they do not create and articulate their role in the future, they cannot expect others to write them in. They must be clear about why faculty colleagues must call upon their skills and experiences, why students and parents must value their work, and why institutional leaders, governing boards, and others outside the academy must support their work.

LOOKING BACK TO MOVE FORWARD

As noted, visioning is a decidedly forward-thinking process. In fact, to have a vision is to hold a picture of what an individual or organization wants to become, or, as Kouzes and Posner (1995) wrote, "an ideal or unique image of the future" (p. 95). The ability to create and sustain vision is essential to the work of educators, leaders, and managers of student affairs because vision provides a blueprint for future action. However, a vision of the future is anchored in the past. Therefore, to understand the importance of vision and the visioning process in student affairs, it is essential to draw upon "that which matters most, to us as individuals, and to us collectively" (Brown, 1997, p. 7).

A vision for student affairs that is clearly communicated, understood, and gracefully articulated will be one that emerges from and is anchored in the core values that have been consistently and persistently present in the profession and have stood the test of time. The philosophical tenets and core values of the profession were first framed in the 1937 and 1949 Student Personnel Point of View statements (National Association of Student Personnel Administrators [NASPA], 1989). These statements clearly articulate a fundamental belief in the holistic development of students, the primacy of student learning, and the importance of environments that support student development. In 1954, Lloyd-Jones and Smith developed the idea of student personnel work as "deeper teaching" performed not by "expert technicians" but by educators who are "somewhat unconventional" and innovative (pp. 12–13). They outlined common beliefs held by student personnel workers of the day, including "(a) a belief in the worth of the individual; that human values are of the greatest importance, that the common good can be promoted best by helping each individual to develop to the utmost in accordance with his [sic] abilities; (b) the belief in the equal dignity of thinking and feeling and working; and that these aspects are inseparable; (c) the belief that the world has a place for everybody; and (d) the belief that what an individual gathers from his [sic] experiences continues on in time; it is not what is imposed, but what is absorbed that persists" (pp. 12–13).

Despite a rapidly changing world and increasingly complex society, these principles and beliefs continue to anchor the work of student affairs educators today. Young (1996) identified the core values of the profession as individuation, community, equality, and justice. These values are rooted in the history of the profession and continue to inform practice today. Effective leadership depends upon the ability to communicate core values in various institutional contexts. The role of educator presumes that these dominant values are reflected in relationships with students, programs delivered, and role modeling. Good management insures that values provide the foundation for professional practice. How, for example, is the value of respect of the whole student reflected in a leader's policy development? What difference does the value of community make in an educator's design of a program on race relations? How might a manager incorporate the value of equality into residence hall roommate assignments?

Current documents of the profession continue to reflect these ideals and espoused core values. Mission statements for divisions of student affairs mirror these ideas and day-to-day work incorporates the principles of good practice suggested by foundational documents and historical tradition. A vision, however, cannot be based solely on what we know. Instead, a lively vision or *compelling vision* (Reisser & Roper, 1999) must build upon the past to create the future. The process of visioning in student affairs, then, becomes the bridge between what we know (history and core values) and what we will become (future aspirations).

CREATING AND SUSTAINING VISION

Creating a vision and engaging others in the visioning process is no small task. Effective leadership in organizations is frequently defined by one's ability to create and sustain a shared vision (Gardner, 1990; Kouzes & Posner, 1995; Nanus, 1992; Senge, 1990). In student affairs work in particular, Reisser and Roper (1999) suggested that a compelling vision "will tell those in and out of student affairs what student affairs stands for and what it aspires to contribute to the mission of the institution" (p. 120). However, although the importance of having a vision is taken for granted, the *process* of creating and sustaining a vision is less clearly understood. There are several possible explanations for this disconnect between rhetoric and reality. As leadership scholar Gardner (1990) suggested, vision is an intangible objective best understood intuitively. In a profession that is increasingly concerned with evidence of outcomes of what is accomplished, proof of effectiveness, and accountability, the "feel-good" nature of visioning seems impractical and irrelevant to some. Brown (1997) captured this sentiment when she wrote, "The instrumental nature of much thinking about vision—vision as positioning or puffery or hype or positive thinking—causes many in higher education to wax cynical about it, believing that it ignores the realities before us" (p. 9). Student affairs administrators have many opportunities to link visions with day-to-day concerns. In fact, the necessity to do so is integral to the ability to be successful and effective. DePree (1997) wrote, "Organizations without vision remain mere organizations, surviving but not living, hitting temporary targets but not moving toward potential" (p. 116).

For a profession such as student affairs that is deeply grounded in practice, visioning creates the very real challenge of linking ideals and dreams with pragmatic actions. It implies taking chances, risks, and venturing into the unknown. For those concerned with the everyday realities of student experiences and campus life, engaging in visioning seems like taking time out from the more immediate, and often pressing, tasks at hand. However, visioning must always be linked to action, and is best understood as a "process of tapping and making collective the meaning in our work lives" (Brown, 1997, p. 7). Visioning in student affairs can focus on more global aspirations (for example, the quality of the student experience) as well as practical considerations (such as customer service). As such, all members of the student affairs division should be engaged in the process of visioning.

As introduced earlier, an important distinction is drawn between vision and visioning. Traditionally, a vision is an object to create and hold and, as such, implies a product. It is typically created by one person and then imparted on others in the organization. By contrast, a living or compelling vision is one that is in the process of constant creation and re-creation. This requires a different style of leadership that focuses less on the vision of one person and more on the process of creating and sharing leadership among all who care about an organization. Senge (1990) suggested that vision is truly shared when "you and I have a similar picture and are committed to one another having it" (p. 206) and that the practice of shared vision "involves the skills of unearthing shared 'pictures of the future'" (p. 9). Engaging in the process of creating and sustaining vision requires student affairs administrators to practice participatory and collaborative forms of leadership. It also involves developing the skills of teamwork, consensus building, and group facilitation, as well as a belief that all in the organization have something to contribute to the vision creation and implementation process. Visioning is a dynamic, inclusive, and shared process facilitated by effective leaders, educators, and managers at all levels of the organization.

A MODEL FOR VISIONING

Engaging in the process of visioning is essential to effective practice in student affairs. Outcomes of visioning should include a greater sense of purpose and direction for work, increased commitment to institutional objectives, personal and professional renewal, and a blueprint for action. Visioning depends upon strong communication skills, imagination, knowledge of the profession, and an ability to work collaboratively with diverse groups of people.

The model for visioning proposed here consists of a five-step process: conceptual grounding, reflection, anticipation, imagination, and action. Thinking through particular questions relevant to each area will provide essential information about developing vision and how to realize the vision.

Conceptual Grounding

Vision incorporates the history and values of the profession as well as the institution and the student affairs division. Also, as Komives and Woodard (1996) pointed out, the field has a growing body of theory upon which to base practice, including reasonably well substantiated research about the psychosocial, intellectual, moral, and ethical development of the individuals who populate our institutions. We have a much better understanding of how characteristics such as gender, ethnicity, age, socioeconomic status, and sexual orientation affect development and learning in these areas. We also have a better understanding of organizations and how the institutional and larger cultures affect their functioning. The visioning process should take into account the historic values of the profession, the most current research and theories about students' development and learning and organizations and their functioning, and our accumulated store of professional and life experience.
Questions include,

- How will the history, heritage, and values of the student affairs profession provide a foundation for vision?
- How does institutional mission influence the visioning process?
- What are the core values of the institution and the organization?
- How will we consciously use a knowledge of theory and research findings to inform decisions and shape processes?

Reflection

Visions emerge from a process of reflection and discernment. A vision-oriented division of student affairs would encourage reflective practice at individual, functional unit, and divisional levels. Individual student affairs administrators need to reflect on their own beliefs, values, and philosophies and articulate their motivations and purposes for engagement in the profession as a foundation for shared organizational visioning. At best, individual vision is in concert with organizational and institutional visions to ensure commitment and purposeful action. Some questions to ask are the following:

- What are relevant individual values and purposes?
- What is fundamentally important to individuals and to the organization?

- What matters in daily work?
- How do responses to these questions relate to professional practice and aspirations?

Anticipation

Knowledge of contemporary issues as well as skill in forecasting future issues is essential to visioning. Reading widely to discern trends that will affect higher education and maintaining professional networks and associations will help in anticipating issues and challenges. Because of the reflective nature of the visioning process, visions are responsive to new conditions, constantly reshaped to incorporate new learning, and anticipatory of future trends. Related questions include,

- What are the issues the profession is likely to encounter in the future?
- What are the results of scanning the environment for evidence of trends, patterns, and future issues?
- How will this information be incorporated into a vision?

Imagination

A vision-oriented division of student affairs would always reflect a shared dream of the ideal that conveys the aspirations and hopes for the work to be done. This picture would be broad enough so that all involved in the division could see and understand their roles in the big picture of student affairs work. Questions related to imagination follow:

- What would the institution look like if it were an ideal environment for student learning and development?
- What would it take to create an institutional community in which all students feel they are full and valued members?
- What are the ideal outcomes of professional practice?
- How can creative thinking and dreaming be incorporated into visioning?
- How can imagination be used to link the ideal picture of the future with everyday practice?

Action

Visioning without action is frustrating to participants because it raises hopes and expectations without possibility of fulfillment. Practice without vision lacks a sense of purpose and results in maintenance of the status quo with little opportunity for creativity or innovation. Vision-based action builds on the foundation created from the first four steps of the model. It includes developing mission, goals, and objectives; developing policy; planning programs; or designing outcomes assessment. The following questions can be used to guide vision-based action:

- How can vision be used to make decisions about how to allocate resources?
- How does vision assist in establishing priorities and in making difficult decisions about what can and cannot be done?
- How can vision help in making connections with colleagues across the institution? How can vision clarify individual roles?
- How can vision be used to increase understanding of students, parents, faculty, institutional leadership, and governing boards of the vital contributions of student affairs to higher education?

Leadership is integral to the process of visioning. Brown (1997) wrote, "Vision emerges from the community under the stewardship of good leadership. Leadership shapes and frames the process that elicits vision" (p. 7). Student affairs leaders need to develop the knowledge and skills to engage those with whom they work in the process of visioning. This is true whether one is advising student organizations, supervising resident assistants, directing specific program areas, or serving as a dean or vice president. Integral to this skill is the ability to translate vision to practice so that a vision becomes a framework for anticipating future issues and responding to change.

ADDRESSING FUTURE ISSUES THROUGH VISIONING

Higher education enters the new century faced with economic uncertainty, eroding public confidence, demands for accountability, and growing numbers of students from historically underrepresented groups. Both supporters and critics of higher education are calling upon colleges and universities to refocus their energies squarely on student learning and to demonstrate their value. Student affairs professional associations have recognized that these challenges present a clear and simple choice: "We can pursue a cause that engages us in the central mission of our institutions or retreat to the margins in the hope that we will avoid the inconvenience of change" (ACPA & NASPA, 1997, n.p.).

As previously described, visioning is what will enable student affairs to be central rather than marginal in defining and shaping the future of higher education. Komives and Woodard (1996) succinctly articulate this challenge: "Student affairs professionals must assertively help to shape the new forms that higher education will take in the future and advocate changes to enhance student learning and development" (p. 537). Although predicting the future is a risky undertaking, there are nevertheless issues and trends present now that will undoubtedly continue into the future (Johnson & Cheatham, 1999). Among the issues that will affect higher education and therefore must be incorporated into the visioning process are (a) changes in student demographics and in the nature of the student experience, (b) renewed focus on learning, (c) increasing emphasis on accountability and assessment, (d) emerging technologies, and (e) community engagement.

Changes in Student Demographics and in the Nature of the Student Experience

Today's college students are increasingly diverse in many ways, including, but not limited to, the following: age, race, ethnicity, socioeconomic status, sexual orientation, language, and ability (Astin, 1998; Levine & Cureton, 1998a, 1998b). (See also Chapter 5 in this volume.) In addition to demographic diversity, students are bringing to higher education a broad range of personal, economic, social, and cultural issues and experiences that must be addressed (Andreas & Schuh, 1999). This range of issues and experiences leads to a variety of situational differences, such as full- or part-time status, degree objective, transferring from one institution to another, intermittent study ("stopping out"), and entering or returning to higher education at various points in life (El-Khawas, 1996). Yet another dimension of diversity results from an array of preferred learning styles and an even wider array of attitudes toward, and motivations for, learning.

Keeling (1999) spoke eloquently about today's "reinvented" students whose lives are dramatically more complicated than those of their predecessors by jobs, debt, family issues, and transportation, for example. The ranking of attending classes and studying among their immediate priorities has clearly changed, "'Student' is only one identity for people who also are employees, wage workers, opinion leaders or followers, artists, friends, children (and sometimes, parents), partners or spouses" (p. 4). The fact that "student" is no longer every student's primary identity reflects far more than demographics: today's students "slot college into their lives, on the one hand, and erase its boundaries, on the other" (p. 4). Higher education attendance for today's (and tomorrow's) students becomes everything that happens, all the sources of learning, all the experiences, all the relationships, all the media that people encounter while they are enrolled in higher education.

What are the implications for visioning the future of student affairs? Of course, there are many. Student affairs administrators must continually scan the environment, both on and off campus, for indications of change in current and prospective students. Administrators can never complacently assume that they know and understand their students. On the contrary, they must examine and reexamine their assumptions. They must share what they know about students with academic colleagues and institutional leaders and be vocal advocates on their behalf. They also must always be designing and redesigning educational environments, policies, programs, and practices to serve the students of today—and tomorrow.

Renewed Focus on Learning

There is a clear consensus among all recent higher education reform agendas that colleges and universities must return to a fundamental focus on student learning by "putting student learning first [and] focusing overwhelmingly on what our students learn and what they achieve" (Wingspread Group on Higher Education, 1993, p. 13). This focus includes not only *what* students should learn but also *how* learning can best be facilitated. Barr and Tagg (1995) argued persuasively that higher education must shift from a "teaching paradigm" to a "learning paradigm," in which the purpose of college is no longer viewed as providing instruction "but to create environments and experiences that bring students to discover and conduct knowledge for themselves, to make students members of communities of learners that make discoveries and solve problems" (p. 15).

The higher education community (Association of American Colleges, 1988; Boyer, 1988; Kellogg Commission on the Future of State and Land-Grant Universities, 1996; Study Group on the Conditions of Excellence in American Higher Education, 1984; Wingspread Group on Higher Education, 1993) has turned much attention to the need to strengthen undergraduate education by "putting student learning first." Angelo (1993) described *higher learning*—the mission of higher education—as an active, interactive process that results in changes in knowledge, understanding, behavior, dispositions, appreciation, and belief that are meaningful and long lasting. He emphasized that active learning has much greater impact than passive learning. Active learning occurs "when students invest physical and mental energy in activities that make their learning meaningful" (Newton & Smith, 1996, pp. 21–22). In this vein, Chickering and Gamson (1987) put forth a set of principles for good practice in undergraduate teaching that encourages student–faculty contact, cooperation among students, active learning, time on task, high expectations, and respect for diverse ways of learning.

In accordance with these and other similar principles, the use of strategies such as cooperative learning, problem-based learning, and learning communities is growing at a remarkable rate (Major, 1998; Shapiro & Levine, 1999). In cooperative learning, students work together to accomplish shared goals. When engaged in cooperative activities, individuals pursue outcomes that are beneficial both to themselves and to other members of the group. "Cooperative learning is the heart of problem-based learning" (Johnson, Johnson, & Smith, 1998, p. 27). Problem-based learning is an institutional strategy in which students tackle conceptualized, ill-structured problems and seek to find meaningful solutions. They actively, and often collaboratively, pursue knowledge and gain problem-solving and critical thinking skills (Major, 1998).

Although there are many different types of learning communities and many definitions of the term, a well-accepted definition was proposed by Gabelnick, MacGregor, Matthews, and Smith (1990):

> Learning communities . . . purposefully restructure the curriculum to link together courses or course work so that students find greater coherence in what they are learning as well as increased intellectual interaction with faculty and fellow students. . . . Learning communities are also usually associated with collaborative and active approaches to learning, some form of team teaching, and interdisciplinary themes. (p. 5)

The renewed emphasis on student learning will undoubtedly shape the development of higher education for the foreseeable future. Visioning for the future of student affairs must, therefore, affirm student learning and development as its primary goal. And student affairs administrators must take the initiative to partner with academic affairs and students to continue to develop and refine optimum learning environments.

Increasing Emphasis on Accountability and Assessment

Accountability has become increasingly prominent on the higher education scene during the past two decades, and this trend will likely continue. (See Chapter 14 in volume.) The value of a college education is increasingly being questioned both inside and outside the academy. A number of reports by higher education experts conclude that the goals of a college education and its outcomes for student are unclear. College graduates sometimes appear not to be well educated and, in some cases, are ill prepared for the world of work (Upcraft & Schuh, 1996). The public is dissatisfied with the rising cost of college, particularly because there is simultaneously increased dissatisfaction with the quality of instruction at many institutions. According to a 1998 survey of state officials in charge of higher education finance, nearly every state may soon link some spending on public colleges to institutional performance (Schmidt, 1998).

The growing press for accountability has led to increased attention to assessment of student outcomes. Student outcomes assessment is a systematic process of gathering, analyzing, and using information about student learning. The forces that have led to a clearer focus on student learning have, rightfully, also encouraged colleges and universities to articulate their desired student learning outcomes and to be accountable for their achievement. Difficult questions are being asked of higher education: What should students expect to learn? What do they learn? How does learning occur? How can a college demonstrate its effectiveness?

As clarion calls for assessment multiply, pressure is increasingly placed on student affairs to measure the extent to which its programs, services, and facilities contribute to student learning (Schuh & Upcraft, 2001, Chapter 13 in this volume; Upcraft & Schuh, 1996). Faculty, academic administrators, and elected officials want to know whether student services and programs are really necessary. As resources decline and demands for accountability become more stringent, institutions tend increasingly to reallocate human and fiscal resources to narrowly defined academic priorities that relate directly to the formal curriculum (Upcraft & Schuh, 1996). Student affairs must conduct ongoing assessment that augments and updates the rich body of existing evidence that out-of-class experiences contribute mightily to student success, learning, personal development, satisfaction, and retention. Student affairs administrators must use assessment to provide evidence that student affairs programs and services make substantial positive contributions to the outcomes that constituents most value from higher education.

Emerging Technologies

There can be no doubt that the information technology revolution continues to change the world in multiple ways. (See Chapter 4 in this volume.) Debates rage about the value of technology in learning—whether it will, in the long run, have a net positive or negative effect. Although the nature of the impact of new and emerging technologies on learning is debatable, the profundity of their impact is not: "Just as the development of the printing press forever changed the teaching enterprise, information technology represents a fundamental change in the basic technology of teaching and learning" (Massey & Zemsky, 1995, p. 1).

The applications of technology in the classroom are expanding rapidly. They range from basic, limited uses (for example, e-mail, course web pages, and class chatrooms) to classroom enhancements (such as PowerPoint, computer simulations, one-way and two-way audiovisual techniques) to sophisticated applications (for example, computer groupware conferencing, computer video and asynchronous computer conferencing, and asynchronous/CD-ROM hybrids) (Upcraft & Terenzini, 1999).

In addition to course-based uses of technology, there is a clear and dramatic increased reliance on technology in administrative and support services and in students' out-of-class experiences. Hardly any aspect of student affairs remains untouched by information technology. Admissions, financial aid, registration, tuition payment, career exploration and search, and academic advising are among the many functions that are often accomplished partially or entirely on-line. As computer labs appear in many campus buildings, as residence halls are networked to the Internet, and as wireless connectivity emerges, students spend increasing amounts of time "cocooning" with their computers. Using computers to retrieve course information, complete assignments, and do research—to say nothing of web-based entertainment, chatrooms, and e-mail communication—takes up greater proportions of students' time (Upcraft & Terenzini, 1999).

As distance education becomes increasingly prominent, students can access courses and even entire academic programs without ever visiting a physical campus. Distance education offered by both traditional and virtual universities dramatically expands access to higher education by freeing it from the constraints of time and place. Phoenix University, a private, for-profit business school with a fully on-line program, enables students from all over the world to earn an academic degree completely via their desktop computers.

Numerous complex questions arise regarding student affairs and the future of technology in higher education. Does technology enhance or detract from learning? How? Will technology increase or decrease the quality of student–faculty, student–advisor, and student–student interactions? How can technology be used most effectively to deliver services and handle administrative functions? Will reliance on technology create a new distinction between the "haves" (that is, those who can afford access to emerging technologies) and the "have-nots"?

In the area of distance learning, questions are already arising about whether a virtual college education can be as rich as a traditional education. And distance educators—whether they are based in for-profit enterprises or "brick-and-mortar" educational institutions—are wondering how student services and programs can be delivered to distance learners. Can academic and career advising be done on-line? Are "staffed" chatrooms a viable way to conduct workshops and discussions on topics ranging from choosing a major to prevention of sexually transmitted diseases to stress management? Can students take service-learning courses as distance learners and engage in reflection on-line?

Community Engagement

Higher education is being called upon to renew its historic commitment to civic responsibility. On July 4, 1999, a distinguished group of college presidents added their voices to the many others who are urging colleges and universities to assume a leadership role in addressing society's increasing problems and in meeting growing human needs: "We challenge higher education to re-examine its public purposes and its commitments to the democratic ideal. We also challenge higher education to become engaged, through actions and teaching, with its communities" (Ehrlich & Hollander, 1999). Colleges and universities are partnering with communities to apply research, as well as technological and human resources, to economic development, housing revitalization, health care, K–12 education, crime control, and a wide range of other areas of concern.

The primary way in which student affairs professionals have become involved in community engagement is by joining with academic colleagues, student leaders, chaplains, and community representatives to develop opportunities for students to participate in service learning. Service learning is "a form of experiential education in which students engage in activities that address human and community needs together with structured opportunities intentionally designed to promote student learning and development" (Jacoby, 1996, p. 5). Although traditional volunteerism is a good thing, all good things cannot be the province of institutions of higher education that must constantly choose among competing priorities. Service learning, with its intentional goals for student learning and development, fits far more clearly into higher education's mission and priorities than do volunteer programs that lack its reflection component.

Among frequently cited benefits to student participants in service learning are the following: developing the habit of critical reflection; deepening their comprehension of course content; integrating theory with practice; increasing their understanding of the complex issues underlying social problems; strengthening their sense of social responsibility; enhancing their cognitive, personal, and spiritual development; heightening their understanding of human difference and commonality; and sharpening their abilities to solve problems creatively and to work collaboratively (Jacoby, 1996).

Community benefits include new energy and assistance to broaden delivery of existing services or to begin new ones, fresh approaches to problem solving, access to institutional resources, and opportunities to participate in teaching and learning. Colleges and universities enjoy improved "town–gown" relationships, additional experiential learning settings for students, and new opportunities for faculty to orient their research and teaching in community contexts (Jacoby, 1996).

To secure the future of service learning among competing institutional priorities, student affairs professionals must ensure that students engage in service-learning activities intentionally designed to achieve specific learning outcomes. For example, as part of new student orientation, a day-long service-learning experience can be an effective means of orienting new students to the community around the campus, acquainting them with the institution's mission of developing students' sense of social responsibility, building connection and community among the students, and encouraging further involvement in service learning. Members of a residence hall floor can develop a sense of community, shared purpose, and commitment to one another and to a cause by participating together in service learning. Judicial offices can use judicially mandated service learning as a powerful educational experience for students who have committed conduct code infractions, as well as a way to provide a form of restitution to the community for inappropriate behaviors. Leadership development programs often engage experienced and emerging student leaders in service learning to enable them to understand through reflective practice the concepts of servant leadership, socially responsible leadership, and effective followership.

Student affairs professionals are working with faculty to create intensive spring break, summer, semester, and year-long service-learning experiences throughout the world. Through such experiences, often called *immersions*, students can develop deep, personal relationships with people different from themselves, their needs, their assets, and the problems they face on a daily basis. Immersions also provide opportunities for more profound and prolonged reflection. Many students who participate in service learning, particularly in immersions, choose to spend a year or two following graduation in national or international service (such as in AmeriCorps°VISTA, Teach for America, Peace Corps) before starting graduate school or a career.

In the conclusion of the "Presidents' Fourth of July Declaration on the Civic Responsibility of Higher Education," the signatories affirmed their belief "that now and through the next century, our institutions must be vital agents and architects of a flourishing democracy" (Ehrlich & Hollander, p. 3). Democracy depends on the development of active citizens who participate in the life of their communities. Engaging students in service learning that promotes a lifelong commitment to participatory democracy is an important role for student affairs professionals that supports institutional missions in unique and powerful ways.

CONCLUSION

The challenge of visioning is that to be effective requires an ability to envision a future not imagined at this moment in time. This is not in any way a crystal ball, but rather a process of connecting past practice to future scenarios. Visioning is both a creative process and one firmly rooted in the everyday realities of professional practice. Envisioning the future of student affairs requires knowledge of the history and core values of the profession, creativity and imagination, and the skills to engage others in the process of anticipating the future and planning accordingly. As DePree (1997) suggested, "Only with vision can we begin to see things the way they can be" (p. 117).

An ability to communicate vision will become increasingly important as the profession moves into the twenty-first century and continues to grapple with the complexities of the times. As leaders, educators, and managers, student affairs administrators must develop a clear vision, articulate it to multiple constituencies, and model it in professional practice. Without vision, higher education will change and respond to future issues without the leadership and expertise of student affairs. A clearly articulated vision, anchored in the core values of the profession and the mission of particular institutions, will ensure that the role of student affairs work in the academy will survive and thrive.

QUESTIONS TO CONSIDER

1. In your current role, how can you work with your colleagues to create a vision?
2. How have you seen vision translated into practice?
3. What is most important to you as you envision your future in student affairs?

REFERENCES

American College Personnel Association (ACPA) & National Association of Student Personnel Administrators (NASPA). (1997). *Principles of good practice for student affairs*. Washington, DC: Author.

Andreas, R. E., & Schuh, J. H. (1999). The student affairs landscape: Focus on learning. In E. J. Whitt (Ed.), *Student learning as student affairs work: Responding to our own imperative* (pp. 1–9). Washington, DC: National Association of Student Personnel Administrators.

Angelo, T. A. (1993). A teacher's dozen: Fourteen general findings from research that can reform classroom teaching and assessment and improve learning. *American Association of Higher Education Bulletin, 13*, 3–8.

Association of American Colleges. (1988). *A new vitality in general education*. Washington, DC: Author.

Astin, A. (1998). The changing American college student: Thirty-year trends, 1966–1996. *Review of Higher Education, 21*, 115–136.

Barr, R. B., & Tagg, J. (1995). From teaching to learning: A new paradigm for undergraduate education. *Change, 27*, 12–25.

Boyer, E. L. (1988). *College: The undergraduate experience in America*. New York: Harper Collins.

Brown, J. S. (1997). On becoming a learning organization. *About Campus, 1*, 5–10.

Chickering, A. W., & Gamson, Z. F. (1987). *Seven principles for good practice in under-*

graduate education. Racine, WI: The Johnson Foundation.

DePree, M. (1997). *Leading without power*. San Francisco: Jossey-Bass.

Ehrlich, T., & Hollander, E. (1999). *President's fourth of July declaration on the civic responsibility of higher education*. Providence, RI: Campus Compact.

El-Khawas, E. (1996). Student diversity on today's campuses. In S. R. Komives, D. B. Woodard, Jr., & Associates, *Student services: A handbook for the profession* (3rd ed., pp. 64–80). San Francisco: Jossey-Bass.

Flexner, S. B. (Ed.). (1987). *The Random House dictionary of the English language* (2nd ed., unabridged). New York: Random House.

Gabelnick, F., MacGregor, J., Matthews, R. S., & Smith, B. L. (Eds.). (1990). *Learning communities: Creating connections among students, faculty, and disciplines*. New Directions for Teaching and Learning, No. 41. San Francisco: Jossey-Bass.

Gardner, J. W. (1990). *On leadership*. New York: The Free Press.

Jacoby, B. (1996). Service-learning in today's higher education. In B. Jacoby & Associates, *Service-learning in higher education: Concepts and practices* (pp. 3–25). San Francisco: Jossey-Bass.

Johnson, C. S., & Cheatham, H. E. (Eds.). (1999). *Higher education trends for the next century: A research agenda for student success*. Washington, DC: American College Personnel Association.

Johnson, D. W., Johnson, R. T., & Smith, K. A. (1998, July/August). Cooperative learning returns to college, *Change*, 27–35.

Keeling, R. P. (1999, February/March). A new definition of college emerges: Everything that happens to. . . . *NASPA Forum*, 4–5.

Kellogg Commission on the Future of State and Land-Grant Universities. (1996). *The student experience: Data related to change* [first working paper]. Washington, DC: National Association of State Universities and Land-Grant Colleges.

Komives, S. R., & Woodard, D. B., Jr. (1996). Building on the past, shaping the future. In S. R. Komives, D. B. Woodard, Jr., & Associates, *Student services: A handbook for the profession* (3rd ed., pp. 536–555). San Francisco: Jossey-Bass.

Kouzes, J., & Posner, B. (1995). *The leadership challenge* (2nd ed.). San Francisco: Jossey-Bass.

Levine, A., & Cureton, J. S. (1998a). Collegiate life: An obituary. *Change, 30*, 12–17, 51.

Levine, A., & Cureton, J. S. (1998b). *When hope and fear collide*. San Francisco: Jossey-Bass.

Lloyd-Jones, E., & Smith, M. (1954). *Student personnel work as deeper teaching*. New York: Harper & Brothers.

Major, C. (1998). What is problem-based learning? *PBL Insight, 1*(1), 5.

Massey, W. F., & Zemsky, R. (1995). *Using technology to enhance academic productivity*. Washington, DC: Educom.

Nanus, B. (1992). *Visionary leadership: Creating a compelling sense of direction for your organization*. San Francisco: Jossey-Bass.

National Association of Student Personnel Administrators. (1989). *Points of view*. Washington, DC: Author.

Newton, F. B., & Smith, J. H. (1996). Principles and strategies for enhancing student learning. In S. C. Ender, F. B. Newton, & R. B. Caple (Eds.), *Contributing to learning: The role of student affairs* (pp. 19–32). New Directions for Student Services, No. 75. San Francisco: Jossey-Bass.

Nuss, E. M. (1996). The development of student affairs. In S. R. Komives & D. B. Woodard, Jr., & Associates, *Student services: A handbook for the profession* (3rd ed., pp. 22–42). San Francisco: Jossey-Bass.

Reisser, L., & Roper, L. D. (1999). Using resources to achieve institutional missions and goals. In G. S. Blimling, E. J. Whitt, & Associates, *Good practice in student affairs: Principles to foster student learning* (pp. 113–131). San Francisco: Jossey-Bass.

Schmidt, P. (1998, July 24). States increasingly link budgets to performance. *The Chronicle of Higher Education*, p. A26.

Schuh, J. H., Upcraft, M. L., & Associates. (2001). *Assessment Practice in Student Affairs: An application manual*. San Francisco: Jossey-Bass.

Senge, P. M. (1990). *The fifth discipline: The art and power of the learning organization*. New York: Doubleday.

Shapiro, N. S., & Levine, J. H. (1999). *Creating learning communities: A practical guide to winning support, organizing for change, and implementing programs*. San Francisco: Jossey-Bass.

Study Group on the Conditions of Excellence in American Higher Education. (1984). *Involvement in learning: Realizing the potential of American higher education*. Washington, DC: National Institute of Education.

Upcraft, M. L., & Schuh, J. H. (1996). *Assessment in student affairs: A guide for practitioners*. San Francisco: Jossey-Bass.

Upcraft, M. L., & Terenzini, P. T. (1999). Looking beyond the horizon: Trends shaping student affairs: Technology. In C. S. Johnson & H. E. Cheatham (Eds.), *Higher education trends for the next century: Research agenda for student success* (pp. 30–36). Washington, DC: American College Personnel Association.

Wingspread Group on Higher Education. (1993). *An American imperative: Higher expectations for higher education*. Racine, WI: The Johnson Foundation.

Young, R. B. (1996). Guiding values and philosophy. In S. R. Komives & D. B. Woodard, Jr., & Associates, *Student services: A handbook for the profession* (3rd ed., pp. 83–105). San Francisco: Jossey-Bass.

RECOMMENDED READING

Palmer, P. (2000). *Let your life speak: Listening for the voice of vocation*. San Francisco: Jossey-Bass.

Quinn, R. (2000). *Change the world: How ordinary people can accomplish extraordinary results*. San Francisco: Jossey-Bass.

Strauss, W. & Howe, N. (2000). *Millenials rising: The next great generation*. New York: Vintage Books.

Vaill, P. (1996). *Learning as a way of being: Strategies for survival in a world of permanent white water*. San Francisco: Jossey-Bass.

APPENDIX A
An Introduction to Legal Research

DONALD D. GEHRING

*R*eading Chapter 3 in this book is a good place to begin legal study of higher education, but it is only a beginning. Entire books have been published that lay good foundation for practitioners interested in the legal aspects of college administration. There are also some excellent subscription services that can be used to keep informed. Many of these books and services are written for the lay reader. All student affairs professionals should have at least one basic text and an updating service as part of their library.

Reading texts and subscription services is an excellent way to develop a basic understanding and keep abreast of current case law. Sometimes, however, more in-depth knowledge is required, and the administrator may want to read the entire case referred to by an author or examine a specific statute or regulation. One need not be an attorney to read the law.

RESOURCES AND HOW TO FIND THE LAW

The law affecting student affairs administration can generally be found in three sources: federal and state statutes, federal regulations, and case law.

Statutes

All federal statutes (laws passed by the Congress) are codified in the *United States Code (LJ.S.C.)*. Commercial printers also publish versions of the Code that contain useful cross indexes and annotations. Many volumes make up the Code, and each volume contains laws related to a specific topic. In some instances several volumes may be devoted to one topic. Each topic is referred to as an Arabic numeral title. For example, Title 42 refers to public health and welfare laws while Title 20 contains the laws related to education. References to Arabic numeral titles should not be confused with references to Roman numeral titles such as Title VI. Title VI, which prohibits discrimination on the basis of race in federally assisted programs, is a part of the Civil Rights Act of 1964. Once that Act was passed by the Congress and signed by the President it became a law and was codified as a specific section of Title 42 (which contains all the federal civil rights laws). Citations to federal statutes will be written with the title number first, the name of the publication (*U.S.C.,* U.S.C.A., or U.S.C.S.) and the section. For example, 42 U.S.C. 2000d refers to Title 42 of the United States Code, Section 2000d. The symbol § is sometimes used and simply means "section." More popular sections such as section 1983 of the Civil Rights Law of 1871 may be referred to simply as § 1983. Each of the published codes will also have index volumes filed at the end of volumes containing the statutes.

State statutes are also codified in several volumes. There are usually one or more index volumes filed at the end of the state code. State statutes are generally cited with an Arabic number representing the chapter or section of the code following an abbreviation for the name of the state statutes. For example *KRS 164.891* refers to Kentucky Revised Statutes Chapter 164 (Colleges and Universities), Section 891 (defines "agents" for purposes of malpractice insurance at the University of Louisville). Administrators who wish to become familiar with their state laws may want to peruse the index volumes for such topics as "Colleges and Universities," "Students," "Education," "Alcoholic Beverages," "Open Public Records Law," or other topics of interest.

The reference room of most college and university libraries will have copies of the United States Code and state statutes. These basic references also can be found in most county courthouses, attorneys' offices, and public libraries.

Regulations

Often when a federal law is enacted it will call for executive agencies (that is, Department of Education) to issue rules to effectuate the law. For example, when Title IX of the Higher Education Amendment of 1972 was made law, it required federal agencies to make rules to implement the law. Those rules or regulations have significant impact on the daily administration of programs in postsecondary education.

Proposed regulations are first published in the *Federal Register (F.R.),* and the public is encouraged to comment on them. Once the comment period has ended, the regulations are again published in the *F.R.* in their final form and then incorporated in the *Code of Federal Regulations (C.F.R.).* Both the *F.R.* and *C.F.R.* usually may be found in the federal documents section or reference room of most college or university libraries. They also will be in the library of a U.S. attorney or federal court house.

References to federal regulations normally will cite the *C.F.R.* Like the U.S. Code, the *C.F.R.* is codified by title, with each title covering a specific topic and designated by an Arabic numeral. For example, Title 34 refers to education while Title 29 contains regulations pertaining to labor. The title number appears first followed by *C.F.R.* (designating the publication) and the specific part to which it refers. Thus, 34 *C.F.R.* 99 refers to Title 34 (education topic) of the Code of Federal Regulations, part 99 (the Buckley Amendment or Family Educational Rights and Privacy Act).

Case Law

Another primary source of law affecting the administration of student affairs programs is case law. Statutes are enacted by the legislative branch of government; regulations are one of the ways the executive branch of government effectuates the law, and when a controversy is settled in court, a judicial interpretation attaches to the constitution, statute, or regulation. The latter is referred to as case law.

Case law becomes very important. For instance, Title VI (part of the Civil Rights Act of 1964 passed by Congress) in essence prohibits discrimination on the basis of race in programs receiving federal financial assistance. However, the case law related to that title has held that an institution may under certain circumstances use race as one of several factors in evaluating candidates for admission without violating Title VI. However, courts also have held that the institution may not operate a quota system in which a specific number of places in an entering class are reserved for members of a particular race. Such a quota system in admissions programs would violate the intent of Title VI.

Cases decided by state courts appear in reports as indicated by the following:

N.E.2d.   Northeastern Reporter, Second Series. Cases decided in the state courts of Massachusetts, Rhode Island, Ohio, Indiana, and Illinois.

A-2d.   Atlantic Reporter, Second Series. Cases decided in the state courts of Maine, New Hampshire, Vermont, Connecticut, New Jersey, Pennsylvania, Delaware, and Maryland.

So.2d.   Southern Reporter, Second Series. Cases decided in the state courts of Florida, Alabama, Mississippi, and Louisiana.

S.E.2d.   Southeastern Reporter, Second Series. Cases decided in the state courts of Virginia, West Virginia, North Carolina, South Carolina, and Georgia.

S.W.2d.   Southwestern Reporter, Second Series. Cases decided in the state courts of Kentucky, Tennessee, Missouri, Arkansas, and Texas.

P.2d.   Pacific Reporter, Second Series. Cases decided in the state courts of Montana, Wyoming, Idaho, Kansas, Colorado, Oklahoma, New Mexico, Utah, Arizona, Nevada, Washington, Oregon, and California.

N.W.2d.   Northwestern Reporter, Second Series. Cases decided in the state courts of Michigan, Wisconsin, Iowa, Minnesota, North Dakota, South Dakota, and Nebraska.

N.Y.S.2d.   New York Supplement, Second Series. Cases decided in certain New York state courts. Some of these cases also may be reported in N.E.2d.

Cal. Rptr.   California Reporter. Cases decided in the state courts of California. Some of these cases also will appear in P.2d. The California Reporter was started in 1960 and California cases decided prior to 1960 can be found in P.2d.

The 2d appearing after the names of the publication simply means second series.

Cases decided by United States District Courts are primarily reported in the *Federal Supplement (F. Supp.)*, although some are also reported in the *Federal Rules Decisions (F.R.D.)*. There are many district courts, and they exercise jurisdiction over a geographic area (for example, Western District of Michigan).

Only 12 Federal United States Courts of Appeals exist and they have jurisdiction over geographic areas as listed in the following:

Circuit	Geographic Area Covered
First	Rhode Island, Massachusetts. New Hampshire, Maine, Puerto Rico
Second	Vermont, Connecticut, New York
Third	Pennsylvania, New Jersey, Delaware, Virgin Islands
Fourth	Maryland, Virginia, West Virginia, North Carolina, South Carolina
Fifth	Mississippi, Louisiana, Texas
Sixth	Ohio, Michigan, Kentucky, Tennessee
Seventh	Indiana, Illinois, Wisconsin
Eighth	Minnesota, North Dakota, South Dakota, Iowa, Nebraska, Missouri, Arkansas
Ninth	California, Oregon, Nevada, Washington, Idaho, Montana, Hawaii, Alaska, Arizona, Guam
Tenth	Colorado, Wyoming, Utah, Kansas, Oklahoma, New Mexico
Eleventh	Alabama, Florida, Georgia
	The District of Columbia is a separate judicial circuit.

Appeals court decisions are currently reported in the second series of the *Federal Reporter* (F.2d.)

The United States Supreme Court is the highest court in the land and its opinions are of great significance. Thus, United States Supreme Court opinions are reported in several sources. The government publishes decisions of the Supreme Court in *United States Reports* (U.S.). Several commercial companies also publish the Court's opinions: *Supreme Court Reporter (S.Ct.); Lawyers Edition* 2d (*L.Ed.*2d); and *United States Law Week (L.W)*.

How to Read a Citation

All published opinions are cited in a similar fashion. The first name generally refers to the person initiating the suit or action, the plaintiff. The second name is the individual defending against the action, the defendant. Next there will be a series of numerals preceding and following the abbreviation for the reporter in which the case appears. The first numbers refer to the volume of the reporter, and the following numbers refer to the page on which the case may be found. Finally, the court (if necessary) and the year of the decision are given. For example, the following diagram demonstrates how to read the citation *Pratz v. Louisiana Polytechnic Institute,* 316 F. Supp. (W.D.LA., 1972).

PLAINTIFF	DEFENDANT	VOLUME	REPORTER	PAGE	COURT	YEAR
↓	↓	↓	↓	↓	↓	↓
Pratz	v. Louisiana Polytechnic Institute	316	F. Supp.	872	W.D.LA.	1972

Thus, in this citation Pratz brought an action against Louisiana Polytechnic Institute. The opinion in that case was given by the United States District Court (only U.S. district court cases are reported in F. Supp.) for the Western District of Louisiana (W.D.LA.) in 1972. The opinion of the court may be found in volume 316 of the *Federal Supplement* on page 872.

Citations in U.S., S. Ct. or L. Ed. list only the year in parentheses, because the United States Supreme Court is assumed to be the court:

Nyquist v. Mauchlet, 97 S. Ct. 2120 (1977)

Citations of *Regional Reporters* for State Supreme Courts list only the name of the state and the year in parentheses:

Melton v. Bow 274 S.E.2d 100 (GA. 1978)

State reporters can be found in attorneys' offices, county courthouses, and law school libraries. *Federal Reporters* will generally be maintained by U.S. attorneys, U.S. courthouse libraries, and law school libraries. They will normally not be kept by local attorneys, except possibly for Supreme Court cases, or by college or university libraries.

American College Personnel Association
Statement of Ethical Principles and Standards*

As presented by the ACPA Standing Committee on Ethics and approved by the ACPA Executive Council, November 1992

PREAMBLE

*T*he American College Personnel Association (ACPA) is an association whose members are dedicated to enhancing the worth, dignity, potential, and uniqueness of each individual within post-secondary educational institutions and thus to the service of society. ACPA members are committed to contributing to the comprehensive education of the student, protecting human rights, advancing knowledge of student growth and development, and promoting the effectiveness of institutional programs, services, and organizational units. As a means of supporting these commitments, members of ACPA subscribe to the following principles and standards of ethical conduct. Acceptance of membership in ACPA signifies that the member agrees to adhere to the provisions of this statement.

This statement is designed to address issues particularly relevant to college student affairs practice. Persons charged with duties in various functional areas of higher education are also encouraged to consult ethical standards specific to their professional responsibilities.

USE OF THIS STATEMENT

The principal purpose of this statement is to assist student affairs professionals in regulating their own behavior by sensitizing them to potential ethical problems and by providing standards useful in daily practice. Observance of ethical behavior also benefits fellow professionals and students due to the effect of modeling. Self-regulation is the most effective and preferred means of assuring ethical behavior. If, however, a professional observes conduct by a fellow pro-

---

*Reprinted with permission of the American College Personnel Association (ACPA).

fessional that seems contrary to the provisions of this document, several courses of action are available.

- **Initiate a private conference.** Because unethical conduct often is due to a lack of awareness or understanding ethical standards, a private conference with the professional(s) about the conduct in question is an important initial line of action. This conference, if pursued in a spirit of collegiality and sincerity, often may resolve the ethical concern and promote future ethical conduct.
- **Pursue institutional remedies.** If private consultation does not produce the desired results, institutional channels for resolving alleged ethical improprieties may be pursued. All student affairs divisions should have a widely-publicized process for addressing allegations of ethical misconduct.
- **Contact ACPA Ethics Committee.** If the ACPA member is unsure about whether a particular activity or practice falls under the provisions of this statement, the Ethics Committee may be contacted in writing. The member should describe in reasonable detail (omitting data that would identify the person(s) as much as possible) the potentially unethical conduct or practices and the circumstances surrounding the situation. Members of the Committee or others in the Association will provide the member with a summary of opinions regarding the ethical appropriateness of the conduct or practice in question. Because these opinions are based on limited information, no specific situation or action will be judged unethical. The responses rendered by the Committee are advisory only and are not an official statement on behalf of ACPA.
- **Request consultation from ACPA Ethics Committee.** If the institution wants further assistance in resolving the controversy, an institutional representative may request on-campus consultation. Provided all parties to the controversy agree, a team of consultants selected by the Ethics Committee will visit the campus at the institution's expense to hear the allegations and to review the facts and circumstances. The team will advise institutional leadership on possible actions consistent with both the content and spirit of the ACPA Statement of Ethical Principles and Standards. Compliance with the recommendations is voluntary. No sanctions will be imposed by ACPA. Institutional leaders remain responsible for assuring ethical conduct and practice. The consultation team will maintain confidentiality surrounding the process to the extent possible.
- **Submit complaint to ACPA Ethics Committee.** If the alleged misconduct may be a violation of the ACPA Statement of Ethical Principles and Standards, the person charged is unavailable or produces unsatisfactory results, then proceedings against the individual(s) may be brought to the ACPA Ethics Committee for review. Details regarding the procedures may be obtained by contacting the Executive Director at ACPA Headquarters.

ETHICAL PRINCIPLES

No statement of ethical standards can anticipate all situations that have ethical implications. When student affairs professionals are presented with dilemmas that are not explicitly addressed herein, five ethical principles may be used in conjunction with the four enumerated standards (Professional Responsibility and Competence, Student Learning and Development, Responsibility to the Institution, Responsibility to Society) to assist in making decisions and determining appropriate courses of action.

Ethical principles should guide the behaviors of professionals in everyday practice. Principles, however, are not just guidelines for reaction when something goes wrong or when a complaint is raised. Adhering to ethical principles also calls for action. These principles include the following:

- **Act to benefit others.** Service to humanity is the basic tenet underlying student affairs practice. Hence, student affairs professionals exist to: [a] promote healthy social, physical, academic, moral, cognitive, career, and personality development of students; [b] bring a developmental perspective to the institution's total educational process and learning environment; [c] contribute to the effective functioning of the institution; and [d] provide programs and services consistent with this principle.
- **Promote justice.** Student affairs professionals are committed to assuring fundamental fairness for all individuals within the academic community. In pursuit of this goal, the principles of impartiality, equity, and reciprocity (treating others as one would desire to be treated) are basic. When there are greater needs than resources available or when the interests of constituencies conflict, justice requires honest consideration of all claims and requests and equitable (not necessarily equal) distribution of goods and services. A crucial aspect of promoting justice is demonstrating an appreciation for human differences and opposing intolerance and bigotry concerning these differences. Important human differences include, but are not limited to, characteristics such as age, culture, ethnicity, gender, disabling condition, race, religion, or sexual/affectional orientation.
- **Respect autonomy.** Student affairs professionals respect and promote individual autonomy and privacy. Students' freedom of choice and action are not restricted unless their actions significantly interfere with the welfare of others or the accomplishment of the institution's mission.
- **Be faithful.** Student affairs professionals are truthful, honor agreements, and are trustworthy in the performance of their duties.
- **Do no harm.** Student affairs professionals do not engage in activities that cause either physical or psychological damage to others. In addition to their personal actions, student affairs professionals are especially vigilant to assure that the institutional policies do not: [a] hinder students' opportunities to

benefit from the learning experiences available in the environment; [b] threaten individuals' self-worth, dignity, or safety; or [c] discriminate unjustly or illegally.

ETHICAL STANDARDS

Four ethical standards related to primary constituencies with whom student affairs professionals work—fellow professionals, students, educational institutions, and society—are specified.

1. **Professional Responsibility and Competence.** Student affairs professionals are responsible for promoting students' learning and development, enhancing the understanding of student life, and advancing the profession and its ideals. They possess the knowledge, skills, emotional stability, and maturity to discharge responsibilities as administrators, advisors, consultants, counselors, programmers, researchers, and teachers. High levels of professional competence are expected in the performance of their duties and responsibilities. They ultimately are responsible for the consequences of their actions or inaction.

   As ACPA members, student affairs professionals will:

   1.1 Adopt a professional lifestyle characterized by use of sound theoretical principles and a personal value system congruent with the basic tenets of the profession.
   1.2 Contribute to the development of the profession (e.g., recruiting students to the profession, serving professional organizations, educating new professionals, improving professional practices, and conducting and reporting research).
   1.3 Maintain and enhance professional effectiveness by improving skills and acquiring new knowledge.
   1.4 Monitor their personal and professional functioning and effectiveness and seek assistance from appropriate professionals as needed.
   1.5 Represent their professional credentials, competencies, and limitations accurately and correct any misrepresentations of these qualifications by others.
   1.6 Establish fees for professional services after consideration of the ability of the recipient to pay. They will provide some services, including professional development activities for colleagues, for little or no remuneration.
   1.7 Refrain from attitudes or actions that impinge on colleagues' dignity, moral code, privacy, worth, professional functioning, and/or personal growth.
   1.8 Abstain from sexual harassment.

1.9 Abstain from sexual intimacies with colleagues or with staff for whom they have supervisory, evaluative, or instructional responsibility.

1.10 Refrain from using their positions to seek unjustified personal gains, sexual favors, unfair advantages, or unearned goods and services not normally accorded those in such positions.

1.11 Inform students of the nature and/or limits of confidentiality. They will share information about the students only in accordance with institutional policies and applicable laws, when given their permission, or when required to prevent personal harm to themselves or others.

1.12 Use records and electronically stored information only to accomplish legitimate, institutional purposes and to benefit students.

1.13 Define job responsibilities, decision-making procedures, mutual expectations, accountability procedures, and evaluation criteria with subordinates and supervisors.

1.14 Acknowledge contributions by others to program development, program implementation, evaluations, and reports.

1.15 Assure that participation by staff in planned activities that emphasize self-disclosure or other relatively intimate or personal involvement is voluntary and that the leader(s) of such activities do not have administrative, supervisory, or evaluative authority over participants.

1.16 Adhere to professional practices in securing positions: [a] represent education and experiences accurately; [b] respond to offers promptly; [c] accept only those positions they intend to assume; [d] advise current employer and all institutions at which applications are pending immediately when they sign a contract; and [e] inform their employers at least thirty days before leaving a position.

1.17 Gain approval of research plans involving human subjects from the institutional committee with oversight responsibility prior to initiation of the study. In the absence of such a committee, they will seek to create procedures to protect the rights and assure the safety of research participants.

1.18 Conduct and report research studies accurately. They will not engage in fraudulent research nor will they distort or misrepresent their data or deliberately bias their results.

1.19 Cite previous works on a topic when writing or when speaking to professional audiences.

1.20 Acknowledge major contributions to research projects and professional writings through joint authorships with the principal contributor listed first. They will acknowledge minor technical or professional contributions in notes or introductory statements.

1.21 Not demand co-authorship of publications when their involvement was ancillary or unduly pressure others for joint authorship.

1.22 Share original research data with qualified others upon request.

1.23 Communicate the results of any research judged to be of value to other professionals and not withhold results reflecting unfavorably on specific institutions, programs, services, or prevailing opinion.

1.24 Submit manuscripts for consideration to only one journal at a time. They will not seek to publish previously published or accepted-for-publication materials in other media or publications without first informing all editors and/or publishers concerned. They will make appropriate references in the text and receive permission to use if copyrights are involved.

1.25 Support professional preparation program efforts by providing assistantships, practica, field placements, and consultation to students and faculty.

As ACPA members, preparation program faculty will:

1.26 Inform prospective graduate students of program expectations, predominant theoretical orientations, skills needed for successful completion, and employment of recent graduates.

1.27 Assure that required experiences involving self-disclosure are communicated to prospective graduate students. When the program offers experiences that emphasize self-disclosure or other relatively intimate or personal involvement (e.g., group or individual counseling or growth groups), professionals must not have current or anticipated administrative, supervisory, or evaluative authority over participants.

1.28 Provide graduate students with a broad knowledge base consisting of theory, research, and practice.

1.29 Inform graduate students of the ethical responsibilities and standards of the profession.

1.30 Assess all relevant competencies and interpersonal functioning of students throughout the program, communicate these assessments to students, and take appropriate corrective actions including dismissal when warranted.

1.31 Assure that field supervisors are qualified to provide supervision to graduate students and are informed of their ethical responsibilities in this role.

2. **Student Learning and Development.** Student development is an essential purpose of higher education, and the pursuit of this aim is a major responsibility of student affairs. Development is complex and includes cognitive, physical, moral, social, career, spiritual, personality, and educational dimensions. Professionals must be sensitive to the variety of backgrounds, cultures, and personal characteristics evident in the student population and use appropriate theoretical perspectives to identify learning opportunities and to reduce barriers that inhibit development.

As ACPA members, student affairs professionals will:

2.1 Treat students as individuals who possess dignity, worth, and the ability to be self-directed.

2.2 Avoid dual relationships with students (e.g., counselor/employer, supervisor/best friend, or faculty/sexual partner) that may involve incompatible roles and conflicting responsibilities.

2.3 Abstain from sexual harassment.

2.4 Abstain from sexual intimacies with clients or with students for whom they have supervisory, evaluative, or instructional responsibility.

2.5 Inform students of the conditions under which they may receive assistance and the limits of confidentiality when the counseling relationship is initiated.

2.6 Avoid entering or continuing helping relationships if benefits to students are unlikely. They will refer students to appropriate specialists and recognize that if the referral is declined, they are not obligated to continue the relationship.

2.7 Inform students about the purpose of assessment and make explicit the planned use of results prior to assessment.

2.8 Provide appropriate information to students prior to and following the use of any assessment procedure to place results in proper perspective with other relevant factors (e.g., socioeconomic, ethnic, cultural, and gender related experiences).

2.9 Confront students regarding issues, attitudes, and behaviors that have ethical implications.

3. **Responsibility to the Institution.** Institutions of higher education provide the context for student affairs practice. Institutional mission, policies, organizational structure, and culture, combined with individual judgment and professional standards, define and delimit the nature and extent of practice. Student affairs professionals share responsibility with other members of the academic community for fulfilling the institutional mission. Responsibility to promote the development of individual students and to support the institution's policies and interests require that professionals balance competing demands.

As ACPA members, student affairs professionals will:

3.1 Contribute to their institution by supporting its mission, goals, and policies.

3.2 Seek resolution when they and their institution encounter substantial disagreements concerning professional or personal values. Resolution may require sustained efforts to modify institutional policies and practices or result in voluntary termination of employment.

3.3 Recognize that conflicts among students, colleagues, or the institution should be resolved without diminishing appropriate obligations to any party involved.

3.4 Assure that information provided about the institution is factual and accurate.

3.5 Inform appropriate officials of conditions that may be disruptive or damaging to their institution.

3.6 Inform supervisors of conditions or practices that may restrict institutional or professional effectiveness.

3.7 Recognize their fiduciary responsibility to the institution. They will assure that funds for which they have oversight are expended following established procedures and in ways that optimize value, are accounted for properly, and contribute to the accomplishment of the institution's mission. They also will assure equipment, facilities, personnel, and other resources are used to promote the welfare of the institution and students.

3.8 Restrict their private interests, obligations, and transactions in ways to minimize conflicts of interest or the appearance of conflicts of interest. They will identify their personal views and actions as private citizens from those expressed or undertaken as institutional representatives.

3.9 Collaborate and share professional expertise with members of the academic community.

3.10 Evaluate programs, services, and organizational structure regularly and systematically to assure conformity to published standards and guidelines. Evaluations should be conducted using rigorous evaluation methods and principles, and the results should be made available to appropriate institutional personnel.

3.11 Evaluate job performance of subordinates regularly and recommend appropriate actions to enhance professional development and improve performance.

3.12 Provide fair and honest assessments of colleagues' job performance.

3.13 Seek evaluations of their job performance and/or services they provide.

3.14 Provide training to student affairs search and screening committee members who are unfamiliar with the profession.

3.15 Disseminate information that accurately describes the responsibilities of position vacancies, required qualifications, and the institution.

3.16 Follow a published interview and selection process that periodically notifies applicants of their status.

4. **Responsibility to Society.** Student affairs professionals, both as citizens and practitioners, have a responsibility to contribute to the improvement of the communities in which they live and work. They respect individuality and recognize that worth is not diminished by characteristics such as age, culture, ethnicity, gender, disabling condition, race, religion, or sexual/affectional orientation. Student affairs professionals work to protect human rights and promote an appreciation of human diversity in higher education.

As ACPA members, student affairs professionals will:

4.1 Assist students in becoming productive and responsible citizens.

4.2 Demonstrate concern for the welfare of all students and work for constructive change on behalf of students.

4.3 Not discriminate on the basis of age, culture, ethnicity, gender, disabling condition, race, religion, or sexual/affectional orientation. They will work to modify discriminatory practices.

4.4 Demonstrate regard for social codes and moral expectations of the communities in which they live and work. They will recognize that violations of accepted moral and legal standards may involve their clients, students, or colleagues in damaging personal conflicts and may impugn the integrity of the profession, their own reputations, and that of the employing institution.

4.5 Report to the appropriate authority any condition that is likely to harm their clients and/or others.

NASPA
Standards of Professional Practice*

*T*he National Association of Student Personnel Administrators (NASPA) is an organization of colleges, universities, agencies, and professional educators whose members are committed to providing services and education that enhance student growth and development. The association seeks to promote student personnel work as a profession which requires personal integrity, belief in the dignity and worth of individuals, respect for individual differences and diversity, a commitment to service, and dedication to the development of individuals and the college community through education. NASPA supports student personnel work by providing opportunities for its members to expand knowledge and skills through professional education and experience. The following standards were endorsed by NASPA at the December 1990 board of directors meeting in Washington, D.C.

1. **Professional Services**
   Members of NASPA fulfill the responsibilities of their position by supporting the educational interests, rights, and welfare of students in accordance with the mission of the employing institution.
2. **Agreement with Institutional Mission and Goals**
   Members who accept employment with an educational institution subscribe to the general mission and goals of the institution.
3. **Management of Institutional Resources**
   Members seek to advance the welfare of the employing institution through accountability for the proper use of institutional funds, personnel, equipment, and other resources. Members inform appropriate officials of conditions which may be potentially disruptive or damaging to the institution's mission, personnel, and property.
4. **Employment Relationship**
   Members honor employment relationships. Members do not commence new duties or obligations at another institution under a new contractual agreement until termination of an existing contract, unless otherwise agreed to by the member and the member's current and new supervisors. Members ad-

*Reprinted with permission of the National Association of Student Personnel Administrators (NASPA)

here to professional practices in securing positions and employment relationships.

5. **Conflict of Interest**

   Members recognize their obligation to the employing institution and seek to avoid private interests, obligations, and transactions which are in conflict of interest or give the appearance of impropriety. Members clearly distinguish between statements and actions which represent their own personal views and those which represent their employing institution when important to do so.

6. **Legal Authority**

   Members respect and acknowledge all lawful authority. Members refrain from conduct involving dishonesty, fraud, deceit, and misrepresentation or unlawful discrimination. NASPA recognizes that legal issues are often ambiguous, and members should seek the advice of counsel as appropriate. Members demonstrate concern for the legal, social codes and moral expectations of the communities in which they live and work even when the dictates of one's conscience may require behavior as a private citizen which is not in keeping with these codes/expectations.

7. **Equal Consideration and Treatment of Others**

   Members execute professional responsibilities with fairness and impartiality and show equal consideration to individuals regardless of status or position. Members respect individuality and promote an appreciation of human diversity in higher education. In keeping with the mission of their respective institution and remaining cognizant of federal, state, and local laws, they do not discriminate on the basis of race, religion, creed, gender, age, national origin, sexual orientation, or physical disability. Members do not engage in or tolerate harassment in any form and should exercise professional judgment in entering into intimate relationships with those for whom they have any supervisory, evaluative, or instructional responsibility.

8. **Student Behavior**

   Members demonstrate and promote responsible behavior and support actions that enhance personal growth and development of students. Members foster conditions designed to ensure a student's acceptance of responsibility for his/her own behavior. Members inform and educate students as to sanctions or constraints on student behavior which may result from violations of law or institutional policies.

9. **Integrity of Information and Research**

   Members ensure that all information conveyed to others is accurate and in appropriate context. In their research and publications, members conduct and report research studies to assure accurate interpretation of findings, and they adhere to accepted professional standards of academic integrity.

10. **Confidentiality**

    Members ensure that confidentiality is maintained with respect to all privileged communications and to educational and professional records considered confidential. They inform all parties of the nature and/or limits of confidentiality. Members share information only in accordance with institutional policies and relevant statutes when given the informed consent or when required to prevent personal harm to themselves or others.

11. **Research Involving Human Subjects**
   Members are aware of and take responsibility for all pertinent ethical principles and institutional requirements when planning any research activity dealing with human subjects. (See Ethical Principles in the Conduct of Research with Human Participants, Washington, D.C.: American Psychological Association, 1982.)

12. **Representation of Professional Competence**
   Members at all times represent accurately their professional credentials, competencies, and limitations and act to correct any misrepresentations of these qualifications by others. Members make proper referrals to appropriate professionals when the member's professional competence does not meet the task or issue in question.

13. **Selection and Promotion Practices**
   Members support nondiscriminatory, fair employment practices by appropriately publicizing staff vacancies, selection criteria, deadlines, and promotion criteria in accordance with the spirit and intent of equal opportunity policies and established legal guidelines and institutional policies.

14. **References**
   Members, when serving as a reference, provide accurate and complete information about candidates, including both relevant strengths and limitations of a professional and personal nature.

15. **Job Definitions and Performance Evaluation**
   Members clearly define with subordinates and supervisors job responsibilities and decision-making procedures, mutual expectations, accountability procedures, and evaluation criteria.

16. **Campus Community**
   Members promote a sense of community among all areas of the campus by working cooperatively with students, faculty, staff, and others outside the institution to address the common goals of student learning and development. Members foster a climate of collegiality and mutual respect in their work relationships.

17. **Professional Development**
   Members have an obligation to continue personal professional growth and to contribute to the development of the profession by enhancing personal knowledge and skills, sharing ideas and information, improving professional practices, conducting and reporting research, and participating in association activities. Members promote and facilitate the professional growth of staff and they emphasize ethical standards in professional preparation and development programs.

18. **Assessment**
   Members regularly and systematically assess organizational structures, programs, and services to determine whether the developmental goals and

needs of students are being met and to assure conformity to published standards and guidelines such as those of the Council for the Advancement of Standards for Student Services/Development Programs (CAS). Members collect data which include responses from students and other significant constituencies and make assessment results available to appropriate institutional officials for the purpose of revising and improving program goals and implementation.

Index